THE YALE EDITION

OF

HORACE WALPOLE'S

CORRESPONDENCE

EDITED BY W. S. LEWIS

VOLUME THIRTY-FIVE

HORACE WALPOLE'S
CORRESPONDENCE

WITH

JOHN CHUTE
RICHARD BENTLEY
THE EARL OF STRAFFORD
SIR WILLIAM HAMILTON
THE EARL AND COUNTESS HARCOURT
GEORGE HARDINGE

EDITED BY W. S. LEWIS
A. DAYLE WALLACE
AND
ROBERT A. SMITH
WITH THE ASSISTANCE OF
EDWINE M. MARTZ

NEW HAVEN
YALE UNIVERSITY PRESS
LONDON · OXFORD UNIVERSITY PRESS

1973

TABLE OF CONTENTS

LIST OF ILLUSTRATIONS

Grateful acknowledgment is made to the National Trust and the British Museum for permission to reproduce Rosalba's drawing, Müntz's painting, and Bentley's sketches and note.

INTRODUCTION

As the correspondents in volumes 15 and 16 were brought together under the category of 'antiquaries,' those in this volume may be classed as 'virtuosi,' although 'lawyer' would suit Hardinge better. Lord Wharncliffe's description of Lord Strafford as 'eminently skilled in architecture and virtu' also fits Chute, Bentley, Lord Harcourt, and Sir William Hamilton. Walpole's attachment to them throve on their common interests in the arts. It remained unbroken with Chute, Strafford, and Hamilton, but wilted away under the pressure of Bentley's improvidence, Harcourt's change of politics, and Hardinge's ceaseless asking for special favours. The letters to Chute, Bentley, and Strafford appear in Walpole's posthumous *Works,* 1798. The disappearance since 1798 of all but three of them (which turned up in the Damer-Waller collection) is one of the unsolved mysteries of Walpole's correspondence.

The results of his friendship with Chute and Bentley may be seen today in Strawberry Hill, for they formed with him 'the Committee' that planned it. Their designs and sketches are now at Farmington, and when they are all reproduced it will be clear that Chute's contribution was greater than was known before his 'Slight Sketches of Architecture' came to light. Walpole's intimacy with him began in 1740 while they were both staying with Mann at Florence. When Chute died, Walpole wrote Mann, 27th May 1776, 'Mr Chute and I agreed invariably in our principles, he was my counsel in my affairs, was my oracle in taste, the standard to whom I submitted my trifles, and the genius that presided over poor Strawberry! His sense decided me in everything, his wit and quickness illuminated everything —I saw him oftener than any man; to him in every difficulty I had recourse, and him I loved to have here, as our friendship was so entire, and we knew one another so entirely, that he alone never was the least constraint to me. We passed many hours together without saying a syllable to each other, for we were both above ceremony. I left him without excusing myself, read or wrote before him, as if he were not present.'

Our introduction to Richard Bentley occurs in Walpole's letter to Montagu of June 23, 1750: 'I have had another of your friends with me there [at Strawberry Hill] some time, whom I adore, Mr Bentley; he has more sense, judgment and wit, more taste and more misfortunes than sure ever met in any man.' Walpole's earliest letter to Bentley, August 5th, 1752, was written while he and Chute were on a 'pilgrimage' to Sussex and Kent, 'This holy land of abbeys and Gothic castles.' 'We bring you,' he wrote Bentley, 'a thousand sketches, that you may show us what we have seen,' and we can picture the Strawberry Committee poring over them when they met as they pored over the engravings of sepulchral monuments in Dugdale's *St Paul's* and Dart's *Westminster* and *Canterbury* to copy and adapt the 'true Gothic' details for Strawberry's embellishments. The Committee saw nothing amiss in converting the tomb of John of Eltham in the Abbey to the chimney-piece in the new library or substituting lath and plaster for stone. Bentley also produced *Designs by Mr R. Bentley for Six Poems by Mr T. Gray*, 1753, a landmark in English book-illustration that was published in London at Walpole's expense. It inspired Gray's 'Stanzas to Mr Bentley' in which the poet pays his tribute to the artist:

> See, in their course, each transitory thought
> Fix'd by his touch a lasting essence take;
> Each dream, in Fancy's airy colouring wrought
> To local symmetry and life awake!

Bentley lived for a while in Jersey to escape his creditors. On his return to England, Walpole wrote Montagu[1] that his history had grown 'woefully bad. Marc Antony [Bentley], though no boy, persists in losing the world two or three times over for every gipsy, that he takes for a Cleopatra. I have laughed, been cool, scolded, represented, begged, and at last spoken very roundly—all with equal success—at present we do not meet—I must convince him of ill usage, before I can make good usage of any service to him. All I have done is forgot, because I will not be enamoured of Hannah Cleopatra [Bentley's wife] too. . . . you may trust me for still being kind to him,' and that he was so appears from George Hardinge's letter to him on July 17, 1780, in which Hardinge tells Walpole he had found out that Walpole was 'still generous to him,' a possible reference to a

---

1. October 2d, 1760.

small sinecure Walpole had secured for him. Bentley was expelled from the house to which he had made such a lasting contribution, the Castle's drawbridge was raised, the portcullis lowered, and he never returned. Yet there is the final short note from him that Walpole kept and that gives a wistful grace to the unhappy conclusion. It was written over twenty years after Bentley left Strawberry forever when he heard at Oxford of Dr Johnson's pending attack on Gray's poems and broke through the long silence to express his indignation.

There is no tension in Walpole's letters to Lord Strafford, which are among the best that he wrote. He was also very fond of Lady Strafford, a beautiful sister of Lady Mary Coke. The first mention of the Straffords is just after Sir Robert Walpole's fall in 1742 when they showed their affection for his youngest son by asking him promptly to dinner. Walpole wrote Bentley from Wentworth Castle, their seat in Yorkshire, 'This place is one of the very few that I really like: the situation, woods, views, and the improvements, are perfect in their kinds: nobody has a truer taste than Lord Strafford.'[2] Bentley's design for a Gothic temple in the 'menagerie' there was executed, but not his design for a chimney-piece, which Strafford found too Jacobean. The Straffords also had a house in Twickenham where they spent much time, a circumstance that deprived us of many of Walpole's sunniest letters that he would otherwise have written. The only letter from Strafford that Walpole apparently kept was sold to Thorpe, the bookseller, in the Strawberry Hill sale, 1842, sixth day, lot 133: 'Twelve letters, notes, and cards addressed by various noblemen to Horace Walpole, namely, Lords Cork, Strafford, Bristol, Huntington, Newnham, etc.'

In Walpole's earliest printed letter to Sir William Hamilton he tells how on returning to Strawberry from a visit at Wentworth Castle he found the cases containing the 13th-century 'shrine of mosaic, three stories high,' that Hamilton had secured for him at Rome. This happy accession sets the tone for the correspondence. Hamilton was minister at Naples for thirty-six years, but unlike Sir Horace Mann he returned to England for visits where he was welcomed warmly by the virtuosi. Although he is remembered today chiefly as the elderly husband of Emma Lady Hamilton (his second wife) and the complaisant friend of Nelson, modern virtuosi honour him for his great collections of Greek vases and his monumental

2. To Bentley, August 1756.

Etruscan, Greek, and Roman Antiquities in four massive folios. Seismologists are also indebted to him for his records of earthquakes and explorations of Vesuvius and Etna, an enthusiasm that Walpole observed with indulgence from afar.

Walpole cuts a rather pathetic figure in his correspondence with Harcourt. He was particularly fond of both Lord and Lady Harcourt, who were some twenty years younger, and loved visiting them. 'I am as interested in Nuneham,' he wrote, 'as in Strawberry.'3 He joined with Sir Joshua Reynolds to write a catalogue of its contents, to which he made several handsome contributions, including the Sheldon Tapestry maps of English counties, for which Harcourt built a special room. Harcourt on his side sent to Strawberry the spurs worn by King William at the Battle of the Boyne that were greeted with gratitude bordering on hysteria. Walpole found in the Harcourts the genius he discerned readily in persons of quality: Harcourt went 'beyond what I have ever seen in etching,'4 Lady Harcourt's verses were written 'with great ease and sense' and a winning modesty. Year after year he begged her to let him print them at Strawberry Hill, but she hung back until Harcourt's return to the Court party had cooled their friendship. Then his and Mason's jibes at 'your wine-merchant' make painful reading, and prove once again that politics may separate the most devoted friends.

Hardinge had some interest in architecture and virtu, enough to write, 'In his [Walpole's] taste for architecture and *virtu* there was both whim and foppery, but still with fancy and with genius,' and to record how on his first day and night at Strawberry Hill, 'with keys of all its treasures' he 'did not and could not go to bed for many hours after midnight' (*post*, Appendix 4), but he appears in this volume more by reason of the extent of the correspondence (72 letters) than for his interest in architecture and virtu. On Appendix 4 he calls Walpole's letters 'delightfully entertaining and clever,' yet he kept only twelve of them, several of which are merely notes.

Hardinge was in his twenties, Walpole in his fifties, when they first met. Dr Warren Smith has pointed out the similarity between the young Hardinge and Boswell: both were lawyers who thrust themselves cheerfully upon eminent elders. Hardinge, a nephew of Walpole's friend and correspondent, Lord Dacre, lacked Boswell's

3. July 1st, 1782, to Harcourt.
4. March 16th, 1763, to Harcourt.

awe of the English upper class and displayed a jocosity that comes as something of a shock even in the present age of easy manners, but Walpole, seduced by his flattery, put up with his cadging, archness, and skipping impertinence until in 1795 he described him to Mary Berry as 'that out-pensioner of Bedlam'[5] and told her how Hardinge continued to bother him with requests for special favours. Walpole's last printed note to him, ca 1789, was inspired by generous and charitable impulses. Mary Beauclerk, the daughter of their neighbour, Lady Di Beauclerk, had eloped with her half-brother, Lord Bolingbroke. Walpole, who had gone to Lady Di at Little Marble Hill to do what he could to alleviate her distress, sent the note and his chaise to Hardinge at his house nearby, urging him to come for ten minutes to advise and comfort their distracted friend.

Hardinge attained sufficient celebrity in his profession to be pilloried by Byron as

> the waggish Welsh Judge, Jefferies Hardsman,
> In his grave office so completely skill'd,
> That when a culprit came for condemnation,
> He had his judge's joke for consolation.[6]

His chief contribution to our work appears in Appendix 4 of this volume, which is one of the few 'characters' of Horace Walpole written by a contemporary.

W. S. L.

5. Sept. 10, 1795.
6. *Don Juan,* Canto XIII, Stanza 88, 5–8.

MANUSCRIPTS AND EDITORIAL METHOD

Of the 293 letters in this volume, 205 are by Walpole of which eight are heretofore unpublished, and four have been printed hitherto only in part. Sixteen of the 88 letters written to Walpole are 'new,' and seven others had been printed only in part. Nearly half of Walpole's previously-printed letters which appear in this volume had first appeared in his *Works*, 1798.

The provenance of Chute's letters to Walpole from Italy is given here in the heading to the first letter, and is not repeated in letters of the same origin; each of the other letters is provided with a heading which outlines the history of the MS, and its previous printings.

Walpole's correspondence with John Chute now numbers 50 letters (besides two written to Chute and Mann together) of which sixteen are given for the first time and eight are here first printed in full.[1] The eighteen letters written by Chute from Italy were kept together with the letters from Horace Mann, in Walpole's collection at Strawberry Hill, and were acquired with them by Richard Bentley the publisher, presumably about 1843. They were bought, along with Mann's letters, in 1934 by W. S. Lewis from the younger Richard Bentley.[2]

Walpole's two letters to Chute that were included in his letters to Mann, 24 June and 12 Oct. 1743 OS, are printed from Walpole's MS transcripts of those letters[3] (two others, 29 Dec. 1741 OS and 10 March 1742 OS, were also written to Chute and Mann). Walpole's other letters were returned to him after Chute's death in 1776.[4] Thirteen of them (five of which are first printed here) were acquired, with the other Walpolian MSS, by the elder Richard Bentley, the publisher, about 1843, and were sold in 1937 to W. S. Lewis by the estate of the younger Richard Bentley. Two letters (3 Nov. 1748 and ?29 July 1756) from Chute to Walpole, and two (30 April 1754 and 3 Oct.

---

1. They were printed in part by Dr John Doran in *Mann and Manners in Florence*, 1876.
2. See MANN i. pp. xlviii–xlix, x. 40–4.
3. See ibid. i. p. xlviii.
4. HW to Lady Ossory 13 July 1776, OSSORY i. 306.

1765) from Walpole to Chute, were 'secured' by Mrs Damer, Walpole's residuary heir, and passed to Sir Wathen Waller after whose sale, 5–6 Dec. 1921, lots 10, 11, two went to the Bodleian Library and two passed through other hands, one (3 Oct. 1765) being later acquired by W. S. Lewis.

Twelve of Walpole's later letters to Chute were printed by Mary Berry in the fifth volume of Walpole's *Works,* 1798; the MSS of these, except for the above-mentioned letter of 3 Oct. 1765 have disappeared. Two letters to Chute were retained by (or returned to) Chute's heirs at the Vyne in Hampshire, and are now in the Hampshire Record Office.

All 35 of Walpole's letters to Richard Bentley were printed by Mary Berry in *Works,* Volume V, but the history of only three are known to us, those of 19 Dec. 1753, 18 May 1754, and 27 July 1754. They and one from Bentley, 7 March 1781, passed from Mrs Damer to Sir Wathen Waller, Bt, and were sold at Sotheby's 5–6 December 1921, lot 8 to an unknown buyer. Dr Toynbee printed them, including passages omitted in *Works,* in the second supplementary volume of his wife's edition. A brief note by Bentley probably to Walpole is in the British Museum, and is the only 'new' letter in the Bentley correspondence.

All but three of Walpole's 57 letters to Lord Strafford were printed in the fifth volume of Walpole's *Works,* 1798; all have disappeared. The three MSS not in *Works,* are those of 28 Aug. 1756, 4 Oct. 1766, and 4 Feb. 1778. The first two passed through the Damer-Waller ownership; the third is in the British Museum.

One letter from Sir William Hamilton 15 Sept. 1771, likewise has a Damer-Waller provenance, but the 14 letters in that correspondence (nine from Walpole and five from Hamilton) come from miscellaneous sources that are given in the headings of the various letters. Six of the letters were dispersed in the Hamilton Sale at Sotheby's in 1886. New material in this correspondence includes two of Walpole's letters and four of Hamilton's, all previously unpublished, and also one letter by Walpole previously printed in part.

Of Walpole's 60 letters to Lord Nuneham, later Lord Harcourt, all but three were kept by the Harcourt family and are now at Stanton Harcourt, Oxon. Crossed-out passages in Walpole's letters of 26 November 1777 and 29 October 1782 have now been restored. Of the three letters not at Stanton Harcourt, that of Feb. 1780 is here printed from Walpole's copy acquired by W. S. Lewis in 1937 from the Bentley estate; the previously unpublished letter by Walpole of ?1 March 1783 was acquired by W. S. Lewis in 1932 from Walter T. Spencer; Walpole's 17 Sept. 1778 is printed from Mitford's edition (1851) of Walpole's correspondence with Mason, the MS having disappeared.

The only two surviving letters from Harcourt to Walpole (ca Jan.– March 1785 and ca June 1795) passed through the Damer-Waller ownership. They were first printed by Dr Toynbee and are now owned by W. S. Lewis. Walpole's one letter to Lady Harcourt is with his others at Stanton Harcourt.

Fifty-four of Walpole's letters to the Harcourts were first published in Peter Cunningham's edition of Walpole's letters, five in the privately printed *Harcourt Papers,* ?1880-1905, which also reprinted seven of the letters published by Cunningham, and gave the omitted part of an eighth.

George Hardinge's 59 letters to Walpole, together with six of Walpole's letters to him, were printed by John Nichols in *Illustrations of the Literary History of the Eighteenth Century,* Volume III, 1818, while six other letters by Walpole to Hardinge (two of them combined as one) had already been printed by Nichols in *Literary Anecdotes of the Eighteenth Century,* Vol. VIII, 1814. Manuscripts of some of these letters survived in the Nichols family; those of 22 March 1777, 10 Sept. 1780, ca June 1781 (a copy), 15 March 1782 (from Walpole), and 23 March 1784 were sold in the J. G. Nichols sale, Sotheby's 18 Nov. 1929, lots 232, 238, 239, to various buyers, while the letters of 13 April 1775, 9 July 1777, and 23 March 1784 (from Hardinge) appeared in the John Boyer Buchanan Nichols sale, 6 Nov. 1951, all being eventually acquired by W. S. Lewis. The MS of Walpole's letter of ca July 1789 (printed by Nichols) also exists, having been sold in 1960 by the Swann Galleries of New York to the Seven Gables Bookshop for W. S. Lewis. Anna Seward's *Letters,* 1811, prints a part omitted by Nichols, of the letter of 4 July 1779. Mrs Toynbee owned the MS of Walpole's letter ca 1784, now untraced and not printed by Nichols. The headings of the individual letters in this correspondence give fuller details.

Biographical notes without references are assumed to be based on the *Dictionary of National Biography, The Complete Peerage* and the *Complete Baronetage,* and also the *History of Parliament* (volumes for 1715–1754 and 1754–1790, by Romney Sedgwick and Sir Lewis Namier and John Brooke respectively). Other sources cited in the footnotes are assumed to have been supplemented by these reference works. Unless otherwise stated, all English books cited were printed in London, and all French books in Paris. Since the English calendar was still unrevised while Chute was in Italy his letters from there are labelled NS (new style) and those from Walpole, in England, OS (old style), the letters appearing in their proper chronological order allowing for the difference in calendar. We have followed our usual practice of modernizing the spelling (except proper names), of retaining Walpole's punctuation but not that of his correspondents, and of using square brackets for editorial emendation (and angular ones for restoration of a mutilated text).

The text of the letters printed in Walpole's *Works*, 1798, contains many blanks or initials where Walpole undoubtedly had spelled out proper names. When the identities are certain, these names are here silently supplied; when they are doubtful, conjectural identifications are given in the notes.

                                                          W.H.S.

ACKNOWLEDGMENTS

Our first expression of indebtedness is due to Viscount Harcourt, K.C.M.G., the owner of Walpole's letters to George Simon, 2nd Earl Harcourt. For upwards of forty years Lord Harcourt has answered our many questions about them and the Harcourt Papers, which are also in his possession at Stanton Harcourt, Oxon. He has done so with unflagging patience, interest and skill, and we are most grateful to him.

For permission to print other letters in this volume we are indebted to the Bodleian Library, the British Museum, the Edinburgh University Library, the Harvard University Library, the late Sir Charles L. Chute, the late Dr James Strachey of London, Mr Robert H. Taylor of Princeton and Mr Morris Wolf of Philadelphia.

Editorial work on the various correspondences in this volume has been in progress, intermittently, for over thirty years. The Chute and Bentley correspondences were started by the late Charles H. Bennett and continued by Messrs Robert A. Smith and A. Dayle Wallace; the Strafford letters were started by Mr Joseph W. Reed Jr and completed by Messrs A. Dayle Wallace and Warren H. Smith. The Hamilton correspondence was almost entirely edited by Mr Wallace. Walpole's correspondence with Lord and Lady Harcourt was begun by Messrs Francis J. Glasheen and Hale Sturges, and continued by Mr Wallace and the late Charles Bennett; the Hardinge letters were begun by Mr Ralph M. Williams and continued by Mr Warren Smith.

Mrs Louis L. Martz assisted in the proof-reading; the references in the notes were verified by Miss Barbara Stoops, Mrs Bryan Wolf, and Mr David Mandel; Mrs Wolf did much of the typing; Mr Mandel '73 was our assistant under Yale's bursary program during the past two years, though earlier bursary aides had occasionally worked, at scattered intervals, upon portions of the volume. Mr Lars E. Troide traced some of the classical quotations in the Hardinge correspondence.

Dr Michael McCarthy of the University of Toronto not only read the proofs of this volume, furnishing us with useful information about the architectural designs of Chute and Bentley, but also supplied photographs of material from the Hampshire Record Office (to which our thanks are likewise due). We also acknowledge information and assistance from Messrs T. S. Blakeney, John Brooke, Robert Halsband, Allen T. Hazen, F. W. Hilles, C. B. Hogan, and the late George Sherburn.

W. S. L.
W. H. S.

CUE-TITLES AND ABBREVIATIONS

Ædes Walpolianæ,
Works ii . . . Horace Walpole, *Ædes Walpolianæ: or, A Description of the Collection of Pictures at Houghton Hall in Norfolk, the Seat of . . . Sir Robert Walpole;* in vol. ii of *The Works of Horatio Walpole, Earl of Orford,* 5 vols, 1798.

Army Lists . . . [Great Britain, War Office], *A List of the General and Field Officers as they Rank in the Army,* 1740–1841.

Bedford Corr . . John Russell, Duke of Bedford, *Correspondence of John Fourth Duke of Bedford,* ed. Lord John Russell, 1842–6, 3 vols.

BERRY . . . *The Yale Edition of Horace Walpole's Correspondence: The Correspondence with Mary and Agnes Berry,* New Haven, 1944, 2 vols.

Bibl. Nat. Cat. . . *Catalogue générale des livres imprimés de la Bibliothèque nationale,* 1897–.

BM Add. MSS . . Additional Manuscripts, British Museum. Film in Yale University Library.

BM Cat. . . . Catalogue of Printed Books in the British Museum.

BM *Cat. of Engraved*
British Portraits . British Museum, Department of Prints and Drawings. *Catalogue of Engraved British Portraits Preserved in the Department of Prints and Drawings in the British Museum,* by Freeman O' Donoghue, 1908–25.

BM, *Satiric Prints* . British Museum Dept. of Prints and Drawings. *Catalogue of Prints and Drawings in the British Museum. Division 1. Political and Personal Satires,* 1870–1954.

CHATTERTON . . *The Yale Edition of Horace Walpole's Correspondence: The Correspondence with Thomas Chatterton . . . ,* New Haven, 1951.

Cobbett, *Parl. Hist.*   .   *The Parliamentary History of England,* ed. William Cobbett and John Wright, 1806–20, 36 vols.

Coke, *Journals*   .   .   *The Letters and Journals of Lady Mary Coke,* Edinburgh, ed. James A. Home, 1889, 4 vols.

Coke, 'MS Journals'   .   Photostats of unpublished journals (1775–91) of Lady Mary Coke in the possession of Lord Home.

COLE   .   .   .   .   *The Yale Edition of Horace Walpole's Correspondence: The Correspondence with the Rev. William Cole,* New Haven, 1937, 2 vols.

Collins *Peerage,* 1812   .   Arthur Collins, *The Peerage of England,* ed. Sir Samuel Egerton Brydges, 1812, 9 vols.

Country Seats   .   .   Horace Walpole's 'Journals of Visits to Country Seats &c,' in *The Walpole Society 1927–1928,* vol. xvi, 1928.

Cunningham   .   .   *The Letters of Horace Walpole, Earl of Orford,* ed. Peter Cunningham, 1858, 9 vols.

Daily Adv. .   .   .   *The Daily Advertiser,* 1731–95. Film in the Yale University Library from the file in the Library of Congress.

DALRYMPLE.   .   .   *The Yale Edition of Horace Walpole's Correspondence: The Correspondence with Sir David Dalrymple* . . . , New Haven, 1951.

Delany Corr.   .   .   *The Autobiography and Correspondence of Mary Granville, Mrs Delany,* ed. the Right Hon. Lady Llanover, 1861, 3 vols; 2d series, 1862, 3 vols.

Des. of SH, 1774 .   .   Horace Walpole, *A Description of the Villa of Horace Walpole* . . . *at Strawberry Hill* . . . *With an inventory* . . . [Strawberry Hill, Printed by Thomas Kirgate, 1774].

'Des. of SH,' *Works* ii   .   .   .   .   Horace Walpole, 'A Description of the Villa of Mr Horace Walpole at Strawberry Hill near Twickenham,' in vol. ii of *The Works of Horatio Walpole, Earl of Orford,* 1798, 5 vols.

DNB . . . . *Dictionary of National Biography*, ed. Leslie Stephen and Sidney Lee, reissue, 1908–9, 22 vols.

Doran . . . John Doran, *'Mann' and Manners at the Court of Florence, 1740–1786*, 1876, 2 vols.

DU DEFFAND . . . *The Yale Edition of Horace Walpole's Correspondence: The Correspondence with Mme du Deffand*, New Haven, 1939, 6 vols.

Enciclopedia italiana . *Enciclopedia italiana*, ed. Gentile and Tumminelli, Milan and Rome, 1929–39, 36 vols.

Foster, *Alumni Oxon* . Joseph Foster, *Alumni Oxonienses: 1500–1714*, Oxford, 1891–2, 4 vols; *1715–1886*, Oxford, 1887–8, 4 vols.

GEC . . . . George Edward Cokayne, *The Complete Peerage*, revised by Vicary Gibbs *et al.*, 1910–59; *The Complete Baronetage*, Exeter, 1900–9, 6 vols.

Geo. III's *Corr.*, ed Fortescue . . . *The Correspondence of King George the Third from 1760 to December 1783 . . .* ed. Sir John Fortescue, 1927–8, 6 vols.

GM . . . . *The Gentleman's Magazine.*

GRAY . . . . *The Yale Edition of Horace Walpole's Correspondence: The Correspondence with Thomas Gray, Richard West, and Thomas Ashton*, New Haven, 1948, 2 vols.

Harcourt Papers . . *The Harcourt Papers*, ed. Edward William Harcourt, Oxford, [1880?–1905], 14 vols.

Hazen, *Bibl. of HW* . Allen T. Hazen, *A Bibliography of Horace Walpole*, New Haven, 1948.

Hazen, *Cat. of HW's Lib.* . . . Allen T. Hazen, *A Catalogue of Horace Walpole's Library*, New Haven, 1969, 3 vols.

Hazen, *SH Bibl.* . . Allen T. Hazen, *A Bibliography of the Strawberry Hill Press*, New Haven, 1942.

Hist. MSS Comm. . Historical Manuscripts Commission.

Historic Doubts . . Horace Walpole, *Historic Doubts on the Life and Reign of King Richard III*, 1768.

Horn, *Diplomatic Representatives* . .	David B. Horn, *British Diplomatic Representatives 1689–1789*, 1932, Camden Society, 3d ser. xlvi.
HW	Horace Walpole.
Isenburg, *Stammtafeln* .	Wilhelm Karl, Prinz von Isenburg, *Stammtafeln zur Geschichte der europaeischen Staaten*, Berlin, 1936, 2 vols.
Journal of the Printing Office . . .	Horace Walpole, *Journal of the Printing-Office at Strawberry Hill*, ed. Paget Toynbee, 1923.
Journals of the House of Commons . .	[Great Britain, Parliament, House of Commons] *Journals of the House of Commons . . . Reprinted by Order of the House of Commons*, 1803, 51 vols.
Journals of the House of Lords . . .	[Great Britain, Parliament, House of Lords], *Journals of the House of Lords*, [ca 1777]– 1891, 123 vols.
La Chenaye-Desbois .	François-Alexandre Aubert de la Chenaye-Desbois and — Badier, *Dictionnaire de la noblesse*, 3d edn, 1863–76, 19 vols.
Last Journals . .	Horace Walpole, *The Last Journals of Horace Walpole during the Reign of George III from 1771–1783*, ed. A. Francis Steuart, 1910, 2 vols.
Leinster Corr. . .	*Correspondence of Emily, Duchess of Leinster*, ed. Brian Fitzgerald, Dublin, 1949–57, 3 vols.
London Past and Present	Henry B. Wheatley and Peter Cunningham, *London Past and Present*, 1891, 3 vols.
MANN	*The Yale Edition of Horace Walpole's Correspondence: The Correspondence with Sir Horace Mann*, New Haven, 1954–71, 11 vols.
MASON . . .	*The Yale Edition of Horace Walpole's Correspondence: The Correspondence with William Mason*, New Haven, 1955, 2 vols.
Mem. Geo. II . .	Horace Walpole, *Memoirs of the Reign of King George the Second*, 2d edn, ed. Henry R. V. Fox, Lord Holland, 1847, 3 vols.

Mem. Geo. III . .	Horace Walpole, *Memoirs of the Reign of King George the Third,* ed. G. F. Russell Barker, 1894, 4 vols.
MONTAGU. . . .	*The Yale Edition of Horace Walpole's Correspondence: The Correspondence with George Montagu,* New Haven, 1941, 2 vols.
MORE	*The Yale Edition of Horace Walpole's Correspondence: The Correspondence with Hannah More . . . ,* New Haven, 1961.
MS Commonplace Book of Verses . .	Horace Walpole, 'A Common Place Book of Verses, Stories, Characters, Letters, &c. &c. with some Particular Memoirs of a Certain Parcel of People' [1740], MS in the possession of W. S. Lewis.
MS Poems . .	Horace Walpole, 'Poems and Other Pieces by Horace Walpole, Youngest Son of Sir Robert Walpole, Earl of Orford,' MS in the possession of W. S. Lewis.
NBG	*Nouvelle biographie générale,* ed. Jean-Chrétien-Ferdinand Hoefer, 1852–66, 46 vols.
Nichols, *Lit. Anec.* .	John Nichols, *Literary Anecdotes of the Eighteenth Century,* 1812–15, 9 vols.
Nichols, *Lit. Illus.*	John Nichols, *Illustrations of the Literary History of the Eighteenth Century,* 1817–58, 8 vols.
OED	*A New English Dictionary on Historical Principles,* ed. Sir James A. H. Murray *et al.,* Oxford, 1888–1928, 10 vols.
OSSORY . . .	*The Yale Edition of Horace Walpole's Correspondence: The Correspondence with the Countess of Upper Ossory,* New Haven, 1965, 3 vols.
P.C.C. . . .	Prerogative Court of Canterbury.
Scots Peerage . .	*The Scots Peerage,* ed. Sir James Balfour Paul, Edinburgh, 1904–14, 9 vols.
SELWYN . . .	*The Yale Edition of Horace Walpole's Correspondence: The Correspondence with George Selwyn . . . ,* New Haven, 1961, 2 vols.
SH	Strawberry Hill.

SH Accounts . . *Strawberry Hill Accounts,* ed. Paget Toynbee, Oxford, 1927.

sold London . . *A Catalogue of the Collection of Scarce Prints* [also MSS and books] *Removed from Strawberry Hill,* 13–23 June 1842. The number following each entry is the lot number in the sale.

sold SH . . . *A Catalogue of the Classic Contents of Strawberry Hill Collected by Horace Walpole,* 25 April–21 May 1842. The roman and arabic numerals which follow each entry indicate the day and lot number of the sale.

S.P. . . . . State Papers. Film in the Yale University Library from the MSS in the Public Record Office in London. The class numbers are followed by the volume numbers in arabic numerals.

Thieme and Becker . Ulrich Thieme and Felix Becker, *Allgemeines Lexikon der bildenden Künstler von der Antike bis zur Gegenwart,* Leipzig, 1907–50, 37 vols.

Toynbee . . . *The Letters of Horace Walpole, Fourth Earl Orford,* ed. Mrs Paget Toynbee, Oxford, 16 vols, 1903–5; *Supplement,* ed. Paget Toynbee, 3 vols, 1918–25.

Venn, *Alumni Cant.* . *Alumni Cantabrigienses,* Part I to 1751, compiled by John Venn and J. A. Venn, Cambridge, 1922–7, 4 vols; Part II 1752–1900, ed. J. A. Venn, Cambridge, 1940–54, 6 vols.

Vict. Co. Hist. . . *The Victoria History of the Counties of England* [with name of county].

Williams's MSS . . A Collection of Sir Charles Hanbury Williams's manuscripts and correspondence owned by W. S. Lewis. The citations are to volumes and folios or pages.

Works . . . *The Works of Horatio Walpole, Earl of Orford,* 1798, 5 vols.

Wright . . . *The Letters of Horace Walpole, Earl of Orford,* ed. John Wright, 1840, 6 vols.

WSL . . . . W. S. Lewis.

LIST OF LETTERS

The dates of the letters to Walpole are in italics. Missing letters are marked by an asterisk after the date. Letters printed here for the first time are marked by a dagger (†); those printed in full for the first time are marked by a double dagger (‡). Page references to earlier editions are given in the preliminary notes to the letters.

LETTERS BETWEEN WALPOLE AND CHUTE

LETTERS BETWEEN WALPOLE AND BENTLEY

LETTERS BETWEEN WALPOLE AND STRAFFORD

LETTERS BETWEEN WALPOLE AND HAMILTON

LETTERS BETWEEN WALPOLE AND LORD NUNEHAM (LATER 2D EARL HARCOURT), AND THE COUNTESS HARCOURT

LETTERS BETWEEN WALPOLE AND HARDINGE

THE CORRESPONDENCE
WITH JOHN CHUTE

HORACE WALPOLE'S CORRESPONDENCE

From CHUTE,[1] Tuesday 22 August 1741 NS

Printed for the first time from the MS now WSL. It was acquired about 1843 (with Sir Horace Mann's letters to HW) by Richard Bentley, the publisher, from Lord Euston, executor to the 6th Earl Waldegrave. Bentley's grandson, the younger Richard Bentley, sold it to WSL in 1934. The rest of Chute's letters to HW, unless otherwise indicated, come from the same source.

The letter was enclosed by Mann to HW 22 Aug. 1741 NS, under the care of Money, the messenger, who returned to England via Hanover. HW presumably did not receive it until he reached London from Paris 14 Sept. OS (MANN i. 114, 115; GRAY i. 11, n. 69).

Florence, August 22d 1741.

Dear Sir,

THOUGH I am persuaded your anxiety on dear Mr Mann's[2] account is long since happily removed, and, I might thence infer, the reason of your obliging command to me in effect ceased, yet you must pardon me if I insist upon my right of punctual and literal obedience to your orders, which were, to write to you as soon as ever I should arrive at Florence; I did so yesterday, and the messenger[3] who will deliver you this sets out so pat today, that everything seems conspiring to give me the pleasure of chattering a quarter of an hour to you upon paper, and for once I cannot forbear. *Per altro,*[4] don't be frightened at the enormous size of my paper,[5] for you'll observe I write wide, and besides, I shan't fill it.[6]

I flew, no doubt, to dear Mr Mann the first minute I could,[7] and to my inexpressible satisfaction found him as well as you yourself can wish him; he is most undoubtedly in a state of much more strong and

1. John Chute (1701–76), youngest son of Edward Chute of the Vyne, Hants; lived in Italy with his cousin Francis Whithed 1740–6; became acquainted with HW and Gray at Florence in 1740; unexpectedly inherited the family estate in 1754; high sheriff of Hants, 1757; remodelled the Vyne, and made designs for SH and other houses (Warren H. Smith, *Originals Abroad*, New Haven, 1952, pp. 157–76; C. W. Chute, *History of The Vyne*, 1888, p. 113; cf. *Correspondence of Thomas Gray*, ed. Toynbee and Whibley, Oxford, 1935, i. 184, n. 1).

2. Horace (later Sir Horace) Mann (1706–86), British representative in Tuscany 1738–86; cr. (1755) Bt; HW's correspondent. He had been operated upon for an anal fistula in July 1741 (Mann to HW 15 July NS—30 July NS, MANN i. 88–9, 94–5, 97).

3. John Money, King's Messenger ca 1734–59 (MANN i. 108, n. 9).

4. 'However.'

5. The letter is written on a gilt-edged sheet measuring about 15 x 11 inches.

6. He did fill it.

7. Mann gives an account of this reunion in his letter to HW 21 Aug. 1741 NS (MANN i. 112).

perfect health than ever he was since I had the happiness of loving, that is knowing him. Judge of the force of my joy at finding him thus when I tell you I had heard nothing of him from the time you left us,[8] except only the night before we left Venice,[9] above a month ago; Mr Smith[10] informed us that the operation was successfully begun,[11] an information which just made room for every anxious thought, and it was accordingly with trembling that I expected the answer to our message, the instant of our arrival here. We caused[12] an hour or more, chiefly about you, and then we left him to finish a charming volume of letter[13] to you, of which I saw some sheets which he called the beginning only. I have not yet been able to examine Dr Co———[14] (I can't spell his name) about Mr Mann, but he looks so purely, and is in such charming spirits, that I can see no room to doubt of his being perfectly re-established.

My important charge[15] I have delivered in perfect health and beauty. I say beauty, because you cannot imagine how extremely like his Papa he is grown; Mr Mann was quite struck at seeing him; you may depend on his attentions and procuring him all the regards that are due to the honourable house of which he is the estimable first fruits, though a little irregularly produced.

Any account of our travels from Venice hither cannot but be tiresome to you, whose steps we followed the most considerable part of the way;[16] so I shall only tell you I am charmed with the Cerigati house[17] at Vicenza, and the paintings of the Palazzo del Thé[18] at

8. HW left Chute and Whithed at Venice 12 July 1741 NS ('Short Notes,' GRAY i. 10 and n. 65; Mann to HW 23 July 1741 NS, MANN i. 94).

9. The exact date of their departure has not been found. Chute was acting as travelling-companion to his young cousin and close friend Francis Whithed (1719–51), of Southwick Park, Hants; M.P. Southampton 1747–51 (see GRAY ii. 18, n. 31).

10. Joseph Smith (ca 1675–1770), British consul at Venice 1744–60; collector (J. F. Revel, 'Le Consul Smith,' L'Œil, Nov. 1963, No. 107, p. 64).

11. On 11 July (Mann to HW 15 July NS, MANN i. 88).

12. Chatted (OED sub 'cause' v. 2).

13. Mann to HW 21 Aug. NS, MANN i. 106–12.

14. Antonio Cocchi (1695–1758), Mann's

physician, who had attended HW during his illness at Reggio in May 1741 (GRAY i. 10, n. 62, 231, n. 9; Mann and Cocchi to HW 18 July NS, MANN i. 89–90).

15. A puppy sired by HW's Patapan (Mann to HW 21 Aug. NS, MANN i. 112).

16. From Venice to Mantua, Chute and Whithed were following the same route HW had taken on his way from Venice to Genoa (whence he sailed to Antibes on his way to Paris), and beyond Bologna their route coincided with that of HW and Gray when they first approached Florence in 1739.

17. I.e., the Palazzo Chiericati, built by Palladio, now the Museo Civico.

18. The Palazzo del Te, a summer residence of the Gonzagas, outside the town of Mantua; decorated by Giulio Romano and others (Selwyn Brinton, The Gonzaga: Lords of Mantua, 1927, pp. 151–6). Illus-

Mantova, but more still with a thing which perhaps you did not see, which is a room, forsaken and neglected, in the Ducal Palace[19] in the town of Mantova; 'tis called Sala di Troia, all painted by Giulio Romano[20] with the most affecting circumstances of the Trojan War, and far beyond anything I have yet seen. If you missed it, you must absolutely come abroad again on purpose, and that soon, for 'tis unfortunately running to ruin very fast.[21] We revisited everything with vast pleasure at Bologna, and amongst the rest your Pallionino,[22] which is extremely prettily done, and which I should have brought with me, if I could have found safe conveyance about our chaise for it; I have notified its being finished to Mr Mann, and it will soon be disposed of according to your directions.

I never saw anything so charming as the Corregio Madonna with St Jerome at Parma;[23] will Sir Robert never buy it?[24]

Cechino[25] is just come in to invite us to a pretty entertainment of music[26] at their villa. He makes a thousand obliging inquiries after you, and gives as many services to you.

Have not you been almost killed with the heats? I own I think you have chosen an improper time to drink so many bumpers to old England. If my Lord Lincoln[27] be with you still, you will oblige me if you present him my respects; and this leads me to tell you the

trations of the building and paintings are in Frederick Hartt, *Giulio Romano*, New Haven, 1958, ii. figs 149–354.

19. The Palazzo Ducale also called the Reggio, or Corte Regio-Ducale (Brinton, op. cit. 147; Hartt, op. cit. ii. figs 355–414).

20. Giulio Pippi (ca 1492–1546), called Giulio Romano; pupil of Raphael; executed many paintings at Mantua for Duke Federigo Gonzaga.

21. The portion of the Palace that contains the Sala di Troia was severely damaged in the sack of Mantua by the Germans in 1630, and was virtually abandoned; the paintings in the Sala di Troia suffered less than the others in this part, and are still well preserved (Brinton, op. cit. 149–50, 229; reproductions are in Hartt, loc. cit., and in G. and A. Pacchioni, *Mantova*, Bergamo, 1930, p. 83).

22. The copy made for HW, by Donato Creti, of Guido Reni's 'Pallione del voto,' a painting on silk at Bologna. HW finally received it in 1743 (Mann to HW 9 May

1741 NS, 14 Aug. 1743 OS, MANN i. 41 and n. 41, ii. 292).

23. In the convent of the sisters of Sant' Antonio (MANN i. 167, n. 28).

24. On HW's recommendation Sir Robert made an offer of £1000 for the painting in 1743, but it was not accepted. It is now in the gallery at Parma (HW to Mann 8 Oct. 1741 and 30 Nov. 1743 OS, MANN i. 167 and n. 31, ii. 351).

25. Cavaliere Francesco Suares de la Concha (1720–77), called 'Cecco' or 'Cecchino'; he had travelled with HW to Venice from Florence (Mann to HW 9 May 1741 NS, MANN i. 39, n. 25).

26. Metastasio's *Demetrio* (ibid. i. 65, 99).

27. Henry Fiennes Clinton (after 1768, Pelham Clinton) (1720–94), 9th E. of Lincoln, 1730; 2d D. of Newcastle-under-Lyne, 1768. HW had gone to Paris from Venice in company with Lincoln and Joseph Spence ('Short Notes,' GRAY i. 10–11).

gallantest thing of our friend Rosa Alba[28] imaginable, who has taken so charming a likeness upon the strength of one transient view she had, of a certain beauty[29] of our acquaintance, in the form of a Juno, to accompany the Diana[30] my Lord bought of her, as I fear will give him a pleasure he may live to repent of—but what am I talking of? For God sake burn my letter.

'Tis full time to remember my promise not to be too long, but I can't release you without a thousand good wishes for your constant happiness and perfect satisfaction in all your schemes, and entreating you to believe me,

Dear Sir, with the sincerest regard, your most obliged,

affectionate, humble servant,

JOHN CHUTE

Mr Whithed's respects attend you.

Did you give me any heads of canes at Venice for Cechino? If you did, I have lost them.[31] Tell dear Patapan I'll kiss him an hour the first time I see him.

To CHUTE, September 1741

Missing; mentioned in HW's letter to Mann ca 5 Oct. 1741 OS (MANN i. 163–4). Written from Paris.

28. Rosalba Carriera (1675–1757), Venetian pastel painter and miniaturist who did a pastel and a sketch of HW at Venice. See C. K. Adams and W. S. Lewis, 'The Portraits of Horace Walpole,' *Walpole Society 1968–1970*, 1970, xlii. 9–10. She also did a sketch of Chute (F. J. B. Watson, 'Two Venetian Portraits,' *Burlington Magazine*, 1969, cxi. 336–7). See illustration.

29. Lady Sophia Fermor (HW). Lady Sophia Fermor (1721–45), m. (1744) John Carteret, E. Granville; lived at Florence with her mother, Lady Pomfret, Dec. 1739–March 1741 (MANN i. 4, nn. 18, 23). For Lincoln's unsuccessful courtship of her, see HW's correspondence with him, printed in SELWYN, esp. pp. 23–4, and

HW to Mann 19 July 1741 (MANN i. 91) and subsequent letters in that correspondence.

30. HW owned a copy of the Juno, which was sold SH xxi. 86 to Lord Lansdowne for 13 gns. Diana was a favourite subject of Rosalba's: in the Dresden Gallery there are eight pastels by her of Diana and a miniature of 'a lady as Diana' (Karl Woermann, *Catalogue of the Royal Picture Gallery in Dresden*, trans. B. S. Ward, Dresden, 1905, pp. 289–94, 298); a 'sketch from the story of Diana and Calisto by Rosalba' was sold SH xxi. 3.

31. These missing heads of canes are also discussed in Mann to HW 27 Aug. 1741 NS (MANN i. 117).

JOHN CHUTE BY ROSALBA CARRIERA

From Chute, ca Sunday 1 October 1741 NS

Printed in full for the first time from MS now WSL; the sixth paragraph is printed in Doran i. 29.
Enclosed in Mann's letter to HW 1 Oct. 1741 NS (Mann i. 153).
Address: To the Honourable Horatio Walpole, Esq., These.
Memoranda by HW (in ink): Cori.

Lady P. not set out. Tr[unks.][1]

Dear Sir,

YOU have been so good to me that undoubtedly I ought to spare you this month at least, but perversely, for that very reason I cannot forbear troubling you. I never had a great opinion of the philosopher's stone, and have all my life been very free in ridiculing the notion that a dirty lump of lead could ever assume the enchanting glitter and colour of fresh minted guineas, but since you have obligingly demonstrated that a letter of mine can produce me one of yours, *procul ite profani,*[2] I declare myself from this time forward an adept, and am resolved to make a venture of my whole stock.

Dear Mr Mann (he'll see my letter, but I will call him so, for all that) is so good as to impart your charming letters as you obligingly permitted him, to my great happiness, but yet I can't be contented without now and then a letter of my own to keep.

I shall write you no news for sundry excellent reasons, whereof, for brevity sake, I shall only mention six: *imprimis,* there is no news, secondly, if there were any, 'twould be bad news, thirdly, I have heard no news, fourthly, if I had heard any, I should not have believed it, fifthly, you would hear it another way, and sixthly, before it came to you, you would be able to contradict it. Tittle-tattle affairs you must not expect from me, for as yet a while I can neither tittle nor tattle myself in any language that's in use at this place; my only means of information, hitherto, is but a sort of eavesdropping, and I

1. Probably notes for HW to Mann 13 Oct. 1741 OS (q.v.), of which HW says that 'the greater part . . . is wanting' (Mann i. 169). 'Cori' is probably Angelo Maria Cori, prompter to the opera, whom HW had perhaps taken as an Italian master about this time (HW to Mann 13 Oct. 1741 OS, 24 Dec. 1741 OS, Mann i. 170, n. 7, 254, n. 32). 'Lady P.' is the Hon. Henrietta Louisa Jeffreys (ca 1700–

61), m. (1720) Thomas Fermor, cr. (1721) E. of Pomfret (GEC vii. 84,n.e). She and her children had returned to England from Italy shortly before 13 Oct., when HW wrote to Mann (Mann i. 170) that 'their trunks are not arrived yet, so they have not made their appearance' in society.

2. 'Begone, ye profane!' (paraphrased from Virgil, *Æneid* vi. 258).

think it can never be worth while to inform you of what I overhear.

I have had the honour of being introduced to the charming Grifone,[3] who is all that ever you can say of her; when she asks me how you do, may I say, at her service? If you commission me, you'll do me great honour, and at the same time please to take notice that whenever she sees me you will be as naturally derived in her imagination as *lucus a non lucendo,*[4] which I think is approved.

Mr Mann goes on purely, except now and then a little headache, which he won't own proceeds from drinking and late setting up with me. I threatened him I would tell you if he took too much of me; you'll mark my generosity, by the way, who am as much interested in his increasing the dose as if I were his apothecary.

The poor Prince's distemper[5] being of a nature to be carried always at his finger's ends, and so not admitting of inquiries much. I who you know am half blind must be ill qualified to give an account of its progress, but I think he does not ferret so much as he did. His Princess,[6] I believe, enjoys perfect health; a circumstance always supposed conducing to which she took care to mark strongly the other night to her whole assembly, by addressing herself to us all, as she sailed in all her floating majesty from the farther end of the gallery to the door of one of her more private apartments, in these terms: *Je ne demande permission à personne;* you know how to accent it, and explain it advantageously, as I did, to the state of her constitution.

I am deeply engaged every morning in the study of medals, and please myself much with the prospect of being able to tumble over your collection[7] judiciously at my return to England, but perhaps

3. Elisabetta Capponi (1714–80), m. (1732) Cavaliere Pietro Grifoni (MANN i. 33, n. 7). She had been HW's *cicisbea* at Florence, and on his departure she presented him with a dog (Patapan) and her portrait, which later hung in his bedchamber at SH. See also HW to Lincoln 31 Jan., 18 and 29 April 1741 NS (SELWYN 12, 14, 16).

4. A phrase used as a generic term for paradoxical or absurd derivations, *non sequiturs* and the like, founded in the derivation of the Latin *lucus* (sacred grove) from the verb *luceo* (to shine), ridiculed by Quintilian; see the discus-

sion in W. F. H. King, *Classical and Foreign Quotations,* 3d edn, 1904, p. 186.

5. Marc-Antoine de Beauvau (1679–1754), Prince de Craon; President of the Council of Regency to the Grand Duke of Tuscany 1737–49 (MANN i. 9, n. 27). His 'distemper' was the itch (Mann to HW 23 July 1741 NS, MANN i. 95, *et passim*).

6. Anne-Marguerite de Ligniville (1686–1772), m. (1704) Marc-Antoine de Beauvau, Prince de Craon (MANN i. 3, n. 8).

7. Chute had doubtless seen some of HW's medals at Florence, but HW apparently had sent others to England that Chute had not seen.

France will run away with them, and England, too, before that time; for *Le Roy le veut* seems of as much weight all over Europe as ever it was under the tottering roof of Versailles; if the poor dear Queen of Hungary[8] be half as much afraid as she seems to have reason to be, *Eau-de-la-Reine*[9] must be quite a drug. I am beginning to talk nonsense, and so 'twould not be improper to think of finishing, which I cannot do without presenting my respects to his little dear Highness,[10] and imparting a passage that imports him something; in the last letter I received from Geofry,[11] who, finding himself a good deal advanced, and having unhappily survived all his children, as well as all hopes of making more, proposes adopting him and settling his fortune upon him, with this only other condition, that he conform himself to the Church of England, as by law established; the former of these conditions I have persuaded him could not with any propriety be complied with by a person of his high birth, and am well assured he will change it into his honouring him with adding his name to the list of his many honourable appellations, which on consideration that it has been borne by the illustrious Plantagenets and Godfrey of Boulogne I have told him may possibly be accepted of; the latter seems to me a bagatelle, but you will favour me with his thoughts upon that head soon. It may seem a little presuming in Geofry (who is only of an obscure good family, and, having passed his whole life in retirement, has never attained any other honour or dignity than that of a Justice of Peace, which has been, as it were, hereditary for some ages to his house) to pretend to take this notice of a Prince, a foreigner that he has not so much as been introduced to; but an estate's a good thing, and I fancy you'll agree with me that the old fellow's offer is not to be slighted. One circumstance I should mention—that his decayed state of health is attributed by all his neighbours to his strenuous endeavours in a county election, and repeated bumpers to Sir R.'s[12] health; if Patapan loves you, as I

8. Maria Theresa (1717–80), m. (1736) Francis of Lorraine, Grand Duke of Tuscany 1737–65, Holy Roman Emperor (as Francis I) 1745–65; Queen of Hungary 1740–80; 'Empress-Queen.' In the War of the Austrian Succession, which had broken out in 1740, Maria Theresa's forces, with the support of England, were opposed to those of France, Spain, Prussia, Bavaria, and Saxony. She appeared on the verge of total defeat at this time; see Mann to HW 24 Sept. 1741 NS (MANN i. 143–4).

9. Eau de la Reine de Hongrie, or Hungary-water, a distillate of rosemary flowers in spirits of wine, used for medicinal purposes (Émile Littré, *Dictionnaire de la langue française*, 1863–77, *sub* 'eau' 21; OED *sub* 'Hungary').

10. Patapan (HW).

11. Mr Chute's cat (HW).

12. Sir Robert Walpole.

cannot doubt, that will have some weight with him. Methinks I hear you cry, *Scriptus et in tergo nec dum finitus,*[13] but pardon me, you mistake, for I am,

Dear Sir, your most obliged, faithful, humble servant,

JOHN CHUTE

Mr Whithed's respects attend you.

To CHUTE, ca Tuesday 13 October 1741 OS

Missing; mentioned in Mann's letter to HW 11 Nov. 1741 NS (MANN i. 181).

From CHUTE, ca Wednesday 15 November 1741 NS

Printed for the first time from MS now WSL.

Dated by Mann's remark in his letter to HW 11 Nov. 1741 NS that Chute 'will answer this post' (MANN i. 181). Mann's letter was not sent till after the 12th (ibid. i. 183).

Address: To the Honourable Horatio Walpole, Esq., These.

Dear Sir,

YOU'RE so good to me, I don't know what in the world to do for you; your charming letter revived my spirits and made me forget the Spaniards were coming[1] all Friday evening; Lord what will become of us? Can you tell? How charming we are, you say, to stay at Florence! You envy us, alas! we are no longer charming;[2] we must not stay at Florence; don't you pity us? Where shall we betake ourselves in our exile? *nous aimons assez les Lucquois,*[3] but they are such terrible politicians, and will tease one so, with neutralities,[4] and

---

13. 'It is written on the back and not yet finished' (Juvenal, *Satires* I. i. 6).

———

1. Spanish and French ships had landed Spanish troops at Orbetello, in southern Tuscany (Mann to HW 11 and 19 Nov. 1741 NS, MANN i. 178, 192).

2. The English at Florence were being regarded with suspicion, because it was mistakenly believed that England approved of the expected Spanish invasion

(Mann to HW 19 Nov. 1741 NS, MANN i. 192 and n. 1).

3. Lucca was considered a safe place of refuge for foreigners in Florence (Mann to HW 11 Nov. 1741 NS, 25 Feb. 1744 NS, MANN i. 178, ii. 398).

4. I.e., George II's agreement with France for the neutrality of Hanover, contradicting England's Austrian alliance (Mann to HW 17 Sept. 1741 NS MANN i. 133 and n. 10).

Admiral Haddocks;[5] I verily believe in my conscience, all is as it should be, but I protest I don't know how; I have but one determination, which, I fancy, you will approve, and that is to stick close to our dear *Ministro,* and in case the King's Arms[6] should grow as unpopular here as Admiral Vernon's Head at Rochester,[7] make our retreat together to regions more worthy of us; but come, I hope 'twill all be better than we fear; perhaps the Spaniards are not coming hither, and then, if they are, the Queen of Spain[8] is not with them, and I don't see why Don Phillip[9] should eat Mr Mann or us any more than his brother[10] did you at Naples,[11] and I think you told me he did but gape at you; at all rates, we won't part with Mr Mann; you see I know how to profit by your pretty epigram,[12] and understand the consequence[13] of keeping good company as well as Dr Hulse[14] or Mr Cheselden.[15]

I have not had the honour of seeing the charming Gryphon[16] since I received yours, but am going presently to our wretched burletta,[17] where I hope to have the pleasure of attending her, with your compliments; if her future sovereign[18] thinks her as handsome as I do, he will be very happy, or very much otherwise, I don't know which.

5. Nicholas Haddock (1686–1746), Vice-Adm., 1741; Adm., 1744; in command of the British fleet in the Mediterranean. He was being blamed for having failed to prevent the descent of the combined Spanish and French squadrons upon Orbetello (H. W. Richmond, *The Navy in the War of 1739–48,* Cambridge, 1920, i. 164–7; Mann to HW 11 and 19 Nov. 1741 NS, MANN i. 180 and n. 13, 194 and n. 20).

6. Mann's house, the Palazzo Manetti, which had the King's arms over the door (MANN i. 27 and n. 2).

7. Edward Vernon (1684–1757), Vice-Adm., 1739; Adm., 1745. After his victory over the Spaniards at Porto Bello in Nov. 1739, his head became a favourite sign for public houses. HW had apparently written Chute a description of some otherwise unknown riots at Rochester in which, he told Lincoln 13 Oct. 1741 OS, 'the sailors of a ship just returned from Vernon, have pulled down all the signs in the town that bore his head' (SELWYN 29).

8. Elizabeth Farnese of Parma (1692–1766), m. (1714) Philip V of Spain.

9. Don Philip (1720–65), Duke of Parma 1749–65, third surviving son of Philip V.

10. Charles (1716–88), K. of Naples 1735–59; K. of Spain (as Charles III) 1759–88.

11. HW had visited Naples in June 1740 (MANN i. 26, n. 1).

12. Verses on Hulse and Cheselden by Dr James Monro, sent to Mann by HW 8 Oct. 1741 OS (MANN i. 168). HW also sent them to Lincoln 13 Oct. OS (SELWYN 30).

13. Written over 'value.'

14. Sir Edward Hulse (1682–1759), M.D.; cr. (1739) Bt; physician to George II.

15. William Cheselden (1688–1752), surgeon and anatomist.

16. Mme Grifoni.

17. Mann calls it the 'worst entertainment' he ever saw, and adds that 'the performers are beginners' (Mann to HW 10 Sept. 1741 NS, MANN i. 128).

18. Apparently Mme Grifoni had no cicisbeo at this time, although by 2 Dec. 1741 Ottavio Mannelli was 'languishing' for her (Mann to HW 2 Dec. NS, MANN i. 202; see also HW to Mann 15 Sept. 1746 OS, MANN iii. 308 and n. 7).

My best compliments to the little dear Knight of the Silver Fleece,[19] and assure him that the stipulations relating to the Malthese cat for me,[20] in no manner whatsoever affect his rights to the full and entire succession of the House of Geoffry.

Mr Whithed is infinitely obliged for your remembrance of him, and means more than I can express in return.

Don't be in any concern for the consequences of our debauches with *our poor Mr Mann*, we have lived three weeks with him, and have been so regular that you can't imagine how fat he grows. He has quite a little plump, round, tight belly, which in his case I think is no bad consequence of a debauch, if we had been guilty of any with him.

Thank you for your good news (is it not good news?) about Cuba;[21] confirm and improve it in your next; and contradict our nasty Berne Gazette,[22] which multiplies the blind in the approaching Parliament.[23]

How charming it would be if Mr Mann can succeed in procuring St Antonio Abbate[24] (I must run over)[25] and Zambecari[26] for Sir R.! I'd give the tip of my little finger to see them arrived safe hither on the way; in the meantime, I wish you joy of the sweet Guido head[27] you are secure of, which I see and kiss through its veil every day; you'll be vastly happy at the unpacking it, which I am vastly glad of,

19. Patapan (HW).

20. Chute had asked for a kitten from a Maltese cat that Mann was to send HW (Mann to HW 11 Nov. 1741 NS, MANN i. 181–2).

21. *Daily Adv.* 8 Oct. 1741 carried the news of Admiral Vernon's capture of Guantánamo in Cuba, and also a false report that General Wentworth's troops were marching on Santiago. See also HW to Lincoln 13 Oct. 1741 OS (SELWYN 29) for further details.

22. The *Gazette de Berne* (1689–1798), a highly undependable source of news (see Mann to HW 15 May 1742 and 15 or 22 April 1743 NS, MANN i. 417 and n. 27, ii. 206).

23. Following the general election in the spring of 1741, Parliament was summoned to meet 25 June, but was four times prorogued and finally met 1 Dec. (*Journals of the House of Commons* xxiv. 3–7; HW to Mann 3 Dec. OS, MANN i.

219 and n. 4). The *Gazette de Berne* had apparently printed estimates of the probable size of the opposition to Sir Robert Walpole.

24. I.e., the Correggio mentioned *ante* 22 Aug. 1741 NS. HW had asked Mann in his letter of 8 Oct. to try to obtain the picture for Sir Robert Walpole (MANN i. 167).

25. Chute here filled the sheet, and completed the letter on a half-sheet.

26. A supposed Domenichino (now attributed to Sassoferrato) of the Virgin and Child, in the Zambeccari palace at Bologna. It finally came to Houghton in 1743 (HW to Mann 8 Oct. 1741 and 14 Aug. 1743 OS, MANN i. 167 and n. 24, ii. 291).

27. A head of Niobe, which also reached England in 1743 (Mann to HW 17 Sept. 1741 and 30 April 1743 NS, MANN i. 138 and n. 54, ii. 214).

for I am without compliment most sincerely, your obliged, humble servant,

J. C.

To CHUTE, Wednesday 25 November 1741 OS

Missing; mentioned in HW's letter to Mann 26 Nov. 1741 OS (MANN i. 212), but apparently written on the 25th (see below, n. 9).

From CHUTE, Monday 25 December 1741 NS

Printed for the first time from MS now WSL.
Sent with Chute's next letter, *post* 1 Jan. 1742 NS, under a single seal.

Florence, December 25th 1741.

Today we should pray.

Dear Sir,

NOTHING less than the satisfaction of being employed, in some sort, in your service,[1] could comfort me for being made wait near three whole days for the pleasure which your experienced goodness made me depend upon for Friday last,[2] and which our journey to Bologna deprived me of till last night; I know you will believe me sincere when I tell you I revisited the charming Domenichino with more than double pleasure, when I considered it as going so soon to give you frequent and sensible satisfaction; but I say no more of that affair because I know Mr Mann has informed you[3] of the result of my negotiation. From the same good author[4] you know all that I could possibly tell you in relation to the Spanish expedition, except this, that I am as anxious on his account, as a thousand friendships I owe him, without one of which I should

1. Chute and Whithed had visited Bologna in the hope of arranging the purchase of the Zambeccari 'Domenichino' (Mann to HW 19 Dec. NS, MANN i. 227–8).

2. When, apparently, the post from England was expected.

3. In a letter to HW 24 Dec. NS (MANN i. 241); he explained that the purchase price had not been settled.

4. In Mann's letters of 17 and 19 Dec. NS (MANN i. 222–3, 226, 228–9).

have loved him, make it fit, as well as unavoidable, I should be. Can one flatter oneself that Tuscany with Florence in it can ever be despised? If so, it may escape; most surely it has no other dependence, except the protection of the Madonna of the Imprunetta,[5] and the inviolable faith of its most honourable guarantee.[6] Sometimes I try to hope that in all events Don Phillip might stand in the light of the King of Naples,[7] and that we should not be indispensably obliged to be uncivil to him, and then you know what I should hope might follow, but alas! I doubt punctilios, which I never understood nor loved, are quite against me, so that all my poor schemes fail me, and I am reduced to take up the parable of Ruth, as you most aptly as well as religiously observe,[8] with only this exception, that the Hebrew lady's zeal was as much inferior to mine and my companion's, as the merit of our dear friend is undoubtedly superior to that of the best mother-in-law that ever lived. By the way, I observe with comfort, that though the date of your letter[9] insinuates that you cried not unto the Lord according to the will of the ruler, yet have you not despised his Word? Search the Scriptures; you may one day find you know not what; this I will affirm, that many holy, yea, many learned men have looked therein, and have not had grace to apply them so well. Lord, what nonsense I am talking! I'll look in your letter and correct my style.

Is it not fair if the women pass over the defects below Monticelli's girdle,[10] that the men should pardon those above the Viscontina's?[11] I am delighted with Heidegger's[12] being past the bloom of his ugliness.

5. A miraculous image revered by the Florentines (SELWYN 3, n. 4).

6. France had guaranteed the security of Tuscany (MANN i. 197, n. 3, 230, n. 2).

7. Who was Don Philip's older brother.

8. In HW to Mann 23 Nov. OS, MANN i. 209.

9. Presumably 25 Nov., which had been appointed by proclamation on 22 Oct. OS as a day of general fast 'to invoke God's blessing on our arms' (*Handlist of Proclamations . . . 1714–1910* [Vol. VIII of the *Bibliotheca Lindesiana*], Wigan, 1913, p. 53). In the absence of HW's letter, many of the allusions in Chute's reply are not wholly clear.

10. Angelo Maria Monticelli (ca 1710–64), male soprano at the London opera

1741–6 (Sir George Grove, *Dictionary of Music and Musicians*, 5th edn, ed. Blom, 1954, v. 859). His popularity with women is mentioned by Mann 7 July 1742 OS, 22 July 1744 OS, MANN i. 487, ii. 481.

11. Caterina Visconti, called 'Viscontina' singer at the London opera; described by Chesterfield as being very fat (Mann to HW 24 June 1741 NS, HW to Mann 12 Nov. 1741 OS, MANN i. 72 and n. 21, 197).

12. John James Heidegger (ca 1659–1749), manager of the opera in London after 1720. His ugliness is mentioned by Pope and Fielding and shown in prints by Hogarth and others (G. F. Russell Barker in DNB).

My dear Sir, I do wish myself, even this very minute, more than a little in England, though not for my Lord Oxford's collection;[13] the sale of which will do me as little good, I am persuaded, as that of his father's[14] collection of Lords would do, if they were put up again.[15] There is this difference, that as I then escaped ruin, I should now be in no danger, and I think you much safer, too, under your own no government,[16] than anybody's else; so buy fine things without fear, and show them me when I come.

We have no confirmation of your Francfort news.[17] I wish we had.

Don't let the Spaniards revenge our keeping out the galleons upon me; in the worst of times I can keep such a lookout, as will secure the prizes you bestow upon me[18] from falling into their hands, and you may depend upon my strictest caution; consider how could I bear to think of a poor, dear letter of yours, with its little ears cropped off! I have not quite that tenderness for Mr P—s,[19] nor have I, God knows, the universal genius of the bright people you mention, but I have an universal curiosity, and, above all, an universal esteem for everything that comes from you. And now I am, dear Sir, for want of time and room, and everything but will to chatter on and entertain you forever,

Your most obliged, faithful, humble servant,

J. CHUTE

Mr Whithed's respects are too big, but must be crowded in this little space.

13. Edward Harley (1689–1741), 2d E. of Oxford, 1724. The sale of his coins (many of which HW bought), portraits, and curiosities was held 8–13 March 1742 (HW to Mann 3 and 22 March OS, MANN i. 357 and n. 35, 373–4).

14. Robert Harley (1661–1724), cr. (1711) E. of Oxford; statesman and collector; prime minister 1711–14.

15. An allusion to Queen Anne's simultaneous creation of twelve peers on 1 Jan. 1712, a political manœuvre of Oxford's (O. B. Miller, *Robert Harley, Earl of Oxford*, Oxford, 1925, p. 36), probably in connection with some remark in HW's missing letter about his father's secure majority in the House of Lords for the forthcoming Parliament.

16. A characteristic phrase of HW's, probably echoed from the missing letter.

17. HW had perhaps mentioned unsubstantiated reports received in London on 25 Nov. by 'private letters' from Holland 'that an express was arrived at The Hague from Germany, importing that there had been a battle between the Bavarians and Austrians, wherein the latter had entirely defeated the former' (*Daily Adv.* 26 Nov. 1741 OS). The same paper also carried a paragraph dated from Frankfurt 26 Nov. NS, describing the opening on 20 Nov. of the conference to elect a new Emperor.

18. HW's letters.

19. Probably an allusion to some comment by HW about William Pulteney (1684–1764), cr. (1742) E. of Bath (leader of the opposition to Sir Robert Walpole), and also the young men in his train, especially Pitt and the Grenvilles.

From CHUTE, Monday 1 January 1742 NS

Printed for the first time from MS now WSL.
Sent with the preceding letter.
Address: To the Honourable Horatio Walpole, Esq., Junior, at the Right Honourable Sir Robert Walpole's house in Downing Street, Westminster. Per L'Inghilterra.

January 1, 1741 [1742].

Dear Sir, once more,

THE enclosed was written a week ago, but unfortunately too late for the post, and as we have lost our dear Mr Mann, who is posted to Leghorne,[1] upon the arrival of a courier[2] from England, I am doubtful whether it may find its way to you, as I am unacquainted with the proper direction,[3] and am forced to trust it alone in the wide world.

There has happened nothing new since last week, except our two operas,[4] which are hardly worth mentioning; how happy should we be if we had the Viscontina, instead of our wretched broken-bellied Bernachi,[5] whose voice is exactly like that of an old lady's old lap-dog, who has caught an asthma of his mistress.

Betange[6] dans le fond was discoursing Doctor Cocchi about the wisdom of the present government of Tuscany, and instanced the poor Prince Craon. 'He is a good man, but I think I have known wiser,' says Cocchi. *Vous avez raison, mais puis il y a la Princesse, qui est fort sage.* I wish you endless happy years, and am with the sincerest regard,

Dear Sir, yours most faithfully.

We expect Mr Mann tomorrow or next day;[7] you can't—yes, *you* can think how we miss him.

1. Where he arrived 30 Dec. (Mann to HW 10 Jan. NS, MANN i. 258 and n. 1).
2. Richard William Haite (ibid. n. 3).
3. The letter is correctly addressed.
4. At the Teatro della Pergola, which opened ca 27 Dec. (Mann to HW 24 Dec. 1741 NS, MANN i. 239 and n. 25).
5. Antonio Bernacchi (1685–1756), singer, teacher, and composer; in 1739 'esteemed the best singer in Italy,' but 'his singing was always much more admired by musicians than by the public' (Sir George Grove, *Dictionary of Music and Musicians*, 3d edn, 1927–8).
6. A Lorrainer, one of the councillors of the finances of Tuscany; not further identified (Mann to HW 21 Jan. 1742 NS, MANN i. 282 and n. 17).
7. He did not return to Florence until ca 15 Jan. (Mann to HW 16 Jan. NS, MANN i. 264).

How terrible it is that we must wait another whole week for the King's speech![8] The choice of the Speaker, who the messenger informs us is Mr Onslow,[9] is a circumstance of good omen.

I open my letter to tell you that I have just had a letter from our agent[10] at Bologna, who tells me that he has the opinions of several persons of approved judgment and integrity at Bologna, amongst whom is Donato Creti,[11] who all declare the picture is not of Dominichino, though without doubt a very good picture, but as the price he had agreed for (upon condition that Monsignor Zambecari[12] produced a satisfactory *fede*[13] of the hand and the originality) is three hundred pistoles, that is, two hundred and twenty-five pounds English, I have determined to write by the first opportunity to suspend all farther proceedings till we can have your determination about it. There is no doubt that it is the picture you saw and liked when we were at Bologna together, but as there is such vehement suspicion of its not being Dominichino's, I could not but think it proper to refer the conclusion of the bargain to your farther deliberations upon it. Enclosed is the letter[14] of Mr Pennee, an English painter whom Mr Mann employed about the purchase. I hope I ha'n't done wrong in suspending the affair; Mr Mann is not yet returned from Leghorn, nor can possibly be informed time enough to write to you about it this week. I will endeavour to manage so as to have the purchase in our power, in case you should determine to have the picture.

I had given Mr Pennee's letter to Palumbo[15] to send to Mr Mann, and cannot now find him to get it again, but the material part of it I have acquainted you with, which certainly makes it very doubtful whether it be of the hand we imagined.

8. The speech from the throne at the opening of Parliament, delivered 4 Dec. OS (*Journals of the House of Lords* xxvi. 7).

9. Arthur Onslow (1691–1768), Speaker of the House of Commons 1728–61. This was the third of his five successive elections as Speaker.

10. Edward Penny (1714–91), painter (Thieme and Becker; Mann to HW 17 and 19 Dec. 1741 NS, MANN i. 226, 227).

11. Donato Creti (1671–1749), painter (Thieme and Becker); he had copied

Guido's 'Pallione' for HW (*ante* 22 Aug. 1741 NS, n. 22; Mann to HW 15 Oct. 1741 NS, MANN i. 162).

12. Monsignore Francesco Zambeccari, a Bolognese collector (Mann to HW 19 Dec. 1741 NS, MANN i. 227 and n. 2); not further identified.

13. Assurance or testimonial.

14. He did not enclose it; see next paragraph.

15. Domenico Palombo, Mann's secretary (Mann to HW 9 May 1741 NS, MANN i. 38 and n. 20).

TO CHUTE, Tuesday 29 December 1741 OS

Printed as part of HW's letter to Mann 29 Dec. 1741 OS, in MANN i. 257.

TO CHUTE, ca Thursday 14 January 1742 OS

Missing; mentioned by Mann to HW 18 Feb. 1742 NS (MANN i. 325) as well as in Chute's reply, 13 Feb. NS. Since HW told Mann, 7 Jan., that he did not write to Chute by that post, it seems likely that he waited until the following Thursday (the 14th), his usual day for writing to Florence (MANN i. 280, 294).

From CHUTE, Tuesday 13 February 1742 NS

Printed for the first time from MS now WSL.

This is the only extant letter from Chute in which the cipher adopted by HW and Mann is used (see MANN i. 115 and 124, n. 1). The expansions here bracketed were noted by HW in the MS.

Address: To the Honourable Horatio Walpole, Esq., Junior.

Florence, Feb. 13th 1742.

Dear Sir,

I AM so vexed about the Domenichino that I cannot begin to you on any other subject; the last page of my last was scratched in such a hurry, for fear of being too late for the post, that I find I did not explain fully to you the state of the case. The connoisseurs consulted by Mr Pennee (of which Donato Creti is one, and another, Ercole Leli,[1] an *intendente*[2] of the first class, etc.) all agree in the opinion that the picture is a copy from Domin[ichino], though a very excellent one they admit it to be, and I hear of nobody that pretends to say where the original is, or ever was to be found. I own the pleasing cloud of my ignorance was so thick as to indulge me with as delightful a degree of admiration of this charming impostor, the

1. Ercole Lelli (1702–66), Bolognese anatomist, painter, and sculptor (NBG; *Enciclopedia italiana*).

2. Connoisseur.

third visit I made it, as either of the former, and till the disgusting
term, copy, saluted my ears, I should, without hesitation, have determined exactly as you do in your last letter, but as the matter stands,
I'm sure of nothing but that it fits not me to decide the contest; there
are gods against us, that's certain; nevertheless, when I remember (as
I do, because I was vastly happy) the approbation and delight with
which I saw you behold it, I must confess I have an impious mind
which inclines me to my own little Cato's[3] side. I should inform you
that the possessor Monsignor Zambecari (who I verily believe sincerely esteems it *originalissimo*) will readily renew the bargain, but
as by your answer my account of the affair seems not quite circumstantial enough for the consequence of the subject, I shall not proceed
any farther at present, and the rather because we expect soon your
answer to what Mr Mann wrote you[4] the next post after mine, concerning a picture of a Sibyl,[5] of so notorious Domenichinality as to
be even superior to all *fedes* and subscriptions, which Mr Pennee
writes me word he could, after all, have procured for our dear Madonna; does not this make you cry out *Proh! Deum atque hominum
FIDEM!*[6] *Consaputo*[7] Pennee will return from Venice perhaps by the
time I can receive your answer, and I think to make him take a little
sketch of the Sibyl, which one may send you by the post, because I
believe in all your journeys to Bologna you never got a sight of it, as
it is in a certain Casa Ratta,[8] which is never shown to strangers. And
now, dear Sir, consider what you thank me so obligingly for, at the
same time you say you won't try to do it, for fishing out a nasty doubt,
which perhaps deprives you of a real satisfaction. Positively, I have

3. I.e., HW himself.

4. 16 Jan. 1742 NS.

5. In 1678, two paintings by Domenichino of a Sibyl were in Bologna (Carlo
Cesare Malvasia, *Felsina pittrice*, Bologna,
1678, ii. 343), one at the Casa Ratta, the
other at the Casa Albergati. The Ratta
family apparently soon sacrificed theirs
(ibid., Bologna, 1841, ii. 243, n. *a*), while
the other was taken to Rome (ibid. ii.
244, n. 2). Reynolds saw a Sibyl at the
Palazzo Ratta in 1752 (*Wallace Collection
Catalogues: Pictures and Drawings*, 16th
edn, 1968, p. 95), which may have been a
duplicate or copy; the Sibyl now in the
Wallace Collection had been in the Or-

léans Collection throughout the 18th century. HW was not interested in the painting and did not mention it to his father
(HW to Mann 18 Feb. OS, MANN i. 339).

6. 'In the name of Gods and men,' a
Ciceronian ejaculation (cf. *Tusculanæ dis-
putationes* V. 48, *Pro Q. Roscio comœdo
oratio* 50), apparently with a pun on
fides in the sense of 'credulity.'

7. 'The well-known.'

8. Some paintings at the Palazzo Ratta
are mentioned in *Pitture, scolture, ed
architetture . . . della città di Bologna*,
Bologna, 1782, pp. 260–1, but the Domenichino is not among them, perhaps an
indication that it had been sold.

so good a will to serve you, though hitherto so ill success, that upon condition of better next time I attempt, I'd renounce your thanks, but not your letters; don't mistake me, for unless you make me happy now and then that way, I've a good mind to say, I will be nothing but your well-wisher as long as I live, and what would you lose then? Or rather, what would you get? Why I'll tell you now; if the minority (for I will always call them so)[9] could be changed into that mind, how charmingly useful might they be to Sir R. while they did nothing at all? Consequently, though good for nothing as a friend, I could make you an excellent foe, still. But hang it, this is nonsense; I don't like it; you shall write on, and I'll always do all I can for you, whether it be nothing or not.

Here I must have a serious paragraph to tell you I am inexpressibly obliged to you for the kind things you say[10] of my brother[11] and his election, in a letter you wrote me by Mr Mann; his fate, perhaps, is decided by this time,[12] though I know nothing of it.

I wish I could help being serious in relation to what you say of 304 [the Prince],[13] but I could never make merry with madness, and really I can make nothing else of the answer; sure this one sally of passion is more than equivalent to kicking a thousand hats, which has been so grievous an imputation to others. An hour's consideration you say was taken; how could he not comply without thinking a minute, or how could he think an hour without complying? Or did

9. Chute is alluding to a vote in the House of Commons 16 Dec. 1741, which the Opposition won by a majority of four (HW to Mann 16 Dec. OS, MANN i. 242–3). This was the first of several adverse votes that led to Sir Robert Walpole's resignation 11 Feb. 1742 ('Short Notes,' GRAY i. 11 and n. 73).

10. In the missing letter of ca 14 Jan. OS.

11. Francis Chute (ca 1696–1745), M.P. Hedon 1741–2; F.R.S.; King's counsel (HW to Mann 5 Sept. 1741 NS, MANN i. 124 and n. 4).

12. Francis Chute and Luke Robinson had been returned as members for Hedon in May 1741, but the defeated candidates, Lord Mountrath and George Berkeley, petitioned the House of Commons against them 11 Dec. 1741 OS; the petition was to be heard 16 Feb. but was deferred until 4 March, when Chute and Robinson

were unseated (HW to Mann 3 Dec. 1741 and 3 March 1742 OS, MANN i. 220 and n. 13, 355 and n. 16).

13. Frederick Louis (1707–51), P. of Wales. HW's missing letter to Chute apparently contained an account of the King's offer to the Prince, 5 Jan., when he promised, in return for his son's acknowledgement of past misdemeanours, to give him an additional £50,000 a year, to pay his debts, and to receive and reward his friends at Court. The Prince replied that he could not approach the King 'whilst Sir Robert Walpole remains about him, nor ever will' (Hist. MSS Comm., *Egmont Diary*, 1920–3, iii. 238–9; J. B. Owen, *The Rise of the Pelhams*, 1957, p. 29). The object of the proposal was to obtain the support of the Prince's followers in Parliament for Sir Robert Walpole.

he consider an hour without thinking at all? What you say of 94
[Duke of Newcastle][14] and 93 [Lord Carteret][15] puts me in mind of
another confidant[16] of 94 [Duke of Newcastle]'s who, though of less
consequence, may be of some weight, and I am sure hung once on
the wrong side.[17] This makes me remember a passage in a collection
which I call my *Musæ pueriles;*[18] it is in verse, or at least in rhythm:

> A stick, a stone, and a feather
> Went into the water together.
> The stick stuck, the feather swam—
> And what was the name of the other?

If you answer me, I won't sell you a bargain. What could 34 [the
King] say on this occasion, or what could he forbear?

If my brother's gout[19] hinders him from attendance in this Parliament, I'll never forgive him if he eats and drinks any more.

Would you think it? I wantonly swallowed two ounces of veal at
supper t'other night, and it weighed a pound in my ankle by morning; it happened just so, when I was with you at Venice. I balked
it next day with bread and butter, and it went to seek for better cheer.

I like Lady T[ownshend]'s[20] remark; was she ever at Florence, where
it is not unusual to meet with marrow-bones in muffs?[21]

Mr Mann tells you all affairs that relate to our Tuscany, and it
will therefore be needless to send those accounts in my letter which
you will be sure to receive with it. And so, my dear good Sir, good

14. Thomas Pelham Holles (1693–
1768), cr. (1715) D. of Newcastle; first lord
of the Treasury 1754–6, 1757–62.

15. John Carteret (1690–1763), 2d Bn
Carteret, 1695; E. Granville, 1744; statesman; opponent of Sir Robert Walpole.
He and Newcastle were on cordial terms
at the time, and engaged in various obscure negotiations for Carteret's inclusion
in the ministry; the historian of the crisis
admits, however, that 'the nature of the
relations . . . between Carteret and Newcastle still remains something of a mystery' (Owen, op. cit. 16, n. 5).

16. Andrew Stone (1703–73), under-sec-
retary of state 1734–51, and confidant of
both the Duke of Newcastle and his
brother, Henry Pelham.

17. Stone was suspected of Jacobitism
(*Mem. Geo. II* i. 303–7), but see Romney

Sedgwick's introduction, *Letters from
George III to Lord Bute*, 1939, pp.
xxvii ff.

18. Not again mentioned; perhaps non-
existent. The 'stick' and the 'feather' are
perhaps intended for Pelham and Newcastle.

19. Chute's eldest brother, Anthony,
was also in Parliament, and later suffered from the gout (MANN iv. 102).

20. Etheldreda or Audrey Harrison (ca
1708–88), m. (1723) Charles Townshend,
3d Vct Townshend, 1738. HW often
quotes her witticisms, which are frequently indelicate.

21. Apparently a reference to something
in the missing letter of ca 14 Jan. OS.
Another remark by Lady Townshend
about a muff is in HW to Mann 8 Oct.
1741 OS (MANN i. 165).

night, good health, and a good majority[22] to you, and that will furnish good news for (I won't say your good) but

Your sincere friend, and most obliged, humble servant,

J. C.

Mr Whithed is most heartily your humble servant, and says he'd go to Bologna again with me for you.

How does dear little Prince Patapan do?

From CHUTE, Monday 5 March 1742 NS

Printed for the first time from MS now WSL.
Appended to Mann's letter to HW 5 March 1742 NS.

Not half so good as you deserve;[1] here, my dear Mr Walpole, I come in, but you must not expect me to say a word about anything but our dear friend who, though weak, is I hope in a very good way;[2] and there is all the reason in the world to conclude the worst is over. I do not forget the satisfaction you said it would have been to you last year if I had been with him. I wish I could do him as much good, as you did me justice in that thought. I cannot be more with him than I was in his health unless he would let me set up with him the nights, which if it could be of any real service to his health, you know he should not hinder me from doing. I have observed him the whole time with all the little skill I have, and think I find him rather better today than ever before since the operation. He says this minute he has an appetite which, as he is very good, and won't eat anything he should not, is no bad sign.

I am to tell you that Prince Craon has been here since he wrote the account above, about the Spaniards,[3] and tells him that they persist in their new intention of passing near this town, on which the government have dispatch[ed] Capponi[4] to expostulate with Mon-

22. I.e., in the House of Commons; see above n. 9.

_____

1. When Chute took over the pen, Mann had just written, 'My dear Mr Chute and Whitehead are vastly good to me.'

2. Mann had had another operation.

3. 'I hear the Spaniards are to pass by the Leghorne gate and round the walls to that of Rome, and so to the *Pace* in order to go out at the gate of St Giorgio.'

4. Probably Gino Pasquale Capponi (1716–81), colonel (Mann to HW 21 Aug. 1741 NS, MANN i. 112 and n. 42).

temar[5] on this fresh insult, as I think they justly enough term it, and from thence he is to proceed directly to acquaint the Great Duke[6] with the affair.

He begs you'll let my Lord Strafford[7] know that his two scagliola pictures[8] in a separate box, were put into a chest of urns that was sent last summer to my Lord Lincoln, and written upon, to my Lord Strafford.

I know 'twill be a satisfaction to you to hear an account how our dear invalid goes on from another hand than his own, and you may depend upon a line or two from me every week till you are convinced past all doubt that he is as well as you and I wish him. Though I love writing to you of all things except hearing from you, I shall be glad when I am come back to my usual three weeks or month's letters. 'Twould be too great a pleasure to correspond so frequently with dear Mr Walpole, for me to expect it unqualified with something to embitter it. Our dear friend says he knows I speak from my heart as indeed I do when I say I am,

My dear Sir,

Yours most faithfully,

J. C.

I must not forget our good-natured friend Whithed's most sincere regards, who loves you and Mr Mann heartily, though he is not here to speak for himself, we having sent him in quality of Mrs Goldsworthy's[9] cicisbé to the academy.[10]

I continue my Carthusian diet, and am grown as fat almost as my brother,[11] though not quite so comely.

5. Don José Carrillo de Albornoz (1663–1747), Duque de Montemar; in command of the Spanish expedition to Italy (Mann to HW 11 Nov. 1741 NS, MANN i. 182 and n. 30).

6. Francis (1708–65) of Lorraine, Grand Duke of Tuscany 1737–65; Holy Roman Emperor (as Francis I) 1745–65. He was married to Maria Theresa and lived at Vienna.

7. William Wentworth (1722–91), 2d E. of Strafford, 1739; HW's correspondent.

8. Mann asked twice again about these pictures (22 April and 12 Aug. 1742 NS, MANN i. 396, ii. 13), but HW apparently did not reply.

9. Philippia Vanbrugh (ca 1716–77), m.

(1734) Burrington Goldsworthy, consul at Leghorn 1736–54 and at Cadiz 1754–62. With an entourage of three children and three servants she had come to Florence to take refuge with Mann after an earthquake at Leghorn (Warren H. Smith, *Originals Abroad*, New Haven, 1952, pp. 13–75; Mann to HW 3 and 6 Feb. 1742 NS, MANN i. 306, 313).

10. I.e., *accadèmia*, a public concert.

11. Anthony Chute (1691–1754) of the Vyne, Hants; M.P. Yarmouth 1737–41, Newport 1741–7 (MANN i. 124, n. 4). Chute was on bad terms with him. HW had met him recently and described him as 'a fat comely gentleman' (HW to Mann 22 Jan. 1742 OS, MANN i. 301).

To CHUTE, Wednesday 10 March 1742 OS.

Printed MANN i. 365–6 as part of HW's letter to Mann 10 March 1742 OS.

From CHUTE, Tuesday 17 April 1742 NS

Printed in full for the first time from MS now WSL; parts of the last three paragraphs were printed in Doran i. 56–7.

Memoranda by HW (in ink):[1] Pr[ince].
                               Lady Eust[on].
                               Brace[girdle].
                               ?Fit[zro]y.

Florence, April 17, 1742.

My dear Sir,

WHAT shall I say to thank you for your goodness in taking notice of me at a time when you might have well neglected people of much greater consequence? The letter[2] of our dear friend's, in the answer[3] to which you bestow so large a piece upon me, was in itself an excuse for passing me quite by, or at least referring me to another time, as I am ashamed to think I have done you so long, directly contrary to the promise I made you of giving you constant accounts, which perhaps was the only way my letters could have been of any consequence; I know you are too good to pass me that reflection, but I am vexed and humble, and must make it for once, even to you, who of all people living have given me most reason to think otherwise, by the punctual notice you have taken of them.

I should now endeavour to tell you why I did not keep my promise, but sincerely, I know not how to go about it,[4] and if you'll guess the

1. These probably refer to a missing letter. Lady Euston was Lady Dorothy Boyle (1724–42), m. (1741) George Fitzroy, styled E. of Euston; Anne Bracegirdle (ca 1663–1748), the actress, was apparently admired by Chute (HW to Mann 26 May 1742 OS, MANN i. 435).

2. Mann and Chute to HW 5 March 1742 NS, MANN i. 340–3.

3. HW to Mann and Chute 10 March OS (MANN i. 362–6).

4. Chute's obscurity in what follows was adopted because of his and Mann's suspicion that Lady Walpole, HW's sister-in-law then living at Florence, had access to Mann's mail through her liaison with Count Richecourt, who as head of finances in Tuscany was virtual ruler of the duchy (Mann to HW 18 March, 20 May 1742 NS, MANN i. 360–1, 422). Chute is here alluding to her vindictiveness towards Sir Robert Walpole and her delight

reason, I'll love you better than ever, if possible; I can only tell you that if the earthquake[5] had come rumbling from Leghorn, or the Spaniards stayed at Florence, they should neither of them have prevented me, unless they had eat me; what's worse than an earthquake and Spaniards?

> Bella per [Emathios] plus quam civilia campos,
> Jusque datum sceleri [canimus], populumque potentem—[6]

that's something like it, but 'tis not the thing, in short, you shall guess, and at the same time imagine your dear Mini[7] and me, whose only comfort has been communicating uneasy thoughts when we were unobserved, almost all day long exposed to the droppings of nonsense[8] on the subject, which, though in itself insipid as water, fell like salt where we were sore, then comes a nasty scurrilous production of Pope's,[9] which puts me in mind of my nasty doctor at Marseilles, who, in allusion to what a nastier servant had (according to the custom of the country) thrown out at window, said to me one day, *Mon Dieu! Monsieur, comme vous faîtes de bile! on en voit partout.* Think of this bastard, begotten in a grotto by the headache upon the gripes, patronized and hawked about, forgive the expression, dear Sir, by those I would honour if I could, for your sake. *Basta,* you'll easily believe, after this, the reason of my silence was that I was both too cross and too dull to think of appearing before you, who have been all life and good humour to me; your letters accordingly in the worst of times have been our only comfort; your last particularly made us all vastly happy; I say all, to do justice to Mr Whithed, who is one of *Orford's crew,* true and tight, and joins

---

in his downfall, which Mann discusses, disguised by cipher and circumlocution, in his letters to HW of 17 April and 20 May NS, and openly in a letter of 7 May sent by a 'safe conveyance' (MANN i. 387–8, 406–7, 422–4).

5. There had been a severe earthquake at Leghorn on 27 Jan. (MANN i. 303, 307–8).

6. Lucan, *Pharsalia* I. 1–2 ('Of wars worse than civil I sing, wars waged over the Emathian plains, of legalized crime, and a powerful people—'). Chute apparently means Lady Walpole was waging war on her father-in-law.

7. Minister (i.e., Mann).

8. By Mrs Goldsworthy, whom Chute detested, and who was friendly with Lady Walpole (Mann to HW 18 March, 1 April 1742 NS, MANN i. 361, 371–2).

9. *Are These Things So? The Previous Question, from an Englishman in His Grotto, to a Great Man at Court,* 1740. This versified attack on Sir Robert Walpole, though intended to be taken for Pope's and even attributed to him on the title-page of a Dublin reprint of 1740, was actually by James Miller (1706–44) (Mann to HW 17 April 1742 NS, MANN i. 387–8 and nn. 2, 4; R. H. Griffith, *Alexander Pope: a Bibliography,* Austin, Texas, 1927, i. pt ii. 415).

in the sincerest congratulations on this last honour,[10] which except the merit of their malice who gave occasion to it, Sir R. must be said to owe singly to his own. This is not at all too much to say, so long as I am persuaded you know it is not more than I think. For my own part, my scheme of politics has ever, in effect, been comprehended in an attachment to one particular house, which I always imagined, as I suppose you do now, was the House of Hanover, but *non saprei*—I feel so much indifference in matters of a certain nature since a certain time, that I am more than half persuaded that the House of Orford all the while went halves at least in my system; howsoever, it is no slight instance of my regard for the former, that I wish, as I do, they had never been parted.

But you'll be justly angry with me for delaying so long to give you the satisfaction of being assured of our good friend's perfect recovery, which I rejoice, as you will believe, in being able to do, though he has not yet ventured abroad, except a little now and then in the garden, but that is owing purely to the season, which is still sick of a lingering winter; in another letter's time 'twill be spring, and I hope to see him as brisk as a bird, but I won't promise for it, unless it be such a sort of one as your last.

We can give no guess at the D[uke] of A[rgyll]'s reasons,[11] if he has any. He puts me in mind of an epitaph that was made upon a covetous Archbishop:[12]

> Here lies his Grace in cold clay clad
> Who died for want of what he had.

Poor man! I hope he'll never go out of place again. And now I have tired you with four sides, to very little purpose (for they no way express my meaning) unless you will be so good as to suppose it this, that I am solicitous for everything that regards your happiness, as becomes one greatly obliged to you and particularly happy in being with the truest regard,

Dear Sir, your most faithful, humble servant,

J. CHUTE

10. Sir Robert Walpole's elevation to the peerage as Earl of Orford, 6 Feb. 1742.

11. For resigning his commissions as colonel of the Royal Horse Guards and Master General of the Ordnance (Mann to HW 25 Feb. 1742 OS, MANN i. 345–6).

12. Richard Bancroft (1544–1610), D.D.; Abp of Canterbury, 1604. The epitaph on him is in William Fairley, *Epitaphiana*, 1873, p. 52.

To CHUTE, ca Monday 3 May 1742 OS

Missing; mentioned by Mann to HW 3 June 1742 NS (MANN i. 432).

To CHUTE, Thursday 3 June 1742 OS

Missing; sent with HW's letter to Mann 3 June 1742 OS (MANN i. 441).

From CHUTE, Sunday 24 June 1742 NS

Printed in full for the first time from MS now WSL; most of the second and sixth paragraphs were printed in Doran i. 76–8.

Charming Terrazzino

Casa Ambrosio,[1] Florence, June 24, 1742.

Dear Sir,

YOUR charming *little* letter[2] was as welcome as anybody's else would have been, though twice as big; I read it over and over, and under and backwards, and forwards and upside down, etc. It was as fat as an ortolan and as delicate too, but then it was gone as soon (I speak the more feelingly as I allow myself but one); you'll excuse me, dear Sir, for remembering with pleasure a certain half hour in the day at Venice when I used to contemplate you, hanging in chains, for want of a better, or perhaps any sort of amusement, this is the part of your time which I think I may most modestly imagine you to bestow, now and then, upon me, let me entreat you, therefore, when you write next, to give me two or three swings extraordinary; a few more last words, indeed you cut yourself down too soon last time; I am sure you could never be half dead. Pardon my placing this little remonstrance at the head of my performance; I have weighty reasons for not risking a point it imports me so much you should remark, at any great distance from the beginning; alas! how many of my betters are never read to the end! and the middle of most

1. Mann's guest-house, the Casa Ambrogi in the Via de' Bardi (GRAY i. 237, n. 4).

2. HW's missing letter of 3 May OS, or a later one.

writings is more properly the centre of the reader's gravity than that of his attention.

Lord, how I wish you were at Florence today! 'Tis San Giovanni![3] the whole town is a *stefanin.*[4] I have just been one of ten thousand gapers to catch St John's wobbling benediction from the top of his tottering tower;[5] if he had danced this dance before King Herod, I can't but think it would have hit his taste as well as the damsel's, for which he swore off his head. We are to have races[6] this afternoon, as I suppose you know, and to crown all, our grand opera, Via della Pergola,[7] begins at night. I'll say how I like it when I have seen it; I have heard it partly at the *prova,*[8] but *non saprei*—we have got Egizziello[9] and that must content us, for I doubt we have nobody else; our first woman, *Sani,*[10] is three parts as ugly as yours;[11] I wish she sung half as well. Your Petraia friends[12] in the midst of all our mirth are obliged to be sorry; the poor Primate[13] is carried off by the smallest pox he ever had in his life; he died at Paris; this will very likely spoil our *partie de campagne* with them, which Mr Mann told you of;[14] I am disappointed, for I am sure we should have talked of you very often, and that I love.

---

3. The feast of St John the Baptist, the patron saint of Florence; one of the two chief Florentine religious festivals.

4. Probably an allusion to the prominence of the Florentine knights of the order of San Stefano, or an allusion to *stefano,* a low word for 'belly.'

5. The Carro della Zecca, or Carro di San Giovanni, a wooden tower ornamented with figures of saints, drawn through the streets by oxen. On top of it rode a prisoner dressed as St John, whose fee was paid partly in money and partly in food and wine, which he consumed during his ride. The impersonation was abolished in 1748, and a wooden statue substituted (Pietro Gori, *Le Feste per San Giovanni,* Florence, 1926, pp. 77–83).

6. For an account of the San Giovanni races in 1741, see Mann to HW 1 July 1741 NS, MANN i. 78–9 and nn. 8, 9.

7. The opera-house was the Teatro della Pergola, built ca 1652 by Ferdinando Tacca; restored 1688 and 1738 (Walther Limburger, *Die Gebäude von Florenz,* Leipzig, 1910, p. 134). See also MANN i. 48, n. 8.

8. Rehearsal.

9. Gioacchino Conti (1714–61), called Gizziello, male soprano (MANN i. 56, n. 15).

10. Probably either Prudenza Sani Grandi of Florence, or Agata Sani (MANN i. 463, n. 23).

11. Caterina Visconti (*ante* 25 Dec. 1741 NS, n. 11).

12. The Prince and Princesse de Craon, whose summer residence was at Petraia near Florence, a villa belonging to the Grand Duke (Mann to HW 23 July 1741 NS, MANN i. 95 and n. 11).

13. François-Vincent-Marc de Beauvau (1713 – 10 June 1742), Primate of Lorraine; the Prince de Craon's second son; a 'young, lusty, ill-looking, proud, debauched, gaming, cheating prelate' (HW's *MS Commonplace Book of Verses* 30; Mann to HW 24 June 1742 NS, MANN i. 12, n. 49, 454 and n. 4).

14. In his letter to HW, 17 June NS (MANN i. 443). The party was postponed until 3 Aug., when Mann, Chute, and Whithed spent the day at Petraia (Mann to HW 5 Aug. NS, MANN ii. 1).

Montemar's affairs by all accounts go ill in Lombardy; they say he retires from the Austrosards,[15] but alas! we poor Tuscans are afraid of even glad tidings, as being in a situation—*a Cæsare posse vel fugiente capi.*[16]

The Suares family have been returned this three or four days; the Vittorina,[17] they say, is grown quite a *bellezza,* but I have only seen her in her trawdrums,[18] and can't perfectly judge; la Signora Madre,[19] by force of talking, travelling or——during her absence, is shrunk to half the quantity; she greeted me with your vastly pretty present[20] in her hand, and you were the first subject of our discourse. Cecchino has been so taken up, I suppose, with his Cecchina,[21] that I have not yet catched him since his return.

I was surprised to see my poor Haydon brother's name[22] in print[23] t'other day; Lord, says I, has he pleaded all his life? And now, perhaps, must go to gaol with his wife[24] for not pleading at last. Your last letters gave us vast comfort, and I am eaten up with zeal for the Lords House;[25] you know I was always religiously inclined; I could not forbear taking up the parable of the great Vernon;[26] this is the Lord's

15. I.e., the combined Austro-Sardinian army.

16. '—a Cæsare possim

Vel fugiente capi' (Lucan, *Pharsalia* V. 783–4).

('I may be captured by Cæsar even when he is fleeing.')

17. Maria Vittoria Suares de la Concha (1725–1806), m. (1745) Pierfrancesco Carducci (Mann i. 38, n. 12).

18. Presumably an article of attire; it also occurs in Mann to HW 8 July 1742 NS (Mann i. 473), spelled tradrums; unexplained.

19. Maria Anna di Valvasone (1697–1773), m. (1716) Balì Baldassare Suares de la Concha; a Florentine beauty of whom HW said that she had 'all the great characteristics of a woman; was talkative, busy, superstitious, silly, lewd, and prodigal of her favours' (Mann to HW 9 May 1741 NS, Mann i. 39 and n. 24). The dash which follows 'or' is Chute's.

20. A 'charming box' (Mann to HW 24 June 1742 NS, Mann i. 456).

21. Or La Cecca (so called from her connection with Cecco Suares), a singer at the burletta; not further identified

(Mann to HW 10 Sept. 1741 NS, Mann i. 128).

22. Francis Chute, recently unseated as M.P. for Hedon (*ante* 13 Feb. 1742 NS, n. 12).

23. Not found; the occasion of his 'not pleading' is unexplained, though Chute may merely be punning on his brother's profession as a lawyer and his loss of his seat in Parliament, which would subject him to debtor's prison if he had debts.

24. Ann Chute (d. ?1754) (Gray ii. 195, 229; *post* 21 May 1754; Mann iii. 92, n. 15).

25. *Sic* in MS; apparently a punning reference to the House of Lords. HW's letter to Mann of 26 May OS (Mann i. 436) tells of the Lords' throwing out the Indemnity Bill, which provided for 'indemnifying such persons as shall . . . make discoveries touching the disposition of public money . . . or concerning other matters relating to the conduct of Robert Earl of Orford' (HW to Mann 13 May 1742 OS, Mann i. 425 and n. 5).

26. Admiral Edward Vernon. HW had ridiculed his quotation of the 'parable' (which Vernon had used in a letter to Newcastle, later printed in the news-

doing, and it is marvellous in our eyes, alas! he spoke before the Lord had done; I trust that is not our case.

In these perilous times, you will imagine we have very few English at Florence; we have only two,[27] who, having very queer names and no less queer dispositions, have determined us to call them Balaam and his ass; did you never hear a story[28] of Swift, and a stammering squire who carried a bully about with him to speak for him? This proxy speaker, thinking to be witty upon the Dean, said to him one day at a full table, 'What do you gentlemen make of that odd story of B. and his ass? I suppose you don't take it in a literal sense.' 'Excuse me, Sir,' says he (devilishly nettled to have Scripture ridiculed by anybody but himself), 'the thing is quite literal, I assure you, and the plainest case in the world; Balaam, Sir, had an impediment in his speech, and his ass spoke for him.' This is just the case of our two countrymen—a prophet and an ass; however, they have got somebody[29] to speak for them both to Mini, and we are vastly civil to them, and Mini carries them out in the coach. He is pure well and was vastly happy with us over your letter[30] yesterday, as I suppose he'll tell you himself; and now, my dear good Sir, if I don't run away from you, I shall lose the race, and you'll be no great gainer if I stay, so let me assure you that I am whatever you please I should be. The Whitheds kiss the Walpoles with all their hearts.

J. C.

To CHUTE, ca Thursday 1 July 1742 OS

Missing; promised by HW to Mann, 30 June 1742 OS (MANN i. 480) and referred to, *post* 29 July NS.

---

papers, about some of the operations before Cartagena in April 1741) in a letter to Mann 29 June 1741 NS, written while he was at Venice with Chute (MANN i. 76 and n. 19).

27. Edward Sainthill (d. 1782) of Bradninch, Devon, and a Mr Cholwick. Sainthill, according to Mann, was 'vastly odd, indeed almost a driveller' (Mann to HW

15 July 1742 NS, MANN i. 483-4 and nn. 20, 21).

28. Not found elsewhere.

29. The Duke of Newcastle had recommended them to Mann (Mann to HW 15 July NS, MANN i. 483).

30. HW to Mann 26 May OS (MANN i. 434-40).

From CHUTE, Sunday 29 July 1742 NS

Printed in full for the first time from MS now WSL; most of the first paragraph and parts of the second and of the postscript are printed in Doran i. 88–
90.

Address: To the Honourable Horatio Walpole, Junior, Esq.

Florence, July 29, 1742.

Dear Sir,

BY A circumstance of good fortune, which I no more comprehend
than I deserve it, I am in possession of two charming letters[1] of
yours, as yet unanswered; I say good fortune, because my conscience
assures me I don't owe them to what I most naturally might, the
neglect of acknowledging any one of your *favours,* that's a silly word
and smells of goose and sausages,[2] but you shall explain it to yourself
by whatever you would have me call them; if that were the case, I
should be ashamed to look either of your letters in the face, which
the Lord forbid. Sometimes I think, or rather fancy, and that pleases
me vastly, that you have mistaken one of our dear Mini's for one of
mine, and that accounts for your loving me so much better than I deserve; I love the thought; why may not it be so? we are three persons in
one mind, and what more natural than a little confusion about our
operations? Forgive me this once for impudently figuring into the
place of the *Dearly Beloved;* I am fully sensible I am nothing but
proceeding, and as fully contented with my station, in my opinion
you have both more merit than if you had begotten me.

Now which of your charming letters shall I speak to first? Jesus! if
all terms are too common to express your friendship to me, what can
be particular enough for my gratitude? If I might but once express it,
I would be contented to be the oddest fellow breathing ever after. I'd
get Chambers's *Dictionary*[3] by heart, if that would do; I am resolved
I'll buy it, if I sell my prints, and I'll thumb it in friendship, like a
boarding-school *Bayly's*[4] in the bawdy words, and for the very same
reason, to be acquainted with the nature of what folks feel for one;

1. Presumably the missing letters of 3
June and ca 1 July OS.

2. Chute implies that 'favours' is a
word over-used by shopkeepers.

3. *Cyclopædia, or an Universal Dic-*
tionary of Arts and Sciences, 1728, by
Ephraim Chambers (ca 1680–1740).

4. *An Universal Etymological English*
Dictionary, 1721, by Nathan Bailey (d.
1742), keeper of a boarding school at
Stepney.

but I hate to joke about a thing so serious to me, and yet if I were grave, perhaps you'd find me more ridiculous; I don't deserve to be so confounded, and to be revenged. If I'm ever in a secret com[mittee] upon your conduct I'll report you for unaccountable good nature. But I must have done; my want of expression, as usual, has produced such an abundance of words, that I shall want room to say half what I would about your last. I'm rejoiced at the other, and well I may, for my own sake, but this obliges me to rejoice on a much better account, for yours; dear Sir, you can't think how it pleases me, that I made you laugh so,[5] that is, I made you happy, for every man's happy while he laughs, 'tis the philosopher's stone, the universal medicine, the *summum bonum* while it lasts, and I should scarcely give the preference to a Turkish Paradise, if I had my choice to laugh to all eternity. Nay, 'tis a Christian one, for what's the reverse of weeping, and wailing, and gnashing of teeth? Why undoubtedly laughing, and giggling, and cracking of sides. Lord! I did not think I was good for so much, and the poor Primate ought (if possible) to be in heaven for leaving us the occasion. In the mind I am in, if you were a King, guess what post I would choose under you; not your prime minister, for I want capacity, love ease and hate the Inquisition; nor your general, for I should never see the danger till I had lost my breeches; not your archbishop, for I can't swear and stare for what I don't believe a word of, besides an archbishop is a sort of a prime minister, too. No, I would be nothing of all these fine things, but you should revive an ancient, laudable usage in my favour, and make me your Majesty's fool. Lord, 'twould be vastly pretty, and dear Mini should be your plenipo and have a peace to make with Prussia; we would hang him round with blue and green and red ribbons,[6] and I'd make you laugh at those who doubted if he deserved them. Apropos I might tell you a pretty thing Mr Villiers[7] said about the King of Poland's[8] accession to the treaty,[9] but Mini told it me, and so he will you too.[10]

I can't quite agree with your sentiment expressed in the words

---

5. At Chute's account of the death of the Primate of Lorraine, *ante* 24 June NS. HW told Mann that he 'never was more diverted' than with Chute's letter (MANN i. 480).

6. Of the Order of the Garter, Thistle, and Bath. Mann was invested with the red ribbon in 1768 (Mann to HW 25 Oct. 1768, MANN vii. 63).

7. Thomas Villiers (1709–86), cr. (1756)

Bn Hyde, (1776) E. of Clarendon; British envoy to Poland 1738–46 (MANN i. 499, n. 15).

8. Frederick Augustus II (1696–1763), Elector of Saxony and King of Poland 1733–63.

9. Of Breslau, concluded 28 July 1742 NS (MANN i. 466, n. 5).

10. See Mann to HW 29 July NS, MANN i. 499.

incolumnis labor[11] etc. If you look upon the affair as I do, *civium ardor prava iubentium,*[12] your memory is good enough to recur instantly to *iustum et tenacem,* and the application makes itself. But I forget and am answering your letter to Mr Mann; I am always getting in his place with you; the truth is, I should envy it anybody but him in the world.

I could have crowded into the other side,

Dear Sir, yours eternally,

J. C.

But Mr Whithed's sincere regards, which could not, without the highest injustice, be excluded, would make my letter overflow; a lucky image for us both.

We all laughed heartily at Balaam's sword,[13] my Lord of Bath's[14] bit, and G. Honywood's[15] fourth passage through the *gens d'armes* to come up with M. Bussy.[16] You have taught me how my letter diverted you so much; to be sure 'twas with the wit I wished for.

Dear Sir, let me hear from you often; you will make me happy even though you were to copy *Tom Thumb;* I won't print you in the jest book, but I believe I shall bind you, and letter you with gold: Mr Walpole's Tom Thumb, Mr Walpole's Cow's-skin, Mr Walpole's Jack the Giantkiller, Pilgrim's Progress, etc., and you shall stand in my library in the post of honour.

From July 1742 until May 1743, there is a gap in Walpole's correspondence with Chute, but Mann's correspondence kept Walpole and

11. 'Unimpeded labour,' 'wholesome exertion.' If the phrase occurred in HW to Mann 30 June OS, HW did not preserve it when he copied the letter, nor is the application of this paragraph to the letter apparent.

12. 'Iustum et tenacem propositi virum
Non civium ardor prava iubentium
. . . Mente quatit solida . . .
    (Horace, *Odes* III, iii. 1–4).
('The man tenacious of his purpose in a righteous cause is not shaken from his resolve by the frenzy of his fellow citizens bidding what is wrong.')

13. This and the rest of this paragraph refer to a missing letter.

14. Pulteney was not created a peer until 14 July OS, but on 24 June HW had written to Mann that Pulteney had 'his warrant in his pocket for Earl of Bath, and kisses hands as soon as the Parliament rises' (MANN i. 467).

15. Possibly General Honywood, i.e., Philip (later Sir Philip) Honywood (d. 1752), K.B., 1743; Lt-Gen., 1735; Gen., 1743 (HW to Mann 24 June 1743 OS, MANN ii. 260, n. 22; GM 1735, v. 738).

16. François de Bussy (1699–1780), French chargé d'affaires at Vienna 1728–33 and at London 1737; minister 1740–3 and minister plenipotentiary 1761–2 to England (MANN ii. 131, n. 21).

Chute in communication with each other. On 19 Aug. 1742 NS, Mann wrote: 'Mr Chute insists on your pointing out to him the exact room you inhabit at Houghton' (MANN ii. 17); Walpole replied on 28 Aug. OS 'my love to Mr Chute,' and pointed out his two windows (ibid. ii. 36). On 30 Sept. NS, Mann quotes Chute, and says that they had identified the windows at Houghton (ibid. ii. 60). On 8 Oct. OS, Walpole wrote 'Sure, if you was ill, Mr Chute would write to me!' (ibid. ii. 71). On 20 Nov. NS, Mann reported Chute's attack of gout (ibid. ii. 100), just before Walpole complained that 'You say nothing of Mr Chute' (ibid. ii. 105). Chute's artistic judgment was utilized by Mann (for instance, ibid. ii. 116, 179), and on 7 Jan. 1743 NS (ibid. ii. 132), Mann wrote 'I sent immediately to the Chutes to share with them the good news [of the defeated attempt to revive the investigation of Sir Robert Walpole].' On 22 Jan. NS, Chute's fever was reported, and, on 26 March NS his gout (ibid. ii. 138, 197); a witticism of Chute's is on ii. 171. Walpole, on 27 Jan. OS, imagines Chute at the theatre in a black domino (ibid. ii. 149).

From CHUTE, Tuesday 7 May 1743 NS

Printed for the first time from MS now WSL.

Florence, May 7th 1743.

Dear Sir,

I DIE with confusion, to approach your presence, till you have asked our dear Mr Mann how much I love you, I have no comfort but my confidence in his answering that terrible question in your last to him[1] by assuring you I have a heart that flutters, he knows how, at a letter from Mr Walpole. Then, for a more *cathegorical* answer as Mrs Goldsworthy says, which I fear you will require, perhaps he will whisper you, if you take him aside into a corner of his letter, that I grow gouty[2] and old and he suspects I have not a great deal to say, that is, allowing for his delicacy, he thinks me a little dull, but very honest,

1. 'I would ask why Mr Chute has left me off? but when he sees what a frippery correspondent I am, he will scarce be in haste to renew with me again' (HW to Mann 4 April 1743 OS, MANN ii. 203–4). Although no letters between Chute and HW have been found from 29 July 1742 NS to 7 May 1743, expressions of regard, news of health, and other mes-sages were transmitted in the Mann correspondence, e.g. Mann to HW 19 Aug. NS, HW to Mann 28 Aug. and 15 Nov. OS, Mann to HW 22 Jan. and 12 Feb. NS, and HW to Mann 24 Feb. OS.

2. '[Mr Chute] eats nothing but milk to keep the gout under' (Mann to HW 7 Jan. 1743 NS, MANN ii. 132).

and recommends me to your good humour; I thank him kindly; 'tis all I have to trust to; your compassion, which in English is fellow-feeling, I depend little upon, for you were never either old or gouty,[3] and so I have only your laugh on my side, *e viva!* I hate a grave forgiving face; it makes one so sensible of one's guilt. I was once caught in a lie by my mother,[4] and when I only expected to be whipped, she made me sensible 'twas impossible she could ever believe a word I should say, and then kissed me; I had much rather have fallen into the hands of my father,[5] who would have knocked me down, for then I should only have hated him; my mother made me hate myself. But really now, what can I do?—Well 'tis a charming thing to have a friend; one may make such use of him sometimes; our little Mini must come up again for me; he has just made my excuse, and now I am going to accuse him; I appeal to you, does not he send you every week a charming fat packet crammed with every earthly thing that can possibly happen here, to divert you? Our loves and our duels, our marriages and our battles are all transmitted you by him as fast as they come about; if a poor countess gets a pox, you know of it before it reaches her husband's ears, and I might as well tell it him as you, when 'tis fifty to one but you both have it another way. Indeed I can't bear to write you letters like the article from Florence in the English Gazette that gives one comfortable hopes from the working of the Electress's[6] physic, when one has seen her go by in a broken couch, stretched upon her back, and knew she had no guts in her. After a few instances of this kind, 'twere too unreasonable to expect you should take me in any more, unless I were to be read, not only written by authority.[7] But this does not clear me; there was nothing, 'tis true,

3. Chute first wrote '—you are neither old nor gouty.'

4. Katharine Keck (living 1713), m. 1 Ferdinando Tracy of Stanway, Glos; m. 2 (1686) Edward Chute (C. W. Chute, *History of the Vyne*, 1888, pp. 82–3; Peter le Neve, *Pedigrees of the Knights*, ed. G. W. Marshall, 1873, p. 418; John Lodge and Mervyn Archdall, *The Peerage of Ireland*, 1789, i. 11).

5. Edward Chute (1658–1722); matriculated Queen's College, Oxford, 1675; barrister of the Middle Temple, 1685, bencher, 1692; high sheriff of Hants, 1699 (C. W. Chute, op. cit. 80, 83; Foster, *Alumni Oxon.*).

6. Anna Maria Luisa de' Medici (1667–18 Feb. 1743), m. (1691) Johann Wilhelm, Elector Palatine (MANN i. 48, n. 11; Mann to HW 18 Feb. 1743 NS, MANN ii. 159). No such article has been found in the *London Gazette*, but the references to her last illness did not indicate its gravity, e.g., 'The Electress Dowager Palatine continues out of order with a cold and slight fever' (news dispatch from Florence, 5 Feb. NS, in *London Gazette* No. 8197, 12–15 Feb. 1743).

7. Alluding to the heading of the *London Gazette*, 'Published by authority.'

for me to say, but I ought to have known how to say that, but I did not, and so I held my tongue. If many authors had been of my mind, I can't but think it would have been no bad expedient for our Austro-britons to have ordered every tart and pie that wore a plain coat, and all trunks and bandboxes that had not embroidered linings, to pay a penny to the Queen of Hungary's poor's box.[8] Messieurs Amiens and Périgord[9] should be only allowed the suit they travel in, to cut off all possible occasions of our plain British paste's disguising itself in French nonsense, and thereby frustrating the end of the act by not incurring the penalty;[10] the force of this law being, as you see, the impossibility of not breaking it, and so contributing to the great end of supporting the balance.[11] Lord! who would have thought it? My empty letter runs over[12] and comes to nothing at last; I set out, I will own it, with a sort of secret satisfaction to reflect that you were tired with not hearing from me; God forbid I should have been all this while writing away my comfort and tiring you with my letter, but you won't tell me so, and besides you'll pay me as well as if it were otherwise; there's the main chance secured, and I had better try to fancy I have amused you, though strictly, I have done nothing but asked your pardon and said I am,

Dear Sir, most sincerely yours, etc.,

J. CHUTE

The Whitheds are always at your service.

8. Referring to the annual subsidy that England had granted for the last three years to Maria Theresa 'for the support of the House of Austria.' In 1741 the amount voted was £300,000, and in 1742 and 1743 it was £500,000 (*Journals of the House of Commons* xxiii. 705, xxiv. 165, 387; HW to Mann 8 April 1742 OS, MANN i. 390 and n. 3).

9. Apparently fictitious names for French provincials.

10. Chute seems to be alluding to a bill recently introduced into Parliament 'for the more effectually preventing the importation and wear of gold or silver thread, lace, fringe, or other work made of gold or silver wire, manufactured in foreign parts,' in which there was a clause providing 'that it shall and may be law-

ful for any person, being a subject of Great Britain, at his arrival from foreign parts, to import, for his own proper use and wear only, two complete suits . . . of apparel, consisting of, or wrought or made up with, gold or silver wire [etc.] . . . manufactured in foreign parts' (*Journals of the House of Commons* xxiv. 462). The bill was passed by the Commons 16 March 1743 and sent to the Lords, where it was tabled (ibid. xxiv. 466; *Journals of the House of Lords* xxvi. 253). The chief provisions of the bill were later embodied in the act of 22 Geo. II (1749), c. 36, which however did not include the clause quoted above.

11. I.e., the balance of trade.

12. On to the fourth side of the folded sheet.

From CHUTE, Tuesday 4 June 1743 NS

Printed for the first time from MS now WSL.
Appended to Mann's letter to HW 4 June 1743 NS.

He says vastly true; I am quite wild about the Rafael;[1] I know the Duke of B[eaufort][2] will buy it. Who would not give all he has sold for fourscore thousand pound[3] for such a heavenly picture? If I was married to a dozen D[uchesse]s,[4] I would permit the whole Conclave, nay the whole universal Church, linkboys and all, to taste their sweet bodies for it. Do but think —— but there's no describing it: in the first place, the most glorious scene of Attic, or Roman, or, what perhaps is more, Rafael architecture; in the middle of the picture, standing before a single pillar like those of the beautiful gate[5] in the cartoon, such a Christ, as beautiful, as graceful, and we may suppose, if his petticoats were off, as well made as his elder brother of the Belvidere, with groups disposed on the sides in all the *grand goût* and ineffable contrast of chosen attitudes that one sees in the cartoon of Paul preaching.[6] Those who write of it from Rome compare it to the 'School of Athens,'[7] which you know I have not yet seen. I only know I felt the same sort of feel at this drawing which I remember to have

1. Mann had said, with reference to the sale of Cardinal Cybo's collection, 'What a pity it is one had not been at Rome with a commission to buy. Mr Chute is quite wild about it, thinking how well some of 'em would have suited your gallery' (Mann to HW 4 June NS, MANN ii. 240). We have erroneously identified (in MANN ii. 235, n. 19), the supposed Raphael, 'Christ Disputing with the Doctors,' with a painting of the same subject by Ghezzi that later belonged to the Duke of Beaufort, but it appears that the art dealer Richard Gaven was trying to sell the 'Raphael' in Poland in 1752, so that it was apparently a different picture (Gaven to Sir Charles Hanbury Williams 14 Sept. 1752, in Williams MSS, now WSL, lxvii. ff. 256–7).

2. Henry Somerset (1707–45), 3d D. of Beaufort, 1714. For anecdotes of his collection of Italian art, see Osbert Sitwell, 'The Red Folder,' in *Sing High Sing Low*, 1944, pp. 30–52.

3. Unexplained probably, like the following sentence, an allusion to the suit for divorce that he had instituted against his wife, thereby losing her very large estate.

4. Beaufort's Duchess was Frances Scudamore (1711–50), whom he married in 1728 and divorced for crim. con. 2 March 1744. She m. 2 (1744) Col. Charles Fitzroy (HW to Mann 10 June 1742 OS, MANN i. 452 and n. 22).

5. The portico of the Court of the Women in the temple at Jerusalem, shown in Raphael's cartoon (one of the seven in the Victoria and Albert Museum) of 'Peter and John healing the lame man' (Richard Cattermole, *The Book of the Cartoons*, 1837, p. 97; A. P. Oppé, *Raphael*, 1909, pp. 160–3).

6. 'Paul preaching at Athens' (ibid. 167–81, with reproduction).

7. Raphael's painting in the Vatican.

felt at the first good print I saw of the above-named cartoon, and shall it never hang in the gallery at Houghton? If I was rich enough to dare at such an acquisition, I would not pay a farthing to a tradesman this seven year, and I would buy it myself.

If I mistake not, there are other things in the list[8] you will receive in this packet that would suit you vastly. I am sure they are tempting names, and I know you are no saint; you may pretend to withstand a Guerchin Seneca,[9] but, if you do, Satan shall buffet you with a Guido Madonna. I wish I was a Gaspar Occhiali,[10] that I might always live in your closet. Oh! but once more, my Lord's gallery, and the Raphael—there's temptation sufficient to give a vandal an erection of virtu. I will not believe the taste that could build Houghton, and, what is more, can make additions to its beauties, is capable of resisting.

I am so heroically contented myself with having no hopes of ever possessing a picture or a statue or anything worth looking at, that I think I deserve to be rewarded by everything that's pretty going always where I wish it; that amounts to dear Mr Walpole's etc., etc.,

J. CHUTE

Give my love to Patapan, and tell him I am going to set for my picture too.[11] Don't let him laugh at me, a young rogue!

To CHUTE, ca Wednesday 1 June 1743 OS

Missing; mentioned in HW's letter to Mann 4 June 1743 OS (MANN ii. 244).

8. Missing.

9. Giovanni Francesco Barbieri (1591–1666), called Guercino. The painting has not been identified.

10. Gaspar Adriaensz van Wittel (1655–1736), called Gaspare Vanvitelli or Gaspare degli Occhiali; architectural painter (Thieme and Becker; *Enciclopedia itali-* *ana*). HW had bought '3 large and 2 small pictures' by him (MANN x. 8).

11. Patapan had been painted by Wootton (HW to Mann 25 April 1743 OS, MANN ii. 220 and n. 25). Chute's picture, which Mann mentions 11 June NS (MANN ii. 243) has not been identified.

To Chute, Saturday 25 June 1743 OS

Printed from HW's MS transcripts (now WSL) of his letters to Mann; see MANN x. 36–44 (Appendix 12). Previously printed (as part of HW's letter to Mann 24 June 1743 OS), *Letters of Horace Walpole . . . to Sir Horace Mann*, ed. Lord Dover, 1833, i. 333–4 (misdated); Wright i. 290–1 (misdated); Cunningham i. 255 (misdated); Toynbee i. 360. It follows HW's postscript to Mann of 'Saturday morning.'

Headed by HW: 'To Mr Chute.'

My dear Sir,

I WISH you joy,[1] and you wish me joy, and Mr Whithed, and Mr Mann and Mrs Bosville[2] etc. etc. etc. Don't get drunk and get the gout. I expect to be drunk with hogsheads of the Mayne-water,[3] and with odes to his Majesty and the Duke[4] and Te Deums.[5] Patapan begs you will get him a dispensation from Rome, to go and hear the thanksgiving at St Paul's. We are all mad, drums, trumpets, bumpers, bonfires! the mob are wild, and cry, 'Long live King George, and the Duke of Cumberland, and Lord Stair[6] and Lord Carteret,[7] and General Clayton[8] that's dead!' My Lord Lovel[9] says, 'Thanks to the gods that *John* has done his duty!'[10]

Adieu! my dear Dukes of Marlborough!

I am ever your

JOHN DUKE OF MARLBOROUGH

1. On the victory at Dettingen, 27 June NS. See HW to Mann 24 June OS.

2. Diana Wentworth (1722–95), m. (1739) Godfrey Bosville of Gunthwaite, Yorks. The Bosvilles were visiting Florence (Mann to HW 4 June 1743 NS, MANN ii. 238–9, and nn. 1 and 2).

3. The French were driven across the Main in the course of the battle.

4. George II and William Augustus (1721–65), Duke of Cumberland, were both in the field at Dettingen. It was the last time that an English king participated personally in a battle.

5. Handel's Te Deum for the victory was performed at the Chapel Royal 27 Nov. 1743 (Paul Henry Lang, *George*

Frideric Handel, New York, 1966, p. 407).

6. John Dalrymple (1673–1747), 2d E. of Stair, 1707; diplomatist and general; one of the commanding officers at Dettingen.

7. Also with the King at Dettingen.

8. Jasper Clayton (d. 1743), Lt-Gen., 1739, was killed at Dettingen (HW to Mann 24 June OS, MANN ii. 258 and n. 4).

9. Thomas Coke (1697–1759), cr. (1728) Bn Lovel, (1744) E. of Leicester.

10. A paraphrase of Addison's *Cato* IV. iv. 71. Lovel apparently used 'John' for 'John Bull' (as also in HW to Mann 3 Oct. 1743 OS), as well as for John, Lord Stair.

From CHUTE, Monday 29 July 1743 NS

Printed for the first time from the MS now WSL.

Dated by Mann's postscript, written 'two days' after Mann's letter to HW 27 July 1743 NS (MANN ii. 275).

Dear Sir,

THIS is the third time my pen has leaped into my hand[1] to pay its honours to yours, full fraught with the reigning topic of all its brethren at the present juncture, but hitherto I have pinched its nib and bid it be quiet till we were satisfied of the safety of all your friends on the banks of the Mayn; I was shocked too much at the imagination of saluting you with my nonsense and *Io pæans* so dreadfully malapropos as an unlucky French bullet might have made them. I felt in my own heart that I had not a stock of public spirit sufficient to make me contented with the sacrifice of one friend, or friend's friend, to the glorious success, had it been the case of drowning the whole French army, and breaking the hearts of the whole French Court.

Your charming letter to Mr Mann by Sunday's post has cleared up all our doubts,[2] and I am at liberty to be as glad as ever I please, and wish you joy without fear or wit, which I have not near enough of to describe my satisfaction. I am glad, vastly glad, for the King and the Duke, and I am glad for the Earl;[3] the Queen of H[ungary] and her L[ord] C[arteret][4] will be glad for themselves. *Bravo maestà! Bravo da vero.* You may tell Mr Pope that

> Now, justly Cæsar scorns the poet's lays;
> *It is* to History he trusts for praise.[5]

We have had an account of the action handed about here from Vienna, which takes as much merit from our countrymen as ever it can; it says we should have come badly off if the Austrians had not been there. I understand nothing in that proposition but that two are not four.

1. Chute's earlier abortive attempts are mentioned in Mann's letters of 23 and 27 July NS (MANN ii. 271, 274).

2. About losses of friends in the Battle of Dettingen. 'I have not so much as an acquaintance hurt' (HW to Mann 24 June OS, MANN ii. 260).

3. Lord Stair.

4. Carteret was Maria Theresa's chief supporter in England. See *post* 15 Aug. 1744 NS and Mann to HW 12 Jan. 1745 NS, MANN ii. 557.

5. *Satires* i. 35–6. 'Cæsar' is George II.

You might have spared your congratulations to Madame Bosvill, for I do not believe she would love you if she knew you, for she does not love the Manns nor the Whitheds nor Chutes, and you shall pardon me for thinking that a shrewd sign in your disfavour; in short, she loves nothing but one thing in the world, and that, the Florentines tell us, she breaks the neck of, every night, at the *mictum*[6] place of the Ponte S[anta] Trinità. Mr Mann invites her and her paramour[7] (who is a saucy pot-bellied purser of a ship) to trot tomorrow night in his orange groves—is not he kind to furnish them with such *comodi* for consummating their unfinished loves? The *beato* Manetti is so taken up with his own Virgin that he won't see them, and, if he should, he can but tell it in heaven.[8] Her husband,[9] whom we call Nykin,[10] declares she came abroad to get him an heir; the devil's in it if she don't succeed; 'tis pity it won't be *cavaliere*.[11]

I wish I could pay you the laugh I owe you for the sow and puggis,[12] and the rest of your diverting Gothic antiquities, and your more diverting modern reflections upon them; but alas! I have no more humour in me than if I were one of the 'CCC monckes that lyvede by hure travayle'—was I always so? or is it owing to my insipid diet? Was anybody ever metamorphosed into a bowl of milk and water? I fancy that's my case. I have a good mind to get drunk with the Captains[13] to the health of the Battle of Oetinghen,[14] and write to you before I give up my wine.

Is Patapan's picture like? My respects to him; I wish him joy, and pray tell him I hope if he goes to St Paul's, he will insist upon a seat in the choir, opposite to my Lord of London's,[15] or in some other distinguished situation suitable to his high blood.

6. Urinal. For a further account of Mrs Bosville's scandalous activity see Mann to HW 13 Aug. and 24 Sept. NS, Mann ii. 286, 309.

7. His name was Prole; perhaps Capt. Henry Prole, d. ca 1763 (Mann to HW 25 June NS, Mann ii. 251 and n. 7).

8. Apparently Chute is referring to a monument with a figure of the Virgin, erected to a member of the Manetti family, from whom Mann rented his house. See Gray i. 237, n. 4; Mann to HW 6 Aug. 1741 NS, Mann i. 100 and n. 5.

9. Godfrey Bosville (1717–84) of Gunthwaite and Thorpe, Yorks (Mann ii. 238, n. 1).

10. An obsolete term of endearment;

the only example given in OED is from Congreve's *Old Bachelor*, 1693.

11. That is, the purser was not a gentleman. The first of the Bosvilles' four children was born in 1745 (Lady Macdonald of the Isles, *The Fortunes of a Family*, Edinburgh, [1927], p. 234).

12. This and the rest of this sentence is unexplained; it apparently refers to a missing letter or portion of a letter to Mann that HW did not transcribe.

13. Probably he means Prole.

14. Chute probably confused Dettingen with Öttingen, also in Bavaria, the capital of a principality.

15. That is, the Bishop's throne.

Mr Whithed is much yours, and rejoices with you and Patapan. I will say no more, for fear of making you sorry, but that I am,

Dear Sir, as much as it is possible to be,

Yours etc. etc.

J. Chute[16]

To Chute, Saturday 20 August 1743 OS

Printed from the MS now wsl. First printed, Wright i. 301–3; reprinted, Cunningham i. 264–6; Toynbee i. 372–4. The MS was apparently among those sold ca 1843 by the 5th D. of Grafton, as executor of the 6th Earl Waldegrave's estate, to Richard Bentley, the publisher; bought by wsl, 1937, from estate of Richard Bentley the younger (MANN x. 40–3).

Houghton, Aug. 20, 1743.

INDEED, my dear Sir, you certainly did not use to be stupid, and till you give me more substantial proofs that you are so, I shall not believe it. As for your temperate diet and milk bringing about such a metamorphosis, I hold it impossible—I have such lamentable proofs every day before my eyes of the stupefying qualities of beef, ale and wine, that I have contracted a most religious veneration for your spiritual *nourriture*. Only imagine that I here every day see men, who are mountains of roast beef, and only seem just roughly hewn out into the outlines of human form, like the giant-rock at Pratolino![1] I shudder when I see them brandish their knives in act to carve, and look on them as savages that devour one another. I should not stare at all more than I do, if yonder alderman at the lower end of the table was to stick his fork into his neighbour's jolly cheek, and cut a brave slice of brown and fat. Why, I'll swear I see no difference between a country gentleman and a sirloin; whenever the first laughs, or the

---

16. A postcript by Mann is printed in MANN ii. 275.

———

1. A colossal crouching figure, called 'Apennin' or 'Giove Pluvio,' carved as though emerging from a rock, at the Grand Duke's villa of Pratolino north of Florence. It was carved by Giovanni Bologna (Jean Bologne) (ca 1524–1608), 1577–81 (Abel Desjardins, *La Vie et l'œuvre de Jean Bologne*, 1883, pp. 95–8, with engraving; Thieme and Becker). HW and Gray had visited Pratolino on their journey from Florence to Bologna in April 1741 (Mann to HW 25 April 1741 NS, MANN i. 31). Chute had accompanied them (SELWYN 16).

latter is cut, there run out just the same streams of gravy! Indeed the sirloin does not ask quite so many questions—I have an aunt[2] here, a family piece of goods, an old remnant of inquisitive hospitality and economy, who to all intents and purposes is as beefy as her neighbours. She wore me so down yesterday with interrogatories, that I dreamt all night she was at my ear with who's, and why's, and when's and where's, till at last in my very sleep I cried out, 'For God in heaven's sake Madam, ask me no more questions!'

Oh! my dear Sir, don't you find that nine parts in ten of the world are of no use but to make you wish yourself with that tenth part! I am so far from growing used to mankind by living amongst them, that my natural ferocity and wildness does but every day grow worse. They tire me, they fatigue me; I don't know what to do with them, I don't know what to say to them; I fling open the windows and fancy I want air; and when I get by myself, I undress myself, and seem to have had people in my pockets, in my plaits and on my shoulders! I indeed find this fatigue worse in the country than in town, because one can avoid it there and has more resources, but it is there too—I fear 'tis growing old—but I literally seem to have murdered a man whose name was ennui, for his ghost is ever before me. They say there is no English word for ennui; I think you may translate it most literally by what is called *entertaining people and doing the honours.* That is, you sit an hour with somebody you don't know and don't care for, talk about the wind and the weather, and ask a thousand foolish questions, which all begin with, *I think you live a good deal in the country,* or *I think you don't love this thing or that.* Oh! 'tis dreadful!

I'll tell you what is delightful! The Dominichin[3]—my dear Sir, if ever there was a Dominichin, if there was ever an original picture this is one. I am quite happy, for my father is as much transported with it, as I am.[4] It is hung in the gallery, where are all his most capital pictures, and he himself thinks it beats all but the two Guidos,

2. Probably Susan Walpole (1687–1763), m. (1707) Anthony Hamond (d. 1743) of Wootton (Mann i. 140, n. 12; Montagu i. 26, n. 12).

3. See *ante* ca 15 Nov. 1741 NS and n. 26. The painting had finally arrived the week before (HW to Mann 14 Aug. OS, Mann ii. 291–2).

4. 'If nature and life can please, the sweet Dominichini must be admired. These two never met in one picture in a higher degree than in Lord Orford's Madonna and Child by him' (HW, 'Ædes Walpolianæ,' *Works* ii. 235).

that of the Doctors[5] and the octagon[6]—I don't know if you ever saw
them. What a chain of thought this leads me into—But why should
I not indulge it? I will flatter myself with your some time or other
passing a few days here with me—Why must I never expect to see
anything but beefs in a gallery which would not yield even to the
Colonna?[7] If I do not most unlimitedly wish to see you and Mr
Whithed in it this very moment, it is only because I would not take
you from our dear Miny. Adieu! you charming people all—Is not
Madam Bosville a beef?

Yours most sincerely,

H. Walpole

From Chute, Tuesday 1 October 1743 NS

Printed for the first time from the MS now wsl.
Enclosed in Mann's letter to HW 1 Oct. 1743 NS (see HW to Mann 12 Oct.
OS, Mann ii. 326 and nn. 1–2).

Dear Sir,

AS I WAS reposing myself after dinner today, as you know we
Florentines are accustomed to do, I dropped asleep with a
Martial in my hand immediately upon reading a certain epigram
entitled *De catella Publii*,[1] and who should I dream of, but Patapan?
'Tis so exactly suited to him, particularly in his present circumstance
of having been lately immortalized by Wotton,[2] that, as much as you
justly despise punning, when you read it, you will own there was
never anything so pat. Methought I was alone with him in the library
at Houghton, which I dreamt of out of the book of prints you sent

---

5. 'Over the farthest chimney [in the
Houghton gallery] is that capital picture,
and the first in this collection, The
Doctors of the Church: they are consulting on the immaculateness of the Virgin,
who is above in the clouds. . . . This picture . . . is by Guido in his brightest
manner' (ibid. 266–8). The painting is
described in *Ermitage impérial: Catalogue
de la galerie des tableaux,* 2d edn, St
Petersburg, 1887, i. 70.
6. 'The Adoration of the Shepherds,

octagon, a most perfect and capital picture of Guido, not inferior to The Doctors' (HW, 'Ædes Walpolianæ,' *Works* ii.
274; *Ermitage impérial,* op. cit. i. 68–9).
7. The Palazzo Colonna at Rome.

———

1. 'On Publius's Lap-dog,' *Epigrams* I.
cix (cx in some editions).
2. John Wootton (ca 1678–1765), animal
painter. See *ante* 4 June 1743 NS and n.
11. The last seven lines of Martial's epigram describe a picture of the dog.

Mr Mann.³ There was he, *collo nixa cubans, capiensque somnos, ut suspiria nulla* etc.,⁴ and dreaming very apropos of pens, ink, and paper, I was naturally led to dream on through a whole translation of the epigram upon Patapan as follows:

Martial l[iber] 1 ep. 110.

Issa est passere nequior Catulli,
*Issa est purior osculo columbæ.*⁵

Pata is frolicksome and smart
As Geoffry once was—(oh! my heart!)
He's purer than a turtle's kiss
And gentler than a little miss.
A jewel for a lady's ear
And Mr Walpole's pretty dear.
He laughs, and cries, with mirth, or spleen,
He does not speak, but thinks, 'tis plain.
One knows his little *guais*⁶ as well
As if he'd little words to tell.
Coil'd in a heap, a plumy wreath,
He sleeps, you hardly hear him breathe.
Then he's so nice, who ever saw
A drop that sulli'd his sofa?
His bended leg (what's this but sense?)
Points out his little exigence.
He looks and points, and whisks about
And says, 'Pray, dear Sir, let me out.'
Where shall we find a little wife
To be the comfort of his life,
To frisk and skip, and furnish means,
Of making sweet Patapanins?
England alas! can boast no she
Fit only for his *cicisbee.*
Must greedy fate then have him all?
No; Wotton to our aid we'll call.

3. Presumably *The Plans, Elevations, and Sections . . . of Houghton,* 1735, published by Isaac Ware with plates after Thomas Ripley and William Kent.

4. 'Resting on his neck and taking repose, so that no breathing—' (Martial I. cix. 8–9).

5. 'Issa is naughtier than Catullus's sparrow, Issa is purer than a dove's kiss.'

6. Griefs.

The immortality's the same
Built on a shadow, or a name.
He shall have one, by Wotton's means,
The other, Wotton for his pains.

I desire Patapan will apologize for my troubling you with my poetical somniculations; it is entirely owing to him; pray tell him so, and that I depend upon Martial and him to recommend my sleeping thoughts more effectually to your notice, than anything I could say, when I was ever so much awake.

I am vastly obliged to you for your thoughts in your last letter upon beef; hitherto you must know, as it was forbidden fruit, I have generally longed for it, and been mighty apt to envy those who were so happy as to stick their knives into sirloins without restraint. But from the image you give me of it, opening its mouth and letting out gravy at each corner, and the danger you lay before my eyes of eating one's self into so strong a likeness of beef as might make one tremble at the sight of a fork, I assure you I loathe it so much that whenever I see beef I shall think of horseflesh, and find nothing more tempting for the future in an oxcheek than in a rump of centaur. No, I'm determined I never will be a beef. What was in my head to invite this monster to Houghton, you would say, when you saw my horns and hoofs; I won't carry him into the gallery, indeed, to chaw his cud over the Guidos and the Dominichino, etc. Dear Sir, you can't imagine how glad I am that the Madonna justifies herself so well; I assure you, I could never account for the fresh pleasure it gave me every day during the considerable time it hung at Mr Mann's, if it was not at least as original as several other established originals here, which have scarce maintained themselves so well upon the test of living amongst them.

You are very good to think of wishing for the Whitheds and Chutes at Houghton; we are impatient to find the moment when we may *godere delle sue grazie*,[7] in the mean time, you will easily believe that we have still stronger inducements than the *délices* of that charming place, even its gallery and all, to wish ourselves there; when you reflect, as I see plainly you sometimes do, that those of this place have been the least powerful motives to moderate our eagerness for Rome.

7. Enjoy its charms.

I might as well have said at once we love you and our dear Mini better than all the pictures and statues in the world.

We have been to see Gaburri's[8] collection of designs which is to be sold[9] and we think there might be a considerable number of very capital ones picked out; the whole is vast, as it includes all masters, even down to this present time; we are informed that the people who have the disposal of them have hopes of selling the whole collection together to the King of Poland; but as there are a great number of examples of all hands, it would not be esteemed one jot less entire for the extraction of three or four examples of all the famous folks; we pretend to propose to them to let us pick out a certain number for you, which might extend to one or two hundred without lessening the profit they may still make of the remainder which will go under the name of Gaburri's entire collection, notwithstanding; as yet they have made no proposal as to price, but we expect soon to hear further from them upon that head; you may imagine we don't press the thing, not to appear too much in love with the particulars. In the meantime Mr Mann desires me to tell you he would be glad to have particular directions from you as soon as possible concerning the number you would choose to have, as well as the price you care to extend to in the purchase; we flatter ourselves they may be induced to conform to a reasonable one upon the consideration which I have already hinted, that whatever they get for this small part of so vast a collection will in all probability be just so much clear profit to them. It seems a good opportunity; for there is certainly a vast number of very fine things in the collection, and we hope there may be means of coming at some of them without an extravagant expense. I wish you good luck in them, and all manner of good things besides, amongst the rest, a good night; and am,

Dear Sir, most absolutely yours,

J. CHUTE

8. Francesco Maria Niccolò Gabburri (1676–1742), collector and author (MANN ii. 296, n. 11). His collection is briefly described in George Vertue's notebooks, *Walpole Society*, 1933–4, xxii. 154–5.

9. For further references to the sale, and Mann's apparently fruitless efforts to buy some drawings for HW, see Mann's letters to HW, 3 Sept., 1 Oct., 19 Nov., and 3 Dec. 1743 NS, and 14 Jan. 1744 NS (MANN ii. 296, 313–4, 338–9, 347, 370).

To Chute, Wednesday 12 October 1743 OS

Printed from HW's MS transcripts, now wsl (see *ante* 25 June 1743 OS); appended to HW's letter to Mann 12 Oct. 1743 OS. Previously printed, *Letters of Horace Walpole . . . to Sir Horace Mann,* ed. Lord Dover, 1833, i. 367–71; Wright i. 314–16; Cunningham i. 275–7; Toynbee i. 388–90.

My dear Sir,

HOW I am obliged to you for your poem! Patapan is so vain with it that he will read nothing else; I only offered him a Martial to compare it with the original, and the little coxcomb threw it into the fire, and told me 'he never heard of a lap-dog's reading Latin; that it was very well for house-dogs and pointers that live in the country and have several hours upon their hands: for my part,' said he,

'I am so nice, who ever saw
A Latin book on my sofa?
You'll find as soon a Bible there,
Or recipes for pastry-ware.
Jesus! D'ye think I ever read
But Crébillon or Calprenède?[1]
This very thing of Mr Chute's
Scarce with my taste and fancy suits.
Oh! had it but in French been writ,
'Twere the genteelest sweetest bit!
One hates a vulgar English poet:
I vow t'ye, I should blush to show it
To women *de ma connaissance,*
Did not that *agréable stance,*
Cher double entendre! furnish means
Of making sweet Patapanins!'

My dear Sir, your translation shall stand foremost in the Patapanianas: I hope in time to have poems upon him,[2] and sayings of his own, enough to make a notable book. *En attendant,* I have sent you some pamphlets to amuse your solitude, for, do you see? as tramontane as I am, and as much as I love Florence, and hate the country;

1. Claude-Prosper Jolyot de Crébillon (1707–77) and Gautier de Costes de la Calprenède (1614–63), novelists.

2. HW's 'Patapan, or the Little White Dog,' 'wrote at Houghton 1743,' is printed in Selwyn 287–306.

while We make such a figure in the world, or at least such a noise in it, one must consider you other Florentines as country gentlemen. Tell our dear *Miny,* that when he unfolds the enchanted carpet, which his brother the wise Galfridus³ sends him, he will find all the kingdoms of the earth portrayed in it. In short, as much history, as was described on the ever memorable and wonderful piece of silk, which the puissant white cat⁴ enclosed in a nutshell, and presented to her paramour prince. In short, in this carpet, which (filberts being out of season) I was reduced to pack up in a walnut, he will find the following immense library of political lore: magazines for Oct. Nov. Dec. with an appendix for the year 1741. All the magazines for 1742 bound in one volume: and nine magazines for 1743.⁵ The life of King Theodore, a certain fairy monarch, with the Adventures of this Prince and the fair Republic of Genoa.⁶ The miscellaneous thoughts of the Fairy Hervey.⁷ The question stated.⁸ Case of the Hanover troops;⁹ and the vindication of the case.¹⁰ Faction detected.¹¹ Con-

3. Galfridus Mann (1706–56), Horace Mann's twin brother; army clothier (MANN i. 24, n. 4). 'Gal is to send me a carpet' (Mann to HW 17 Sept. 1743 NS, MANN ii. 303). The books mentioned below were to be packed with it.

4. See the story of the white cat in the fairy tales (HW). 'La Chatte blanche,' in the *Contes des fées* of Marie-Catherine Le Jumel de Barneville (1650 or 1651–1705), m. (ca 1665) François de la Motte, Baron d'Aulnoy, was a favourite of HW's, who refers frequently to it and other tales by her; see COLE i. 90, GRAY i. 200, MASON i. 329, and MANN ii. 238 (and n. 13, which corrects earlier biographical notes on her). HW owned a translation, *Tales of the Fairies,* 3 vols, 1721 (Hazen, *Cat. of HW's Lib.,* No. 1776).

5. HW seems to have sent a two-year file of a single magazine, presumably GM.

6. An anonymous *History of Theodore I* [Theodore (1694–1756), Baron de Neuhoff, self-styled] *King of Corsica, Containing . . . the Rise and Consequence of the Troubles in Corsica, and the Resolution of Its Inhabitants to Shake off the Government of the Genoese,* 1743. HW's copy is now WSL (Hazen, op. cit. No. 1608:5).

7. John Hervey (1696–1743), summoned to Parliament (1733) as Lord Hervey of Ickworth. HW's copy of *Miscellaneous Thoughts on the Present Posture Both of Our Foreign and Domestic Affairs,* 1742, now WSL, is inscribed by HW, 'By John Lord Hervey, son to the Earl of Bristol, and lately Lord Privy Seal.' See Hazen, op. cit. No. 1608:90.

8. *The Question Stated with Regard to Our Army in Flanders,* 1743. HW wrote on the title-page of his copy (now WSL), 'By Lord Hervey.' See ibid. No. 1608:28.

9. *The Case of the Hanover Forces in the Pay of Great Britain,* 1742, by Edmund Waller corrected by Lord Chesterfield (HW to Mann 9 Dec. 1742 OS, MANN ii. 123 and n. 5). HW's copies of two editions are now WSL (Hazen, op. cit. No. 1608:43 and 46).

10. *A Vindication of a Late Pamphlet, Entitled the Case of the Hanover Forces,* 1743, attributed to Chesterfield and Waller in S. L. Gulick, Jr, 'A Chesterfield Bibliography to 1800,' *Papers of the Bibliographical Society of America,* 1935, xxix. 93. HW's copy is now WSL (Hazen, op. cit. No. 1608:43).

11. John, Lord Perceval, *Faction Detected by the Evidence of Facts,* 1743, 'a vast pamphlet in favour of the new ad-

gratulatory letter to Lord Bath.[12] The Mysterious Congress;[13] and four Old England journals.[14] Tell Mr Mann, or Mr Mann tell himself, that I would send him nothing but this enchanted carpet, which he can't pretend to return—I will accept nothing under enchantment. Adieu All! continue to love

THE TWO PATAPANS

During the second long interval in Walpole's correspondence with Chute, messages and news of health continued to be exchanged between them in the Walpole-Mann correspondence. On 28 Jan. 1744 NS Mann wrote, 'Poor Mr Chute has got the gout and is bad. We are willing to attribute it to his dining and eating all kinds of things [at] Prince Craon's.' On 4 Feb. NS he wrote, 'Mr Chute is almost well. He has been once at the opera in a chair and a domino to hide his legs.' In his letter to Mann of 24 Jan. OS, when Walpole thought that the French fleet might be threatening Leghorn, he wrote as an aside, 'My dear Mr Chute, I trust to your friendship to comfort our poor Miny.' 18 Feb. NS Mann wrote, 'Poor Mr Chute has had a relapse and is now confined with the gout.' 9 Feb. OS, after Walpole had received the first news of Chute's illness, he wrote, 'I am very unhappy for Mr Chute's gout, or for anything that disturbs the peace of people I love so much, and that I have such vast reason to love.' 16 Feb. OS, when the Young Pretender had escaped from Rome into France, and the English were expecting an invasion, Walpole wrote, 'My best love to the Chutes [i.e., Chute and Whithed]; tell 'em I never knew how little I was a Jacobite, till it was almost my interest to be one.' 1 March OS Walpole interpolated another aside: 'My dear Chutes, I hope you will still return to your own England.' 6 May NS Mann wrote, referring to Sir William Maynard, a visitor to Florence whom HW had recommended, 'Mr Chute intended to tell you

ministration' (HW to Mann 3 Oct. OS, MANN ii. 318). HW's copy is Hazen, op. cit. No. 2844.

12. *A Congratulatory Letter to a Certain Right Honourable Person upon His Late Disappointment*, listed in GM Sept. 1743 (xiii. 504). HW attributes it to Sir Charles Hanbury Williams in his biographical account of Williams, but the attribution is doubtful; see SELWYN 315 and n. 48. Mann and Chute thought it was by HW (Mann to HW 17 March 1744 NS, MANN ii. 411).

13. *The Mysterious Congress. A Letter from Aix la Chappel, Detecting the Late*

Secret Negotiations There, listed in GM Oct. 1743 (xiii. 560). According to the title-page the author was 'a nobleman distinguished for integrity and consummate knowledge in public affairs.' Two copies that belonged to HW are now WSL (Hazen, op. cit. No. 1608:26 and 44).

14. One of them probably contained HW's 'The Dear Witches,' published 18 June 1743 (Mann to HW 17 March 1744 NS, MANN ii. 411 and n. 2). For this and HW's other contributions to *Old England, or the Constitutional Journal* (1743–9), see Hazen, *Bibl. of HW* 153–4, and GRAY i. 13–14.

. . . from the beginning, that unless you ordered it absolutely, he would not love him, as he believes he is the only fool you ever interested yourself for.' Walpole replied, 29 May OS, 'I am very sorry I recommended such a troublesome booby to you. Indeed, dear Mr Chute, I never saw him, but was pressed by Mr Selwyn, whose brother's friend he is, to give him that letter to you.' Two other asides occur in Walpole's letters to Mann. On 18 June OS Walpole wrote, referring to Joseph Smith, British consul at Venice, 'My dear Mr Chute, how we used to enjoy the title-page of his understanding! Do you remember how angry he was, when showing us a Guido after pompous rooms full of Sebastian Riccis, which he had a mind to establish for capital pictures, you told him he had now made amends for all the rubbish he had showed us before?' 22 July OS Walpole wrote, 'My dear Chutes, stay for me: I think the first gale of peace will carry me to you. Are you as fond of Florence as ever? Of me you are not, I am sure, for you never write me a line.' The following letter was written before this hint could have been received.

From CHUTE, Saturday 15 August 1744 NS

Printed for the first time from the MS now WSL.

Florence, August 15, 1744.

Dear Sir,

IT IS such an age that I am indebted to you and Patapan for the prettiest letter in the world, as I must confess it, though the rogue was a little smart upon my homespun Muse, that I am heartily ashamed to appear before either of you in the guilty shape of a letter from Mr Chute at last; but I will not die in my sins, and therefore have determined that this courier[1] shall carry my act of contrition, and lay it at both your feet; you may kick it and he bite it if you please, upon condition you read it at last, and one time or other before you die send me a pardon under your hands and seals. If you find your heart hardened against me, do but once reflect how much better is one dull letter than a dozen I might have written in all this time, if I had been good. What shall I say more? I will adjure you by the victory of Veletri,[2] by those first fruits of our dear Mini's naval expedition,[3] by the Spanish cavalry quite ruined, and a king of a

---

1. Probably Samuel Cox (MANN ii. 486, n. 1).

2. 11 Aug. NS (ibid., n. 2).

3. Mann had 'sent four ships to Nettuno etc. to assist the Queen's army' (Mann to HW 21 July 1744 NS, MANN ii. 476).

pair of Sicilies[4] scuttling through a back door in a pair of slippers,[5] to believe I love you entirely as well as if I had tired you two and fifty times since this day twelvemonth.

If ever you should be so good as to write to me again, tell me what you think of my living forever at Florence; do you not believe I propose at last to become *fin senatore fiorentino?*[6] I will tell you as a secret that my other half[7] is within a very little of *fin cicisbeo;* it is in the Pepi's[8] power with a single hair to tie him fast at her girdle all next Carnival at least, and if he should not stop there—if you do not hear of me at Rome in the winter, you know the reason.

We have at present numbers of English here who are all amazed what can keep us so long here; they think it the dullest place they ever saw, but as the major part of them are of a taste which prefers the Venuses of the Via del Giardino[9] to her of the Tribune[10] and even to such as she of the corner of the Nunziata,[11] I don't dispute with them, but pick my teeth and say in English, *non saprei*—apropos of odd English, I took a certain *gobbino*[12] baronet[13] into my bosom at his first arrival, because he came to me in the name of the Walpole[14] to which it seems he is not known, and after a little time he began to hiss and look livid, as if he would have stung me, so I shook him off as I could, notwithstanding his letter, and was sure you would forgive me, because he is a fool.

The great establishment of Uguccioni's[15] great friend[16] has almost

4. Charles, K. of the Two Sicilies, later Charles III of Spain.

5. For an account of Charles's undignified escape from the Austrians at Velletri, see Mann to HW 16 Aug. NS, MANN ii. 487 and n. 9.

6. An English gentleman at Florence being in love with a very handsome lady there said, if her parents would consent to let him marry her, he would settle there, turn Roman Catholic, and become *fin senatore fiorentino* ['at last a Florentine senator'] (HW).

7. Mr Whitehed (HW).

8. Probably Ottavia Macinghi (1717–77), m. (1735) Francesco Gaspero Pepi (MANN i. 111, n. 27).

9. Now an extension of the Via dell' Ulivo. Prostitutes evidently lurked there.

10. The Venus de' Medici, which still stands in the Tribune, in the Uffizi.

11. Madame Grifoni (HW). The Palazzo Grifoni is in the Piazza della SS. Annunziata (Walther Limburger, *Die Gebäude von Florenz*, Leipzig, 1910, p. 79).

12. 'Little hunchback.'

13. Sir William Maynard (1721–72), 4th Bt, 1738; M.P. Essex 1759–72. For his behaviour in Florence see Mann to HW 21 Jan. and 6 May 1744 NS (MANN ii. 371–2, 439–40).

14. For HW's letter of recommendation, Dec. 1743, see MANN ii. 367, and for his explanation of it, ibid. ii. 451.

15. Giovanni Battista Maria Uguccioni (1710–82); Florentine senator, 1761; a close friend of Lady Pomfret and her daughter, Lady Sophia Fermor (Mann to HW 10 Sept. 1741 NS, MANN i. 129 and n. 15).

16. Lady Carteret (HW). Lady Sophia Fermor had married Lord Carteret 14 April 1744.

turned his little brain; he has had five letters from milords and miladies by this courier and thinks of nothing less than my Lady P[omfret]'s[17] making my Lady C[arteret] make her Lord C[arteret] make his Q[ueen] of H[ungary][18] make her G. D[uke] of T[uscany] make his Toussain[19] make his C[oun]t Richcourt[20] make him something or another, he knows not what.[21]

I am sure you remember Pitchfork Antenore and I suppose Mr Mann told you some time since how she picked up a *sposo* no bigger than a sausage in the spring;[22] I am to tell you she has lain in above a month, strange effects of *salsiciotti!*[23] Where was her pitchfork then? but alas, it would not have done, *naturam expellas furca licet*[24]—her husband may add it to his coat, a proper bearing for a *coin en herbe*.

I am afraid of being too late for Mr Mann's *plico*[25] and too long for your patience, so I wish you good night with all my heart and am

Dear Mr Walpole's most etc., etc., etc.,

J. CHUTE[26]

Mr Whithed is entirely at your service.

17. The expansions in this paragraph were made by HW in the MS.

18. See *ante* 29 July 1743 NS, n. 4.

19. First minister to the Great Duke (HW). Franz Joseph (d. 1762), Freiherr von Toussaint, Imperial cabinet secretary and finance minister (MANN i. 235, n. 3).

20. Chief minister at Florence (HW). Emmanuel-François-Joseph-Ignace de Nay (1694–1759), Comte de Richecourt; head of finances in Tuscany (ibid. i. 24, n. 9). Toussaint was Richecourt's patron at the Imperial Court.

21. 'Uguccioni is quite mad about Lady Carteret. He is persuaded if he was not a Catholic that he should have a great place . . .' (Mann to HW 16 June 1744 NS, MANN ii. 455). The remainder of Mann's sentence gives the chain of influence that Chute has here imitated.

22. 'The great bouncing Antinori is married to little Boccineri' (Mann to HW 28 April 1744 NS, MANN ii. 435). Maria

Maddalena Antinori (1725–1802), m. (1744) Domenico Andrea Bocchineri (1712–76) (ibid., n. 17). The nickname is unexplained, but her father boasted that she was 'so strong that she would make nothing of jumping upon a man's shoulders' (Mann to HW 21 March 1749 NS, MANN iv. 36–7).

23. Sausages.

24. Chute is paraphrasing Horace, *Epistolæ* I. x. 24: 'Naturam expelles furca, tamen usque recurret' ('You can drive out nature with a fork, but it keeps coming back').

25. Packet of letters.

26. HW wrote to Mann from Houghton 1 Sept. OS, 'Thank dear Mr Chute for his letter; I will answer it very soon; but in the country I am forced to let my pen lie fallow between letter and letter' (MANN ii. 506). No reply from HW has been found.

From Chute, Tuesday 5 January 1745 NS

Printed in full for the first time from the MS now WSL; part of the first paragraph printed in Doran i. 208–9.

Mann received the letter too late to send it with his letter of 5 Jan., and it was not sent until 12 Jan. (Mann to HW 12 Jan. NS, Mann ii. 560).

Florence, Jan. 5, 1745.

Dear Sir,

I AM resolved my letter shall begin with something new, and therefore date it at this end; I dare say this is the first 1745 you have ever seen in your life; well, I swear 'tis an odd thing to look a new year thus in the face. If I were to live to write 1800 a new century! Jesus! how it would make one stare, if one was not to be blind first! I wonder what sort of a world it will be then. Will there be a bruin of Brandeburg[1] to roar and ramp and suck his bloody paws as he does now, or will the Queen of H[ungary] lead one muzzled in a cord, and make him leap over her sceptre for the Emperor Joseph?[2] Will the King of France bestow his favours on a *Duc* or a *Duchesse,* or send both to the devil and turn saint again? Who will be Czar of Moscovy, who King of England, and who King of him in those days? Apropos I must tell you what a strange dream I had last night; excuse me, I know dreams are nonsense; but this may be as capable of diverting from the oddness of it, as any of the extreme common things which befall me waking.

I thought I was invited to the Tribune to the *nozze* of the Venus of Medicis,[3] who seemed to have lost something of that animated grace which made Mr Richardson think she was stepping from her pedestal and advancing towards him.[4] I soon saw that this was oc-

1. Frederick II of Prussia.
2. Maria Theresa's son Joseph (1741–90) was elected Holy Roman Emperor as Joseph II upon the death of his father, Francis I, in 1765.
3. What follows is an allegorical description of the marriage of Lady Sophia Fermor to Lord Carteret (later Lord Granville) in April 1744.
4. Chute is probably thinking of the description of the Venus in *An Account of Some of the Statues, Bas-Reliefs, Drawings, and Pictures in Italy,* 1722, edited

by Jonathan Richardson (1665–1745), the painter, from materials collected by the younger Jonathan Richardson (1694–1771); Richardson says:

'This figure is, I think, take it all together, the best in the Tribunal, and . . . 'tis so light, 'tis leaping off its pedestal' (p. 57).

Though Richardson's account is somewhat confusing, the context shows that he is referring to the Venus and not to another statue.

casioned by a great swelling dirty purse hung round her neck tied
with strings of a greenish blue, for I could not see distinctly which
colour they were or whether either or not, but upon the middle, or
more properly the belly, of this crammed purse was embroidered in
gold the figure 3.[5] Bianchi[6] told me *qui dentro c'e Volcano ma non si
mostra più.*[7] Looking round to see the rest of my old acquaintance, I
found them strangely changed; amongst them there was one Gothic
figure dressed as I at first thought in a ruff, but I found upon a nearer
view it was the circle of a mahogany *chaise-percée,* which he wore
exactly in the manner of that uncouth ornament of the court of
K. James I. *Cosa mai e questo? Signor Bianchi. C'e il Signor Presidente,
e questo,—che so lo—forte saran le arme della sua moglie.*[8] After this
the scene was all confusion, in the midst of which I could distinguish
Patapan in his own dear little shape barking with all his might at
the Presidente della Seggetta.[9] What followed was a huddle: as usual
in dreams most of the statues were out of their places; some were
riding on horseback and some rowing in boats, and everything so
changed that I began to dream it was nothing but a dream. When I
rose I recollected on an article in the Mantua Gazette of yesterday,
which I fancy our dear Mini will have mentioned to you, from which
all this might be tolerably well traced allowing a little for an extravagant brain in its night revels. I long, of all things, for the next post
to contradict the Mantua gazetteer, or at least give us the comfort

5. An allusion to an article on the
change of ministers in England that appeared in the *Gazzetta di Mantova,* which,
as Chute explains below, inspired his
dream. Mann clipped the first paragraph
and sent it to HW in his letter of 5 Jan.
The pertinent passage is as follows, in
translation (the Italian text is printed in
MANN ii. 556): 'London 11 December [NS].
On 5 December Lord Carteret, Earl of
Granville, renounced the seals, and his
office of secretary of state was conferred
upon Lord Harrington, whereupon the
King granted to the former a pension of
£3000 sterling. The Earl of Bath has
been made Lord President; the Duke of
Marlborough Master of the Horse; and
the Duke of Richmond, who had that office, has been appointed Viceroy of Ireland.' Granville had resigned 24 Nov. OS
and was succeeded by Harrington, but the

rest of the report was untrue, including
the grant of a pension to Granville. The
changes following Granville's resignation
are given by HW to Mann 24 Dec. OS,
MANN ii. 550-1.

6. Giovanni Francesco Bianchi Buona-
vita (1670-1752), keeper of the Uffizi
(MANN i. 213, n. 11).

7. 'Vulcan is in here, but he doesn't
show himself any more.' Vulcan, Venus's
unsightly husband, is Lord Granville, who
was thirty years older than his wife.

8. 'But what is this, Signor Bianchi?
It's the Lord President, and that—I'm
sure of it—is his wife's coat of arms.'
Lady Bath's 'low' birth—her father, John
Gumley, was a rich merchant and com-
missary-general to the Army—was often
alluded to in satires on Lord Bath (see
GEC *sub* Bath).

9. Close-stool.

of knowing his information is not quite true; for I cannot endure the thoughts of any part of a close-stool in the Tribune.

I have almost finished my sheet with an idle dream. That may truly be called nothing at all, but if one was to wait till anything happens really here worth your notice, one should write so very seldom that even the indulgent disposition of Pope Patapan and his legate *a latere*,[10] which has lately been so favourable to me, would be exhausted and deliver me up at last to the devil a word more from them.

The thoughts of this made me have so much mind to write, though so nothing had I to say, that I had almost determined once to seal up a sheet of paper with my name and etc., etc. and my *baisepieds* to Pope Pat and nothing else; this perhaps is not much better—I am almost afraid 'tis worse, so I will have done and wish you good night and good year, and everything that you can wish yourself.

I am dear Mr Walpole's most truly etc., etc.,

J. CHUTE

Mr Whithed salutes you with much warmth, though

> Not with half the warmth and life
> With which he kissed *Vincenzo's* wife.[11]

For six months the correspondence between Walpole and Chute was again suspended, and again news and messages were transmitted in the correspondence with Mann. 'Mr Chute . . . is confined to his house, trying to avoid a fit of the gout, with which he is threatened' (Mann 12 Jan. NS). 'Thank Mr Chute for his letter [5 Jan. NS]; I will answer it very soon' (Walpole 1 Feb. OS). 'Mr. Chute will excuse me yet; the first moment I have, I will write' (Walpole 28 Feb. OS). 'Mr Chute and Whithed leave me [to go to Rome] the day after tomorrow, which design they had concealed to me, out of a kind motive' (Mann 25 May NS). 'I am inconsolable for the loss of the Chutes, who departed last Thursday.

10. A papal legate of the highest class (OED *sub* 'legate' sb. 1, 1c).

11. Chute is paraphrasing Prior's 'The Ladle':

'Jove kissed the farmer's wife, you say.
He did—but in an honest way:
Oh! not with half that warmth and life,
With which he kissed Amphitryon's wife.'

'Vincenzo's wife' is perhaps Maria Maddalena Gerini (1717–75), m. (1733) Vincenzo Riccardi (1703–52), Marchese di Chianni (MANN i. 37, n. 5). Whithed's mistress, Angiola Lucchi, by whom he had had a daughter in March 1744, seems to have been unmarried (Mann to HW 14 Jan. and 10 March 1744 NS, MANN ii. 368, 406).

. . . After having been four years constantly with people, one is very awkward without them. . . . Mr Chute went away vastly afflicted for the death of his favourite brother [Francis Chute], a confirmation of which he received the night before he set out. I am in great hopes the journey will divert his melancholy. They . . . will be in Rome in about ten days' (Mann 1 June NS). 'The Chutes are well at Rome, and salute you most affectionately' (Mann 15 June NS).

From Chute, Saturday 26 June 1745 NS

Printed in full for the first time from the MS now wsl; printed, with omissions that include the entire sixth paragraph, in Doran i. 216–18.

Sent to Mann, who enclosed it in his letter to HW of 29 June NS: 'Here is a letter from Mr Chute at Rome. . . . I have introduced the Chutes to my friend the Cardinal [Albani], who has introduced them to everybody, so that they are in all the high Roman world' (Mann iii. 59).

Rome, June 26, 1745.

My dear Sir,

I WRITE to you now, because you are the only person in the world who can enter truly into the distress which stares you in the face at the top of my letter; do but think I am no longer at Florence; I have left Mr Mann; I need say no more to entitle me to your compassion. You know what I have left, and 'tis my only comfort, to think you will love me, and write to me, because you pity me.

As this is the first of my letters which he is, unfortunately, not present at, I may permit myself to do justice to his goodness for me, which has as much exceeded all I could expect, as it really does what I pretend to deserve. I know I owe the beginning of his friendship to you, and I leave you to account for that, but the unwearied continuance of it for four years together, I can give no account of at all, except I can suppose he has looked into my heart, which, of all others, is undoubtedly the most estimable part of me; this I ought not to say to you, because you are capable of thinking it a real merit, which I ascribe to myself; do so, and censure me as vain, provided you believe me sincerely so.

My dear Sir, can you forgive my not writing to you when all mankind did?[1] Mr Mann promised me to mention me, and I know he

---

1. On the death of Sir Robert Walpole, 18 March 1745 OS.

did;[2] the reason I did not mention myself was truly this, I despaired of saying anything you could bear in the shape of consolation, 'twas folly even to think my letter could do you any good, and I found the great melancholy occasion[3] much too serious for me to compliment about. It will be infinitely good in you, if you admit this an excuse for my being silent, where everything was to be said.

I must thank you ten thousand times for a kind paragraph in your last to Mr Mann which he would not let me lose; it really did me good; my loss[4] is inexpressible on all accounts, nor am I able to find the least comfort in being one horrid step nearer to a mouldering estate, which has lost the only chance of ever being repaired.[5]

I would never have believed some few years ago, that it was possible for me to look with such an eye of indifference upon Rome as I do; hitherto nothing has made any impression upon me; all statues appear like those at High Park Corner,[6] and a Raphael or a Domenichino is no more than Queen Anne's head at an ale-house door. I have indeed seen very few as yet and though I am in the lodging[7] you had last, which is close by the Villa Medici, I have passed but five minutes there, and when it was too dark to enjoy anything but the solitude of the place, which reduced all the charming people there to downright Gothic sprites.[8]

We talk of nothing here but Silesia,[9] the news of the defeat having reached us but on Wednesday last; all parties agree that our L[orrain][10] hero has been duped. There was another *batterie* in a *Bäut*

2. 'Mr Chute assures you of his best respects' (4 May NS, MANN iii. 38).

3. Lord Orford's death (HW).

4. His brother's death (HW). HW wrote to Mann 29 April OS, referring to Francis Chute's recent death, 'My dear child, you have nothing but misfortunes of your friends to lament! You have [a] new subject by the loss of poor Mr Chute's brother. It really is a great loss! He was a most rising man, and one of the best natured and most honest that ever lived' (MANN iii. 39).

5. The Vyne was owned by Chute's elder brother Anthony, for whom Chute had little love. Francis Chute would have inherited it had he survived Anthony.

6. Chute means Hyde Park Corner, where mortuary monuments were made

and sold (MANN iii. 66, n. 12). ('High Park,' probably a phonetic spelling, occurs in Etherege's *Man of Mode* III. iii.).

7. Not identified.

8. The Villa Medici, now the seat of the Accademia di Francia, at that time contained a large collection of antique and Renaissance statues, most of which were removed to Florence in 1769 and 1775 by Leopold II, the Grand Duke (Gaetano Moroni, *Dizionario di erudizione storico-ecclesiastica*, Venice, 1840–61, xcix. 271–2).

9. Frederick II's defeat of the Austrian army at Hohenfriedberg 4 June 1745 NS (Mann to HW 29 June NS, MANN iii. 58 and n. 13).

10. Expanded by HW in MS. Charles Alexander (1712–80) of Lorraine, brother

like that of Tournay;[11] but I will not say any more of that affair, since whatever can be news to you from hence, you will have from our dear Min at the same time you receive this. The K[ing] of P[russia] immediately dispatched a courier with his success to the E[lector] of B[avaria][12] and hence Acquavivians[13] begin to draw consequences, which make our *geniali* grave.

There is just arrived a new French minister here;[14] the Pope[15] despised the former[16] so much they were forced to recall him;[17] on his pressing a little too importunately for an audience some time ago, the Pope came out at last in a passion and said, *Coglioncello,*[18] *non sai, che quando non voglio sentire, non voglio sentire.*[19]

I trembled for Mr Conway[20] when I heard the Duke was in so much danger, and am charmed not to find him in the dreadful list;[21] the poor M. de Beaveau,[22] Prince Craon's youngest son, is there. He

of Grand Duke Francis; general in the Austrian army; governor-general of Flanders 1744–80 (Mann i. 205, n. 27).

11. I.e., the battle of Fontenoy (near Tournai), 11 May NS, in which the British forces under the Duke of Cumberland were defeated by the French under Marshal Saxe (HW to Mann 11 May OS, Mann iii. 42 and nn. 1–2). What word Chute was aiming at in *Bäut* is not clear, but he probably referred to the French cannon in the 'Redoubt d'Eu,' which 'played a great part in the battle' (F. H. Skrine, *Fontenoy*, 1906, p. 154).

12. 'Bavaria' expanded by HW in MS. The 18-year-old Elector was Maximilian Joseph (1727–77), Elector of Bavaria 1745–77. Bavaria was at that time supposedly neutral, the Elector having signed a treaty of peace with Maria Theresa 22 April 1745 NS (HW to Mann 15 April OS, Mann iii. 34 and n. 14).

13. Party of Cardinale Acquaviva, minister of Spain (HW). Trajano Acquaviva (1695–1747), cardinal, 1732; ambassador from Spain to the papal court (Gray i. 220, n. 13; Michael Ranfft, *Merkwürdige Lebensgeschichte aller Cardinäle*, Regensburg, 1768–73, ii. 476).

14. Frédéric-Jérôme de Roye de la Rochefoucauld (1701–57), Abp of Bourges, 1729; cardinal, 1747; ambassador from France to the papal court 1745–8 (NBG;

Michael Ranfft, *Neue genealogisch-historische Nachrichten*, 1757–8, viii. 472–6).

15. Benedict XIV (Prospero Lambertini) (1675–1758), pope 1740–58.

16. Claude-François Rogier de Beaufort-Montboissier de Canilliac (1693–1761), abbé; chargé d'affaires at the papal court 1742 – 17 June 1745 (*Recueil des instructions données aux ambassadeurs . . . Rome*, vol. iii, ed. Gabriel Hanotaux and Jean Hanoteau, 1913, p. 199 n. 1).

17. He again served as chargé d'affaires for ten months in 1748–9 (ibid.).

18. Diminutive of *coglioni*, testicles; a term of abuse, especially as applied to a frivolous and presumptuous young man (cf. *Vocabolario degli accademici della Crusca*, Florence, 1863–93).

19. 'I don't know, but when I don't want to hear, I don't want to hear.'

20. Hon. Henry Seymour Conway (1719–95), then a lieutenant-colonel and one of the Duke of Cumberland's aides-de-camp; later secretary of state and field marshal; HW's cousin and correspondent.

21. For a list of the British officers killed at Fontenoy see HW to Mann 11 May 1745 OS (Mann iii. 42–3).

22. Alexandre (1725–45), Comte de Beauvau; colonel in the French army; d. 13 May NS of wounds received at Fontenoy (Mann to HW 15 June 1745 NS, Mann iii. 54 and n. 5).

writes me in answer to my compliment on the occasion, *Ma consolation ne peut être que l'ouvrage du temps,*[23] *il émousse la pointe de
tous les sentiments, et il détruit enfin la plus vive douleur que les
événements, dont il est le père, avaient fait naître.* 'Tis very true, but
I should never have thought of saying it so finely. Time nor his sons
shall never *émousse* the point of what makes me dear Mr Walpole's
etc., etc., etc.,

J. CHUTE

To CHUTE, Friday 12 July 1745 OS

Missing; sent with HW's letter to Mann of this date. 'My dear child, your
expressions about me in Mr Chute's letter are so tender and kind that I can only
thank you for them. They proceed totally from your affection for me, which is
my greatest happiness' (Mann to HW 17 Aug. NS, MANN iii. 90).

From CHUTE, Saturday 28 August 1745 NS

Printed in full for the first time from the MS now WSL; the third and fifth
paragraphs, and parts of the first and fourth, are printed in Doran i. 197–8.

Rome, Aug. 28, 1745.

My dear Sir,

YOUR charming dismal letter found me already meditating a
refuge[1] under the short russet mantle[2] of our common grandam
Geneva, for indeed the waters of Babylon[3] had even compassed me
about, it was one wave tossing another, because of the noise of the

23. Prince Craon is fourscore (HW).
This is a mistake; he was only 75 at the
time of his death in 1754.

---

1. From this sentence and the reference
below to Lake Geneva, it appears that
HW had suggested that Chute join him
in a Swiss refuge if the French invaded
England in support of the Young Pretender.
2. 'But look, the morn, in russet mantle
clad' (*Hamlet* I. i. 166). Geneva as a centre

of Protestantism would be a likely refuge
for exiled English Protestants seeking
their 'grandam.' This and the 'waters of
Babylon,' probably echo HW's missing
letter.
3. 'By the waters of Babylon we sat
down and wept' (Psalm 137.1), a favourite
allusion of HW's. This allusion and the
one below follow the wording of the version in the Book of Common Prayer
rather than the Authorized Version.

water-pipes.[4] The Pretendentino was landed in Scotland,[5] was met by 20, by 40,000 Highlanders on the shore, was marched to Edinburgh,[6] was master of it, on his march to London—*caro fratello Duchino,*[7] *non iscrivo più*—*a rivederci a St Giam's;*[8] Abbé Grant[9] had letters in his pocket from seventy lords who would live and die with the boy;[10] my *Lord* Dunbar[11] had sent a Monsignore to school me for my neglect of him; I was to expect all the punishments our dying laws stretched by a future chancellor could bequeath me.[12] Your letter which should have been my only comfort, increased my confusion, all was over, I saw no resource, our army lost, at least, if not beaten, our allies some making emperors and others making butter; the old Opposition making mischief, and the new m[inisters] making nothing at all of the public affairs. What could I think? what could I do! I had once almost resolved to turn abbate and address a sonnet to the Pope's great dog. I might have driven a pretty trade in nails, hair, and the other holy excrements you mention; I would slip in now and then an antique, as a votive Priapus, and though you seem not to think of making your court to the ladies with relics, there are some of this latter sort not unworthy to find a place in the good

4. 'One deep calleth another, because of the noise of the water-pipes' (Psalm 42.7).

5. Charles Edward had sailed from Belle-Île 16 July NS and landed at Eriskay in the Hebrides 3 Aug. NS (MANN iii. 85, n. 28, 87, n. 10).

6. Charles Edward did not reach Edinburgh until 17 Sept. OS (*The Lyon in Mourning*, ed. Henry Paton, Edinburgh, 1895–6, i. 211). Chute is echoing the rumours current at Rome.

7. The Young Pretender's brother, the titular Duke of York.

8. 'Dear little brother Duke, I write no more until we meet at St James's.'

9. Peter Grant (d. 1784), Scottish abbé at Rome 1737–84 (DNB).

10. 'There is at Rome an Abbé Grant, whom I have formerly had occasion to mention to your Grace, and with whom several English correspond, as a man of learning; many not knowing, I am persuaded, that he is totally in the Pretender's interest, and that he cultivates their acquaintance and correspondence for his service. That person lately told an Englishman [Chute] at Rome, that he

had received an account of the project in favour of the Pretender's eldest son from Lord Egglington, and that eighty lords were concerned in it. Abbé Grant held out a letter at the same time. . . . The said Englishman could not persuade him to show him the subscription' (Mann to Newcastle 31 Aug. 1745 NS, S.P. 98/50, f. 232).

11. Hon. James Murray (ca 1690–1770), titular Earl of Dunbar (cr. by the Pretender, 1721); governor to Charles Edward, and the old Pretender's chief adviser at Rome (HW to Mann 2 May 1740 NS, MANN i. 18 and n. 4).

12. I.e., if the Stuarts regained the throne Chute would be attainted and his brother's estate forfeited. '[Dunbar], not being used to the contempt the Chutes have shown him, has done all he can to discredit them, seeing that they were well introduced, by telling everybody they were of the meanest extraction, and that Mr Chute was Mr Whithed's governor' (Mann to HW 26 Oct. 1745 NS, MANN iii. 136).

graces of some of our fair patronesses of the coalition.[13] I wish I could find the *natura femminile* Mr Wright[14] talks of in some collection; I would give it my patron to get blessed by the Pope and send it you for an incentive to your particular devotions; you might place it just over your *prie-dieu*, at the foot of a Santissima which I shall get you from Lucca, and she shall be called la Madonna della Bocca di Verità.[15] But you put me quite out of conceit with all this pretty scheme as you go on; you talk of cheerful hours together in a box upon the lake; my guardian angel had dressed up Geneva like an old beldame which he knows I hate, for the good of my soul, and now comes the devil in the shape of you and our dear Mini (for he will be of the *partie*) to tempt me out of my salvation. I was presently lulled into a reverie (which is always giving him an advantage) which I confess I was ashamed of when I waked, for I found my public spirit had quite given way to my private interest; I once cried out in my sleep—*Scelera ipsa nefasque hac mercede placent*[16] and so I went on till I came to—*quod* MIHI *res acta est*,[17] here I started at the crime my *amour propre* had plunged me in, and was as much confounded as the monk who had persuaded himself of the plurality of worlds from a text in St Matthew,—*nonne decem sunt mundi?*[18] but was struck dumb with the context—*sed ubi sunt novem?*

I see and contemplate every day the likenesses you mention, but alas! they are all amongst the mighty dead. I can find no Camillus[19] nor would he do now if we had him; a Fabius[20] lately was our point, and him we had,[21] but would not have him. I visit his image at the Villa Montalta[22] often, and in vain break out, oh!

---

13. I.e., the wives of the heads of the government, including the Duchesses of Newcastle and Bedford.

14. Possibly Fortunatus Wright (d. 1757) (DNB; MANN i. 423, n. 7).

15. 'The Madonna of the Mouth of Truth'; probably an allusion to the church of Santa Maria in Cosmedin at Rome, called Bocca della Verità from a marble slab that containe an opening from which, traditionally, a perjurer is unable to withdraw his hand.

16. Lucan, *Pharsalia* I. 37–8 (*ipsa* substituted for *ista*): 'Even such crimes and such guilt are a welcome price to pay.'

17. Ibid. I. 45 (*mihi* substituted for *tibi*): 'What was done was done for me.'

18. Not Matthew, but Luke 17.17; the correct reading of the verse in the Vulgate is 'Nonne decem mundati sunt? et novem ubi sunt?' ('Were not the ten [lepers] cleansed? But where are the nine?')

19. Marcus Furius Camillus (d. ?365 B.C.), Roman military hero.

20. Quintus Fabius Maximus Cunctator (d. 203 B.C.).

21. I.e., Sir Robert Walpole, whose policy of trying to avoid war had resembled Fabius's strategy in preserving his army.

22. The Villa Montalto Peretti, also called the Villa Negroni (Ridolfino Venuti, *Accurata, e succinta descrizione . . . di Roma moderna*, Rome, 1767, i. 165–8).

Utinam posses iterum tu, Maxime, nasci!
Cui res cunctando restituenda foret.[23]

They tell us when the election[24] is done, we are to have a vast army in Flanders, and besides that we are to have peace with the King of Prussia; these are very pleasing dreams, if one was asleep enough to enjoy them. I own my fears disturb my rest.

The triumphs of even our victorious fleet are not so complete as you make me imagine. I blush more for Commodore Cooper's[25] bombs at Savona[26] which did not do what they might, than for the poor Duke who was so near doing more than he could at Fontenoy. We must wait with patience for the arrival of Admiral Vernon with twenty men-of-war, who, they face me down here, is to bring our government's answer to the Genoese remonstrance. In the mean time we content ourselves with plundering poor harmless merchant vessels, and brag of the *miglione di scudi* which our captains run away with. This keeps one in countenance, for riches are respectable.

Mr Whithed makes you his compliments; he would have been charmed with putting an argument on foot with the Princess Borghese[27] which she is so well skilled in the handling of, but she has done with the subject, and exhibits herself no more to the English.

I am ever yours,

J. CHUTE

The history of Walpole's acquisition of the Boccapadugli eagle (see DU DEFFAND i. 405 n. 4), which Chute purchased for him, is told in the Walpole-Mann correspondence:

'Mr Chute has pressed me to mention to you a most beautiful antique eagle that has lately been found at Rome. . . . The demand is 250 crowns, but Mr Chute believes . . . that he could get it for 100 zecchins

23. Ovid, *Fasti* II. 241–2 (*utinam* etc. substituted for *ut posses olim tu*): 'Oh that you, Maximus, might be born again! to save the state by biding your time.'

24. Of Grand Duke Francis as Holy Roman Emperor. He was crowned 4 Oct. NS (Mann to HW 31 Aug. NS, MANN iii. 95 and n. 1).

25. Thomas Cooper (d. 1770), com-

mander of the Genoese squadron (MANN iii, 64, n. 4).

26. Cooper bombarded Savona 25 July NS (Mann to HW 27 July and 10 Aug. NS, MANN iii. 76, n. 10, 81, n. 4).

27. Agnese Colonna (1702–80), m. (1723) Principe Camillo Borghese; friend of Lady Walpole and Lady Pomfret (MANN i. 12, n. 51). For her earlier attentions to the English, see SELWYN 5, nn. 17, 19.

ready money. . . . I have not time to say half Mr Chute writes in its praise' (Mann 13 July 1745 NS, Mann iii. 65–6).

'I don't know what to say to Mr Chute's eagle; I would fain have it; I can depend upon his taste—but would not it be folly to be buying curiosities now? How can I tell that I shall have anything in the world to pay for it, by the time it is bought? You may present these reasons to Mr Chute; and if he laughs at them, why then he will buy the eagle for me—if he thinks them of weight, not' (Walpole 26 July OS, ibid. iii. 79).

'I have just received an answer from Mr Chute to the reasons you give against buying the eagle. He desires me to tell you that he does not approve of them, but is doing his best to get it as cheap as he can' (Mann 7 Sept. NS, ibid. iii. 100).

'Mr Chute by his last letter tells me that he was sure I should be pleased to know that he then wrote like his namesake the Evangelist, with his eagle by his side, which had cost 200 crowns, or 100 *ruspi,* which he most willingly had given' (Mann 12 Oct. NS, ibid. iii. 121). It was nearly two years before Walpole received the eagle; see his letter to Mann of 26 June 1747 OS, ibid. iii. 420.

To Chute, April 1746 OS

Missing; mentioned in HW's letter to Mann 16 May 1746 OS (Mann iii. 256). It contained 'farther particulars' of the battle of Culloden, described in HW's letter to Mann 25 April 1746 OS (Mann iii. 247–9).

Chute and Whithed had returned to Florence in January 1746, and in May they began their journey back to England, by way of Bologna, Milan, Venice, Vienna, Dresden, and Berlin. They reached London shortly before 1 October (Mann to Walpole 18 Jan., 24 May, 31 May, 9 Aug. NS; Walpole to Mann 2 Oct. OS, Mann iii. 196, 252, 257, 279, 316–17).

In May 1747 Walpole leased the house at Twickenham that became Strawberry Hill. He wrote to Mann 2 Oct. 1747 (Mann iii. 442), 'The Chuteheds have been extremely good, and visited and stayed with me at Twickenham—I am sorry I must at your expense be so happy. If I were to say all I think of Mr Chute's immense honesty, his sense, his wit, and his knowledge, and his humanity, you would think I was writing a dedication. I am happy in him; I don't make up to him for you, for he loves nothing a quarter so well, but I try to make him regret you less—do you forgive me?'

From CHUTE, Thursday 3 November 1748 OS

Printed from photostat of the MS in the Bodleian Library; first printed, Toynbee *Supp.* ii. 88–9. The MS was bequeathed by Mrs Damer to Sir Wathen Waller in 1828; sold Sotheby's 5 Dec. 1921 (Waller sale), lot 11.

Memoranda by HW (in ink):[1] Richm[ond] Buck.
　　　　　　　　　　　　　Uncle Hor[ace] Cook
　　　　　　　　　　　　　anticip. Marriage
　　　　　　　　　　　　　Tom ?Ventem
　　　　　　　　　　　　　Cutting her flowers
　　　　　　　　　　　　　killing own salad.

Bond Street, November 3d 1748.

I DESIGNED myself the pleasure of visiting you and your plantations[2] (which I suppose before this time in a condition to receive company) some days ago, but have been detained in town on account of a commission of Mr Mann's, in whose behalf I am determined to exert all my skill in heraldry; you can never comprehend what I mean, unless his brother has told you what a beast Rinuccini, who was here last year,[3] has been to him since his return to Florence; he (having taken part, I know not how, in the fracas, which the Boccaneri's f— match[4] occasioned) has made it his business, underhand to abuse and vilify Mr Mann wherever he went, and amongst other things has possessed them with a notion that he is not *cavaliere*.[5] I am at present bent upon vindicating his *diritti cavaliereschi*,[6] at all rates, and expect to make out something at the Heralds' Office to-

---

1. Probably notes for a missing letter. The first four lines have been struck out, which implies that HW used them in his reply. There is also a drawing in pencil; see below, n. 2.

2. HW's *Strawberry Hill Accounts* (ed. Toynbee, Oxford, 1927, pp. 36–8) show that he was at the height of his enthusiasm for planting during the autumn of 1748.

3. The Marchese Folco Rinuccini (1719–60) was in London Sept.–Dec. 1746 (Mann to HW 26 Feb. 1743 NS, HW to Mann

15 Sept. 1746, 25 Dec. 1746 OS, MANN ii. 169 and n. 12, iii. 307, 348).

4. For an account of Madame Bocchineri's scandalous conduct in Mann's garden, which was commemorated by a 'vile poet' in a sonnet Mann was falsely suspected of having approved of, see Mann to HW 13 Aug. 1748 NS (MANN iii. 497–9).

5. Well-born.

6. Chivalric rights. Chute's discoveries about Mann's distinguished ancestry were described by HW to Mann 4 June 1749 OS (MANN iv. 64–5).

morrow morning to that effect. As soon as that is over, I am at your service, and if you have no objection to Monday morning, I hope by that time to be with you; Mr Whithed remembers you in all his letters; he proposes being in town by the tenth of this month.

Addio, yours ever etc., etc.,

John Chute

Mrs Le Neve[7] has been very ill, but I have just heard from her that she is a great deal better.

Gray does not go till Saturday.[8] Do let us have a little dry weather.

———————

Somewhat after this time, Walpole formed the 'Committee' for gothicising Strawberry Hill. Its members were Chute, Bentley, and Walpole himself. Walpole wrote to Mann 10 Jan. 1750 (MANN iv. 111): 'I am going to build a little Gothic Castle at Strawberry Hill.' On 23 June he wrote to Montagu of Bentley's staying at Strawberry Hill, so that the Committee was probably formed about this time. The methods of the Committee have been discussed by W. S. Lewis in 'The Genesis of Strawberry Hill,' *Metropolitan Museum Studies,* vol. v pt i, June, 1934, and in *Collector's Progress.* Chute's sketches and designs (now WSL) show that he had a much greater share in the designing of Strawberry than had been realized.

———————

To Chute, Tuesday 30 March 1751

Printed for the first time from MS now WSL. For the history of the MS see *ante* 20 Aug. 1743 OS.

Arlington Street, March 30, 1751.

My dearest Sir,

AS YOU know the extreme friendship I have for you, and the great regard I had for poor Mr Whithed, you will easily believe the anguish I feel for his death[1] and for your affliction. I don't write

7. Isabella Le Neve (ca 1686–1759), for many years governess-companion to Sir Robert Walpole's children, and after 1745 a member of HW's household (MONTAGU i. 62, n. 27; MANN ii. 36, n. 37, v. 316, 353, n. 5).

8. After an absence of seven months at Stoke, London, SH, etc., Gray returned to Cambridge 5 Nov. 1748 (*Correspondence of Thomas Gray,* ed. Toynbee and Whibley, Oxford, 1935, i. p. iii).

———

1. Whithed's death on 30 March precipitated the 'Nicoll affair' in which HW

now to tell you this, but to press you in the most earnest manner to come to town—in short, to leave a place where everything must inevitably heighten your concern. I can't expect to replace him, but at least you will in me see one who loves you as sincerely as he did, and who will omit nothing that is possible to alleviate your grief—Indeed it is a sad invitation, but in coming to me, you will come where misfortunes are felt, and consequently pitied. Before you receive this, my brother will be no more![2] The unhappy are only fit for one another: I can't love you better, or more than I have ever done since I knew you, but as you will at least want more attention, I shall do everything in my power to prevent your missing Mr Whithed so much as I fear you will. I shall never have a home that will not be yours—we have both seen enough of the world, to care little about it, or how soon we have done with it—but among the very few satisfactions that remain for either of us, I am persuaded we have mutually that of knowing each other's friendship—You have lost what you loved the best, what have I to lose? Adieu! my dear Sir, I feel for you, I pity you, I grieve with you, I want to see you!

Yours ever

Hor. Walpole

From Chute, ca Wednesday 13 December 1752

Missing. See next letter.

---

and Chute were concerned. See GRAY, Appendix 1.

2. Robert Walpole (1701–51), 2d E. of Orford, HW's eldest brother, died the next day 'of an abscess in his back' (*Daily Adv.* 2 April 1751). HW's mild unhappiness on his loss was not comparable to Chute's grief for the death of Whithed.

To Chute, Thursday 14 December 1752

Printed for the first time from the MS now wsl. For the history of the MS see *ante* 20 Aug. 1743 OS.

White's,[1] Dec. 14, 1752, NS.[2]

My dear Sir,

I WRITE you a line only to thank you for yours: there is nothing new: no governor, no preceptor.[3] There is a letter advertised to come out in a day or two to Mr Stone,[4] but as the name is printed at length, I suppose it is Grub-Street:[5] if it should be by Earl or Bishop,[6] I will certainly send it you. All the world is gone a-Christmassing: I can't be in the fashion, for my workmen will never finish.[7] Lady Archibald Hamilton[8] is gathered to the Duchesses of Cleveland and Portsmouth,[9] and is to be buried at Paris,[10] perhaps at Val-de-Grâce.[11] Lady Mary was in town t'other day and hearing you are in Hampshire, asked if she might not hope to see you, as you are within so few miles.[12] Good night.

Yours ever

H. W.

1. HW wrote to Montagu from White's at the same time (MONTAGU i. 144–5).
2. The 'New Style' in dating, which had been in use in most of Europe since the 16th century, was finally adopted in England in Sept. 1752, eleven days being dropped from the calendar.
3. Lord Harcourt, governor to the Prince of Wales (later George III), and Thomas Hayter, Bp of Norwich, the Prince's preceptor, had resigned, the former on 5 Dec. and the latter on the 6th, precipitating a minor political crisis. They were succeeded by Lord Waldegrave and John Thomas, Bp of Peterborough, whose appointments were known by 17th Dec. See HW to Mann 11 Dec. 1752 (MANN iv. 342–8 and notes) for full details.
4. *A Letter to Andrew Stone, Esq.* was announced in the *Daily Advertiser* 14 Dec. as to be published 'on Saturday next' (16 Dec.), but it did not appear until 11 Jan. (*Daily Adv.*). Stone was sub-governor to the Prince, and the resignations were partly the result of his suspected Jacobitism; see MANN, loc. cit.
5. I.e., a eulogy of Stone by an anonymous hack; a satire would have been advertised as 'A Letter to A—— S——,' to lessen the risk of prosecution for libel. HW's prediction was correct; the pamphlet is grossly flattering. No author's name is given in HW's copy, now wsl.
6. I.e., by Harcourt or Hayter.
7. The remodelling of SH; see above, p. 66.
8. Lady Jane Hamilton (d. 6 Dec. 1752), m. (1719) Lord Archibald Hamilton; supposed mistress of Frederick, Prince of Wales and mother of Sir William Hamilton.
9. Mistresses of Charles II.
10. She died at Paris, and was buried in Montmartre cemetery (*Scots Peerage*, i. 62).
11. In which were entombed the hearts (and occasionally, the bodies) of many royal personages.
12. Lady Mary Churchill, HW's half-

To Chute, ?March 1753

Printed for the first time from the MS now wsl. For the history of the MS see *ante* 20 Aug. 1743 OS.

The date is conjectural. On 4 March, HW wrote to Mann from SH: 'Mr Chute and I are come hither for a day or two to inspect the progress of a Gothic staircase' (MANN iv. 361).

Address: To Mr Chute.

My dear Sir,

IF IT will not be inconvenient or disagreeable to you, I shall beg you will go to Strawberry Hill with me tomorrow in a post-chaise.[1] My own is left there, or I should offer you that. The reason of my proposing this, is out of delicacy to poor Mr Bentley,[2] whom I must carry in my chariot, whom I cannot ask to hire a chaise, and it saves him a confusion, not to hire one for him. I know your good nature will feel all this better than I can express it, and consequently will easily forgive this note. Good night. We go between eleven and twelve.

To Chute, Saturday 4 August 1753

Printed from *Works* v. 407–11; reprinted, Wright iii. 12–16; Cunningham ii. 345–9; Toynbee iii. 176–81. HW's account of Stowe in this letter should be compared with new material in *Apollo*, June 1973, xcvii. 542–604.

Stowe,[1] Aug. 4, 1753.

My dear Sir,

YOU would deserve to be scolded, if you had not lost almost as much pleasure as you have disappointed me of.[2] Whether George Montagu[3] will be so content with your commuting punishments, I

sister, lived at Chalfont Park in south-west Bucks, some twenty miles from the Vyne.

---

1. HW is asking Chute to hire a post-chaise (to attend a meeting of the Committee at SH) because there was room for only two in HW's chariot, and he did not want the impecunious Bentley to be embarrassed.

2. Richard Bentley (1708–82), HW's cor-

respondent, and, like Chute, a member of the 'Committee' for SH.

---

1. Stowe, Bucks, Lord Temple's seat.

2. In not accompanying Mr Walpole on a visit to Mr George Montagu at Great-worth (HW). This was the house Montagu rented near Brackley, Northants (MONTAGU i. 146, n. 1).

3. George Montagu (ca 1713–80), HW's correspondent.

don't know: I should think not: he *cried and roared all night*[4] when I delivered your excuse. He is extremely well-housed, after having roamed like a Tartar about the country[5] with his whole personal estate at his heels. There is an extensive view, which is called pretty: but Northamptonshire is no county to please me. What entertained me was, that he who in London was grown an absolute recluse, is over head and ears in neighbours, and as popular as if he intended to stand for the county, instead of having given up the town. The very first morning after my arrival, as we were getting into the chaise to go to Wroxton,[6] they notified a Sir [Harry Danvers],[7] a young squire, booted and spurred, and buckskin-breeched. 'Will you drink any chocolate?'—'No; a little wine and water, if you please.'—I suspected nothing but that he had rode till he was dry. 'Nicolò, get some wine and water.' He desired the water might be warm—I began to stare—Montagu understood the dialect, and ordered a negus.—I had great difficulty to keep my countenance, and still more when I saw the baronet finish a very large jug indeed. To be sure, he wondered as much at me who did not finish a jug; and I could not help reflecting, that living always in the world makes one as unfit for living out of it, as always living out of it does for living in it. Knightley,[8] the knight of the shire, has been entertaining all the parishes round with a turtle-feast, which, so far from succeeding, has almost made him suspected for a *Jew*,[9] as the country parsons have not yet learned to wade into green fat.

The roads are very bad to Greatworth, and such numbers of gates, that if one loved punning one should call it the *Gate House*. The proprietor[10] had a wonderful invention: the chimneys, which are of

4. A phrase of Mr Montagu's (HW).
5. He had come to Greatworth *via* Bruern Abbey, Oxon, and Roel, Glos (HW to Montagu 22 May 1753, MONTAGU i. 146).
6. Lord Guilford's seat near Banbury, Oxon; see below.
7. Sir Henry Danvers (1731–53), 4th Bt, of Culworth, Northants. He died suddenly a few days later. See HW to Montagu 16 Aug. 1753 (MONTAGU i. 155).
8. Valentine Knightley (1718–54) of Fawsley; M.P. Northants 1748–54 (George Baker, *The History and Antiquities of the County of Northampton*, 1822–41, i. 383).

9. A violent wave of anti-semitism, occasioned by the passage of a bill for the naturalization of the Jews in the last session of Parliament, was sweeping England during the summer of 1753 with the special encouragement of the lower clergy. The agitation became so intense that the government repealed the bill a few months later; see the account in *Mem. Geo. II* i. 357–67, and *post* HW to Bentley Sept. 1753.
10. Charles Howe (1661–1742), who built the house early in the century. It was destroyed by fire in 1793 (Baker, op. cit. i. 509).

stone, have niches and benches in them, where the man used to sit and smoke. I had twenty disasters, according to custom; lost my way, and had my French boy almost killed by a fall with his horse: but I have been much pleased. When I was at Park Place[11] I went to see Sir H. Englefield's,[12] which Mr C[hurchill][13] and Lady M[ary] prefer, but I think very undeservedly, to Mr Southcote's.[14] It is not above a quarter as extensive, and wants the river. There is a pretty view of Reading seen under a rude arch, and the water is well disposed. The buildings are very insignificant, and the house far from good. The town of Henley has been extremely disturbed with an engagement between the ghosts of Miss Blandy and her father,[15] which continued so violent, that some bold persons, to prevent farther bloodshed, broke in, and found it was two jackasses which had got into the kitchen.

I felt strangely tempted to stay at Oxford and survey it at my leisure; but, as I was alone, I had not courage.[16] I passed by Sir James Dashwood's,[17] a vast new house, situated so high that it seems to stand for the county as well as himself. I did look over Lord Jersey's,[18]

11. Conway's seat in Berks, near Henley-on-Thames.

12. Whiteknights (HW). It was the seat of Sir Henry Englefield (d. 1780), 6th Bt, in Berks, near Reading. HW describes the owner as 'one of the first improvers on the new style [in gardening],' who 'selected with singular taste that chief beauty of all gardens, prospect and fortunate points of view' ('Essay on Modern Gardening,' *Works* ii. 541). The house was rebuilt and the gardens and park further remodelled later in the century (*Vict. Co. Hist. Berks* iii. 210–11).

13. HW's brother-in-law, Charles Churchill (?1720–1812), of Chalfont Park, Bucks; M.P. (MANN i. 222, n. 26).

14. Woburn Farm, on the Thames between Chertsey and Weybridge, Surrey; the seat of Philip Southcote (d. 1758), 'first designer of the *ferme ornée*' (COLE ii. 275, n. 15).

15. Mary Blandy of Henley was hanged 6 April 1752, having been convicted of poisoning her father, Francis Blandy, who opposed her marriage to William Henry Cranstoun. See DNB and references in MONTAGU i. 142, n. 10.

16. HW seems to have felt similar emo-

tions the following year when he wrote to Bentley 9 July 1754 that he had not yet been to see the tomb he had erected to his mother in Westminster Abbey; 'none of my acquaintance were in town, and I literally had not courage to venture alone among the Westminster boys at the Abbey.'

17. Kirtlington Park, Oxon, the seat of Sir James Dashwood (1715–79), 2d Bt, M.P. Oxon 1740–54, 1761–8 (MONTAGU i. 320 n. 3). HW's note in *Works*, presumably written after Chute's death in 1776, reads erroneously 'At High Wycombe'; but, as Mrs Toynbee pointed out, HW was probably thinking of Sir Francis Dashwood's seat at West Wycombe Park. Kirtlington had been begun in 1742, and was sufficiently completed for occupancy by 1746, though decoration continued for three decades. See the account and illustrations in Christopher Hussey, *English Country Houses, Early Georgian, 1715–1760*, 1955, pp. 170–4; and *Country Life*, 1912, xxxi. 542–9.

18. Middleton (HW). Near Middleton Stony, Oxon; seat of William Villiers (ca 1712–69), 3d E. of Jersey, 1721. The house, built in the mid-17th century, had been

which was built for a hunting-box, and is still little better. But now I am going to tell you how delightful a day I passed at Wroxton. Lord Guildford[19] has made George Montagu so absolutely viceroy over it, that we saw it more agreeably than you can conceive; roamed over the whole house, found every door open, saw not a creature, had an extreme good dinner, wine, fruit, coffee and tea in the library, were served by fairies, tumbled over the books, said one or two talismanic words, and the cascade played, and went home loaded with pineapples and flowers.—You will take me for Monsieur de Coulanges,[20] I describe eatables so feelingly;[21] but the manner in which we were served made the whole delicious. The house was built by a Lord Downe[22] in the reign of James I;[23] and though there is a fine hall[24] and a vast dining-room[25] below, and as large a drawing-room above,[26] it is neither good nor agreeable; one end of the front was never finished, and might have a good apartment. The library is added by this Lord, and is a pleasant chamber. Except loads of old portraits, there is no tolerable furniture. A whole-length of the first Earl of Downe[27] is in the Bath robes, and has a coif under the hat and feather.[28] There is a charming picture of Prince Henry[29] about

much repaired and enlarged by Lord Jersey; it burned in 1755 (not 1753 as usually stated) and was replaced by a new house (J. P. Neale, *Views of the Seats of Noblemen and Gentlemen*, 2d ser., Vol. V, 1829; *London Evening Post* 1–3 May 1755).

19. Francis North (1704–90), 7th Bn North; cr. (1752) E. of Guilford; Montagu's cousin by marriage (MONTAGU ii. 352).

20. Philippe-Emmanuel (1631–1716), Marquis de Coulanges; cousin of Mme de Sévigné (DU DEFFAND ii. 139, n. 8).

21. HW has in mind a letter from Coulanges to Mesdames de Sévigné and de Grignan 20 June 1695: 'Nous vous donnâmes aussi un très-bon soupé; et ce fut dans l'enthousiasme du veau, du bœuf et du mouton, qui se trouvèrent au suprême degré de bonté, que je fis en soupant ce triolet, qui me parut avoir approbation. . . .

Quel veau! quel bœuf! et quel mouton! Rôti, soyez exquis et blond . . .

(*Recueil de lettres choisies pour servir de suite aux lettres de Madame de Sévigné à Madame de Grignan*, 1751, p. 305; HW's

copy is Hazen, *Cat. of HW's Lib.*, No. 951).

22. Sir William Pope (1573–1631), K.B., 1603; cr. (1628) E. of Downe.

23. It was completed in 1618 (F. G. Brabant, *Oxfordshire*, 1933, p. 290).

24. 'The Great Hall . . . is a very remarkable apartment, with . . . enwreathed columns beautifully sculptured to support its carved oak gallery' (Charles Latham, *In English Homes*, 1904–9, i. 167; photographs on pp. 168, 170–2).

25. 'The dining-room has fine oak panelling, and a plaster ceiling with a strange pattern of musical instruments' (Brabant, op. cit. 291; photographed in Latham, op. cit. i. 167).

26. Described in Latham, op. cit. i. 173.

27. William Pope (1573–1631), cr. 1628 E. of Downe.

28. Probably the portrait attributed to Marcus Gheeraerts by Lionel Cust, 'Marcus Gheeraerts,' *Walpole Society 1913–1914*, iii. 32 (photograph, Plate XVIII). A number of other portraits by Gheeraerts at Wroxton are also described and illustrated in this article.

29. Henry Frederick (1594–1612), P. of Wales.

twelve years old, drawing his sword to kill a stag, with a Lord Harrington;[30] a good portrait of Sir Owen Hopton,[31] 1590; your *pious* grandmother, my Lady Dacre,[32] which I think like you; some good Cornelius Johnsons;[33] a Lord North[34] by Riley,[35] good; and an extreme fine portrait by him of the Lord Keeper:[36] I have never seen but few of the hand, but most of them have been equal to Lely and the best of Sir Godfrey.[37] There is too a curious portrait of Sir Thomas Pope,[38] the founder of Trinity College, Oxford, said to be by Holbein. The chapel is new, but in a pretty Gothic taste, with a very long window of painted glass,[39] very tolerable. The frieze is pendent, just in the manner I propose for the eating-room[40] at Strawberry Hill. Except one scene, which is indeed noble, I cannot much commend the without-doors. This scene consists of a beautiful lake entirely shut in with wood: the head falls into a fine cascade, and that into a

30. John Harington (1592–1614), 2d Bn Harington of Exton, 1613. (See OSSORY iii. 189, nn. 7, 8).

31. Sir Owen Hopton (1519–91), Kt, 1561; Lieutenant of the Tower of London 1570–90 (*Miscellanea genealogica et heraldica*, ed. J. J. Howard, 1900, 3d ser. iii. 10). Anne, wife of the 1st E. of Downe (see n. 27 above), was his daughter.

32. His great-grandmother: Dorothy North (ca 1605–98), m. 1 (1625) Richard Lennard, 13th Lord Dacre; m. 2 (1650), as his second wife, Chaloner Chute, Speaker of the House of Commons, Chute's great-grandfather; her daughter, Catherine Lennard, married the younger Chaloner Chute, and was John Chute's grandmother (GEC; *Vict. Co. Hist. Hants* iv. 161; C. W. Chute, *History of The Vyne*, 1888, pp. 69, 73, 77–8).

33. Cornelius Johnson (or Jonson van Ceulen) (1593–ca 1664), born in London of Flemish parents (A. J. Finberg, 'A Chronological List of Portraits by Cornelius Johnson, or Jonson,' *Walpole Society*, 1921–2, x. 6–7). Finberg (pp. 9–10, 14–16) lists eight portraits by him at Wroxton, including that of Lady Dacre.

34. Probably Dudley North (ca 1602–77), 4th Lord North. Latham (op. cit. i. 174) says that 'one of the most interesting portraits at Wroxton is of him.'

35. John Riley (1646–91), whom HW considered 'one of the best native painters that has flourished in England' (*Anecdotes, Works* iii. 372).

36. Francis North (1637–85), cr (1683) Bn of Guilford; lord keeper of the Great Seal 1682–5. He acquired Wroxton by his marriage to Lady Frances Pope, sister and co-heir of Thomas, 4th E. of Downe. Riley's portrait of him at Wroxton was engraved by J. S. Agar and published in 1818 in Lodge's *Portraits* (*BM Cat. of Engraved British Portraits* ii. 398).

37. Kneller.

38. Sir Thomas Pope (1508–59), Kt, 1536; founded Trinity College, Oxford, 1555; uncle of the 1st E. of Downe (George Baker, *The History and Antiquities of the County of Northampton*, 1822–41, i. 707). The portrait at Wroxton, 'plausibly attributed to Holbein' (H. E. D. Blakiston in DNB), was engraved by William Skelton and published in 1821 (*BM Cat. of Engraved British Portraits* iii. 494). It does not appear in catalogues of Holbein's paintings.

39. By Bernhard van Linge (fl. 1622–32), Dutch glass-painter in England. It represented 'stories from the Bible' (*Anecdotes, Works* iii. 158; Thieme and Becker). Sanderson Miller placed the glass in a new chancel (W. Hawkes, 'Miller's Work at Wroxton,' *Cake and Cockhorse*, Banbury Hist. Soc., 1969, iv. 99–106).

40. The Great Parlour, or Refectory, completed in 1754 (W. S. Lewis, 'The Genesis of Strawberry Hill,' *Metropolitan Museum Studies*, 1934, vol. v pt i. 70).

serpentine river, over which is a little Gothic seat[40a] like a round temple, lifted up by a shaggy mount. On an eminence in the park is an obelisk erected to the honour and at the expense of 'optimus' and 'munificentissimus' the late Prince of Wales, 'in loci amœnitatem et memoriam adventus eius.'[41] There are several paltry Chinese buildings and bridges, which have the merit or demerit of being the progenitors of a very numerous race all over the kingdom: at least they were of the very first. In the church is a beautiful tomb of an Earl and Countess of Downe,[42] and the tower is in a good plain Gothic style, and was once, they tell you, still more beautiful; but Mr Miller,[43] who designed it, unluckily once in his life happened to think rather of beauty than of the water-tables, and so it fell down the first winter.[44]

On Wednesday morning we went to see a sweet little chapel at Steane,[45] built in 1620 by Sir T. Crewe,[46] Speaker in the time of the first James and Charles. Here are remains of the mansion-house, but quite in ruins:[47] the chapel is kept up by my Lady Arran,[48] the last of the race. There are seven or eight monuments. On one is this epitaph, which I thought pretty enough:

> *Conjux casta, parens felix, matrona pudica,*
> *Sara viro, mundo Martha, Maria Deo.*[49]

On another is the most affected inscription I ever saw, written by

40a. The seat, designed by Sanderson Miller, is illustrated in Miller, loc. cit.

41. 'For the pleasantness of the place and in memory of his visit.' In June 1805 an inscription was added to the obelisk commemorating a visit of 'Georgius Walliæ Princeps Frederici nepos' (George, Prince of Wales, Frederick's grandson) (*History, Gazetteer, and Directory of the County of Oxford,* Peterborough, 1852, p. 634).

42. Anne Hopton (1561–1625), m. 1 (ca 1585) Henry, 3d Lord Wentworth (d. 1593); m. 2 (1595) Sir William Pope, cr. (1628) E. of Downe (GEC; *History, Gazetteer, and Directory of the County of Oxford,* Peterborough, 1852, p. 635).

43. Sanderson Miller (1717–80), amateur architect (MONTAGU i. 156, n. 3).

44. It was built in the spring of 1747 and the stone octagon on its top collapsed in Dec. 1748 (Hawkes, loc. cit.; information from Mr Michael McCarthy). Letters (one misdated) to Miller from

his friends on this misfortune are printed in Lilian Dickins and Mary Stanton, *An Eighteenth-Century Correspondence,* New York, 1910, pp. 277–8.

45. In Northants near Brackley.

46. Sir Thomas Crewe (1565–1633), Kt, 1623; speaker of the House of Commons 1623–6.

47. 'The manor-house . . . was deserted and taken down between 1740 and 1750' (George Baker, *The History and Antiquities of the County of Northampton,* 1822–41, i. 686).

48. Elizabeth Crewe (ca 1680–1756), m. (1705) Charles Butler, cr. (1693) E. of Arran.

49. 'Chaste wife, happy parent, virtuous matron; Sarah to her husband, Martha to the world, Mary to God.' The epitaph is that of Sir Thomas Crewe's wife, Temperance Bray (ca 1581–1619) (Baker, op. cit. i. 687).

two brothers[50] on their sister;[51] they say, *This agreeable mortal translated her into immortality such a-day:*[52] but I could not help laughing at one quaint expression, to which time has given a droll sense: *She was a constant lover of the best.*[53]

I have been here[54] these two days, extremely amused and charmed indeed. Wherever you stand you see an Albano landscape. Half as many buildings I believe would be too many, but such a profusion gives inexpressible richness.[55] You may imagine I have some private reflections entertaining enough, not very communicable to the company: the Temple of Friendship, in which, among twenty memorandums of quarrels,[56] is the bust of Mr Pitt:[57] Mr James Grenville[58] is now in the house,[59] whom his uncle disinherited[60] for his attachment

50. Sir Thomas Crewe's sons, John (ca 1598–1679) and Nathaniel (living 1651) (ibid. i. 685, 688).

51. Temperance Crewe (ca 1609–34), m. John Browne of Eydon (ibid.).

52. 'This becoming mortall translated her into immortalitye Sept. 22. 1634 aged 25 yeares' (ibid. i. 688).

53. 'A constant lover of the best. Of a disposition amiable and cheerfull: and a witt high and pleasant. Her spirite of a dayntye elevation,' etc. (ibid.). HW may have had in mind the anonymous 'drolleries,' *The Constant Lovers; with the Humours of Sir Timothy Littlewit and his Man Trip*, 1714, and *The Constant Lovers, or The False Friend*, 1719.

54. At Stowe.

55. Francesco Albani or Albano (1578–1660) was mentioned in the dedicatory verses to B. Seeley's *Stowe*, 1744, often reprinted:

'. . . when Poussin's or Albano's hand
On glowing canvas the rich landscape plann'd'

(HW's copy, Hazen, *Cat. of HW's Lib.*, No. 2387:4, of the 1768 edn has his note on p. 4 attributing these verses to 'Hannah Chamber Countess Temple'). HW repeated his remarks about Stowe to Montagu 24 Sept. 1762 (MONTAGU ii. 44). See also ibid. ii. 313–17. For a list of the buildings see ii. 44, n. 7. For another reference by HW to Albano's landscapes see *post* HW to Bentley 5 Aug. 1752.

56. HW is referring to the shifting political alliances of the late owner of Stowe and builder of its gardens, Sir

Richard Temple (1675–1749), cr. (1714) Bn and (1718) Vct Cobham. He broke with Sir Robert Walpole in 1733 and later quarrelled with the Pelhams and Carteret. Christopher Hussey points out that Stowe's embellishment expressed Cobham's Whig politics (*Country Life* 12 Sept., 19 Sept., 26 Sept. 1947, cii. 526–9, 578–81, 626–9; also idem, *English Gardens and Landscapes 1700-1750*, 1967, pp. 100–3).

57. William Pitt (1708–78), cr. (1766) E. of Chatham; later secretary of state. This bust and the others in the Temple of Friendship are attributed to Michael Rysbrack in George Bickham, *Beauties of Stowe*, 1750, p. 54; but are not included in the discussion of his work at Stowe in M. I. Webb, *Michael Rysbrack, Sculptor*, 1954. Hussey, *English Gardens*, p. 102 attributes the busts to Rysbrack and Scheemakers.

58. Hon. James Grenville (1715–83), nephew of Lord Cobham; M.P.; a lord of trade and deputy-paymaster of the forces 1746–55; a lord of the Treasury 1756–61; cofferer of the Household 1761–3. HW, in his *Memoirs* for 1751, writes 'James, the youngest of the three had all the defects of his brothers, and had turned them to the best account' (*Mem. Geo. II* i. 136).

59. That is, as a guest. On Cobham's death in 1749 his estates had passed to his sister, Hester Grenville, Cts Temple, and on her death in 1752 to her eldest son, Richard, Earl Temple.

60. In 1746, for adhering to Pitt when

to that very Pylades[61] Mr Pitt. He broke with Mr Pope, who is deified in the Elysian Fields,[62] before the inscription for his head was finished.[63] That of Sir J. Barnard,[64] which was bespoke by the name of a bust of my Lord Mayor, was by a mistake of the sculptor done for Alderman Perry.[65] The statue of the King,[66] and that 'honori, laudi, virtuti divæ Carolinæ,'[67] make one smile, when one sees the ceiling where Britannia rejects and hides the reign of King ———.[68] But I have no patience at building and planting a satire! Such is the Temple of Modern Virtue in ruins![69] The Grecian Temple[70] is

the latter accepted the pay office and changed his politics (*Grenville Papers,* ed. W. J. Smith, 1852–3, i. 424–5; L. M. Wiggin, *The Faction of Cousins,* New Haven, 1958, pp. 113–15).

61. HW usually uses this only as a synonym for devoted friendship, as in his frequent references to himself and Mann as Orestes and Pylades, but here he seems to be implying other details of myth as well.

62. A part of the gardens containing the Temple of British Worthies, in which Pope's bust stands (J. A. Temple, *The Temple Memoirs,* 1925, pp. 169–70). This, and the other busts in the Temple, are usually attributed to Rysbrack, but M. I. Webb, although accepting most of them, expresses grave doubts about the bust of Pope (Webb, op. cit. 136).

63. HW seems to be mistaken in assuming a breach between Cobham and Pope; there is no other indication that their friendship, which began about 1725, was ever broken (Norman Ault, *New Light on Pope,* 1949, p. 355; information from Professor George Sherburn). HW may have been misled by a cryptic couplet appended to Pope's bust in 1750, and perhaps still there in 1753 (quoted in Bickham, op. cit. 39), in the absence of a formal inscription; the latter, highly laudatory, was not added until the late 1760s (Seeley's *Stowe,* 1762, p. 26 and Thomas Martyn, *The English Connoisseur,* 1766, ii. 108, both of which mention the bust as being 'without any inscription'; Seeley's *Stowe,* 1768, p. 22, which gives the inscription).

64. Sir John Barnard (1685–1764), Kt, 1732; M.P.; lord mayor of London 1737–8 (A. B. Beaven, *The Aldermen of the City of London,* 1908–13, ii. 126; DNB).

65. Micajah Perry (d. 1753), M.P.; lord mayor 1738–9 (Beaven, loc. cit.). If HW means that the bust called Barnard's in the Temple of British Worthies actually represents Perry, the mistake is not noted in the descriptions of Stowe. There was no inscription on the bust at this time (Bickham, op. cit. 45).

66. 'The next object of view is a Corinthian column, on which is the statue of his present Majesty, with this inscription: GEORGIO AUGUSTO' (ibid. 19).

67. 'To the honour, praise, and virtue of the divine Caroline.' The inscription was curtailed to *Divæ Carolinæ* sometime in the 1760s (Bickham, op. cit. 21; Seeley's *Stowe,* 1762, p. 21; 1768, p. 7).

68. '[In the] emblematic painting on the ceiling [of the Temple of Friendship] . . . sits Britannia: upon one side is held the glory of her annals on cartoons, whereon these words are written, "The Reigns of Queen Elizabeth and Edward III," and on the other is offered "The Reign of ———," which she frowns upon and puts by. The name is artfully covered with Britannia's hand; but it is an easy matter to guess what reign is meant. . . . Never accept it, honest Lady, till corruption is at an end, and public spirit revive' (Bickham, op. cit. 54). The Temple was destroyed by fire about 1947 (*Country Life* cii. 581).

69. 'Another thing very observable near this Temple [of Ancient Virtue] is a heap of artificial ruins, which forms an admirable contrast with this fine building. . . . These ruins, and the old statue just close to them, are intended to show us the shattered state of modern virtue, which as early almost as its birth, becomes withered and decrepit' (Bickham, op. cit. 30). The name was still preserved in 1762,

glorious: this I openly worship: in the heretical corner of my heart I adore the Gothic building,[71] which by some unusual inspiration Gibbs[72] has made pure and beautiful and venerable. The style has a propensity to the Venetian or mosque-Gothic, and the great column[73] near it makes the whole put one in mind of the Place of St Mark. The windows are throughout consecrated with painted glass; most of it from the Priory at Warwick, a present from that foolish [Mr Wise],[74] who quarrelled with me (because his father was a gardener) for asking him if Lord Brook had planted much.[75]—Apropos to painted glass, I forgot to tell you of a sweet house which Mr Montagu carried me to see, belonging to a Mr Holman, a Catholic, and called Warkworth.[76] The situation is pretty, the front charming, composed of two round and two square towers. The court within is incomplete on one side; but above-stairs is a vast gallery with four bow-windows and twelve other large ones, all filled with the arms of the old peers of England, with all their quarterings entire. You don't de-

but by 1768 the Temple had been demoted to merely 'a ruin' (Seeley's *Stowe*, 1762, p. 22; 1768, p. 17). HW has noted in his copy of the 1768 edn (now WSL), 'This used to be called the Temple of Modern Virtue, in ruins.'

70. 'Originally designed by Kent from the measurements of the Maison Carrée at Nismes, but left unfinished till 1763' (J. A. Temple, op. cit. 172). According to the Stowe MSS at the Huntington Library and the Lyttelton MSS at Hagley Hall (information from Mr Michael McCarthy), it was designed by Lord Temple, with ornaments by Borra; it was begun 1749 and finished 1763 as 'Temple of Concord and Victory'; it is illustrated in *Country Life*, 1947, cii. 627.

71. Called the Temple of Liberty and dedicated 'to the liberty of our ancestors' (Bickham, op. cit. 46–7). 'The Gothic Temple is a large building of red stone, 70 feet high, upon a rising ground, adorned in the Gothic way with carved work and painted glass. . . . You enter a circular room, the dome of which is ornamented with the descents of the Temple family. On the second storey is a gallery' (Seeley's *Stowe*, 1768, p. 30; HW added 'It was designed by Gibbs'). It is illustrated in *Country Life*, 1947, cii. 628.

72. James Gibbs (1682–1754) designed

the Pillar (see next note) and other structures at Stowe. His designing the Gothic temple is established by L. Whistler, 'Authorship of the Stowe Temples,' *Country Life*, 1950, cviii. 1003.

73. 'Lord Cobham's Pillar, 115 feet high; adorned with a statue of his lordship on the summit. This monument was designed by Gibbs' (Seeley's *Stowe*, 1797, p. 29). The pillar was built 1746–7 (MSS in Huntington Library cited by Mr Michael McCarthy). The column is illustrated in *Country Life*, 1947, cii. 628.

74. Left blank in *Works*. Previous editors have inserted 'Greathead' but HW calls Wise by name in writing the story to Lady Ossory 10 June 1777 (OSSORY i. 353–4). He was Matthew Wise (d. 1776), of the Priory, Warwick, eldest son of Henry Wise (1653–1738), gardener to William III, Anne, and George I. The elder Wise purchased the Priory in 1709 (*Vict. Co. Hist. Warwick* vi. 162).

75. At Warwick Castle; Francis Greville (1719–73), 8th Bn Brooke, cr. (1746) E. Brooke, (1759) E. of Warwick.

76. HW seems to have mistaken the name of the proprietor. Warkworth had belonged to the Holmans, a Catholic family, since 1629, but in 1746 it came into the possession of Francis Eyre (ca 1732–1804), a pamphleteer and apologist

serve, after deserting me, that I should tempt you to such a sight; but this alone is worth while to carry you to Greatworth.[77]

Adieu, my dear Sir! I return to Strawberry tomorrow, and forgive you enough not to deprive myself of the satisfaction of seeing you there whenever you have nothing else to do.

Yours ever,

Hor. Walpole

To Chute, Tuesday 30 April 1754

Printed from Toynbee iii. 228–9 and *Supp.* ii. 94; printed in part in *Works* v. 411–12; Wright iii. 53–4; Cunningham ii. 382–3. The MS passed from HW to Mrs Damer, and was bequeathed by her to Sir Wathen Waller, 1st Bt; sold Sotheby's 5 Dec. 1921 (first Waller Sale) lot 10 to 'Hunt'; not further traced.

Arlington Street, April 30, 1754.

'MY GOD! Farinelli,[1] what has this nation done to the King of Spain,[2] that the moment we have anything dear and precious he should tear it from us?'—This is not the beginning of my letter to you, nor does it allude to *Mr Bentley:*[3] much less is it relative to the captivity of the ten tribes; nor does *the King* signify Ben-hadad or Tiglath-pileser;[4] nor Spain, Assyria, as Dr Pocock[5] or Warburton,[6]

for Catholicism, nephew of William Holman (d. 1740). Warkworth was sold in 1805 and the house demolished in 1806 (Baker, op. cit. i. 739–41; GM 1804, lxxiv pt. ii. 1072–3).

77. Chute was about to leave for a visit to Montagu on 16 Aug. 1753 (MONTAGU i. 155).

———

1. Carlo Broschi (1705–82), called Farinelli, Neapolitan male soprano; came to London in 1734; went to Madrid in 1737 where he became a favourite of both Philip V and Ferdinand VI (HW to Mann 5 Nov. 1741 and 30 June 1742 OS, MANN i. 190 and n. 4, 478 and n. 27).

2. Ferdinand VI (1713–59), K. of Spain 1746–59.

3. Who had retired to Jersey sometime in the autumn of 1753 to escape his creditors and his wife (see *post* HW to Bentley 19 Dec. 1753).

4. In 1 Kings 15.18 and 2 Kings 15.29.

5. Probably Richard Pococke (1704–65), D.C.L.; traveller and divine; Bp of Ossory 1756–65, of Meath, 1765. HW describes him in a note in his copy (now WSL) of John Nichols, *Biographical and Literary Anecdotes*, 1782, p. 171, as 'a man of great virtue, learning, simplicity and modesty, but of very slow parts, and utterly ignorant of the world,' and gives two anecdotes of him. HW probably has in mind Pococke's *A Description of the East*, 1743–5, which abounds, particularly in the chapters on the Near East, in somewhat far-fetched derivations of modern place names from Biblical ones, and in conjectures about probable equivalents where no possible philological connection existed. HW's copy of the book is Hazen, *Cat. of HW's Lib.*, No. 1099.

6. William Warburton (1698–1779), D.D., Bp of Gloucester, 1759; editor of

misled by dissimilitude of names, or by the Septuagint, may, for very good reasons, imagine—but it is literally the commencement of my Lady Rich's[7] epistle to Farinelli, on the recall of General Wall,[8] as she relates it herself. It serves extremely well for my own lamentation, when I sit down by the waters of Strawberry, and think of ye, O Chute and Bentley!

I have seen *Creusa*,[9] and more than agree with you: it is the only new tragedy that I ever saw, and really liked. The plot is most interesting, and, though so complicated, quite clear and natural. The circumstance of so much distress being brought on by characters, every one good, yet acting consistently with their principles towards the misfortunes of the drama, is quite new and pleasing. Nothing offended me but that lisping Miss Haughton,[10] whose every speech is inarticulately oracular.

I have been forced to agree with Clermont[11] for seventy pound:[12]

Pope, 1751. HW, who considered Warburton 'all-arrogant and absurd' (GRAY i. 39), is here alluding to his *Divine Legation of Moses*, 1738–41 (see HW to Montagu 11 May 1769, MONTAGU ii. 278).

7. One of the daughters and co-heiresses of the Lord Mohun killed in a duel with Duke Hamilton (Mary Berry). Elizabeth Griffith (ca 1692–1773), m. (1714) Sir Robert Rich, 4th Bt. Her penchant for singers is mentioned by HW to Mann 22 July 1744 OS, MANN ii. 481.

8. Richard Wall (1694–1778), born in Ireland, diplomatist and lieutenant-general in the Spanish service; ambassador to England 1747–April 1754, when he was recalled to Madrid to become secretary of state for foreign affairs (MANN iii. 504, n. 10, iv. 426, n. 10).

9. By William Whitehead (1715–85); poet laureate, 1757. *Creusa*, based on the *Ion* of Euripides, was first performed at Drury Lane 20 April 1754 with Garrick and Mrs Pritchard in the leading parts, and was acted nine times that season (John Genest, *Some Account of the English Stage*, Bath, 1832, iv. 388), and three times in 1755 (*London Stage 1660–1800*, pt 4, ed. G. W. Stone, Carbondale, Ill., 1962, i. 420–4, 426–7, 471, 479). William Mason thought that the play had been unduly neglected, remarking that 'there is hardly a single tragedy of English manufacture, in which the three unities are

more accurately observed,' but added that the catastrophe 'does not satisfy' (Mason's memoirs of Whitehead in Whitehead's *Poems*, Vol. III, 1788, pp. 74–6).

10. In the rôle of the 'Pythia' (Genest, op. cit. iv. 388). 'Mrs Haughton, formerly of Drury Lane playhouse,' died 6 Dec. 1771 (GM 1771, xli. 571). She acted at Drury Lane 1753–62 (Dougald MacMillan, *Drury Lane Calendar 1747–1776*, Oxford, 1938, pp. 333, 89). When Garrick revived *Creusa* the following season, Whitehead wrote to Dodsley from Leipzig 1 April 1755, 'I still find the "Pythia" does not please; though she plays the part sensibly, yet everybody tells me she seems to have no idea of the fury and vehemence of her character where she is to assume an air of inspiration' (Ralph Straus, *Robert Dodsley*, 1910, p. 111).

11. Jean-François Clermont (1717–1807), called Ganif; French painter in England for many years, returning to France in 1754 (*Anecdotes, Works* iii. 449; *SH Accounts*, ed. Toynbee, Oxford, 1927, 74). He 'painted in grotesque, foliages with birds and monkeys' (*Works*, loc. cit.).

12. On 2 July 1754 HW paid Clermont £73 10s. for painting the Library ceiling at SH (*SH Accounts* 5). For a further account of the ceiling see *post* HW to Bentley 17 March 1754. HW's pencil sketch for the ceiling is now WSL.

I have beat down fifty, but could not get it lower. The last time I went to Strawberry, I found the stucco men as busy as so many Irish bees, plastering up eggs and anchors for the frieze of the eating-room,[13] but I soon made them destroy all they had done.

I was last night at a little ball at Lady Anne Furnese's[14] for the new Lords, Dartmouth[15] and North;[16] but nothing passed worth relating: indeed the only event since you left London was the tragi-comedy that was acted last Saturday at the opera. One of the dramatic guards fell flat on his face and motionless in an apoplectic fit.[17] The Princess[18] and her children were there. Miss Chudleigh,[19] who *apparemment* had never seen a man fall on his face before, went into the most theatric fit of kicking and shrieking that ever was seen. Several other women, who were preparing their fits, were so distanced, that she had the whole house to herself, and indeed such a confusion for half an hour I never saw! The next day, at my Lady Townshend's, old Charles Stanhope[20] asked what these fits were called? Charles Townshend[21] replied, '*The true convulsive fits, to be had only of the maker.*'[22] As we were talking of it, in came Lord Pultney[23] (you

13. Later called the Refectory or Great Parlour; 'hung with paper in imitation of stucco' ('Des. of SH,' *Works* ii. 401).

14. Lady Anne Shirley (1708–79), m. (1729, as his fourth wife) Sir Robert Furnese (d. 1733), 2d Bt.

15. William Legge (1731–1801), 2d E. of Dartmouth, 1750; F.R.S. and F.S.A., 1754; P.C., 1765; secretary for the Colonies 1772–5; lord privy seal 1775–82. He took his seat in the House of Lords for the first time when the new Parliament assembled 31 May 1754 (*Journals of the House of Lords* xxviii. 270).

16. Frederick North (1732–92), styled Lord North 1752–90; first lord of the Treasury 1770–82; 2d E. of Guilford, 1790. His stepmother, Lady Guilford, was a stepdaughter of Lady Anne Furnese. Like Dartmouth he had recently come of age, and had been elected M.P. for Banbury, Oxon.

17. 'On Saturday [27 April] there was a very crowded audience at the King's Theatre in the Haymarket, and the weather being warm, one of the ladies of honour to her Royal Highness the Princess of Wales fainted away, as did one of the soldiers on the stage' (*Daily Adv.* 29

April 1754). The opera was Metastasio's *Attilio Regalo*, with music by Niccolò Jomelli (1714–74) (*The London Stage*, op. cit. i. 423; Alfred Loewenberg, *Annals of Opera*, 2d edn, Geneva, 1955, i. 220–1; Sir George Grove, *Dictionary of Music*, 5th edn, ed. Blom, 1954, iv. 654).

18. The Princess of Wales, mother to his present Majesty (HW). Augusta (1719–72) of Saxe-Gotha, m. (1736) Frederick, P. of Wales.

19. Elizabeth Chudleigh (ca 1720–88), maid of honour to the Princess of Wales; m. 1 (privately, 1744) Hon. Augustus Hervey, 3d E. of Bristol, 1755; m. 2 (illegally, 1769) Evelyn Pierrepont (1711–73) 2d D. of Kingston-upon-Hull, 1726; found guilty of bigamy, 1776.

20. Charles Stanhope (1673–1760), of Elvaston, a retired politician (HW to Montagu 6 Dec. 1753, MONTAGU i. 158 and n. 15).

21. Hon. Charles Townshend (1725–67), statesman and wit.

22. The language of quack advertisements.

23. Lord Bath's only son, William Pulteney (?1731–63), styled Vct Pulteney 1742–63; M.P.

remember the fracas he occasioned two years ago by repeating what my Lady[24] had said of Miss Chudleigh and the Duke of Kingston, and how that wise Duke went to challenge my Lady);[25] the discourse naturally stopping short, Lord Pultney for want of something to say, began to talk the town news, and mentioned the soldier's fit—we stared at one another; he recollected what this led to, and I never saw a poor young man so distressed!

Adieu, my dear Sir! Today looks summerish, but we have no rain yet.

Yours ever,

H. W.

To Chute, Tuesday 14 May 1754

Printed from *Works* v. 412–3. Reprinted, Wright iii. 54–5; Cunningham ii. 383–4; Toynbee iii. 230–1.

Arlington Street, May 14, 1754.

My dear Sir,

I WROTE to you the last day of last month: I only mention it, to show you that I am punctual to your desire. It is my only reason for writing today, for I have nothing new to tell you. The town is empty, dusty, and disagreeable; the country is cold and comfortless; consequently I daily run from one to t'other, as if both were so charming that I did not know which to prefer. I am at present employed in no very lively manner; in reading a treatise on commerce, which Count Perron[1] has lent me, of his own writing: this obliges me to go through with it, though the subject and the style of the French would not engage me much. It does not want sense.

T'other night a description was given me of the most extraordinary

24. Lady Townshend.
25. This story has not been found elsewhere. Miss Chudleigh had been the Duke's mistress for several years; in 1752 they were constantly seen together (*Letters from Lady Jane Coke to . . . Mrs Eyre . . . 1747–1758*, ed. Mrs Ambrose Rathborne, 1899, p. 110–1). Lord Bath had befriended Miss Chudleigh ca 1740, and

was said to have been responsible for her Court appointment in 1743.

1. Carlo Francesco, Conte di Perrone, envoy extraordinary from Sardinia to England 1749–55 (*Repertorium der diplomatischen Vertreter aller Länder*, Vol. II, ed. Friedrich Hausmann, Zurich, 1950, p. 365). The treatise was probably not published; it has not been found.

declaration of love that ever was made. Have you seen young Ponia-towski?[2] He is very handsome. You *have* seen the figure of the Duchess of G[ordon],[3] who looks like a raw-boned Scotch metaphysician that has got a red face by drinking water. One day at the Drawing-Room, having never spoken to him, she sent one of the foreign ministers to invite Poniatowski to dinner with her for the next day. He bowed, and went. The moment the door opened, her two little sons,[4] attired like Cupids with bows and arrows, shot at him, and one of them literally hit his hair, and was very near putting his eye out, and hindering his casting it to the couch

Where she, another sea-born Venus, lay.[5]

The only company besides this Highland goddess were two Scotchmen, who could not speak a word of any language but their own Erse; and to complete his astonishment at this allegorical entertainment, with the dessert there entered a little horse, and galloped round the table; a hieroglyphic I cannot solve. Poniatowski accounts for this profusion of kindness by his great-grandmother being a G[ordon];[6] but I believe it is to be accounted for by * * * *[7]

Adieu, my dear Sir!

Yours ever,

Hor. Walpole

From Chute, Monday 20 May 1754

Missing. Chute sent it by his servant immediately after the death on 20 May of his childless elder brother Anthony (1691–1754), owner of the Vyne, who died intestate, thus making Chute his heir (Mann i. 124, n. 4; GM 1754, xxiv. 244).

2. Stanislaus, the late ill-fated King of Poland (HW). Stanislas Augustus Poniatowski (1732–98), K. of Poland 1764–95 as Stanislas II.

3. Lady Catherine Gordon (1718–79), m. 1 (1741) Cosmo George Gordon, 3d D. of Gordon (d. 1752); m. 2 (1756) Staats Long Morris.

4. Alexander Gordon (1743–1827), styled M. of Huntly 1743–52, 4th D. of Gordon, 1752; and Lord William Gordon (1744–1823) (Scots Peerage iv. 554–6).

5. Quotation not found.

6. Lady Catherine Gordon (living 1687), dau. of George Gordon, 2d M. of Huntly (great-great-great-grandfather of the 4th D. of Gordon; m. (ca 1653) Count Andreas Morsztyn, Polish statesman and poet. Their grand-daughter, Constance Czartoryska, married Count Stanislas Poniatowski (1678–1762), father of Stanislas Augustus (J. M. Bulloch in Scottish Notes and Queries, 1898, xii. 8–9, 38; 1902, 2d ser., iv. 17; Scots Peerage iv. 545, 548).

7. So printed by Miss Berry in Works v. 413.

To Chute, Tuesday 21 May 1754

Printed from photostat of the MS in the possession (1955) of Sir Charles L. Chute, Bt, of the Vyne, Hants. Previously printed, C. W. Chute, *History of The Vyne*, 1888, pp. 106–9; Toynbee iii. 235–8.

This is probably the letter mentioned by HW in his memoranda on his letter from Mann 3 May 1754 (MANN iv. 427); HW replied to that letter on the 23d.

Endorsement in an unidentified hand: Horace Walpole's letter [of] *condolence* to John Chute on the death of his brother Anthony, 1754.

Arlington Street, May 21, 1754.

My dearest Sir,

DON'T be surprised if I write you a great deal of incoherent nonsense![1] The triumph of my joy is so great that I cannot think with any consistence! unless you could know how absolutely persuaded I was that your brother would disinherit you, nay, though the best I almost hoped, was, that he would outlive you (forgive me) you cannot judge of my surprise and satisfaction—I am sure the frame-maker[2] could not when Francesco[3] brought me your letter, and told me in Italian the good news, I started up and embraced him—and put myself into such an agitation, that I believe I shall not get it off without being bloodied. I have hurried to Mrs Chute[4] to embrace her too, but was not so lucky to find her. I am overjoyed that you will not come away, without leaving her there—I would not trust a cranny of the house, into which a will might be thrust, in any other hands—well! it was so unexpected! on not hearing from you, I concluded all went ill, and that you would not tell me of some new brutality—how kind you was to conceal his illness, I should have lived in agonies of apprehensions for the consequence—you are in the right to believe I should be overjoyed—

1. HW's jubilation is explained by the Nicoll affair of 1751 (GRAY, Appendix 1). He considered himself indirectly responsible for Chute's having become involved in that quarrel, which had produced such a coldness between Chute and his brother that HW had expected Chute to be disinherited.

2. Probably the man who made the black and gold frames for the Blue Bedchamber mentioned by HW to Bentley

post 18 May 1754. Among Chute's drawings (now WSL) are two labelled by HW 'Gothic frames.'

3. Chute's Italian servant, Francesco Martelli (living 1774; he probably survived Chute) (MANN iv. 119, n. 2, vii. 569).

4. I.e., Francis Chute's widow (*ante* 24 June 1742 NS, n. 24). In 1751 she had lodgings in Somerset House in the Strand (GRAY ii. 229).

think of the obligations I have to you; remember that in the transports of your grief for Mr Whithed, your first thought was to serve
me and my family;[5] recollect the persecutions you have suffered on
my account; judge how great and continued my fears were that you
might still be an essential sufferer from that era, and then imagine
how unmixed my joy must be, at deliverance from such fears! how
impatient I am to be quite secure! that I may crowd into the papers
the most exaggerated paragraph of your good fortune that I can
devise[6]—my uncle[7] shall read it in every journal. How strange, that
I should live to be glad that he is alive! but it is comfortable that he
is yet to have this mortification!—and Harrison;[8] you don't tell me
that you will discard him; I expect an absolute promise of that—I
distrust the goodness of your heart, lest it should dispose you to forgiveness—do you know that I relent so little, that I would give much
to have Mr and Mrs Atkyns[9] go down to the Vine today with a will
in their pockets for your brother to sign, and find him dead and you
in possession.

An de ma vie! am I in the right to take it for my motto? Erasmus
Shorter![10] Henry Pelham![11] Antony Chute! where could I have
chosen three other such hatchments! nay, my dear Sir, even things
apparently ill, have had their good fortune—if you had not been
laid up three months with the gout, you would now have been

5. By suggesting the match between
Lord Orford and Whithed's fiancée, the
wealthy heiress, Margaret Nicoll (GRAY
ii. 194).

6. The following appeared in the *Daily
Advertiser* and the *Whitehall Evening
Post* for 28 May, apparently at HW's insti-
gation: 'Last week died at his seat in
Hampshire, Anthony Chute, Esq., of the
Vine. By his death an estate of £4000 a
year, and a very considerable personal
estate, devolves to his only brother, John
Chute, Esq., of Argyle Buildings.'

7. Horatio Walpole (1678–1757), cr.
(1756) Bn Walpole of Wolterton; statesman and diplomatist; brother of Sir
Robert Walpole; 'Old Horace.' HW had
suspected his uncle of conspiring to marry
his son Richard to Miss Nicoll, and on 22
June 1751 broke with him in a letter
concluding, 'There are no terms on which

I should not disdain your friendship'
(GRAY ii. 205–6).

8. A clergyman who held a living from
Anthony Chute and who had been Miss
Nicoll's trustee (GRAY ii. 195–7). Not
further identified.

9. John Tracy Atkyns (d. 1773), barrister, son of Chute's half-brother John
Tracy, m. (1735) Katherine Lindsey (d.
1788) (GRAY ii. 199, n. 29, 201, n. 34).

10. HW's uncle, who died intestate 23
Nov. 1753, his fortune being divided
among HW, his brother, Sir Edward Walpole, and three Conway cousins (GRAY i.
25 and n. 163).

11. Pelham had died 6 March 1754. On
the following day HW wrote Mann an
account of his last illness and the political
confusion that his death had caused, and
concluded with the remark that he would
not indulge 'any immoderate grief; consequently I am *as well as can be expected.*'

returned from the Vine, and the Atkynses and Tracys[12] might have been there in your place!

I can scarce contain from divulging my joy till I hear farther: I have stifled Mr Mann[13] with it, and nobody was ever more pleased to be so stifled—he begs me to leave one paragraph to his satisfaction. I must tell you, that great part of my own, is, that this event will prolong your life at least twenty years; your brother was a perpetual gouty thorn in your sides. I am going to notify it to Gray,[14] and to our poor Cliquetée[15]—it will make his bleak rocks and barren mountains smile![16] I am going to write it to G. Montagu—[17] I am sure he will be truly happy.

My only present anxiety, after that of the desire of *certain certainty,* is, lest you should not come to town on Sunday night, Sir George and Lady Lyttelton[18] are engaged to be at Strawberry on Monday and Tuesday, and I cannot bear to lose a minute of seeing you—I have as many questions to ask, as if the only material one were not answered—if it should happen so unluckily that you should not come till Monday, I beg and insist that you will come the next minute to Strawberry—I am really in a fever, and you must not wonder at any vehemence in a light-headed man, in whose greatest intermissions there is always vehemence enough. Take care that I do not meet with the least drawback or disappointment in the plenitude of my satisfaction. The least that I intend to call you is a fortune of five thousand pounds a year and seventy thousand pounds in money—you shall at least exceed Woolterton![19] This is for the public—with regard to myself, I don't know that I shall, but if I should grow to love you less, you will not be surprised—you know the partiality I have to the afflicted, the disgraced, and the oppressed, and must recollect how many titles to my esteem you will lose, when you are rich Chute of the Vine, when you are courted by chancellors

12. John Tracy Atkyns's brother, Robert Tracy (1706–67), of Stanway, Glos, M.P. Tewkesbury 1734–41; Worcester City 1748–54; and his wife, Anna Maria Hudson (GRAY ii. 199 and nn. 28 and 30).

13. I.e., Galfridus Mann, who lived at Richmond.

14. Gray replied from Cambridge 23 May to HW's missing letter (GRAY ii. 82).

15. Bentley (HW to Montagu 26 July 1755, MONTAGU i. 172 and n. 9). If HW

wrote to him at this time, the letter is missing.

16. Addison, *A Letter from Italy,* l. 140.

17. Which he did (MONTAGU i. 161–2).

18. Sir George Lyttelton (1709–73), Bt, cr. (1756) Bn Lyttelton, writer and statesman; m. (1749 as his second wife) Elizabeth Rich (ca 1716–95).

19. Wolterton, 'Old' Horace's estate in Norfolk.

of the Exchequer, for your interest in Hampshire; by a thousand nephew *Tracys* for your estate, and by my Lady *Brown*[20] for her daughter.[21] Oh! you will grow to wear a slit gouty shoe, and a gold-headed cane with a spying glass; you will talk stocks and actions with Sir R. Brown, and be obliged to go to the South Sea House, when one wants you to whisk in a comfortable way to Strawberry. You will dine at Farley[22] in a swagging coach with fat mares of your own, and have strong port of a thousand years old got on purpose for you at Hackwood, because you will have lent the Duke[23] thirty thousand pounds—oh! you will be insupportable, shan't you? I find I shall detest you!—*en attendant,* I do wish you joy!

Yours ever

H. W.

PS. Pray mind how I direct to you![24]—I would not be so insolent as to frank to you[25] for all the world.—When the rich citizens, who get out of their coaches *backwards,* used to dine with my father, my mother called them *rump-days*—take notice, I will never dine with you on *rump-days.*—I hope your brother won't open this letter!

2d PS. I always thought Sophy had a good heart and indeed had no notion that a cat could have a bad one, but I must own that she is shocked to death with envy, on my telling her, that the first thing you would certainly do, would be to give her sister Luna a diamond pompon and a bloodstone *Torcy.*[26]

20. Margaret Cecil (ca 1696–1782), m. Sir Robert Brown (d. 1760), cr. (1732) Bt, merchant and M.P.

21. The Browns' only surviving daughter died unmarried ca July 1755 (*post* HW to Bentley 17 July 1755; HW to Montagu 17 July 1755, Montagu i. 170; William Betham, *The Baronetage of England,* 1801–5, iii. 219).

22. Farley (now Farleigh) House, near Basingstoke; Lord Portsmouth's seat.

23. Charles Powlett (1685 – 26 Aug. 1754), 3d D. of Bolton, 1722; a notorious libertine and a political opponent of Sir Robert Walpole; Chute's neighbour at Hackwood Park, near Basingstoke.

24. HW probably wrote 'To John Chute, Esq., of the Vine, near Basingstoke, Hants.'

25. As a wealthy squire Chute could afford to pay the postage.

26. As C. W. Chute says in *History of The Vyne,* 1888, p. 109, HW seems to be punning (inexplicably) on the names of Simon Arnauld (1618–99), Marquis de Pomponne, and his son-in-law Jean-Baptiste Colbert (1665–1746), Marquis de Torcy. They appear in Mme de Sévigné's letters.

To Chute, ca Thursday 4 July 1754

Missing; mentioned in HW's memoranda on his letter from Mann 14 June 1754 (Mann iv. 436); it presumably concerned Chute's forthcoming visit to SH, for which see *post* HW to Bentley 9 July 1754.

Walpole paid a brief visit to Chute at the Vyne early in June, and, in July, Chute and Gray visited Strawberry Hill (Walpole to Montagu 8 June 1754, Montagu i. 162; *post*, Walpole to Bentley 9 July 1754). In October Walpole made a longer visit at the Vyne, and later he and Chute visited Belhus, the seat of Thomas Barrett Lennard (later Lord Dacre), near Aveley in Essex (HW to Mann 6 Oct. 1754, to Bentley 3 Nov. 1754). Chute seems to have spent most of December at Strawberry Hill (Walpole to Mann 1 Dec. and to Bentley 24 Dec. 1754), and further references to him in the Bentley and Mann correspondences (23 Feb., 22 April, 15 June, and 16 July 1755) show that his meetings with Walpole were so frequent that probably few if any letters passed between them. Gray wrote to Walpole 22 July 1755 (Gray ii. 83) that Chute would write by the 'next post,' but it is doubtful that he did so.

From Chute, ca Saturday 27 September 1755

Missing.

To Chute, Monday 29 September 1755

Printed from the MS now wsl. First printed, Wright iii. 156–7; reprinted, Cunningham ii. 471–2; Toynbee iii. 350–2, all lacking the postscript. For the history of the MS see *ante* 20 Aug. 1743 OS.

There are two sketches on the back, of a Gothic column and (probably) a picture frame, presumably by Chute.

Arlington Street, Sept. 29, 1755.

I SHOULD not answer your letter so soon, *as you write so often,* if I had not something particular to tell you. Mr Fox[1] is to be secretary of state. The history of this event in short is this; George

---

1. Henry Fox (1705–74), cr. (1763) Bn Holland; M.P.; secretary at war 1746–55; secretary of state for the south, Nov. 1755 – Nov. 1756; paymaster-general 1757–65;

Elector of Hanover, and Thomas King of England[2] have been exceedingly alarmed. By some strange misapprehension, the Russian and Hessian treaties,[3] the greatest blessings that were ever calculated for this country, have been totally, and almost universally disapproved. Mr *Legge*[4] grew *conscientious* about them; the Speaker,[5] constitutional; Mr Pitt,[6] patriot; Sir George Lee,[7] scrupulous; Lord Egmont,[8] uncertain; the Duke of Devonshire[9] something that he meant for some of these; and my *uncle*, I suppose, *frugal*[10]—Now you know, let a Parliament be ever so ready to vote for anything, yet if everybody in both Houses is against a thing, why the Parliament itself can't carry a point against both Houses—This made such a dilemma, that after trying everybody else, and being ready to fling up themselves, King Thomas and his Chancellor[11] offered Mr Fox the honour of defending and saving them. He, who is all Christian charity, and forgiving everybody but himself and those who dissuaded him, for not taking the seals before,[12] consented to undertake the cause of the treaties, and is to have the management of the House of Commons as long as he can keep it.[13] In the mean time to

HW's correspondent. For details of the negotiations with him at this time, see MANN iv. 502, nn. 16–20.

2. The Duke of Newcastle, first lord of the Treasury.

3. The treaty with Hesse-Cassel, signed at Hanover 18 June 1755, and the treaty with Russia, signed at St Petersburg 30 Sept. 1755, were negotiated by George II for the protection of Hanover in the expected war with France. Fox presented the treaties to the House of Commons 26 Nov. 1755, and on 15 Dec. the sums to be paid to the Landgrave and Empress were finally voted (*Journals of the House of Commons* xxvii. 308, 339). For a more detailed account of the crisis see HW to Mann 21 Aug. and 29 Sept. 1755 (MANN iv. 493, 501) and *Mem. Geo. II* ii. 33–45.

4. Henry Bilson Legge (1708–64), M.P.; chancellor of the Exchequer 1754–5, 1756–7, 1757–61. He had refused to sign the Hessian treaty (MANN iv. 493, n. 23; *Mem. Geo. II* ii. 35–6), and was forced to resign in November.

5. Arthur Onslow.

6. For his opposition, see MANN iv. 501, n. 13.

7. (?1700–58), D.C.L., 1729; Kt, 1752; M.P. At this time he was treasurer of the Household to the Ps of Wales; he was

being considered for the Exchequer in place of Legge during the summer (MANN iv. 493, n. 25).

8. John Perceval (1711–70), 2d E. of Egmont; another member of the Princess's faction with whom Newcastle was negotiating at the time.

9. William Cavendish (?1698–5 Dec. 1755), 3d D. of Devonshire, 1729.

10. HW frequently alludes to 'Old' Horace's parsimony. He was connected with Pitt at this time; see *Mem. Geo. II* ii. 37.

11. Philip Yorke (1690–1764), cr. (1733) Bn and (1754) E. of Hardwicke; lord chancellor 1737–56; closely allied to Newcastle.

12. In March 1754, when HW had been one of those who advised him to refuse the seals as secretary of state; see HW to Fox 13 March 1754 (SELWYN 122–3 and nn. 1, 4, 5, 6). Fox's acceptance at this time marks the beginning of HW's political alienation from him; see SELWYN, Appendix 7.

13. With the secretaryship Fox became leader of the House of Commons until his resignation in Nov. 1756. HW was somewhat more optimistic about Fox's prospects in his letter to Mann 29 Sept. (MANN iv. 502).

THE VYNE BY MÜNTZ

give his new friends all the assistance he can, he is endeavouring to bring the Bedfords[14] to Court; and if any other person in the world hates King Thomas, why Mr F. is very willing to bring them to Court too. In the mean time Mr Pitt is scouring his old Hanoverian trumpet, and Mr Legge is to accompany him with his hurdy-gurdy.

Mr Mann[15] did not tell me a word of his intending you a visit. The reason the Dacres[16] have not been with you, is, they have been at Court;[17] and as at present there are as many royal hands to kiss as a Japanese idol has, it takes some time to slabber through the whole ceremony.

I have some thoughts of going to the Bath for a week;[18] though I don't know whether my love for my country, while my country is in a quandary, may not detain me hereabouts. When Mr Müntz[19] has done, you will be so good as to packet him up and send him to Strawberry: I rather wish you would bring him yourself; I am impatient for the drawing you announce to me.[20] A commission has passed the Seals, I mean of secrecy, for I don't know whether they must not be stole, to get you some swans;[21] and as in this age one

14. John Russell (1710–71), 4th D. of Bedford, leader of a Whig faction that was strongly anti-Newcastle. In an undated entry before 12 Nov. 1755 HW wrote in his memoirs, 'Fox would have engaged him [Bedford] to accept the privy seal, which he had prepared the Duke of Marlborough to cede; but the Duke of Bedford had resolution enough to refuse any employment for himself' (*Mem. Geo. II* ii. 47). A letter from Fox to Lord Gower, 14 Oct. 1755, asking him to sound out Bedford as to his willingness to accept the privy seal, and Bedford's reply to Gower rejecting the proposal, are printed in Bedford's *Correspondence*, ed. Lord John Russell, 1842–6, ii. 168–71.

15. I.e., Galfridus Mann.

16. Thomas Barrett Lennard (1717–86), 17th Bn Dacre, 1755; m. (1739) Anna Maria Pratt (d. 1806). Chute was distantly related to Lord Dacre (*ante* 4 Aug. 1753, n. 32).

17. The King had arrived at Kensington Palace 16 Sept. after his return from Hanover, and on the 17th and 18th there was a 'great Court' at Kensington (*Daily Adv.* 17, 18, 19 Sept. 1755). Lord Dacre had succeeded to the peerage 26 June

during the King's absence, and may have been among the first to pay his compliments.

18. Apparently with George Selwyn to visit 'Gilly' Williams. The latter wrote to Selwyn 16 Oct. 1755, 'Try if you can't revive those intentions [of visiting Bath] in Mr Walpole, say everything of this place it deserves, and give it the thousand things which it wants' (MS now WSL). The excursion did not take place, nor did HW visit Bath until October 1766.

19. Johann Heinrich Müntz (1727–98), a Swiss painter who had come to SH from Jersey early in June and had been at the Vyne since mid-July (*post* HW to Bentley 3 Nov. 1754, 10 June, 5 July, and 4 Aug. 1755; Gray to HW 22 July 1755, Gray ii. 83 and n. 9). He remained in HW's employ until 1759, when he was dismissed 'for very impertinent behaviour' (Gray i. 34 and n. 233).

20. Probably the 'View of the Vine in Hampshire, the seat of John Chute, Esq., by Müntz' that later hung in HW's bedchamber ('Des. of SH,' *Works* ii. 452). It is now at the Vyne. See illustration.

21. HW probably had in mind the swans in the Thames, whose beaks were marked to show that they were owned

ought not to despair of anything where robbery is concerned, I have some hopes of succeeding. If you should want any French ships for your water, there are great numbers to be had cheap and small enough.[22] Adieu!

Yours ever

H. W.

PS.[23] I perceive I have writ in such a hurry, that, as the girls say, I must beg you would excuse this scrawl.

To Chute, Monday 20 October 1755

Printed from the MS now WSL. First printed Wright iii. 163–4; reprinted, Cunningham ii. 477–8; Toynbee iii. 357–8. For the history of the MS see *ante* 20 Aug. 1743 OS.

Arlington Street, Oct. 20, 1755.

YOU know, my dear Sir, that I don't love to have you taken unprepared: the last visit I announced to you was of the Lord Dacre of the South,[1] and of the Lady Baroness, his spouse: the next company you may expect will be composed of the Prince of Soubise[2] and twelve thousand French; though as winter is coming on, they will scarce stay in the country, but hasten to London. I need not protest to you I believe, that I am serious, and that an invasion[3] before Christmas will certainly be attempted; you will believe me at the first word. It is a little hard however! they need not envy

by the Crown or a corporation. It is not known whether he yielded to the temptation.

22. HW told Mann the same day that 'we take, from men of war and Domingomen, down to colliers and cockboats' (MANN iv. 500). Chute enlarged the water at the Vyne ('Some Account . . . of the Vyne,' MS by C. W. Chute in Hampshire Record Office).

23. The postscript has not previously been printed.

———

1. So called to distinguish this barony from that of Dacre of Gilsland (or the North). The southern Dacres had seats in Essex, Sussex, and Kent (GEC iv. 21 note g).

2. Charles de Rohan (1715–87), Prince de Soubise; general; Maréchal de France, 1758.

3. The French preparations for invasion are the subject of HW's letter to Mann of 27 Oct. 1755. Such reports at that time were greatly exaggerated, but by 5 Feb. 1756 Newcastle had received information that 60,000 men were quartered in the French ports on the Channel (Julian S. Corbett, *England in the Seven Years' War,* 1907, i. 86–8).

us General Braddock's[4] laurels; they were not in such quantity!

Parliamentary and subsidiary politics[5] are in great ferment; I could tell you much if I saw you; but I will not while you stay there —yet as I am a true friend and not to be changed by prosperity, I can't neglect offering you my services when I am *censé* to be well with a minister. It is so long since I was, and I believe so little a while that I shall be so (to be sure I mean that he will be minister)[6] that I must *faire valoir* my interest while I have any—in short, shall I get you one of these new independent companies?[7]—hush! don't tell Mr Müntz how powerful I am; his warlike spirit will want to coincide with my ministerial one; and it would be very inconvenient to the Lords Castlecomers,[8] to have him knocked on the head, before he had finished all the Strawberries and Vines that we lust after.

I had a note from Gray,[9] who is still at Stoke, and he desired I would tell you that he has continued pretty well. Do come[10]—adieu!

Yours ever

H. W.

Lottery tickets rise:[11] subsidiary treaties under par—I don't say, no price.[12]

Lord Robert Bertie[13] with a company of the Guards *has thrown* himself into Dover Castle;[14] don't that sound very war-ful?

4. Maj.-Gen. Edward Braddock (1695–1755), commander-in-chief in North America 1754–5; defeated and mortally wounded in battle with the French and Indians at Fort Duquesne, 9 July 1755.

5. Relating to the Hessian and Russian treaties (see postscript and *ante* 29 Sept. 1755, n. 3).

6. Fox's appointment as secretary of state was announced 14 Nov. (GM 1755, xxv. 523). HW expected him to be minister only a short time.

7. 'Last Thursday orders were sent to the War Office to make out commissions for twelve independent companies, to consist of 100 men each, which are now raising with all possible expedition' (*Daily Adv.* 20 Oct. 1755). The officers are listed in *Daily Adv.* 22 Oct.

8. HW explained this favourite 'Strawberry proverb' to Mary Berry 20 Aug.

1789 (BERRY i. 55–6). See also MONTAGU ii. 311.

9. 14 Oct. (GRAY ii. 86).

10. Chute may have come to SH before 16 Nov. (see *post* HW to Bentley 16 Nov. 1755).

11. From a low of £8 16s. on 8 Oct. to £10 8s. 10d. on the 20th; they had reached £12 12s. by the end of the month (GM 1755, xxv. 480).

12. That is, unpopular as they were, they might well be (as they were) approved by Parliament.

13. (1721–82), 5th son of the 1st D. of Ancaster; Col. of the 7th Foot (Royal Fusiliers) 1754–76, and of the second troop of Horse Guards 1776–82; Gen., 1777; M.P. Whitchurch 1751–4, Boston 1754–82.

14. No mention of Bertie's regiment of foot (not guards) as being quartered at

To Chute, Tuesday 8 June 1756

Printed from the MS now wsl. First printed, Wright iii. 222–4; reprinted, Cunningham iii. 17–18, Toynbee iii. 430–2. For the history of the MS see *ante* 20 Aug. 1743 OS.

During the long interval that preceded this letter, HW and Chute, as usual, saw much of each other, as references in HW's other correspondences show. HW wrote to Bentley 6 Jan. 1756, 'Mr Chute is at the Vine, but I don't expect to hear from him: no post but a dove can get from thence.'

Arlington Street, June 8th 1756.

My dear Sir,

PRAY have a thousand masses said in your divine chapel[1] *à l'intention* of your poor country: I believe the occasion[2] will disturb the founder of it,[3] and make him shudder in his shroud for the ignominy of his countrymen. By all one learns, Byng,[4] Fowke[5] and *all* the officers at Gibraltar were infatuated! They figured Port Mahon lost, and Gibraltar a-going! a-going! Lord Effingham,[6] Cornwallis,[7] Lord Rob. Bertie,[8] all, all signed the council of war,[9] and are in as bad odour as possible. The King says it will be his

this time at Dover Castle has been found, but on 13 Oct. it was reviewed in the 'Old Park' near Canterbury (*Daily Adv.* 14 Oct.).

———

1. 'The most heavenly chapel in the world' (HW to Mann 16 July 1755). See HW's account of the Vyne, *post* Appendix 1.

2. Byng's retreat from Minorca.

3. William Sandys (ca 1470–1540), of the Vyne cr. (1523) Bn Sandys; who held various offices under Henry VIII and attended him at the Field of the Cloth of Gold in 1520. He built the present chapel at the Vyne in the early years of the sixteenth century (C. W. Chute, *History of The Vyne*, 1888, p. 20).

4. Adm. John Byng (1704–57), then about to undergo the investigation which led to his execution for failing to relieve Minorca.

5. Thomas Fowke (d. 1765), Lt-Gen., 1754; Col. of the 14th Foot, 1755; governor of Gibraltar 1742–56; in Aug. 1756 he was court-martialled and dismissed

from the service, being restored in 1761 (Mann iv. 560, n. 1).

6. Thomas Howard (ca 1714–63), 2d E. of Effingham, 1743; Col. (1754–60) of the 34th Foot, assigned to Minorca 1752–6 (*Historical Record of the Thirty-Fourth . . . Regiment of Foot*, 1844, pp. 29–32).

7. Edward Cornwallis (d. 1776), brother of Bp (later Abp) Frederick Cornwallis; at this time Col. of the 24th Foot, also assigned to Minorca; Lt-Gen., 1760 (GM 1776, xlvi. 47; *Court and City Register*, 1756, p. 159; 1772, p. 173).

8. Byng had received orders from the Admiralty, dated 31 March, to land Bertie's Royal Fusiliers at Minorca in case it was attacked by the French (*The Trial of the Honourable Admiral Byng*, Lacy's edn, 1757, pt ii, Appendix, pp. 20–1).

9. Fowke had received orders from Lord Barrington, the secretary at war, to send a detachment of troops from Gibraltar to reinforce the garrison at Port Mahon. On 4 May 1756 Fowke called a council of war at Gibraltar, which decided 'that the

death, and that he neither eats nor sleeps—all our trust is in Hanoverians![10]

The Prince has desired to be excused living at Kensington, but accepts the £40,000 a year;[11] £5000 is given to Prince Edward,[12] and an establishment[13] is settling; but that too will meet with difficulties. I will be more circumstantial when we meet.

My uncle has chosen no motto nor supporters[14] yet—one would think there were fees to pay for them! Mr Fox said to him, 'Why don't you take your family motto?'[15] He replied, 'Because *my nephew* would say I think I speak as well as my brother.'—I *believe he means me*. I like his awe. The Duke of Richmond[16] taking me for his son, reproached himself to Lady Caroline Fox[17] for not wishing me joy. She is so sorry she undeceived him!

Charles Townshend has turned his artillery upon his own court: he says, 'Silly fellow for silly fellow, I don't see why it is not as well to be governed by my uncle with a blue ribband as by my cousin with a green one.'[18]

I have passed today one of the most agreeable days of my life; your righteous spirit will be offended with me—but I must tell you:

sending such a detachment from hence to Minorca, at this time, instead of being useful to his Majesty's service, would be diminishing the strength of the garrison of Gibraltar . . . without any reasonable prospect or hope of their being of any assistance to Minorca' (ibid. 22). Fowke's disobedience seems to have been wilful and the result of excessive caution. The commanding officers of the troops under orders for Minorca, including Effingham, Cornwallis, and Bertie, were invited by Fowke to join the Gibraltar officers 'ostensibly to strengthen the character of the council, but in reality to implicate as many persons as possible' (Brian Tunstall, *Admiral Byng and the Loss of Minorca*, 1928, p. 71). The minutes of the council of war had been received in London 31 May (MANN iv. 560, n. 2).

10. Contingents of Hessian and Hanoverian troops had landed in England on 15 and 20 May respectively, to help defend England against an expected invasion (MANN iv. 526, n. 5; 550, nn. 6, 7).

11. Offered to him by the King on his coming of age, together with an invitation to live at Kensington; for further details see MANN iv. 562–3 and the references cited in nn. 20, 21.

12. Edward Augustus (1739–67), cr. (1760) D. of York.

13. I.e., a household; the arrangements dragged on for several months; for details see *Mem. Geo. II* ii. 204–8, 221–3, 249–50, 258–9.

14. 'Old' Horace Walpole had been created Baron Walpole of Wolterton on 4 June.

15. *Fari quæ sentiat* ('-To say what he thinks'), which 'Old' Horace did select as his motto.

16. Charles Lennox (1735–1806), 3d D. of Richmond; married, in 1757, Conway's step-daughter, after which he became a close friend of HW.

17. Lady Georgiana Caroline Lennox (1723–74), m. (1744) Henry Fox, cr. (1763) Bn Holland; cr. (1762) Bns Holland, s.j.; the D. of Richmond's sister.

18. By Newcastle, a Knight of the Garter, as by Bute, a Knight of the Thistle. Newcastle was a half-brother of Townshend's grandmother; Bute, a first cousin of Townshend's wife, Lady Dalkeith.

my Lord and Lady Bath[19] carried my Lady Hervey[20] and me to dine with my Lady Allen[21] at Blackheath.[22] What added to the oddness of the company in which I found myself was her sister Mrs Cleveland,[23] whose bitterness against my father and uncle for turning out her husband[24] you have heard—but she is very agreeable—I had a little private satisfaction in very naturally telling my Lord Bath how happy I have made his old printer Franklyn.[25] The Earl was in extreme good humour, repeated epigrams, ballads, anecdotes, stories, which as Madame Sévigné says put one in mind *de sa défunte veine*.[26] The Countess was not in extreme good humour, but in the best-humoured ill humour in the world; contested everything with great drollery, and combatted Mrs Cleland on Madame Maintenon's character with as much satire and knowledge of the world as ever I heard in my life. I told my Lord Bath General Wall's foolish vain motto, *Aut Cæsar aut nihil*[27]—He replied, 'He is an impudent fellow, he should have taken *Murus Aheneus!*'[28] Doddington[29] has translated well the motto on the caps of the Hanoverians, *Vestigia nulla retrorsum*,[30] *They never mean to go back again.*

19. Anna Maria Gumley (ca 1694–1758), m. (1714) William Pulteney, cr. (1742) E. of Bath.

20. Mary Lepell (1700–68), m. (1720) John Hervey, styled Bn Hervey of Ickworth; HW's correspondent.

21. Margaret Du Pass (d. 1758), m. (1707) Joshua Allen, 2d Vct Allen.

22. Near Greenwich, south-east of London.

23. I.e., Cleland; the widow of William Cleland (ca 1674–1741), the friend of Pope. HW describes the sisters in his marginal notes to Chesterfield's *Miscellaneous Works*: 'Mrs Cleland was sister of Lady Allen, both of Jewish and Flemish extraction. Both had parts, both were very satirical. Mrs Cleland was very affected, but had less parts than her sister. She was wife of Pope's friend, Mr Cleland. Lady Allen kept a sort of academy of *beaux esprits*, and was much connected with Lionel, Duke of Dorset, Lord Chesterfield, Lord Bath, Lord Lyttelton, and Lady Hervey' (*Miscellanies of the Philobiblon Society*, 1867–8, xi. 60–1). For a further character of Mrs Cleland, see Chesterfield's letter introducing her to Mme de Tencin in his *Letters*, ed. Dobrée, 1932, ii.

516–18. Their father was a famous converted Jew of the Restoration, for whom see James Picciotto, *Sketches of Anglo-Jewish History*, 1875, pp. 34, 54.

24. Cleland was dismissed from his post of surveyor of the land tax in May 1741, a few months before his death; see Pope's *Correspondence*, ed. Sherburn, Oxford, 1956, iv. 377–8.

25. Richard Francklin (d. 1765), printer of the *Craftsman*, to which Bath contributed many of his diatribes against Sir Robert Walpole. He was a tenant of HW's at Twickenham, where he occupied the cottage across the road from SH (Cole i. 85; Montagu ii. 147; Mann iv. 374).

26. Not found in Mme de Sévigné's letters, nor elsewhere.

27. Correctly *Aut Cæsar aut nullus* (A. Chassart and H. Tausin, *Dictionnarie des devises*, 1878, i. 29).

28. 'Wall of brass' (Horace, *Epistles* I. i. 60). It was actually the motto of the Irish family of Reynell.

29. George Bubb Dodington (1691–1762), cr. (1761) Bn Melcombe; M.P.; wit and politician.

30. 'Their foot prints do not return' (Horace, *Epistles* I. i. 74–5).

Saunders the new Admiral[31] told the King yesterday in a very odd phrase, that they *should screw his heart out,* if Byng is not now in the harbour of Mahon—The world condemns extremely the rashness of superseding Admirals on no information but from our enemies.[32] The ministry tremble for Thursday sennight (*inter alia*) when the King is to desire the Parliament to adjourn again.[33] I believe altogether it will make a party.[34] Adieu!

Yours ever

H. W.

To Chute, Friday 23 ?July 1756

Printed for the first time from the MS now wsl. For the history of the MS see *ante* 20 Aug. 1743 OS.

The month and year are conjectured on the assumption that this belongs with the following letter. The paper is also of a type that HW used frequently during 1757; and we also know that Chute was confined with the gout in London at this time (Gray ii. 92).

Strawberry Hill, Friday 23d.

My dear Sir,

I AM vastly comforted to hear you are better; that is, I would think so, but would not have you; I had rather you would believe yourself ill enough to call in Dr Addington:[1] there is no such thing as works of supererogation about health.

Was you ever more drowned than you was yesterday? I *sailed* in the evening to Clivden, where I found the face of the lady of the house[2] hissing in the midst of many waters like a red hot poker: we

---

31. Sir Charles Saunders (ca 1713–75), K.B., 1761, had been made Rear-Adm., 4 June, and was being sent to the Mediterranean as second-in-command under Hawke to supersede Byng and West; see Mann iv. 561–2 and nn. 13–15.

32. All the accounts of the so-called Battle of Port Mahon (20 May) so far received in England had come from France; see HW to Mann 14 June 1756 (Mann iv. 561, especially nn. 9 and 12)

33. Parliament, which had been adjourned to Friday 18 June, met on that day and was prorogued without incident

to 15 July and so repeatedly until 2 Dec. (*Journals of the House of Commons* xxvii. 619–20).

34. A favourite expression of HW; see *post* HW to Bentley 6 March 1755, n. 19, 19 Oct. 1755, 16 Nov. 1755.

---

1. Anthony Addington (1713–90), M.D., 1744. He practised in London after 1754, and was Chatham's physician.

2. Catherine Raftor (1711–85), m. (1732) George Clive; actress, whom HW had settled at Little SH by Nov. 1754 (*post* HW to Bentley 3 Nov. 1754).

touched a card *à votre intention.* I don't think anything will do you so much good as *les amusements des eaux de Straberri.*

Adieu! yours ever

H. W.

From CHUTE, Thursday ?29 July 1756

Printed from a photostat of the MS now in the Bodleian Library. First printed, Toynbee *Supp.* iii. 140. For the history of the MS see *ante* 3 Nov. 1748.

The day of the month is conjectured on the assumption that this and the preceding letter belong together.

Thursday night, [?29] July 1756.

My dear Sir,

PRAY make yourself quite easy about me; I am certainly much better than I was yesterday; I rested well, but towards morning had my usual sweat; I have seen the doctor, who finds me better than when I went out of town; but yet with some remain of fever; though by my own feel I should think myself quite free at present; he has ordered me to continue the lemon draughts, will see me tomorrow again, and then thinks he shall give me the bark: you shall hear from me again very soon, and I am persuaded the account will be, as you wish it.

Adieu,
Yours ever,

J. CHUTE

To Chute, Sunday 27 February 1757

Printed from the MS now wsl. First printed Wright iii. 275; reprinted, Cunningham iii. 63, Toynbee iv. 37–8. The MS was sold, June 1958, by J. K. Fletcher to wsl; a MS copy (on paper watermarked 1831) was among the papers acquired by wsl from the estate of Richard Bentley, the younger, in 1937, so that at one time the original was perhaps with the other Chute letters in that collection (see *ante* 20 Aug. 1743 OS) but was later separated from them after the copy was made.

Dated by comparison with HW to Mann 3 March 1757 (Mann v. 62–5) which discusses and dates the same events mentioned here.

Address: To Mr Chute.

Sunday night very late.

My dear Sir,

I SHOULD certainly have been with you tonight as I desired G. M.[1] to tell you, but every six hours produce such new wonders, that I don't know when I shall have a moment to see you. Will you, can you believe me, when I tell you that the four persons[2] of the court martial whom Keppel[3] named yesterday to the House as commissioning him to ask for the bill,[4] now deny they gave him such commission[5]—though Norris,[6] one of them, was twice on Friday with Sir Richard Lyttelton,[7] and once with G. Grenville[8] for the same purpose! I have done nothing but traverse the town tonight from Sir R. Lyttelton's to the Speaker's,[9] to Mr Pitt's,[10] to Mr Fox's, to Doddington's, to Lady Hervey's,[11] to find out and try how to defeat the evil of this, and to extract if possible some good from it—alas!

1. Presumably, as earlier editors have assumed, George Montagu.

2. Rear-Adm. Henry Norris, and Captains Charles Holmes, Francis Geary, and John Moore (Mann v. 64, n. 17).

3. Capt. (later Adm.) Augustus Keppel (1725–86), cr. (1782) Vct Keppel; M.P.; a member of the court martial on Byng.

4. Absolving the members of the court martial on Admiral Byng from their oath of secrecy. For these events see HW to Mann 3 March 1757 and the references there given.

5. This was true only of one of them, Capt. Holmes (Mann v. 64, n. 18).

6. Rear-Adm. Henry Norris (d. 1764), Vice-Adm., 1759 (Mann v. 64, n. 17; GM 1764, xxxiv. 302).

7. (d. 1770), K.B. 1753; army officer and M.P. (Montagu i. 110, n. 35).

8. George Grenville (1712–70), M.P.; treasurer of the navy 1754, 1756–62; first lord of the Treasury 1763–5.

9. Arthur Onslow.

10. See Pitt to HW 27 Feb. 1757.

11. Presumably to consult with her son Augustus, with whom HW was working closely to secure mercy for Byng (*Augustus Hervey's Journal*, ed. Erskine, 1953, pp. 239–41).

alas! that what I meant so well, should be likely only to add a fortnight[12] to the poor man's misery! Adieu!

Yours ever

H. W.

To Chute, Tuesday 12 July 1757

Printed from *Works* v. 414. Reprinted, Wright iii. 304–5, Cunningham iii. 89–
90, Toynbee iv. 73–4.

Strawberry Hill, July 12, 1757.

IT WOULD be very easy to persuade me to a *Vine-voyage*,[1] without
your being so indebted to me, if it were possible. I shall represent
my impediments, and then you shall judge. I say nothing of the
heat of this magnificent weather, with the glass yesterday up to three-
quarters of sultry. In all English probability this will not be a
hindrance long; though at present, so far from travelling, I have made
the tour of my own garden but once these three days before eight at
night, and then I thought I should have died of it. For how many
years we shall have to talk of the summer of fifty-seven!—But
hear: my Lady Ailesbury[2] and Miss Rich[3] come hither on Thursday[4]
for two or three days; and on Monday next the Officina Arbuteana
opens in form.[5] The Stationers' Company, that is, Mr Dodsley,[6] Mr
Tonson,[7] etc. are summoned to meet here on Sunday night. And
with what do you think we open? *Cedite*, Romani *Impressores*[8]—
with nothing under Graii *Carmina*.[9] I found him in town last week:

12. Byng had been respited for two
weeks while the bill for absolution from
oaths of secrecy was being considered. HW
had been responsible for persuading Keppel and Dashwood to propose the bill
(*Mem. Geo. II* ii. 327–8, 331–2).

1. To visiting Mr Chute at the Vine, his
seat in Hampshire (HW).

2. Caroline Campbell (1721–1803), m. 1
(1739) Charles Bruce, 3d E. of Ailesbury,
1741; m. 2 (1747) Hon. Henry Seymour
Conway.

3. Mary Rich d. (1769), the Conways'
friend (*Annual Register*, 1769, xii. 174),

dau. of Field Marshal Sir Robert Rich.

4. See Lady Ailesbury to HW 6 [7] July
1757.

5. I.e., the printing was to begin (actually it was started on Saturday the 16th);
the press had been erected on 25 June
(*Journal of the Printing Office* 3).

6. Robert Dodsley (1703–64), publisher.

7. Jacob Tonson (d. 1767), publisher.

8. 'Give place, ye Roman printers': paraphrased from Propertius (*Cedite Romani
scriptores*), *Elegies* ii. xxxiv. 65.

9. Gray's *The Bard* and *The Progress of
Poesy*. See Hazen, *SH Bibl.* 23.

he had brought his two odes to be printed. I snatched them out of Dodsley's hands, and they are to be the first-fruits of my press. An edition of Hentznerus,[10] with a version by Mr Bentley and a little preface of mine, were prepared, but are to wait—Now, my dear Sir, can I stir?

> Not ev'n thy virtues, tyrant, shall avail![11]

Is not it the plainest thing in the world that I cannot go to you yet, but that you must come to me?

I tell you no news, for I know none, think of none. Elzevir,[12] Aldus[13] and Stephens[14] are the freshest personages in my memory. Unless I was appointed printer of the *Gazette,* I think nothing could at present make me read an article in it. Seriously, you must come to us, and shall be witness that the first holidays we have I will return with you. Adieu!

Yours ever,

HOR. WALPOLE

To CHUTE, Tuesday 26 July 1757

Printed from *Works* v. 415–16. Reprinted, Wright iii. 307–8, Cunningham iii. 92–3, Toynbee iv. 76–7.

Strawberry Hill, July 26, 1757.

I LOVE to communicate my satisfactions to you. You will imagine that I have got an original portrait of John Guttemburg,[1] the first inventor of printing, or that I have met with a little *boke* called *Eneydos,*[2] which I am going to translate and print—No, no; far beyond any such thing! Old Lady Sandwich[3] is dead at Paris, and my

10. *A Journey into England,* by Paul Hentzner (1558–1623), was the second production of the Press (ibid. 31–3).

11. *The Bard,* l. 6.

12. Louis Elzevir (1540–1617), Dutch publisher.

13. Aldus Manutius (1450–1515), Venetian printer.

14. HW translates the name of the Estienne family of printers, who flourished in Paris and Geneva during the 16th and 17th centuries.

———

1. Johan Gutenberg (ca 1397–1468).

2. A French romance translated and printed by William Caxton.

3. Daughter of the famous Wilmot, Earl of Rochester (HW). Elizabeth Wilmot (1674–1757), m. (1689) Edward Montagu, 3d E. of Sandwich.

Lord[4] has given me her picture of Ninon L'Enclos;[5] given it me in the prettiest manner in the world.[6]—I beg, if he should ever meddle in any election in Hampshire, that you will serve him to the last drop of your shrievalty. If you reckon by the thermometer of my natural impatience, the picture would be here already, but I fear I must wait some time for it.

The press goes on as fast as if I printed myself. I hope in a very few days to send you a specimen,[7] though I could wish you was at the birth of the first produce. Gray has been gone these five days. Mr Bentley has been ill, and is not recovered of the sweating-sickness, which I now firmly believe was only a hot summer like this, and England, being so unused to it, took it for a malady. Mr Müntz is not gone; but pray don't think that I keep him: he has absolutely done nothing this whole summer but paste two chimney-boards. In short, instead of Claud Lorrain,[8] he is only one of Bromwich's men.[9]

You never saw anything so droll as Mrs Clive's countenance, between the heat of the summer, the pride in her legacy,[10] and the efforts to appear concerned.

We have given ourselves for a day or two the air of an earthquake, but it proved an explosion of the powder-mills at Epsom.[11] I asked Louis[12] if it had done any mischief: he said, 'Only blown a man's head off'; as if that was a part one could spare!

Yours ever,

HOR. WALPOLE

4. Lady Sandwich's grandson, the politician John Montagu (1718–92), 4th E. of Sandwich.

5. Ninon de Lenclos (1620–1705), courtesan. The portrait, which HW finally received in June 1758, is reproduced from a copy pasted in HW's extra-illustrated Des. of SH, 1784 (now WSL) as the frontispiece to Vol. II of Julia Pardoe, Louis XIV, 1886. For further details see HW to Lady Hervey 13 Sept. 1757 (MORE 6, and n. 2) and MONTAGU ii. 54, n. 22.

6. See Sandwich to HW 22 July 1757, offering him the picture.

7. HW apparently did so 4 Aug., with a missing letter; see post 4 Aug. 1757.

8. Claude Lorrain (1600–82), landscape painter.

9. Thomas Bromwich (d. 1787), a fash-ionable decorator who kept a shop on Ludgate Hill (Thomas Gray, Correspondence, ed. Toynbee and Whibley, Oxford, 1935, ii. 761; GM 1787, lvii pt ii. 646).

10. A legacy of £50 left her by John Robarts [1686 – 15 July 1757], the last Earl of Radnor of that family (HW). He lived at Twickenham.

11. 'Last night [18 July] about half an hour past nine o'clock, a powder mill near Leatherhead was blown up by an explosion of thirty-six barrels of gun powder. The flash and report were seen and heard at Clapham. There was only one man killed, whose head was blown quite from his body' (London Chronicle 16–19 July 1757, ii. 64).

12. HW's Swiss servant, d. 1767.

PS. I hope Dr Warburton will not think I encroach either upon his commentatorship or private pretensions, if I assume these lines of Pope, thus altered,[13] for myself:

> Some have for wits and then for poets pass'd,
> Turn'd *printers* next, and prov'd plain fools at last.

To Chute, Thursday 4 August 1757

Missing; HW told Montagu the same day, when mentioning news of the battle of Hastenbeck: 'I know no more particulars—if I did, I should say as I have just said to Mr Chute, I am too busy about *something*, to have time to write them' (MONTAGU i. 214). The letter presumably enclosed a copy of Gray's *Odes*, which HW sent to several other correspondents that day; a copy now at the Vyne is presumably, though not certainly, the one sent (Hazen, *SH Bibl.* 27).

To Chute, Thursday 29 June 1758

Printed from *Works* v. 416. Reprinted, Wright iii. 367, Cunningham iii. 146–7, Toynbee iv. 152.

Strawberry Hill, June 29, 1758.

THE Tower guns have sworn through thick and thin that Prince Ferdinand[1] has entirely demolished the French,[2] and the City bonfires all believe it.[3] However, as no officer is yet come, nor confirmation,[4] my crackers suspend their belief. Our great fleet is

13. From *Essay on Criticism* i. 36–7.

1. Prince Ferdinand (1721–92), of Brunswick; commander-in-chief of the Allied army in Germany.
2. At the Battle of Crefeld 23 June 1758. The first news reached London on 27 June in 'a letter from Mr Cressener'; see MANN v. 220, n. 1.
3. 'Tuesday night [27 June], upon account of Prince Ferdinand's victory, there were bonfires and illuminations in many parts of London and Westminster. Two fine E. O. tables, which were lately detected and secured, were erected on a scaffold twenty feet high, at the corner of

Bow Street, Covent Garden, and burnt, on account of the glorious defeat of the French by Prince Ferdinand' (*London Chronicle* 27–29 June 1758, iii. 614).
4. It had reached London, but not Twickenham: 'Yesterday [28 June] two expresses arrived, one from Prince Ferdinand of Brunswick, with the particulars of the battle fought between the army under his command and the French. We are informed that the French have lost 7,776 men, killed, wounded, and taken prisoners; twelve cannon, two pair of kettle-drums, four pair of colours and standards, with their tents and baggage; and the Hanoverians had 1,400 men

stepped ashore again near Cherbourg;[5] I suppose, to singe half a yard more of the coast. This is all I know; less, as you may perceive, than anything but the *Gazette*.[6]

What is become of Mr Montagu?[7] Has he stolen to Southampton, and slipped away a-volunteering like Norborne Berkeley,[8] to conquer France in a dirty shirt and a frock? He might gather forty load more of laurels in my wood. I wish I could flatter myself that you would come with him.

My Lady Suffolk[9] has at last entirely submitted her barn to our *ordination*.[10] As yet it is only in *Deacon's orders;* but will very soon have our last imposition of hands. Adieu! Let me know a word of you.

Yours ever,

Hor. Walpole

killed and wounded. The Hanoverian left wing was not engaged' (ibid. iii. 613, *sub* 29 June). Details were published in a *Gazette Extraordinary* on the 30th.

5. HW is following the newspapers: 'Yesterday [27 June] it was reported that an express was arrived from the Duke of Marlborough, with an account that our troops were landed at Cherburg' (*London Chronicle* 27–29 June 1758, iii. 609, *sub* 28 June). This was exaggerated; the English expedition, after withdrawing from St-Malo, 11 June, merely made a feint at Cherbourg (among other places) before returning to Spithead 1 July; the full-scale descent on Cherbourg did not begin until 7 Aug. (MANN v. 212–13, nn. 1–3, 214, n. 12; 221, n. 3; 225, n. 1, 226, n. 3).

6. The *London Gazette* No. 9803, 24–27 July 1758, to which HW is apparently referring, contained only (*sub* 'Whitehall, June 27') the vague early reports of the battle and did not mention the supposed

landing at Cherbourg. A *London Gazette Extraordinary* on the battle was not published until 30 June.

7. Mr George Montagu (HW). He was attending his brother, who was ill (MONTAGU i. 221).

8. (1717–70), 4th Bn Botetourt, 1764; M.P., groom of the Bedchamber 1760–4; gov. of Virginia 1768–70. HW wrote to Conway 4 June that Berkeley had 'converted a party of pleasure into a campaign, and is gone with the expedition, without a shirt but what he had on, and what is lent him.'

9. Henrietta Hobart (ca 1688–1767), m. 1 (1706) Charles Howard, 9th E. of Suffolk; m. 2 (1735) Hon. George Berkeley; George II's mistress; lived at Marble Hill, Twickenham 1724–67.

10. In Bentley's MS book of designs (now WSL) is his drawing for Lady Suffolk's 'priory,' a Gothic barn.

To Chute, Tuesday 22 August 1758

Printed from the MS now wsl. First printed Wright iii. 384–5; reprinted, Cunningham iii. 164, Toynbee iv. 177–8. For the history of the MS see *ante* 20 Aug. 1743 OS. Before this letter was written, HW had visited Chute at the Vyne (HW to Montagu 20 Aug., Montagu i. 222).

Arlington Street, Aug. 22d 1758.

BY MY ramble into Warwickshire[1] I am so behindhand in politics, that I don't know where to begin to tell you any news, and which by this time would not be news to you. My table is covered with gazettes, victories and defeats, which have come in such a lump, that I am not quite sure whether it is Prince Ferdinand or Prince Boscawen[2] that has taken Louisbourg,[3] nor whether it is the late Lord Howe[4] or the present[5] that is killed at Cherbourg.[6] I am returning to Strawberry,[7] and shall make Mr Müntz's German and military *sangfroid* set the map in my head to rights.

I saw my Lord Lyttelton and Miller[8] at Ragley; the latter put me out of all patience. As he has heard me talked of lately, he thought it not below him to consult me on ornaments for my Lord's house— I, who know nothing but what I have purloined from Mr Bentley and you, and who have not forgot how little they tasted your real taste and charming plan,[9] was rather tart—to my comfort, I have seen the plan of their hall, it is stolen from Houghton,[10] and mangled

1. To visit the Hertfords at Ragley.
2. Edward Boscawen (1711–61), Adm.; M.P.; in command of the fleet that besieged Louisbourg.
3. Which capitulated 26 July; the news reached London 18 Aug. (*London Gazette Extraordinary* 18 Aug. 1758; GM 1758, xxviii. 392).
4. George Augustus Howe (?1724–58), 3d Vct Howe; army officer; M.P.; killed near Fort Ticonderoga on 6 July; the news had reached London 21 Aug. (Mann v. 233, and nn. 6–8; Selwyn 148, nn. 2, 4).
5. Richard Howe (1726–99), 4th Vct Howe; cr. an English Vct (1782) and (1788) E. Howe; naval officer; M.P.
6. HW is, of course, joking; the new Lord Howe was in command of the attack on Cherbourg 6 Aug. News of the successful demolition of the works there had reached London 19 Aug. (Selwyn

148, nn. 6, 7). HW discusses these various events in a somewhat similar vein to Selwyn 22 Aug. (Selwyn 148–9).
7. HW had stopped there on the 20th on his way to London from Ragley (Montagu i. 222).
8. Sanderson Miller, the amateur architect (*ante* 4 Aug. 1753, n. 43). Some of his most successful work was at Lyttelton's house, Hagley.
9. Chute's designs for the façade of Hagley, in the Italian Renaissance style, ca 1752, are now wsl; one is reproduced in Christopher Hussey, *English Country Houses, Early Georgian, 1715–1760*, 1955, p. 196. Other designs are in the Hampshire County Record Office.
10. HW is not referring to rooms called 'hall' but to the design of the entire Hagley Hall, which is basically similar to Houghton.

frightfully; and *both* their eating-room and salon are to be stucco with pictures.[11]

I have not time or paper to give you a full account of a vast treasure that I have discovered at Lord Hertford's[12] and brought away with me—If I were but so *lucky* as to be thirty years older, I might have been much luckier—in short, I have got the remains of vast quantities of letters and state papers of the two Lords Conway,[13] Secretaries of State—forty times as many have been using for the oven and the house, by sentence of a steward during my Lord's minority. Most of what I have got, are, gnawed by rats, rotten, or not worth a straw—and yet I shall save some volumes of what is very curious and valuable—three letters of Mr Garrard, Master of the Charterhouse,[14] same of Lord Strafford,[15] and two of old Lenox the Duchess,[16] etc., etc., etc. In short, if I can but contrive to live thirty years extraordinary, in lieu of those I have missed, I shall be able to give the world some treasures from the press at Strawberry.[17] Do tell one a little of your motions and good night.

Yours ever

H. W.

From Chute, ca Wednesday 31 January 1759

Missing; mentioned in HW's letter of 2 Feb.

11. Illustrated in Hussey, op. cit. 198. The stucco was by Vassali (G. W. Beard, 'Hagley Hall,' *Connoisseur Year-Book*, 1954, pp. 13, 16, 17).

12. Francis Seymour Conway (1718–94), 2d Bn Conway, cr. (1750) E. and (1793) M. of Hertford; HW's cousin and correspondent.

13. Edward Conway (ca 1564–1631), cr. (1625) Bn and (1627) Vct Conway, secretary of state 1623–8; and Edward Conway (ca 1623–83), 3d Vct Conway, cr. (1679) E. of Conway, secretary of state 1681–3. A selection of these papers (now in the British Museum and Public Record Office) was published by Marjorie Hope Nicolson under the title *Conway Letters*, 1930. HW gives a similar account of their

discovery and contents to Montagu, 20 Aug. 1758 (Montagu i. 223–4).

14. George Garrard (b. ca 1580), Master of the Charterhouse 1637–50 (Foster, *Alumni Oxon.;* [Robert Smythe], *Historical Account of the Charter-House*, 1808, p. 236).

15. Sir Thomas Wentworth (1593–1641), cr. (1628) Vct Wentworth, (1640) E. of Strafford. 'Three letters' according to HW to Montagu 20 Aug. 1758 (Montagu i. 224).

16. Frances Howard (d. 1639), m. 1 Henry Pranell; m. 2 (1601) Edward Seymour, 1st E. of Hertford; m. 3 (1621) Ludovic Stuart, Duke of Lennox and Richmond.

17. HW never printed any of the Conway papers.

To Chute, Thursday 1 February 1759

Printed from the MS now WSL. First printed, Wright iii. 429–30; reprinted, Cunningham iii. 204–5, Toynbee iv. 234–5. For the history of the MS see *ante* 20 Aug. 1743 OS.

Arlington Street, Feb. 1, 1759.

WELL! my dear Sir, I am now convinced that both Mr Keate's[1] panic and mine were ill-founded—but pray another time don't let him be afraid of being afraid for fear of frightening me; on the contrary, if you will dip your gout in lemonade, I hope I shall be told of it—if you have not had it in your stomach, it is not your fault—drink brandy and be thankful. I would desire you to come to town, but I must rather desire you not to have a house to come to. Mrs H. Grenville[2] is passionately enamoured of yours,[3] and begged I would ask you what will be the lowest price, with all the particulars, which I assured her you had stated very ill for yourself. I don't quite like this commission; if you part with your house in town, you will never come hither—at least stow your cellars with drams and gunpowder as full as Guy Fawkes's[4]—you will be drowned if you don't blow yourself up—I don't believe that the Vine is within the verge of the rainbow—seriously it is too damp for you.

Colonel Campbell[5] marries the Duchess of Hamilton[6] forthwith. The House of Argyle is content, and think that the head of the Hamiltons had purified the blood of Gunning—but I should be afraid that his Grace was more likely to corrupt blood than to mend it.[7]

Never was anything so crowded as the House last night for the

1. George Keate (1729–97), miscellaneous writer. His and HW's panic was apparently produced by one of Chute's attacks of the gout.

2. Margaret Eleanor ('Peggy') Banks (d. 1793), m. (1757) Hon. Henry Grenville; she had been a celebrated beauty (BERRY i. 2, n. 4).

3. Chute's town house was in Tilney Street (see address *post* 4 Nov. 1759). Mrs Grenville changed her mind and took another house before HW had a chance to receive Chute's reply (*post* 6 Feb. 1759).

4. (1570–1606), conspirator in the Gunpowder Plot.

5. John Campbell (1723–1806), styled M. of Lorne 1761–70, 5th D. of Argyll, 1770; Col. of the 14th Dragoons 1757–65; Field Marshal, 1796; M.P.; Lady Ailesbury's brother.

6. Elizabeth Gunning (1733–90), m. 1 (1752) James Hamilton (1724–58), 6th D. of Hamilton; m. 2 (3 Feb. 1759) John Campbell, 5th D. of Argyll, 1770.

7. HW described Hamilton at the time of his marriage as 'hot, debauched, extravagant, and equally damaged in his fortune and person' (MANN iv. 302) and two years earlier as the prime example of the frequenters of 'bagnios and taverns' (ibid. iv. 155).

Prussian cantata[8]—the King was hoarse and could not go to sing his own praises. The dancers seemed transplanted from Sadler's Wells;[9] there were milkmaids riding on dolphins; Britain and Prussia kicked the King of France off the stage, and there was a *petit maître* with his handkerchief full of holes; but this vulgarism happily was hissed.

I am deeper than ever in Gothic antiquities; I have bought a monk of Glastonbury's chair[10] full of scraps of the psalms, and some seals of most reverend illegibility. I pass all my mornings in the thirteenth century, and my evenings with the century that is coming on. Adieu!

Ego Ethelwulf ✠ Signavi

To Chute, Friday 2 February 1759

Printed from the MS now wsl. First printed, Wright iii. 430–1; reprinted, Cunningham iii. 205–6, Toynbee iv. 235–6. For the history of the MS see *ante* 20 Aug. 1743 OS.

Arlington Street, Feb. 2d 1759.

My dear Sir,

I AM glad to see your writing again, and can now laugh very cordially at my own fright, which you take a great deal too kindly. I was not quite sure you would like my proceedings,[1] but just then I could not help it, and perhaps my natural earnestness

8. 'For this night only. At the King's Theatre in the Hay-Market, this day, being the 31st instant, will be performed a grand musical entertainment, with choruses, etc. called, *Il tempio della gloria: or, The Glorious Alliance of His Majesty George the Second, King of Great Britain, with Frederick the IIId* [sic] *King of Prussia*. With new decorations and new dances, and all the characters dressed suitable to the subject. The music newly composed by Sig. [Gioacchino] Cocchi [ca 1715–1804]' (*Daily Adv.* 31 Jan. 1759). HW mentions it to Conway 19 Jan. 1759. For

Cocchi, see *Enciclopedia dello spettacolo*, Rome, 1954–62, iii. 1006–8.

9. At that time a music-hall.

10. 'A very ancient chair of oak, which came out of Glastonbury Abbey; on it are carved these sentences, *Joannes Arthurus Monacus Glastonie, salvet eum Deus: Da pacem, Domine: Sit Laus Deo*. Lord Bathurst had several chairs copied from this' ('Des. of SH,' *Works* ii. 455).

1. HW had apparently sent a physician to the Vyne (*post* 6 Feb. 1759).

had more merit than my friendship—and yet it is worth my while
to save a friend, if I think I can; I have not so many! You yourself
are in a manner lost to me! I must not, cannot repine at your
having a fortune that delivers you from uneasy connections with
a world that is sure to use ill those that have any dependence on it;
but undoubtedly some of the satisfaction that you have acquired,
is taken out of my scale—I will not however moralize, though I
am in a very proper humour for it, being just come home from an
outrageous crowd at Northumberland House, where there were five
hundred people that would have been equally content or discontent
with any other five hundred. This is pleasure! you invite so many
people to your house, that you are forced to have constables at your
door to keep the peace; just as the royal family when they hunted,
used to be attended by surgeons. I allow honour and danger to keep
company with one another, but diversion and breaking one's neck
are strangely ill-matched.

Mr Spence's *Magliabechi*[2] is published today from Strawberry;
I believe you saw it, and shall have it, but 'tis not worth sending
you on purpose. However it is full good enough for the generality
of readers. At least there is a proper dignity in *my* saying so, who
have been so much abused in all the magazines lately for my *Catalogue*.[3] The chief points in dispute lie in a very narrow compass;
they think I don't understand English, and I am sure they don't;
yet they will not be convinced, for I shall certainly not take the
pains to set them right. Who *Them* are I don't know—the highest
I believe are Dr Smollet[4] or some chaplain of my uncle.

Adieu! I was very silly to alarm you so, but the wisest of us from
Solomon to old Carr's cousin[5] are poor souls—maybe you don't

2. *A Parallel in the Manner of Plutarch
between a Most Celebrated Man of Florence* [Antonio Magliabechi (1633–1714)]
and One Scarce Ever Heard of in England
by the Rev. Joseph Spence (1699–1768).
See Hazen, *SH Bibl.* 44–6.

3. The *Catalogue of the Royal and
Noble Authors.* The *Monthly Review* for
Dec. 1758 is on the whole complimentary
in tone, though with reservations, e.g.,
'His manner of writing, though sometimes incorrect, is in general easy and
elegant: and his reflections, though not
always just, seldom fail to be agreeable'
(xix. 557). The review was by Owen Ruff-
head (B. C. Nangle, *The Monthly Review*

First Series . . . *Indexes of Contributors
and Articles*, Oxford, 1934, p. 73). The
reviewer in the *Critical Review* for Dec.
1758 (vi. 483–90), whom HW took to be
Smollett, finds fault with HW's unfriendly
treatment of Mary Queen of Scots and of
the later Stuarts, and in general repre-
hends the 'singularity' of many of HW's
opinions.

4. Tobias George Smollett (1721–71) was
editor and in large part author of the
Critical Review.

5. This is probably an allusion to the
family of Robert Carr (d. 1755), curate of
Twickenham ca 1735–55 (R. S. Cobbett,
Memorials of Twickenham, 1872, p. 68).

know anything of Carr's cousin. Why then, Carr's cousin was,—I don't know who, but Carr was very ill and had a cousin, as I may be, to sit up with her. Carr had not slept for many nights—at last she dozed—her cousin jogged her; 'Cousin;—cousin'—'well,' said Carr, 'what would you have?'—'Only, Cousin, if you die, where will you be buried?'—This resemblance mortifies me ten times more than a thousand reviews could do. There is nothing in being abused by Carr's cousin, but it is horrid to be like Carr's cousin! good night.

From CHUTE, ca Sunday 4 February 1759

Missing; implied in the following letter.

To CHUTE, Tuesday 6 February 1759

Printed from a photostat of the MS in the possession (1933) of Sir Charles L. Chute, Bt, of the Vyne, Hants. First printed, C. W. Chute, *History of the Vyne*, 1888, p. 114; reprinted, Toynbee iv. 239.

Endorsed (in an unidentified hand): 'From Horace Walpole to John Chute.'

The lower edge of the leaf is roughly torn, perhaps indicating that part of the MS is missing.

Arlington Street, Feb. 6, 1759.

MRS H. GRENVILLE is a foolish gentlewoman and don't know her own mind—before it was possible for me to receive your answer, she fixed herself in Clifford Street.

I find instead of a physician, it would have been a shorter way to send you a housekeeper, as all La Cour's[1] prescriptions are at last addressed to the confectioner, not to the apothecary.

I don't approve your changing your arms[2] for those of Chelsea

1. Philip de la Cour (Abraham Gomes Ergas) (ca 1710–80 or 1786), M.D. (Leyden, 1733), licentiate of the Royal College of Physicians, 1751 (William Munk, *Roll of the Royal College of Physicians, of London*, 1878, ii. 178, and GM 1780 p. 543, where the date of his death is given as 1780, but see GM 1786, lvi pt i. 82, 96; Lucien Wolf, *Essays in Jewish History*, ed. Cecil Roth, 1934, p. 169). He had treated Chute in 1756 (GRAY ii. 93 and n. 1).

2. In the absence of Chute's letter this passage cannot be wholly understood. The present arms of the Chute family are:

College,[3] nor do I understand what *the chief* means, I mean, the bearing on it. The crest[4] I honour, it is as *anciently* a coat; the late Lord Hervey said, his arms should be *a cat,* scratchant, with this motto, *for my friends where they itch, for my enemies where they are sore.*

To Chute, Tuesday 13 March 1759

Printed from the MS now WSL. First printed Wright iii. 438; reprinted, Cunningham iii. 215, Toynbee iv. 250–1. For the history of the MS see *ante* 20 Aug. 1743 OS.

Arlington Street, March 13, 1759.

I AM puzzled to know how to deal with you: I hate to be officious, it has a horrid look; and to let you alone till you die at the Vine of mildew, goes against my conscience. Don't it go against yours to keep all your family there till they are mouldy? instead of sending you a physician, I will send you a dozen braziers; I am persuaded that you want to be dried and aired more than physicked. For God's sake don't stay there any longer—*Mater Cyrene, Mater, quæ gurgitis huius ima tenes,*[1] send him away— Nymphs and Jew-doctors![2] I don't know what I shall pray to next against your obstinacy.

No more news yet from Guardaloupe![3] a persecution seems to be raising against General Hobson[4]—I don't wonder! Wherever Com-

---

'Quarterly, 1 and 4, gules, three swords barwise points to the dexter proper, pommels and hilts or, and (for distinction) a canton ermine' (A. C. Fox-Davies, *Armorial Families,* 1929–30, ii. 2087).

3. I.e., Chelsea Hospital, a royal hospital for old and disabled soldiers, erected on the site of Chelsea College, founded by James I in 1609 and later abandoned. HW, whose childhood was largely spent at Orford House in Chelsea, may be joking about some proposed rearrangement of the swords on the bearing.

4. The present crest is 'On a wreath of the colours, a dexter cubit arm in armour, the hand in a gauntlet grasping a broken sword in bend sinister proper, pommel

and hilt gold, and (for distinction) the arm encircled in a wreath of laurel vert' (Fox-Davies, loc. cit.).

---

1. Virgil, *Georgics* iv. 321–2 ('Mother Cyrene, Mother who dwellest in this flood's depths–').

2. La Cour.

3. Reports of an attack, 23 Jan., upon Basse-Terre, on Guadeloupe, and of its occupation the following day, were published in a *London Gazette Extraordinary* on 7 March; see also MANN v. 277, n. 1.

4. Peregrine Thomas Hopson, Major-Gen., 1757, was in command of the attack on Basse-Terre. He died at Guadeloupe 27 Feb. 1759 (MANN v. 252, n. 14, 290, n.

modore Moore[5] is, one may expect treachery and blood.[6] Good
night!

⟨H. W.⟩[7]

To Chute, Sunday 4 November 1759

Printed for the first time from the MS now WSL. For the history of the MS see
ante 20 Aug. 1743 OS.
   Address: To John Chute Esq. in Tilney Street near Lord Chesterfield's London. Free. Hor. Walpole.
   Postmark: 5 NO.

Strawberry Hill, Nov. 4th 1759.

WELL, how delightful! how the deuce did you contrive to get
such proportion? you will certainly have all the women with
short legs come to you to design high-heeled shoes for them. The
cloister,[1] instead of a wine-cellar, has the air of a college. It has
already passed the Seals. Mr Müntz has commended it in a piece of
every language, and Mr Bentley is at this moment turning it outside inwards.—I assure you, Mr Chute, you shall always have my
custom. You shall design every scrap of the ornaments; and if ever
I build a palace or found a city, I will employ nobody but you. In
short, you have found a proportion and given a simplicity and lightness to it, that I never expected. I have but one fault to find, and
that is no bigger than my little finger; I think the buttresses too
slight; and yet I fear, widening them would destroy the beauty of
the space round the windows. There is another thing which is more
than a fear, for it seems an impossibility, that is, of getting pictures

2). The 'persecution' was for the failure of
an attack on Martinique earlier in Jan.,
also reported in the *London Gazette Extraordinary* 7 March. As HW points out
(*Mem. Geo. II* iii. 170) the *Gazette* was
weighted against him in favour of Moore.
   5. Sir John Moore (1718–79), cr. (1766)
Bt; Adm., 1778; in command of the fleet
at Guadeloupe.
   6. Moore, after supporting the request
for absolution from the oath of secrecy at
Byng's court martial in 1757 (*ante* 27 Feb.
1757) had declined to give any evidence

for mercy. HW attributed this to treachery
and a desire to make his court to the
government (*Mem. Geo. II* ii. 364–5, iii.
170).
   7. The signature has been cut away.

   1. Chute's second design for the exterior
of the cloister at SH is reproduced in
WSL, 'Genesis of SH,' *Metropolitan Museum Studies*, 1934, v pt i. 73. His third
design, also WSL, shows enlarged buttresses
in response to this letter.

over the windows within; and if I can't, what shall I do with the spaces?

I shall be in town on Wednesday; I dine at Lord Bath's, and if you could call upon one between three and four, you would certainly find me. The weather is so warm that I am almost writing to you under a tree, that is, I am writing by a fire that is so hot I cannot bear it. Adieu!

Yours ever

H. W.

To Chute, ca Tuesday 17 September 1765

Missing; listed in 'Paris Journals' (DU DEFFAND v. 376).

To Chute, Thursday 3 October 1765

Printed from the MS now wSL. Previously printed, Toynbee vi. 308–11 and *Supp.* ii. 128; previously printed in part, *Works* v. 417–19, Wright v. 77–9, Cunningham iv. 411–13. The MS passed from HW to Mrs Damer, and was bequeathed by her to Sir Wathen Waller, 1st Bt; sold Sotheby's 5 Dec. 1921 (Waller sale), lot 11, to Maggs; sold by Maggs to wSL, June 1932.

Paris,[1] Oct. 3d 1765.

I DON'T know where you are, nor when I am likely to hear of you. I write at random, and, as I talk, the first thing that comes into my pen.

I am, as you certainly conclude, much more amused than pleased. At a certain time of life, sights and new objects may entertain one, but new people cannot find any place in one's affection. New faces with some name or other belonging to them, catch my attention for a minute—I cannot say many preserve it. Five or six of the women that I have seen already, are very sensible.[2] The men are in

1. Where HW had been since 13 Sept. ('Paris Journals,' DU DEFFAND v. 260).

2. Particularly Mmes de Rochefort, Geoffrin, de Mirepoix and de Bentheim, whom HW had met by this time; he was already acquainted with Mme du Deffand but had not yet become a habitué of her salon.

general much inferior, and not even agreeable. They sent us their best, I believe, at first, the Duc de Nivernois.[3] Their authors, who, by the way are everywhere, are worse than their own writings, which I don't mean as a compliment to either.[4] In general, the style of conversation is solemn, pedantic, and seldom animated, but by a dispute. I was expressing my aversion to disputes: Mr Hume,[5] who very gratefully admires the tone of Paris, having never known any other tone, said with great surprise, 'Why what do you like, if you hate both disputes and whisk?'

What strikes me the most upon the whole is, the total difference of manners between them and us, from the greatest object to the least. There is not the smallest similitude in the twenty-four hours. It is obvious in every trifle. Servants carry their Lady's train and put her into her coach with their hat on. They walk about the streets in the rain with umbrellas to avoid putting on their hats; driving themselves in open chaises in the country without hats, in the rain too, and yet often wear them in a chariot in Paris when it does not rain. The very footmen are powdered from the break of day, and yet wait behind their master, as I saw the Duc of Praslin's[6] do, with a red pocket handkerchief about their necks. Versailles like everything else is a mixture of parade and poverty;[7] and in every instance exhibits something most dissonant from our manners. In the colonnades, upon the staircases, nay in the antechambers of the royal family, there are people selling all sorts of wares. While we were waiting in the Dauphin's[8] sumptuous bedchamber, till his dressing-room door should be opened, two fellows were sweeping it, and dancing about in sabots to rub the floor.

You perceive that I have been presented.[9] The Queen[10] took great notice of me; none of the rest said a syllable. You are let into

3. Louis-Jules-Barbon Mancini-Mazarini (1716–98), Duc de Nivernais, who later translated HW's *Essay on Modern Gardening*. He had been ambassador to England 1762–3.

4. See also HW to Montagu 22 Sept. 1765 (Montagu ii. 176), for further sentiments on this subject.

5. David Hume (1711–76), the philosopher, was in Paris as secretary to Hertford's embassy.

6. César-Gabriel de Choiseul (1712–85), Duc de Praslin: secretary of state for foreign affairs, with whom HW had dined two days before; see below.

7. 'Parade and Poverty the land divide
And Parsimony ministers to Pride.'
(HW's 'Paris Journals,' du Deffand v. 357).

8. Louis (1729 – 20 Dec. 1765).

9. 1 Oct. ('Paris Journals,' du Deffand v. 266). See HW to Lady Hervey 3 Oct. and to Conway 6 Oct. 1765 for further details of HW's presentation.

10. Marie-Catherine-Sophie-Félicité (Leszczyńska) (1703–68), m. (1725) Louis XV (1710–74), K. of France 1715–74.

the King's bedchamber just as he has put on his shirt; he dresses
and talks good-humouredly to a few, glares at strangers, goes to Mass,
to dinner and a-hunting. The good old Queen, who is like Lady
Primrose[11] in the face, and Queen Caroline[12] in the immensity of
her cap, is at her dressing-table, attended by two or three old ladies,
who are languishing to be in Abraham's bosom, as the only man's
bosom to whom they can hope for admittance. Thence you go to
the Dauphin, for all is done in an hour. He scarce stays a minute;
indeed poor creature, he is a ghost and cannot possibly last three
months. The Dauphiness[13] is in her bedchamber, but dressed and
standing: looks cross, is not civil, and has the true Westphalian
grace and accents. The four Mesdames,[14] who are clumsy plump
old wenches, with a bad likeness to their father, stand in a bedchamber in a row, with black cloaks and knotting bags, looking
good-humoured, not knowing what to say, and wriggling as if they
wanted to make water. This ceremony too is very short: then you
are carried to the Dauphin's three boys, who you may be sure only
bow and stare. The Duke of Berry[15] looks weak and weak-eyed: the
Count de Provence[16] is a fine boy; the Count d'Artois,[17] well enough.
The whole concludes with seeing the Dauphin's little girl[18] dine,
who is as round and fat as a pudding.

I dined at the Duc of Praslin's, with four and twenty ambassadors
and envoys, who never go but on Tuesdays to Court. He does the
In the Queen's antechamber we foreigners and foreign ministers
were shown the famous beast of the Gévaudan,[19] just arrived, and
covered with a cloth which two chasseurs lifted up. It is an absolute
wolf, but uncommonly large, and the expression of agony and fierce-
ness remains strongly imprinted on its dead jaws.

I dined at the Duc of Praslin's, with four and twenty ambassadors
and envoys, who never go but on Tuesdays to Court. He does the

11. Anne Drelincourt (d. 1775), m. (1739) Hugh Primrose, 3d Vct Primrose.

12. Caroline (1683–1737), m. (1705) George II of England.

13. Marie-Josèphe (1731–67) of Saxony, m. (1747) Louis, Dauphin.

14. Louis XV's unmarried daughters: Marie-Adélaïde (1732–1800); Victoire-Lou-ise-Marie-Thérèse (1733–99); Sophie-Phil-ippine-Élisabeth-Justine (1734–82); and Louise-Marie (1737–87).

15. Louis-Auguste (1754–93), who be-came Louis XVI.

16. Louis-Stanislas-Xavier (1755–1824), who became Louis XVIII, 1814.

17. Charles-Philippe (1757–1836), who became Charles X, 1824.

18. Marie-Adélaïde-Clotilde-Xavière (1759–1802), m. (1775) Charles Emmanuel, P. of Piedmont, later Charles Emmanuel IV of Sardinia.

19. Cole describes this over-sized wolf, which for some months had ravaged the countryside of Auvergne and the Gévau-dan, in his *Journals of My Journey to Paris*, 1931, p. 210. See also HW to Lady Hervey 3 Oct., to Conway 6 Oct., to Anne Pitt 8 Oct., and to Lady Mary Coke 15 Oct. 1765.

honours sadly, and I believe nothing else well, looking important and empty.[20] The Duc de Choiseul's[21] face, which is quite the reverse of gravity, does not promise much more. His wife[22] is gentle, pretty, and very agreeable; the Duchess of Praslin,[23] jolly, red-faced, looking very vulgar, and being very attentive and civil. I saw the Duc de Richlieu[24] in waiting, who is pale except his nose which is red, much wrinkled, and exactly a remnant of that age which produced General Churchill,[25] Wilkes the player,[26] the Duke of Argyle[27] etc.

The enclosed letter for Martinelli[28] has been in England, and followed me hither; I don't know where he lives or would not trouble you with it. Adieu!

Yours ever

H. W.

To Chute, ca Sunday 13 October 1765

Missing; listed in 'Paris Journals' (DU DEFFAND V. 376).

To Chute, Tuesday 29 October 1765

Missing; listed in 'Paris Journals' (DU DEFFAND V. 377).

20. 'The Duc de Praslin is as like his own letters in d'Éon's book as he can stare; that is, I believe, a very silly fellow. His wisdom is of the grave kind' (HW to Conway 6 Oct. 1765).

21. Étienne-François de Choiseul-Stainville (1719–85), Duc de Choiseul, principal minister; 'a little volatile being, whose countenance and manner had nothing to frighten me for my country' (ibid.).

22. Louise-Honorine Crozat du Châtel (1735–1801), m. (1750) Étienne-François, Duc de Choiseul; the 'grand'maman' of Mme du Deffand's letters.

23. Anne-Marie de Champagne-la-Suze (1713–84), m. (1732) César-Gabriel de Choiseul, Duc de Praslin.

24. Louis-François-Armand Vignerot du Plessis (1696–1788), Duc and Maréchal de Richelieu.

25. Charles Churchill (ca 1679–1745), army officer; M.P.

26. Robert Wilkes (ca 1665–1732), actor.

27. John Campbell (1680–1743), 2d D. of Argyll.

28. Vincenzo Martinelli (1702–85), Florentine writer who spent much of his life in London (Enciclopedia italiana).

To Chute, ca Tuesday 26 November 1765

Missing; listed in 'Paris Journals' (DU DEFFAND v. 377).

To Chute, ca Friday 29 November 1765

Missing; listed in 'Paris Journals' (DU DEFFAND v. 378).

To Chute, Tuesday 7 January 1766

Printed from *Works* v. 420–2. Reprinted, Wright v. 111–14, Cunningham iv. 456–8, Toynbee vi. 389–92.

Misdated in *Works:* 'January 1765.' Here dated by the contents; see notes below.

Paris, January 1765 [1766].

IT IS in vain, I know, my dear Sir, to scold you, though I have such a mind to it—nay, I must. Yes, you that will not lie a night at Strawberry in autumn for fear of the gout, to stay in the country till this time, and till you caught it![1] I know you will tell me, it did not come till you had been two days in town. Do, and I shall have no more pity for you, than if I was your wife, and had wanted to come to town two months ago.

I am perfectly well, though to be sure Lapland is the torrid zone in comparison of Paris. We have had such a frost for this fortnight, that I went nine miles to dine in the country today, in a villa[2] exactly like a greenhouse, except that there was no fire but in one room. We were four[3] in a coach, and all our chinks stopped with furs, and yet all the glasses were frozen. We dined in a paved hall painted in fresco, with a fountain at one end; for in this country they live in a perpetual opera, and persist in being young when

1. HW wrote to Lady Hervey 11 Jan. 1766: 'I have never heard from Mr Chute this century, but am glad the gout is rather his excuse than the cause, and that it lies only in his pen' (MORE 97).

2. The house of the Marquis de Prie, Bois Prévu, near Rueil ('Paris Journals,' DU DEFFAND v. 293).

3. HW was accompanied by 'Mrs Shirley, her companion, and M. Dangeul' (ibid.).

they are old, and hot when they are frozen. At the end of the hall sat shivering three glorious macaws, a vast cockatoo, and two poor perroquets, who squalled like the children in the wood after their nursery fire! I am come home, and blowing my billets between every paragraph, yet can scarce move my fingers. However, I must be dressed presently, and go to the Comtesse de la Marche,[4] who has appointed nine at night for my audience.[5] It seems a little odd to us to be presented to a Princess of the Blood at that hour—but I told you, there is not a tittle in which our manners resemble one another. I was presented to her father-in-law the Prince of Conti[6] last Friday. In the middle of the levee entered a young woman, too plain I thought to be anything but his near relation. I was confirmed in my opinion, by seeing her, after he had talked to her, go round the circle and do the honours of it. I asked a gentleman near me if that was the Comtesse de la Marche? He burst into a violent laughter, and then told me, it was Mademoiselle Auguste,[7] a dancer!—Now, who was in the wrong?

I give you these as samples of many scenes that have amused me, and which will be charming food at Strawberry. At the same time that I see all their ridicules, there is a *douceur* in the society of the women of fashion that captivates me. I like the way of life, though not lively; though the men are posts and apt to be arrogant, and though there are twenty ingredients wanting to make the style perfect. I have totally washed my hands of their *savants* and philosophers, and do not even envy you Rousseau,[8] who has all the *charlatanerie* of Count St Germain[9] to make himself singular and

4. Fortunée-Marie d'Este (1731–1803), m. (1759) Louis-François-Joseph de Bourbon, Comte de la Marche, Prince de Conti, 1776.

5. 'At half an hour after 8 was carried with Mr Craufurd by Chevalier Lorenzi to be presented to the Comtesse de la Marche; she offered to salute us: the hall and antechamber hung in black, but not her room' (ibid.).

6. Louis-François de Bourbon (1717–76). HW was presented to him 3 Jan. but had already supped with him at Mme de Luxembourg's 17 Dec. (ibid. v. 286, 292).

7. Probably the Mlle Augusta who danced at Venice in 1757 (Taddeo Weil, *I teatri musicali veneziani del settecento*,

Venice, 1897, p. 211), and who was probably the Mlle or Mme Auguste who danced at Drury Lane 1752–4 (*The London Stage 1660–1800*, pt 4, ed. G. W. Stone, Carbondale, Ill., 1962, i. 318, 376).

8. Who had set out for England 4 Jan.; see HW to Lady Mary Coke of that date (MORE 94).

9. The Comte de Saint-Germain (d. 1784), a celebrated adventurer who had been in England in the mid-1740's and later lived much at the French Court. He was very wealthy, but the source of his wealth and even his true name remain unknown. See MANN iii. 181–2 and nn. 29–35, and (for HW's long accounts of him) MANN x. 20–1 (Appendix 6).

talked of. I suppose Mrs ———,[10] my Lord ———,[11] and a certain lady friend of mine[12] will be in raptures with him, especially as conducted by Mr Hume. But however I admire his parts, neither he nor any *Genius* I have known has had common sense enough to balance the impertinence of their pretensions. They hate priests, but love dearly to have an altar at their feet; for which reason it is much pleasanter to read them than to know them. Adieu, my dear Sir!

Yours ever,

Hor. Walpole

January 15.

THIS has been writ this week, and waiting for a conveyance, and as yet has got none.[13] Favre[14] tells me you are recovered, but you don't tell me so yourself. I enclose a trifle that I wrote lately,[15] which got about and has made enormous noise in a city where they run and cackle after an event, like a parcel of hens after an accidental husk of a grape. It has made me the fashion, and made Madame de Boufflers[16] and the Prince of Conti very angry with me;[17] the former intending to be rapt to the Temple of Fame by clinging to Rousseau's Armenian robe. I am peevish that with his parts he should be such a mountebank: but what made me more peevish was, that after receiving Wilkes with the greatest civilities,[18] he paid court to Mr Hume by complaining of Wilkes's visit and intrusion.

Upon the whole, I would not but have come hither; for, since

10. Presumably, as assumed by earlier editors, Elizabeth Robinson (1720–1800), m. (1742) Edward Montagu.

11. Presumably Lord Lyttelton.

12. Probably, as suggested by Cunningham and Toynbee, Lady Hervey, who was a friend of Hume.

13. The letter was finally sent on the 18th 'by Rochester postillion' ('Paris Journals,' du Deffand v. 379).

14. HW's servant in Arlington Street.

15. The letter from the King of Prussia to Rousseau (HW). HW wrote it, 23 Dec. 1765, and it had been circulating in Paris since 28 Dec. (More 99, n. 10). Copies of it are in HW's letters to Con-

way 12 Jan., to Anne Pitt 19 Jan., and to Cole 25 Feb. 1766.

16. Marie-Charlotte-Hippolyte de Campet de Saujon (1725–1800), m. (1746) Édouard, Comte (Marquis, 1751) de Boufflers-Rouverel; Conti's mistress.

17. They had rebuked HW on the 14th at Mme de Luxembourg's ('Paris Journals,' du Deffand v. 295).

18. Wilkes had been in France and Switzerland since the preceding June. On 25 Aug. 1765 Rousseau was expecting a visit from him at Motier (Horace Bleackley, *Life of John Wilkes*, 1917, p. 172; Jean-Jacques Rousseau, *Correspondance générale*, ed. Théophile Dufour, Paris, 1924–34, xiv. 110).

I am doomed to live in England, it is some comfort to have seen that the French are ten times more contemptible than we are. I am a little ungrateful; but I cannot help seeing with my eyes, though I find other people make nothing of seeing without theirs. I have endless histories to amuse you with when we meet, which shall be at the end of March.[19] It is much more tiresome to be fashionable than unpopular; I am used to the latter, and know how to behave under it: but I cannot stand for member of Parliament of Paris. Adieu!

To Chute, ca Monday 17 February 1766

Missing; listed in 'Paris Journals' (DU DEFFAND v. 379).

To Chute, Friday 10 October 1766

Printed from *Works* v. 419–20; reprinted, Wright v. 161–2, Cunningham v. 16–17, Toynbee vii. 49–50.

Bath, Oct. 10, 1766.

I AM impatient to hear that your charity to me[1] has not ended in the gout to yourself—all my comfort is, if you have it, that you have good Lady Brown[2] to nurse you.

My health advances faster than my amusement. However, I have been at one opera, Mr Wesley's.[3] They have boys and girls with charming voices, that sing hymns, in parts, to Scotch ballad tunes; but indeed so long, that one would think they were already in eternity, and knew how much time they had before them. The chapel is very neat,[4] with true Gothic windows (yet I am not converted);

---

19. HW did not return until late April ('Paris Journals,' DU DEFFAND v. 314).

------

1. Chute had accompanied HW to Bath at the beginning of October and remained until the 7th (MONTAGU ii. 228).
2. I.e., Margaret, Lady Brown. See *ante* 21 May 1754.
3. John Wesley (1703–91). HW had

probably attended his service 9 Oct., when Wesley noted in his journal: 'In the evening I preached again [as he had done on the 5th] at my Lady's chapel [Lady Huntingdon's Chapel] to another numerous congregation' (John Wesley, *Journal*, ed. Curnock, 1909–16, v. 189).
4. Lady Huntington's chapel in Harlequin Row, built the preceding year ([A.

but I was glad to see that luxury is creeping in upon them before persecution: they have very neat mahogany stands for branches,[5] and brackets of the same in taste. At the upper end is a broad *haut-pas* of four steps, advancing in the middle; at each end of the broadest part are two of *my* eagles[6] with red cushions for the parson and clerk. Behind them rise three more steps, in the midst of which is a third eagle for pulpit. Scarlet armed-chairs to all three. On either hand a balcony for elect ladies. The rest of the congregation sit on forms. Behind the pit, in a dark niche, is a plain table within rails; so you see the throne is for the apostle. Wesley is a lean elderly man, fresh-coloured, his hair smoothly combed, but with a *soupçon* of curl at the ends. Wondrous clean, but as evidently an actor as Garrick. He spoke his sermon, but so fast and with so little accent, that I am sure he has often uttered it, for it was like a lesson. There were parts and eloquence in it; but towards the end he exalted his voice, and acted very vulgar enthusiasm; decried learning, and told stories, like Latimer,[7] of the fool of his college,[8] who said, 'I *thanks* God for everything.' Except a few from curiosity, and *some honourable women,* the congregation was very mean. There was a Scotch Countess of B——,[9] who is carrying a pure rosy vulgar face to heaven, and who asked Miss Rich, if that was *the author of the poets.* I believe she meant me and the *Noble Authors.*

C. H. Seymour], *Life and Times of Selina, Countess of Huntingdon,* 1840, i. 466–8; illustrated in Bryan Little, *The Buildings of Bath,* 47–1947, plate 51). It is described in 1801 as displaying 'taste and elegance in the interior part. The ground floor is intersected by a light iron railing into several divisions, each well-furnished with seats covered with red cloth; a handsome gallery runs round, supported by fluted pillars, every two of which form an arch with the side of the gallery. The communion table is placed in a circular recess at one end, with a fine toned organ directly over it; at the other end, two steps higher than the floor, there are two reading-desks, each supported by a spread eagle, behind these the throne rises six steps higher still, with another reading-desk, borne by a spread eagle also, that stands on its summit. These ornaments unite to make the whole to have a pleasing effect on the eye of the beholder' (*The Historic and Local New Bath Guide,* Bath, [1801], pp. 51–2).

5. I.e., candelabra.

6. Resembling HW's Roman eagle; see *ante* pp. 63–4.

7. Hugh Latimer (ca 1485–1555), D.D.; Bp of Worcester. HW may have in mind an anecdote told by Latimer in his last sermon before Edward VI, 1550: 'And it is with me as it is with a scholar of Cambridge, who being demanded of his tutor how he understood his lesson, and what it meant: I know (quoth he) what it meaneth, but I cannot tell, I cannot express it' (Latimer, *Fruitfull Sermons,* 1635, f. 113v.; HW's copy is now WSL, see Hazen, *Cat. of HW's Lib.,* No. 1332).

8. Wesley was a fellow of Lincoln College, Oxford.

9. Probably, as assumed by earlier editors, Agnes Steuart (d. 1778), m. (1739) Henry David Erskine, 10th E. of Buchan. They were Methodist converts.

The Bedfords[10] came last night. Lord Chatham was with me yester-day two hours;[11] looks and walks well, and is in excellent political spirits.

Yours ever,

Hor. Walpole

To Chute, ca Thursday 27 August 1767

Missing; listed in 'Paris Journals' (du Deffand v. 385).

To Chute, ca Wednesday 2 September 1767

Missing; listed in 'Paris Journals' (du Deffand v. 385).

To Chute, ca Wednesday 23 September 1767

Missing; listed in 'Paris Journals' (du Deffand v. 385).

To Chute, Wednesday 30 August 1769

Printed from *Works* v. 422–4; reprinted, Wright v. 248–50, Cunningham v. 182–4, Toynbee vii. 307–9.

Paris, August 30, 1769.

I HAVE been so hurried with paying and receiving visits, that I have not had a moment's worth of time to write. My passage[1] was very tedious, and lasted near nine hours for want of wind—But I need not talk of my journey; for Mr Morrice,[2] whom I met on the road, will have told you that I was safe on terra firma.

<hr>

10. The 4th D. of Bedford m. (1737) Gertrude Leveson Gower (1715–94).

11. HW gives an account of this conversation in *Mem. Geo. III* ii. 261–2.

1. On 18 Aug. ('Paris Journals,' du Deffand v. 324; see also HW to Montagu 18 Aug. 1769, Montagu ii. 282–3).

2. Probably Humphrey Morice (1723–85), M.P.

Judge of my surprise at hearing four days ago that my Lord D——
and my Lady[3] were arrived here. They are lodged within a few
doors of me. He is come to consult a Doctor Pomme,[4] who has
proscribed wine, and Lord D—— already complains of the violence
of his appetite. If you and I had *pommed* him to eternity, he would
not have believed us. A man across the sea tells him the plainest
thing in the world; that man happens to be called a doctor; and
happening for novelty to talk common sense, is believed, as if he
had talked nonsense! and what is more extraordinary, Lord D——
thinks himself better, *though* he is so.

My dear old woman[5] is in better health than when I left her, and
her spirits so increased, that I tell her she will go mad with age.
When they ask her how old she is, she answers, 'J'ai soixante et mille
ans.' She and I went to the boulevard last night after supper, and
drove about there till two in the morning. We are going to sup in
the country[6] this evening, and are to go tomorrow night at eleven to
the puppet-show.[7] A protégé of hers[8] has written a piece for that
theatre. I have not yet seen Madame du Barri,[9] nor can get to see
her picture[10] at the Exposition at the Louvre, the crowds are so
enormous that go thither for that purpose. As royal curiosities are
the least part of my virtu, I wait with patience. Whenever I have
an opportunity I visit gardens, chiefly with a view to Rosette's[11]
having a walk. She goes nowhere else, because there is a distemper
among the dogs.

There is going to be represented a translation of *Hamlet;*[12] who,
when his hair is cut, and he is curled and powdered, I suppose will
be exactly *Monsieur le Prince Oreste.*[13] T'other night I was at

3. Lord and Lady Dacre *(ante* 29 Sept.
1755) as 'Paris Journals,' op. cit. v. 326
makes clear; HW called on them on the
27th and 29th (ibid. v. 326, 327). See also
HW to Montagu 7 Sept. 1769 (MONTAGU ii.
290).

4. Pierre Pomme (1735–1812) (NBG).

5. Mme du Deffand (HW).

6. At Gennevilliers ('Paris Journals,' DU
DEFFAND v. 327).

7. Apparently at the Foire St-Ovide
(ibid.).

8. Not identified.

9. Jeanne Bécu (1743–93), m. (1768)
Guillaume, Comte du Barry; mistress of
Louis XV. HW finally saw her at Ver-
sailles 17 Sept. (ibid. v. 330).

10. Two portraits of Mme du Barry,
one as a man, the other as a woman, by
Henri-François Drouais (d. 1775) were the
sensation of the salon of 1769; see Charles
Vatel, *Histoire du Madame du Barry*,
1883, i. 279–83; Edmond and Jules de-
Goncourt, *La du Barry*, new edn, 1880,
pp. 72–7.

11. A favourite dog of Mr Walpole's
(HW).

12. An adaptation by Jean-François
Ducis (1733–1816); HW attended the first
performance 30 Sept. ('Paris Journals,' op.
cit. v. 332 and n. 34a).

13. In *Oreste*, a tragedy by Voltaire.

Mérope.[14] The Dumenil[15] was as divine as Mrs Porter;[16] they said her familiar tones were those of a *poissonnière*. In the last act, when one expected the catastrophe, Narbas, more interested than anybody to see the event, remained coolly on the stage to hear the story. The Queen's maid of honour entered without her handkerchief, and with her hair most artfully undressed, and reeling as if she was maudlin, sobbed out a long narrative,[17] that did not prove true;[18] while Narbas, with all the good breeding in the world, was more attentive to her fright than to what had happened. So much for propriety. Now for probability. Voltaire has published a tragedy, called *Les Guèbres*.[19] Two Roman colonels open the piece: they are brothers, and relate to one another, how they lately in company destroyed, by the Emperor's mandate, a city of the Guèbres, in which were their own wives and children, and they recollect that they want prodigiously to know whether both their families did not perish in the flames. The son of the one and the daughter of the other are taken up for heretics, and, thinking themselves brother and sister, insist upon being married, and upon being executed for their religion. The son stabs his father, who is half a Guèbre too. The high-priest rants and roars. The Emperor arrives, blames the pontiff for being a persecutor, and forgives the son for assassinating his father (who does not die) because—I don't know why, but that he may marry his cousin.—The grave-diggers in *Hamlet* have no chance, when such a piece as the *Guèbres* is written agreeably to all rules and unities. Adieu, my dear Sir! I hope to find you quite well at my return.

Yours ever,

Hor. Walpole

14. Also by Voltaire; first performed in 1743. HW had attended 27 Aug. (ibid. v. 326).

15. Marie-Françoise Dumesnil (1713–1803). Her performance in *Mérope* is described in Voltaire's *Appel à toutes les nations*, in *Œuvres complètes*, ed. Moland, 1877–85, xxiv. 220.

16. Mary Porter (d. 1765), actress. HW frequently expresses his admiration of her as a tragedian.

17. Isménie tells how Mérope's son Égisthe, who has been threatened with death by the tyrant Polyphonte unless Mérope will marry him, kills Polyphonte with an axe.

18. HW is mistaken; Isménie's narrative is true.

19. Written in August 1768, first published pseudonomously in Geneva in 1769 and reprinted in Paris about July; it was never performed (Voltaire, op. cit. vi. 483–5). Voltaire presented a copy to Mme du Deffand in July 1769 (Mme du Deffand, *Correspondance complète*, ed. Sainte-Aulaire, 1866, i. 244–6).

To Chute, Tuesday 9 July 1771

Printed from *Works* v. 424–5. Reprinted, Wright v. 303–4, Cunningham v. 314–15, Toynbee vii. 56–8.

Amiens, Tuesday evening, July 9, 1771.

I AM got no farther yet, as I travel leisurely, and do not venture to fatigue myself. My voyage was but of four hours. I was sick only by choice and precaution, and find myself in perfect health. The enemy, I hope, has not returned to pinch you again, and that you defy the foul fiend. The weather is but lukewarm, and I should choose to have all the windows shut, if my smelling was not much more summerly than my feeling; but the frowsiness of obsolete tapestry and needlework is insupportable.[1] Here are old fleas and bugs talking of Louis Quatorze like tattered refugees in the Park, and they make poor Rosette attend to them whether she will or not. This is a woeful account of an evening in July, and which Monsieur de St Lambert has omitted in his *Seasons*,[2] though more natural than anything he has placed there. If the Grecian religion had gone into the folly of self-mortification, I suppose the devotees of Flora would have shut themselves up in a nasty inn, and have punished their noses for the sensuality of having smelt to a rose or a honeysuckle. This is all I have yet to say; for I have had no adventure, no accident, nor seen a soul but my cousin R—— W——,[3] whom I met on the road and spoke to in his chaise. Tomorrow I shall lie at Chantilly, and be at Paris early on Thursday.[4] The C[hurchills][5] are there already. Good night—and a *sweet* one to you!

1. HW was staying at the Aux Bons Enfants, which he described in the 'Paris Journals' as 'a very bad inn' (DU DEFFAND v. 334).

2. *Les Saisons*, 1769, by Jean-François (1716–1803), Marquis de Saint-Lambert. For HW's opinion of it, see DU DEFFAND ii. 213–14.

3. Expanded by Wright and later editors to Richard Walpole; but it was the Hon. Robert Walpole (1736–1810), whose arrival from France on 11 July was re-ported in the *London Chronicle* 11–13 July 1771, xxx. 46.

4. HW went through to Paris the following day; see below. Presumably he stayed again at the Hôtel du Parc-Royal, Rue du Colombier ('Paris Journals,' DU DEFFAND v. 266).

5. HW's sister and brother-in-law, with whom he spent the day at Mme du Deffand's on the 11th ('Paris Journals,' DU DEFFAND v. 334).

Paris, Wednesday night, July 10.

I was so suffocated with my inn last night, that I mustered all my resolution, rose with the *alouette,* and was in my chaise by five o'clock this morning. I got hither by eight this evening, tired, but rejoiced, have had a comfortable dish of tea, and am going to bed in clean sheets. I sink myself even to my dear old woman and my sister; for it is impossible to sit down and be made charming at this time of night after fifteen posts, and after having been here twenty times before.

At Chantilly I crossed on the Countess of W——,[6] who lies there tonight on her way to England. But I concluded she had no curiosity about me—and I could not brag of more about her—and so we had no intercourse. I am woebegone to find my Lord F——[7] in the same hotel. He is as starched as an old-fashioned plaited neck-cloth, and come to suck wisdom from this curious school of philosophy. He reveres me because I was acquainted with his father;[8] and that does not at all increase my partiality to the son.

Luckily, the post departs early tomorrow morning. I thought you would like to hear I was arrived well. I should be happy to hear you are so; but do not torment yourself too soon, nor will I torment you. I have fixed the 26th of August for setting out on my return.[9] These jaunts are too juvenile. I am ashamed to look back and remember in what year of Methuselah I was here first.[10] Rosette sends her blessing to her daughter. Adieu!

Yours ever,

Hor. Walpole

6. Not identified. The only Countesses of W. living in 1771 were two countesses of Westmeath, one of Wemyss, and two of Westmorland. HW was uncle of Lady Waldegrave.

7. HW to Lady Ossory 11 Aug. 1771 shows that this was James Ogilvy (1750–1811), 7th E. of Findlater, 1770.

8. James Ogilvy (ca 1714–70), 6th E. of Findlater. HW describes himself as having been 'very intimate' with him when he was Lord Deskford; they had become acquainted in Rome in 1740 (HW to Conway 23 April 1740; to Dalrymple 10 Feb. 1781, Dalrymple 151; Mann i. 7, n. 16).

9. He did not leave Paris until 2 Sept. ('Paris Journals,' du Deffand v. 342).

10. In 1739.

To Chute, ca Sunday 14 July 1771

Missing; listed in 'Paris Journals' (du Deffand v. 393).

From Chute, Tuesday 30 July 1771

Missing. Date given in following letter.

To Chute, Monday 5 August 1771

Printed from *Works* v. 425–8; reprinted, Wright v. 308–11, Cunningham v. 320–3, Toynbee vii. 64–7.

Paris, August 5, 1771.

IT IS a great satisfaction to me to find by your letter of the 30th that you have had no return of your gout. I have been assured here that the best remedy is to cut one's nails in hot water.—It is, I fear, as certain as any other remedy! It would at least be so here, if their bodies were of a piece with their understandings; or if both were as curable, as they are the contrary. Your prophecy, I doubt, is not better founded than the prescription. I may be lame; but I shall never be a duck, nor deal in the garbage of the alley.[1]

I envy your *Strawberry-tide,* and need not say how much I wish I was there to receive you. Methinks I should be as glad of a little grass, as a seaman after a long voyage. Yet English gardening gains ground here prodigiously—not much at a time indeed—I have literally seen one that is exactly like a tailor's paper of patterns. There is a Monsieur Boutin,[2] who has tacked a piece of what he calls an English garden to a set of stone terraces with steps of turf. There are three or four very high hills, almost as high as, and exactly in the shape of, a tansy pudding. You squeeze between these and a

1. Chute had apparently 'prophesied' something about HW's engaging in stock-jobbing; 'lame ducks' were unsuccessful speculators and 'the alley' 'Change Alley.'
2. Simon-Charles Boutin (d. 1794) (du

Deffand iv. 378, n. 3). HW had visited his garden 28 July ('Paris Journals,' du Deffand v. 336); for a plan and further details see HW to Lady Ossory 11 Aug, 1771, Ossory i. 55–7.

river, that is conducted at obtuse angles in a stone channel, and supplied by a pump; and when walnuts come in, I suppose it will be navigable. In a corner enclosed by a chalk wall are the samples I mentioned: there is a stripe of grass, another of corn, and a third *en friche,* exactly in the order of beds in a nursery. They have translated Mr Whateley's book,[3] and the Lord knows what barbarism is going to be laid at our door. This new *anglomanie* will literally be *mad English.*

New *arrêts,*[4] new retrenchments,[5] new misery, stalk forth every day. The Parliament of Besançon is dissolved; so are the *Grenadiers de France.* The King's tradesmen are all bankrupt, no pensions are paid, and everybody is reforming their suppers and equipages. Despotism makes converts faster than ever Christianity did. Louis Quinze is the true *Rex Christianissimus,* and has ten times more success than his dragooning great-grandfather.[6] Adieu, my dear Sir!

Yours most faithfully,

Hor. Walpole

Friday 9th.

This was to have gone by a private hand, but cannot depart till Monday; so I may be continuing my letter till I bring it myself. I have been again at the Chartreuse;[7] and though it was the sixth time, I am more enchanted with those paintings[8] than ever. If it is not the first work in the world, and must yield to the Vatican, yet in simplicity and harmony it beats Raphael himself. There is a vapour over all the pictures that makes them more natural than any representation of objects—I cannot conceive how it is effected! you see them through the shine of a southeast wind. These poor folks do not know the inestimable treasure they possess—but they are perishing these pictures, and one gazes at them as at a setting sun.[9] There is the purity of Racine in them, but they give me more

---

3. *Observations on Modern Gardening,* 1770, by Thomas Whately (d. 1772). HW discusses it in his 'Essay on Modern Gardening,' *Works* ii. 540–3.

4. Many of these are summarized in the *Mercure historique et politique,* 1771, clxxi. 83–96.

5. Some of these are mentioned by HW to Conway 30 July 1771.

6. Louis XIV.

7. On the 6th ('Paris Journals,' DU DEFFAND v. 337).

8. 'La Vie de Saint-Bruno,' by Eustache le Sueur (1616–55). See GRAY i. 169–70.

9. The pictures were bought by Louis XVI in 1776, were transferred to canvas in 1777, and are now in the Louvre (GRAY, loc. cit. nn. 17 and 19).

pleasure—and I should much sooner be tired of the poet than of the painter.

It is very singular that I have not half the satisfaction in going into churches and convents that I used to have. The consciousness that the vision is dispelled, the want of fervour so obvious in the religious, the solitude that one knows proceeds from contempt, not from contemplation, make those places appear like abandoned theatres destined to destruction. The monks trot about as if they had not long to stay there; and what used to be holy gloom is now but dirt and darkness. There is no more deception, than in a tragedy acted by candle-snuffers. One is sorry to think that an empire of common sense would not be very picturesque; for, as there is nothing but taste that can compensate for the imagination of madness, I doubt there will never be twenty men of taste for twenty thousand madmen. The world will no more see Athens, Rome, and the Medici again, than a succession of five good emperors, like Nerva, Trajan, Adrian, and the two Antonines.

August 13.

Mr Edmondson[10] has called on me; and as he sets out tomorrow, I can safely trust my letter to him.

I have, I own, been much shocked at reading Gray's death[11] in the papers. 'Tis an hour that makes one forget any subjects of complaint, especially towards one with whom I lived in friendship from thirteen years old.[12] As self lies so rooted in self, no doubt the nearness of our ages made the stroke recoil to my own breast; and having so little expected his death, it is plain how little I expect my own. Yet to you, who of all men living are the most forgiving, I need not excuse the concern I feel. I fear, most men ought to apologize for their want of feeling, instead of palliating that sensation when they have it. I thought that what I had seen of the world had hardened my heart; but I find it had formed my language, not extinguished my tenderness. In short, I am really shocked—nay, I am hurt at my own weakness, as I perceive that when I love anybody, it is for my life; and I have had too much reason not to

10. Perhaps Joseph Edmondson (d. 1786), the genealogist.

11. Gray died on 30 July; HW learned of it on 11 Aug. ('Paris Journals,' DU DEFFAND v. 338).

12. They had been at Eton together since 1727, but evidently did not become close friends until about 1730.

wish that such a disposition may very seldom be put to the trial.
You at least are the only person to whom I would venture to make
such a confession.

Adieu, my dear Sir!—Let me know when I arrive, which will
be about the last day of the month,[13] when I am likely to see you.
I have much to say to you. Of being here I am most heartily tired,
and nothing but this dear old woman should keep me here an
hour—I am weary of them to death—but that is not new!

Yours ever,

Hor. Walpole

To Chute, ca Tuesday 29 August 1775

Missing; listed in 'Paris Journals' (du Deffand v. 396).

To Chute, ca Tuesday 12 September 1775

Missing; listed in 'Paris Journals' (du Deffand v. 396). This is HW's last
recorded letter to Chute, who died 26 May 1776; see HW to Mann 27 May 1776
for HW's lament on the occasion.

13. He did not reach London until 6 Sept. ('Paris Journals,' du Deffand v. 342).

THE CORRESPONDENCE
WITH RICHARD
BENTLEY

BENTLEY'S SKETCHES AND NOTE

From Bentley, ? 1752

There is no certainty that this brief unpublished note by Bentley was addressed to HW. It was received by the British Museum from the Iolo Williams bequest in May, 1963. It is conjecturally dated on the assumption that it was written to HW when Bentley was working for HW on the illustrations to Gray's poems, since the two Chinese boxes in this drawing suggest those in the 'Mandarin Cats' (see illustration opposite Montagu i. 134).

Dear Sir:

[Drawings, in ink, follow; see illustration opposite].

and am vastly sorry I cannot have the pleasure of attending you tomorrow; I am

Your most obedient servant

R. Bentley

It was impossible for me to give you earlier notice.

To Bentley,[1] Wednesday 5 August 1752

Printed from *Works* v. 261–9; reprinted, Wright ii. 435–46, Cunningham ii. 296–305, Toynbee iii. 108–21.

Battel,[2] Wednesday, August 5, 1752.

HERE we[3] are, my dear Sir, in the middle of our pilgrimage; and lest we should never return from this holy land of abbeys and Gothic castles, I begin a letter to you, that I hope some charitable monk, when he has buried our bones, will deliver to you. We have had piteous distresses, but then we have seen glorious sights! You shall hear of each in their order.

Monday, wind S.E.—at least that was our direction.—While they were changing our horses at Bromley, we went to see the Bishop of Rochester's palace; not for the sake of anything there was to be

---

1. Only son of Dr Bentley, the celebrated commentator (?HW). See *ante* HW to Chute ? March 1753, n. 2.

2. I.e., Battle, Sussex.

3. Chute was accompanying HW on this 'pilgrimage' through Kent and Sussex.

seen, but because there was a chimney, in which had stood a flower-pot, in which was put the counterfeit plot against Bishop Sprat.[4] 'Tis a paltry parsonage,[5] with nothing of antiquity but two panes of glass, purloined from Islip's[6] chapel in Westminster Abbey, with that abbot's rebus, an eye and a slip of a tree.[7] In the garden there is a clear little pond, teeming with gold-fish. The Bishop[8] is more prolific than I am.[9]

From Sevenoak we went to Knowle.[10] The park is sweet, with much old beech, and an immense sycamore before the great gate, that makes me more in love than ever with sycamores. The house is not near so extensive as I expected: the outward court[11] has a beautiful decent simplicity that charms one. The apartments are many, but not large. The furniture throughout, ancient magnificence; loads of portraits, not good, nor curious; ebony cabinets, embossed silver in vases, dishes, etc. embroidered beds, stiff chairs, and sweet bags lying on velvet tables, richly worked in silk and gold. There are two galleries,[12] one very small; an old hall,[13] and a spacious great drawing-room. There is never a good staircase. The first little room you enter has sundry portraits of the times; but they seem to have been bespoke by the yard, and drawn all by the same painter:[14] one should be happy if they were authentic; for among

4. Thomas Sprat (1635–1713), Dean of Westminster 1683–1713; Bp of Rochester 1684–1713, was the victim of a plot (1692) to implicate him in a supposed conspiracy to restore James II, but was released when it was discovered that the incriminating paper was a forgery. See DNB and Sprat's own 'Relation' of the plot. The flower pot and the counterfeit paper were at Matson; see *post* HW to Bentley Sept. 1753.

5. It had been much enlarged and altered from time to time, especially by Bishop Wilcocks, the then incumbent. Sprat himself had rebuilt the chapel. The palace was demolished in 1774 and a new one completed by 1776 (Edward Hasted, *History . . . of Kent,* 2d edn, Canterbury, 1797–1801, i. 558).

6. John Islip (d. 1532), abbot of Westminster.

7. The chapel, which still bears Islip's name, contains a cornice with two rebuses: an eye and a slip of a tree, and an eye and a tree with a man slipping from it

(Jocelyn Perkins, *Westminster Abbey,* 1937, p. 51).

8. Joseph Wilcocks (1673–1756), Bp of Gloucester 1721–31, Rochester 1731–56.

9. HW, however, had told Montagu in June that his goldfish at SH 'breed with me excessively and are grown to the size of small perch' (Montagu i. 134).

10. Knole, Kent, seat of the Duke of Dorset.

11. The Green Court, described in V. Sackville-West, *Knole,* National Trust [1955], p. 15.

12. There are actually three galleries: the Brown, the Leicester, and the Cartoon.

13. Built about 1460, although it was much altered and improved in the later 16th century (V. Sackville-West, op. cit. 17).

14. Presumably the series of historical portraits now hanging in the Brown Gallery; they were formerly confidently attributed to Holbein and his pupils, but

them there is Dudley Duke of Northumberland,[15] Gardiner[16] of Winchester, the Earl of Surry[17] the poet, when a boy, and a Thomas Duke of Norfolk; but I don't know which.[18] The only fine picture is of Lord Goring[19] and Endymion Porter[20] by Vandyke. There is a good head of the Queen of Bohemia,[21] a whole-length of Duc d'Espernon,[22] and another good head of the Clifford Countess of Dorset,[23] who wrote that admirable haughty letter[24] to Secretary Williamson,[25] when he recommended a person to her for member for Appleby: 'I have been bullied by an usurper, I have been neglected by a court, but I won't be dictated to by a subject:—your man shan't stand. Ann Dorset, Pembroke and Montgomery.' In the chapel is a piece of ancient tapestry: Saint Luke in his first profession is holding an urinal. Below stairs is a chamber of poets and players,[26] which is proper enough in that house; for the first Earl

are now tentatively assigned to John Van Belcamp, a copyist living in the reign of Charles I (ibid. 20).

15. John Dudley (1502–53), cr. (1551) D. of Northumberland.

16. Stephen Gardiner (ca 1483–1555), Bp of Winchester.

17. Henry Howard (ca 1517–47), styled E. of Surrey. For another portrait of him at Knole, see below, n. 34.

18. According to Lionel Sackville-West's *Knole House*, Sevenoaks, 1906, p. 30, this was Thomas Howard (1538–72), 4th D. of Norfolk, 1554.

19. George Goring (1608–57), styled Lord Goring 1644–57.

20. Endymion Porter (1587–1649), groom of the Bedchamber to Prince Charles. At least four portraits of Porter by Van Dyck are known, and two of Goring, but this double portrait has not been traced (Lionel Cust, *Anthony van Dyck*, 1900, pp. 275, 279, 281). Probably what HW saw was a double portrait of Mountjoy Blount, Earl of Newport, and Lord Goring, now hanging in the Cartoon Gallery at Knole and described merely as 'after Van Dyck,' although earlier attributions were more definite (Lionel Sackville-West, op. cit. 96; V. Sackville-West, op. cit. 33).

21. Elizabeth Stuart (1596–1662), dau. of James I; m. (1613) Frederick V, K. of Bohemia and Elector Palatine. The portrait, attributed to Honthorst, hung in the

'Parlour Passage' in 1906 (Lionel Sackville-West, op. cit. 101).

22. Jean-Louis de Nogaret (1554–1642), Duc d'Épernon; favourite of Henri III. The painting, by Porbus, now hangs in the Great Hall (ibid. 24).

23. Anne Clifford (1590–1676), Bns Clifford, s.j.; m. 1 (1609) Richard Sackville, 3d E. of Dorset; m. 2 (1630) Philip Herbert, E. of Pembroke and Montgomery. The head, attributed to Cornelis van Ceulen Janssens, was hanging in the Brown Gallery in 1906 (ibid. 29); it has not been located in more recent guides to Knole. Another portrait, full-length, hanging in the Ball-Room, is reproduced in V. Sackville-West, *Knole and the Sackvilles*, 1922, facing p. 56; see also idem, *Knole*, National Trust, [1955], p. 30.

24. This letter was first printed by HW in the *World* for 5 April 1753. It is not now considered authentic; see George L. Williamson, *Lady Anne Clifford*, Kendal, 1922, pp. 285–302 and Wallace Notestein, *Four Worthies*, New Haven, 1957, pp. 158–60.

25. Sir Joseph Williamson (1633–1701), secretary of state 1674–8.

26. Later known as the 'Poets' Parlour and now the dining room (V. Sackville-West, *Knole*, National Trust, [1955], p. 35).

wrote a play,[27] and the last Earl was a poet,[28] and I think married a player.[29] Major Mohun[30] and Betterton[31] are curious among the latter, Cartwright[32] and Flatman[33] among the former. The arcade is newly enclosed, painted in fresco, and with modern glass of all the family matches. In the gallery is a whole-length of the unfortunate Earl of Surry,[34] with his device a broken column, and the motto *Sat superest*.[35] My father had one of them, but larger, and with more emblems, which the Duke of Norfolk[36] bought at my brother's sale.[37] There is one good head of Henry VIII[38] and divers of Cranfield Earl of Middlesex,[39] the citizen who came to be Lord Treasurer,[40] and

27. Thomas Sackville (d. 1608), cr. (1567) Bn Buckhurst and (1604) E. of Dorset, was joint author (with Thomas Norton) of *Gorboduc*. He is in HW's *Catalogue of the Royal and Noble Authors, Works* i. 330–3.

28. Charles Sackville (1638–1706), 6th E. of Dorset, 1677, wrote verses. See ibid. i. 425–6, 530.

29. Dorset's third wife, Ann Roche, is not known to have been an actress, but was a woman of obscure connections (GEC; V. Sackville-West, *Knole and the Sackvilles*, 1922, pp. 140–1).

30. Michael Mohun (ca 1620–84) was an actor who became a Major in the Royalist army. At the Restoration he returned to the stage. The portrait 'painted in his shirt, having a sword in his hand to defend himself' was hanging in the billiard room in 1816 (John Bridgman, *Historical . . . Sketch of Knole*, 1817, p. 42), but is not mentioned in later descriptions.

31. Thomas Betterton (? 1635–1710), the Restoration actor. The portrait, by Kneller, was still in the 'Poets' Parlour' in 1906 (Lionel Sackville-West, op. cit. 96).

32. William Cartwright (d. 1687), actor and bookseller. The portrait, by Riley, was still in the 'Poet's Parlour' in 1906 (ibid. 97). HW, in calling him a poet, seems to have confused him with William Cartwright (1611–43), dramatist, poet, and divine; but if the attribution to Riley is correct, it must be the later Cartwright.

33. Thomas Flatman (1637–88), poet and painter. The portrait, by himself, was still in the 'Poets' Parlour' in 1906 (ibid.).

34. Henry Howard, who was executed in 1547. The painting, which was originally attributed to Holbein, then to Holbein or Morone, hangs in the Cartoon Gallery (ibid. 75; V. Sackville-West, *Knole*, National Trust, [1955], p. 33). This portrait, and the several other similar ones, are probably by Guillim Scrots (E. A. Waterhouse, *Painting in Britain: 1530–1790*, 1953, p. 12 and plate 9).

35. 'Enough is left.'

36. Edward Howard (1686–1777), 9th D. of Norfolk, 1732.

37. Robert, 2d E. of Orford. In 1748, and just after his death in 1751, there were sales of the pictures that his father had kept in London and Chelsea (MANN iv. 261, nn. 28, 29, viii. 441, n. 13). According to Dallaway's note to HW's *Anecdotes of Painting*, the picture 'was purchased in 1720, at the sale of the Arundel Collection at Strafford House . . . for Sir Robert Walpole, who made a present of it to the late Edward, Duke of Norfolk' (*Anecdotes*, ed. Wornum, 1876, i. 138n, which says that the picture was then at Arundel Castle). HW mentions seeing it at Worksop in 1769 (COLE i. 192). See also the description of it in M. A. Tierney, *History and Antiquities of . . . Arundel*, 1834, i. 90–2.

38. Probably the portrait now in the Cartoon Gallery, described as 'after Holbein' (V. Sackville-West, *Knole*, National Trust, [1955], p. 33).

39. Lionel Cranfield (1575–1645), cr. (1622) E. of Middlesex; two portraits of him by Mytens, one in the Great Hall, and one in the Leicester Gallery, and another by ?Russell are mentioned ibid. 18, 20, 27.

40. 1621–4.

was very near coming to be hanged.[41] His Countess,[42] a bouncing kind of lady-mayoress, looks pure awkward amongst so much good company. A visto cut through the wood has a delightful effect from the front; but there are some trumpery fragments of gardens that spoil the view from the state apartments.

We lay that night at Tunbridge[43] town, and were surprised with the ruins of the old castle.[44] The gateway is perfect, and the enclosure formed into a vineyard by a Mr Hooker[45] to whom it belongs, and the walls spread with fruit, and the mount on which the keep stood, planted in the same way. The prospect is charming, and a breach in the wall opens below to a pretty Gothic bridge of three arches over the Medway. We honoured the man for his taste—not but that we wished the committee at Strawberry Hill were to sit upon it, and stick cypresses among the hollows—But, alas! he sometimes makes eighteen sour hogsheads, and is going to disrobe *the ivy-mantled tower*,[46] because it harbours birds!

Now begins our chapter of woes. The inn was full of farmers and tobacco; and the next morning, when we were bound for Penshurst, the only man in the town who had two horses would not let us have them, because the roads, as he said, were so bad. We were forced to send to the Wells for others, which did not arrive till half the day was spent—we all the while up to the head and ears in a market of sheep and oxen. A mile from the town we climbed up a hill to see Summer Hill,[47] the residence of Grammont's[48] Princess of Babylon.[49] There is now scarce a road to it: the Paladins of those

41. In 1624 he was found guilty of mismanaging his various offices, was dismissed from them, heavily fined, and imprisoned in the Tower for two weeks.

42. Probably Ann Brett (d. 1670), Middlesex's second wife, whose portrait, attributed variously to Mytens and the school of Van Dyck, hangs in the Leicester Gallery (Lionel Sackville-West, op. cit. 48; V. Sackville-West, *Knole*, National Trust, [1955], p. 28). She was a niece of the Countess of Buckingham, mother of James I's favourite, whose family origins are obscure.

43. Or Tonbridge.

44. Partly Norman, but enlarged in the 13th century; the ruins are still standing.

45. John Hooker (d. 1765), who had

purchased the Castle and other property in Tonbridge in 1739 (Edward Hasted, *History . . . of Kent,* 2nd edn, Canterbury, 1797–1801, v. 219; GM 1765, xxxv. 443).

46. A phrase from Gray's 'Elegy Written in a Country Church-Yard,' which had been completed in June 1750 (GRAY ii. 43).

47. Or Somerhill.

48. Philibert (1621–1707), Comte de Gramont. His memoirs, published by HW in 1772, were by Anthony Hamilton.

49. Lady Margaret de Burgh (d. 1698), dau. of 1st M. of Clanricarde, m. 1 (1660) Charles Maccarty, styled Vct Muskerry; m. 2 (1676) Robert Villiers, self-styled Vct Purbeck: m. 3 Robert Fielding. She was very ugly, and was called 'the Princess of

times were too valorous to fear breaking their necks; and I much apprehend that *la Muskerry*[50] and the fair Mademoiselle Hamilton[51] must have mounted their palfreys and rode behind their gentlemen-ushers upon pillions to the Wells. The house is little better than a farm, but has been an excellent one, and is entire, though out of repair.[52] I have drawn the front of it[53] to show you, which you are to draw over again to show me. It stands high, commands a vast landscape beautifully wooded,[54] and has quantities of large old trees to shelter itself, some of which might be well spared to open views.

From Summer Hill we went to Lamberhurst to dine; near which, that is, at the distance of three miles, up and down impracticable hills, in a most retired vale, such as Pope describes in the last *Dunciad,*

Where slumber abbots, purple as their vines,[55]

we found the ruins of Bayham Abbey,[56] which the Barrets and Hardings[57] bid us visit. There are small but pretty remains,[58] and a neat little Gothic house built near them by their nephew Pratt.[59] They

Babylon' from a costume she wore at a masquerade to which she had been invited as a joke (Anthony Hamilton, *Mémoires du Comte de Gramont*, SH, 1772, pp. 96–7, 105).

50. Printed *Monsery* in *Works* and later editions; corrected by Mrs Toynbee.

51. Elizabeth Hamilton (1641–1708), m. (1663) Philibert, Comte de Gramont.

52. The house was built by the 4th E. of Clanricarde in the reign of James I. Its ruinous state is mentioned in a description of 1767, while Hasted states at the end of the century that 'the state apartment of this large and venerable mansion is noble and spacious, and retains its original form, as well as much of its gilding and other decorations, and the whole, by a repair made with a proper attention to the style of its architecture, might be rendered a most magnificent residence' (Hasted, op. cit. v. 197, 233; T. B. Burr, *History of Tunbridge Wells,* 1766, p. 234). The house was occupied by members of the Woodgate family at this time (Hasted, op. cit. v. 236).

53. A rough drawing by Walpole of Summer Hill was inserted by him in his own copy of Grammont (his own edi-

tion). It is now WSL. HW noted on it later: 'Summer Hill near Tunbridge. This view was taken about 1750. It was then a farm house.'

54. 'The country around it [Somerhill] is so wildly beautiful as to make it one of the most pleasing romantic retirements in nature' (Burr, loc. cit.).

55. *Dunciad* iv. 302 (read 'wines' for 'vines').

56. For an account and illustrations of the ruins, see *Country Life,* 1943, xciv. 596–9.

57. Nicholas Hardinge (1699–1758), clerk to the House of Commons 1731–48, and his wife (m. 1738), Jane Pratt. She and Mrs Barrett Lennard (for whom see *ante* HW to Chute 29 Sept. 1755, n. 16) were daughters of Lord Chief Justice Sir John Pratt, who had purchased Bayham Abbey about 1714 (Hasted, op. cit. v. 304; *Country Life,* 1943, xciv. 598).

58. According to Hasted and others even the roof remained on the Abbey until it was removed by Sir John Pratt for building materials (op. cit. v. 305).

59. John Pratt (d. 1797) of Bayham Abbey, son of Mrs Hardinge's and Mrs Barrett Lennard's half-brother, John

have found a tomb of an abbot, with a crosier, at length on the stone.

Here our woes increased. The roads grew bad beyond all badness, the night dark beyond all darkness, our guide frightened beyond all frightfulness. However, without being at all killed, we got up, or down, I forget which,[60] it was so dark, a famous precipice called Silver Hill,[61] and about ten at night arrived at a wretched village called Rotherbridge.[62] We had still six miles hither,[63] but determined to stop, as it would be a pity to break our necks before we had seen all we intended. But, alas! there was only one bed to be had: all the rest were inhabited by smugglers, whom the people of the house called mountebanks; and with one of whom the lady of the den told Mr Chute he might lie. We did not at all take to this society, but, armed with links and lanthorns, set out again upon this impracticable journey. At two o'clock in the morning we got hither to a still worse inn, and that crammed with excise officers, one of whom had just shot a smuggler. However, as we were neutral powers, we have passed safely through both armies hitherto, and can give you a little farther history of our wandering through these mountains, where the young gentlemen are forced to drive their curricles with a pair of oxen. The only morsel of good road we have found, was what even the natives had assured us was totally impracticable; these were eight miles to Hurst Monceaux.[64] It is seated at the end of a large vale, five miles in a direct line to the sea, with wings of blue hills covered with wood, one of which falls down to the house in a sweep of 100 acres. The building for the convenience of water to the moat sees nothing at all; indeed it is entirely imagined on a plan of defence, with drawbridges actually in being, round towers, watch-towers mounted on them, and battlements pierced for the passage of arrows from long bows. It was

Pratt, of Wilderness, Kent (Collins, *Peerage*, 1812, v. 265). His house is mentioned in Burr, op. cit. 250 and Hasted, loc. cit.: it is perhaps the one still standing, much altered, near the ruins.

60. HW says, *post, sub* 'Friday,' correctly, that they 'floundered down' the hill.

61. 'Silver Hill is in Sussex about two miles north of Robertsbridge where the London-Battle-Hastings road starts to descend to the Rother Valley' (see G. P.

Johnston in *Notes and Queries*, 1939, clxxvii. 337).

62. Or Robertsbridge.

63. I.e., Battle Abbey.

64. Hurstmonceaux or Herstmonceux, Sussex. For an account of the history of the structure and of its restoration 1913–35 see H. Avray Tipping, *English Homes*, Periods I and II, vol. ii, 1937, pp. 281–306. See also Edmund Venables, 'The Castle of Herstmonceux and Its Lords,' *Sussex Archæological Collections*, Vol. IV, 1851, pp. 125–202.

built in the time of Henry VI[65] and is as perfect as the first day.[66]
It does not seem to have been ever quite finished, or at least that age
was not arrived at the luxury of whitewash; for almost all the walls,
except in the principal chambers, are in their native *brickhood*.[67]
It is a square building, each side about two hundred feet in length;
a porch and cloister, very like Eton College; and the whole is much
in the same taste, the kitchen extremely so, with three vast funnels
to the chimneys going up on the inside. There are two or three
little courts for offices, but no magnificence of apartments. It is
scarcely furnished with a few necessary beds and chairs: one side
has been sashed, and a drawing-room and dining-room and two or
three rooms wainscoted by the Earl of Sussex,[68] who married a
natural daughter[69] of Charles II. Their arms with delightful carv-
ings by Gibbons,[70] particularly two pheasants, hang over the chimneys. Over the great drawing-room chimney is the coat-armour of the
first Leonard Lord Dacre,[71] with all his alliances. Mr Chute was
transported, and called cousin with ten thousand quarterings.[72]
The chapel is small, and mean: the Virgin and seven long lean
saints, ill done, remain in the windows. There have been four more,
but seem to have been removed for light; and we actually found
St Catherine, and another gentlewoman with a church in her hand,
exiled into the buttery. There remain two odd cavities, with very
small wooden screens on each side the altar, which seem to have
been confessionals. The outside is a mixture of grey brick and stone,
that has a very venerable appearance. The drawbridges are romantic
to a degree; and there is a dungeon,[73] that gives one a delightful
idea of living in the days of soccage and under such goodly tenures.
They showed us a dismal chamber which they called *Drummer's*

65. About 1440 (Tipping, op. cit. 282).
66. The interior was demolished in 1777
to provide building materials for a new
mansion (Venables, op. cit. 165–6).
67. It is an early example of brick-work.
'We have no important brick building
earlier than Herstmonceux lying south
of the Thames' (Tipping, op. cit. 290).
68. Thomas Lennard (1654–1715), 15th
Bn Dacre, cr. (1674) E. of Sussex.
69. Anne Palmer (1662–1722), otherwise
Fitzroy, dau. of Charles II by Barbara, Ds
of Cleveland; Sussex married her in 1674.

70. Grinling Gibbons (1648–1720), wood-
carver.
71. Henry Lennard (1570–1616), 12th
Bn Dacre, 1612.
72. Chute's paternal grandmother was
a dau. of the 13th Bn Dacre.
73. Venables, op. cit. 182 quotes a description of it as 'an octagonal room, in
the midst of which is a stone post with
a long chain, and in a corner of the
room, a door into a privy, a commendable
attention to cleanliness.'

Hall,[74] and suppose that Mr Addison's comedy[75] is descended from it. In the windows of the gallery over the cloisters, which leads all round to the apartments, is the device of the Fienneses,[76] a wolf holding a baton with a scroll, *Le roy le veut*—an unlucky motto, as I shall tell you presently, to the last peer[77] of that line. The estate is two thousand a year, and so compact as to have but seventeen houses upon it. We walked up a brave old avenue to the church, with ships sailing on our left hand the whole way. Before the altar lies a lank brass knight, hight William Fienis, chevalier, who obiit c.c.c.c.v. that is in 1405.[78] By the altar is a beautiful tomb, all in our trefoil taste, varied into a thousand little canopies and patterns, and two knights reposing on their backs. These were Thomas Lord Dacre, and his only son Gregory,[79] who died sans issue.[80] An old grey-headed beadsman of the family talked to us of a blot in the scutcheon; and we had observed that the field of the arms was green instead of blue, and the lions ramping to the right, contrary to order. This and the man's imperfect narrative let us into the circumstances of the personage before us; for there is no inscription. He[81] went in a Chevy-Chase style to hunt in *a Mr Pelham's* park at Lawton:[82] the keepers opposed, a fray ensued, a man[83] was killed. The haughty baron took the death upon himself, as most

74. It was above the porter's lodge in the great gateway tower, 'tradition having marked it out as the principal scene of the pranks of a ghostly drummer, by whom the slumber of the inhabitants were wont to be disturbed' (Venables, op. cit. 174).

75. *The Drummer*, acted in 1715.

76. Some of this glass, apparently of the 15th century, was at Belhus, Essex (*Country Life*, 1920, xlvii. 694).

77. The last peer of the Fiennes line was Gregory (1539–94), 10th Bn Dacre; HW's anecdote, however, concerns his father, Thomas, 9th Bn Dacre; see below nn. **79, 81.**

78. This brass is described and the inscription (which HW quotes somewhat inaccurately) given in Venables, op. cit. 194.

79. HW is mistaken; the monument, erected about 1534, commemorates Thomas Fiennes (ca 1472–1533), 8th Bn Dacre and his son Sir Thomas Fiennes (d. 1528). It is described in Venables, op.

cit. 191–3, and illustrated facing p. 191; see also ibid. 153–5. HW has confused them with the 8th Bn's grandson and successor Thomas Fiennes (ca 1516–41), 9th Bn Dacre and his 2d, but first surviving son, Gregory (1539–94), 10th and last Bn Dacre of the Fiennes line.

80. He had a dau. who died young, so that the barony passed to his sister Margaret (1541–1612), who carried it into the Lennard family.

81. That is, correctly, Thomas, 9th Bn Dacre, not the one on the tomb.

82. Laughton Place, Sussex, seat of the Pelham family. The then occupant was Sir Nicholas Pelham (ca 1515–59), Kt, 1549 (Arthur Collins, *Historical and Genealogical History of the . . . Family of Pelham*, 1755, p. 554). The incident, which occurred in 1541, is described in Holinshed's *Chronicles of England, Scotland, and Ireland* 1807–8, iii. 821–2.

83. John Busbrig (Holinshed, loc. cit.).

secure of pardon: but however, though there was no Chancellor of the Exchequer[84] in the question, he was condemned to be hanged:[85] *Le roy le vouloist.*

Now you are fully master of Hurst Monceaux, I shall carry you on to Battel—By the way, we bring you a thousand sketches, that you may show us what we have seen. Battel Abbey stands at the end of the town exactly as Warwick Castle does of Warwick; but the house of Webster have taken due care that it should not resemble it in anything else. A vast building, which they call the old refectory, but which I believe was the original church, is now barn, coach-house, etc. The situation is noble, above the level of abbeys: what does remain of gateways and towers is beautiful, particularly the flat side of a cloister, which is now the front of the mansion-house. A Miss of the family has clothed a fragment of a portico with cockle-shells! The grounds, and what has been a park, lie in a vile condition. In the church[86] is the tomb of Sir Antony Browne,[87] Master of the Horse for life to Harry VIII, from whose descendants the estate was purchased.[88] The head of John Hammond,[89] the last abbot, is still perfect in one of the windows. Mr Chute says, 'What charming things we should have done if Battel Abbey had been to be sold at Mrs Chenevix's,[90] as Strawberry was!' Good night!

Tunbridge, Friday.

We are returned hither, where we have established our headquarters. On our way, we had an opportunity of surveying that formi-

84. Henry Pelham had been chancellor of the Exchequer since 1743.

85. At Tyburn 29 June 1541 (Holinshed, loc. cit.).

86. The parish church of St Mary.

87. Sir Anthony Browne (d. 1548), K.G. His tomb is illustrated and described in Edward Blore, *Monumental Remains of Noble and Eminent Persons*, 1826, part 30; and in Mackenzie Walcott, *Battle Abbey*, 1870, pp. 86–7.

88. It is said on the tomb of the first Lord Montacute, at Coudray in Sussex, that he built the magnificent house at Battel, of which I suppose the ruinous apartment still remaining was part (HW). HW has apparently confused an inscrip-

tion on a portrait (now destroyed) of Sir Anthony Browne and the inscription on the tomb (which was at nearby Midhurst, not at Cowdray) of his son, Anthony Browne (ca 1528–92), cr. (1554) Vct Montagu. The former reads in part 'he began a stately house [at Battle] since proceeded on by his son and heir'; the latter does not mention the house at Battle (Mrs Charles Roundell, *Cowdray*, 1884, pp. 20, 30).

89. Died 1546 (Walcott, op. cit. 39). He became abbot in 1529.

90. The toyshop of Elizabeth Deard, m. Paul Daniel Chenevix (Mann ii. 366, n. 12; Selwyn 54, n. 9). HW leased Strawberry Hill from her (Gray 17, n. 112).

dable mountain, Silver Hill, which we had floundered down in the dark: it commands a whole horizon of the richest blue prospect you ever saw. I take it to be the individual spot to which the Duke of Newcastle carries the smugglers, and, showing them Sussex and Kent, says, 'All this will I give you, if you will fall down and worship me.'[91] Indeed one of them, who exceeded the tempter's warrant, hangs in chains on the very spot where they finished the life of that wretched custom-house officer[92] whom they were two days in murdering.

This morning we have been to Penshurst[93]—but, oh! how fallen!— The park seems to have never answered its character: at present it is forlorn; and instead of Sacharissa's[94] cypher carved on the beeches, I should sooner have expected to have found the milkwoman's score. Over the gate is an inscription, purporting the manor to have been a boon from Edward VI to Sir William Sydney.[95] The apartments are the grandest I have seen in any of these old palaces, but furnished in a tawdry modern taste. There are loads of portraits; but most of them seem christened by chance, like children at a foundling hospital. There is a portrait of Languet,[96] the friend of Sir Philip Sydney;[97] and divers of himself and all his great kindred, particularly his sister-in-law[98] with a vast lute, and Sacharissa,[99] charmingly handsome. But there are really four very great curiosities, I believe as old portraits as any extant in England: they are, Fitzallen Archbishop of Canterbury,[100] Humphry Stafford the first Duke of

91. Matthew 4:9. The allusion is unexplained.

92. Not identified.

93. The seat of the Sidneys, in Kent.

94. Lady Dorothy Sidney (1617–84), m. 1 (1639) Henry, Bn Spencer, cr. (1643) E. of Sunderland; m. 2 (1652) Robert Smythe; the poet Waller's 'Sacharissa.'

95. Sir William Sidney (ca 1481–1553) (Philip Sidney, *Memoirs of the Sidney Family*, 1899, p. 6). The inscription is printed in J. P. Neale, *Views of the Seats of Noblemen and Gentlemen*, 2d ser., 1824–9, iv. [No. 18].

96. Hubert Languet (1518–81), statesman and Huguenot. The portrait is reproduced in A. H. Bill, *Astrophel*, New York, 1937, facing p. 146.

97. Languet's *Epistolæ politicæ et historicæ ad Phl. Sydnæm* was published in 1633.

98. Barbara Gamage (d. 1621), m. (1584) Robert Sidney, cr. (1618) E. of Leicester. The portrait, probably by Marcus Gheeraerts, is reproduced in Lionel Cust, 'Marcus Gheeraerts,' *Walpole Society*, 1913–14, iii. Plate xxxvi(b); the identity of the person represented is now considered doubtful (ibid. 39).

99. By Van Dyck. She is shown as a shepherdess (Lionel Cust, *Anthony Van Dyck*, 1900, pp. 121, 196).

100. Thomas Fitzalan or Arundel (1353–1414), Abp of Canterbury 1396–1414. This 'portrait' is still at Penshurst (Waterhouse, op. cit. 25).

Buckingham,[101] T. Wentworth,[102] and John Foxle;[103] all four with the dates of their commissions as constables of Queenborough Castle, from whence I suppose they were brought. The last is actually receiving his investiture from Edward III, as Wentworth is in the dress of Richard III's time. They are really not very ill done.[104] There are six more,[105] only heads; and we have found since we came home, that Penshurst belonged for a time to that Duke of Buckingham.[106] There are some good tombs in the church, and a very Vandal one, called *Sir Stephen of Penchester*.[107] When we had seen Penshurst, we borrowed saddles, and, bestriding the horses of our post-chaise, set out for Hever to visit a tomb of Sir Thomas Bullen Earl of Wiltshire,[108] partly with a view to talk of it in Anna Bullen's walk[109] at Strawberry Hill. But the measure of our woes was not full; we could not find our way, and were forced to return; and again lost ourselves in coming from Penshurst, having been directed to what they called a better road than the execrable one we had gone.

101. Humphrey Stafford (1402–60), cr. (1444) D. of Buckingham.

102. Thomas Wentworth was constable of Queenborough Castle in the first year (1483–4) of Richard III's reign (John Harris, *History of Kent,* 1719, p. 377).

103. John Foxley was constable of Queenborough in the 36th year (1362–3) of Edward III's reign (ibid. 376).

104. In Harris's *History of Kent,* he gives from Philpot a list of the constables of Queenborough Castle, p. 376; the last but one of whom, Sir Edward Hobby, is said to have collected all their portraits, of which number most probably were these ten (HW). The 'portraits' were, in fact, painted for Hoby in 1593 (Waterhouse, op. cit. 25–6). HW mentions them in *Anecdotes of Painting* (*Works* iii. 57), by which time he realized that they were not all originals, but, misled by Vertue, introduced a new confusion by attributing them to Lucas Cornelii.

105. When Vertue visited Penshurst in 1728, there were sixteen heads in this series ('Vertue Note Books, Vol. II,' *Walpole Society* 1931–2, xx. 51–2); they are now widely scattered (Waterhouse, loc. cit.).

106. It was given to him by Henry VI, and remained in the hands of the Buckinghams until the execution of the 3d Duke in 1522 (H. A. Tipping, *English Homes,* Period I, Vol. I, 1921, p. 172).

107. Sir Stephen de Pencester (d. 1299), warden of the Cinque Ports. 'In the chancel . . . is a very ancient figure in stone of a knight in armour. . . . It was formerly laid on an altar tomb in the chancel, but is now placed erect against the door on the south side, with these words painted on the wall above it, Sir Stephen de Penchester' (Hasted, op. cit. iii. 255). His family had been the original proprietors of the manor of Penshurst (ibid. 230–1).

108. Thomas Boleyn (ca 1478–1539), cr. (1529) E. of Wiltshire; father of Anne Boleyn. His tomb was described in Hasted, op. cit. iii. 193.

109. On 25 June 1752, HW 'paid for the wood walk' £9 13s. 6d. (HW's *Strawberry Hill Accounts,* ed. Toynbee, Oxford, 1927, p. 4). Dr Toynbee conjectures (ibid. 58) that this was the winding walk in the serpentine wood bordering the lawn at SH. Daniel Lysons, *Environs of London,* iii. 561 says, of Twickenham manor-house, that 'tradition reports it to have been the residence of one of Henry VIII's queens.'

Since dinner we have been to Lord Westmorland's[110] at Mere-worth,[111] which is so perfect in a Palladian taste, that I must own it has recovered me a little from Gothic. It is better situated than I had expected from the bad reputation it bears, and has some prospect, though it is in a moat, and mightily besprinkled with small ponds.[112] The design, you know, is taken from the Villa del Capra by Vicenza,[113] but on a larger scale; yet, though it has cost an hundred thousand pounds, it is still only a fine villa: the finishing of in and outside has been exceedingly expensive. A wood that runs up a hill behind the house is broke like an Albano landscape[114] with an octa-gon temple and a triumphal arch;[115] but then there are some dismal clipt hedges, and a pyramid, which by a most unnatural copulation is at once a grotto and a greenhouse. Does it not put you in mind of the proposal for your drawing a garden-seat, Chinese on one side and Gothic on the other? The chimneys, which are collected to a centre, spoil the dome of the house, and the hall is a dark well. The gallery[116] is eighty-two feet long, hung with green velvet[117] and pictures, among which is a fine Rembrandt,[118] and a pretty La Hire.[119] The ceilings are painted,[120] and there is a fine bed of silk and gold tapestry. The attic is good, and the wings[121] extremely pretty, with porticos formed on the style of the house. The Earl has built a new church, with a steeple which seems designed for the latitude of Cheapside,[122] and is so tall, that the poor church curtseys under it,

110. John Fane (1686–1762), 7th E. of Westmorland, 1736.

111. The house, built by Colin Camp-bell ca 1720–3, is described and illustrated by H. A. Tipping in *Country Life*, 1920, xlvii. 808–16, 876–83, 912–19; and in Christopher Hussey, *English Country Houses: Early Georgian 1715–1760*, 1955, pp. 58–65.

112. The moat was filled in during the 19th century and the ponds, too, have dis-appeared (Hussey, op. cit. 58, 65).

113. Now known as the Villa Rotonda, built at Vicenza by Palladio for the Marchese Capra.

114. See *ante* HW to Chute, 4 Aug. 1753, for a similar mention of Albano in connection with the landscape at Stowe.

115. Both still standing (Hussey, op. cit. 65).

116. Illustrated in *Country Life*, op. cit. 815, 846; and Hussey, op. cit. 61.

117. Which remained until ca 1930 (Hussey, op. cit. 61).

118. 'An Old Lady Seated in a Chair' (J. P. Neale, *Views of the Seats of Noble-men and Gentlemen*, 2d ser., 1824–9, ii. [plate 19]).

119. Laurent de la Hire (1606–56), painter to Louis XIV. His painting was an 'Assumption of the Virgin' (ibid.). Neither picture appears to be still at Mereworth.

120. By Francesco Sleter (Hussey, op. cit. 61).

121. That is, pavilions; there are no wings to the house.

122. The steeple was modelled after that of St-Martin's-in-the-Fields, by James Gibbs (Marcus Whiffen, *Stuart and Geor-gian Churches*, 1947–8, p. 42). The church, built 1744–6, is illustrated ibid., plate 41, and *Country Life*, op. cit. 916.

like Mary Rich[123] in a vast high-crown hat: it has a round portico like St Clement's,[124] with vast Doric pillars supporting a thin shelf. The inside is the most abominable piece of tawdriness that ever was seen, stuffed with pillars painted in imitation of verd antique, as all the sides are like Siena marble:[125] but the greatest absurdity is a Doric frieze, between the triglyphs of which is the Jehovah, the I.H.S. and the dove. There is a little chapel with Nevil tombs, particularly of the first Fane Earl of Westmorland,[126] and of the founder of the old church, and the heart of a knight who was killed *in the wars*. On the Fane tomb is a pedigree of brass in relief, and a genealogy of virtues to answer it. There is an entire window of painted-glass arms, chiefly modern, in the chapel, and another over the high altar. The hospitality of the house was truly Gothic; for they made our postilion drunk, and he overturned us close to a water, and the bank did but just save us from being in the middle of it. Pray, whenever you travel in Kentish roads, take care of keeping your driver sober.

Rochester, Sunday.

We have finished our progress sadly! Yesterday, after twenty mishaps, we got to Sissinghurst to dinner. There is a park in ruins, and a house in ten times greater ruins, built by Sir John Baker,[127] Chancellor of the Exchequer to Queen Mary. You go through an arch[128] of the stables to the house, the court of which is perfect and

123. See *ante* HW to Chute 12 July 1757, n. 3; she was Lady Lyttelton's sister.

124. HW seems to have confused St Clements Danes with its neighbour, St Mary-le-Strand, which had a round portico designed by James Gibbs, resembling that of Mereworth Church. St Clements, however, formerly had a half-domed portico over the southwest door, removed in 1813 (Elizabeth and Wayland Young, *Old London Churches*, 1956, p. 144).

125. The interior is illustrated in Whiffen, op. cit., facing p. 38 and *Country Life*, op. cit. 916.

126. Sir Francis Fane (ca 1580–1629), cr. (1624) E. of Westmorland. H. A. Tipping points out that HW is mistaken; the tomb is that of his father Sir Thomas Fane and his mother Mary Nevil; the 1st Earl and his brother kneel below and are commemorated in inscriptions on the plinths of the columns (*Country Life*, op. cit. 917; illustrated ibid. 916).

127. Died 1558. The house, built ca 1535–40, was largely demolished in 1763, but the remains have been restored since 1930 by Sir Harold Nicolson and his wife, V. Sackville-West. See her account and the illustration in *Country Life*, 1942, xcii. 410–13, 458–61, 506–9. The estate was owned at this time by the Mann family, although probably not, as Miss Sackville-West states (apparently on the basis of Hasted, op. cit. vii. 102) by HW's correspondent Sir Horace.

128. In a tower which is still standing.

very beautiful.[129] The Duke of Bedford has a house at Cheneys in Buckinghamshire, which seems to have been very like it, but is more ruined.[130] This has a good apartment, and a fine gallery a hundred and twenty feet by eighteen, which takes up one side: the wainscot is pretty and entire; the ceiling vaulted, and painted in a light genteel grotesque. The whole is built for show; for the back of the house is nothing but lath and plaster. From thence we went to Bocton-Malherbe,[131] where are remains of a house of the Wottons,[132] and their tombs in the church: but the roads were so exceedingly bad, that it was dark before we got thither—and still darker before we got to Maidstone. From thence we passed this morning to Leeds Castle.[133] Never was such disappointment![134] There are small remains: the moat is the only handsome object, and is quite a lake, supplied by a cascade which tumbles through a bit of a romantic grove. The Fairfaxes[135] have fitted up a pert bad apartment in the fore-part of the castle, and have left the only tolerable rooms for offices. They had a gleam of Gothic in their eyes; but it soon passed off into some modern windows, and some that never were ancient.[136] The only thing that at all recompensed the fatigues we have undergone, was a picture of the Duchess of Buckingham,[137] *la Ragotte*, who is mentioned in Grammont[138]—I say us; for I trust that Mr Chute

129. Shown in an engraving reproduced in *Country Life*, op. cit. 458. It was demolished in 1763.

130. HW had visited Chenies, four miles east of Amersham, Bucks, in 1749; he describes its ruinous condition in a letter to George Montagu (MONTAGU i. 102). One wing, however, is still standing (*Royal Commission on Historical Monuments . . . Buckinghamshire*, 1912–13, i. 90).

131. I.e. Boughton Malherbe.

132. For an account of this family, which flourished under the Tudors, see Hasted, op. cit. v. 400–3; the manor and other estates had been purchased by Galfridus Mann in 1750 (ibid. v. 405).

133. The Castle, which was extensively restored and rebuilt in the 19th century, is described and illustrated in H. A. Tipping, *English Homes*, Period I, Vol. I, 1921, pp. 201–19.

134. Twenty-six years later, HW advised Conway against visiting Leeds Castle on

a projected tour of Kent, with the comment that it was 'not worth seeing' (HW to Conway 21 Aug. 1778).

135. Leeds had belonged to the Colepepers, but passed to the Fairfaxes as the result of Catherine Colepeper's marriage to the 5th Lord Fairfax about 1685.

136. 'That part at the far side of the square, opposite the entrance, contains the state or principal apartments, which has had a handsome uniform front of rustic stonework added to it; the windows of it, though sashed, are arched in the Gothic taste, and the parapet is embattled' (Hasted, op. cit. v. 491).

137. Mary Fairfax (1638–1704), m. (1657) George Villiers, 2d D. of Buckingham. The portrait was still in the house in 1921 (Tipping, op. cit. 216).

138. 'Comme la Duchesse de Buckingham était une petite ragote à peu près de sa figure' (Anthony Hamilton, *Mémoires du Comte de Grammont*, SH, 1772, p. 268).

is as true a bigot to Grammont as I am. Adieu! I hope you will be as weary with reading our history, as we have been in travelling it.

Yours ever,

HOR. WALPOLE

To BENTLEY, September 1753

Printed from *Works* v. 274–80; reprinted, Wright iii. 18–25, Cunningham ii. 351–7, Toynbee iii. 184–93.

Arlington Street, September 1753.

My dear Sir,

I AM going to send you another volume of my travels; I don't know whether I shall not, at last, write a new *Camden's Britannia;*[1] but lest you should be afraid of my itinerary, I will at least promise you that it shall not be quite so dry as most surveys, which contain nothing but lists of impropriations and glebes, and carucates,[2] and transcripts out of Domesday, and tell one nothing that is entertaining, describe no houses nor parks, mention no curious pictures, but are fully satisfied if they inform you, that they believe that some nameless old tomb belonged to a Knight Templar, or one of the crusado, because he lies cross-legged. Another promise I will make you is, that my love of abbeys shall not make me hate the Reformation till that makes me grow a Jacobite like the rest of my antiquarian predecessors; of whom, Dart[3] in particular wrote Billingsgate against Cromwell and the regicides;[4] and Sir Robert Atkins[5] concludes his summary of the Stuarts with saying, *that it is*

1. *Britannia, sive florentissimorum regnorum Angliæ, Scotiæ, Hiberniæ, et insularum adjacentium ex intima antiquitate chorographica descriptio,* 1586, by William Camden (1551–1623).

2. A measure of land (OED).

3. Rev. John Dart (d. 1730) wrote on Canterbury Cathedral and Westminster Abbey.

4. This passage occurs in Dart's *Westmonasterium* under 'Persons Removed after Burial': 'Oliver Cromwell, the Arch-Rebel. He died of an ague the third of Sept. 1658. His body, for the stench, was

buried privately, on Feb. 26. . . . That infamous wretch Bradshaw, president of the mock-court of justice, where he impudently insulted and gave sentence of death against his Sovereign. He was a dark melancholy miscreant, and as well qualified to kill his Prince or his father in private, as to give judgment in public' (John Dart, *Westmonasterium* [?1742], ii. 143). For HW's copy, see Hazen, *Cat. of HW's Lib.,* No. 566.

5. Sir Robert Atkyns (1647–1711) published a topographical work on Gloucester in 1712.

no reason, because they have been so, that this family should always continue unfortunate.[6]

I have made my visit at Hagley[7] as I intended. On my way I dined at Park Place, and lay at Oxford. As I was quite alone, I did not care to see anything; but as soon as it was dark I ventured out, and the moon rose as I was wandering among the colleges, and gave me a charming venerable Gothic scene, which was not lessened by the monkish appearance of the old fellows stealing to their pleasures. Birmingham is large, and swarms with people and trade, but did not answer my expectation from any beauty in it: yet new as it is, I perceived how far I was got back from the London hegira; for every ale-house is here written *mug-house,* a name one has not heard of since the riots in the late King's time.[8]

As I got into Worcestershire, I opened upon a landscape of country which I prefer even to Kent, which I had reckoned the most beautiful county in England: but this, with all the richness of Kent, is bounded with mountains. Sir George Lyttelton's house is immeasurably bad and old:[9] one room at the top of the house, which was reckoned a *conceit* in those days, projects a vast way into the air. There are two or three curious pictures, and some of them extremely agreeable to me for their relation to Grammont: there is *le sérieux Lyttelton,*[10] but too old for the date of that book;[11] Mademoiselle

6. 'It is remarkable of this royal family, that the witty king was overreached by the wit of the Spanish ambassador; that the religious king was murdered by rebellious saints; the voluptuary was conspired against by men of no religion; and the best friend was betrayed and forsaken by them whom he most entirely loved. It does not hence follow that this family will always be unfortunate' (Atkyns, *The Ancient and Present State of Gloucestershire,* 1758 [reprint of 1712 edn], p. 89). For HW's copy of the 2d edn, 1768, see Hazen, *Cat. of HW's Lib.,* No. 423.

7. Hagley Park, Lyttelton's seat. HW had been there sometime between 1 Sept., when he was still in London, and 11 Sept., when he expected to reach Matson (Selwyn 120).

8. Political clubs of Hanoverian sympathies in the early 18th century were called 'mug-house clubs' (OED).

9. It was of regional 'black and white' (Christopher Hussey, *English Country*

Houses, Early Georgian 1715–1760, 1955, p. 195). The new house was begun the following year; Chute had contributed plans which had been rejected (see *ante* HW to Chute 22 Aug. 1758 and nn. 9, 10).

10. Sir Charles Lyttelton (1629–1716), 3d Bt, 1693. In Gramont's memoirs, Miss Hobart tells Miss Temple, Lyttelton's future wife, that 'le très sérieux Chevalier Lyttelton sent dégourdir sa gravité naturelle en faveur de vos attraits' (SH edn, 1772, p. 203).

11. HW is apparently referring to the portrait of Lyttelton by John Riley and Johann Baptist Closterman, painted sometime in the 1680's (C. H. Collins Baker, *Lely and the Stuart Portrait Painters,* 1912, ii. 29, 44, 45), and hence represents Lyttelton as older than at the period of Gramont. There is another portrait of him at Hagley, by Roland Lefebvre, painted about 1665 (ibid. ii. plate facing p. 4).

Stuart,[12] Lord Brounker,[13] and Lady Southesk;[14] besides, a portrait
of Lord Clifford the treasurer,[15] with his staff, but drawn in armour
(though no soldier) out of flattery to Charles II, as he said the most
glorious part of his life was attending the King at the battle of
Worcester. He might have said that it was as *glorious* as any part of
his Majesty's life. You might draw, but I can't describe the enchanting scenes of the park: it is a hill of three miles, but broke into all
manner of beauty; such lawns, such wood, rills, cascades, and a
thickness of verdure quite to the summit of the hill, and commanding such a vale of towns and meadows, and woods extending quite
to the Black Mountain in Wales, that I quite forgot my favourite
Thames!—Indeed, I prefer nothing to Hagley but Mount Edgecumbe.[16] There is extreme taste in the park: the seats are not the
best, but there is not one absurdity. There is a ruined castle, built
by Miller,[17] that would get him his freedom even of Strawberry: it
has the true rust of the Barons' Wars. Then there is a scene of a
small lake with cascades[18] falling down such a Parnassus! with a
circular temple[19] on the distant eminence; and there is such a fairy
dale, with more cascades gushing out of rocks! and there is a

12. Frances Theresa Stewart or Stuart
(1647–1702), m. (1667) Charles Stuart, 3d
D. of Richmond and 6th D. of Lennox,
1660; one of the principal characters in
the Gramont. The portrait is by Jacob
Huysmans (Collins Baker, op. cit. i. 213
and plate facing p. 208); it was formerly
attributed to Lely or Greenhill (Joseph
Heely, *Letters on the Beauties of Hagley,
Envil, and the Leasowes*, 1777, i. 105).

13. Henry Brouncker (ca 1627–88), 3d
Vct Brouncker, 1684, who had bequeathed
his estate to Sir Charles Lyttelton; the
portrait is by Lely (Collins Baker, op. cit.
ii. 129). His passion for Miss Jennings is
discussed by Gramont, SH, 1772, pp.
230–2.

14. Lady Anna or Anne Hamilton (d.
1695), m. (ca 1660) Robert Carnegie, 3d E.
of Southesk. The portrait is attributed
to Lely in Heely, op. cit. i. 105; it is not
mentioned by Collins Baker, loc cit. Her
relations with the Duke of York are discussed in Gramont, SH, 1772, pp. 138–40.

15. Thomas Clifford (1630–73), cr. (1672)
Bn Clifford of Chudleigh; treasurer of
the Household 1668–72; member of the

'Cabal.' The portrait is attributed to
'Old Stone' in Heely, op. cit. i. 104, but
this seems unlikely; it is not mentioned
by Collins Baker, loc. cit.

16. Near Plymouth, seat of HW's
friends, the Edgcumbes. HW had visited
it in 1745 (MANN iii. 92, 101).

17. In 1748 (Hussey, op. cit. 195; illustration ibid. 196; information from Mr
Michael McCarthy).

18. One of these artificial cascades is
thus described by Heely, op. cit. 150:
'from a sort of cavernous hollow, worked
into a precipice above, rudely decorated
with glassy cinders, and misshapen stones,
the cascade, which before only filled the
ear with its soothing murmurs, now
breaks full on the eye.' HW mentions
'the artificial cascatelle of Hagley, played
for moments to entertain visitors' in a
letter to Mason 18 Feb. 1776 (MASON i.
241).

19. The Ionic rotunda was designed by
John Pitt (G. W. Beard and J. H. Folkes,
'John Chute and Hagley Hall,' *Architec-
tural Review*, 1952, cxi. 199–200).

hermitage,[20] so exactly like those in Sadeler's[21] prints, on the brow of a shady mountain, stealing peeps into the glorious world below! and there is such a pretty well under a wood, like the Samaritan woman's in a picture of Nicolò Poussin![22] and there is such a wood without the park, enjoying such a prospect! and there is such a mountain on t'other side of the park commanding all prospects, that I wore out my eyes with gazing, my feet with climbing, and my tongue and my vocabulary with commending! The best notion I can give you of the satisfaction I showed, was, that Sir George proposed to carry me to dine with my Lord Foley;[23] and when I showed reluctance, he said, 'Why, I thought you did not mind any strangers, if you were to see anything!' Think of my not minding strangers! I mind them so much, that I missed seeing Hartlebury Castle, and the Bishop of Worcester's[24] chapel of painted glass[25] there, because it was his public day when I passed by his park.—Miller has built a Gothic house[26] in the village at Hagley for a relation of Sir George: but there he is not more than Miller; in his castle he is almost Bentley. There is a genteel tomb in the church to Sir George's first wife,[27] with a Cupid and a pretty urn in the Roman style.[28]

20. 'This hermitage, or call it what you will, is well enough adapted to the scenery about it, being rudely formed with chumps of wood, and jagged old roots, jambed together, and its interstices simply filled with moss; the floor is neatly paved with small pebbles, and a matted couch goes round it' (Heely, op. cit. 191–2).

21. Jan Sadeler (1550–1600); for a note on his prints of hermits see Montagu ii. 276, n. 3.

22. Nicolas Poussin (ca 1594–1665). HW is apparently thinking of his painting (or probably of a print after it) of 'Christ and the Samaritan Woman,' now in the Esterházy Gallery, Vienna (Émile Magne, *Nicolas Poussin*, Brussels and Paris, 1914, p. 210).

23. Thomas Foley (ca 1703–66), 2d Bn Foley, 1733. His seat was Witley Court, Worcs.

24. Isaac Maddox (1697–1759), Bp of St Asaph, 1736, of Worcester, 1743. Hartlebury Castle, about ten miles north of Worcester, is the seat of the bishops of Worcester.

25. The chapel had been rebuilt by Maddox with glass painted by John Rowell (d. 1756) of Reading, the design of the east window having been made by the Bishop's friend, Dr Wall, of the Worcester porcelain factory. All of it, except for some armorial glass in the side top lights, has disappeared (*Country Life*, 1971, cl. 741).

26. Rockingham Hall, now destroyed, which Miller rebuilt about 1751 for Adm. Thomas Smith (ca 1707–62), Lyttelton's illegitimate half brother (*An Eighteenth-Century Correspondence*, ed. Dickins and Stanton, New York, 1910, p. 275; Maud Wyndham, *Chronicles of the Eighteenth Century*, 1924, ii. 77 and both vols *passim* for an account of Adm. Smith, superseding DNB).

27. Lucy Fortescue (ca 1718–47), m. (1742) George Lyttelton.

28. It is described by Bp Pococke as 'an urn on a pedestal with a bas-relief of a lady on a couch, with a statue of Hymen on the right kneeling on an extinct torch, wringing his hands and weeping' (quoted in Dickins and Stanton, op. cit. 292). It was designed by Sanderson Miller.

You will be diverted with my distresses at Worcester. I set out
boldly to walk down the High Street to the cathedral: I found it
much more peopled than I intended, and, when I was quite embarked, discovered myself up to the ears in a contested election. A
new candidate[29] had arrived the night before, and turned all their
heads. Nothing comforted me, but that the opposition is to Mr
T——;[30] and I purchased my passage very willingly with crying, 'No
T——! No Jews!'[31] However, the inn where I lay was Jerusalem itself, the very headquarters, where T—— the Pharisee was expected;
and I had scarce got into my room, before the victorious mob of his
enemy, who had routed his advanced guard, broke open the gates of
our inn, and almost murdered the ostler—and then carried him off
to prison for being murdered.

The cathedral is pretty, and has several tombs, and clusters of light
pillars of Derbyshire marble, lately cleaned. Gothicism and the
restoration of that architecture, and not of the bastard breed, spreads
extremely in this part of the world. Prince Arthur's[32] tomb, from
whence we took the paper for the hall and staircase,[33] to my great
surprise, is on a less scale than the paper, and is not of brass but
stone, and that wretchedly whitewashed. The niches are very small,

29. Henry Crabb Boulton (d. 1773), a
director (and later Chairman) of the East
India Company; he captured one of the
Worcester seats at the general election of
1754 and retained it until his death
(W. R. Williams, *Parliamentary History of
the County of Worcester*, Hereford, 1897,
p. 104). He had announced his candi-
dacy in an advertisement dated London,
Sept. 6; in a further advertisement, dated
Worcester, Sept. 10, he describes having
'this day been met and escorted into'
Worcester (*Daily Adv.* 7, 13 Sept. 1753),
when HW's encounter with his supporters
undoubtedly took place.

30. Expanded by previous editors to
Trevis, but the person meant was Chute's
nephew, Robert Tracy, M.P. for Worcester city until 1754 when he was defeated
by Boulton (*ante* HW to Chute 21 May
1754, n. 12; Williams, op. cit. 103–4). HW
had quarrelled with him during the
Nicoll affair in 1751 (GRAY ii. 199–202,
227, 229). For his unsuccessful attempt
to get the government to underwrite his
election expenses in this contest, see Sir

Lewis Namier, *Structure of Politics at
the Ascension of George III*, 2d edn, 1957,
p. 197 and nn. 1, 2.

31. For a note on the wave of anti-
semitism sweeping England in the summer of 1753, see *ante* HW to Chute 4
Aug. 1753.

32. Arthur (1486–1502), son of Henry
VII.

33. 'This hall is united with the staircase, and both are hung with Gothic paper, painted by one Tudor, from the
screen of Prince Arthur's tomb in the
cathedral of Worcester' ('Des. of SH,'
Works ii. 401). The design had been taken
from a plate of the screen in Francis Sand-
ford, *A Genealogical History of the Kings
of England*, 1677; in HW's copy (Hazen,
Cat. of HW's Lib., No. 581), now WSL,
there are markings on the plate by HW
and (probably) Bentley. There is a similar plate in William Thomas, *A Survey
of the Cathedral-Church of Worcester*,
1737, of which HW also owned a copy
(Hazen, op. cit. No. 641).

and the long slips in the middle are divided every now and then with the trefoil. There is a fine tomb for Bishop Hough,[34] in the Westminster Abbey style; but the obelisk at the back is not loaded with a globe and a human figure, like Mr Kent's[35] design for Sir Isaac Newton:[36] an absurdity which nothing but himself could surpass, when he placed three busts at the foot of an altar—and, not content with that, placed them at the very angles—where they have as little to do as they have with Shakespeare.[37]

From Worcester I went to see Malvern Abbey.[38] It is situated halfway up an immense mountain of that name: the mountain is very long, in shape like the prints of a whale's back: towards the larger end lies the town. Nothing remains but a beautiful gateway and the church,[39] which is very large: every window has been glutted with painted glass, of which much remains,[40] but it did not answer: blue and red there is in abundance, and good faces; but the portraits are so high, I could not distinguish them. Besides, the woman who showed me the church would pester me with Christ and King David, when I was hunting for John of Gaunt and King Edward.[41] The greatest curiosity, at least what I had never seen before, was, the whole floor and far up the sides of the church has been, if I may call it so, wainscoted with red and yellow tiles, extremely polished, and diversified with coats of arms, and inscriptions, and mosaic.[42] I have since found the same at Glocester, and have even been so fortunate as to purchase from the sexton about a dozen, which think what an acquisition for Strawberry![43] They are made of the natural earth

34. John Hough (1651–1743), Bp of Oxford 1690–9, of Lichfield and Coventry 1699–1717, of Worcester 1717–43. The tomb, erected in 1746, was by Roubiliac (K. A. Esdaile, *The Life and Works of Louis François Roubiliac*, 1928, p. 57; photograph of detail, plate xiv *b*).

35. William Kent (?1686–1748). (Margaret *Jourdain, Work of William Kent*, 1948, *Addendum*).

36. The monument to Newton in Westminster Abbey, designed by Kent and executed by Michael Rysbrack in 1731; it is described by M. I. Webb, *Michael Rysbrack, Sculptor*, 1954, pp. 82–4; a photograph is on p. 60 and reproductions of drawings for it by Kent and Rysbrack on p. 65.

37. The monument to Shakespeare in Westminster Abbey, designed by Kent and

executed by Scheemaker. The three heads represent three royal characters from the plays.

38. Correctly Malvern Priory.

39. Both of which still remain; the church was thoroughly restored in 1861 (*Vict. Co. Hist. Worcs* iv. 127).

40. This glass, mostly of the fifteenth century, is fully described and illustrated in G. McN. Rushforth, *Medieval Christian Imagery as Illustrated by the Painted Windows of Great Malvern Priory Church*, Oxford, 1936.

41. For the 'portrait' of Edward the Confessor in the Malvern glass, see ibid. 123–4 and fig. 54. There appears to have been no portrait of John of Gaunt.

42. These are described in *Vict. Co. Hist. Worcs* iv. 130.

43. These tiles from Gloucester Cathe-

of the country, which is a rich red clay, that produces everything. All the lanes are full of all kind of trees, and enriched with large old apple trees, that hang over from one hedge to another. Worcester city is large and pretty. Glocester city is still better situated, but worse built, and not near so large. About a mile from Worcester you break upon a sweet view of the Severn. A little farther on the banks is Mr Lechmere's house;[44] but he has given strict charge to a troop of willows never to let him see the river: to his right hand extends the fairest meadow covered with cattle that ever you saw: at the end of it is the town of Upton, with a church half ruined,[45] and a bridge of six arches,[46] which I believe with little trouble he might see from his garden.

The vale increases in riches to Glocester. I stayed two days at George Selwyn's house called Matson, which lies on Robin Hood's Hill:[47] it is lofty enough for an Alp, yet is a mountain of turf to the very top, has wood scattered all over it, springs that long to be cascades in twenty places of it; and from the summit it beats even Sir G. Lyttelton's views, by having the city of Glocester at its foot, and the Severn widening to the horizon. His house is small, but neat.[48] King Charles lay here at the siege;[49] and the Duke of York,[50] with typical fury, hacked and hewed the window-shutters of his chamber,[51] as a memorandum of his being there. Here is a good picture of Dudley Earl of Leicester[52] in his later age, which he gave

dral were inlaid in the floor of the China Closet at SH ('Des. of SH,' *Works* ii. 405; HW to Charles Churchill 27 March 1764). Some of the remaining tiles at Gloucester are described in H. J. L. J. Massé, *The Cathedral Church of Gloucester*, 3d edn, 1908, pp. 58–9, 84–5.

44. Severn End, seat of Edmund Lechmere (1710–1805), M.P. Worcestershire 1734–47. The house, which burned down in 1895 but has been restored, is described in *Vict. Co. Hist. Worcs* iv. 90–3.

45. The old church was demolished and a new one built 1756–7 (ibid. iv. 216).

46. Built in the reign of James I and washed away in 1852 (ibid. iv. 213).

47. Properly Robins Wood Hill, named for the Robins family, lessees of Matson and neighbouring manors in the sixteenth century (*Country Life*, 1950, cviii. 1990, 1992).

48. For a description and illustrations, see the article by Arthur Oswald in *Country Life*, 1950, cviii. 1990–4.

49. Charles I's siege of Gloucester, 1643.

50. Who became James II.

51. These marks are on the window-sill of an attic bedroom (*Country Life*, 1950, cviii. 1992). Selwyn told Wraxall that James II told his grandfather that 'my brother and I were generally shut up in a chamber on the second floor at Matson during the day, where you will find that we have left the marks of our confinement inscribed with our knives on the ledges of all the windows' (Sir N. W. Wraxall, *Historical and Posthumous Memoirs*, ed. H. B. Wheatley, 1884, ii. 288).

52. Robert Dudley (1532 or 1533–88), cr. (1564), E. of Leicester.

to Sir Francis Walsingham,[53] at whose house in Kent[54] it remained till removed hither; and what makes it very curious, is, his age marked on it, 54 in 1572.[55] I had never been able to discover before in what year he was born. And here is the very flower-pot and counterfeit association, for which Bishop Sprat was taken up,[56] and the Duke of Marlborough sent to the Tower.[57] The reservoirs on the hill supply the city. The late Mr Selwyn[58] governed the borough by them—and I believe by some wine too. The Bishop's house[59] is pretty, and restored to the Gothic by the last Bishop.[60] Price[61] has painted a large chapel window[62] for him, which is scarce inferior for colours, and is a much better picture than any of the old glass. The eating-room is handsome. As I am a Protestant Goth, I was glad to worship Bishop Hooper's room,[63] from whence he was led to the stake: but I could almost have been a Hun, and set fire to the front of the house, which is a small pert portico, like the conveniencies at the end of a London garden. The outside of the cathedral is beautifully light; the pillars in the nave outrageously plump and heavy. There is a tomb of one Abraham Blackleach,[64] a great curiosity; for, though the figures of him and his wife[65] are cumbent, they are very graceful, designed by Vandyck,[66] and well executed.

53. (ca 1530–90), statesman.

54. Scadbury Park, Chislehurst, which had belonged to Selwyn's father.

55. This is an error; Leicester was only 41 or 42 in 1572.

56. For this plot, see ante HW to Bentley 5 Aug. 1752 and n. 4.

57. Marlborough's was one of the signatures attributed to the forgery. He was in the Tower 5 May–15 June 1692.

58. George Selwyn's father, Col. John Selwyn (1688–1751), M.P. Truro 1715–21, Whitchurch 1727–34, Gloucester 1734–51.

59. The Bishop, 1752–9, was James Johnson (1705–74), later (1759–74), Bp of Worcester. This was the old abbot's lodging, much altered and rebuilt by various bishops; it was replaced by a modern house in 1857–62 (T. D. Fosbrooke, *Original History of . . . Gloucester*, 1819, pp. 98, 100–101; Massé, op. cit. 115).

60. Martin Benson (1689–1752), D.D., Bp of Gloucester 1735–52.

61. William Price (1703–65), the younger, glass-painter, who later did work at SH in 1754 and 1759 (HW, *Strawberry Hill Accounts*, ed. Paget Toynbee, Ox-

ford, 1927, pp. 5, 7, 73–4, 100–1). An article on the Prices and an incomplete list of their works is in *The Antiquaries Journal*, 1953, xxxiii. 184–92.

62. This window, which has disappeared, was 'descriptive of the resurrection' (Thomas Rudge, *History and Antiquities of Gloucester*, Gloucester, [? 1833], p. 306).

63. John Hooper (1495–1555), Bp of Gloucester, 1550; burned at the stake for heresy in Gloucester 9 Feb. 1555. He was lodged at the house of Robert Ingram (now No. 52 Westgate), opposite St Nicholas's church, when he was returned to Gloucester for execution and led to the stake from there (Fosbrooke, op. cit. 93; John Hooper, *Later Writings*, ed. Charles Nevinson, Cambridge, 1852, p. xxv; *England*, ed. Findlay Muirhead, 1924, p. 269).

64. Died 1639 (*Transactions of the Bristol and Gloucestershire Archæological Society*, 1879–80, iv. 235).

65. Gertrude Elton (ibid. 1933, lv. 48).

66. HW repeats this attribution in *Anecdotes of Painting, Works* iii. 223, but

Kent designed the screen;[67] but knew no more there than he did anywhere else how to enter into the true Gothic taste. Sir Christopher Wren, who built the tower of the great gateway at Christ Church, has catched the graces of it as happily as you could do: there is particularly a niche between two compartments of a window, that is a masterpiece.

But here is a *modernity*, which beats all antiquities for curiosity: Just by the high altar is a small pew hung with green damask, with curtains of the same; a small corner cupboard, painted, carved and gilt, for books, in one corner, and two troughs of a bird-cage, with seeds and water. If any mayoress on earth was small enough to enclose herself in this tabernacle, or abstemious enough to feed on rape and canary, I should have sworn that it was the shrine of the queen of the aldermen. It belongs to a Mrs Cotton,[68] who, having lost a favourite daughter, is convinced her soul is transmigrated into a robin-redbreast; for which reason she passes her life in making an aviary of the cathedral of Glocester. The chapter indulge this whim, as she contributes abundantly to glaze, whitewash and ornament the church.

King Edward II's tomb is very light and in good repair. The old wooden figure of Robert,[69] the Conqueror's unfortunate eldest son, is extremely genteel, and, though it may not be so ancient as his death,[70] is in a taste very superior to anything of much later ages. Our Lady's Chapel has a bold kind of portal, and several ceilings of chapels, and tribunes in a beautiful taste: but of all delight, is what they call the abbot's cloister. It is the very thing that you would build, when you had extracted all the quintessence of trefoils, arches, and lightness. In the church is a star-window of eight points, that is prettier than our rose-windows.

A little way from the town are the ruins of Lantony Priory:[71] there remains a pretty old gateway, which G. Selwyn has begged, to erect

---

it has not been generally accepted. A photograph of the monument is in *Transactions of the Bristol and Gloucestershire Archæological Society*, 1904, xxvii. 319; and an engraving of the effigies in Fosbrooke, op. cit., facing p. 127.

67. It was erected in 1741 and removed in 1820 (H. Haines, *Guide to the Cathedral Church of Gloucester*, 3d edn, [1884], p. 9).

68. Not further identified.

69. Robert (ca 1054–1134), Duke of Normandy.

70. It probably dates from the end of the twelfth or the early thirteenth century (Kate Norgate in DNB). A photograph is in Massé, op. cit. 87).

71. Llanthony Priory (*secunda*), founded in 1136 as a refuge for the monks of Llanthony in Wales.

on the top of his mountain,⁷² and it will have a charming effect.

At Burford I saw the house⁷³ of Mr Lenthal,⁷⁴ the descendant of the Speaker.⁷⁵ The front is good; and a chapel connected by two or three arches, which let the garden appear through, has a pretty effect; but the inside of the mansion is bad and ill-furnished. Except a famous picture of Sir Thomas More's family,⁷⁶ the portraits are rubbish, though celebrated.⁷⁷ I am told that the Speaker, who really had a fine collection, made his peace by presenting them to Cornbury,⁷⁸ where they were, well known, till the Duke of Marlborough bought that seat.⁷⁹

I can't go and describe so known a place as Oxford, which I saw pretty well on my return. The whole air of the town charms me; and what remains of the true Gothic *un-Gibbs'd*,⁸⁰ and the profusion of painted glass, were entertainment enough to me. In the Picture Gallery are quantities of portraits; but in general they are not only not so much as copies, but *proxies*—so totally unlike they are to the persons they pretend to represent. All I will tell you more of Oxford is, that Fashion has so far prevailed over her collegiate sister, Custom, that they have altered the hour of dinner from twelve to one. Does not it put one in mind of reformations in religion? One don't abolish Mahommedism; one only brings it back to where the impostor himself left it.—I think it is at the South Sea House, where they have

72. This scheme apparently fell through; the gateway is still with the rest of the Priory ruins. There is a print of it in Fosbrooke, op. cit., facing p. 147.

73. Burford Priory, Oxon. The house, which has been much altered, is described and illustrated in *Country Life*, 1911, xxix. 306–15.

74. William Lenthall (ca 1706–81) (GM 1781, li. 492).

75. William Lenthall (1591–1662), speaker of the Long Parliament, 3 Nov. 1640–20 April 1653.

76. A version of the Holbein painting. It was sold by the Lenthalls in 1833, and in 1910 was acquired by Sir Hugh P. Lane. A full history and description is in A. B. Chamberlain, *Hans Holbein the Younger*, New York, 1913, pp. 301–2, and the painting reproduced, ibid. plate 76.

77. Some of them are described in GM 1799, lxix pt ii. 644.

78. Then the seat of Edward Hyde (1609–74), cr. (1661) E. of Clarendon, Charles II's chief minister.

79. Charles Spencer (1706–58), 2d D. of Marlborough, bought Cornbury in 1751 (V. J. Watney, *Cornbury*, 1910, pp. 191, 194). HW repeats this anecdote in a marginal note to his copy, now WSL, of James Granger's *Biographical History of England*, Vol. I, pt ii, 1769, p. 379, but it has not been confirmed. The portraits, which HW had seen at Cornbury in 1736, remained there until 1763, when they were divided between the Duchess of Queensbury and Lady Hyde (MONTAGU i. 5 and n. 11; BERRY i. 152 and n. 38).

80. Mr Walpole means, unaltered by the architect Gibbs (HW). James Gibbs did not work in Gothic at Oxford, but HW was under the mistaken impression that he had designed the new buildings at All Souls; see *Anecdotes of Painting*, *Works* iii. 433 and note.

been forced to alter the hours of payment, instead of from ten to twelve, to from twelve to two; so much do even moneyed citizens sail with the current of idleness!

Was not I talking of religious sects? Methodism is quite decayed in Oxford, its cradle. In its stead, there prevails a delightful fantastic system, called the sect of the Hutchinsonians,[81] of whom one seldom hears anything in town. After much inquiry, all I can discover is, that their religion consists in driving Hebrew to its fountainhead, till they find some word or other in every text of the Old Testament, which may seem figurative of something in the New, or at least of something that may happen God knows when, in consequence of the New. As their doctrine is novel, and requires much study, or at least much invention, one should think that they could not have settled half the canon of what they are to believe—and yet they go on zealously, trying to make and succeeding in making converts.—I could not help smiling at the thoughts of *etymological salvation;* and I am sure you will smile when I tell you, that according to their gravest doctors, *Soap is an excellent type of Jesus Christ,*[82] *and the York Buildings waterworks*[83] *of the Trinity.*—I don't know whether this is not as entertaining as the passion of the Moravians for the *little side-hole!*[84] Adieu! my dear Sir!

Yours ever,

Hor. Walpole

81. Followers of John Hutchinson (1674–1737), a religious symbolist.

82. 'Mal. iii. 2. "Who may abide the day of his coming? And who shall stand when he appears? For his is like the refiner's fire, and like fuller's . . . soap, etc." The idea is . . . here . . . applied to an agent, a person who was to make persons and things pure and clear, so a refiner, a purifier, who in a spiritual sense was to refine and to make the souls of men pure, clean, etc.' (*Works* of John Hutchinson, 1748–9, iv. 362).

83. On the Thames in London.

84. Some Moravian churches in the period 1745–9 were characterized by extravagant conceptions 'as regarded the atonement in general, and Christ's wounded side in particular' (*New Schoff-Herzog Encyclopedia of Religious Knowledge*, New York, [1908–12], xii. 92). They had been somewhat in the public eye in 1749 when Parliament recognized them as an old Episcopal church; see J. T. Hamilton, *The Recognition of the Unitas Fratum as an Old Episcopal Church*, Bethlehem, Pa, 1925.

From Bentley, ca Wednesday 12 December 1753

Missing; mentioned in following letter.

To Bentley, Wednesday 19 December 1753

Printed from Toynbee iii. 200–3 and *Supp.* ii. 93. Previously printed in part, *Works* v. 281–2, Wright iii. 31–3, Cunningham ii. 362–4. The MS was among those which passed from HW to Mrs Damer, who bequeathed it to Sir Wathen Waller, 1st Bt; sold Sotheby's 5 Dec. 1921 lot 8 to an unknown purchaser.

Arlington Street, December 19, 1753.

I LITTLE thought when I parted with you,[1] my dear Sir, that your absence could indemnify me so well for itself; I still less expected that I should find you improving daily: but your letters grow more and more entertaining, your drawings more and more picturesque; you write with more wit, and paint with more *melancholy,* than ever anybody did: your woody mountains hang down *somewhat so poetical,* as Mr Ashe[2] said, that your own poet Gray will scarce keep tune with you.[3] All this refers to your cascade scene[4] and your letter. For the library, it cannot have the Strawberry imprimatur: the double arches and double pinnacles are most ungraceful; and the doors below the book-cases in Mr Chute's design had a conventual look,[5] which yours totally wants.[6] For this time, we shall put your

1. Bentley had gone to Jersey because of debt.

2. A nurseryman at Twickenham. He had served Pope. Mr Walpole telling him he would have his trees planted irregularly, he said, 'Yes, Sir, I understand: you would have them hang down somewhat poetical' (HW). He was probably Thomas Ashe or Ash (HW's *Strawberry Hill Accounts,* ed. Paget Toynbee, Oxford, 1927, pp. 45–6).

3. HW had published, through Dodsley, *Designs by Mr R. Bentley for Six Poems by Mr T. Gray* on 29 March 1753 ('Short Notes', Gray i. 24 and nn. 160, 161). The original drawings are now wsl.

4. Not identified, unless it was one of the two 'landscapes in soot water' which hung in the Green Closet ('Des. of SH,' *Works* ii. 434; sold SH xviii. 99).

5. A sketch by Chute for the presses at SH, inspired by a print in Dugdale's *St Paul's* is now wsl in a volume of drawings and sketches by Chute (Hazen, *Cat. of HW's Lib.*, No. 3490); other sketches are at the Vyne drawn by Chute on the end pages of Chute's copy of Scamozzi's *Cinq ordres d'architecture.*

6. Bentley's rejected design is reproduced in wsl, 'Genesis of SH,' *Metropolitan Museum Studies,* v pt i, 1934, p. 66.

genius in commission, and, like some other regents, execute our own plan without minding our sovereign. For the chimney, I do not wonder you missed our instructions: we could not contrive to understand them ourselves; and therefore, determining nothing but to have the old picture[7] stuck in a thicket of pinnacles, we left it to you to find out *the how*. I believe it will be a little difficult; but as I suppose *facere quia impossibile est,* is full as easy as *credere,* why— you must do it.

The present journal of the world and of me stands thus: King George II does not go abroad[8]—Some folks fear nephews, as much as others hate uncles.[9] The Castle of Dublin has carried the Armagh election by one vote only[10]—which is thought equivalent to losing it by twenty. Mr Pelham has been very ill, I thought of St Patrick's fire,[11] but it proved St Antony's. Our House of Commons, mere poachers, are piddling with the torture of Leheup,[12] who extracted so much money out of the lottery.

The robber of *Po Yang*[13] is discovered, and I hope will be put to death, without my pity interfering, as it has done for Mr Shorter's

7. 'The Marriage of Henry VI,' which hung over the chimney in the Library; it is now in the Toledo Museum of Art, Toledo, Ohio. For a discussion, see Gray ii. 68, n. 12 and illustration.

8. No other reference to George II's intention of going abroad at this time has been found.

9. I.e., George II feared his nephew, Frederick II of Prussia, as much as HW hated his uncle, 'Old Horace.'

10. On 10 Dec. when the Irish House of Commons voted 120–119 that William Brownlow, the sitting member for Armagh, was duly elected (Ireland, Parliament, House of Commons, *Journals,* Vol. IX, 1757, p. 189). The news was reported in the *Daily Adv.* 18 Dec.

11. Alluding to the disturbances and opposition to government, which took place in Ireland during the viceroyalty of Lionel [Cranfield Sackville (1688–1765), 7th E. of Dorset, cr. (1720)] Duke of Dorset (HW). For the Irish crisis at this time, see HW to Mann 6 Dec. 1753 (Mann iv. 401–2).

12. Peter Leheup (d. 1774), one of the

commissioners of the lottery for the purchase of the Sloane Museum and the Harleian MSS, was under investigation for various illegal practices connected with the management of the lottery. Accounts of the commissioners had been ordered by the House of Commons on 4 and 13 Dec. and referred to a committee on the 14th and 17th; the committee was increased on the 19th. It reported in great detail 14 March 1754, presenting resolutions condemning Leheup, who was then prosecuted by the Attorney-General before the King's Bench 19 April 1755, found guilty and fined £1000 (*Journals of the House of Commons* xxvi. 870, 872, 873, 874, 879, 987–1001; GM 1755, xxv. 184, 233; 1774, xliv. 142). An account of the debate on 14 Dec. is in Cobbett, *Parl. Hist.* xv. 193–226. Leheup's uncle had married the sister of 'Old Horace Walpole's wife (*Miscellanea genealogica et heraldica,* 1908, 4th ser. ii. 114–115, 157).

13. Mr Walpole had given this Chinese name to a pond of gold-fish at Strawberry Hill (HW).

servant,[14] or Lady [Caroline] [Petersham]'s,[15] as it did for Maclean.[16] In short, it was a heron. I like this better than thieves, as I believe the gang will be more easily destroyed, though not mentioned in the King's Speech[17] or Fielding's treatises.[18]

Lord Clarendon,[19] Lord Thanet,[20] and Lord Burlington,[21] are dead. The second sent for his tailor, and asked him if he could make him a suit of mourning in eight hours: if he could, he would go into mourning for his brother Burlington[22]—but that he did not expect to live twelve hours himself. Lord Burlington has left everything he had to his Countess[23] for her life, then to Lady Hartington,[24] and then to her son.[25] The Marquis[26] is not mentioned in the will. Can one doubt but he must have seen something in his son-in-law to merit such very marked omission? or can one more doubt that a capricious mother-in-law, an indulgent rich wife, and independent son, will find some opportunity to try all the *candour* of a Cavendish?[27]

14. A Swiss servant of Erasmus Shorter's, maternal uncle to Mr Walpole, who was not without suspicion of having hastened his master's death (Mary Berry). For this affair, see MONTAGU i. 157, GRAY i. 25, n. 163, and *ante* HW to Chute 21 May 1754.

15. Lady Caroline Fitzroy (1722–84), m. (1746) William Stanhope, styled Vct Petersham 1742–56, 2d E. of Harrington, 1756. HW mentions her and Miss Ashe as 'the principal persons who have been to comfort and weep over' Maclaine after his arrest in 1750 (MANN iv. 169).

16. A celebrated highwayman (HW). James Maclaine (1724–50), the highwayman who had robbed HW among others.

17. In a speech to Parliament 15 November 1753 the King had said: 'It is with the utmost regret I observe, that the horrid crimes of robbery and murder are of late rather increased than diminished,' etc. (*Journals of the House of Commons* xxvi. 841).

18. Henry Fielding's treatises, chiefly *An Inquiry into the Causes of the Late Increase of Robbers*, 1751.

19. Henry Hyde (1672 – 10 Dec. 1753), 4th E. of Clarendon, 1723.

20. Sackville Tufton (1688 – 4 Dec. 1753), 7th E. of Thanet, 1729.

21. Richard Boyle (1694 – 3 Dec. 1753), 3d E. of Burlington, 1704.

22. The Countesses of Thanet and Burlington were sisters (HW). The former was Lady Mary Savile (1700–51), m. (1722) Sackville Tufton, 7th E. of Thanet.

23. Lady Dorothy Savile (1699–1758), m. (1721) Richard Boyle, 3d E. of Burlington.

24. Lady Charlotte Elizabeth Boyle (1731–54), Bns Clifford s.j., dau. of Lord Burlington; m. (1748) William Cavendish, styled M. of Hartington 1729–55; 4th D. of Devonshire, 1755.

25. William Cavendish (1748–1811), styled M. of Hartington 1755–64; 5th D. of Devonshire, 1764.

26. William Cavendish (ca 1720–64), styled M. of Hartington 1729–55; 4th D. of Devonshire, 1755.

27. This passage is partially explained by the character of Lord Hartington in HW's 'foul copy' of *Mem. Geo. II*, much curtailed in the printed version (i. 196): 'The Marquis [of Hartington] was more fashioned [than his father], but with an impatience to do everything, and a fear to do anything, and he was always in a hurry to do nothing. His discretion was so great that he would sooner whisper to a man's prejudice, than openly deliver

There are two more volumes come out of *Sir Charles Grandison*.²⁸ I shall detain them till the last is published, and not think I postpone much of your pleasure. For my part, I stopped at the fourth; I was so tired of sets of people getting together, and saying, 'Pray, Miss, with whom are you in love?' and of mighty good young men that convert your *Mr M——'s*²⁹ in the twinkling of a sermon!—You have not been much more diverted, I fear, with Hogarth's book³⁰—'Tis very silly!—*Palmyra*³¹ is come forth, and is a noble book; the prints finely engraved, and an admirable dissertation before it. My wonder is much abated: the Palmyrene empire which I had figured, shrunk to a small trading city with some magnificent public buildings out of proportion to the dignity of the place.

The operas succeed pretty well; and music has so much recovered its power of charming, that there is started up a burletta at Covent Garden, that has half the vogue of the old *Beggar's Opera*: indeed there is a soubrette, called the Nicolina,³² who, besides being pretty, has more vivacity and variety of humour than ever existed in any creature.

Yours ever,

H. W.

a harmless opinion; and these whispers had the more effect, as he was too civil ever to own himself an enemy. Nor was this all malice; if he had had reflection enough to design all the mischief he did, he would have been less capable of doing it. It is the tales of the gentle and the good that stab.' Lord Holland, the editor of the *Memoirs*, attributes HW's hostility to Lord Hartington at this time, in contrast to his later admiration for him, to Lord Hartington and his father having taken the side of 'Old Horace' in the Nicoll affair (*Mem. Geo. II* i. 196, n. 3). See also *post* HW to Bentley 6 March 1754 and n. 8.

28. By Samuel Richardson (1689–1761). Vols V–VI were published 11 Dec. (W. M. Sale, Jr, *Samuel Richardson: A Bibliographical Record*, 1936, p. 76).

29. 'Name scored through in the original' (Toynbee *Supp*. ii. 93).

30. *The Analysis of Beauty* (HW). It was published 1 Dec. 1753 (*Daily Adv.* 30 Nov. 1753). HW's copy, with a few notes and markings by him, is now WSL (Hazen, *Cat. of HW's Lib.*, No. 3880).

31. Robert Wood's *The Ruins of Palmyra*. The earliest advertisement found is in *London Gazette*, Nos 9320, 9322, 13–17, 20–4 Nov. 1753. HW's copy is Hazen, *Cat. of HW's Lib.*, No. 3548.

32. Signora Nicolina Giordani acted the part of 'Spiletta' in *Gli amanti gelosi*, an Italian burletta by Giuseppe Giordani and Gioacchino Cocchi (ca 1715–1804), first given 17 Dec. 1753 at Covent Garden (MANN iv. 410, n. 24; *The London Stage 1660–1800*, pt 4 ed. G. W. Stone, Carbondale, Ill., 1962, i. 397–8; *Enciclopedia dello spettacolo*, Rome, 1954–62, iii. 1006–7, v. 1309; Sir George Grove, *Dictionary of Music*, 5th edn, ed. Blom, 1954, iii. 647).

To Bentley, Saturday 2 March 1754

Printed from *Works* v. 283–5; reprinted, Wright iii. 37–9, Cunningham ii. 368–70, Toynbee iii. 209–12.

Arlington Street, March 2, 1754.

AFTER calling two or three times without finding him, I wrote yesterday to Lord Granville,[1] and received a most gracious answer, but desiring to see me. I went. He repeated all your history with him, and mentioned your vivacity at parting; however, consented to give you the apartment,[2] with great good humour, and said he would write to his bailiff; and added, laughing, that he had an old cross housekeeper, who had regularly quarrelled with all his grantees. It is well that some of your desires, though unfortunately the most trifling, depend on me alone, as those at least are sure of being executed. By Tuesday's coach there will go to Southampton, two orange-trees, two Arabian jasmines, some tuberose roots, and plenty of cypress seeds, which last I send you in lieu of the olive-trees, none of which are yet come over.

The weather grows fine, and I have resumed little flights to Strawberry. I carried G. Montagu thither, who was in raptures, and screamed, and whooped, and hollaed, and danced, and crossed himself a thousand times over. He returns tomorrow to Greatworth, and I fear will give himself up entirely to country *squirehood*. But what will you say to greater honour which Strawberry has received? Nolkejumskoi[3] has been to see it, and liked the windows and staircase. I can't conceive how he entered it. I should have figured him like Gulliver cutting down some of the largest oaks in Windsor Forest to make jointstools, in order to straddle over the battlements and peep in at the windows of Lilliput. I can't deny myself this reflection (even though he liked Strawberry), as he has not employed you as an architect.[3a]

1. John Earl Granville, then secretary of state, had an estate in Jersey (HW). Granville (see *ante* Chute to HW 13 Feb. 1742 NS, n. 15) was at this time lord president of the Council, not secretary of state; he had inherited the ancestral Carteret estates in Jersey in 1715 and was Bailiff of the Island.
2. Perhaps in the Manoir de St Ouen, ancestral seat of the Carterets in Jersey. A description and photograph are in R. C. F. Maugham, *The Island of Jersey Today*, [1938], pp. 61–3.
3. Cant name for William Duke of Cumberland (HW).
3a. Bentley's (unexecuted) design for a palace for the Duke of Cumberland at Windsor is now WSL.

Still there is little news. Today it is said that Lord George Sackville[4] is summoned in haste from Ireland,[5] where the grand juries are going to petition for the resitting of the Parliament.[6] Hitherto they have done nothing but invent satirical healths, which I believe gratify a taste more peculiar to Ireland than politics, drinking. We have had one considerable day in the House of Commons here. Lord Egmont, in a very long and fine speech, opposed a new **Mutiny Bill** for the troops going to the East Indies[7] (which I believe occasioned the reports with you of an approaching war). Mr Conway got infinite reputation by a most charming speech[8] in answer to him, in which he displayed a system of military learning, which was at once new, striking, and entertaining. I had carried Monsieur de Gisors[9] thither, who began to take notes of all I explained to him: but I begged he would not; for, the question regarding French politics, I concluded the Speaker[10] would never have done storming at the Gaul's collecting intelligence in the very senate-house. Lord Holderness[11] made a magnificent ball for these foreigners last week:[12] there were 140 people, and most stayed supper. Two[13] of my Frenchmen learnt country-dances, and succeeded very well. T'other

4. Lord George Sackville (from 16 Feb. 1770, Germain) (1716–85), cr. (1782) Vct Sackville; army officer, statesman.

5. Where he was chief secretary to his father, the Lord Lieutenant. It was mentioned in the *Daily Adv.* 4 March that he was expected in London 'this week.'

6. The Irish Parliament had adjourned 24 Dec. 1753 until 15 Jan. 1754, then again until 5 Feb. 1754, and then through a series of prorogations until 7 Oct. 1755. For the disturbances in Ireland at this time, see HW to Mann 28 Jan. 1754 (MANN iv. 409–10 and nn. 17–21), and HW to Anne Pitt 10 Feb. 1754 (MORE 5 and n. 10).

7. '19th [Feb. 1754]. There was a debate on the bill for subjecting to military law the troops going to the East Indies; but it passed on a division of 245 to 50' (*Mem. Geo. II* i. 369; *Journals of the House of Commons* xxvi. 961). The debate is reported in Cobbett, *Parl. Hist.* xv. 250–87. Egmont's speech is ibid. xv. 250–68. There is a brief summary of Egmont's speech, after the Comte de Gisors's notes,

in C.-F.-M. Rousset, *Le Comte de Gisors*, 1868, pp. 58–9.

8. Conway's speech is outlined in Cobbett, *Parl. Hist.* xv. 282–7.

9. Louis-Marie Fouquet (1732–58), Comte de Gisors, son of the Maréchal de Belle-Isle, who had been recommended to HW by Anne Pitt (MORE 2–4).

10. Arthur Onslow.

11. Robert Darcy (1718–78), 4th E. of Holdernesse, 1722.

12. Gisors wrote to his mother on the 24th: 'Mercredi [20 Feb.] . . . il y a eu en très beau bal chez milady Holderness qui a été, si j'ose le dire, un peu en ma faveur. Il y avait plus de cent personnes dont je ne vous dirai pas les noms . . . ni ne vous ferai le détail du souper magnifiquement servi' (quoted by Rousset, op. cit. 65–6). Gisors's journal mentions that dancing continued until 5 A.M. (ibid. 67).

13. Gisors was accompanied by the Chevalier de Keralio, apparently the Chevalier Louis-Félix Guinement de Keralio (1731–93), soldier and author, and a M. de Grandpré (ibid. 50, 66).

night they danced minuets for the entertainment of the King at the masquerade;[14] and then he sent for Lady Coventry[15] to dance: it was quite like Herodias—and I believe if he had offered her a boon, she would have chosen the head of *St John*—I believe I told you of her passion for the young Lord B——.[16]

Dr Meade[17] is dead, and his collection going to be sold[18]—I fear I have not virtue enough to resist his miniatures—I shall be ruined![19]

I shall tell you a new instance of the *Sortes Walpolianæ:* I lately bought an old volume of pamphlets;[20] I found at the end a history of the Dukes of Lorrain, and with that an account of a series of their medals,[21] of which, says the author, there are but two sets in England. It so happens that I bought a set above ten years ago at Lord Oxford's sale;[22] and on examination I found the Duchess,[23] wife of Duke René,[24] has a head-dress, allowing for being modernized, as the medals are modern, which is evidently the same with that figure in my 'Marriage of Henry VI'[25] which I had imagined was of her. It is said to be taken from her tomb at Angiers; and that

14. On 25 Feb. (*Daily Adv.* 23, 25 Feb. 1754). Gisors's attendance is mentioned by Rousset, op. cit. 64, 69.

15. Maria (Mary) Gunning (1732–60), m. (1752) George William Coventry, 6th E. of Coventry, 1751. Gisors mentions promenading with her at the masquerade for an hour until she was brusquely reclaimed by her husband (ibid. 64).

16. Frederick St John (1734–87), 2d Vct Bolingbroke, 1751. For further developments in this affair, see *post* HW to Strafford 4 July 1757.

17. Richard Mead (1673 – 16 Feb. 1754), M.D.; collector.

18. The sale of his pictures was first advertised in the *Daily Advertiser* 27 Feb. 1754; the sale took place 20–22 March. His books were sold in Nov. 1754 and April 1755; his prints and drawings, 13–28 Jan. 1755; his medals and sculpture, 11–19 Feb. and 11–15 March 1756; some odds and ends, 25–26 March 1756; and his collection of pamphlets in 1783 (Frits Lugt, *Catalogue des ventes*, The Hague, 1938, Nos 830, 858, 871, 912; British Museum, *List of Catalogues of English Book Sales 1676–1900*, 1915, pp. 65, 66, 85).

19. HW told Bentley *post* 18 May 1754 that all the miniatures had been sold to the late Prince of Wales, but HW later

bought two (among other things) at the sales of his collections in 1755 (MANN iv. 470, n. 18).

20. For a description of this volume, see Hazen, *Cat. of HW's Lib.*, No. 683. The previous owner, Samuel Gale, had died in Jan. 1754, and HW had apparently bought it at Osborn's shop (information kindly supplied by Professor Allen T. Hazen).

21. Augustin Calmet, *Dissertation upon the High Roads of the Duchy of Lorraine*, translated by S. Fraser, 1729. An appendix to this is a dissertation upon the medals of the Dukes and Duchesses of Lorraine (information kindly supplied by Professor Hazen).

22. In March 1742 (*ante* Chute to HW 25 Dec. 1741 NS, n. 13; MANN i. 374, n. 17); they were sold SH x. 94.

23. Isabelle (1410–53), daughter of Charles II, Duc de Lorraine, m. (1420) René I, Duc de Bar et de Lorraine; K. of Sicily 1435–42 (GRAY ii. 69, nn. 4, 5).

24. René I (1409–80), Duc de Bar, 1419, de Lorraine, 1431, d'Anjou, 1435; Comte de Provence, 1435; King of Sicily 1435–42 (GRAY ii. 69, n. 5). HW's MS account of René is printed in MORE Appendix 10.

25. For a discussion of the personages supposedly represented in this picture, see GRAY ii. 68–80.

I might not decide too quickly *en connoisseur,* I have sent to Angiers[26] for a draught of the tomb.

Poor Mr Chute was here yesterday, the first going out after a confinement of thirteen weeks; but he is pretty well. We have determined upon the plan for the library,[27] which we find will fall in exactly with the proportions of the room, with no variations from the little door-case of St Paul's,[28] but widening the larger arches. I believe I shall beg your assistance again about the chimney-piece and ceiling; but I can decide nothing till I have been again at Strawberry. Adieu! my dear Sir,

Yours ever,

Hor. Walpole

From Bentley, ca Saturday 2 March 1754

Missing; mentioned in following letter.

To Bentley, Wednesday 6 March 1754

Printed from *Works* v. 285–7; reprinted, Wright iii. 39–42, Cunningham ii. 370–3, Toynbee iii. 212–15.

Arlington Street, March 6, 1754.

My dear Sir,

YOU will be surprised at my writing again so very soon; but unpleasant as it is to be the bearer of ill news,[1] I flattered myself that you would endure it better from me, than to be shocked with it from an indifferent hand, who would not have the same management

26. Nothing further is known of this commission; Gray wrote to HW on 3 March, jokingly urging him to send to Angiers for the windows from a chapel in a church there containing portraits of Duchesse Isabelle amongst others (GRAY ii. 69).

27. At Strawberry Hill (HW).

28. Old St Paul's; the design was based on engravings in Dugdale's *History of St Paul's;* see *ante* HW to Bentley 19 Dec. 1753, n. 5.

1. This is an ironic letter on the death [that day] of Henry Pelham, first lord of the Treasury and chancellor of the Exchequer, with whom Mr Walpole was on ill terms (HW). The 'ill terms' were the result of Pelham's not acceding to HW's request about his sinecures in 1752 (HW to Pelham 25 Nov. 1752; Fox to HW 23 Nov. 1752. SELWYN 119; and HW's account of his interview with Pelham, printed Toynbee iii. 132).

for your tenderness and delicacy as I naturally shall, who always feel
for you, and on this occasion with you! You are very unfortunate:
you have not many real friends, and you lose—for I must tell it you,
the chief of them! indeed, the only one who could have been of real
use to you—for what can *I* do, but wish, and attempt, and miscarry?—or from whom could I have hoped assistance for you, or
warmth for myself and my friends, but from the friend I have this
morning lost?—But it is too selfish to be talking of our losses, when
Britain, Europe, the world, the King, Jack Roberts,[2] Lord Barnard,[3]
have lost their guardian angel.—What are private misfortunes to the
affliction of one's country? or how inglorious is an Englishman to
bewail himself, when a true patriot should be acting for the good of
mankind!—Indeed, if it is possible to feel any comfort, it is from
seeing how many true Englishmen, how many *true Scotchmen,*[4] are
zealous to replace the loss, and snatch at the rudder of the state,
amidst this storm and danger! Oh! my friend, how will your heart
glow with melancholy admiration, when I tell you, that even the
poor Duke of Newcastle himself conquers the torrent of his grief, and
has promised Mrs Betty Spence,[5] and Mr Graham the apothecary,[6]
that, rather than abandon England to its evil genius, he will even
submit to be lord treasurer himself! My Lord Chancellor,[7] too, is
said to be willing to devote himself in the same manner for the
good of his country. Lord Hartington[8] is the most inconsolable of
all; and when Mrs Molly Bodens[9] and Mrs G[arrick][10] were entreated
by some of the cabinet council to ask him whom he wished to have
minister, the only answer they could draw from him was, *A Whig!*

2. John Roberts [ca 1712–72], Esquire,
secretary to Mr Pelham (HW).

3. Henry Vane [(ca 1705–58), 3d Bn
Barnard], afterwards [cr. 3 April 1754]
Earl of Darlington (HW). At this time he
was a lord of the Treasury.

4. I.e., William Murray (1705–93), cr.
(1756) Bn and (1776) E. of Mansfield, at
this time solicitor-general, who was talked
of as a successor to Pelham; see HW to
Mann 7 March 1754 (Mann iv. 411–12)
and *Mem. Geo. II* i. 379–80.

5. Companion to the Duchess of Newcastle (HW). Elizabeth Spence (d. 1764), a
sister of Thomas Spence (d. 1737), serjeant-
at-arms to the House of Commons (*London Chronicle* 25–27 Oct. 1764, xvi. 402;
HW to Hertford 1 Nov. 1764).

6. Daniel Graham (d. 1778), apothecary

to the King (More 28, n. 6). Several letters
from him to Newcastle are in the Newcastle Papers in the British Museum.

7. Philip Earl of Hardwicke (HW). He
was lord chancellor 1737–56 (*ante* HW to
Chute 29 Sept. 1755, n. 11). HW told
Mann the following day that both he and
Newcastle were being talked of for lord
treasurer (Mann iv. 412).

8. William, afterwards fourth Duke of
Devonshire (HW).

9. Companion of Lady Burlington, Lord
Hartington's mother-in-law (HW).

10. Eva Maria Veigel (1725–1822), called
Violette, m. (1749) David Garrick. She had
lived with Lord and Lady Burlington before her marriage, and the latter had provided her with an income (Mann iv. 74,
nn. 28–9).

a Whig![11] As for Lord B.[12] I may truly say, he is humbled and licks the dust; for his tongue, which never used to hang below the waistband of his breeches, is now dropped down to his shoe-buckles; and had not Mr Stone assured him, that if the worst came to the worst, they could but make their fortunes under another family,[13] I don't know whether he would not have despaired of the commonwealth. But though I sincerely pity so good a citizen, I cannot help feeling most for poor Lord Holderness, who sees a scheme of glory dashed which would have added new lustre to the British annals, and have transmitted the name of D'Arcy down to latest posterity. He had but just taken Mr Mason the poet into his house[14] *to write his deserts;* and he had just reason to expect that the Secretary's office[15] would have gained a superiority over that of France and Italy, which was unknown even to Walsingham.

I had written thus far, and perhaps should have elegized on for a page or two farther, when Harry,[16] who has no idea of the dignity of grief, blundered in, with satisfaction in his countenance, and thrust two packets from you into my hand.—Alas! he little knew that I was incapable of tasting any satisfaction but in the indulgence of my concern.—I was once going to commit them to the devouring flames, lest any light or vain sentence should tempt me to smile; but my turn for true philosophy checked my hand, and made me determine to prove that I could at once launch into the bosom of pleasure and be insensible to it.—I have conquered; I have read your letters, and yet think of nothing but Mr Pelham's death! Could Lady [Catherine][17] do thus? Could she receive a love-letter from Mr [Brown],[18] and yet think only on her breathless lord?

11. See HW's character of Hartington, quoted *ante* HW to Bentley 19 Dec. 1753, n. 27, for his aversion to expressing opinions. HW adds that Sir Robert Walpole having set up Hartington's father, the 3d Duke of Devonshire, as the standard of Whiggism, the Duke 'was constantly bigotted to whoever passed for the head of the Whigs' (*Mem. Geo. II* i. 196).

12. Lord Barnard. HW wrote of him in a note to 'Patapan,' 1743: 'If ever he had attempted to speak, he would have been prevented by a monstrous tongue, that always lolled out of his mouth' (SELWYN 303, n. 57).

13. The Stuarts, in reference to Stone's supposed Jacobitism.

14. William Mason (1725–97), divine and poet; later HW's correspondent. He had apparently just become Holdernesse's private secretary (Thomas Gray, *Correspondence*, ed. Toynbee and Whibley, Oxford, 1935, i. 389, n. 4), and became his chaplain in Nov. 1754 after taking orders.

15. Holdernesse was secretary of state for the South 1751–4 and for the North 1754 – March 1761.

16. Henry Jones, HW's 'steward and butler' ca 1752–62 (MONTAGU i. 132 and n. 1; GRAY ii. 85 and n. 1).

17. Lady Catherine Pelham (ca 1701–80), m. (1726) Henry Pelham.

18. Wright expands this silently to 'Brown' and Cunningham and Mrs Toyn-

Thursday 7.

I wrote the above last night, and have stayed as late as I could this evening, that I might be able to tell you who the person is in whom all the world is to discover the proper qualities for replacing the national loss. But, alas! the experience of two whole days has showed that the misfortune is irreparable; and I don't know whether the elegies on his death will not be finished before there be any occasion for congratulations to his successor. The mystery is profound. How shocking it will be if things should go on just as they are! I mean by that, how mortifying, if it is discovered, that when all the world thought Mr Pelham did and could alone maintain the calm and carry on the government, even he was not necessary, and that it was the calm and the government that carried on themselves! However, this is not my opinion.—I believe all this *will make a party*.[19]

Good night! There are two more new plays: *Constantine*,[20] the better of them, expired the fourth night at Covent Garden. *Virginia*,[21] by Garrick's acting and popularity, flourishes still: he has written a remarkably good epilogue to it.[22] Lord Bolingbroke[23] is come forth in five pompous quartos,[24] two and a half new and most unorthodox.[25] Warburton is resolved to answer, and the bishops not to answer him.[26] I have not had a moment to look into it. Good night!

Yours ever,

Hor. Walpole

bee follow him, but no other reference to any connection between Lady Catherine Pelham and Mr Brown has been found.

19. Mr Walpole, when young, loved faction; and Mr Bentley one day saying, 'that he believed certain opinions would make a sect,' Mr W. said eagerly, 'Will they make a party?' (HW).

20. By Philip Francis (ca 1708–73), divine and author, first performed at Covent Garden 23 Feb. (John Genest, *Some Account of the English Stage*, Bath, 1832, iv. 397–8; Allardyce Nicoll, *A History of English Drama 1660–1900*, Cambridge, 1952–67, iii. 261).

21. By Samuel Crisp (d. 1783), first performed at Drury Lane 25 Feb. (Genest, op. cit. 386–7). There is a full account of the

play in Frances Burney, *Early Diary*, ed. A. R. Ellis, 1913, ii. 325–32.

22. The epilogue was 'written by Mr Garrick,' and 'spoken by Mrs Cibber' (Samuel Crisp, *Virginia*, 1754, p. 75).

23. Henry St John (1678–1751), cr. (1712) Vct Bolingbroke.

24. *Works*, ed. David Mallet; advertised as published 6 March (*Daily Adv.*; *Whitehall Evening Post*). HW's copy is Hazen, *Cat. of HW's Lib.*, No. 3159.

25. For some of their contents see Mann iv. 454, n. 11.

26. In this year and the next Warburton published *A View of Lord Bolingbroke's Philosophy in Four Letters to a Friend*.

To Bentley, Sunday 17 March 1754

Printed from *Works* v. 287–90; reprinted, Wright iii. 45–8, Cunningham ii. 375–7, Toynbee iii. 219–22.

Arlington Street, March 17, 1754.

IN THE confusion of things, I last week hazarded a free letter to you by the common post. The confusion is by no means ceased. However, as some circumstances may have rendered a desire of intelligence necessary,[1] I send this by the coach, with the last volume of *Sir Charles Grandison*,[2] for its chaperon.

After all the world had been named for Chancellor of the Exchequer, and my Lord Chief Justice Lee,[3] who is no part of the world, really made so *pro tempore*;[4] Lord Hartington went to notify to Mr Fox,[5] that the cabinet council having given it as their unanimous opinion to the King, that the Duke of Newcastle should be at the head of the Treasury, and he (Mr Fox) Secretary of State with the management of the House of Commons; his Grace, who had submitted to so *oracular* a sentence, hoped Mr Fox would not refuse to concur in so salutory a measure; and assured him, that *though* the Duke would reserve the sole disposition of the secret-service money, his Grace would bestow his entire confidence on Mr Fox, and acquaint him with the most minute details of that service. Mr Fox bowed and obeyed—and, as a preliminary step, received the Chancellor's[6] absolution. From thence he attended his—and our new master.[7]—But either grief for his brother's death, or joy for it, had so

1. HW apparently means that his letter, if sent by the common post, might be opened by the government in the hopes of finding intelligence about Fox's intentions as a result of his breach with Newcastle (see below).

2. Vol. VII of Sir Charles Grandison was published 14 March 1754 (W. M. Sale, Jr, *Samuel Richardson: A Bibliographical Record*, 1936, p. 76). An advertisement for it in the *Daily Adv.* 14 March 1754 erroneously calls it Vol. VI and announces its publication 'tomorrow.'

3. Sir William Lee (1688 – 8 April 1754), Kt, 1737; lord chief justice of the Court of King's Bench 1737–54.

4. His appointment was announced *sub*

Whitehall, 9 March, in the *London Gazette* No. 9352, 5–9 March 1754.

5. On 12 March (SELWYN 122–3, nn. 1, 4, 6 and references there cited). HW had advised Fox to have nothing to do with Newcastle in the new ministry (ibid. 123); his accounts of the negotiation, more full there than in any other source, probably came directly from Fox in an interview on the 13th (ibid. 123).

6. With whom he was at variance (HW). Fox's interview with him had taken place in the morning of the 13th (Lord Ilchester, *Henry Fox*, 1920, i. 204; *Mem. Geo. II* i. 382).

7. On the 13th (SELWYN 123, n. 7).

intoxicated the new *maire du palais,* that he would not ratify any one of the conditions he had imposed: and though my Lord Hartington's virtue interposed, and remonstrated on the purport of the message he had carried, the Duke persisted in assuming the whole and undivided power himself, and left Mr Fox no choice, but of obeying or disobeying, as he might choose. This produced the next day a letter from Mr Fox,[8] carried by my Lord Hartington, in which he refused Secretary of State, and pinned down the lie with which the new ministry is to commence. It was tried to be patched up at the Chancellor's on Friday night,[9] though ineffectually; and yesterday morning Mr Fox in an audience desired to remain Secretary at War.[10] The Duke immediately kissed hands[11]—declared, in the most unusual manner, universal minister. Legge was to be Chancellor of the Exchequer;[12] but I can't tell whether that disposition will hold, as Lord Duplin[13] is proclaimed the acting favourite. The German Sir Thomas Robinson[14] was thought on for the Secretary's seals; but has just sense enough to be unwilling to accept them[15] under so ridiculous an administration.—This is the first act of the comedy.

On Friday this august remnant of the Pelhams went to Court for the first time. At the foot of the stairs he cried and sunk down: the yeomen of the guard were forced to drag him up under the arms. When the closet-door opened, he flung himself at his length at the King's feet, sobbed, and cried, 'God bless your Majesty! God preserve your Majesty!' and lay there howling and embracing the King's knees, with one foot so extended, that my Lord C[oventry],[16]

8. Printed Ilchester, op. cit. i. 206–7 and, with slight verbal differences, *Mem. Geo. II* i. 385–6.

9. The 15th, in a conference of three hours (Ilchester, op. cit. 207).

10. Which he had been since May 1746. Accounts of his interview with the King are ibid. i. 208–9 and *Mem. Geo. II* i. 386–7.

11. His appointment was announced *sub* Whitehall 16 March in the *London Gazette* No. 9354, 12–16 March 1754.

12. His appointment was recommended in the Cabinet Minutes of the 12th (MANN iv. 417, n. 6), but not formally announced (*sub* Whitehall 6 April) until the *London Gazette* No. 9360, 2–6 April.

13. Thomas Hay (1710–87), styled Vct Dupplin 1719–58; 9th E. of Kinnoull,

1758. His appointment as a lord of the Treasury was announced *sub* Whitehall, 6 April, in the *London Gazette* No. 9360, 2–6 April 1754.

14. Sir Thomas Robinson (1695–1770), K.B., 1742, cr. (1761) Bn Grantham; minister at Vienna 1730–48. HW calls him 'German' to distinguish him from 'Long Sir Thomas' Robinson.

15. Robinson reluctantly accepted the seals as secretary for the southern department; his appointment was announced *sub* St James's, 23 March, and he was sworn in on the 28th (*London Gazette* Nos 9356, 9358, 19–23, 26–30 March 1754). See HW's comments on the appointment in *Mem. Geo. II* i. 388.

16. George William Coventry (1722–1809), 6th E. of Coventry, 1751, the only

who was *luckily* in waiting, and begged the standers-by to retire, with 'For God's sake, gentlemen, don't look at a great man in distress,' endeavouring to shut the door, caught his Grace's foot, and made him roar out with pain.

You can have no notion of what points of ceremony have been agitated about the tears of the family. George Selwyn was told that my Lady Catherine had not shed one tear: 'And pray,' said he, 'don't she intend it?' It is settled that Mrs [Watson][17] is not to cry till she is brought to bed.[18]

You love George Selwyn's bons mots: this crisis has redoubled them: here is one of his best. My Lord Chancellor is to be Earl of Clarendon:[19]—'Yes,' said Selwyn, from the very summit of the whites of his demure eyes; 'and I suppose he will get the title of Rochester[20] for his son-in-law, my Lord A[nson].'[21] Do you think he will ever lose the title of Lord Rochester?

I expected that we should have been overrun with elegies and panegyrics: indeed I comforted myself, that one word in all of them would atone for the rest—the *late* Mr Pelham. But the world seems to allow that their universal attachment and submission was universal interestedness: there has not been published a single encomium:[22] Orator Henley[23] alone has held forth in his praise:[24]— yesterday it was on *charming Lady Catherine*.[25] Don't you think it should have been in these words, in his usual style?

lord of the Bedchamber whose title began with a 'C.'

17. Grace Pelham (ca 1731–77), Henry Pelham's daughter, m. (1752) Hon. Lewis Watson (before 1746, Monson) cr. (1760) Bn Sondes. Her name and date of birth have frequently been confused with those of her elder sister Frances (GEC; MONTAGU ii. 72).

18. Her first child was born 18 April 1754: Lewis Thomas Watson (1754–1806), 2d Bn Sondes, 1795; M.P. Hedon 1776–80. Her tears are alluded to, *post* HW to Strafford 25 June 1768.

19. So the newspapers reported (*Whitehall Evening Post* 7–9 March 1754), but the Chancellor became Earl of Hardwicke, instead, on 2 April.

20. The second son of the first Earl of Clarendon had been cr. Earl of Rochester in 1682 after the Wilmot line became extinct.

21. George Anson (1697–1762), cr. (1747) Bn Anson; Adm.; m. (1748) Elizabeth Yorke, the Chancellor's daughter. Selwyn's joke contrasts Anson's alleged impotence with the vigour of the notorious Wilmot, Earl of Rochester.

22. The first one, *An Ode on the Death of the Right Hon. Henry Pelham*, was published 18 March (*Daily Adv.* 18 March 1754).

23. John Henley (1692–1756), eccentric London preacher.

24. On Sunday 10 March; Henley describes his projected sermon in a 'news item' signed 'J. H.' in the *Daily Adv.* 8 March and in his advertisement ibid. 9 March.

25. Henley's advertisement for his sermon of 17 March is headed 'More on R. H. H. Pelham; Charming Lady C.' (ibid. 16 March).

'Oratory-Chapel.—Right reason; madness; charming Lady Catherine; hell-fire,'[26] etc.

Monday, March 18.

Almost as extraordinary news as our political, is, that it has snowed ten days successively, and most part of each day: it is living in Muscovy, amid ice and revolutions: I hope lodgings will begin to let a little dear in Siberia! Beckford[27] and Delaval,[28] two celebrated partisans, met lately at Shaftesbury, where they oppose one another:[29] the latter said,

Art thou the man, whom men fam'd Beckford call?

T'other replied,

Art thou the much more famous Delaval?

But to leave politics, and change of ministries, and to come to something of *real* consequence, I must apply you to my library ceiling; of which I send you some rudiments. I propose to have it all painted by Clermont;[30] the principal part in chiaroscuro, on the design which you drew for the Paraclete:[31] but as that pattern would be surfeiting so often repeated in an extension of 20 feet by 30, I propose to break and enliven it by compartments in colours, according to the enclosed sketch, which you must adjust and dimension. Adieu!

Yours ever,

Hor. Walpole

---

26. For other examples of Henley's style, see Mann ii. 465, n. 13; Selwyn 56, n. 37.

27. William Beckford (1709–70), lord mayor of London 1762–3, 1769–70; M.P.

28. Francis Blake Delaval (1727–71), K.B., 1761; M.P. Hindon 1751–4, Andover 1754–68.

29. Beckford had been M.P. for Shaftesbury 1747–54, but in the present election was a candidate in London at Petersfield. Delaval was contesting Andover at the time.

30. For him and his charges for painting the Library ceiling, see *ante* HW to Chute 30 April 1754 and nn. 11, 12.

31. The hall at SH was named Paraclete 'in memory of Eloisa's cloister' (HW to Mann 27 April 1753, Mann iv. 372).

From Bentley, ca Thursday 18 April 1754

Missing; mentioned *post* 18 May 1754.

To Bentley, ca May 1754

Missing; mentioned *post* 18 May 1754.

From Bentley, Wednesday 8 May 1754

Missing; mentioned in following letter.

To Bentley, Saturday 18 May 1754

Printed from Toynbee iii. 231–4 and *Supp.* ii. 95. Previously printed in part, *Works* v. 290–3; Wright iii. 55–8; Cunningham ii. 384–6. The MS was among those which passed from HW to Mrs Damer, who bequeathed it to Sir Wathen Waller, 1st Bt; sold Sotheby's 5 Dec. 1921 (first Waller sale) lot 8 to an unknown purchaser.

Arlington Street, May 18, 1754.

My dear Sir,

UNLESS you will be exact in dating your letters, you will occasion me much confusion. Since the undated one which I mentioned in my last, I have received another as unregistered, with the fragment of the rock, telling me of one which had set sail on the 18th, I suppose of last month, and been driven back: this I conclude was the former. Yesterday, I received a longer, tipped with May 8th. You must submit to this lecture, and I hope will amend by it. I cannot promise that I shall correct myself much in the intention I had of writing to you seldomer and shorter at this time of year. If you could be persuaded how insignificant I think all I do, how little important it is even to myself, you would not wonder that I have not much *empressement* to give the detail of it to anybody else.

Little excursions to Strawberry, little parties to dine there, and many jaunts to hurry Bromwich,[1] and the carver,[2] and Clermont, are my material occupations. Think of sending these 'cross the *sea!* —The times produce nothing: there is neither party, nor controversy, nor gallantry, nor fashion, nor literature—the whole proceeds like farmers regulating themselves, their business, their views, their diversions, by the almanac. Mr Pelham's death has scarce produced a change; the changes in Ireland,[3] scarce a murmur. Even in France the squabbles of the Parliament and clergy are under the same opiate influence.—I don't believe that Mademoiselle Murphy[4] (who is delivered of a prince,[5] and is lodged openly at Versailles) and Madame Pompadour[6] will mix the least grain of ratsbane in one another's tea. I, who love to ride in the whirlwind,[7] cannot record the yawns of such an age!

The little that I believe you would care to know relating to the Strawberry annals, is, that the great tower[8] is finished on the outside, and the whole whitened, and has a charming effect, especially as the verdure of this year is beyond what I have ever seen it: the grove nearest the house comes on much; you know I had almost despaired of its ever making a figure. The bow-window room[9] over the supper-parlour is finished; hung with a plain blue paper, with a chintz bed[10] and chairs; my father and mother over the chimney in the Gibbons

1. Thomas Bromwich (d. 1787), a fashionable decorator and paperhanger (GM 1787, lvii pt ii. 646; *SH Accounts*, ed. Toynbee, Oxford, 1927, pp. 66–7). At some time between 22 Feb. and 15 May 1754 HW had paid him £77 17s. 2d. for 'papering staircase, pink room, green closet and garrets' (ibid. 5).

2. Perhaps George Murray (d. 1761), master sculptor and master carver to the King, 1760, who received £8 sometime between 22 Feb. and 15 May 1754 'for the chimney piece for the little parlour' (ibid. 5; Rupert Gunnis, *Dictionary of British Sculptors 1660–1851*, Cambridge, Mass., 1954, p. 268).

3. For these see HW to Mann 24 April 1754 (MANN iv. 425–6 and nn. 3–8).

4. An Irish woman for a short time mistress to Louis XV (HW). Marie-Louise Morphy (ca 1738–1815), m. 1 (1755) Jacques de Beaufranchet d'Ayat; m. 2 (ca 1759) François-Nicolas Le Normant, cr. (1765) Comte de Flaghac; m. 3 (before 1798) Louis-Philippe Dumont; Louis XV's mistress 1753–5 (MANN iv. 542, n. 14).

5. It was a daughter, not a son. She was Agathe-Louise de Saint-Antoine de Saint André (d. 1774), m. (1773) Louis-René-Mans de la Tour de Charce (Comte de Fleury, *Louis XV intime et les petites maîtresses*, 1909, pp. 130–7; *Répertoire . . . de la Gazette de France*, ed. de Granges de Surgères, 1902–6, iii. 252). HW is probably following a newspaper report.

6. Jeanne-Antoinette Poisson (1721–64), m. (1741) Charles-Guillaume Le Normand d'Etiolles; cr. (1745) Marquise de Pompadour; mistress of Louis XV.

7. Addison, *The Campaign*, l. 292; Pope, *Dunciad*, iii. 264.

8. Not the Round Tower, which was not begun until 1760, but the square tower at the south-east corner of the house.

9. The Blue Bedchamber.

10. For which HW paid £38 7s. 6d. on 15 May (*SH Accounts* 5).

frame,[11] about which you know we were in dispute what to do. I have fixed on black and gold, and it has a charming effect over *your chimney with the two dropping points,* which is executed exactly;[12] and the old grate of Henry VIII[13] which you bought, is within it. In each panel round the room is a single picture;[14] Gray's,[15] Sir Charles Williams's,[16] and yours,[17] in their black and gold frames;[18] mine[19] is to match yours; and, on each side the door, are the pictures of Mr Churchill and Lady Mary, with their son,[20] on one side, Mr Conway and Lady Ailesbury[21] on the other. You can't imagine how new and pretty this furniture is.—I believe I must get you to send me an attestation under your hand that you knew nothing of it, that Mr Rigby[22] may allow that at least this one room was by my own direction. As the library and great parlour grow finished, you shall have exact notice.

From Mabland[23] I have little news to send you, but that the obelisk is danced from the middle of the rabbit-warren into his neighbour's garden, and he pays a ground-rent for looking at it there. His shrubs are hitherto unmolested,

11. The frame and picture by Eccardt and Wootton (now wsl) are reproduced in MANN iii. 511.

12. A plate of the chimney-piece in the Blue Bedchamber is in 'Des. of SH,' *Works* ii. facing p. 435.

13. Rather Henry VII. It is mentioned by Montagu to HW, ca April 1754 (MONTAGU i. 161), and is presumably the 'chimney-back, which I had bought for having belonged to Harry VII' (HW to Mann 6 Oct. 1753, MANN iv. 396). HW had previously referred to it as a 'grate' (ibid. iv. 395). It was later in the Great North Bedchamber ('Des. of SH,' *Works* ii. 494).

14. All by Eccardt.

15. Painted in 1748; sold SH xxii. 30; now in the National Portrait Gallery. It is reproduced in GRAY ii. 22.

16. Sir Charles Hanbury Williams (1708–59), K.B., 1744; politician, diplomatist, wit, and poet; HW's correspondent. The portrait, which has not been located, was sold SH xxii. 29 to G. M. Dartry, Esq. Williams is holding his 'Isabella, or the Morning.'

17. Reproduced in Wright ii. facing p.

435; sold SH xxii. 31 to 'Money'; it has not been located.

18. 'Carved after those to Lombard's prints from Vandyck, but with emblems peculiar to each person' ('Des. of SH,' *Works* ii. 436).

19. Painted about 1755 and sold SH xxii. 28; now in the National Portrait Gallery. It is reproduced in MONTAGU i. 269.

20. Charles Churchill (1747–83 *or* 85), their eldest son (MANN iii. 371, n. 18; 'Des. of SH,' *Works* ii. 436). The painting, in which the attitudes and dress were taken from a Rubens at Blenheim, was sold SH xxii. 36 and is now wsl.

21. This picture, in which the attitudes and dress were taken from Watteau ('Des. of SH,' *Works* ii. 436), was sold SH xxii. 35 and is now owned by Major Campbell-Johnston.

22. Richard Rigby (1722–88), politician, M.P. HW had been intimate with him since 1744, but their friendship eventually cooled.

23. HW's name for Lord Radnor's house, next to SH. For various details of his grounds, see MONTAGU i. 53 and n. 2; MANN iv. 382; and HW to Conway 8 Nov. 1752.

Et Maryboniacos[24] gaudet revirescere lucos![25]

The town is as busy again as ever on the affair of Canning,[26] who has been tried for perjury.[27] The jury would have brought her in guilty of perjury, but not wilful, till the judge[28] informed them that that would rather be an Irish verdict; they then brought her in simply guilty, but recommended her. In short, nothing is discovered; the most general opinion is that she was robbed, but by some other gipsy.[29] For my own part, I am not at all brought to believe her story, nor shall, till I hear that living seven-and-twenty days without eating[30] is among one of those secrets for doing impossibilities, which I suppose will be at last found out. You know my system is, that everything will be found out, and about the time that I am dead, even some art of living forever.

You was in pain for me, and indeed I was in pain for myself, on the prospect of the sale of Dr Mead's miniatures. You may be easy: it is more than I am quite; for it is come out that the late Prince of Wales had bought them every one.[31]

I have not yet had time to have your granite examined, but will next week. If you have not noticed to your sisters[32] any present of ormer shells,[33] I shall contradict myself, and accept them for my Lady Lyttelton,[34] who is making a grotto. As many as you can send con-

24. Lord Radnor's garden was full of statues, etc., like that at Marybone (HW).

25. 'And he rejoices in the Marybone groves' recovery of their verdure.' This may be an ill-remembered paraphrase of Ovid, *Metamorphoses* ii. 408: 'læsaque iubet revirescere silvas' ('and bids the damaged forests grow green again').

26. Elizabeth Canning (1734–73) had, according to her own story, been kidnapped in January 1753. The affair had caused a great stir and a vigorous pamphlet controversy in the winter and spring of 1753.

27. The trial lasted from 29 April to 8 May; it is fully reported in T. B. Howell, et al., *Complete Collection of State Trials*, 1809–28, xix. 283–692.

28. Sir William Moreton (?1696–1763), Kt, 1755; recorder of London; M.P. (Howell, op. cit. xix. 669).

29. Elizabeth Canning had accused Mary Squires, a gipsy, of assaulting and robbing her at the time of her kidnapping. She had been tried 21–26 Feb. and condemned

to death, but pardoned in view of later evidence (Howell, op. cit. xix. 261–76; DNB *sub* Elizabeth Canning).

30. Elizabeth Canning had asserted that she had subsisted during her confinement of 27 days on a pitcher 'not quite full of water,' twenty-four pieces of bread, and 'a penny mince pie' (Howell, op. cit. xix. 264).

31. But see *ante* HW to Bentley 2 March 1754, n. 19.

32. Elizabeth Bentley, m. 1 Humphrey Ridge; m. 2 Rev. James Favell, D.D. (Richard Cumberland, *Memoirs*, 1806, i. 17–18; Venn, *Alumni Cantab.*); and Joanna Bentley (d. 1775), m. (1728) Rev. Denison Cumberland, D.D., Bp of Clonfert, 1763, of Kilmore, 1772; mother of Richard Cumberland, the dramatist (GM 1775, xlv. 351).

33. A shell-fish especially abundant in Guernsey (OED).

34. The second Lady Lyttelton (*ante* HW to Chute 21 May 1754, n. 18).

veniently, and anything for the same use, will be very acceptable. You will laugh when I tell you that I am employed to reconcile Sir George and Moore;[35] the latter has been very flippant, nay[36] impertinent, on the former's[37] giving a little place to Bower,[38] in preference to him.[39]—Think of my being the mediator!

The Parliament is to meet for a few days the end of this month,[40] to give perfection to the Regency Bill.[41] If the King dies before the end of this month, the old Parliament revives, which would make tolerable confusion, considering what sums have been laid out on seats in this.—Adieu! This letter did not come kindly; I reckon it rather extorted from me, and therefore hope it will not amuse. However, I am in tolerable charity with you, and

Yours ever,

Hor. Walpole

From Bentley, June 1754

Missing; mentioned by HW to Montagu 29 June 1754 (Montagu i. 162).

35. Author of *The World*, and some plays and poems. Moore had written in defence of Lord Lyttelton against the *Letters to the Whigs* [1747–8]; which were not known to be Mr Walpole's (HW). Edward Moore (1712–57), whose poetical defence, *The Trial of Selim the Persian for divers High Crimes and Misdemeanours* was published in May 1748 (Hazen, *Bibl. of HW* 34). HW was connected with Moore at this time by his own writings for the *World*.

36. *Works* reads 'say.'

37. *Works* reads 'latter's.'

38. Archibald Bower (1686–1766), author of a *History of the Popes*, had been given the post of clerk of the buck-warrant by Lyttelton in April 1754. For HW's later relations with Bower see HW to Mann 23 Feb. 1756 (Mann iv. 531–4).

39. According to Dr Johnson, Moore had been paid for the *Trial of Selim* 'with kind words, which, as is common, raised great hopes, that at last were disappointed' (Johnson's *Lives of the Poets*, ed. G. B. Hill, Oxford, 1905, iii. 448). Lyttelton had been of no assistance in Fielding's unsuccessful attempt to get Moore the post of deputy licencer of the stage in Aug. 1749, but had exerted himself in organizing the *World* for Moore's benefit (R. M. Davis, *The Good Lord Lyttelton*, Bethlehem, Pa, 1939, p. 223).

40. 31 May–5 June (Mann iv. 434, n. 13, 435).

41. 24 Geo. II, c. 24. Section 18 had provided that if there was no Parliament in being which had met and sat at the succession of a minor to the throne, the old Parliament should revive, even though dissolved.

To Bentley, Tuesday 9 July 1754

Printed from *Works* v. 293–5; reprinted Wright iii. 67–9, Cunningham ii. 393–5, Toynbee iii. 248–50.

Strawberry Hill, July 9, 1754.

I ONLY write a letter for company to the enclosed one.[1] Mr Chute is returned from the Vine, and gives you a thousand thanks for your letter;[2] and if ever he writes, I don't doubt but it will be to you. Gray and he come hither tomorrow, and I am promised Montagu and the Colonel[3] in about a fortnight[4]—How naturally my pen adds, but when does Mr Bentley come? I am sure Mr Wicks[5] wants to ask me the same question every day—*Speak to it, Horatio!*[6] —Sir Charles Williams brought his eldest daughter[7] hither last week: she is one of your real admirers, and, without its being proposed to her, went on the bowling-green, and drew a perspective view of the castle from the angle, in a manner to deserve the thanks of the *committee:*[7a] she is to be married to my Lord Essex[8] in a week, and I begged she would make you overseer of the works at Cashiobury.[9] Sir Charles told me, that on the Duke of Bedford's wanting a Chinese house at Woburn,[10] he said, 'Why don't your Grace speak to Mr Walpole? He has the prettiest plan in the world for one.'[11]— 'Oh,' replied the Duke, 'but then it would be too dear!' I hope this

1. Missing; it was presumably from George Montagu. HW had promised on 29 June to send a letter for him to Bentley the first time he wrote (Montagu i. 162).

2. Missing; Bentley had probably written to Chute congratulating him on his brother Anthony's death; see *ante* HW to Chute 21 May 1754.

3. Charles Montagu [d. 1777], brother of George, and afterwards General, and Knight of the Bath [1771] (HW). For him see Montagu i. 31, n. 14.

4. They did not come until late October (*post* HW to Bentley 3 Nov. 1754; Montagu i. 165 and n. 1).

5. Probably the same as the 'Mr Weekes' mentioned *post* HW to Bentley 24 April 1755, whom HW identifies as a Twickenham carpenter employed at SH.

6. *Hamlet* I. i. 42.

7. Frances Hanbury Williams (1735–59), m. (1 Aug. 1754) William Anne Holles Capel, 4th E. of Essex.

7a. Mr Walpole in these letters calls the Strawberry committee those of his friends who had assisted in the plans and Gothic ornaments of Strawberry Hill (Mary Berry).

8. William Anne Holles Capel (1732–99), 4th E. of Essex, 1743.

9. Cassiobury Park, Essex's seat in Herts. Bentley is not known to have designed anything there.

10. Woburn Abbey, Bedford's seat in Bedfordshire.

11. Bentley's drawing of a proposed Chinese building for SH is reproduced in wsl; 'Genesis of SH,' *Metropolitan Museum Studies*, vol. v pt i, 1934, p. 68. Two more Chinese designs for SH and three for Holland House are also wsl.

was very great economy, or I am sure ours would be very great extravagance—Only think of a plan for poor little Strawberry giving the alarm to thirty thousand pounds a year!—My dear Sir, it is time to retrench!—Pray send me a slice of granite[12] no bigger than a Naples biscuit.

The monument for my mother is at last erected:[13] it puts me in mind of the manner of interring the Kings of France: when the reigning one dies, the last before him is buried.[14] Will you believe that I have not yet seen the tomb? None of my acquaintance were in town, and I literally had not courage to venture alone among the Westminster boys at the Abbey; they are as formidable to me as the ship-carpenters at Portsmouth.[15] I think I have showed you the inscription,[16] and therefore I don't send it you.

I was reading t'other day the life of Colonel Codrington,[17] who founded the library at All Souls': he left a large estate for the propagation of the Gospel, and ordered that three hundred Negroes should constantly be employed upon it:[18] did one ever hear a more truly Christian charity, than keeping up a perpetuity of three hundred slaves to look after the Gospel's estate? How could one intend a religious legacy, and miss the disposition of that estate for delivering three hundred Negroes from the most shocking slavery imagable? Must devotion be twisted into the unfeeling interests of trade? I must revenge myself for the horror this fact has given me, and tell you a story of Gideon.[19] He breeds his children Christians: he had a

12. Mr Walpole had commissioned Mr Bentley to send him a piece of the granite found in the island of Jersey, for a side-board in his dining-room. It is now at Strawberry Hill (Mary Berry).

13. For an account of this monument, see 'Short Notes,' Gray i. 26 and n. 170.

14. The coffin of the last king of France stood on the first steps leading to the high altar of the Church of St-Denis until replaced by his successor (William Cole, *Journal of My Visit to Paris*, ed. F. G. Stokes, 1931, p. 308). HW had seen that of Louis XIV when he visited St-Denis with Gray in April 1739 (Gray i. 163).

15. This unexplained incident apparently occurred in August 1745; see Fox to HW 22 July 1746 (Selwyn 103 and n. 12).

16. Which is printed in *Works* i. 131; there is a MS copy in HW's *MS Poems* 226. It was written at Florence in 1740 (ibid. 225).

17. Christopher Codrington (1668–1710), wit and scholar, commander-in-chief of the Leeward Islands. HW was probably reading the account of him in the second volume (1748) of the *Biographia Britannica* (see following note); HW's set is Hazen, *Cat. of HW's Lib.*, No. 2041.

18. 'By his last will, he bequeathed his two plantations in Barbadoes, and part of the island of Barbuda, to the Society for the Propagation of the Gospel in foreign parts. And desired, that the plantations should continue entire; and three hundred Negroes, at least, should always be kept thereon' (*Biographia Britannica*, 1747–66, ii. 1375). The slaves were branded with 'Society' on the chest (*Country Life*, 1972, clii. 1753).

19. Sampson Gideon [1699–1762], a noted rich Jew (HW).

mind to know what proficience his son[20] had made in his new religion; 'so,' says he, 'I began, and asked him, who made him? He said, "God." I then asked him, who redeemed him? He replied very readily, "Christ." Well, then I was at the end of my interrogatories, and did not know what other question to put to him—I said, "Who —who—" I did not know what to say—at last I said, "Who gave you that hat?" "The Holy Ghost," said the boy.'—Did you ever hear a better catechism?—The great cry against Nugent[21] at Bristol was for having voted for the Jew Bill:[22] one old woman said, 'What, must we be represented by a Jew and an Irishman?' He replied, with great quickness, 'My good dame, if you will step aside with me into a corner, I will show you that I am *not* a Jew, and that *I am* an Irishman.'

The Princess[23] has breakfasted at the long Sir Thomas Robinson's[24] at Whitehall:[25] my Lady T[ownshend] will never forgive it.[26] The second Dowager of Somerset[27] is gone to know whether all her letters from the living to the dead have been received.[28] Before I bid you good-night, I must tell you of an admirable curiosity: I was looking over one of our antiquarian volumes,[29] and in the description of Leeds is an account of Mr Thoresby's[30] famous museum there— What do you think is one of the rarities? *A knife taken from one of*

20. Sampson Gideon (1745–1824), cr. (1789) Bn Eardley of Spalding; M.P.
21. Robert Nugent (1709–88), cr. (1767) Vct Clare, (1776) E. Nugent; M.P. St Mawes 1741–54, 1774–84, Bristol 1754–74.
22. The bill for the naturalization of the Jews, passed in the spring of 1753 and was repealed in the autumn (*ante* HW to Chute 4 Aug. 1753, n. 9). Nugent's speech in support of the Bill 17 April 1753 is printed by Claud Nugent, *Memoir of Robert, Earl Nugent*, 1898, pp. 42–6; he also voted for the repeal (ibid. 62). His support for the Bill is mentioned in a Bristol election broadside of March 1754 (ibid. 64).
23. Of Wales (HW).
24. Sir Thomas Robinson (?1702–77), cr. (1731) Bt; M.P.; amateur architect.
25. Formerly No. 5 Whitehall Gardens, the smaller half of Holdernesse House, which Robinson had purchased in 1749, demolished and rebuilt (London County Council, *Survey of London*, xiii [Parish of St Margaret, Westminster], pt ii, 1930, pp. 157–8).
26. Lady Townshend occupied the other (and larger) half of Holdernesse House (ibid. 153).
27. Frances Thynne (HW). (1699–7 July 1754), m. (1715) Algernon Seymour, styled M. of Hertford, 7th D. of Somerset, 1748; the patroness of Thomson, Watts, and Shenstone. For her biography, see H. S. Hughes, *The Gentle Hertford*, New York, 1940. HW calls her the 'second' to distinguish from the widow of the 6th (the Proud) Duke, who was still living.
28. The Duchess had become very religious in her later years, but no letters 'from the living to the dead' are mentioned in her biography.
29. Presumably Thoresby's *Ducatus Leodiensis: or, The Topography . . . of Leedes*, 1715 (Hazen, *Cat. of HW's Lib.*, No. 612; n. 31 below).
30. Ralph Thoresby (1658–1725), antiquary.

the Mohocks!³¹ Whether *tradition is infallible or not,* as you say, I think so authentic a relique will make their history indisputable—Castles, Chinese houses, tombs, Negroes, Jews, Irishmen, princesses, and Mohocks—what a farrago do I send you! I trust that a letter from England to Jersey has an imposing air, and that you don't presume to laugh at anything that comes from your mother island. Adieu!

Yours ever,

Hor. Walpole

To Bentley, Thursday 11 July 1754

Missing; mentioned *post* 27 July 1754.

From Bentley, Monday 15 July 1754

Missing; mentioned *post* 27 July 1754.

To Bentley, Tuesday 23 July 1754

Missing; mentioned *post* 27 July 1754.

To Bentley, Saturday 27 July 1754

Printed from Toynbee *Supp.* i. 67–9. The MS was among those that passed from HW to Mrs Damer; bequeathed by her to Sir Wathen Waller, 1st Bt; sold Sotheby's 5 Dec. 1921 (first Waller sale) lot 8 to an unknown purchaser.

Arlington Street, Saturday, July 27, 1754.

THOUGH I wrote to you but last Tuesday, besides a letter on the 11th, I must send away another tonight in haste; as I am uneasy at the last paragraph of your great dispatch of the 15th,

31. '*A knife* taken from one of the *Mohawks* at *London,* An. 1710, Don. D. *Jo. Cookson Lond.*' (Thoresby, op. cit. 486).

which I received but this morning at Strawberry Hill, from whence I am just arrived on business. I don't want tenderness for you, my dear Sir, so much as to make a merit of more than I had: I do assure you, I wrote no such letter to Mr Seward[1] as his wife mentioned to you, and I very much fear it was some wicked art of Miss Vavassor's.[2] Keep on your guard, till I am able to tell you farther. I am going to write to Seward, to desire he will send me *that letter*. As I have received no answer from him to *that* inquiry, he must have been desired to direct to some other place than Arlington Street, which may give a clue to an *éclaircissement*. I shall not grieve if I can detect Miss Vavassor in counterfeiting my hand; it will be such a check on her ecclesiastic processes, as can only effectuate that return, about which you seem to make to yourself your old visions, overlooking what I said to you about Doctors' Commons. Without her iniquity will be so good as to entrap itself, I don't see upon what foundation we can build, though sure nobody ever meditated more schemes than I do for seeing you, though unfortunately mine prove to have as little stability as yours.

As I have not yet received Mabland,[3] which I suppose travels at its leisure, I have nothing to soften a little stock of peevishness, which is very ready to break out. In the first place, my chairs![4] if you had taken a quarter of the time to draw what they might be, that you have employed to describe what they must not be, I might possibly have had some begun by this time. Would not one think that it was I who make charming drawings and designs and not you? I shall have very little satisfaction in them, if I am to invent them! My idea is, a black back, higher, but not much higher than common chairs, and extremely light, with matted bottoms. As I found yours came

1. Presumably the Mr S. mentioned *post* HW to Bentley 11 Nov. 1754, 9 Jan. and 18 Sept. 1755. From the last reference, it appears that he lived at Southampton.

2. Presumably the 'Miss ——' to whom overtures were being made in April 1755 to prevent her raising impediments to Bentley's return to England (*post* HW to Bentley 13 April 1755). Why she was pursuing Bentley in the ecclesiastical courts does not appear, but it suggests that the reasons for his exile in Jersey were not wholly financial. Nearly all the passages in this correspondence relating to Bent-

ley's private affairs were omitted when the letters were published by Miss Berry.

3. Apparently a book of Bentley's drawings, from the references to it, *post* HW to Bentley 5 July and 18 Sept. 1755.

4. For the Refectory or Great Parlour, 'black, of a gothic pattern, designed by Mr Bentley and Mr Walpole' ('Des. of SH,' *Works* ii. 402). HW paid Hallet £30 for them 20 Sept. 1755 (*SH Accounts,* ed. Toynbee, Oxford, 1927, p. 6). Four of the eight which were sold SH xix. 49–52 are now WSL. The design copied a stained-glass window at SH (album now WSL of Bentley's drawings, annotated by HW).

not, I have been trying to make out something like the windows—
for example

[here⁵ is a drawing of a chair with a back resembling a
three-light ecclesiastical window]

I would have only a sort of black sticks, pierced through: you must
hatch this egg soon, for I want chairs in the room extremely.

In the next place, you send me a letter to Captain Lis⁶ to take
care of fish and fowls for you, at the very time you believe him
sailed, and without allowing me any time to get them ready. However, as I have a little more thought and contrivance than you
(luckily for us both!) I have written to him⁷ to advertise me against
his next sailing, and then you shall have bantams and gold-fish: for
the latter, (for their sakes) I must insist on their being delivered
to the Governor;⁸ I can't allow you to reserve one for yourself, to
be kept in a pan like a water souchy.⁹ I told you I was peevish—now
you will believe it.

I will not insist on any particular colour for the granite. I was
afraid you could not find pieces large enough to answer my dimen-
sions, but I perceive that my Lilliputian castle might stand upon
one of your shelfs of Brobdignag granite. I do not mean to put you
to any expense about it, my dear Sir, but desire to pay for everything
of that kind, exclusively of your quarters—I would certainly give
you no commissions upon any other condition. I shall now bid you
good-night, and go write to Seward.

Yours ever,

H. W.

PS. You shall have Indian ink and colours soon.

5. So printed Toynbee *Supp.*, instead of
a cut.

6. John and 'Ph.' Lys are mentioned in
a list of ship captains in A. C. Saunders,
Jersey in the 18th and 19th Centuries, Jersey, 1930, pp. 29–30.

7. HW's letter is missing.

8. Gen. John Huske (ca 1692–1761) was
governor of Jersey (*Court and City Register*, 1754, p. 163; DNB).

9. 'Fish (properly perch) boiled and
served in its own liquor' (OED). HW also
uses the phrase to mean sodden mass
(ibid.).

From Bentley, October 1754

Missing; mentioned *post* 11 Nov. 1754.

From Bentley, Sunday 3 November 1754

Missing; mentioned *post* 20 November 1754.

To Bentley, Sunday 3 November 1754

Printed from *Works* v. 295–8; reprinted, Wright iii. 75–8, Cunningham ii. 400–3, Toynbee iii. 257–61.

Strawberry Hill, November 3, 1754.

I HAVE finished all my parties, and am drawing towards a conclusion here: the Parliament meets in ten days:[1] the House, I hear, will be extremely full—curiosity drawing as many to town as party used to do. The minister[2] in the House of Lords is a new sight in these days.[3]

Mr Chute and I have been at Mr Barret's[4] at Belhouse;[5] I never saw a place for which one did not wish, so totally void of faults. What he has done is in Gothic,[6] and very true, though not up to the perfection of the committee. The hall is pretty;[7] the great dining-

1. Parliament met on 14 Nov. 1754 (*Journals of the House of Commons* xxvii. 13).

2. The Duke of Newcastle (HW).

3. Except for the Earl of Wilmington's tenure (1742–3) as a figurehead first lord of the Treasury, the first lord had sat in the House of Commons since Sir Robert Walpole came to power in 1721.

4. Afterwards Lord Dacre (HW). He and Chute were distantly related (*ante* HW to Chute 4 Aug. 1753).

5. Properly Belhus, near Aveley, Essex. The house, built in the reign of Henry VIII, somewhat renovated in the early eighteenth century, and 'gothicized' by

Barrett, is illustrated and described by H. A. Tipping in *Country Life*, 1920, xlvii. 656–62, 690–6. HW paid another visit in 1761, described in his *Country Seats* 34.

6. Barrett had been remodelling Belhus with the advice of Sanderson Miller since 1745 (*An Eighteenth-Century Correspondence*, ed. Lilian Dickins and Mary Stanton, New York, 1910, pp. 111, 310–13). Miller's active work there had started in 1751 (information from Mr Michael McCarthy).

7. It had been 'fitted up' in 1745 (ibid. 111); there are photographs of it in *Country Life*, op. cit. xlvii. 660, 661.

room[8] hung with good family pictures;[9] among which is his ancestor, the Lord Dacre, who was hanged.[10] I remember, when Barret was first initiated in the College of Arms by the present Dean of Exeter[11] at Cambridge,[12] he was overjoyed at the first ancestor he *put up*, who was one of the murderers of Thomas Becket.[13] The chimney-pieces, except one little miscarriage into total Ionic[14] (he could not resist statuary and Siena marble),[15] are all of a good King James I Gothic. I saw the heronry so fatal to Po Yang,[16] and told him that I was persuaded they were descended from Becket's assassin, and I hoped from my Lord Dacre too. He carried us to see the famous plantations and buildings of the last Lord Petre.[17] They are the Brobdignag of bad taste. The unfinished house is execrable, massive, and split through and through: it stands on the brow of a hill, rather to see *for* a prospect than to see one, and turns its back upon an outrageous avenue, which is closed with a screen of tall trees, because he would not be at the expense of beautifying the back front of his house. The clumps are gigantic, and very ill placed.

George Montagu and the Colonel have at last been here,[18] and have screamed with approbation through the whole *Cu*-gamut.[19] In-

8. Formerly the Hall of the old house; redecorated in 1752 (Dickins and Stanton, op. cit. 190, 311–12); there is a photograph of it in *Country Life*, op. cit. xlvii. 692.

9. Described in HW's *Country Seats*, loc. cit.; several of them are illustrated in the article in *Country Life*.

10. Thomas Fiennes, 9th Bn Dacre; for the incident, see *ante* HW to Bentley 5 Aug. 1752 and nn. 79, 82–5.

11. Dr Charles Lyttelton (HW). (1714–68), antiquary; Dean of Exeter 1747–62; Bp of Carlisle 1762–8; HW's early friend and correspondent.

12. HW may be referring to the Society of Antiquaries, of which Lyttelton and Barrett were fellows.

13. Thomas à Becket (ca 1118–70), Abp of Canterbury; saint. His murderer, from whom Barrett was descended, was Hugh de Morville (d. 1204), whose daughter Ada married as her second husband Thomas de Multon, great-great-great-grandfather of the wife of the 1st Bn Dacre (see GEC ix. *sub* Multon of Gilsland; iv. *sub*

Dacre; and DNB *sub* Hugh de Morville). There seem to have been other connections between the Multons and the Dacres in the 13th century as well.

14. In the North or Tapestry Room, illustrated in *Country Life* xlvii. 657. It had been recently completed by the joint efforts of Barrett and Miller (ibid. 662).

15. Apparently an allusion to Barrett's Italian tour in 1749–50; see the HW-Mann correspondence for these years, for details.

16. HW's gold-fish pond; see *ante* HW to Bentley 19 Dec. 1753.

17. Robert James Petre (1713–42), 8th Bn Petre, 1713. His unfinished house, Thorndon Hall, near Brentwood, Essex, was pulled down and a new one built in 1764 by James Paine for the 9th Bn Petre.

18. They were at SH by 24 Oct. (HW to Conway 24 Oct. 1754).

19. Mr George Montagu, who used many odd expressions, called his own family the Montagus the *Cu's* (HW).

deed, the library is delightful. They went to the Vine,[20] and approved as much. Do you think we wished for you? I carried down incense and mass-books, and we had most Catholic enjoyment of the chapel.[21] In the evenings, indeed, we did *touch a card*[22] a little to please George—so much, that truly I have scarce an idea left that is not spotted with clubs, hearts, spades and diamonds. There is a vote of the Strawberry committee for great embellishments to the chapel,[23] of which it will not be long before you hear something. It will not be longer than the spring, I trust, before you see something of it. In the mean time, to rest your impatience, I have enclosed a scratch of mine,[24] which you are to draw out better, and try if you can give yourself a perfect idea of the place. All I can say is, that my sketch is at least more intelligible than Gray's was of Stoke,[25] from which you made so like a picture.[26]

Thank you much for the box of Guernsey lilies, which I have received. I have been packing up a few seeds, which have little merit but the merit they will have with you, that they come from the Vine and Strawberry. My chief employ in this part of the world, except surveying my library, which has scarce anything but the painting to finish, is planting at Mrs Clive's,[27] whither I remove all my superabundancies. I have lately planted the green lane, that leads from her garden to the common: 'Well,' said she, 'when it is done, what shall we call it?'—'Why,' said I, 'what would you call it but Drury Lane?' I mentioned desiring some samples of your Swiss's[28] abilities: Mr Chute and I even propose, if he should be tolerable, and would continue reasonable, to tempt him over hither, and make him work upon your designs—upon which, you know, it is not easy to make you work. If he improves upon our hands, do you think we shall purchase the fee-simple of him for so many years, as Mr Smith did of Canaletti?[29] We will *sell to the English.* Can he

20. On 26 Oct. (HW to Conway 24 Oct. 1754).

21. For a description of the chapel at the Vyne, see C. W. Chute, *A History of the Vyne*, 1888, pp. 11–28.

22. An expression of Mr Montagu's (HW).

23. For these, see HW's 'Inventionary of alterations to be made at the Vine, 1 July 1755' (*post* Appendix 1).

24. Missing.

25. Gray's sketch of Stoke Manor House,

now WSL, is reproduced in Gray ii. 59.

26. Bentley followed Gray's sketch in the headpiece for 'A Long Story' in *Designs by Mr R. Bentley for Six Poems by Mr T. Gray*, 1753. Bentley's original drawings are now WSL.

27. Little Strawberry Hill.

28. Mr Müntz, a Swiss painter (HW).

29. Mr Smith, the English consul at Venice, had engaged Canaletti [Antonio Canal (1697–1768)] for a certain number of years to paint exclusively for him

paint perspectives, and cathedral-aisles, and holy glooms? I am sure you could make him paint delightful insides of the chapel at the Vine,[29a] and of the library here. I never come up the stairs without reflecting how different it is from its primitive state, when my Lady T[ownshend] all the way she came up the stairs, cried out, 'Lord God! Jesus! what a house! It is just such a house as a parson's, where the children lie at the feet of the bed!' I can't say that today it puts me much in mind of another speech of my Lady's, 'that it would be a very pleasant place, if Mrs Clive's face did not rise upon it and make it so hot!' The sun and Mrs Clive seem gone for the winter.

The West Indian war[30] has thrown me into a new study: I read nothing but American voyages, and histories of plantations and settlements.[31] Among all the Indian nations, I have contracted a particular intimacy with the Ontaouanoucs, a people with whom I beg you will be acquainted: they pique themselves upon speaking the purest dialect.[32] How one should delight in the grammar and dictionary of their Crusca![33] My only fear is, that if any of them are taken prisoners, General Braddock is not a kind of man[34] to have proper attentions to so polite a people; I am even apprehensive that he would damn them, and order them to be scalped, in the very worst plantation-accent. I don't know whether you know that none of the people of that immense continent have any labials: they tell you *que c'est ridicule* to shut the lips, in order to speak.[35] Indeed I

at a fixed price, and sold his pictures at an advanced price to English travellers (Mary Berry). See *ante* Chute to HW 22 Aug. 1741 NS. K. T. Parker, in *The Drawings of Antonio Canaletto*, 1948, p. 10, doubts the accuracy of these statements by HW and Mary Berry. Smith made the collection of Canaletto which was bought by George III and is now at Windsor Castle.

29a. Müntz went to the Vyne in 1755, and stayed about six months without painting the chapel; this was done later by Roma whose receipt is dated 5 Oct. 1771 (Hampshire County Record Office 31M57/639-27v., courtesy of Mr Michael McCarthy).

30. The clashes with the French and Indians in North America. See HW to Mann 6 Oct. 1754, Mann iv. 448, 449-50.

31. HW's sources for this paragraph were Charlevoix's *Histoire et description*

générale de la Nouvelle France, 1744 (of which there is no copy recorded in HW's library), and Cadwallader Colden's *History of the Five Indian Nations of Canada*, 2d edn, 1750 (Hazen, *Cat. of HW's Lib.*, No. 1400).

32. Charlevoix, in his account of the Hurons, mentions that 'quelquesuns se donnent le nom de Ontaouonoués, c'est-à-dire ceux, qui parlent la meilleure langue' (op. cit. i. 184).

33. Alluding to the dictionary of the Accademia della Crusca at Florence.

34. For anecdotes of Braddock's brutality, see HW to Mann 21 and 28 Aug. 1755, Mann v. 492-3, 494-5. He was to command the troops being sent to America to drive the French from their recent encroachments in the Mississippi valley.

35. 'They [the Five Nations] have no labials in their language, nor can they

was as barbarous as any polite nation in the world, in supposing that there was nothing worth knowing among these charming savages. They are in particular great orators, with this little variation from British eloquence, that at the end of every important paragraph they make a present;[36] whereas we expect to receive one. They begin all their answers with recapitulating what has been said to them; and their method for this is, the respondent gives a little stick to each of the bystanders, who is, for his share, to remember such a paragraph of the speech that is to be answered.[37] You will wonder that I should have given the preference to the Ontaouanoucs, when there is a much more extraordinary nation to the north of Canada, who have but one leg, and p— from behind their ear; but I own I had rather converse for any time with people who speak like Mr Pitt, than with a nation of jugglers, who are only fit to go about the country, under the direction of T[aaffe] and M[ontagu].[38] Their existence I do not doubt; they are recorded by Père Charlevoix,[39] in his much-admired history of New France, in which there are such outrageous legends of miracles for the propagation of the Gospel, that his fables in natural history seem strict veracity.

Adieu! You write to me as seldom as if you were in an island

pronounce perfectly any word wherein there is a labial, and when one endeavours to teach them to pronounce these words, they tell one they think it ridiculous that they must shut their lips to speak' (Colden, op. cit. 15).

36. Although Colden does not specifically discuss this custom, nearly every paragraph of the Indian speeches he quotes concludes with a statement of the gift given to confirm the words.

37. 'They commonly repeat over all that has been said to them, before they return any answer, and one may be surprised at the exactness of these repetitions. They take the following method to assist their memories: the *sachem*, who presides at these conferences, has a bundle of small sticks in his hand; as soon as the speaker has finished any one article of his speech, this sachem gives a stick to another *sachem*, who is particularly to remember that article, and so when another article is finished, he gives a stick to another to take care of that other, and so on. In like manner, when the speaker answers,

each of these has the particular care of the answer resolved on to each article, and prompts the orator, when his memory fails him, in the article committed to his charge' (ibid. 100–1).

38. Two English gentlemen who were shut up in Fort l'Évêque for cheating a Jew (HW). They were Theobald Taaffe (ca 1708–80), M.P., and Edward Wortley Montagu (1713–76), M.P. For the incident, which occurred in 1751, see MANN iii. 450, n. 13, iv. 287–9 and nn. 13–25 and v. 473, n. 14.

39. Pierre-Francois-Xavier de Charlevoix (1682–1761), author of *Histoire et description générale de la Nouvelle France*, 1744. The passage HW refers to is as follows: 'Elle [a female slave of the Eskimos] avait vu dans son pays deux hommes d'une grandeur et d'une grosseur monstreuses, qui rendaient leurs excréments par la bouche, et urinaient par-dessous l'épaule. Elle dit encore que parmi ses compatriotes il y avait une autre sorte d'hommes, qui n'ont qu'une jambe . . .' (*Histoire*, i. 17).

where the Duke of N[ewcastle] was sole minister, parties at an end, and where everything had done happening.

Yours ever,

Hor. Walpole

PS. I have just seen in the advertisements that there are arrived two new volumes of Madame de Sévigné's letters.[40]—Adieu, my American studies!—adieu, even my favourite Ontaouanoucs!

To Bentley, Monday 11 November 1754

Printed from *Works* v. 298–9; reprinted, Wright iii. 79–80, Cunningham ii. 404–5, Toynbee iii. 262–3.

Arlington Street, Nov. 11, 1754.

IF YOU was dead, to be sure you would have got somebody to tell me so. If you was alive, to be sure in all this time you would have told me so yourself. It is a month today since I received a line from you. There was a Florentine ambassador here in Oliver's reign, who with great circumspection wrote to his Court, 'Some say the Protector is dead, others say he is not: for my part, I believe neither one nor t'other.'[1] I quote this sage personage, to show you that I have a good precedent, in case I had a mind to continue neutral upon the point of your existence. I can't resolve to believe you dead, lest I should be forced to write to Mr S.[2] again to bemoan you; and on the other hand, it is convenient to me to believe you living, because I have just received the enclosed from your sister,[3] and the money from Ely. However, if you are actually dead, be so good as to order

40. *Lettres nouvelles . . . Pour servir de supplément à l'édition de Paris en six volumes,* 1754. These letters had been extracted from a new 'complete' edition of Mme de Sévigné's *Lettres,* 1754, to go with a reprint of the original six-volume edition, also published in 1754 (Mme de Sévigné, *Lettres,* ed. Monmerqué, 1862–6, xi. 444, 446). HW's set is Hazen, *Cat. of HW's Lib.,* No. 950; his set of the second edition, 1738, of the six-volume edition is ibid., No. 949. He discusses and quotes from the new letters *post* 11 Nov., 20 Nov and 24 Dec. The advertisement which he saw has not been found.

1. HW's source for this anecdote, which he also relates in his letter to Mann 2 Aug. 1750 OS (Mann iv. 170), has not been found. The Florentine resident in England at the time of Cromwell's death was Giovanni Salvetti Antelminelli, resident 1657–80 (ibid. n. 43).

2. Presumably Mr Seward as *ante* HW to Bentley 27 July 1754.

3. Probably Mrs Cumberland.

your executor to receive the money and to answer your sister's letter. If you are not dead, I can tell you who is, and at the same time whose death is to remain as doubtful as yours till tomorrow morning. Don't be alarmed! it is only the Queen Dowager of Prussia.[4] As *excessive* as the concern for her is at Court, the whole royal family, out of great consideration for the mercers, lacemen, etc. agreed not to shed a tear for her till tomorrow morning, when the Birthdays[5] will be over; but they are all to rise by six o'clock tomorrow morning to cry quarts. This is the sum of all the news that I learnt today on coming from Strawberry Hill, except that Lady Betty Waldegrave[6] was robbed t'other night in Hyde Park,[7] under the very noses of the lamps and the patrol. If anybody is robbed at the ball at Court tonight,[8] you shall hear in my next dispatch. I told you in my last that I had just got two new volumes of Madame Sévigné's letters; but I have been cruelly disappointed; they are two hundred letters[9] which had been omitted in the former editions, as having little or nothing worth reading. How provoking, that they would at last let one see that she could write so many letters that were not worth reading! I will tell you the truth: as they are certainly hers, I am glad to see them, but I cannot bear that anybody else should. Is not that

4. Sophia Dorothea (1687–1757), sister of George II, m. (1706) Frederick William I (1688–1740), King of Prussia. This erroneous rumour of her death is mentioned in the *Whitehall Evening Post* 5–7 Nov. 1754.

5. George II's birthday, on 10 Nov., was being celebrated on Monday, 11 Nov.

6. Lady Elizabeth Leveson Gower (1724–84), m. (1751) Col. John Waldegrave, 3d E. Waldegrave, 1763 (Ossory i. 275, n. 1).

7. 'On Tuesday night [5 Nov.] the Hon. Lady Elizabeth Waldegrave, Lady of the Bedchamber to the Princess Amelia, and Mrs Russell, belonging also to her Royal Highness, going in a coach to Kensington, were robbed near the Gore by two footpads, soon after eight o'clock. They took from Lady Waldegrave a gold watch, and from Mrs Russell a purse of money' (*Daily Adv.* 7 Nov.; *Whitehall Evening Post* 5–7 Nov. 1754). The latter paper amended its account on 7–9 Nov. by repeating that 'it was by two highwaymen, who waited till the House-Guard patrol were passed, then dismounted, tied their horses to the rail by the road-side, then attacked and made off with their booty.'

8. 'On Monday night [11 Nov.] there was a grand ball at St James's. The King came into the room soon after nine o'clock, when the ball was opened. His Majesty withdrew soon after eleven, and the Prince of Wales and Prince Edward continued dancing country dances till near twelve, when the ball ended. The quality, especially the ladies, made a most brilliant appearance, the dresses being as rich as art could invent, and chiefly of British manufacture. The Right Hon. the Lord Mayor was there, and received some very high compliments' (*Daily Adv.* 13 Nov. 1754).

9. According to the 'Notice bibliographique' in Monmerqué's edition of Mme de Sévigné's *Lettres*, there were only 86 letters in the *Lettres nouvelles:* there were, however, 158 more letters in the collected edition of 1754, from which these were taken, than there had been in the previous collected edition (Monmerqué, op. cit. xi. 442, 444, 446).

true sentiment? How would you like to see a letter of hers, describing a wild young Irish lord, a Lord P[owerscourt],[10] who has lately made one of our ingenious wagers, to ride I don't know how many thousand miles in an hour, from Paris to Fontainebleau?[11] But admire the *politesse* of that nation: instead of endeavouring to lame his horse, or to break his neck, that he might lose the wager, his antagonist and the spectators showed all the attention in the world to keep the road clear, and to remove even pebbles out of his way. They heaped coals of fire upon his head with all the good breeding of the Gospel. Adieu!—If my letters are short, at least my notes are long.

Yours ever,

Hor. Walpole

To Bentley, Wednesday 20 November 1754

Printed from *Works* v. 300–2; reprinted, Wright iii. 81–4, Cunningham ii. 406–8, Toynbee iii. 265–7.

Arlington Street, November 20, 1754.

IF THIS does not turn out a scolding letter, I am much mistaken. I shall give way to it with the less scruple, as I think it shall be the last of the kind; not that you will mend, but I cannot support a commerce of visions! and therefore, whenever you send me mighty cheap schemes for finding out longitudes[1] and philosophers' stones, you

---

10. Edward Wingfield (1729–64), 2d Vct Powerscourt, 1751.

11. 'Lord Powerscourt, of the kingdom of Ireland, lately laid a wager with the Duke of Orléans, that he would ride on his own horses from Fontainebleau to Paris, which is 42 English miles, in two hours, for 1000 *louis d'ors*. The king was pleased to order the Marshalsea guards to clear the way, which was lined with crowd of Parisians, and to be present when his Lordship set out. He was to mount only three horses, but did it with two; both which, however, he killed. He performed the wager in one hour, thirty-seven minutes, and twenty-two seconds'

(GM 1754, xxiv. 529). The first reports of this event, differing somewhat from the GM account, were printed in the *Daily Adv.* 6 Nov. and *Whitehall Evening Post* 5–7 Nov. from 'letters from Paris, dated October 27th,' which said the wager had taken place the preceding day. More details in the *Whitehall Evening Post* 12–14 Nov. are closer to the account in GM.

1. Parliament in 1713 had offered a reward of up to £20,000 for an accurate method of determining longitude, but none had yet been devised (see DNB *sub* John Harrison 1693–1776).

will excuse me if I only smile, and don't order them to be examined
by my council.—For heaven's sake, don't be a projector! Is not it
provoking, that, with the best parts in the world, you should have
so gentle a portion of common sense? But I am clear, that you never
will know the two things in the world that import you the most to
know, yourself and me.—Thus much by way of preface: now for
the detail.

You tell me in your letter of November 3d, that the quarry of
granite might be rented at twenty pounds or twenty shillings, I don't
know which, no matter, per annum. When I can't get a table out of
it, is it very likely you or I should get a fortune out of it? What
signifies the cheapness of the rent? The cutting and shippage would
be articles of some little consequence! Who should be supervisor?
You, who are so good a manager, so attentive, so diligent, so expeditious, and so accurate? Don't you think our quarry would turn
to account? Another article, to which I might apply the same questions, is the project for importation of French wine: it is odd that a
scheme so cheap and so practicable should hitherto have been totally
overlooked—One would think the breed of smugglers was lost, like
the true spaniels, or genuine golden pippins! My dear Sir, you know
I never drink three glasses of any wine—Can you think I care
whether they are sour or sweet, cheap or dear?—or do you think
that I, who am always taking trouble to reduce my trouble into as
compact a volume as I can, would tap such an article as importing
my own wine?[2] But now comes your last proposal about the Gothic
paper. When you made me fix up mine, unpainted, engaging to
paint it yourself, and yet could never be persuaded to paint a yard of
it, till I was forced to give Bromwich's man God knows what to do
it,[3] would you make me believe that you will paint a room eighteen
feet by fifteen?[4]—But, seriously, if it is possible for you to lay aside
visions, don't be throwing continual discouragements in my way. I
have told you seriously and emphatically, that I am labouring your
restoration: the scheme is neither facile nor immediate:—but, for

2. HW, however, had asked Mann in
1754 to send him a case of drams (Mann
iii. 177) and in 1758 a case of liqueurs
(Mann v. 203).

3. Probably the Gothic paper on the
staircase; HW had paid Bromwich
£77 17s. 2d. earlier in the year for various

work including the paper on the staircase (SH Accounts, ed. Toynbee, Oxford,
1927, p. 5).

4. This was probably the Little Parlour, which was 18 x 13 and hung with
Gothic paper ('Des. of SH,' Works ii. 418).

God's sake, act like a reasonable man. You have a family to whom
you owe serious attention. Don't let me think, that if you return,
you will set out upon every wild-goose chase, sticking to nothing,
and neglecting chiefly the talents and genius which you have in such
excellence, to start projects, which you have too much honesty and
too little application ever to thrive by. This advice is, perhaps,
worded harshly: but you know the heart from which it proceeds, and
you know that, with all my prejudice to it, I can't even pardon your
wit, when it is employed to dress up schemes that I think romantic.
The glasses and Ray's *Proverbs*[5] you shall have, and some more gold-
fish, when I have leisure to go to Strawberry; for you know I don't
suffer any fisheries to be carried on there in my absence.

I am as newsless as in the dead of summer: the Parliament produces nothing but elections: there has already been one division on
the Oxfordshire of two hundred and sixty-seven Whigs to ninety-
seven Tories:[6] you may calculate the burial of that election easily
from these numbers. The Queen of Prussia is not dead, as I told you
in my last. If you have shed many tears for her, you may set them
off to the account of our son-in-law the Prince of Hesse,[7] who is
turned Roman Catholic. One is in this age so unused to conversions
above the rank of a house-maid turned Methodist, that it occasions
as much surprise as if one had heard that he had been initiated in
the Eleusinian mysteries. Are not you prodigiously alarmed for the
Protestant interest in Germany?

We have operas, burlettas, cargos of Italian dancers, and none
good but the Mingotti,[8] a very fine figure and actress. I don't know a
single bon mot that is new: George Selwyn has not waked yet for
the winter. You will believe that, when I tell you, that t'other night
having lost eight hundred pounds at hazard, he fell asleep upon the
table with near half as much more before him, and slept for three

5. *A Collection of English Proverbs*, first
published in 1670 by John Ray (1627–
1705), the naturalist.

6. This division occurred on 18 Nov.
(*Journals of the House of Commons* xxvii.
18). For a full history of the Oxfordshire
Election of 1754, see R. J. Robson, *The
Oxfordshire Election of 1754*, 1949.

7. Friedrich Wilhelm (1720–85), Landgrave of Hesse-Cassel (1760) as Friedrich
II; m. (1740) Mary, dau. of George II.
His conversion, which had happened four
years before, was reported in the *Whitehall Evening Post* 12–14 Nov. 1754.

8. Regina Valentini (1722–1808), m.
Pietro Mingotti; soprano. Dr Burney describes her as having 'revived the favour
of our lyric theatre, with considerable
splendour' (Charles Burney, *General History of Music*, ed. Mercer, 1935, ii. 852;
Sir George Grove, *Dictionary of Music
and Musicians*, 5th edn, ed. Blom, 1954,
v. 784–5). The opera season had begun on
9 Nov. (Burney, loc. cit.).

hours, with everybody stamping the box close at his ear. He will say prodigiously good things when he does wake. In the mean time, can you be *content* with one of Madame Sévigné's best bons mots, which I have found amongst her new letters? Do you remember her German friend the Princess of Tarente,[9] who was always in mourning for some sovereign prince or princess? One day Madame de Sévigné happening to meet her in colours, made her [a] low curtsey, and said, 'Madame, je me réjouis de la santé de l'Europe.'[10] I think I may apply another of her speeches, which pleased me, to what I have said to you in the former part of my letter. Mademoiselle du Plessis[11] had said something she disapproved: Madame Sévigné said to her, 'Mais que cela est sot, car je veux vous parler doucement.'[12] Adieu!

Yours ever,

Hor. Walpole

From Bentley, Friday 22 November 1754

Missing; mentioned *post* 13 Dec. 1754.

From Bentley, Friday 6 December 1754

Missing; mentioned *post* 24 December 1754.

9. Amelie of Hesse-Cassel (1625–93), m. (1648) Henri-Charles de la Trémoïlle, Prince de Tarente (Mme de Sévigné, *Lettres*, ed. Monmerqué, 1862–6, ii. 229, n. 4).

10. This is in a letter to Mme de Grignan, 4 Oct. 1684 (ibid. vii. 299). The 'low curtsey' is HW's addition.

11. Mlle du Plessis d'Argentré, Mme de Sévigné's neighbour in Brittany, whom she frequently ridiculed (ibid. ii. 229, n. 3 *et passim*).

12. In a letter to Mme de Grignan, 16 Oct. 1680 (ibid. vii. 110).

To Bentley, Friday 13 December 1754

Printed from *Works* v. 302–4; reprinted, Wright iii. 87–9, Cunningham ii. 411–13, Toynbee iii. 271–4.

Arlington Street, Friday, December 13, 1754.

IF WE do not make this effort to recover our dignity, we shall only sit here to register the arbitrary edicts of one too powerful a subject!'—*Non riconosci tu l'altero viso?*[1] Don't you at once know the style? Shake those words altogether, and see if they can be anything but the *disjecti membra* of Pitt!—In short, about a fortnight ago,[2] this bomb burst. Pitt, who is well, is married,[3] is dissatisfied—not with his bride, but with the Duke of N.; has twice[4] thundered out his dissatisfaction in Parliament, and was seconded by Fox.[5] The event was exactly what I dare say you have already foreseen. Pitt *was to be* turned out; overtures were made to Fox;[6] Pitt is *not* turned out; Fox is quieted with the dignity of cabinet-councillor, and the Duke of N. remains affronted—and omnipotent. The commentary on this text is too long for a letter; it may be developed some time or other.[7] This scene has produced a diverting interlude: Sir George Lyttelton, who could not reconcile his content with Mr Pitt's discontents, has been very ill with the cousinhood. In the grief of his heart he thought of resigning his place;[8] but *somehow or other,*[9] stumbled upon a negotiation for introducing the Duke of Bedford into the ministry again, to balance the loss of Mr Pitt. Whatever persuaded him, he thought this treaty so sure of success, that he lost no time to be the agent of it himself; and whether commissioned or non-commissioned, as both he and the Duke of N. say, he carried

1. 'Don't you recognize the proud face?'

2. 25 Nov. 1754. HW repeats this quotation from Pitt's speech in *Mem. Geo. II* i. 408; and Fox, who claims to have 'verified' Pitt's words, gives virtually the same ones (James, 2d E. Waldegrave, *Memoirs,* 1821, p. 147).

3. Pitt had married, 15 Nov., Lady Hester Grenville (1720–1803), cr. (1761) Bns Chatham, s.j.

4. Pitt had denounced the ministry in a second speech on the 25th (*Mem. Geo. II* i. 409–10; Waldegrave, op. cit. 149); and on the 27th had attacked the Jacobites with some slightly veiled references to

Attorney-General Murray (ibid. 151–2; *Mem. Geo. II* i. 412–13).

5. On the 25th (ibid. i. 416; Waldegrave, op. cit. 149; Lord Ilchester, *Henry Fox,* 1920, i. 363).

6. These are discussed by Ilchester, op. cit. i. 231–9.

7. I.e., in HW's memoirs; he discusses these events in *Mem. Geo. II* i. 417–20.

8. Lyttelton was cofferer of the Household.

9. Through HW himself, who told Conway, who told Lyttelton, who approached the Duke of Bedford. See *Mem. Geo. II* i. 414–17 for an account of this 'interlude.'

carte blanche to the Duke of B[edford], who bounced like a rocket, frightened away poor Sir George, and sent for Mr Pitt to notify the overture. Pitt and the Grenvilles¹⁰ are outrageous; the Duke of N. disclaims his ambassador, and everybody laughs. Sir George came hither yesterday, to *expectorate* with me, as he called it. Think how I pricked up my ears, as high as King Midas, to hear a Lyttelton vent his grievances against a Pitt and Grenvilles! Lord Temple has named Sir George the *apostolic nuncio;* and George Selwyn says, 'that he will certainly be invited by Miss A—¹¹ among the foreign ministers.' These are greater storms than perhaps you expected yet: they have occasioned mighty bustle, and whisper, and speculation; but you see

*Pulveris exigui iactu composta quiescunt!*¹²

You will be diverted with a collateral incident.—met Dick Edgecumbe,¹³ and asked him with great importance if he knew whether Mr Pitt was out. Edgecumbe, who thinks nothing important that is not to be decided by dice, and who consequently had never once thought of Pitt's political state, replied, 'Yes.'—'Ay! how do you know?'—'Why, I called at his door just now, and his porter told me so.' Another political event is, that Lord E[gmont] comes into place;¹⁴ he is to succeed Lord Fitzwalter,¹⁵ who is to have Lord Grantham's pension,¹⁶ who is dead immensely rich¹⁷—I think this

---

10. George Grenville and his brothers, Richard Grenville Temple (1711–79), 1st E. Temple, 1752, and James Grenville (1715–83), M.P.

11. Probably Elizabeth Ashe, m. 1 (1751) Edward Wortley Montagu, by whom she was soon deserted; m. 2 (1761) Capt. Robert Faulknor; the 'Pollard' Ashe. Despite her marriage to Wortley Montagu, she seems to have continued to be known as Miss Ashe. She is reported to have been for some years the mistress of Count Haszlang, the Bavarian minister (MONTAGU i. 106, n. 13).

12. 'They may be laid to rest by the scatterings of a little dust' (Virgil, *Georgics* iv. 87).

13. Richard Edgcumbe (1716–61), 2d Bn Edgcumbe, 1758; M.P.; HW's friend and occasional correspondent.

14. Egmont was to become treasurer of the Household, at the request of the Princess of Wales, but was so overwhelmed by an attack by Charles Townshend in the debate on 11 Dec. that he declined the appointment (*Mem. Geo. II* i. 421–2). The news, as HW reports it, was given in the *Whitehall Evening Post* 10–12 Dec.

15. Benjamin Mildmay (1672–1756), 19th Bn Fitzwalter, cr. (1730) E. Fitzwalter; treasurer of the Household 1737–55.

16. Henry Nassau d' Auverquerque (ca 1672 – 5 Dec. 1754), cr. (1698) E. of Grantham, had enjoyed a pension of £1,000 per annum since 1709 in consideration of his father's services in subduing Ireland (GEC vi. 81 n. *e*).

17. 'We hear that by the will of the late Earl of Grantham, Lord Fordage [*sic*], eldest son of Earl Cowper, who married his Lordship's daughter, becomes possessed of £100,000 ready money, and £4000 per annum, and a reversion of £100,000 after the death of Lady Frances Elliot, his Lordship's other daughter' (*Daily Adv.* 11 Dec. 1754).

is the last of the old Opposition of any name except Sir John Bernard[18]—If you have curiosity about the Ohio, you must write to France: there I believe they know something about it: here it was totally forgot, till last night, when an express arrived with an account of the loss of one of the transports off Falmouth,[19] with eight officers and sixty men on board.

My Lady T[ownshend] has been dying, and was woefully frightened, and *took* prayers; but she is recovered now, even of her repentance. You will not be undiverted to hear that the mob of Sudbury have literally sent a *card* to the mob of Bury, to offer their assistance at a contested election there:[20] I hope to be able to tell you in my next that Mrs H[olman][21] has sent cards to both mobs for her assembly.

The shrubs shall be sent, but you must stay till the holidays; I shall not have time to go to Strawberry sooner. I have received your second letter, dated November 22d, about the Gothic paper. I hope you will by this time have got mine, to dissuade you from that thought. If you insist upon it, I will send the paper: I have told you what I think, and will therefore say no more on that head; but I will transcribe a passage which I found t'other day in Petronius, and thought not unapplicable to you: 'Omnium herbarum succos Democritus expressit; et ne lapidum virgultorumque vis lateret, ætatem inter experimenta consumpsit.'[22] I hope Democritus could not draw charmingly, when he threw away his time in extracting tints from flints and twigs!

I can't conclude my letter without telling you what an escape I had at the sale of Dr Meade's library, which goes extremely dear.[23] In the catalogue I saw Winstanley's views of Audley Inn,[24] which

18. I.e., Sir John Barnard (*ante* HW to Chute 4 Aug. 1753, n. 64).

19. This was a false report; it was the *Olive Branch*, a merchantman bound for Spain, that sank off Falmouth, not one of the transports going to America (*Daily Adv.* 14 Dec. 1754; *Whitehall Evening Post* 12–14 Dec. 1754).

20. At the Bury St Edmunds election in April 1754, Augustus John Hervey, later 3d E. of Bristol, and his uncle Felton Hervey had tried for second place in the poll. This double return was voided by the House of Commons on 2 Dec. and a new election ordered (*Journals of the House of Commons* xxvii. 38) at which Felton was returned. Details of the

original contest are in W. S. Childe-Pemberton, *The Earl Bishop*, New York, [1925], i. 35–9, 42–6. The 'card' from the mob at Sudbury, which HW probably saw in a newspaper, has not been found.

21. Who had a passion for holding assemblies; see MONTAGU i. 127, n. 11.

22. 'Democritus extracted the juice of every plant on earth, and spent his whole life in experiments to discover the virtues of stones and twigs' (Petronius, *Satyricon* 88).

23. The sale of the first part of his library produced £2,475 18s. 6d. (GM 1754, xxiv. 577).

24. . . . *Ground-platts, General and Particular Prospects of . . . Audley End,*

I concluded was, as it really was, a thin dirty folio worth about fifteen shillings. As I thought it might be scarce, it might run to two
or three guineas: however, I bid Graham²⁵ *certainly* buy it for me.
He came the next morning in a great fright, said he did not know
whether he had done very right or very wrong, that he had gone as
far as *nine-and-forty guineas*—I started in such a fright! Another
bookseller had luckily had as unlimited a commission, and bid fifty
—when my Graham²⁶ begged it might be adjourned, till they could
consult their principals. I think I shall never give an unbounded
commission again, even for views of *Les Rochers!*²⁷ Adieu! Am I
ever to see any more of your *hand-drawing?* Adieu!

Yours ever,

HOR. WALPOLE

To BENTLEY, Tuesday 24 December 1754

Printed from *Works* v. 304–6; reprinted, Wright iii. 89–92, Cunningham ii.
413–15, Toynbee iii. 274–7.

Strawberry Hill, December 24, 1754.

My dear Sir,

I RECEIVED your packet of December 6th, last night, but intending to come hither for a few days, had unluckily sent away
by the coach in the morning a parcel of things for you; you must
therefore wait till another bundle sets out, for the new letters of Madame Sévigné. Heaven forbid that I should have said they were bad! I

Littlebury, [1676–88], a set of 24 plans
and views of Audley End by Henry Winstanley (1644–1703), engineer and engraver. Mead's copy was lot 440, 3 Dec.
1754. HW secured a copy in 1757 at the
sale of Vertue's prints and drawings for
£3 10s. (Hazen, *Cat. of HW's Lib.*, No.
3480).

25. Josiah Graham, a bookseller at the
corner of Craven Street in the Strand;
published the 2d edn of HW's *Letter
from Xo Ho*, 1757 (H. R. Plomer *et al.*,
*A Dictionary of the Printers and Book-
sellers . . . 1726 to 1775*, Oxford, 1932, p.
107; Hazen, *Bibl. of HW* 41).

26. The successful bidder at £50, according to HW's note in his own copy of
Gough's *British Topography* in the Huntington Library, was Thomas Barrett of
Lee in Kent, the father of HW's friend
and correspondent of the same name
(Hazen, *Cat. of HW's Lib.*, No. 3480).

27. Mme de Sévigné's seat in Bretagne
(HW). HW does not seem to have acquired a drawing of Les Rochers until
1786 when he obtained one 'done on the
spot by Mr Hinchliffe, son of the Bishop
of Peterborough' ('Des. of SH,' *Works* ii.
427) sold SH xi. 4.

only meant that they were full of family details, and mortal dis-
tempers, to which the most immortal of us are subject; and I was
sorry that the profane should ever know that my divinity was ever
troubled with a sore leg, or the want of money; though indeed the
latter defeats Bussy's[1] ill-natured accusation of avarice; and her tear-
ing herself from her daughter,[2] then at Paris, to go and save money
in Bretagne to pay her debts, is a perfection of virtue which com-
pletes her amiable character. My Lady Hervey has made me most
happy, by bringing me from Paris an admirable copy of the very
portrait that was Madame de Simiane's:[3] I am going to build an altar for it, under the title of *Notre Dame des Rochers!*

Well! but you will want to know the contents of the parcel that
is set out. It contains another parcel, which contains I don't know
what; but Mr C[umberland][4] sent it, and desired I would transmit
it to you. There are Ray's proverbs in two volumes interleaved; a
few seeds, mislaid when I sent the last; a very indifferent new tragedy, called *Barbarossa,* now running, the author[5] unknown, but
believed to be Garrick himself:[6] there is not one word of Barbarossa's
real story, but almost the individual history of Merope; not one new
thought, and, which is the next material want, but one line of perfect nonsense;

> And rain down transports in the shape of sorrow.[7]

To complete it, the manners are so ill observed, that a Mahometan
princess royal is at full liberty to visit her lover in Newgate, like

1. Roger de Rabutin (1618–93), Comte
de Bussy-Rabutin, cousin and correspondent of Mme de Sévigné.

2. Françoise-Marguerite de Sévigné
(1648–1705), m. (1669) François de Castel-
lane-Adhémar de Monteil, Comte de
Grignan.

3. Françoise-Pauline de Castellane-Ad-
hémar de Monteil de Grignan (1674–
1737), m. (1695) Louis de Simiane du
Claret, Marquis de Truchenu et d'Esparron; grand-daughter of Mme de Sévigné. The portrait, which HW placed in
the Long Gallery, was sold SH xxi. 81.

4. Presumably the Rev. Denison Cumberland (ca 1708–74), D.D., 1761; Bp of
Clonfert, 1763; of Kilmore, 1772; Bentley's
brother-in-law (*Record of Old Westmin-
sters,* ed. G. F. Russell Barker and A. H.
Stenning, 1928, i. 237); or his son, Richard

Cumberland (1732–1811), the dramatist,
Bentley's nephew.

5. It was written by Dr Browne (HW).
John Brown (1715–66), author of the *Estimate of the Manners and Principles of
the Times* (1757). *Barbarossa* was first
performed at Drury Lane on 17 Dec. and
published 28 Dec. (John Genest, *Some
Account of the English Stage,* Bath, 1832,
iv. 405–6; *Daily Adv.* 21, 23 Dec. 1754).

6. Garrick wrote the prologue and the
epilogue (*London Stage 1660–1800,* pt 4,
ed. G. W. Stone, Carbondale, Ill., 1962, i.
458).

7. 'Selim. Now, swelling heart,
  Indulge the luxury of grief! Flow
    tears!
  And rain down transport in the shape
    of sorrow!'
          (*Barbarossa,* Act III).

the banker's daughter in *George Barnwell*.[8] I have added four more *Worlds*,[9] the second of which will, I think, redeem my Lord Chesterfield's character with you for wit, except in the two stories, which are very flat: I mean those of two misspelt letters. In the last *World*,[10] besides the hand, you will find a story of your acquaintance: *Boncœur* means Norborne Berkeley,[11] whose horse sinking up to his middle in Woburn Park, he would not allow that it was anything more than a little damp. The last story of a highwayman happened almost literally to Mrs Cavendish.[12]

For news, I think I have none to tell you. Mr Pitt is gone to the Bath, and Mr Fox to Newcastle House; and everybody else into the country for the holidays. When Lord Bath was told of the first determination of turning out Pitt, and letting Fox remain, he said, it put him in mind of a story of the Gunpowder Plot.[13] The Lord Chamberlain was sent to examine the vaults under the Parliament House, and, returning with his report, said, he had found five-and-twenty barrels of gunpowder; that he had removed ten of them, and hoped the other fifteen would do no harm—Was ever anything so well and so just?

The Russian ambassador[14] is to give a masquerade for the birth of the little great prince:[15] the King lends him Somerset House: he wanted to borrow the palace over against me,[16] and sent to ask it of the cardinal-nephew,[17] who replied, 'Not for half Russia.'

8. *The London Merchant, or The History of George Barnwell*, by George Lillo.

9. Numbers 92, 98, 100, and 101 of the third volume of that periodical paper (HW).

10. No. 103 by Mr Walpole (HW).

11. 'When Boncœur shivers on your dreary hill, where for twenty years you have been vainly endeavouring to raise reluctant plantations, and yet profess that only some of the trees have been a little kept back by the late dry season, he is not polite; he is more; he is kind.'

12. Probably Elizabeth Cavendish (d. 1779), dau. of Lord James Cavendish, 3d son of 1st D. of Devonshire; m. (1732) Richard Chandler, later Cavendish (SELWYN 270, n. 13). In the story, the victim is a man. Maclaine, the highwayman in question, writes two letters of excuses for his conduct, and offers to let his victim buy back part of what has been stolen.

13. Of 1605.

14. Count Petr Grigor'evich Chernyshev, Russian ambassador to England 1746–55 (*Repertorium der diplomatischen Vertreter aller Länder*, Vol. II, ed. Friedrich Hausmann, Zurich, 1950, p. 320).

15. The present Czar, Paul I (Mary Berry). Paul I (1754–1801) succeeded Catherine II in 1796. HW describes the masquerade *post* HW to Bentley 8 Feb. 1755.

16. The house in Arlington Street (later No. 17) built by Henry Pelham in 1743 on the site of Sir Robert Walpole's old house where HW had been born. It was across the street from HW's house (GRAY i. 3, n. 1, 12, n. 76; MANN ii. 231 and n. 9).

17. Henry, Earl of Lincoln, nephew to the Duke of Newcastle, to whose title he succeeded (HW). Lincoln, who had married Pelham's daughter, had presumably inherited the house, but lived in Palace Yard.

The new madness is Oratorys. Macklin[18] has set up one, under the title of The British Inquisition:[19] Foote[20] another, against him: and a third man has advertised another today.[21] I have not heard enough in their favour to tempt me to them: nor do I in the world know enough to compose another paragraph. I am here quite alone; Mr Chute is setting out for his Vine; but in a day or two I expect Mr Williams,[22] George Selwyn, and Dick Edgecumbe.[23] You will allow that when I do admit anybody within my cloister, I choose them well. My present occupation is putting up my books; and thanks to arches, and pinnacles, and pierced columns, I shall not appear scantily provided! Adieu!

Yours ever,

Hor. Walpole

To Bentley, Thursday 9 January 1755

Printed from *Works* v. 307–9; reprinted, Wright, iii. 93–6, Cunningham ii. 416–19, Toynbee iii. 278–82.

Arlington Street, January 9, 1755.

I USED to say that one could not go out of London for two days, without finding at one's return that something very extraordinary had happened; but of late the climate had lost its propensity to odd accidents. Madness be praised, we are a little restored to the want of our senses! I have been twice this Christmas at Straw-

18. Charles Macklin (ca 1697–1797), actor.

19. In Hart Street, Covent Garden; it began on 21 Nov. 1754 (DNB *sub* Macklin).

20. Samuel Foote (1720–77), actor and dramatist. 'On Monday night [16 Dec.] Mr Foote made his appearance at the Theatre in the Haymarket for the first time, on his plan of oration. There was a very crowded house, the stage being half full. He made a polite humorous apology to the audience for his appearance in that manner, was very severe and satiric on the Inquisitor [Macklin] for his ingratitude to him, spoke with great respect of the law and gospel, but mimicked some of the members, who by their af-

fected voices and gestures were remarkable, as also some of the gentlemen of the Robinhood Society' (*Daily Adv.* 18 Dec. 1754).

21. This advertisement has not been found. The first one in the *Daily Adv.* for any but Macklin's and Foote's is in the issue of 2 Jan. for a course of comic lectures in the Little Theatre in the Haymarket beginning 8 Jan.

22. George James ['Gilly'] Williams, Esq. (HW), (1719–1805), wit; M.P.

23. These three composed HW's 'out-of-town' parties at SH at Christmas and Easter for many years, and were painted by Reynolds (Montagu i. 417).

berry Hill for a few days, and at each return have been not a little surprised: the first time, at the very unexpected death of my Lord Albemarle,[1] who was taken ill at Paris, going home from supper, and expired in a few hours; and last week at the far more extraordinary death of [Lord Montfort].[2] He himself, with all his judgment in bets,[3] I think would have betted any man in England against himself for self-murder: yet after having been supposed the sharpest genius of his time, he, by all that appears, shot himself on the distress of his circumstances;[4] an apoplectic disposition I believe concurring, either to lower his spirits, or to alarm them. Ever since Miss ——[5] lived with him, either from liking her himself, as some think, or to tempt her to marry his Lilliputian figure, he has squandered vast sums at [Horseheath],[6] and in living. He lost twelve hundred a year by Lord Albemarle's death, and four by Lord Gage's,[7] the same day. He asked immediately for the government of Virginia[8] or the Foxhounds,[9] and pressed for an answer with an eagerness that surprised the Duke of N[ewcastle] who never had a notion of pinning down the relief of his own or any other man's wants to a day. Yet that seems to have been the case of [Lord Montfort], who determined to throw the die of life or death, Tuesday was sennight, on the answer he was to receive from Court; which did not prove favourable. He consulted indirectly, and at last pretty

1. William Anne van Keppel (1702 – 22 Dec. 1754), 2d E. of Albemarle, at this time ambassador to France. News of his death reached London by messenger on 26 Dec. (*Daily Adv.* 27 Dec. 1754).

2. Henry Bromley (1705 – 1 Jan. 1755); cr. (1741) Bn Montfort. According to Cole's 'Athenæ Cantabrigienses,' Bentley had lived 'some time' at Holt Castle, Worcs, by Montfort's permission (J. B. Nichols, *Illustrations of the Literary History of the Eighteenth Century*, 1817–58, viii. 572).

3. For some of these, see MANN iv. 74.

4. His son informed Newcastle in 1756 that he had 'debts to the amount of above £30,000, and my estate out of repair and in a very ruinous condition' (MANN iv. 461, n. 17).

5. Perhaps Miss Middleton, niece of Conyers Middleton, later wife of Jeremiah Lagden. She 'lived for some time as housekeeper of Horseth Hall' (COLE i. 364). Montfort's wife had died in 1733.

6. Montfort's seat near Linton, Cambs.

7. Thomas Gage (ca 1695 – 21 Dec. 1754), cr. (1720) Vct Gage. Why Montfort should have lost these incomes by their deaths is not clear.

8. Vacant by Albemarle's death and worth £1,650 a year (MANN iv. 461, n. 15). Montfort is mentioned as having 'half asked it,' along with other candidates in Newcastle's list of vacant employments 28 Dec. 1754 (BM Add. MSS 32737 f. 514). There are no letters from Montfort to Newcastle concerning either of the vacant posts in the Newcastle papers, and the only references to his suicide there are general expressions of shock and references to vacancies in Cambridgeshire occasioned by his death.

9. Master of the Harriers and Foxhounds, worth £2,000 a year, and vacant by the death of Lord Gower. The King had determined to 'sink it' (BM Add. MS 32737, ff. 485, 518).

directly, several people on the easiest method of finishing life;[10] and seems to have thought that he had been too explicit; for he invited company to dinner for the day after his death, and ordered a supper at White's; where he supped too the night before. He played at whisk till one in the morning; it was New Year's morning: Lord Robert Bertie drank to him a happy New Year; he clapped his hand strangely to his eyes! In the morning he had a lawyer and three witnesses, and executed his will, which he made them read twice over, paragraph by paragraph: and then asking the lawyer, if that will would stand good, though a man were to shoot himself? and being assured it would; he said, 'Pray stay while I step into next room';—went into next room, and shot himself.[11] He clapped the pistol so close to his head, that they heard no report. The housekeeper heard him fall, and, thinking he had a fit, ran up with drops, and found his skull and brains shot about the room!—You will be charmed with the friendship and generosity of Sir ——.[12] [Lord Montfort] a little time since opened his circumstances to him. Sir —— said, '[Montfort], if it will be of any service to you, you shall see what I have done for you'; pulled out his will, and read it, where he had left him a vast legacy. The beauty of this action is heightened by Sir ——'s life not being worth a year's purchase. I own I feel for the distress this man must have felt, before he decided on so desperate an action. I knew him but little; but he was good-natured and agreeable enough, and had the most compendious understanding I ever knew. He had affected a finesse in money matters beyond what he deserved, and aimed at reducing even natural affections to a kind of calculations like Demoivre's.[13] He was asked, soon after his daughter's[14] marriage, if she was with child:—He replied, 'Upon my word, I don't know; I have no bet upon it.' This and poor [Drum-

10. 'One now hears so many stories of his having talked within these [?]ten days about *shooting through the head*, that it is astonishing that none of his friends took any care to have him watched' (Hardwicke to Newcastle 3 Jan. 1754[5], Add. MSS 32852, ff. 65–6).

11. Similar details of Montfort's suicide are in a letter from Lady Hervey to Edmund Morris 7 Jan. 1755 (*Letters of Mary Lepel*, Lady Hervey, ed. Croker, 1821, pp. 206–7).

12. Not identified. Wright and later editors have identified him as Sir Francis (presumably for Sir Francis Wyndham,

Montfort's brother-in-law), but he died in 1719.

13. Abraham Demoivre (or Moivre) (1667–1754), mathematician who did much work in the theory of probabilities and life-contingencies. According to Mrs Montagu, Montfort always carried Demoivre's *Probabilités de la vie humaine* in his pocket (E. J. Climenson, *Elizabeth Montagu*, 1906, ii. 67, which see for fuller details of Montfort's suicide).

14. Hon. Francis Bromley (d. 1768), m. (1747) Charles Sloane Cadogan, 3d Bn Cadogan, 1776, cr. (1800) E. Cadogan.

lanrig]'s[15] self-murder have brought to light another, which happening in France had been sunk; ———'s.[16] I can tell you that the
ancient and worshipful company of lovers are under a great dilemma, upon a husband and a gamester killing themselves: I don't
know whether they will not apply to Parliament for an exclusive
charter for self-murder.

On the occasion of [Lord Montfort]'s story, I heard another more
extraordinary. If a man insures his life, this killing himself vacates
the bargain. This (as in England almost everything begets a contradiction) has produced an office for insuring in spite of self-murder;
but not beyond three hundred pounds. I suppose voluntary deaths
were not then the *bon ton* of people in higher life. A man went and
insured his life, securing this privilege of a *free-dying* Englishman.
He carried the insurers to dine at a tavern, where they met several
other persons. After dinner he said to the life-and-death brokers,
'Gentlemen, it is fit that you should be acquainted with the company: these honest men are tradesmen, to whom I was in debt, without any means of paying, but by your assistance; and now I am your
humble servant!' He pulled out a pistol and shot himself. Did
you ever hear of such a mixture of honesty and knavery?

Lord Rochford[17] is to succeed as Groom of the Stole. The Duke of
Marlborough is Privy Seal,[18] in the room of Lord Gower,[19] who is
dead; and the Duke of Rutland[20] is Lord Steward. Lord Albemarle's
other offices and honours[21] are still *in petto*. When the King first

15. Probably, as Mrs Toynbee assumed,
Henry Douglas (1722 – 19 Oct. 1754), styled
E. of Drumlanrig, who shot himself, al-
though it was probably by accident; see
GEC X. 700 n.*b*.

16. Not identified; Mrs Toynbee as-
sumes it to have been Bland, but he did
not commit suicide until Sept. 1755.

17. William Henry Nassau de Zuylestein
(1717–81), 4th E. of Rochford, at this
time envoy to Sardinia; Groom of the
Stole and first lord of the Bedchamber
1755–60. The King had determined to
appoint him on learning of Albemarle's
death, and despite opposition from the
ministers, had signed his letter of recall
3 Jan. Rochford reached England 28 Feb.,
received the gold key on 2 March, and
was sworn in on the 3d (MANN iv. 460, n.
13, 469, n. 11; *London Evening Post* 27
Feb.–1 March, 1–4 March 1755).

18. His appointment was announced in
the *London Gazette* No. 9440, 7–11 Jan.
1755, but the promotion had been decided before Gower's death (Hardwicke
to Newcastle 26 Dec. 1754, BM Add. MSS
32737, f. 485; Newcastle to Marlborough
27 Dec. 1754, ibid. f. 493).

19. John Leveson Gower (1694 – 25 Dec.
1754), 2d Bn Gower, cr. (1746) E. Gower.

20. John Manners (1696–1779), 3d D. of
Rutland; his promotion was part of the
plan formed before Gower's death (Newcastle to Marlborough 27 Dec. 1754, loc.
cit.). His appointment was announced
in the *London Gazette* No. 9441, 11–14
Jan. 1755, *sub* Whitehall, 14 Jan.; he
held the post until 1761.

21. Governor of Virginia, Col. of the
Coldstream Guards, ambassador to France,
and Knight of the Garter.

saw this Lord Albemarle,[22] he said, 'Your father had a great many good qualities, but he was a sieve!'—It is the last receiver into which I should have thought his Majesty would have poured gold! You will be pleased with the monarch's *politesse*. Sir John Bland[23] and Offley[24] made interest to play at Twelfth Night, and succeeded— not at play, for they lost £1400 and £1300. As it is not usual for people of no higher rank to play, the King thought they would be bashful about it, and took particular care to do the honours of his house to them, set only to them,[25] and spoke to them at his levee next morning.

You love new nostrums and inventions: there is discovered a method of inoculating the cattle for the distemper—it succeeds so well that they are not even marked. How we advance rapidly in discoveries, and in applying everything to everything! Here is another secret, that will better answer your purpose, and I hope mine too. They found out lately at the Duke of Argyle's,[26] that any kind of ink may be made of privet: it becomes green ink by mixing salt of tartar. I don't know the process; but I am promised it by Campbell,[27] who told me of it t'other day, when I carried him the true genealogy of the Bentleys, which he assured me shall be inserted in the next edition of the Biographia.[28]

There sets out tomorrow morning, by the Southampton wagon, such a cargo of trees for you, that a detachment of Kentishmen

---

22. George Keppel (1724–72), styled Vct Bury, who succeeded his father as 3d E. of Albemarle in 1754.

23. Sir John Bland (ca 1722–55), 6th Bt, a notorious gamester.

24. John Offley (?1717–84), surveyor of the King's private roads 1756–7; groom of the Bedchamber 1757–62; man of fashion; M.P. Bedford 1747–54, Orford 1754–68, East Retford 1768–74.

25. The King traditionally played at hazard in the Great Council Chamber on Twelfth Night (*Daily Adv.* 7 Jan. 1755).

26. Archibald Campbell (1682–1761), cr. (1706) E. of Ilay; 3d D. of Argyll, 1743. He was interested 'in philosophical experiments, mechanics, natural history' (Lady Louisa Stuart, 'Memoir' of John, Duke of Argyll in Lady Mary Coke, *Letters and Journals*, ed. Home, Edinburgh, 1889–96, i. xxiv).

27. John Campbell (1708–75), LL.D., called by HW 'one of the ablest and most beautiful writers of this country' (*Catalogue of the Royal and Noble Authors, Works*, i. 506); contributed to the early volumes of *Biographia Britannica*.

28. The article on Bentley (not written by Campbell) in the first edition of the *Biographia Britannica* (Vol. II, 1748) described him as 'by birth, a Yorkshireman, and son (as I have been informed) of —— Bentley, a tradesman, viz. either a tanner, or a blacksmith, at Wakefield, in the West Riding of Yorkshire' (p. 734). This is only slightly modified in the main article on Bentley in the second edn (Vol. II, 1780, pp. 224–5), but completely corrected in a long footnote at the end of the article (p. 242) from information apparently supplied by Richard Cumberland, not HW.

would be furnished against an invasion[29] if they were to unroll the bundle. I write to Mr S——[30] to recommend great care of them. Observe how I answer your demands: are you as punctual? The forests in your landscapes do not thrive like those in your letters. Here is a letter from G. Montagu;[31] and then I think I may bid you good-night!

Yours ever,

Hor. Walpole

To Bentley, late January 1755

Missing. HW says *post* 6 March that he had written Bentley three letters between those of 9 Jan. and 6 March; in that of 8 Feb. he mentions having promised Bentley a description of the Russian ambassador's masquerade. This promise is not in any surviving letter, and the long space between the preceding and following letter makes it likely that one intervened between them.

To Bentley, Saturday 8 February 1755

Printed from *Works* v. 310; reprinted, Wright iii. 99–100, Cunningham ii. 422–3, Toynbee iii. 285–6.

Arlington Street, Feb. 8, 1755.

My dear Sir,

BY THE wagon on Thursday there set out for Southampton, a lady whom you must call *Phillis,* but whom George Montagu and the gods would name *Speckle-belly.* Peter[1] begged her for me, that is for you, that is, for Captain Dumaresque,[2] after he had been asked

29. An allusion to the story of the men of Kent going out to meet William the Conqueror with green boughs and obtaining in consequence a confirmation of their old liberties from the new king. See *post* HW to Hamilton 18 Feb. 1776, n. 17.

30. Probably the Mr Seward mentioned *ante* HW to Bentley 27 July 1754.

31. Mentioned by HW to Montagu, 7 Jan. 1755, Montagu i. 167.

1. Probably HW's coachman; see Montagu i. 196.

2. Perhaps 'le Capitaine Jean Dumaresq, l'officier le plus ancien de la garnison' who was deputy-gov. of Jersey 1752–3 (*Société jersiaise*, 1905, v. 9); he is perhaps the John Dumaresque, 'oldest commander in the Navy,' who d. 15 Jan. 1763 in Beverley, Yorks (GM 1763, xxxiii. 46). The family were very prominent in Jersey in

three guineas for another. I hope she will not be poisoned with salt-water, like the poor Poyangers.³ If she should, you will at least observe, that your commissions are not still-born with me, as mine are with you. I *draw*⁴ a spotted dog the moment you desire it.

George Montagu has intercepted the description I promised you of the Russian masquerade: he wrote to beg it, and I cannot transcribe from myself.⁵ In few words, there were all the beauties, and all the diamonds, and not a few of the uglies of London. The Duke,⁶ like Osman the Third,⁷ seemed in the centre of his new seraglio, and I believe my Lady⁸ and I thought that my Lord [Anson] was the chief eunuch.⁹ My Lady Coventry was dressed in a great style, and looked better than ever. Lady Betty Spencer,¹⁰ like Rubens's wife¹¹ (not the common one with the hat),¹² had all the bloom and bashfulness and wildness of youth, with all the countenance of all the former Marlboroughs. Lord Delawar¹³ was an excellent mask, from a picture at Kensington of Queen Elizabeth's porter.¹⁴ Lady Caroline Petersham, powdered with diamonds and crescents for a Turkish slave, was still extremely handsome. The hazard was excessively deep, to the astonishment of some Frenchmen of quality who are here, and

the 17th and 18th centuries, but had English branches.

3. Mr Walpole having called his gold-fish-pond *Poyang*, calls the gold-fish *Poyangers* (Mary Berry).

4. Alluding to Mr Bentley's dilatoriness in exercising his pencil at the request of Mr Walpole (HW).

5. HW's description and Montagu's request are both missing from the Montagu correspondence. The masquerade, which took place 5 Feb., is described at some length in the *London Evening Post* 6–8 Feb. 1755.

6. William, Duke of Cumberland (HW). He wore 'a Turkish dress, with a large bunch of diamonds in his turban' (*London Evening Post* 6–8 Feb. 1755).

7. Osman III (1696–1757), sultan of Turkey.

8. Apparently, from the context, Elizabeth Yorke (1725–60), m. (1748) George Anson, cr. (1747) Bn Anson; although 'my Lady' in HW's letters is usually Lady Townshend.

9. HW told Mann 10 Sept. 1761 (MANN v. 528) that this description of Anson was

attributed to the Tripolitan ambassador. For a similar allusion to Anson, see *ante* HW to Bentley 17 March 1754 and n. 21.

10. Lady Elizabeth Spencer (1737–1831), m. (1756) Henry Herbert, 10th E. of Pembroke.

11. Ruben's second wife, Helena Fourment (m. 1630) was one of his favourite subjects. The costume was probably taken from one of the two portraits then at Blenheim (Edward Dillon, *Rubens*, 1909, pp. 163–4 and plates CCCXLIX and CCCLIII).

12. Probably the *Chapeau de Paille*, now in the National Gallery, London, although the subject is Susanna, not Helena Fourment (ibid. 160 and plate CCIX).

13. John West (1693–1766), 7th Bn de la Warr, 1723, cr. (1761) E. de la Warr.

14. 'Queen Elizabeth's Giant Porter,' attributed to Federico Zuccaro, now in the Guard Room at Hampton Court. De la Warr had worn the same costume at a masquerade in 1749 (MANN iv. 49 and n. 23).

who I believe, from what they saw that night, will not write to their Court to dissuade their armaments, on its not being worth their while to attack so beggarly a nation. Our fleet is as little despicable; but though the preparations on both sides are so great, I believe the storm will blow over. They insist on our immediately sending an ambassador to Paris; and to my great satisfaction, my cousin and friend Lord Hertford is to be the man.[15] This is still an entire secret here, but will be known before you receive this. The weather is very bitter, and keeps me from Strawberry. Adieu!

Yours ever,

Hor. Walpole

To Bentley, Sunday 23 February 1755

Printed from *Works* v. 311–13; reprinted, Wright iii. 100–3, Cunningham ii. 423–5, Toynbee iii. 286–9.

Arlington Street, Feb. 23, 1755.

My dear Sir,

YOUR *Argosie* is arrived safe; thank you for shells, trees, cones; but above all, thank you for the landscape.[1] As it is your first attempt in oils, and has succeeded so much beyond my expectation (and being against my advice too, you may believe the sincerity of my praises), I must indulge my *Vasari-hood,* and write a dissertation upon it. You have united and mellowed your colours, in a manner to make it look like an old picture; yet there is something in the tone of it, that is not quite right. Mr Chute thinks that you should have exerted more of your force in tipping with light the edges on which the sun breaks: my own opinion is, that the result of the whole is not natural, by your having joined a Claude Lorrain summer sky to a wintry sea, which you have drawn from the life. The water breaks finely, but the distant hills are too strong, and the outlines much

15. He did not go until 1763 because of deteriorating relations with France, and the Seven Years' War. See *post* 6 March 1755.

_____

1. It is now at Strawberry Hill (HW). Probably the 'landscape, view in Jersey, by Mr. Bentley, in oil' in which Bentley 'has represented himself and his second wife on the seashore' which hung in the Red Bedchamber ('Des. of SH,' *Works* ii. 438). It was sold SH xxii. 2 from the Plaid Bedchamber, described as 'A View in Jersey, 1754.'

too hard. The greatest fault is the trees (not apt to be your stum-bling-block): they are not of a natural green, have no particular re-semblance, and are out of all proportion too large for the figures. Mend these errors, and work away in oil. I am impatient to see some Gothic ruins of your painting. This leads me naturally to thank you for the sweet little *cul-de-lampe* to the *Entail:*[2] it is equal to any-thing you have done in perspective and for taste; but the boy is too large.

For the block of granite I shall certainly think a louis well be-stowed—provided I do but get the block, and that you are sure it will be equal to the sample you sent me. My room remains in want of a table; and as it will take so much time to polish it, I do wish you would be a little expeditious in sending it.

I have but frippery news to tell you; no politics; for the rudiments of a war, that is not to be a war, are not worth detailing. In short, we have acted with spirit, have got ready 30 ships of the line, and conclude that the French will not care to examine whether they are well manned or not.[3] The House of Commons *bears* nothing but elections; the Oxfordshire till seven at night three times a week:[4] we have passed ten evenings on the Colchester election,[5] and last Mon-day sat upon it till near two in the morning. Whoever stands a con-tested election, and pays for his seat, and attends the first session, surely buys the other six very dear!

The great event is the catastrophe of Sir John Bland,[6] who has *flirted* away his whole fortune at hazard. He t'other night exceeded what was lost by the late Duke of Bedford,[7] having at one period of

2. It is reproduced in W. S. Lewis's *Bentley's Designs for Walpole's Fugitive Pieces*, Farmington, 1936, p. 18.

3. One current rumour was that 'it is said the French have offered to settle all things *bona fide* according to the Treaty of Utrecht; but that our Court insists on being paid the expenses occasioned by their faithless behaviour' (*Whitehall Eve-ning Post* 25–27 Feb. 1755).

4. Hearings on the Oxfordshire election had been proceeding before the whole House since 3 Dec. 1754; the matter was not determined until 23 April (*Journals of the House of Commons* xxvii. 41, 291–2).

5. The Committee of Privileges and Elections, of which HW was apparently a member, was holding hearings on the Colchester election; it finally reported on it 12 March, the report was considered on the 13th, and the return surrendered in favour of the petitioner, Isaac Martin Rebow, on the 14th (ibid. xxvii. 15, 21, 199, 205–13).

6. See n. 10 below.

7. Wriothesley Russell (1708–32), 3d D. of Bedford, 1711. For his extravagance and debts, which nearly ruined his estate, see Gladys Scott Thomson, *The Russells in Bloomsbury*, 1940, pp. 157–8, 187–8; and idem, *Letters of a Grandmother*, 1943, *passim*.

the night (though he recovered the greatest part of it) lost two-and-thirty thousand pounds. The citizens put on their double-channeled pumps[8] and trudge to St James's Street, in expectation of seeing judgments executed on White's—angels with flaming swords, and devils flying away with dice-boxes, like the prints in Sadeler's Hermits.[9] Sir [John] lost this immense sum to a Captain O'Brien,[10] who at present has nothing but a few debts and his commission.

Garrick has produced a detestable English opera,[11] which is crowded by all true lovers of their country. To mark the opposition to Italian operas, it is sung by some cast singers,[12] two Italians,[13] and a French girl,[14] and the chapel boys;[15] and to regale us with sense, it

8. 'What are English channelshoes? Sewed shoes have the seam that unites the sole and upper sunk into a channel cut in the sole . . . As it cannot be cut in thin poor leather, it indicates a good article' (Leslie's *Illustrated Newspaper* 10 Oct. 1874, quoted OED *sub* 'channel' 9b, where the only other recorded use of the word is also from 1874).

9. For other references to these prints, see *ante* HW to Bentley Sept. 1753 and MONTAGU ii. 276 and n. 3.

10. Previous editors have assumed that this was Gen. John Scott, a successful gambler (BERRY ii. 68, n. 22, 258), but a letter from Lady Essex to Sir Charles Hanbury Williams 20 Feb. 1755, makes it clear that it was Murrough O'Brien (1726–1808), Capt. in the 1st Foot Guards, later (1777) 5th E. of Inchiquin, cr. (1800) M. of Thomond: 'Sir John Bland played at White's last week with Captain O'Brien, and lost £32,000 in one night. Capt. O'B. let him win it back to £6,000; which debt still remains against him, and I believe is likely to do so' (quoted by Earl of Ilchester and Mrs Langford-Brooke, *Life of Sir Charles Hanbury-Williams*, 1929, p. 305). In 1793 Inchiquin himself related a somewhat distorted version of the event to Joseph Farington (*The Farington Diary*, [1922–8], i. 92).

11. *The Fairies*, first performed 3 Feb. at Drury Lane and repeated eight times (*The London Stage 1660–1800*, pt 4, ed. G. W. Stone, Carbondale, Ill., 1962, i. 467 *et passim*; John Genest, *Some Account of the English Stage*, Bath, 1832, iv. 407), with music and text by John Christopher

Smith (1712–95), organist and composer (Sir George Grove, *Dictionary of Music and Musicians*, 5th edn, ed. Blom, 1954, vii. 854–5; Alfred Loewenberg, *Annals of Opera*, 2d edn, Geneva, 1955, p. 228). The dialogue, completed for *A Midsummer Night's Dream* with the addition of some 27 songs, was commonly attributed to Garrick, but he repudiated the authorship in a letter to James Murphey French in Dec. 1756 (Genest, loc. cit.; Loewenberg, loc. cit.).

12. I.e. worn-out (OED). The principal English singers were John Beard (ca 1717–91) tenor; Atkins, Chamnys, and Mrs Jefferson (Grove, op. cit. i. 517; Genest, loc. cit.).

13. 'Signor Curioni' and 'Signora Passerini' (Genest, loc. cit.). A Rosa Curioni sang at London 1754–5 and at Venice in 1757 (Grove, op. cit. ii. 562); Dr Burney mentions 'the Passerini' as singing in 1753 and 1754 (*A General History of Music*, ed. Mercer, 1935, ii. 852). Guadagni (Gaetano Guadagni ca 1725–92) is mentioned by G. W. Stone, loc. cit.

14. Probably the 'Miss Poitier, a singer at Drury Lane' who married, early in 1755, Joseph Vernon (ca 1738–82), tenor and composer (Grove, op. cit. viii. 755). A 'Miss Vernon' sang the part of Helena (Genest, loc. cit.), and is also called 'Miss Potier' (G. W. Stone, loc. cit.).

15. I.e., the choristers of the Chapel Royal. Among the children and youths who sang in the opera were 'Master Reinholt' (Frederick Charles Reinhold 1737–1815, later an organist and bass according to Grove, op. cit. vii. 116), 'Master More'

is Shakespeare's *Midsummer Night's Dream,* which is forty times more nonsensical than the worst translation of any Italian opera-books—But such sense and such harmony are irresistible!

I am at present confined with a cold, which I caught by going to a fire in the middle of the night, and in the middle of the snow, two days ago. About five in the morning Harry waked me with a candle in his hand, and cried, 'Pray, your honour, don't be frightened!' 'No, Harry, I am not; but what is it that I am not to be frightened at?' 'There is a great fire here in St James's Street.'—I rose, and indeed thought all St James's Street was on fire, but it proved in Bury Street.[16] However, you know I can't resist going to a fire; for it is certainly the only horrid sight that is fine. I slipped on my slippers, and an embroidered suit that hung on the chair, and ran to Bury Street, and stepped into a pipe that was broken up for water It would have made a picture—the horror of the flames, the snow, the day breaking with difficulty through so foul a night, and my figure, party per *pale,*[17] mud and gold. It put me in mind of Lady Margaret Herbert's[18] providence, who asked somebody for a *pretty* pattern for a nightcap. 'Lord,' said they, 'what signifies the pattern of a nightcap?'—'Oh, child,' said she, 'but you know, in case of fire.' There were two houses burnt, and a poor maid; an officer[19] jumped out of window, and is much hurt, and two young beauties[20] were conveyed out the same way in their shifts. There have been two more great

or 'Moore,' and 'Master Evans' but none of them appears in the list of the children of the Chapel Royal in John Chamberlayne, *Magnæ Britaniæ Notitia,* 1755, pt ii. Book III, 113.

16. 'Yesterday morning [20 Feb.], about five o'clock, a fire broke out at Mr Thompson's, an embroiderer in Bury Street, St James's, which entirely consumed the same, and damaged several other houses adjoining' (*Daily Adv.* 21 Feb. 1755). 'The fire . . . between three and four in the morning . . . was first discovered by Mr Swan, a gentleman who lodged there, who hearing of the crackling of the ceiling, alarmed the whole house, and made his escape out of the dining-room window; three young ladies (his sisters) who lay in a back-house, got out of a back window in their shifts. . . . One Mr Forbes jumped out of a two pair of stairs window, and is so much bruised that his life is in great

danger' (*London Evening Post,* 20–22 Feb. 1755). Similar details are in GM 1755, xxv. 90.

17. In heraldry: divided by a vertical line through the middle. For a further discussion of HW's use of the term in this letter, see Norman Pearson, 'Neglected Aspects of Horace Walpole,' *Fortnightly Review,* 1909, xcii. 494.

18. Lady Margaret Herbert (d. 1752), dau. of 8th E. of Pembroke (Collins, *Peerage,* 1812, iii. 142–3).

19. Mr Forbes (above, n. 16). He died of his bruises 10 March (GM 1755, xxv. 138).

20. Actually three, the Miss Swans (above, n. 16). They were possibly the three Miss Swans of Swinderby, Lincs: Alice, (1737–after 1769), m. Rev. Henry Hoggart; Elizabeth (1739–after 1769); and Anne, m. (after 1769) James Yates (*Harleian Society Publications,* 1904, lii. 941).

fires. Alderman Belchier's[21] house at Epsom,[22] that belonged to the Prince, is burnt, and Beckford's fine house[23] in the country, with pictures and furniture to a great value.[24] He says, 'Oh! I have an odd fifty thousand pounds in a drawer: I will build it up again: it won't be above a thousand pounds apiece difference to my thirty children.'[25] Adieu!

Yours ever,

HOR. WALPOLE

From BENTLEY, ca February 1755

Two letters missing; mentioned *post* 6 March 1755.

21. William Belchier (d. 1772), banker; M.P. Southwark 1747–61; a common councilman, not an alderman, of London (A. B. Beaven, *Aldermen of the City of London,* 1908–13, i. 306, 307).

22. Durdans, built in the late 17th century by George, E. of Berkeley, which at one time had been lent or leased to Frederick, P. of Wales, although he never owned it (*Vict. Co. Hist. Surrey* iii. 276). 'On Thursday morning [20 Feb.] a fire broke out in the upper part of the house of William Belchier, Esq.; at Epsom in Surrey (late the Prince of Wales's hunting seat) which in about two hours entirely consumed the same. The house and furniture was insured at £5,500' (*London Evening Post* 20–22 Feb. 1755; see also ibid. 18–20 Feb. and GM 1755, xxv. 90).

23. Fonthill, Wilts, which burned during the night of 12–13 Feb. 1755. A long description of the fire is in an 'Extract of a letter from Salisbury, Feb. 17' in *London Evening Post* 18–20 Feb.; and various ad-

ditional details ibid. 25–27 Feb.; *Whitehall Evening Post* 15–18, 25–27 Feb.; and GM 1755, xxv. 90.

24. The first reports placed the loss at '£30,000 only six of which were insured,' including 'most of the rich furniture, together with the fine organ, which is said to have cost near £5,000' (GM 1755, xxv. 90). Later reports, however, mentioned that 'all Mr Beckford's books, writings, and plate, were saved during the fire, except one large piece, which weighed about 400 ounces, and has since been found in melted pieces among the rubbish.' Beckford had meanwhile 'sent down orders for all the outwork to go on the same as if the accident had never happened, and is already come to a resolution to rebuild the house in a most elegant manner, and as soon as possible' (*London Evening Post* 25–27 Feb. 1755).

25. Beckford's only child, William, was born in 1759.

To Bentley, Thursday 6 March 1755

Printed from *Works* v. 313–14; reprinted, Wright iii. 103–4, Cunningham ii. 425–6, Toynbee iii. 289–91.

Arlington Street, March 6, 1755.

My dear Sir,

I HAVE to thank you for two letters and a picture. I hope my thanks will have a more prosperous journey than my own letters have had of late. You say you have received none since January 9th. I have written three since that. I take care, in conjunction with the times, to make them harmless enough for the post. Whatever secrets I may have (and you know I have no propensity to mystery) will keep very well till I have the happiness of seeing you, though that date should be farther off than I hope. As I mean my letters should relieve some of your anxious or dull minutes, I will tempt no postmasters or secretaries to retard them.

The state of affairs is much altered since my last epistle that persuaded you of the distance of a war. So haughty and so ravenous an answer came from France,[1] that my Lord Hertford does not go. As a *little* islander, you may be very easy: Jersey is not prey for such fleets as are likely to encounter in the Channel in April. You must tremble in your *Bigendian* capacity[2] if you mean to figure as a good citizen. I sympathize with you extremely in the interruption it will give to our correspondence. You, in an inactive little spot, cannot wish more impatiently for every post that has the probability of a letter, than I, in all the turbulence of London, do constantly, never-failingly, for letters from you. Yet by my busy, hurried, amused, irregular way of life, you would not imagine that I had much time to care for my friends. You know how late I used to rise: it is worse and worse: I stay late at debates and committees; for, with all our tranquillity and my indifference, I think I am never out of

1. 'France sent a haughty answer, accompanied with these inadmissable proposals; that each nation should destroy all their forts on the south of the Ohio, which would leave them in possession of all the north side of that river; and whereas the Five Nations were allotted to the division of England by the Treaty of Utrecht, and the French had built forts amongst them contrary to that treaty, and we agreeably to it, they demanded that we should destroy such forts, while they should be permitted to maintain theirs' (*Mem. Geo. II* ii. 2).

2. The Bigendians, in *Gulliver's Travels*, pt i, were exiled for heresy.

the House of Commons: from thence, it is the fashion of the winter to go to vast assemblies, which are followed by vast suppers, and those by balls. Last week I was from two at noon till ten at night at the House: I came home, dined, new-dressed myself entirely, went to a ball at Lord Holderness's,[3] and stayed till five in the morning. What an abominable young creature! But why may not I be so? Old Haslang[4] dances at sixty-five;[5] my Lady Rochford[6] without stays, and her husband the new Groom of the Stole,[7] dance. In short, when secretaries of state, cabinet councillors, foreign ministers, dance like the universal ballet in the *Rehearsal*,[8] why should not I—see them? In short, the true definition of me is, that I am a dancing senator—Not that I do dance, or do anything by being a senator: but I go to balls, and to the House of Commons—to look on: and you will believe me when I tell you, that I really think the former the more serious occupation of the two; at least the performers are most in earnest. What men say to women, is at least as sincere as what they say to their country. If perjury can give the devil a right to the souls of men, he has titles by as many ways as my Lord Huntingdon[9] is descended from Edward III.[10]

Yours ever,

Hor. Walpole

3. 'Yesterday [26 Feb.] the . . . Earl of Holdernesse gave a great entertainment to a great number of the nobility and foreign ministers' (*Whitehall Evening Post* 25–27 Feb. 1755).

4. Joseph Xaver (ca 1700–83), Freiherr (later Graf) von Haszlang, Bavarian minister to England 1741–83 (Montagu i. 185, n. 25).

5. He was only about fifty-five.

6. Lucy Young (ca 1723–73), m. (1740) William Henry Nassau de Zuylestein, 4th E. of Rochford.

7. He had returned to England from Turin 28 Feb., received the gold key as Groom of the Stole 2 March, and been sworn in on the 3d (*ante* HW to Bentley 9 Jan. 1755, n. 17).

8. In Buckingham's *Rehearsal*, Act V, there is a 'grand dance,' in which, presumably, everybody joins.

9. Francis Hastings (1729–89), 10th E. of Huntingdon, 1746.

10. The Hastingses were descended from four of Edward IV's sons, chiefly through various branches of the Nevills and Beauforts. HW was descended from the Hastingses, and therefore was familiar with their pedigree.

To Bentley, Thursday 27 March 1755

Printed from *Works* v. 314–16; reprinted, Wright iii. 106–9, Cunningham ii.
428–30, Toynbee iii. 293–6.

Arlington Street, March 27, 1755.

YOUR chimney[1] is come, but not to honour: the caryatides are
fine and free, but the rest is heavy: Lord Strafford is not at all
struck with it, and thinks it old-fashioned: it certainly tastes of Inigo
Jones. Your myrtles I have seen in their pots, and they are magnificent,
but I fear very sickly. In return I send you a library. You will receive
some time or other, or the French for you, the following books: a
fourth volume of Dodsley's *Collection of Poems*,[2] the worst tome of
the four; three volumes of *Worlds;* Fielding's travels,[3] or rather an
account how his dropsy was treated and teased by an innkeeper's wife
in the Isle of Wight;[4] the new letters of Madame de Sévigné;[5] and
Hume's history of Great Britain;[6] a book which, though more decried than ever book was, and certainly with faults, I cannot help
liking much. It is called Jacobite—but in my opinion is only not
George-abite: where others abuse the Stuarts, he laughs at them: I
am sure he does not spare their ministers. Harding,[7] who has the
history of England at the ends of his Parliament fingers, says, that
the *Journals*[8] will contradict most of his facts. If it is so, I am sorry;
for his style, which is the best we have in history, and his manner,
imitated from Voltaire, are very pleasing. He has showed very
clearly that we ought to quarrel originally with Queen Elizabeth's
tyranny for most of the errors of Charles I. As long as he is willing

1. A design for a chimney-piece, which,
at Mr Walpole's desire, Mr Bentley had
made for Lord Strafford (HW). It is perhaps the 'Design for a Chimney in the
Style of Architecture in the Reign of
James the First' now WSL.

2. Published 18 March (*Daily Adv.* 17,
18 March 1754).

3. Henry Fielding's *A Journal of a Voyage to Lisbon* was published 25 Feb. 1755
(W. L. Cross, *The History of Henry Fielding*, New Haven, 1918, iii. 84, 326).

4. Considerable space is given to an
account of the Fieldings' stay at the
Humphrys' house in the Isle of Wight;

but his dropsy, from which he was suffering, is not mentioned in this connection.

5. For these, see *ante* HW to Bentley
3, 11, 20 Nov. and 24 Dec. 1754.

6. The first volume of Hume's History,
covering the reigns of James I and Charles
I had been published 20 Nov. 1754 (*Daily
Adv.* 18, 19 Nov. 1754; T. E. Jessop, *A
Bibliography of David Hume*, 1938, p. 28,
which does not give a precise date).

7. Nicholas Hardinge, clerk to the House
of Commons 1731–48 (*ante* 5 Aug. 1752,
n. 57).

8. I.e. the journals of the House of
Lords and House of Commons.

to sacrifice some royal head, I would not much dispute with him which it should be. I incline every day to lenity, as I see more and more that it is being very partial to think worse of some men than of others. If I was a king myself, I dare say I should cease to love a republic. My Lady ——9 desired me, t'other day, to give her a motto for a ruby ring, which had been given by a handsome woman of quality to a fine man: he gave it to his mistress, she to Lord ——,10 he to my Lady; who, I think, does not deny that it has not yet finished its travels. I excused myself for some time, on the difficulty of reducing such a history to a poesy—at last I proposed this:

This was given by woman to man—and by man to woman.

Are you most impatient to hear of a French war, or the event of the Mitchell election?11 If the former is uppermost in your thoughts, I can tell you, you are very unfashionable. The Whigs and Tories in Rome, Athens, and Jerusalem, never forgot national points with more zeal, to attend to private faction, than we have lately. After triumphs repeated in the committee,12 Lord Sandwich and Mr Fox were beaten largely on the report.13 It was a most extraordinary day! The Tories, who could not trust one another for two hours, had

9. Previous editors have assumed, probably correctly, that this was Lady Rochford, who was well known for her gallantries; see MONTAGU i. 42, n. 18; MANN iv. 58.

10. Possibly Sackville Tufton (1733–86), 8th E. of Thanet. Lord Chesterfield wrote to his son in 1758: 'Your friend Lady Rochford is gone into the country with her Lord to negotiate, coolly and at leisure, their intended separation. My Lady insists upon my Lord's dismissing the Batotti [the Banti, see MANN iv. 378, n. 2, where 53–6 should be 153–6], as ruinous to his fortune; my Lord insists, in his turn, upon my Lady's dismissing Lord Thanet; my Lady replies, that that is unreasonable, since Lord Thanet creates no expense to the family, but rather the contrary. My Lord confesses there is some weight in the argument; but then pleads sentiment; my Lady says a fiddlestick for sentiment, after having been married so long' (Chesterfield, Letters, ed. Dobrée, 1932, v. 2316).

11. For a note on the Parliamentary contest over this election, in which Fox, Bedford and their friends opposed Legge, Newcastle, and theirs, see GRAY i. 26, n. 172. HW became deeply involved in the proceedings, during the course of which he had a serious, although obscure quarrel with his nephew, Lord Orford (ibid. and SELWYN 169, n. 2). HW's account of the part played by the 'Tories,' to which he alludes below, is severely criticized by Sir Lewis Namier in Personalities and Powers, 1955, pp. 67–70, from accounts in Sir Roger Newdigate's pocket diaries.

12. Where they carried at least two divisions, one on 28 Feb. when some twenty 'Tories' voted with Fox, and the other on 12 March, the last day of consideration in committee, by 158–141 although the Tories, by a previous decision, left before the division (Namier, op. cit. 67, 68). The report, accordingly, had favoured their candidates.

13. 24 March, by 207–183 on the motion that Clive (Sandwich's and Fox's candidate) was duly elected, as the committee had recommended (Journals of the House of Commons xxvii. 263).

their last consult at the Horn Tavern[14] just before the report, and all but nine or ten voted in a body (with the Duke of Newcastle) against agreeing to it: then Sir John Philipps,[15] one of them, moved for a void election,[16] but was deserted by most of his clan.[17] We now begin to turn our hands to foreign war. In the Rebellion, the ministry was so unsettled, that nobody seemed to care who was king. Power is now so established, that I must do the engrossers the justice to say, that they seem to be determined that *their own king*[18] shall continue so. Our fleet is great and well manned; we are raising men and money, and messages have been sent to both Houses from St James's, which have been answered by very zealous *cards*.[19] In the mean time, sturdy mandates are arrived from France; however, with a codicil of moderation, and power to Mirepoix[20] still to treat. He was told briskly—'Your terms must come speedily; the fleets will sail very quickly; war cannot then be avoided.'

I have passed five entire days lately at Dr Meade's sale,[21] where, however, I bought very little: as extravagantly as he paid for everything, his name has even resold them with interest. Lord Rocking-

14. In Fleet Street. Sixty-eight of them had met on the 24th at 11 A.M. 'Sir J. Philips proposed to disappoint both parties by voting against both and making it a void election. Sir Charles Mordaunt, Mr Northey, Mr Crolle, R[oger] N[ewdigate], Mr Bertie, against it. Nothing in the evidence to warrant it. Mr Beckford for it. Came away without any joint resolution' (Sir Roger Newdigate's diary, quoted by Namier, op. cit. 69).

15. (ca 1701–64), 6th Bt; M.P.; HW's distant cousin.

16. He had proposed this, but been opposed, at the 'Tory' meeting (n. 14 above); but nevertheless divided the House on the motion that Simon Luttrell, Newcastle's candidate, had been duly elected, and lost 201–178 (*Journals of the House of Commons* xxvii. 263; Namier, op. cit. 69. See also Rigby to Bedford, 24 March [1755] *Bedford Corr.* ii. 156–7.

17. Sir Lewis Namier describes the actual cause of the 'Tories': 'Some . . . were engaged on either side; a few political leaders such as Philipps, Beckford, and Fazakerley, thought of political manœuvres; but the great body of independent country gentlemen deemed it proper to

judge the case on its merits. Their behaviour was highly respectable but politically ineffective' (ibid. 70).

18. Presumably Newcastle, who had prevailed against Fox (*Mem. Geo. II* ii. 10–14). 10–14).

19. Messages from the King informing the Houses 'that the present situation of affairs makes it requisite to augment his forces by land and sea' were received 25 March and answered immediately, *nem. con.*, by addresses stating that they would 'with the utmost zeal and affection for his royal person, family, and government, effectively enable his Majesty to make such augmentation of his forces by sea and land . . . as shall be found necessary in the present conjuncture' (*Journals of the House of Commons* xxvii. 265; *Journals of the House of Lords* xxviii. 386, where the phrasing is somewhat different).

20. Gaston-Charles-Pierre de Lévis de Lomagne (ca 1699–1757), Marquis (Duc, 1751) de Mirepoix; French ambassador to England 1749–55.

21. The sale of Mead's miniatures, bronzes and sculptures, 11–15 March. For HW's purchases, see MANN iv. 470, n. 18.

ham[22] gave two hundred and thirty guineas for the Antinous[23]—the dearest bust that, I believe, was ever sold; yet the nose and chin were repaired, and very ill. Lord Exeter[24] bought the Homer[25] for one hundred and thirty. I must tell you a piece of fortune: I supped the first night of the sale at Bedford House, and found my Lord Gower[26] dealing at silver pharaoh to the women. 'Oh!' said I laughing, 'I laid out six-and-twenty pounds this morning, I will try if I can win it back;' and threw a shilling upon a card: in five minutes I won a 500-leva, which was twenty-five pounds eleven shillings. I have formerly won a 1000-leva, and another 500-leva.[27]—With such luck, shall not I be able to win you back again?

Last Wednesday I gave a feast in form to the Harrises.[28] There was the Duke of Grafton,[29] Lord and Lady[30] Hertford, Mr Conway, and Lady Ailesbury. In short, all the Conways in the world, my Lord Orford,[31] and the Churchills. We dined in the drawing-room[32] below stairs, amidst the Eagle, Vespasian, etc.[33] You never saw so Roman a banquet; but with all my virtu, the bridegroom seemed the most venerable piece of antiquity.[34] Good-night! The books go to Southampton on Monday.

Yours ever,

Hor. Walpole

22. Charles Watson Wentworth (1730–82), 2d M. of Rockingham; first lord of the Treasury 1765-6, 1782.

23. A beautiful youth, favourite of the Emperor Hadrian, who died 130 A.D.

24. Brownlow Cecil (1725–93), 9th E. of Exeter.

25. Five years later he presented it to the British Museum; for details, see Lort to HW 14 March 1762, Chatterton 153 and n. 87.

26. Granville Leveson Gower (1721–1803), 2d E. Gower, cr. (1786) M. of Stafford; the Ds of Bedford's brother.

27. In 1748 (Mann iii. 494).

28. John Harris (ca 1690–1767), m. (10 March 1755) Hon. Anne Seymour Conway (d. 1774), HW's cousin and H. S. Conway's and Hertford's sister.

29. Charles Fitzroy (1683–1757), 2d D. of Grafton, Lady Hertford's father.

30. Lady Isabella Fitzroy (1726–82), m. (1741) Francis Seymour Conway, 2d Bn Conway, cr. (1750) E. and (1793) M. of Hertford.

31. HW's nephew, George Walpole (1730–91), 3d E. of Orford, 1751.

32. I.e., the Great Parlour.

33. The Boccapadugli eagle which HW had acquired in 1747 and the bust of Vespasian which he purchased at Cardinal Ottoboni's sale at Rome in 1740 (Gray i. 232 and n. 15; Dalrymple 12, nn. 4, 5; Mann iii. 420). HW later moved them both to the Gallery.

34. He was about 65.

To Bentley, Sunday 13 April 1755

Printed from *Works* v. 317–19; reprinted, Wright iii. 109–12, Cunningham ii. 430–3, Toynbee iii. 296–300.

Strawberry Hill, April 13, 1755.

IF I DID not think that you would expect to hear often from me at so critical a season, I should certainly not write to you tonight: I am here alone, out of spirits, and not well. In short, I have depended too much upon my constitution being like

Grass, that escapes the scythe by being low;[1]

and having nothing of the oak in the sturdiness of my stature, I imagined that my mortality would remain pliant as long as I pleased. But I have taken so little care of myself this winter, and kept such bad hours, that I have brought a slow fever upon my nights, and am worn to a skeleton: Bethel[2] has plump cheeks to mine. However, as it would be unpleasant to die just at the beginning of a war, I am taking exercise and air, and much sleep, and intend to see Troy taken. The prospect thickens: there are certainly above twelve thousand men at the Isle of Rhé;[3] some say twenty thousand. An express was yesterday dispatched to Ireland, where it is supposed the storm will burst; but unless our fleet can disappoint the embarkation, I don't see what service the notification can do: we have quite disgarnished that kingdom of troops;[4] and if they once land, ten thousand men may walk from one end of the island to the other. It begins to be thought that the King will not go abroad:[5] that he cannot, everybody has long thought. You will be entertained with a prophecy which my Lord Chesterfield has found in the 35th chapter of Ezekiel, which clearly promises us victory over the French, and expressly relates to this war, as it mentions the two countries (Nova

1. Quotation not found.

2. Mrs Bethel, who had a face like an axe (Montagu i. 41). For a probable identification see Selwyn 105, n. 5.

3. Or Ré, an island off the west coast of France, opposite La Rochelle. An intelligence report received 30 March had said that orders had been sent to Brest to embark the troops on 10 April and that the men of war would be ready to sail on the

15th (Mann iv. 474, n. 1). HW says in *Mem. Geo. II* ii. 20 that the report that 20,000 French were ready to embark for the Isle of Ré arrived 10 April.

4. Eight regiments which had been brought from Ireland to England are listed in GM April 1755, xxv. 185.

5. He set out for Hanover 28 April (*Daily Adv.* 29 April 1755).

Scotia and Acadia)[6] which are the point in dispute. You will have no difficulty in allowing that *mounseer* is typical enough of France: except Cyrus, who is the only heathen prince mentioned by his right name, and that before he had any name, I know no power so expressly described.

2. Son of man, set thy face against *Mount Seir,* and prophesy against it.

3. And say unto it, Thus saith the Lord God: Behold, *O Mount Seir,* I am against thee; and I will stretch out mine hand against thee, and I will make thee most desolate.

4. I will lay thy cities waste, and thou shalt be desolate, etc.

10. Because thou hast said, These two nations and these two countries shall be mine, and we will possess it, etc.

I am disposed to put great trust in this prediction; for I know few things more in our favour. You will ask me naturally, what is to become of you? Are you to be left to all the chance of war, the uncertainty of packets, the difficulty of remittance, the increase of prices?—My dear Sir, do you take me for a prime minister, who acquaints the *states* that they are in damned danger, when it is about a day too late? Or shall I order my *chancellor* to assure you that this is numerically the very day on which it is fit to give such notification, and that a day sooner or a day later would be improper?—But not to trifle politically with you, your redemption is nearer than you think for, though not complete: the terms a little depend upon yourself. You must send me an account, strictly and upon your honour, what your debts are: as there is no possibility for the present but of compounding them, I put my friendship upon it, that you answer me sincerely. Should you, upon the hopes of facilitating your return, not deal ingenuously with me, which I will not suspect, it would occasion what I hope will never happen. Some overtures are going to be made to Miss ——,[7] to ward off impediments from her. In short, though I cannot explain any of the means, your fortune wears another face; and if you send me immediately, upon your honour, a faithful account of what I ask, no time will be lost to labour your return, which I wish so much, and of which I have said so little lately, as I have had better hopes of it. Don't joke with me upon this head, as you sometimes do: be explicit, be open in the

6. Acadia was merely another name for Nova Scotia.

7. Probably Miss Vavassor as *ante* HW to Bentley 27 July 1754.

most unbounded manner, and deal like a man of sense with a heart that deserves you should have no disguises to it. You know me and my style: when I engage earnestly as I do in this business, I can't bear not to be treated in my own way.

Sir Charles Williams is made ambassador to Russia;[8] which concludes all I know. But at such a period, two days may produce much, and I shall not send away my letter till I am in town on Tuesday. Good-night!

Thursday 17th.

All the officers on the Irish establishment are ordered over thither immediately:[9] Lord Hartington has offered to go directly,[10] and sets out with Mr Conway this day sennight. The journey to Hanover is positive: what if there should be a crossing-over and figuring-in[11] of kings? I know who don't think all this very serious; so that, if you have a mind to be in great spirits, you may quote Lord H———.[12] He went to visit the Duchess of Bedford t'other morning, just after Lord Anson had been there and told her his opinion. She asked Lord H——— what news? He knew none. 'Don't you hear there will be certainly war?' 'No, Madam: I saw Mr Nugent yesterday, and he did not tell me anything of it.'[13] She replied, 'I have just seen a man who must know, and who thinks it unavoidable.' 'Nay, Madam, perhaps it may: *I don't think a little war would do us any harm.*' Just as if he had said, losing a little blood in spring is very wholesome; or that a little hissing would not do the Mingotti[14] any harm!

I went t'other morning to see the sale of Mr Pelham's plate,[15]

8. Sir Charles Hanbury Williams was appointed ambassador to Russia 10 April 1755 (D. B. Horn, *British Diplomatic Representatives*, 1932, p. 115).

9. 'His Excellency the Marquis of Hartington, Lord Lieutenant of Ireland, has ordered all such officers of his Majesty's forces upon the establishment of Ireland as are absent, and not on the recruiting service, to repair forthwith to their respective posts in that kingdom' (*Daily Adv.* 16 April 1755).

10. As viceroy (HW). Conway went with him as secretary. The *Whitehall Evening Post* 15–17 April reported that he would embark in 'about ten days' and the *Daily Adv.* 25 April, that he would set out on the 27th, but he apparently did not

leave until 29 April (*Daily Adv.* 1 May 1755); he arrived in Dublin 5 May (Conway to HW 8 May 1755).

11. Dance terms. HW uses the same image to Mann on 22 April (MANN iv. 474).

12. Previous editors, following Wright, have assumed that this was Lord Hertford, but the remark seems out of character.

13. Robert Nugent was at this time a lord of the Treasury and therefore in a position to learn such news early.

14. For the hissing of the Mingotti, see *post* HW to Bentley 19 Oct. 1755.

15. Pelham's plate was sold at auction by Mr Prestage of Savile Row 16–17 April, but had been on view since the 14th (*Daily Adv.* April 1755 *passim*).

with G. Selwyn—'Lord!' says he, 'how many toads have been eaten off those plates!' Adieu! I flatter myself that this will be a comfortable letter to you: but I must repeat, that I expect a very serious answer, and very sober resolutions. If I treat you like a child, consider you have been so. I know I am in the right—more delicacy would appear kinder, without being so kind. As I wish and intend to restore and establish your happiness, I shall go thoroughly to work. You don't want an apothecary, but a surgeon—but I shall give you over at once, if you are either froward or relapse.

Yours till then,

Hor. Walpole

To Bentley, Thursday 24 April 1755

Printed from *Works* v. 319–21; reprinted, Wright iii. 113–15, Cunningham ii. 434–5, Toynbee iii. 302–3.

Arlington Street, April 24, 1755.

I DON'T doubt but you will conclude that this letter, written so soon after my last, comes to notify a great sea-victory, or defeat; or that the French are landed in Ireland, and have taken and fortified Cork; that they have been joined by all the wild Irish, who have proclaimed the Pretender, and are charmed with the prospect of being governed by a true descendant of the Mac-na-O's; or that the King of Prussia, like an unnatural nephew, has seized his uncle[1] and Schutz[2] in a post-chaise, and obliged them to hear the rehearsal of a French opera of his own composing—No such thing! If you will be guessing, you will guess wrong—all I mean to tell you is, that thirteen gold-fish, caparisoned in coats of mail, as rich as if Mademoiselle Scudéri[3] had invented their armour, embarked last Friday on a secret expedition; which, as Mr Weekes[4] and the wisest

1. George II.
2. Augustus Schutz (1690–1757), Keeper of the Privy Purse and Master of the Robes to George II (Montagu i. 112, n. 4).
3. Madeleine de Scudéry (1607–1701), novelist who wrote in a florid style.

4. A carpenter at Twickenham, employed by Mr Walpole (HW). Probably the same as Wicks, mentioned *ante* 9 July 1754.

politicians of Twickenham concluded, was designed against the island of Jersey—but to their consummate mortification, Captain Chevalier[5] is detained by a law-suit, and the poor Chinese adventurers are now frying under deck below bridge.—In short, if your governor[6] is to have any gold-fish, you must come and manage their transport yourself. Did you receive my last letter? If you did, you will not think it impossible that you should preside at such an embarkation.

The war is quite gone out of fashion, and seems adjourned to America: though I am disappointed, I am not surprised. You know my despair about this eventless age! How pleasant to have lived in times when one could have been sure every week of being able to write such a paragraph as this!—'We hear that the *Christians* who were on their voyage for the recovery of the Holy Land, have been massacred in Cyprus by the natives, who were provoked at a rape and murder committed in a church by some young noblemen belonging to the nuncio—' or—'Private letters from Rome attribute the death of his Holiness to poison, which they pretend was given to him in the sacrament, by the Cardinal of St Cecilia, whose mistress he had debauched. The same letters add, that this Cardinal stands the fairest for succeeding to the papal tiara; though a natural son of the late Pope is supported by the whole interest of Arragon and Naples.'—Well! since neither the Pope nor the Most Christian King[7] will play the devil, I must condescend to tell you flippancies of less dignity. There is a young Frenchman here, called Monsieur Hérault.[8] Lady [Caroline Petersham][9] carried him and his governor to sup with her and Miss [Ashe][10] at a tavern t'other night. I have long said that the French were relapsed into barbarity, and quite ignorant of the world—You shall judge: in the first place, the young man was bashful: in the next, the governor, so ignorant as not to have heard of women of fashion carrying men to a tavern, thought it incumbent upon him *to do the honours* for his pupil, who was as

5. Probably either John or Abraham Chevalier (A. C. Saunders, *Jersey in the 18th and 19th Centuries*, Jersey, 1930, pp. 30, 191).

6. Capt. Jean Dumaresq, the deputy governor (*ante* HW to Bentley 8 Feb. 1755, n. 2).

7. Louis XV.

8. Probably Jean-Baptiste-Martin Hé-

rault (1737–59), only surviving son of the late intendant of Paris (La Chenaye-Desbois x. 575).

9. The name is omitted in *Works* but the assumption of earlier editors that it was Lady Caroline Petersham is probably correct; the anecdote is in character.

10. Who was a close friend of Lady Caroline.

modest and as much in a state of nature as the ladies themselves, and hazarded some familiarities with Lady [Caroline]. The consequence was, that the next morning she sent a card to both, to desire they would not come to her ball that evening, to which she had invited them, and to beg the favour of them never to come into her house again. Adieu! I am prodigal of my letters, as I hope not to write you many more.

Yours ever,

Hor. Walpole

To Bentley, April–May 1755

Missing; from the following letter it is clear that HW wrote to Bentley between his letters of 24 April and 6 May.

To Bentley, Tuesday 6 May 1755

Printed from *Works* v. 321–2; reprinted, Wright iii. 116–18, Cunningham ii. 436–8, Toynbee iii. 304–6.

Arlington Street, May 6, 1755.

My dear Sir,

DO YOU get my letters? or do I write only for the entertainment of the clerks of the post office? I have not heard from you this month! It will be very unlucky, if my last to you has miscarried, as it required an answer, of importance to you, and very necessary to my satisfaction.

I told you of Lord P[oulett]'s[1] intended motion.[2] He then re-

1. John Poulett (1708–64), 3d E. Poulett.
2. For the House of Lords to address the King not to go to Hanover. Poulett, who had been first lord of the Bedchamber, had resigned 6 March (Mann iv. 469, n. 12), piqued at the appointment of Rochford, a younger lord, as Groom of the Stole in preference to him, and took this means of showing his resentment. He had given notice early in April of his intentions of making the motion 16 April, but on that day his courage failed him; see the account of proceedings in the Lords on 16 April in Rigby to Bedford 17 April 1755, *Bedford Corr.* i. 160–2.

pented, and wrote to my Lady Yarmouth[3] and Mr Fox[4] to mediate his pardon. Not contented with his reception,[5] he determined to renew his intention. Sir Cordel Firebrace[6] took it up, and intended to move the same address in the Commons, but was prevented by a sudden adjournment. However, the last day but one[7] of the session, Lord P[oulett] read his motion, which was a speech. My Lord Chesterfield (who of all men living seemed to have no business to defend the Duke of N[ewcastle] after much the same sort of ill-usage) said the motion was improper, and moved to adjourn.[8] T'other Earl said, 'Then, pray, my Lords, what is to become of my motion?' The House burst out a-laughing: he divided it,[9] but was single. He then advertised his papers as lost.[10] Legge, in his punning style, said, 'My Lord P[oulett] has had a stroke of an apoplexy; he has lost both his speech and motion.' It is now printed;[11] but not having succeeded in prose, he is turned poet[12]—you may guess how good!

3. Amalie Sophie Marianne von Wendt (1704–65), m. (1727) Adam Gottlieb, Oberhauptmann von Wallmoden; cr. (1740) Cts of Yarmouth, s.j.; George II's mistress.

4. Fox was a friend of Poulett, and had endeavoured to dissuade him from making his motion. He later did approach the King in Poulett's behalf (Earl of Ilchester, *Henry Fox*, 1920, pp. 249–50).

5. Fox left a memorandum of it: 'When the letter was obtained, which was wrote at Mr Fox's request, the King said, "Would you advise one to thank Lord Poulett for not hitting me a slap in the face?" ' (quoted by Ilchester, op. cit. i. 250).

6. Sir Cordell Firebrace (1712–59), 3d Bt; M.P.

7. 24 April. HW gives a similar account of the scene that day in *Mem. Geo. II* ii. 21.

8. Chesterfield explained himself to Dayrolles 2 May 1755: 'You have certainly heard of, and probably seen, Lord Poulett's extraordinary motion, which he made in the House of Lords, just before the rising of the Parliament, when it could not possibly have any good effect, and must necessarily have some bad ones. It was an indecent, ungenerous, and malignant question, which I had no mind should either be put or debated, well knowing the absurd and improper things that

would be said both for and against it, and therefore I moved the House to adjourn, and so put a quiet end to the whole affair' (Chesterfield, *Letters*, ed. Dobrée, 1932, v. 2142-3).

9. On the motion for adjournment (*Journals of the House of Lords* xxviii. 412).

10. 'The Earl of Poulett having lost the copy of a motion made on Thursday last, the 24th instant, in the House of Lords, together with some other papers thereto relating, offers the reward of twenty guineas to any one that brings those papers to his Lordship's house in York Buildings; and will prosecute anyone who shall print any of those papers, excepting the motion itself' (*Daily Adv.* 26 April 1755).

11. The motion is advertised as to be published 1 May 1755 in the *Daily Adv.* 30 April; a second edn was published 6 May (*Daily Adv.* 6 May). It is reprinted in Cobbett, *Parl. Hist.* xv. 521–3. A letter to the lord mayor of London and an 'Introductory Speech to the Motion,' presumably intended to be made by Poulett, was also printed as *Sibylline Leaves, or Anonymous Papers*, on 15 May (*Daily Adv.* 15 May 1755). HW's copy (Hazen, *Cat. of HW's Lib.*, No. 1608:50:4) is now WSL.

12. HW writes that Poulett's 'patriotism

The Duke[13] is at the head of the Regency[14]—you may guess if we are afraid! Both fleets are sailed.[15] The night the King went, there was a magnificent ball and supper at Bedford House.[16] The Duke was there: he was playing at hazard with a great heap of gold before him: somebody said, he looked like the prodigal son and the fatted calf both. In the dessert was a model of Walton Bridge[17] in glass. Yesterday I gave a great breakfast at Strawberry Hill to the Bedford court. There were the Duke and Duchess, Lord Tavistock[18] and Lady Caroline,[19] my Lord and Lady[20] Gower, Lady Caroline Egerton,[21] Lady Betty Waldegrave,[22] Lady Mary Coke,[23] Mrs Pitt,[24] Mr Churchill and Lady Mary, Mr Bap. Leveson,[25] and Colonel Sebright.[26] The first thing I asked Harry was, 'Does the sun shine?' It did; and Strawberry was all gold, and all green. I am not apt to think people really like it, that is, understand it; but I think the flattery of yesterday was sincere; I judge by the notice the Duchess took of your drawings. Oh! how you will think the shades of Strawberry extended! Do you observe the tone of satisfaction with which I say this, as thinking it near? Mrs Pitt brought her French horns: we placed them in the corner of the wood, and it was delightful. Poyang has great custom: I have lately given Count Perron[27] some gold-

... vented itself in reams of papers without meaning, and of verses without metre, which were chiefly addressed to the mayor of Bridgewater, where the Earl had been dabbling in an opposition' (*Mem. Geo. II* ii.18).

13. William Duke of Cumberland (HW).

14. Appointed 26 April (*London Evening Post* 29 April – 1 May 1755).

15. The French fleet sailed 3 May (Georges Lacour-Gayet, *La Marine militaire de la France sous le règne de Louis XV*, 1902, p. 238; the English, on 27 April (*Daily Adv.* 1 May).

16. 'On Monday night [28 April] his Grace the Duke of Bedford gave a grand entertainment, with a ball, to near 400 persons of quality and distinction' (*Daily Adv.* 30 April).

17. A bridge 'of a very peculiar design and exceedingly steep,' opened at Walton-on-Thames in Aug. 1750. It was replaced shortly after 1780. See the contemporary account and engraving in GM 1750, xx. 587–90 and E. W. Brayley, *A Topographical History of Surrey*, [1841–8], ii. 341.

18. Francis Russell (1739–67), styled M. of Tavistock, Bedford's son.

19. Lady Caroline Russell (1743–1811), m. (1762) George Spencer, 3d D. of Marlborough.

20. Lady Louisa Egerton (1723–61), m. (1748) Granville Leveson Gower, 2d E. Gower. Lord Gower was brother of the Ds of Bedford and Lady Gower a niece of the Duke.

21. Lady Carolina Egerton (1724–92), Lady Gower's sister (Collins, *Peerage*, 1812, iii. 208; GM 1792 lxii pt ii. 868).

22. The Duchess of Bedford's sister.

23. Lady Mary Campbell (1727–1811), m. (1747) Edward Coke, styled Vct Coke; HW's correspondent.

24. Anne Pitt (1712–81), William Pitt's sister and HW's correspondent.

25. Hon. Baptist Leveson Gower (?1703–82), Lord Gower's uncle; M.P.

26. John (later Sir John) Sebright (1725–94), 6th Bt, 1761; army officer and M.P.; see BERRY i. 286, n. 22.

27. The Sardinian envoy to England 1749–55 (*ante* HW to Chute 14 May 1754, n. 1).

fish, which he has carried in his post-chaise to Turin: he has already carried some before. The Russian minister[28] has asked me for some too, but I doubt their succeeding there; unless, according to the universality of my system, everything is to be found out at last, and practised everywhere.

I have got a new book that will divert you, called *Anecdotes littéraires*:[29] it is a collection of stories and bons mots of all the French writers; but so many of their bons mots are impertinencies, follies, and vanities, that I have blotted out the title, and written *Misères des savants*. It is a triumph for the ignorant. Gray says, very justly, that learning never should be encouraged, it only draws out fools from their obscurity; and you know, I have always thought a running footman as meritorious a being as a learned man. Why is there more merit in having travelled one's eyes over so many reams of papers, than in having carried one's legs over so many acres of ground? Adieu, my dear Sir! Pray don't be taken prisoner to France, just when you are expected at Strawberry!

Yours ever,

Hor. Walpole

To Bentley, Tuesday 10 June 1755

Printed from *Works* v. 323–6; reprinted, Wright iii. 119–23, Cunningham ii. 439–43, Toynbee iii. 307–12.

Strawberry Hill, June 10, 1755.

MR MÜNTZ[1] is arrived. I am sorry I can by no means give any commendation to the hasty step you took about him. Ten guineas were a great deal too much to advance to him, and must

28. Chernyshev (*ante* HW to Bentley 24 Dec. 1754, n. 14). He was about to return permanently to Russia.

29. First published in 1750, compiled by the Abbé Guillaume-Thomas-François Raynal (1713–96). HW's copy of the second edn in three vols, 1752 (now wsl) is Hazen, *Cat. of HW's Lib.*, No. 1165. It has four short notes by HW and marginal markings throughout in addition to the alteration of the title-page mentioned below.

———

1. Upon Mr Bentley's recommendation, Mr Walpole had invited Mr Müntz from Jersey, and he lived for some time at Strawberry Hill (Mary Berry).

raise expectations in him that will not at all answer. You have entered into no written engagement with him, nor even sent me his receipt for the money. My good Sir, is this the sample you give me of the prudence and providence you have learned? I don't love to enter into the particulars of my own affairs; I will only tell you in one word, that they require great management. My endeavours are all employed to serve you; don't, I beg, give me reasons to apprehend that they will be thrown away. It is much in obscurity whether I shall be able to accomplish your re-establishment; but I shall go on with great discouragement, if I cannot promise myself that you will be a very different person after your return. I shall never have it in my power to do twice what I am now doing for you; and I choose to say the worst beforehand, rather than to reprove you for indolence and thoughtlessness hereafter, when it may be too late. Excuse my being so serious, but I find it is necessary.

You are not displeased with me, I know, even when I pout: you see I am not quite in good humour with you, and I don't disguise it; but I have done scolding you for this time. Indeed I might as well continue it; for I have nothing else to talk of but Strawberry, and of that subject you must be well wearied. I believe she alluded to my disposition to *pout,* rather than meant to compliment me, when my Lady Townshend said to somebody, t'other day, who told her how well Mrs Leneve was, and in spirits, 'Oh! she must be in spirits: why, she lives with Mr Walpole, who is spirit of hartshorn!'

Princess Emily[1a] has been here:—Liked it? Oh no!—I don't wonder;—I never liked St James's.—She was so inquisitive and so curious in prying into the very offices and servants' rooms, that her Captain Bateman[2] was sensible of it, and begged Catherine[3] not to mention it. He addressed himself well, if he hoped to meet with taciturnity! Catherine immediately ran down to the pond, and whispered to all the reeds, 'Lord! that a princess should be such a gossip!' —In short, Strawberry Hill is the puppet-show of the times.

I have lately bought two more portraits of personages in Gram-

---

1a. Princess Amelia Sophia Eleanora (1711–86), dau. of George II.

2. Nathaniel Bateman (d. 1761), later Lt-Col.; equerry and gentleman usher to

Ps Amelia (GM 1761, xxxi. 188; *Court and City Register,* 1755, p. 103).

3. HW's housekeeper; the only references to her are in this letter and *post* 15 Aug. 1755.

mont, Harry Jermyn,[4] and Chiffinch:[5] my Arlington Street is so full of portraits, that I shall scarce find room for Mr Müntz's works.

Wednesday, 11th.

I was prevented from finishing my letter yesterday, but what do you think? By no less magnificent a circumstance than a deluge. We have had an extraordinary drought, no grass, no leaves, no flowers; not a white rose for the festival of yesterday![6] About four arrived such a flood, that we could not see out of the windows: the whole lawn was a lake, though situated on so high an Ararat: presently it broke through the leads, drowned the pretty blue bedchamber, passed through ceilings and floors into the little parlour, terrified Harry, and opened all Catherine's water-gates and *speech-gates*.—I had but just time to collect two dogs, a couple of sheep, a pair of bantams, and a brace of gold-fish; for, in the haste of my zeal to imitate my ancestor Noah, I forgot that fish would not easily be drowned. In short, if you chance to spy a little ark with pinnacles sailing towards Jersey, open the skylight, and you will find some of your acquaintance. You never saw such desolation! A pigeon brings word that Mabland has fared still worse: it never came into my head before, that a rainbow-office for insuring against water might be very necessary. This is a true account of the late deluge.

Witness our hands,
Horace Noah
Catherine Noah, her X mark
Henry Shem
Louis Japhet
Peter Ham, etc.

I was going to seal my letter, and thought I should scarce have anything more important to tell you than the history of the flood, when a most extraordinary piece of news indeed arrived—nothing

4. Henry Jermyn (ca 1636–1708), cr. (1685) Bn Dover and 1689 (in the Jacobite peerage) E. of Dover; 3d Bn Jermyn, 1703. HW was apparently mistaken in the subject of the portrait, since no picture of this Harry Jermyn is mentioned in 'Des. of SH.' HW did own a portrait of his uncle, Henry Jermyn, Earl of St Albans, favourite and reputedly husband of Queen Henrietta Maria, attributed to Old Stone

which later hung in the Gallery at SH ('Des. of SH,' *Works* ii. 464) and was sold SH xxi. 64.

5. William Chiffinch (ca 1602–88), closet-keeper to Charles II. The portrait, attributed to Riley, later hung in the Gallery at SH ('Des. of SH,' *Works* ii. 467; sold SH xxi. 107).

6. The Pretender's birthday (HW).

less than a new gunpowder plot[7]—last Monday was to be the fatal day—There was a ball at Kew—Vanneschi[8] and his son, directors of the Opera, two English lords and two Scotch lords are in confinement at Justice Fielding's.[9]—This is exactly all I know of the matter; and this weighty intelligence is brought by the waterman from my housemaid in Arlington Street, who sent Harry word that the town is in an uproar; and to confirm it, the waterman says he heard the same thing at Hungerford Stairs. I took the liberty to represent to Harry, that the ball at Kew was this day sennight for the Prince's birthday;[10] that, as the Duke was at it, I imagined the Scotch lords would rather have chosen that day for the execution of their tragedy; that I believed Vanneschi's son was a child, and that peers are generally confined at the Tower, not at Justice Fielding's; besides, that we are much nearer to Kew than Hungerford Stairs are.—But Harry, who has not at all recovered the deluge, is extremely disposed to think Vanneschi very like Guy Fawkes; and is so persuaded that so dreadful a story could *not* be invented, that I have been forced to believe it too: and in the course of our reasoning and guessing, I told him, that though I could not fix upon all four, I was persuaded that the late Lord Lovat[11] who was beheaded must be one of the Scotch peers, and Lord A[nson]'s son who is not begot, one of the English.—I was afraid he would think I treated so serious a business too ludicrously, if I had hinted at the scene of distressed friendship that would be occasioned by Lord H[ardwicke]'s examining his intimate Vanneschi. Adieu! my dear Sir—Mr Fox and Lady Caroline, and Lord and Lady Kildare[12] are to dine here today; and if they tell Harry or me any more of the plot, you shall know it.

7. For more accurate details of this 'plot,' see the latter part of this letter.

8. Abate Francesco Vaneschi (fl. 1732–59), manager of the opera (HW to Conway 19 Jan. 1759, n. 11). For his quarrels and difficulties at this time, which led to his bankruptcy the following year, and which probably gave rise to the 'plot,' see especially Charles Burney, *General History of Music*, ed. Mercer, 1935, ii. 855. His son, if he had one, is unidentified.

9. Sir John Fielding (d. 1780), the blind magistrate.

10. 'The ball Wednesday night [4 June] at Kew, on account of his Royal Highness the Prince of Wales's birthday, was very brilliant, and was opened by his Royal Highness and Princess Augusta, and Prince Edward danced with the Right Hon. Lady Jane Scott. His Royal Highness gave a very grand supper, and about five the ball ended' (*London Evening Post* 7–10 June 1755).

11. Simon Fraser (ca 1667–1747), 11th Bn Lovat; executed for participation in the '45.

12. James Fitzgerald (1722–73), 20th E. of Kildare, cr. (1761) M. of Kildare and (1766) D. of Leinster; m. (1747) Lady Emilia Mary Lennox (1731–1814). She m. 2 (1774) William Ogilvie.

Wednesday night.

Well! now for the plot: thus much is true. A laundry-maid of the Duchess of Marlborough,[13] passing by the Cocoa-Tree,[14] saw two gentlemen go in there, one of whom dropped a letter; it was directed, *To You*. She opened it. It was very obscure, talked of designs at Kew miscarried, of new methods to be taken; and as this way of correspondence had been repeated too often, another must be followed; and it told *You* that the next letter to him should be in a bandbox at such a house in the Haymarket. The Duchess concluded it related to a gang of street-robbers, and sent it to Fielding. He sent to the house named, and did find a box and a letter, which, though obscure, had treason enough in it. It talked of a design at Kew miscarried; that the Opera was now the only place, and consequently the scheme must be deferred till next season, especially as *a certain person* is abroad. For the other great person (the Duke), they are sure of him at any time. There was some indirect mention too of gunpowder. Vanneschi and others have been apprehended: but a conclusion was made, that it was a malicious design against the Lord High Treasurer of the Opera and his administration, and so they have been dismissed.[15] Macnamara,[16] I suppose you Jerseyans know, is returned with his fleet to Brest, leaving the transports sailing to America. Lord Thanet and Mr Stanley[17] are just gone to Paris, I believe to inquire after the war.

The weather has been very bad for showing Strawberry to the

13. Elizabeth Trevor (d. 1761), m. (1732) Charles Spencer, 2d D. of Marlborough.
14. A Tory coffee-house, formerly the resort of Jacobites.
15. 'We hear that a treasonable letter was found in a house at Westminster discovered by means of one dropped in the street; in consequence of which some persons were taken into custody, who being examined by Mr Fielding, there was such strong reasons to suspect that the former letter was maliciously conveyed into the said house with an intention either to asperse the character of a particular person, or to disturb the peace and tranquillity of the government, that all the persons were immediately discharged' (*London Evening Post* 10–12 June 1755). A more detailed account, very similar to HW's, is in GM 1755, xxv. 280–1.

16. The French admiral (HW). John MacNamara (ca 1690–1756), known as the Comte de Macnamara, a Frenchman of Irish birth; lieutenant-général des armes navales, 1752; Vice-Adm., 1756 (MANN iv. 482, n. 8). He had returned to Brest with nine ships on 20 May (Georges Lacour-Gayet, *La Marine militaire de la France sous le règne de Louis XV*, 1902, p. 238).
17. Hans Stanley (1721–80) M.P.; diplomatist. He wrote to Lord Huntingdon 4 July from Paris: 'I am come to pass a month at this place with Lord Thanet and Mr Dawkins in virtue of a sudden resolution taken *entre le poire et le fromage*' (Hist. MSS Comm., *Hastings MSS*, Vol. III, 1934, p. 100).

Kildares; we have not been able to stir out of doors: but to make me amends, I have discovered that Lady Kildare is a true Sévignist. You know what pleasure I have in any increase of our sect; I thought she grew handsomer than ever as she talked with devotion of *Notre Dame des Rochers.* Adieu, my dear Sir!

Yours ever,

Hor. Walpole

PS. Tell me if you received this; for in these gunpowder-times to be sure the clerks of the post office are peculiarly alert.

To Bentley, Saturday 5 July 1755

Printed from *Works* v. 326–8; reprinted, Wright iii. 126–8, Cunningham ii. 445–7, Toynbee iii. 315–18.

Strawberry Hill, July 5, 1755.

YOU vex me exceedingly. I beg, if it is not too late, that you would not send me these two new quarries of granite; I had rather pay the original price and leave them where they are, than be encumbered with them. My house is already a stone-cutter's shop, nor do I know what to do with what I have got. But this is not what vexes me, but your desiring me to traffic with Carter,[1] and showing me that you are still open to any visionary project! Do you think I can turn broker, and factor, and I don't know what? And at your time of life do you expect to make a fortune by becoming a granite-merchant? There must be great demand for a commodity that costs a guinea a foot, and a month an inch to polish! You send me no drawings, for which you know I should thank you infinitely, and are hunting for everything that I would thank you for letting alone. In short, my dear Sir, I am determined never to be a projector, nor to deal with projects. If you will still pursue them, I must beg you will not only not employ me in them, but not even let me know that

1. Probably Thomas Carter (d. 1795), a marble-mason famous for his chimney-pieces and monuments. He was later employed for the chimney-pieces in the Gallery at SH and executed the monument to Speaker Chute at the Vyne (Rupert Gunnis, *Dictionary of British Sculptors 1660–1851,* Cambridge, Mass., 1954, pp. 84–6; *SH Accounts,* ed. Toynbee, Oxford, 1927, pp. 10, 120–1).

you employ anybody else. If you will not be content with my plain rational way of serving you, I can do no better; nor can I joke upon it. I can combat any difficulties for your service, but those of your own raising. Not to talk any more crossly, and to prevent, if I can for the future, any more of these expostulations, I must tell you plainly, that with regard to my own circumstances, I generally drive to a penny, and have no money to spare for visions. I do and am doing all I can for you; and let me desire you once for all, not to send me any more persons or things without asking my consent, and staying till you receive it. I cannot help adding to the chapter of complaint* * * *.[2]

These, my dear Sir, are the imprudent difficulties you draw me into, and which almost discourage me from proceeding in your business. If you anticipate your revenue, even while in Jersey, and build castles in the air before you have repassed the sea, can I expect that you will be a better economist either of your fortune or your prudence here? I beg you will preserve this letter, ungracious as it is, because I hope it will serve to prevent my writing any more such—

Now to Mr Müntz:—Hitherto he answers all you promised and vowed for him: he is very modest, humble, and reasonable; and has seen so much and knows so much of countries and languages, that I am not likely to be soon tired of him. His drawings are very pretty: he has done two views of Strawberry[3] that please me extremely: his landscape and trees are much better than I expected. His next work is to be a large picture from your Mabland[4] for Mr Chute, who is much content with him: he goes to the Vine in a fortnight or three weeks. We came from thence the day before yesterday. I have drawn up an *inventionary*[5] of all I propose he should do there; the computation goes a little beyond five thousand pounds; but he does not go half so fast as my impatience demands: he is so reasonable, and will think of dying, and of the gout, and of twenty disagreeable things that one must do and have, that he takes no joy in planting and future views, but distresses all my rapidity of schemes. Last week

2. An omission so indicated in *Works*.

3. Müntz's drawing of the shell bench and bridge at SH, in HW's extra-illustrated copy of the 1784 'Des. of SH,' is dated 1755, and is reproduced in WSL's 'Genesis of SH,' *Metropolitan Museum Studies*, 1934, v pt i. 87. A drawing of the view from SH, from the same 'Des. of SH,' is in MONTAGU i. 53.

4. A book of drawings; see *ante* HW to Bentley 27 July 1754.

5. See Appendix 1.

we were at my sister's at Chaffont[6] in Buckinghamshire, to see what
we could make of it; but it wants so much of everything, and would
require so much more than an inventionary of five thousand pounds,
that we decided nothing, except that Mr Chute has designed[7] the
prettiest house in the world for them. We went to see the objects of
the neighbourhood, Bulstrode[8] and Latimers.[9] The former is a melancholy monument of Dutch magnificence: however, there is a brave
gallery of old pictures,[10] and a chapel with two fine windows of
modern painted glass. The ceiling[11] was formerly decorated with the
assumption, or rather *presumption,* of Chancellor Jeffries,[12] to whom
it belonged; but a very judicious fire hurried him somewhere else.
Latimers belongs to Mrs Cavendish.[13] I have lived there formerly
with Mr Conway,[14] but it is much improved since; yet the river stops
short at an hundred yards just under your eye, and the house has
undergone Batty Langley-discipline:[15] half the ornaments are of
his bastard Gothic,[16] and half of Hallet's mongrel Chinese. I want
to write over the doors of most modern edifices, *Repaired and beau-
tified, Langley and Hallet*[17] *churchwardens.* The great dining-room

6. Lady Mary Churchill's place, called
Chalfont Park, near Chalfont St Peter's,
Bucks. The estate had been purchased earlier in the year by the trustees of Charles
Churchill, senior's, estate, for Charles,
junior, and Lady Mary. It was sold again
in 1792 (*Vict. Co. Hist. Bucks* iii. 196).
It is not clear whether Lady Mary was
living there earlier, or whether her house
was elsewhere.

7. This plan has apparently not survived.

8. Seat of the D. of Portland in Bucks,
built in 1686 by Jeffreys, and purchased
by the 1st E. of Portland in 1706. It was
sold by the Portlands in 1810 to the D.
of Somerset, who pulled it down *(Vict. Co.
Hist. Bucks* iii. 278, 280). In 1763 HW told
Montagu 'I have been often at Bulstrode
from Chaffont, but I don't like it. It is
Dutch and trist' (MONTAGU ii. 104). He
paid another visit in 1770, described in
his *Country Seats* 68.

9. Near Chesham, Bucks. It had been in
the Cavendish family since 1615. It was
rebuilt in an Elizabethan style in the
mid-19th century (*Vict. Co. Hist. Bucks*
iii. 204, 209). There is an engraving in

George Lipscomb, *History . . . of Buckingham,* 1847, iii. facing p. 268.

10. Some of them are described by HW
in *Country Seats* 68; a longer list is in
Lipscombe, op. cit. iv. 507.

11. Of the chapel.

12. George Jeffreys (1648–89), cr. (1685)
Bn Jeffreys; lord chancellor, 1685.

13. Elizabeth Cavendish (*ante* HW to
Bentley 24 Dec. 1754, n. 12).

14. Conway had rented Latimers 1749–
50; HW had visited him there in Sept.
1749 and doubtless at other times as well
(MONTAGU i. 102; Conway to HW 14 Sept.
1749 OS, 28 June, 17 July, 29 Oct. 1750
OS).

15. (1696–1751), architect and writer.

16. As advocated in his *Gothic Architecture Improved by Rules and Proportions,* 1747.

17. William Hallet (1707–81), fashionable cabinet maker (Ralph Edwards, *Dictionary of English Furniture,* revised edn,
1954, ii. 252). On 20 Sept. 1755 HW paid
him £73 11*s.* 4*d.* for the 'Gothic lanthorn'
and various pieces of furniture for the
Refectory (*SH Accounts,* ed. Toynbee,
Oxford, 1927, pp. 6, 82).

is hung with the paper of my staircase, but not shaded properly like mine. I was much more charmed lately at a visit I made to the Cardigans[18] at Blackheath.[19] Would you believe that I had never been in Greenwich Park? I never had, and am transported! Even the glories of Richmond and Twickenham hide their diminished rays.—Yet nothing is equal to the fashion of this village: Mr Müntz says we have more coaches than there are in half France. Mrs Pritchard[20] has bought Ragman's Castle,[21] for which my Lord Litchfield[22] could not agree. We shall be as celebrated as Baiæ or Tivoli; and, if we have not such sonorous names as they boast, we have very famous people: Clive and Pritchard, actresses; Scott[23] and Hudson,[24] painters; my Lady Suffolk, famous in her time; Mr Hickey,[25] the impudent lawyer, that Tom Hervey wrote against;[26] Whitehead,[27] the poet—and Cambridge,[28] the everything. Adieu! my dear Sir—I know not one syllable of news.

Yours ever,

Hor. Walpole

18. George Brudenell (1712–90), 4th E. of Cardigan, cr. (1766) D. of Montagu; m. (1730) Lady Mary Montagu (ca 1711–75).

19. Where Lady Cardigan owned a house 'adjoining to Greenwich Park, on the west side' (Daniel Lysons, *Environs of London*, 1792–6, iv. 462).

20. Hannah Vaughan (1711–68), m. William Pritchard; actress.

21. For an account of this house and its occupants, see R. S. Cobbett, *Memorials of Twickenham*, 1872, pp. 246–8.

22. George Henry Lee (1718–72), 3d E. of Lichfield.

23. Samuel Scott (ca 1710–72), architectural and landscape painter; for his house see Cobbett, op. cit. 293.

24. Thomas Hudson (1701–79), portrait painter. For his house see Cobbett, op. cit. 291–2.

25. Joseph Hickey (ca 1714–94), attorney (GM 1794, lxiv pt ii. 769); for his house at Twickenham see Cobbett, op. cit. 292–3.

26. HW identifies the Hon. Thomas Hervey (1699–1775), pamphleteer, as the author of *A Letter to a Gentleman in the Country, Concerning the Acquittal of Joseph Hickey, Attorney, upon an Indictment for Perjury, before the Lord Chief Justice Lee on Thursday the 11th Instant*, 1751, and *The Case of John Hamilton, against Joseph Hickey, Attorney*, published in Sept. 1751 (GM 1751, xxi. 430), in notes on the title pages of his copies of those pamphlets (now WSL; Hazen, *Cat. of HW's Lib.*, No. 1608:28). Hickey's son, however, describes his father's antagonist as 'a Mr Hervey, who had risen to eminence in the profession [of law], and by it had acquired a large fortune' and gives other details that do not fit Tom Hervey (William Hickey, *Memoirs*, ed. Spencer, 1913–25, i. 5–6).

27. For his house see Cobbett, op. cit. 340–2.

28. Richard Owen Cambridge (1717–1802). He purchased his house at Twickenham, near Richmond Bridge, in 1751 (ibid. 236).

To BENTLEY, Thursday 17 July 1755

Printed from *Works* v. 329–31; reprinted, Wright iii. 130–3, Cunningham ii. 449–52, Toynbee iii. 320–3.

Strawberry Hill, July 17, 1755.

TO BE sure, war is a dreadful calamity, etc.! But then it is a very comfortable commodity for writing letters and writing history; and as one did not contribute to make it, why, there is no harm in being a little amused with looking on: and if one can but keep the Pretender on t'other side Derby, and keep Arlington Street and Strawberry Hill from being carried to Paris, I know nobody that would do more to promote peace, or that will bear the want of it with a better grace than myself. If I don't send you an actual declaration of war[1] in this letter, at least you perceive I am the harbinger of it. An account arrived yesterday morning, that Boscawen had missed the French fleet, who are got into Cape Breton; but two of his captains attacked three of their squadron and have taken two,[2] with scarce any loss. This is the third time one of the French captains[3] has been taken by Boscawen.

Mr Conway is arrived from Ireland, where the triumphant party are what parties in that situation generally are, unreasonable and presumptuous. They will come into no terms without a stipulation that the Primate[4] shall not be in the Regency. This is a bitter pill

1. England did not formally declare war until 17 May 1756; France issued a conditional declaration 21 Dec. 1755 and a more formal one 9 June 1756 (MANN iv. 524 and notes, 556, n. 13, 571, n. 6).

2. 'By letters received by the *Gibraltar* man of war, from Vice-Admiral Boscawen, dated off Louisbourg the 22d of June 1755, there is an account that on the 10th of that month the *Alcide*, a French man of war of 64 guns and 480 men, commanded by M. Hocquart, and the *Lys*, commanded by M. Lageril . . . having eight companies of land forces on board, being separated from the French squadron commanded by M. Bois de Lamothe, fell in with the English fleet off the Banks of Newfoundland, and that a skirmish happened between the said French men of war and his Majesty's ships the *Dunkirk* and De-

fiance, in which the *Alcide* and *Lys* were taken. The French ship the *Dauphin Royal*, which had been in company with the two above mentioned, disappeared in the fog' (*Daily Adv.* 16 July 1755). See also HW to Mann 16 July 1755 (MANN iv. 484 and notes).

3. Toussaint Hocquart de Blincourt (1700–72), Capt., 1746 (MANN iv. 484, n. 4), whom Boscawen had also captured in 1744 and 1747 (Cecil Aspinall-Oglander, *Admiral's Wife*, 1940, p. 17, 43, 169, 183, 195; E. J. Climenson, *Elizabeth Montagu*, 1906, ii. 74).

4. Dr Stone (HW). George Stone (ca 1708–64), D.D.; Abp of Armagh 1747–64. For details of this Irish political crisis, see HW's letters from Conway in 1755, and MANN iv. 315–16.

to digest—but must not it be swallowed? Have we heads to manage a French war and an Irish civil war too?

There are little domestic news. If you insist upon some, why, I believe I could persuade somebody or other to hang themselves; but that is scarce an article uncommon enough to send cross the sea. For example, the rich [Crowley][5] whose brother[6] died of the smallpox a year ago, and left him £400,000 had a fit of the gout last week, and shot himself. I only begin to be afraid that it should grow as necessary to shoot one's self here, as it is to go into the army in France. Sir Robert Browne has lost his last daughter,[7] to whom he could have given eight thousand pounds a year. When I tell these riches and madnesses to Mr Müntz, he stares so, that I sometimes fear he thinks I mean to impose on him. It is cruel to a person who collects the follies of the age for the information of posterity, to have one's veracity doubted: it is the truth of them that makes them worth notice. Charles Townshend marries the great Dowager Dalkeith:[8]—his parts and presumption are prodigious. He wanted nothing but independence to let him loose: I propose great entertainment from him; and now, perhaps, the times will admit it! There may be such things again as parties—odd evolutions happen. The ballad I am going to transcribe for you is a very good comment on so commonplace a text. My Lord Bath, who was brought hither by my Lady Hervey's and Billy Bristow's[9] reports of the charms of the

5. John Crowley (ca 1720 – 5 July 1755), heir to a great iron-mongering fortune (*The East Anglian*, 1869, iii. 97; 1891–2, iv. (n.s.). 159; GM 1755, xxv. 333; *Daily Adv.* 7 July 1755). See also CHATTERTON 76–7 and nn. 25–6 for further details of the family. His suicide is not mentioned in the obituaries in the newspapers, but on 15 July Henry Harris wrote to Sir Charles Hanbury Williams that 'Crowley's next brother having succeeded to £14,000 per annum, found life so *troublesome* that he last week shot himself'; and Selina, Cts of Huntingdon told her son on the 21st that she had heard by that day's post that 'John Crowley has shot himself' (Williams's MSS, now WSL, lxiii, f. 265; Hist. MSS Comm., *Hastings MSS*, Vol. III, 1934, p. 100). He and his brother were apparently at Eton with

HW (*Eton College Register 1698–1752*, ed. R. A. Austen-Leigh, Eton, 1927, p. 91).

6. Ambrose Crowley (ca 1718–54) (*The East Anglian*, loc. cit.; GM 1754, xxiv. 244; *Daily Adv.* 23 May 1754).

7. The second of two daughters (William Betham, *Baronetage of England*, 1801–5, iii. 219).

8. Lady Caroline Campbell (1717–94), m. 1 (1742) Francis Scott, styled E. of Dalkeith; m. 2 (18 Sept. 1755) Charles Townshend; cr. (1767) Bns of Greenwich, s.j. See HW's comments on the approaching marriage in his letter to Montagu 26 July 1755 (MONTAGU i. 171).

9. William Bristow (d. 1758), 'brother of the Countess of Buckingham, friend of Lord Bath, and a great pretender to taste' ('Des. of SH,' *Works* ii. 514; MONTAGU i. 169, n. 5).

place, has made the following stanzas, to the old tune which you remember of Rowe's[10] ballad on Doddington's Mrs Strawbridge:[11]

I.

Some talk of Gunnersbury,[12]
    For Sion[13] some declare;
And some say, that with Chiswick House[14]
    No villa can compare;
But all the beaux of Middlesex,
    Who know the country well,
Say, that Strawberry Hill, that Strawberry
    Doth bear away the bell.

II.

Though Surry boasts its Oatlands,[15]
    And Claremont[16] kept so gim;[17]
And though they talk of Southcote's,[18]
    'Tis but a dainty whim;
For ask the gallant Bristow,
    Who does in taste excel,
If Strawberry Hill, if Strawberry
    Don't bear away the bell.

Can there be an odder revolution of things, than that the printer[19] of the *Craftsman* should live in a house of mine, and that the author of the *Craftsman* should write a panegyric on a house of mine?

10. Nicholas Rowe (1674–1718).

11. (d. 1742), Dodington's mistress to whom he had given a bond of £10,000 'to be paid if he married anybody else' (HW to Lady Ossory 1 Feb. 1787, Ossory ii. 556, where other details are given). HW in that letter, in *Mem. Geo. II* i. 440, and in 'Des. of SH,' *Works* ii. 513, attributes the original ballad to Dodington himself. HW quotes Bath's stanzas to Montagu 17 July 1755 (Montagu i. 169) and, with three more composed by himself in 'Des. of SH,' *Works* ii. 513–14.

12. At Ealing, Middlesex; bought by Ps Amelia in 1761 (Montagu i. 169, n. 6).

13. Sion or Syon House, Isleworth, seat of the E. (now D.) of Northumberland (ibid. n. 7).

14. Built 1725–7 by the 3d E. of Bur-lington and William Kent (ibid. i. 28, n. 25); now public property (*Short Guide to London*, ed. Russell Muirhead, 1956, p. 52).

15. Near Weybridge; seat of the E. of Lincoln and later of the D. of York; burned 1794 (Montagu i. 169, n. 8).

16. Built by Vanbrugh for himself, purchased by Newcastle in 1714; after his death Clive pulled down the house and built a new one (ibid. i. 71, n. 36 *post* HW to Hamilton 19 June 1774).

17. 'Spruce, smart' (obs.—OED).

18. Woburn Farm, Chertsey, Surrey, seat of Philip Southcote (d. 1758), first designer of the *ferme ornée* (Montagu i. 71, n. 34).

19. Richard Francklin (see *ante* HW to Chute 8 June 1756, n. 25).

I dined yesterday at Wanstead:[20] many years have passed since I saw it. The disposition of the house and the prospect are better than I expected, and very fine: the garden, which they tell you cost as much as the house, that is, £100,000 (don't tell Mr Müntz) is wretched; the furniture fine, but totally without taste: such continences and incontinences of Scipio[21] and Alexander, by I don't know whom! such flame-coloured gods and goddesses, by Kent![22] such family-pieces, by—I believe the late Earl[23] himself, for they are as ugly as the children that he really begot! The whole great apartment is of oak, finely carved, unpainted, and has a charming effect. The present Earl[24] is the most generous creature in the world: in the first chamber I entered he offered me four marble tables that lay in cases about the room: I compounded, after forty refusals of everything I commended, to bring away only a haunch of venison: I believe he has not had so cheap a visit a good while. I commend myself, as I ought; for, to be sure, there were twenty ebony chairs, and a couch, and a table, and a glass, that would have tried the virtue of a philosopher of double my size! After dinner we dragged a gold-fish-pond for my Lady F——[25] and Lord S.[26] I could not help telling my Lord Tilney, that they would certainly burn the poor fish for the gold, like old lace. There arrived a Marquis St Simon,[27] from Paris, who understands English, and who has seen your book of designs for Gray's Odes:[28] he was much pleased at meeting me, to whom the in-

20. Near Walthamstow, Essex, designed for Sir Richard Child (after 1734 Tylney) (1680–1750), 2d Bt, cr. (1718) Vct Castlemaine and (1731) E. Tylney, by Colin Campbell. It was begun in 1715 and demolished in 1822. Descriptions, with illustrations from contemporary prints and paintings, are in Fiske Kimball, 'Wanstead House,' *Country Life*, 1933, lxxiv. 605–7, and Geoffrey Atwell, 'Wanstead House,' *Essex Review*, 1954, lxiii. 67–82. The gardens are described in *Country Life*, 1950, cviii. 294–8.

21. The continence of Scipio was a favourite topic with HW; see Ossory i. 265–6, n. 1.

22. Kent adorned the ceiling of the Great Hall with a symbolic painting of 'Morning, Noon, Evening, and Night' (Atwell, op. cit. 70).

23. Richard Child, cr. (1731) E. Tylney of Castlemaine (n. 20 above).

24. John Tylney (to 1734, Child) (1712–84), 2d E. Tylney of Castlemaine, 1750.

25. Previous editors, following Wright, have assumed that this was Lady Fitzroy, i.e. Elizabeth Cosby (d. 1788), m. 1 (1734) Lord Augustus Fitzroy; m. 2 James Jeffreys. Although she was correctly styled Lady Augustus Fitzroy, she was apparently usually known, being mother of the heir apparent to a dukedom, as Lady Fitzroy. See Montagu i. 108, n. 27.

26. Not identified.

27. Maximilien-Henri (1720–99), Marquis de Saint-Simon; writer. For HW's subsequent relations with him, see the following letter.

28. *Designs by Mr R. Bentley for Six Poems by Mr T. Gray*, 1753.

dividual cat[29] belonged—and you may judge whether I was pleased with him. Adieu! my dear Sir.

Yours ever,

Hor. Walpole

From Bentley, Wednesday 30 July 1755

Missing; mentioned *post* 4 August 1755.

From Bentley, Friday 1 August 1755

Missing; mentioned *post* 4 August 1755.

To Bentley, Monday 4 August 1755

Printed from *Works* v. 331–4; reprinted, Wright iii. 135–8, Cunningham ii. 453–6, Toynbee iii. 326–9.

Strawberry Hill, August 4, 1755, between
11 and 12 at night.

I CAME from London today, and am just come from supping at Mrs Clive's, to write to you by the fire-side. We have been exceedingly troubled for some time with St Swithin's diabetes,[1] and have not a dry thread in any walk about us. I am not apt to complain of this malady, nor do I: it keeps us green at present, and will make our shades very thick, against we are fourscore, and fit to enjoy them. I brought with me your two letters of July 30 and August 1; a sight I have not seen a long time!—But, my dear Sir, you have been hurt at my late letters. Do let me say thus much in excuse for

29. Selima, the subject of Gray's 'On the Death of a Favourite Cat, Drowned in a Tub of Gold Fishes,' 1747.

1. The meteorological records in the GM mention rain on 13 days since 15 July (GM 1755, xxv. 295, 343).

myself. You know how much I value, and what real and great satisfaction I have in your drawings. Instead of pleasing me with so little trouble to yourself, do you think it was no mortification to receive everything but your drawings? to find you full of projects, and, I will not say, with some imprudences!—But I have done on this subject—my friendship will always be the same for you; it will only act with more or less cheerfulness, as you use your common sense or your disposition to chimerical schemes and carelessness. To give you all the present satisfaction in my power, I will tell you* * * * * *2

I think your good nature means to reproach me with having dropped any hint of finding amusement in contemplating a war. When one would not do anything to promote it, when one would do anything to put a period to it, when one is too insignificant to contribute to either, I must own I see no blame in thinking an active age more agreeable to live in, than a soporific one.—But, my dear Sir, I must adopt *your* patriotism—Is not it laudable to be revived with the revival of British glory? Can I be an indifferent spectator of the triumphs of my country? Can I help feeling a tattoo at my heart, when the Duke of Newcastle makes as great a figure in history as Burleigh3 or Godolphin4—nay, as Queen Bess herself?— She gained no battles in person; she was only the actuating genius. You seem to have heard of a proclamation of war, of which we have not heard; and not to have come to the knowledge of taking of Beau Séjour5 by Colonel Monckton.6 In short, the French and we seem to have crossed over and figured in, in politics. Mirepoix complained grievously that the Duke of N[ewcastle] had overreached him—But he is to be forgiven in so good a cause! It is the first person he ever deceived!—I am preparing a new folio for heads of the heroes that are to bloom in mezzotinto from this war. At present my chief study is West Indian history. You would not think me very ill-natured if you knew all I feel at the cruelty and villainy of European settlers— But this very morning I found that part of the purchase of Maryland

2. Omission so indicated in *Works*.

3. William Cecil (1521–98), cr. (1571) Bn Burghley; lord high treasurer 1572–98 and chief minister of Queen Elizabeth.

4. Sidney Godolphin (1645–1712), cr. (1684) Bn and (1706) E. of Godolphin; first lord of the Treasury 1690–6; lord high treasurer 1700–1, 1702–10, the financial organizer of Marlborough's victories.

5. News of the surrender of Fort Beau Séjour on the Bay of Fundy on 16 June was printed in the *London Gazette* No. 9497, 26–29 July 1755.

6. Hon. Robert Monckton (1726–82), Lt-Col., 1751; sent to Nova Scotia, 1752; second in command at Quebec, 1759; Lt-Gen., 1770.

from the savage proprietors (for *we* do not massacre, *we* are such good Christians as only to cheat) was a quantity of vermilion and a parcel of Jew's-harps![7]

Indeed, if I pleased, I might have another study; it is my fault if I am not a commentator and a corrector of the press. The Marquis de St-Simon, whom I mentioned to you, at a very first visit proposed[8] to me to look over a translation he had made of *The Tale of a Tub* —the proposal was soon followed by a folio, and a letter of three sides to press me seriously to revise it. You shall judge of my scholar's competence. He translates *L'Estrange,*[9] *Dryden* and others, *l'étrange, Dryden,* etc. Then in the description of the tailor as an idol, and his goose as the symbol;[10] he says in a note, that the *goose* means the dove, and is a concealed satire on the Holy Ghost.—It put me in mind of the Dane, who talking of orders to a Frenchman, said— 'Notre Saint Esprit est un éléphant.'[11]

Don't think, because I prefer your drawings to everything in the world, that I am such a churl as to refuse Mrs B[entley]'s[12] partridges: I shall thank her very much for them. You must excuse me, if I am vain enough to be so convinced of my own taste, that all the neglect that has been thrown upon your designs cannot make me think I have overvalued them. I must think that the states of Jersey who execute your town-house,[13] have much more judgment than all our connoisseurs. When I every day see Greek, and Roman, and Italian, and Chinese, and Gothic architecture embroidered and inlaid upon one another, or called by each other's names, I can't help thinking that the grace and simplicity and truth of your taste, in whichever you undertake, is real taste. I go farther: I wish you would know in what you excel, and not be hunting after twenty things unworthy your genius. If flattery is my turn, believe this to be so.

Mr Müntz is at the Vine, and has been some time. I want to know

---

7. HW's source for this has not been found. The 'Narrative' on which accounts of the settlement of Maryland are usually based, mentions only axes, hoes, and cloth as payment for the first lands.

8. St-Simon's letter to HW of 19 July is now WSL.

9. Sir Roger L'Estrange (1616–1704), pamphleteer and fabulist. This passage is in the 'Author's Apology.'

10. In Section 2 of *The Tale of a Tub.*

11. The Order of the Elephant is the chief Danish order of knighthood, as the Ordre du Saint-Esprit was the chief French order.

12. Called 'Hannah Bernard' or 'Hannah Cliquetis'; her real name is unknown (Montagu i. 308, n. 2).

13. Bentley's design for a town-house at St Helier, Jersey, is now WSL.

more of this history[14] of the German: I do assure you, that I like both his painting and behaviour—but if any history of any kind is to accompany him, I shall be most willing to part with him. However I may divert myself as a spectator of broils, believe me I am thoroughly sick of having anything to do in any. Those in a neighbouring island[15] are likely to subside—and, contrary to custom, the *priest*[16] himself is to be the *sacrifice*.

I have contracted a sort of intimacy with Garrick, who is my neighbour.[17] He affects to study my taste: I lay it all upon you—he admires you. He is building a grateful temple to Shakespeare: I offered him this motto: '*Quod spiro et placeo, si placeo tuum est.*'[18] Don't be surprised if you should hear of me as a gentleman coming upon the stage next winter for my diversion.—The truth is, I make the most of this acquaintance to protect my poor neighbour at *Clivden*—you understand the conundrum, *Clive's den.*

Adieu, my dear Sir! Need I repeat assurances? If I need, believe that nothing that can tend to your recovery has been or shall be neglected by me. You may trust me to the utmost of my power—beyond that, what can I do? Once more, adieu!

Yours ever,

HOR. WALPOLE

To BENTLEY, Friday 15 August 1755

Printed from *Works* v. 334–6; reprinted, Wright iii. 138–40, Cunningham ii. 456–8, Toynbee iii. 329–32.

Strawberry Hill, August 15, 1755.

My dear Sir,

THOUGH I wrote to you so lately, and have certainly nothing new to tell you, I can't help scribbling a line to you tonight,[1] as I am going to Mr Rigby's for a week or ten days, and must thank you

14. HW perhaps means *the* history of *this* German. Bentley had evidently promised an account of Müntz.

15. Ireland.

16. The Primate of Ireland (HW). He was Abp Stone.

17. Garrick had purchased Hampton House in 1754 (Carola Oman Lenanton, *David Garrick*, 1958, pp. 161–2).

18. 'Breath of song and power to please, if please I may, are alike yours' (Horace, *Odes* IV. iii. 24).

1. Rigby wrote to the D. of Bedford 21 Aug.: 'The night before last Mr Walpole came down here for a few days, and as he generally has a good deal of political in-

first for the three pictures. One of them charms me, the Mount Orgueil,[2] which is absolutely fine; the sea, and shadow upon it, are masterly. The other two I don't, at least won't, take for finished. If you please, Elizabeth Castle[3] shall be Mr Müntz's performance: indeed I see nothing of you in it. I do *reconnaître* you in the Hercules and Nessus;[4] but in both, your colours are dirty, carelessly dirty: in your distant hills you are improved, and not hard. The figures are too large—I don't mean in the Elizabeth Castle, for there they are neat; but the centaur, though he dies as well as Garrick can, is outrageous. Hercules and Deianira are by no means so: he is sentimental, and she most improperly sorrowful. However, I am pleased enough to beg you would continue. As soon as Mr Müntz returns from the Vine you shall have a supply of colours. In the mean time, why give up the good old trade of drawing? Have you no Indian ink, no soot-water, no snuff, no coat of onion, no juice of anything? If you love me, draw: you would, if you knew the real pleasure you can give me. I have been studying all your drawings; and next to architecture and trees, I determine that you succeed in nothing better than animals. Now (as the newspapers say) the late ingenious Mr Seymour[5] is dead, I would recommend horses and greyhounds to you. I should think you capable of a landscape or two with delicious bits of architecture. I have known you execute the light of a torch or lanthorn so well, that if it was called Schalken,[6] a housekeeper at Hampton Court or Windsor, or a Catherine at Strawberry Hill, would show it, and say it cost ten thousand pounds. Nay, if I could believe that you would ever execute any more designs I proposed to you, I would give you a hint for a picture that struck me t'other day in Péréfixe's life of Henry IV.[7] He says, the King was often seen

telligence, I think my sending it can but give you the same trouble as reading a newspaper, and you may put equal confidence in it too, if you please.' There follows a report of items of Irish news heard from HW (*Bedford Corr.* ii. 165–6).

2. Which HW later hung in the Gallery at SH ('Des. of SH,' *Works* ii. 466; sold SH xxi. 102). HW describes it in his sketch of Bentley as 'very good' (Appendix 2). A water-colour by Müntz of Mont Orgueil, 1754, is in HW's extra-illustrated *Des. of SH*, 1784, now WSL.

3. A fortress on a rock near St Helier, Jersey. HW describes the painting as by Müntz, in the Red Bedchamber, in 'Des.

of SH' (*Works* ii. 437) but in his account of Bentley, he wrote: 'a small long view of Elizabeth Castle . . . begun by him, but finished by Mr Müntz' (Appendix 2). This may be the view likewise pasted into HW's extra-illustrated *Des. of SH*, 1784.

4. Not mentioned in 'Des. of SH' or HW's account of Bentley.

5. James Seymour (1702–52), painter of horses and hunting subjects.

6. Godfried Schalcken (1643–1706), Dutch painter, famous for his pictures with artificial sources of light.

7. *Histoire du Roy Henry le Grand*, 1661, by Hardouin de Beaumont de Péréfixe (1605–71). HW's copy of the Paris,

lying upon a common straw-bed among the soldiers, with a piece of brown bread in one hand, and a bit of charcoal in t'other, to draw an encampment, or town that he was besieging.[8] If this is not character and a picture, I don't know what is.

I dined today at Garrick's: there were the Duke of Grafton, Lord and Lady Rochford,[9] Lady Holderness,[10] the crooked Mostyn,[11] and Dabreu[12] the Spanish minister; two regents, of which one is Lord Chamberlain,[13] the other Groom of the Stole;[14] and the wife[15] of a Secretary of State. This is being *sur un assez bon ton* for a player! Don't you want to ask me how I like him? Do want, and I will tell you—I like her[16] exceedingly; her behaviour is all sense, and all sweetness too. I don't know how, he does not improve so fast upon me: there is a great deal of parts and vivacity and variety, but there is a great deal too of mimicry and burlesque. I am very ungrateful, for he flatters me abundantly; but unluckily I know it. I was accustomed to it enough when my father was first minister: on his fall I lost it all at once: and since that, I have lived with Mr Chute, who is all vehemence; with Mr Fox, who is all disputation; with Sir Charles Williams, who has no time from flattering himself; with Gray, who does not hate to find fault with me; with Mr Conway, who is all sincerity; and with you and Mr Rigby, who have always laughed at me in a good-natured way. I don't know how, but I think I like all this as well—I beg his pardon, Mr Raftor[17] does flatter me;

1662, quarto edn is Hazen, *Cat. of HW's Lib.*, No. 930.

8. 'Durant la guerre on l'a veu faire le camarade avec le soldat, s'asseoir au corps de garde, s'y coucher sur la paillasse, tenir d'une main un morceau de pain bis qu'il mangeoit, et de l'autre un charbon pour desseigner un campement et des tranchées' (Péréfixe, op. cit., Amsterdam, 1678, pp. 550–1, in a section entitled 'Recueil de quelques belles actions et paroles memorables du Roi Henry le Grand, lesquelles n'ont point esté inserées en sa vie'). There is no evidence that Bentley ever drew the scene.

9. Who were old friends of Garrick.

10. Mary Doublet (ca 1720–1801), m. (1743) Robert Darcy, 4th E. of Holdernesse, 1722.

11. The Mostyns who are often mentioned in Garrick's *Letters*, ed. Little and Kahrl, Cambridge, Mass., 1963, are Ann and Elizabeth Mostyn, presumably nieces

of Mrs Garrick's patroness, Lady Burlington (ibid. i. 176, n. 3, and *passim*). Elizabeth apparently succeeded Ann (d. 1759) as housekeeper of Hampton Court, and d. 1785 (ibid.; *Court and City Register* 1759, p. 79; GM 1759, xxix. 346; 1785, lv pt i. 78). Since the Garricks lived near Hampton Court, Ann Mostyn, who became housekeeper ca 1754, would be their neighbour (*Court and City Register*, 1754, p. 78).

12. Felix de Abreu y Bertodano, Spanish envoy to England 1754–60 (MANN iv. 561, n. 8).

13. Grafton.

14. Rochford.

15. Lady Holdernesse.

16. Mrs Garrick.

17. James Raftor (d. 1790) lived with Mrs Clive, his sister or half-sister (GM 1790, lx pt ii. 861; MONTAGU i. 264, n. 10).

but I should be a cormorant for praise, if I could swallow it whole as he gives it me.

Sir William Yonge,[18] who has been extinct so long, is at last dead; and the war, which began with such a flirt of vivacity, is I think gone to sleep. General Braddock has not yet sent over to claim the surname of Americanus.[19] But why should I take pains to show you in how many ways I know nothing?—Why; I can tell it you in one word—why, Mr [Cambridge] knows nothing!—I wish you good-night!

Yours ever,

Hor. Walpole

From Bentley, Saturday 23 August 1755

Missing; mentioned *post* 18 September 1755.

To Bentley, Thursday 28 August 1755

Printed from *Works* v. 336–8; reprinted Wright iii. 145–7, Cunningham ii. 462–4, Toynbee iii. 338–41.

Arlington Street, August 28, 1755.

OUR piratic laurels, with which the French have so much reproached us, have been exceedingly pruned! Braddock is defeated and killed,[1] by a handful of Indians and by the baseness of his own troops, who sacrificed him and his gallant officers. Indeed, there is some suspicion that cowardice was not the motive, but resentment at having been drafted from Irish regiments.—Were such a desertion universal, could one but commend it? Could one blame men who should refuse to be knocked on the head for sixpence a day,[2]

18. (ca 1693 – 10 Aug. 1755), 4th Bt; M.P.; F.R.S.; had held many offices under Sir Robert Walpole.

19. Braddock had been defeated and killed 9 July, but the news had not yet reached England; see the following letter.

———

1. At the Battle of the Monongahela 9 July; he died of his wounds on the 13th.

The news, which reached London 22 Aug., was published in the *London Gazette* No. 9505, 23–26 Aug. 1755. For further details see HW to Mann 28 Aug. 1755, Mann iv. 494–5.

2. A private soldier in an English regiment of foot received 8 *d.* a day plus 6 *d.* a day subsistence allowance, in an Irish regiment 7 *d.* a day plus 5 *d.* subsistence

and for the advantage and dignity of a few ambitious? But in this case, one pities the brave young officers, who cannot so easily disfranchise themselves from the prejudices of glory!—Our disappointment is greater than our loss: six-and-twenty officers are killed, who, I suppose, have not left a vast many fatherless and *widowless*, as an old woman told me today with great tribulation. The ministry have a much more serious affair on their hands—Lord L[incoln] and Lord A[shburnham][3] have had a dreadful quarrel![4] *Coquus teterrima belli causa!*[5] When Lord [Montfort] shot himself,[6] Lord L[incoln] said, 'Well, I am very sorry for poor [Montfort]! but it is the part of a wise man to make the best of every misfortune—I shall now have the best cook in England.' This was uttered before Lord A[shburnham]. Joras,[7] who is a man of extreme punctilio, as cooks and officers ought to be, would not be hired till he knew whether this Lord [Montfort][8] would retain him. When it was decided that he would not, Lord L[incoln] proposed to hire Joras. Lord A[shburnham] had already engaged him. Such a breach of friendship was soon followed by an expostulation (there was jealousy of the Duke of Newcastle's favour already under the coals): in short, the nephew earl[9] called the favourite earl[10] such gross names, that it was well they were ministers! otherwise, as Mincing says, '*I vow, I believe they must have fit.*'[11] The public, that is, half a dozen toad-eaters, have great hopes that the present unfavourable posture of affairs in America will tend to cement this breach, and that *we* shall all unite hand and heart against the common enemy.

(table of 'Daily Pay of the Land Forces' preceding the title-page of [Great Britain, War Office], *List . . . of the Officers*, 1756), but this was reduced by various deductions.

3. John Ashburnham (1724–1812), 2d E. of Ashburnham, 1737. Mrs Toynbee wrongly guessed Lord Anson.

4. 'A great quarrel has happened between two very wise lords, Lord Lyncon [*sic*] and Lord Ashburnham, which should have a French cook. No water language was ever worse than what passed between them. This gives much uneasiness to the Duke of Newcastle and their intimate friends, it is very unlucky to have these two sorrowful things happen at pretty near the same time' (MS letter Hon. Audrey Townshend to her father, Charles, 3d Vct Townshend 27 Aug. 1755, Raynham

Hall, Norfolk. Transcript kindly furnished by Mr T. S. Blakeney, of North Walls, Chichester, Sussex).

5. 'A cook was the shameful cause of war,' an adaptation of Horace, *Satires* I. iii. 107.

6. 1 Jan. 1755 (*ante* 9 Jan. 1755).

7. The name of the cook in question (HW).

8. Thomas Bromley (1733–99), 2d Bn Montfort, 1755.

9. Lord Lincoln.

10. Lord Ashburnham was 'the chief favourite of the Duke of Newcastle whom he afterwards abandoned being a very prudent and interested man' (*Mem. Geo. III* ii. 134n).

11. Congreve, *The Way of the World*, III iii.

I returned the night before last from my peregrination. It is very unlucky for me that no crown of martyrdom is entailed on zeal for antiquities; I should be a rubric martyr of the first class. After visiting the new salt-water baths at Harwich,[12] (which, next to horse-racing, grows the most fashionable resource for people *who want to get out of town, and who love the country and retirement!*) I went to see Orford Castle,[13] and Lord Hertford's at Sudborn.[14] The one is a ruin, and the other ought to be so. Returning in a one-horse chair over a wild vast heath, I went out of the road to see the remains of Buttley Abbey;[15] which however I could not see: for, as the keys of Orford Castle were at Sudborn, so the keys of Buttley were at Orford! By this time it was night; we lost our way, were in excessive rain for above two hours, and only found our way to be overturned into the mire the next morning going into Ipswich. Since that I went to see an old house[16] built by Secretary Naunton.[17] His descendant,[18] who is a strange retired creature, was unwilling to let us see it; but we did, and little in it worth seeing. The house never was fine, and is now out of repair;[19] has a bed with ivory pillars and loose rings, presented to the secretary by some German prince or German artist; and a small gallery of indifferent portraits, among

12. Advertisements for these from the *Ipswich Journal* for 1753 describing 'a new-invented salt-bath . . . with various contrivances to change the water whenever desired,' and 'a crane chair . . . for such who have not the strength or courage to leap in' are mentioned in the *Essex Review*, 1943, lii. 153. Hot and cold baths made by Griffith Davis are also mentioned in Philip Morant, *History . . . of . . . Essex,* 1768, i. 500, and [P. Muilman], *A New and Complete History of Essex,* Chelmsford, 1772, vi. 100; the latter describes Harwich as 'now deemed a very genteel bathing place, and much resorted to.' A more detailed description of the baths at a later date is in G. A. Cooke, *Topographical and Statistical Description of the County of Essex,* [1823], pp. 47–8.

13. At Orford, Suffolk.

14. Sudbourne, an estate near Orford which Hertford had purchased in 1753 in an attempt to gain control of the Parliamentary borough (see Hertford to HW 1 Sept. 1755, n. 6).

15. Correctly Butley Priory, near Or-

ford, once a large and prosperous Augustinian house; the gatehouse, converted into a mansion, was the chief remain (John Kirby, *The Suffolk Traveller,* 2d edn, 1764, p. 120).

16. Letheringham, near Wickham Market, Suffolk, the seat first of the Wingfields, then of the Nauntons (Frank Groome to Mrs Toynbee 13 Oct. 1900, MS now WSL).

17. Sir Robert Naunton [1563–1635], Master of the Court of Wards. He wrote anecdotes of Queen Elizabeth and her favourites (Mary Berry). HW's copy of Naunton's *Fragmenta regalia,* 1642, is Hazen, *Cat. of HW's Lib.,* No. 1340.

18. William Naunton (d. 1758), descended from Naunton's brother (GM 1758, xxviii. 452; John Nichols, *History and Antiquities of the County of Leicester,* 1795–1815, iii. pt i. *513, *516).

19. It was demolished about 1770 during litigation over the succession to the estate (DNB *sub* Naunton; Nichols, loc. cit.).

which there are scarce any worth notice but of the Earl of North-umberland,[20] Anna Bullen's lover, and of Sir Antony Wingfield;[21] who having his hand tucked into his girdle, the housekeeper told us, had had his fingers cut off by Harry VIII. But Harry VIII was not a man *pour s'arrêter à ces minuties-là!* While we waited for leave to see the house, I strolled into the churchyard, and was struck with a little door open into the chancel, through the arch of which I dis-covered cross-legged knights and painted tombs! In short, there are no less than eight considerable monuments,[22] very perfect, of Wing-fields, Nauntons, and a Sir John Boynet[23] and his wife, as old as Richard II's time. But what charmed me still more, were two figures of Secretary Naunton's father and mother[24] in the window in painted glass, near two feet high, and by far the finest painting on glass I ever saw. His figure, in a puffed doublet, breeches and bonnet, and cloak of scarlet and yellow, is absolutely perfect: her shoulder is damaged. This church, which is scarce bigger than a large chapel, is very ruinous, though containing such treasures! Besides these, there are brasses on the pavement with a succession of all the won-derful head-dresses, which our *plain virtuous* grandmothers invented to tempt our rude and simple ancestors.—I don't know what our nobles might be, but I am sure the milliners three or four hundred years ago must have been more accomplished in the arts, as Prynne[25]

20. Henry Percy (ca 1502–37), 5th E. of Northumberland, 1527.

21. Sir Anthony Wingfield (ca 1485–1552), K.G., 1541; controller of the House-hold, 1550. His third daughter, Elizabeth, married William Naunton and carried Letheringham into that family (W. A. Copinger, *The Manors of Suffolk*, Man-chester, 1905–11, iv. 307).

22. These, and the church, went rapidly to ruin during the later eighteenth cen-tury, and were also much mutilated dur-ing the disputed succession to the estate. Finally, in 1789, church and monuments were sold to the contractor for a new church, and the monuments beaten to powder and sold for tarras (Nichols, loc. cit.). Descriptions of them, plates some of the best, and transcripts of many inscrip-tions are ibid. iii. *513–*16 and in Rich-ard Gough, *Sepulchral Monuments in Great Britain*, 1786–96, i. 218, ii. 27–8.

23. This seems to be an error; HW may have misread an inscription or accidentally

confused several of them when remember-ing his visit. None of the descriptions of the monuments mention one to such a person and his wife (whom HW identi-fies below as Dame Winifred Boynet). There were, however, various monuments there (most of them apparently without legible inscriptions) to members of the Boville or Boiville family (the name is spelled many ways, once as Boynet in a seventeenth-century source) who held the estates from the twelfth to early four-teenth centuries. An heiress had, however, carried Letheringham to the Wingfields well before this time of Richard II, and several of the Wingfield monuments date from his reign (sources cited in the pre-ceding note, and, for the Boville geneal-ogy, Copinger, op. cit. iv. 4–6, 306–7).

24. Henry Naunton (d. 1599), m. Eliza-beth Asheby (ibid. iv. 308).

25. William Prynne (1600–69), Puritan pamphleteer.

calls them, of crisping, curling, frizzling, and frouncing, than all the tirewomen[26] of Babylon, modern Paris, or modern Pall Mall. Dame Winifred Boynet, whom I mentioned above, is accoutred with the coiffure called piked horns, which, if there were any signs in Lothbury and Eastcheap, must have brushed them about strangely, as their Ladyships rode behind their gentlemen ushers! Adieu!

Yours ever,

HOR. WALPOLE

To BENTLEY, Thursday 18 September 1755

Printed from *Works* v. 338–40; reprinted, Wright iii. 148–51, Cunningham ii. 464–6, Toynbee iii. 341–4.

Strawberry Hill, September 18, 1755.

My dear Sir,

AFTER an expectation of six weeks, I have received a letter from you, dated August 23d. Indeed I did not impute any neglect to you; I knew it arose from the war; but Mr S——[1] tells me the packets will now be more regular—Mr S—— tells me!—What, has he been in town, or at Strawberry?—No; but I have been at Southampton: I was at the Vine; and on the arrival of a few fine days, the first we have had this summer, after a deluge, Mr Chute persuaded me to take a jaunt to Winchester and Netley Abbey, with the latter of which he is very justly enchanted.

I was disappointed in Winchester: it is a paltry town, and small: King Charles II's house[2] is the worst thing I ever saw of Sir Christopher Wren, a mixture of a town-hall and an hospital; not to mention the bad choice of the situation in such a country; it is all *ups* that should be *downs*. I talk to you as supposing that you never have been at Winchester, though I suspect you have, for the entrance of

26. An archaic term for ladies' maids (OED).

1. Probably Mr Seward. See *ante* 27 July 1754 and n. 1.
2. Winchester Palace, begun in 1683, but left unfinished after Charles's death in 1685. It was subsequently used as a barracks and burned in 1894. A full account, plans, and prints are in 'The Royal Palaces of Winchester, Whitehall, Kensington and St James's,' *Wren Society*, 1930, vii. 11–69, illustrations, pp. 231–3, and plates I–V.

the cathedral is the very idea of that of Mabland. I like the smugness of the cathedral, and the profusion of the most beautiful Gothic tombs. That of Cardinal Beaufort³ is in a style more free and of more taste than anything I have seen of the kind. His figure confirms me in my opinion that I have struck out the true history of the picture that I bought of Robinson;⁴ and which I take for the marriage of Henry VI.⁵ Besides the monuments of the Saxon kings,⁶ of Lucius,⁷ William Rufus,⁸ his brother,⁹ etc. there are those of six such great or considerable men as Beaufort, William of Wickham,¹⁰ him of Wainfleet,¹¹ the Bishops Fox¹² and Gardiner,¹³ and my Lord Treasurer Portland¹⁴—How much power and ambition under half a dozen stones! I own, I grow to look on tombs as lasting mansions, instead of observing them for curious pieces of architecture!—Going into Southampton, I passed Bevismount, where my Lord Peterborough¹⁵

Hung his trophies o'er his garden gate;¹⁶

3. Henry Beaufort (ca 1375–1447), Bp of Lincoln 1398–1404, of Winchester 1404–47; cardinal, 1426. His chantry is in the south aisle of the retro-choir.

4. Perhaps William Robinson (ca 1720–75) of the Board of Works, who built SH, although there is no other evidence of his selling pictures.

5. This picture, which hung over the fireplace in the Library at SH and is now in the Toledo Museum of Art, is reproduced in Gray ii. facing p. 68. Gray, in his letter of 3 March 1754, concluded that Beaufort was not shown in the picture (ibid. ii. 75), but HW, arguing in the *Anecdotes of Painting* for Beaufort's representation, stated that the face in the picture was 'very like the image on his tomb at Winchester' (*Works* iii. 38). The effigy on Beaufort's tomb at Winchester, however, was not placed there until the reign of Chalres II (John Vaughan, *Winchester Cathedral*, [1919], p. 52). HW later (1777) acquired another portrait he believed to be Beaufort which did not so closely resemble the supposed portrait in 'The Marriage of Henry VI' (Cole ii. 31, 219, 221; Chatterton 184).

6. In the Mortuary Chests on the top of the choir screen; see the description in Vaughan, op. cit. 15–28.

7. The legendary 'first Christian king in Britain.' A tomb was formerly shown as his.

8. William II (d. 1100), K. of England 1087–1100; buried at Winchester but the tomb shown as his is doubtful; see Vaughan, op. cit. 83–7.

9. Richard, D. of Beorn. For his tomb see ibid. 82–3.

10. William of Wykeham (1324–1404), Bp of Winchester 1367–1404.

11. William of Waynefleet (ca 1395–1486), Bp of Winchester 1447–86.

12. Richard Foxe or Fox (ca 1448–1528), Bp of Bath and Wells 1492–4, of Durham 1494–1501, of Winchester 1501–28.

13. Stephen Gardiner.

14. Richard Weston (1577–1635), cr. (1633) E. of Portland; lord high treasurer 1628–35.

15. Charles Mordaunt (ca 1658–1735), 3d E. of Peterborough, 1697.

16. Altered from Pope, *Epistles of Horace* I. i. 8. 'Warton has preserved the tradition that Pope was alluding to the entrance of Lord Peterborough's lawn at Bevismount, near Southampton' (Alexander Pope, *Imitations of Horace*, ed. John Butt, 1939, p. 278, n. 7).

but General Mordaunt[17] was there, and we could not see it. We walked long by moonlight on the terrace along the beach—Guess, if we talked of and wished for you! The town is crowded; sea-baths are established there too. But how shall I describe Netley to you? I can only, by telling you that it is the spot in the world for which Mr Chute and I wish. The ruins are vast,[18] and retain fragments of beautiful fretted roofs pendent in the air, with all variety of Gothic patterns of windows wrapped round and round with ivy—many trees are sprouted up amongst the walls, and only want to be increased with cypresses! A hill rises above the Abbey, encircled with wood: the fort,[19] in which We would build a tower for habitation, remains with two small platforms. This little castle is buried from the Abbey in a wood, in the very centre, on the edge of the hill: on each side breaks in the view of the Southampton sea, deep blue, glistering with silver and vessels; on one side terminated by Southampton, on the other by Calshot Castle; and the Isle of Wight rising above the opposite hills.—In short, they are not the ruins of Netley, but of Paradise—Oh! the purple abbots,[20] what a spot had they chosen to slumber in! The scene is so beautifully tranquil, yet so lively, that they seem only to have *retired into* the world.

I know nothing of the war, but that we catch little French ships like crawfish. They have taken one of ours[21] with Governor Lyttelton[22] going to [South Carolina]. He is a very worthy young man, but so stiffened with Sir [George]'s[23] old fustian, that I am persuaded he is at this minute in the citadel of Nantes comparing himself to Regulus.

Gray has lately been here. He has begun an ode,[24] which if he

---

17. Sir John Mordaunt (1697–1780), K.B., 1749, nephew of Lord Peterborough; Gen.; M.P.

18. A description and photograph of the Abbey ruins are in *Vict. Co. Hist. Hants* iii. 472–6. See also E. H. Jones, *John Adams's Guide to Netley Abbey*, revised edn, Southampton, n.d. and George Guillaume, *Architectural Views and Details of Netley Abbey*, Southampton, 1848.

19. Built in 1545 and maintained until after 1627; it subsequently was turned into a private residence (*Vict. Co. Hist. Hants* iii. 477).

20. Cf. Pope's *Dunciad* iv. 302.

21. 'The *Blandford* man of war, bound for Carolina, was taken so long ago as the 13th ult. by Count du Guay's squadron and carried into Nantes the 5th inst.' (*Public Adv.* 17 Sept.).

22. William Henry Lyttelton (1724–1808), cr. (1794) Bn Lyttelton; governor of South Carolina 1755–60. His appointment as governor was announced in the *London Gazette* No. 9444, 21–5 Jan., *sub* St James's 23 Jan. His release, and arrival in London are in the *Whitehall Evening Post* 18–20 Sept.

23. Lyttelton's brother, Sir George Lyttelton.

24. *The Bard*.

finishes equally, will, I think, inspirit all your drawing again. It is founded on an old tradition of Edward I[25] putting to death the Welsh bards. Nothing but you, or Salvator Rosa,[26] and Nicolò Poussin, can paint up to the expressive horror and dignity of it. Don't think I mean to flatter you; all I would say is, that now the two latter are dead, you must of necessity be Gray's painter. In order to keep your talent alive, I shall next week send you flake white, brushes, oil, and the enclosed directions from Mr Müntz, who is still at the Vine, and whom, for want of you, we labour hard to form. I shall put up in the parcel two or three prints of my Eagle,[27] which, as you never would draw it, is very moderately performed; and yet the drawing was much better than the engraving. I shall send you too a trifling snuff-box, only as a sample of the new manufacture at Battersea,[28] which is done with copper-plates. Mr Chute is at the Vine, where I cannot say any works go on in proportion to my impatience. I have left him an *inventionary*[29] of all I want to have done there; but I believe it may be bound up with the century of projects of that foolish Marquis of Worcester,[30] who printed a catalogue of titles of things, which he gave no directions to execute, nor I believe could. Adieu!

Yours ever,

Hor. Walpole

25. Edward I subdued Wales, 1277–82.

26. (1615–73), landscape painter.

27. Two engravings of HW's eagle were made by Charles Grignion (1717–1810) after a drawing by Samuel Wale (d. 1786). HW sent copies to Mann, 16 July (Mann iv. 485). See ibid. iii. p. vii for a description and iii. 66 for an illustration.

28. For the enamel manufacture at Battersea, see William Chaffers, *Marks and Monograms of . . . Pottery Porcelain*, ed. Littlefield, 14th edn, 1932, pp. 974–9.

29. See Appendix 1.

30. *A Century of the Names and Scantlings of Such Inventions as at Present I Can Call to Mind to Have Tried and Perfected*, 1663, by Edward Somerset (1603–67), 2d M. of Worcester, 1646. HW's copy is Hazen, *Cat. of HW's Lib.*, No. 1608:4:3.

To Bentley, Tuesday 30 September 1755

Printed from *Works* v. 340–1; reprinted, Wright iii. 157–9, Cunningham ii. 472–3, Toynbee iii. 352–3.

Arlington Street, September 30, 1755.

SOLOMON says, somewhere or other, I think it is in Castelvetro's, or Castelnuovo's, edition[1]—is not there such a one?—that the infatuation of a nation for a foolish minister is like that of a lover for an ugly woman: when once he opens his eyes, he wonders what the devil bewitched him. This is the text to the present sermon in politics, which I shall not divide under three heads, but tell you at once, that no minister was ever nearer the precipice than ours has been. I did tell you, I believe, that Legge had refused to sign the warrant for the Hessian subsidy:[2] in short, he heartily resented the quick coldness that followed his exaltation,[3] waited for an opportunity of revenge, found this; and to be sure no vengeance ever took speedier strides. All the world revolted against subsidiary treaties;[4] nobody was left to defend them but Murray,[5] and he did not care to venture. Offers of graciousness, of cabinet councillor, of Chancellor of the Exchequer, were made to right and left. Dr Lee[6] was conscientious; Mr Pitt might be brought in compliment to his M[ajesty] to digest one—But a system of subsidies!—Impossible! In short, the very first ministership was offered to be made over to my Lord Granville—He begged to be excused—he was not fit for it.— Well! you laugh: all this is fact. At last we were forced to strike sail to Mr Fox: he is named for secretary of state, with not only the lead, but the power of the House of Commons. You ask, in the room of which secretary? What signifies of which? Why, I think of Sir Thomas Robinson,[7] who returns to his Wardrobe, and Lord Barrington[8]

1. HW is punning on 'Oldcastle' and 'Newcastle.'
2. One of the 'subsidiary treaties' (see below).
3. To the chancellorship of the Exchequer.
4. 'One subsidiary treaty was hurried on with Hesse; another with Russia, to keep the King of Prussia in awe' (*Mem. Geo. II* ii. 34–5). Copies of the Hessian treaty of 18 June 1755 and of the Russian treaty, signed at St Petersburg 30

Sept., are in *Journals of the House of Commons* xxvii. 308–15 *sub* 26 Nov.
5. William Murray, later Lord Mansfield.
6. Sir George Lee.
7. Robinson had been Master of the Great Wardrobe 1749–54, and returned to it 1755–60.
8. William Wildman Barrington Shute (1717–93), 2d Vct Barrington, 1734; secretary at war 1755–61.

comes into the War Office. This is the present state of things in this grave reasonable island: the union hug like two cats over a string; the rest are arming for opposition—But I will not promise you any more warlike winters; I remember how soon the campaign of the last was addled.

In Ireland, Mr Conway has pacified all things: the Irish are to get as drunk as ever to the glorious and immortal memory of King George, and the prerogative is to be exalted as high as ever, by being obliged to give up the Primate.⁹—There! I think I have told you volumes: yet I know you will not be content; you will want to know something of the war and of America: but I assure you it is not the *bon ton* to talk of either this week. We think not of the former, and of the latter we should think to very little purpose, for we have not heard a syllable more; Braddock's defeat still remains in the situation of the longest battle that ever was fought with nobody. Content your English spirit with knowing that there are very near three thousand French prisoners in England, taken out of several ships.

Yours ever,

Hor. Walpole

From Bentley, September–October 1755

Two letters missing; mentioned in the following letter.

To Bentley, Sunday 19 October 1755

Printed from *Works* v. 342–4. Reprinted, Wright iii. 160–3, Cunningham ii. 474–7, Toynbee iii. 354–7.

Arlington Street, October 19, 1755.

DO YOU love royal quarrels? You may be served—I know you don't love an invasion—nay, that even passes my taste; *it will make too much party.*¹ In short, the Lady Dowager Prudence¹ᵃ begins

---

9. Abp George Stone was excluded from the regency in May 1756.

1. See *ante* HW to Chute 8 June 1756, n. 4.

1a. The Princess of Wales.

to step a little over the threshold of that discretion which she has always hitherto so sanctimoniously observed. She is suspected of strange whims; so strange, as neither to like more German subsidies or more German matches. A strong faction, professedly against the treaties, openly against Mr Fox, and covertly under the banners of the aforesaid *Lady Prudence,* arm from all quarters against the opening of the session. Her Ladyship's eldest boy declares violently against being *bewolfenbuttled*[2]—a word which I don't pretend to understand, as it is not in Mr Johnson's new dictionary.[3] There! now I have been as enigmatic as ever I have accused you of being; and hoping you will not be able to expound my German hieroglyphics, I proceed to tell you in plain English that we are going to be invaded. I have within this day or two seen grandees of ten, twenty, and thirty thousand pounds a year, who are in a mortal fright: consequently, it would be impertinent in much less folk to tremble—and accordingly they don't. At Court there is no doubt but an attempt will be made before Christmas.—I find valour is like virtue: impregnable as they boast themselves, it is discovered that on the first attack both lie strangely open! They are raising more men, camps are to be formed in Kent and Sussex, the Duke of Newcastle is frightened out of his wits, which though he has lost so often you know he always recovers, and as fresh as ever. Lord E[gmont] despairs of the commonwealth; and I am going to fortify my castle of Strawberry, according to an old charter I should have had, for embattling and making a deep ditch—But here am I laughing, when I really ought to cry both with my public eye and my private one. I have told you what I think ought to sluice my public eye: and your private eye too will moisten, when I tell you that poor Miss Harriet Montagu[4] is dead. She died about a fortnight ago; but having nothing else to tell you, I would not send a letter so far with only such melancholy news—and so, you will say, I stayed till I could tell still more bad news. The truth is, I have for some time had two letters of yours to answer: it is three weeks since I wrote to you, and one begins to doubt whether one shall ever be to write again. I will hope all my best hopes, for I have no sort of intention at this time of day of finishing either as a martyr

2. George II had met and been much struck by Sofie Karoline (1737–1817) of Brunswick-Wolfenbüttel, suggesting her as a wife for his grandson, but the Princess, fearful of losing her influence over the Prince, prejudiced him against her, and he refused to enter into any marital negotiations (James, Earl Waldegrave, *Memoirs from 1754 to 1758,* 1821, pp. 39–41; MANN iv. 494).

3. Published 15 April 1755.

4. Sister to Mr George Montagu (HW).

or a hero.—I rather intend to live and record both those professions, if need be—and I have no inclination to scuttle barefoot after a Duke of Wolfenbuttle's army, as Philip de Comines[5] says he saw their Graces of Exeter[6] and Somerset[7] trudge after the Duke of Burgundy's.[8] The invasion, though not much in fashion yet, begins like Moses's rod[9] to swallow other news, both political and *suicidical*. Our politics I have sketched out to you, and can only add, that Mr Fox's ministry does not as yet promise to be of long duration. When it was first thought that he had got the better of the Duke of Newcastle, Charles Townshend said admirably, that he was sure the Duchess,[10] like the old Cavaliers, would make a vow not to shave her beard till the Restoration.[11]

I can't recollect the least morsel of a fess or chevron of the Boynets: they did not happen to enter into any extinct genealogy for whose welfare I interest myself. I sent your letter to Mr Chute, who is still under his own vine: Mr Müntz is still with him, recovering of a violent fever.—Adieu! If memoirs don't grow too memorable, I think this season will produce a large crop.

Yours ever,

Hor. Walpole

PS. I believe I scarce ever mentioned to you last winter the follies of the Opera: the impertinences of a great singer were too old and too common a topic. I must mention them now, when they rise to any improvement in the character of national folly. The Mingotti, a noble figure, a great mistress of music, and a most incomparable actress, surpassed anything I ever saw for the extravagance of her humours. She never sung above one night in three, from a fever upon her temper; and never would act at all when Ricciarelli,[12] the first

5. Philippe de Comines (1445–1509), French chronicler.

6. Henry Holand (1430–75), 2d D. of Exeter, 1447; attainted in 1461.

7. Edmund Beaufort (ca 1439–71), titular D. of Somerset 1464–71.

8. 'J'ay veu ung duc de Cestre [Exeter] aller à pied sans chausses aprés le train dudict duc [Charles (1433–77), Duc de Bourgogne], pourchassent sa vie de maison en maison, sans se nommer. . . . Ceulx de Sombresset et aultres y estoient' (*Mémoires de Philippe de Commynes*, ed. B. de Mandrot, 1901–3, i. 195).

9. It was Aaron's rod, not Moses's, that swallowed up the other rods (Exodus 7.12).

10. Of Newcastle.

11. The Parliamentarians were supposed to have taken such oaths, alluded to in Samuel Butler's *Hudibras*, Pt I, Canto i, i. 269–70:

' 'Twas [his beard] to stand fast
    As long as monarchy should last.'

12. Probably Giuseppe Ricciarelli. For his quarrel with the Mingotti, see HW to Mann 27 May 1756 (MANN iv. 557).

man, was to be in dialogue with her. Her fevers grew so high, that the audience caught them, and hissed her more than once: she herself once turned and hissed again— Tit pro tat geminat τὸν δ' ἀπαμειβομένη.¹³ —Well, among the treaties which a Secretary of State has negotiated this summer, he has contracted for a *succedaneum* to the Mingotti. In short, there is a woman hired to sing when the other shall be out of humour!

Here is a *World*¹⁴ by Lord Chesterfield: the first part is very pretty, till it runs into witticism. I have marked the passages I particularly like.

You would not draw Henry IV at a siege for me: pray don't draw Louis XV.¹⁵

To Bentley, Friday 31 October 1755

Printed from *Works* v. 344–5. Reprinted in Wright iii. 166–7, Cunningham ii. 480–1, misdated and headed 'To Sir Horace Mann,' Toynbee iii. 360–2.

Strawberry Hill, October 31, 1755.

AS THE invasion is not ready, we are forced to take up with a victory. An account came yesterday, that General Johnson¹ had defeated the French near the lake St Sacrement,² had killed one thousand,³ and taken the lieutenant-general who commanded them prisoner; his name is Dieskau,⁴ a Saxon, an esteemed *élève* of Marshal Saxe.⁵ By the printed account, which I enclose, Johnson showed great generalship and bravery.⁶ As the whole business was done by irregu-

13. 'Tit for tat repeats and answering him.' The Greek is a Homeric tag.
14. Number 146, of the fifth volume (HW).
15. Alluding to the subject Mr Walpole had proposed to him for a picture, in Letter XXVII and to the then expected invasion of England by Louis XV (HW).

1. Maj.-Gen. William Johnson (1715–74); cr. (27 Nov. 1755) Bt; superintendent of Indian affairs in North America 1755–74. His account of the Battle of Lake George, 8 Sept., is in BM Add. MSS 20662, f. 155.
2. Renamed Lake George by Johnson

(L. P. Gipson, *British Empire before the American Revolution*, New York, 1936–70, vi. 167).
3. The total French loss was 100 killed and 130 wounded (ibid. vi. 174).
4. Lt.-Gen. Baron Ludwig August von Dieskau (1701–67) (*Neue genealogisch-historische Nachrichten*, 1768, pp. 821–3).
5. Hermann-Maurice Saxe (1696–1750), Comte de Saxe; Maréchal de France. Dieskau had been a cavalry commander under him.
6. 'There is certain advice from Boston in New England, that on the 7th of September, upon the approach of General Johnson, with the New England forces

lars, it does not lessen the faults of Braddock, and the panic of his troops. If I were so disposed, I could conceive that there are heroes in the world who are not quite pleased with this extra-martinette success[7]—but we won't blame those Alexanders, till they have beaten the French in Kent! You know it will be time enough to abuse them, when they have done all the service they can! The other enclosed paper is another *World*,[8] by my Lord Chesterfield; not so pretty, I think, as the last; yet it has merit. While England and France are at war, and Mr Fox and Mr Pitt going to war, his Lordship is coolly amusing himself at picquet at Bath[9] with a Moravian baron,[10] who would be in prison, if his creditors did not occasionally release him to play with and cheat my Lord Chesterfield, as the only chance they have for recovering their money!

We expect the Parliament to be thronged, and great animosities. I will not send you one of the eggs that are laid; for so many political ones have been addled of late years, that I believe all the state game-cocks in the world are impotent.

I did not doubt but you would be struck with the death of poor Bland.[11] I, t'other night, at White's, found a very remarkable entry in our very—very remarkable wager-book: 'Lord [Montfort] bets Sir [John Bland] twenty guineas that Nash[12] outlives Cibber!'[13] How odd that these two old creatures, selected for their antiquities, should live to see both their wagerers put an end to their own lives! Cibber is within a few days of eighty-four, still hearty, and clear, and well. I told him I was glad to see him look so well: 'Faith,' said he, 'it is very well that I look at all!'—I shall thank you for the ormer shells and roots; and shall desire your permission to finish my letter already. As

towards Crown Point, near the great carrying-place, he was vigorously attacked by 2000 French; upon which our advanced guard gave way, in order to bring the French and their Indians from their lurking-places behind trees and bushes, which had its effect, and, by the intrepid behaviour of these New Englandmen, the French, after an obstinate fight of near a whole day, were entirely defeated, with the loss of their artillery and baggage' (*Daily Adv.* 31 Oct. 1755).

7. Alluding to William Duke of Cumberland (HW).

8. Number 148, of the fifth volume (HW).

9. Where he had gone about 19 Sept. (Chesterfield's *Letters*, ed. Dobrée, 1932, pp. 2159, 2163).

10. Not identified.

11. Sir John Bland took his own life in France on 3 Sept. 1755.

12. Richard Nash (1674–1761), 'Beau Nash.'

13. Colley Cibber (1671–1757), actor and dramatist. The exact reading of the entry is 'Nov. 4th, 1754. Lord Montfort wagers Sir John Bland one hundred guineas, that Mr Nash outlives Mr Cibber' (W. B. Boulton, *The History of White's*, 1892, ii. 33).

the Parliament is to meet so soon, you are likely to be overpowered with my dispatches.—I have been thinning my wood of trees, and planting them out more into the field: I am fitting up the old kitchen for a china-room: I am building a bedchamber for myself over the old blue-room, in which I intend to die, though not yet; and some trifles of this kind, which I do not specify to you, because I intend to reserve a little to be quite new to you. Adieu!

Yours ever,

Hor. Walpole

From Bentley, November 1755

Missing; mentioned *post* 16 Nov. 1755.

From Bentley, Wednesday 5 November 1755

Missing; mentioned *post* 17 December 1755.

To Bentley, Sunday 16 November 1755

Printed from *Works* v. 345–7. Reprinted, Wright iii. 172–4, Cunningham ii. 485–7, Toynbee iii. 368–70.

Arlington Street, November 16, 1755.

NEVER was poor invulnerable immortality so soon brought to shame! Alack! I have had the gout! I would fain have persuaded myself that it was a sprain; and, then, that it was only the gout come to look for Mr Chute at Strawberry Hill: but none of my evasions will do! I was, certainly, lame for two days; and though I repelled it—first, by getting wet-shod, and then by spirits of camphor; and though I have since tamed it more rationally by leaving off the little wine I drank, I still know where to look for it whenever I have an occasion for a political illness.—Come, my constitution is not very much broken, when in four days after such a mortifying attack, I could sit in the House of Commons, full as possible, from two at noon till past five in the morning, as we did but last Thursday.[1] The new Opposition attacked the Address.—Who are the new Opposition?—Why, the old Opposition: Pitt and the Grenvilles; indeed, with Legge instead of Sir George Lyttelton. Judge how entertaining it was to me, to hear Lyttelton answer Grenville, and Pitt Lyttelton! The debate, long and uninterrupted as it was, was a great deal of it extremely fine: the numbers did not answer to the merit: the new friends, the Duke of Newcastle and Mr Fox, had 311 to 105. The bon mot in fashion is, that the staff was very good, but they wanted private men. Pitt surpassed himself, and then I need not tell you that he surpassed Cicero and Demosthenes. What a figure would they, with their formal, laboured, cabinet orations, make *vis-à-vis* his manly vivacity and dashing eloquence at one o'clock in the morning, after sitting in that heat for eleven hours! He spoke above an hour and a half, with scarce a bad sentence: the most admired part was a comparison he drew of the two parts of the new administration, to the conflux of the Rhone and the Saône; 'the latter a gentle, feeble, languid stream, languid but not deep; the other a boisterous and overbearing torrent: but they join at last; and long may they continue united, to the comfort of each other, and to the glory, honour and happiness of this nation!' I hope you are not mean-spirited enough to dread an invasion, when the senatorial contests are reviving in the temple of Concord.—*But will it make a party?*[2] Yes, truly; I never saw so promising a prospect. Would not it be cruel, at such a period, to be laid up?

I have only had a note from you to promise me a letter; but it is not arrived:—but the partridges are, and well; and I thank you.

England seems *returning:*[3] for those who are not in Parliament, there are nightly riots at Drury Lane, where there is an anti-Gallican party against some French dancers.[4] The young men of quality have

1. HW gives further details of the debate on 13 Nov. in his letter to Conway 15 Nov. 1755.

2. See *ante* HW to Chute 8 June 1756 and HW to Bentley 6 March 1754, n. 19, 19 Oct. 1755.

3. He means the disposition towards mobs and rioting at public places, which was then common among young men, and had been a sort of fashion in his early youth (Mary Berry).

4. 'Mr Noverre . . . exhibits this evening his *Chinese Festival,* at the Theatre Royal in Drury Lane, in pursuance of a contract made above a year ago with the managers of the said theatre, who beg leave to assure the public, that the insinuation of their engaging at this time an extraordinary number of French dancers is groundless, they having at present as few of that nation as any other theatre now has, or perhaps had. Mr

protected them till last night, when, being Opera night,[5] the galleries were victorious.

Montagu writes me many kind things for you: he is in Cheshire, but comes to town this winter. Adieu! I have so much to say, that I have time to say but very little.

Yours ever,

Hor. Walpole

PS. G. Selwyn hearing much talk of a sea war or a continent, said, 'I am for a sea-war and a *continent* admiral.'

To Bentley, Wednesday 17 December 1755

Printed from *Works* v. 347–9. Reprinted, Wright iii. 178–81, Cunningham ii. 490–3, Toynbee iii. 375–8.

Arlington Street, December 17, 1755.

AFTER an immense interval, I have at last received a long letter from you, of a very old date (November 5th), which amply indemnifies my patience; nay, almost makes me amends for your blindness; for I think, unless you had totally lost your eyes, you would not refuse me a pleasure so easy to yourself, as now and then sending me a drawing.—I can't call it laziness—one may be too idle to amuse one's self; but sure one is never so fond of idleness as to prefer it to the power of obliging a person one loves! And yet I own your letter has made me amends; the wit of your pen recompenses the stupidity of your pencil; the *cæstus* you have taken up supplies a little the *artem* you have relinquished. I could quote twenty passages that have charmed me; the picture of Lady Prudence[1] and her family; your idol that gave you hail when you prayed for sunshine; misfortune the teacher of superstition; unmarried people being the fashion

Noverre and his brothers are Swiss, of a Protestant family in the canton of Bern, his wife and his [*sic*] sisters, German. There are about sixty performers concerned in the entertainment, more than forty of which are English, assisted only by a few French figures (five men and four women) to complete the ballet, as usual' (*Daily Adv.* 8 Nov. 1755).

5. The gentry apparently deserted Drury Lane on opera nights at Haymarket.

1. The Princess of Wales; see *ante* 19 Oct. 1755.

in heaven; the *Spectator-hacked* phrases; Mr Spence's blindness to Pope's mortality; and above all, the criticism on the Queen in *Hamlet* is most delightful. There never was so good a ridicule of all the formal commentators on Shakespear, nor so artful a banter on him himself for so improperly making her Majesty deal in *doubles entendres* at a funeral! In short, I never heard as much wit except in a speech with which Mr Pitt concluded the debate t'other day on the treaties.[2] His antagonists endeavour to disarm him; but as fast as they deprive him of one weapon, he finds a better—I never suspected him of such an universal armoury—I knew he had a Gorgon's head composed of bayonets and pistols, but little thought that he could tickle to death with a feather. On the first debate on these famous treaties, last Wednesday, Hume Campbell,[3] whom the Duke of N[ewcastle] had retained as the most abusive counsel he could find against Pitt (and hereafter perhaps against Fox), attacked the former for *eternal invectives*. Oh! since the last philippic of Billingsgate memory, you never heard such an invective as Pitt returned—Hume Campbell was annihilated! Pitt like an angry wasp seems to have left his sting in the wound—and has since assumed a style of delicate ridicule and repartee.—But think how charming a ridicule must that be that lasts and rises, flash after flash, for an hour and a half! Some day or other perhaps you will see some of the glittering splinters that I gathered up.[4] I have written under his print these lines, which are not only full as just as the original, but have not the tautology of *loftiness* and *majesty*:

> Three orators in distant ages born,
> Greece, Italy, and England did adorn:
> The first in loftiness of thought surpass'd,
> The next in language, but in both the last:
> The pow'r of Nature could no farther go;
> To make a third, she join'd the former two.[5]

Indeed we have wanted such an entertainment to enliven and make the fatigue supportable. We sat on Wednesday till ten at night; on Friday[6] till past three in the morning; on Monday till between nine

2. The treaties of subsidy with the Landgrave of Hesse and the Empress of Russia for defending Hanover.

3. Hon. Alexander Hume-Campbell (1708–60), M.P. Berwickshire 1734–60.

4. They were used in the memoirs. See *Mem. Geo. II* ii. 112–6.

5. Paraphrased from Dryden's *Under Mr Milton's Picture*, beginning 'Three poets, in three distant ages born.' The other orators are Demosthenes and Cicero; see preceding letter.

6. The *Whitehall Evening Post* 11–13 Dec. reported they sat until six A.M.

and ten. We have profusion of orators, and many very great, which is surprising so soon after the leaden age of the late Right Honourable Henry Saturnus!⁷ The majorities are as great as in Saturnus's *golden* age.

Our changes are begun; but not being made at once, our very changes change! Lord Duplin and Lord Darlington are made joint Paymasters:⁸ George Selwyn says, that no act ever showed so much the Duke of Newcastle's absolute power, as his being able to make Lord Darlington *a paymaster*.⁹ That so often *repatrioted* and *reprostituted* prostitute Doddington is again to be treasurer of the Navy:¹⁰ and he again drags out Harry Furnese¹¹ into the Treasury. The Duke of Leeds¹² is to be cofferer, and Lord Sandwich emerges so far as to be chief justice in eyre.¹³ The other parts by the comedians—I don't repeat their names, because perhaps the fellow that today is designed to act Guildenstern, may tomorrow be destined to play *half* the part of the second grave-digger. However, they are all to kiss hands on Saturday. Mr Pitt told me today that he should not go to Bath till next week. 'I fancy,' said I, 'you scarce stay to kiss hands.'

With regard to the invasion, which you are so glad to be allowed to fear, I must tell you that it is quite gone out of fashion again, and I really believe was dressed up for a vehicle (as the apothecaries call it) to make us swallow the treaties. All along the coast of France they are much more afraid of an invasion than we are!

As obliging as you are in sending me plants, I am determined to thank you for nothing but drawings. I am not to be bribed to silence, when you really disoblige me. Mr Müntz has ordered more cloths for you. I even shall send you books unwillingly; and indeed why should I? As you are stone-blind, what can you do with them? The few I shall send you, for there are scarce any new, will be a pretty dialogue by Crébillon;¹⁴ a strange imperfect poem, written by Voltaire when he was very young,¹⁵ which with some charming strokes has a great deal of humour *manqué* and of impiety *estropiée;* and an historical

7. Mr Pelham (HW).
8. Of the Forces.
9. See GRAY ii. 87–8.
10. Bubb Dodington had been treasurer of the Navy 1744–9.
11. Henry Furnese (after 1688–1756), M.P.
12. Thomas Osborne (1713–89), 4th D. of Leeds, 1731.
13. It was Lord Sandys, not Lord Sandwich, who became chief justice in eyre. HW lists all the new appointments in his letter to Mann of 21 Dec. 1755, MANN iv. 517–18.
14. *La Nuit et le moment*, 1755 (Conway to HW 27 Nov. 1755).
15. *La Pucelle d'Orléans*, published about Oct. 1755 (Georges Bengesco, *Voltaire: Bibliographie de ses œuvres*, 1882–90, i. 126).

romance, by him too, of the last war,[16] in which is so outrageous a
lying anecdote of old Marlborough,[17] as would have convinced her,
that when poets write history they stick as little to truth in prose as
in verse. Adieu!

Yours ever,

Hor. Walpole

To Bentley, Tuesday 6 January 1756

Printed from *Works* v. 349–50. Reprinted, Wright iii. 186–7, Cunningham ii.
497–8, Toynbee iii. 384–5.

Strawberry Hill, January 6, 1756.

I AM quite angry with you; you write me letters so entertaining,
that they make me almost forgive your not drawing: now, you
know, next to being disagreeable there is nothing so shocking as
being too agreeable. However, as I am a true philosopher, and can
resist anything I like, when it is to obtain anything I like better, I
declare, that if you don't coin the vast ingot of colours and cloth that
I have sent you, I will burn your letters unopened.

Thank you for all your concern about my gout—but I shall not
mind you; it shall appear in my stomach, before I attempt to keep
it out of it by a fortification of wine: I only drank a little two days
after being very much fatigued in the House, and the worthy pioneer
began to cry *Swear* from my foot the next day. However, though I
am determined to feel young still, I grow to take the hints age gives
me—I come hither oftener, I leave the town to the young; and
though the busy turn that the world has taken draws me back into it,
I excuse it to myself, and call it retiring into politics. From hence I
must retire, or I shall be drowned; my cellars are four feet under
water, the Thames gives itself Rhône airs, and the meadows are more
flooded than when you first saw this place and thought it so dreary.

16. *Histoire de la guerre de 1741*, 1755
(ibid. i. 364).

17. Perhaps the following: 'La hauteur
d'une anglaise avec la reine Anne donna
la paix à l'Europe: la Duchesse de Mal-
bouroug avait révolté l'esprit de la reine,
et lassé sa patience; les Torris en pro-
fitèrent. La reine changea de ministres et
de maximes; l'Angleterre si longtemps
acharnée contre la France fut la première
à faire sa paix' (*Histoire de la guerre de
1741*, 1756 edn, p. 24).

We seem to have taken out our earthquake[1] in rain: since the third week in June, there have not been five days together of dry weather. They tell us that at Colnbrook and Staines they are forced to live in the first floor. Mr Chute is at the Vine, but I don't expect to hear from him; no post but a dove can get from thence. Every post brings new earthquakes;[2] they have felt them in France, Sweden, and Germany:—what a convulsion there has been in nature! Sir Isaac Newton, somewhere in his works, has this beautiful expression, 'The globe will want *manum emendatricem.*'[3]

I have been here this week with only Mr Müntz; from whence you may conclude I have been employed—Mémoires thrive apace. He seems to wonder (for he has not a little of your indolence, I am not surprised you took to him) that I am continually occupied every minute of the day, reading, writing, forming plans: in short, you know me. He is an inoffensive good creature, but had rather ponder over a foreign gazette than a palette.

I expect to find George Montagu in town tomorrow: his brother has at last got a regiment.[4] Not content with having deserved it, before he got it, by distinguished bravery and indefatigable duty, he persists in meriting it still. He immediately, unasked, gave the chaplainship (which others always sell advantageously) to his brother's parson[5] at Greatworth. I am almost afraid it will make my commendation of this really handsome action look interested, when I add, that he has obliged me in the same way, by making Mr Mann his clothier,[6] before I had time to apply for it. Adieu! I find no news in town.

Yours ever,

Hor. Walpole

1. Alluding to the catastrophic earthquake at Lisbon on 1 Nov.

2. Since Christmas, there had been accounts of earthquakes in the *Daily Adv.* for 25, 26, 29, 30 Dec., and 1, 3, 5 Jan.

3. 'The amending hand.'

4. Charles Montagu was appointed, 30 Dec. 1755, Col. of the 61st Foot, which became the 59th Foot ca 1757 (*Army Lists,* 1756, p. 81; 1758, p. 121).

5. James Miller (fl. 1756–80), appointed chaplain of the 61st Foot 15 Jan. 1756 (ibid. 1756, p. 81). He appears for the last time in the *List* for 1780, p. 130.

6. Galfridus Mann (1706–56). See Montagu i. 182.

To Bentley, August 1756

Printed from *Works* v. 270–4. Reprinted, Wright iii. 234–40, Cunningham iii. 27–32, Toynbee iii. 442–8.

Wentworth Castle, August [1756].

I ALWAYS dedicate my travels to you. My present expedition has been very amusing: sights are thick sown in the counties of York and Nottingham: the former is more historic, and the great lords live at a prouder distance: in Nottinghamshire there is a very Heptarchy of little kingdoms elbowing one another, and the barons of them want nothing but small armies to make inroads into one another's parks, murder deer, and massacre park-keepers.—But to come to particulars: the Great Road as far as Stamford is superb: in any other country it would furnish medals, and immortalize any drowsy monarch in whose reign it was executed. It is continued much farther, but is more rumbling. I did not stop at Hatfield and Burleigh to see the palaces of my great-uncle-ministers,[1] having seen them before.[2] Bugden Palace[3] surprises one prettily in a little village; and the remains of Newark Castle, seated pleasantly, began to open a vein of historic memory. I had only transient and distant views of Lord Tyrconnel's[4] at Belton, and of Belvoir.[5] The borders of Huntingdonshire have churches instead of milestones—but the richness and extent of Yorkshire quite charmed me.—Oh! what quarries for working in Gothic! This place is one of the very few that I really like:[6] the situation, woods, views, and the improvements are perfect in their kinds: nobody has a truer taste than Lord Strafford. The house is a pompous front screening an old house: it was built by the last Lord[7] on a design of the Prussian architect Bott,[8] who is mentioned in the King's *Mémoires de Brandenburg*,[9] and is not ugly: the one pair of stairs is entirely engrossed by a gallery of 180 feet, on the plan of

1. HW's descent from Lord Burghley was outlined by HW to Cole 5 June 1775 (Cole i. 374).

2. In an unrecorded tour. HW saw Hatfield again in 1761 and Burghley in 1763 (*Country Seats* 35, 58–9).

3. Or Buckden, in Hunts.

4. Sir John Brownlow (d. 1754) cr. (1718) Vct Tyrconnel. His sister Anne, Lady Cust, had inherited Belton.

5. Near Grantham in Leics.

6. A full history and description of Wentworth Castle are in *Country Life*, 1924, lvi. 588–96, 634–42.

7. Thomas Wentworth (1672–1739), cr. (1711) E. of Strafford.

8. Johann Bott (1670–1745).

9. Frederick the Great, *Mémoires pour servir à l'histoire de la maison de Brandenbourg*.

Building in Strafford's Menagerie
at Wentworth Castle Yorkshire
By mr Bentley 1756.

BENTLEY'S DESIGN FOR A TEMPLE IN
LORD STRAFFORD'S MENAGERIE

that in the Colonna palace at Rome: it has nothing but four modern
statues, and some bad portraits; but, on my proposal, is going to have
books at each end. The hall is pretty, but low; the drawing-room
handsome: there wants a good eating-room, and staircase; but I have
formed a design for both, and I believe they will be executed—That
my plans should be obeyed when yours are not! I shall bring you a
ground-plot for a Gothic building, which I have proposed that you
should draw for a little wood, but in the manner of an ancient market-cross.[10] Without doors all is pleasing: there is a beautiful (artificial) river[11] with a fine semicircular wood overlooking it, and the
temple of Tivoli placed happily on a rising towards the end. There
are obelisks, columns, and other buildings, and above all, a handsome
castle, in the true style, on a rude mountain, with a court and towers;
in the castle-yard, a statue of the late Lord who built it. Without the
park is a lake on each side, buried in noble woods.—Now contrast all
this, and you may have some idea of Lord Rockingham's.[12] Imagine
a most extensive and most beautiful modern front erected before
the great Lord Strafford's old house, and this front almost blocked
up with hills, and everything unfinished round it, nay within it. The
great apartment, which is magnificent, is untouched: the chimney-
pieces lie in boxes unopened. The park is traversed by a common
road between two high hedges—not from necessity—Oh! no; this
Lord loves nothing but horses, and the enclosures for them take place
of everything. The bowling-green behind the house contains no less
than four obelisks, and looks like a Brobdignag ninepin-alley: on
a hill near, you would think you saw the York Buildings waterworks[13] invited into the country. There are temples in corn-fields;
and in the little wood, a window-frame mounted on a bunch of
laurel, and intended for an hermitage. In the inhabited part of the
house, the chimney-pieces are like tombs; and on that in the library
is the figure of this Lord's grandfather[14] in a nightgown of plaster and
gold. Amidst all this litter and bad taste, I adored the fine Vandyck

10. Bentley drew this, after Chichester
Cross, and it was erected. See Montagu i.
295 and n. 15, and Berry i. 66–7. See also
illustration.

11. Lady Louisa Stuart, seeing Wentworth Castle, twenty-two years later, did
not agree: 'I did not like the water which,
though *serpentine*, does not look natural;
and then there is a kind of canal that

comes across down to it that has an
ill effect' (*Gleanings from an Old Port-
folio*, ed. A. G. C. Clarke, Edinburgh,
1895–8, i. 11).

12. Wentworth Woodhouse, between
Barnsley and Rotherham.

13. Shaped like an obelisk.

14. Sir William Wentworth (d. 1692)
(GEC).

of Lord Strafford and his secretary,[15] and could not help reverencing his bedchamber. With all his faults and arbitrary behaviour one must worship his spirit and eloquence: where one esteems but a single royalist, one need not fear being too partial. When I visited his tomb in the church (which is remarkably neat and pretty, and enriched with monuments) I was provoked to find a little mural cabinet, with his figure three feet high kneeling. Instead of a stern bust (and his head would furnish a nobler than Bernini's[16] Brutus) one is peevish to see a plaything that might have been bought at Chenevix's. There is a tender inscription to the second Lord Strafford's wife,[17] written by himself—but his genius was fitter to coo over his wife's memory, than to sacrifice to his father's.

Well! you have had enough of magnificence; you shall repose in a desert.—Old Wortley Montague[18] lives on the very spot where the dragon of Wantley did[19]—only I believe the latter was much better lodged.—You never saw such a wretched hovel, lean, unpainted, and half its nakedness barely shaded with harrateen stretched till it cracks.—Here the miser hoards health and money, his only two objects: he has chronicles in behalf of the air, and battens on Tokay, his single indulgence, as he has heard it is particularly salutary. But the savageness of the scene would charm your Alpine taste: it is tumbled with fragments of mountains, that look ready laid for building the world. One scrambles over a huge terrace, on which mountain ashes and various trees spring out of the very rocks; and at the brow is the den, but not spacious enough for such an inmate. However, I am persuaded it furnished Pope with this line, so exactly it answers to the picture:

On rifted rocks, the dragon's late abodes.[20]

I wanted to ask if Pope had not visited Lady Mary Wortley[21] here during their intimacy—but could one put that question to *Avidien*[22]

15. Sir Philip Mainwaring (1589–1661), secretary to the 'great' E. of Strafford. It is one of Van Dyck's most famous paintings. See Lionel Cust, *Anthony Van Dyck*, 1900, p. 130. In the *Anecdotes of Painting*, HW called it 'the finest picture in my opinion of this master' (*Works* iii. 223).

16. Giovanni Lorenzo Bernini (1598–1680).

17. Henrietta Mary Stanley (1630–85), m. (1655) Lord William Wentworth (1626–95), 2d E. of Strafford, 1641. She was buried at York Minster, but this inscrip-

tion is among the Strafford tombs at Wentworth Woodhouse church.

18. Edward Wortley Montagu (1678–1761), husband of Lady Mary Wortley Montagu.

19. Wharncliffe is the scene of the ballad, 'The Dragon of Wantley' (Thomas Percy, *Reliques of Ancient English Poetry*, ed. H. B. Wheatley, 1876–77, iii. 281).

20. *The Messiah*, l. 71.

21. Lady Mary Pierrepont (1689–1762), m. (1712) Edward Wortley Montagu.

22. Edward Wortley Montagu and Lady

himself? There remains an ancient odd inscription here, which has such a whimsical mixture of devotion and romanticness that I must transcribe it: 'Preye for the soul of Sir Thomas Wortley,[23] knight of the body to the Kings Edward IV, Richard III, Henry VII, Henry VIII, whose faults God pardon. He caused a lodge to be built on this crag in the midst of Wharncliff' (the old orthography) 'to hear the harts bell, in the year of our Lord 1510.'—It was a chase, and what he meant to hear was the noise of the stags.

During my residence here I have made two little excursions; and I assure you it requires resolution: the roads are insufferable: they mend them—I should call it spoil them—with large pieces of stone. At Pomfret I saw the remains of that memorable castle 'where Rivers, Vaughan, and Grey[24] lay shorter by the head';[25] and on which Gray says,

> And thou, proud boy, from Pomfret's walls shalt send
> A groan, and envy oft thy happy grandsire's end![26]

The ruins are vanishing, but well situated; there is a large demolished church, and a pretty market-house. We crossed a Gothic bridge of eight arches at Ferrybridge, where there is a pretty view, and went to a large old house of Lord Huntingdon's at Ledstone, which has nothing remarkable but a lofty terrace, a whole-length portrait of his grandfather[27] in tapestry, and the having belonged to the great Lord Strafford. We saw that monument of part of poor Sir John Bland's extravagance, his house and garden,[28] which he left orders to make without once looking at either plan. The house is a bastard

Mary are savagely satirized as Avidien and his wife in Pope's *Second Satire of the Second Book of Horace*.

23. Presumably the Thomas Wortley who was knighted in 1482; another was knighted in 1497 (W. A. Shaw, *Knights of England*, 1906, ii. 20, 31).

24. '. . . the duke of Gloucester sent the lorde Ryvers, the lord Richard [Grey] and sir Thomas Vaughan . . . into the North-parties into diverse prisones, but at last al came to Pomfret where they al foure were beheaded without judgment' (Edward Hall, *The Union of the two Noble and Illustre Famelies of Lancastre and York*, 1548, AA. vi). Anthony Wydevill (ca 1440–83), 2d E. Rivers, 1469, brother of Edward IV's Queen (Elizabeth) was beheaded at Pontefract (Pomfret) Castle, 25 June 1483,

having been arrested with the others by Richard III's orders when they were escorting young Edward V from Ludlow. Grey (K.B., 1475) and Vaughan (Kt, 1475) were executed about the same time.

25. 'her brother Rivers
    'Ere this lies shorter by the head at Pomfret'
(Nicholas Rowe, *Jane Shore* I. i. 4–5). HW paraphrases the lines in *Catalogue of the Royal and Noble Authors* (*Works* i. 287).

26. Gosse prints these lines among the MS readings of *The Bard* (*Works of Thomas Gray*, New York, 1895, i. 45).

27. Theophilus Hastings (1650–1701), 7th E. of Huntingdon, 1656; he had married the heiress of Ledston, Yorkshire.

28. Kippax Park, near Pomfret.

Gothic, but of not near the extent I had heard. We lay at Leeds, a
dingy large town; and through very bad black roads, for the whole
country is a colliery, or a quarry, we went to Kirkstall Abbey, where
are vast Saxon ruins, in a most picturesque situation, on the banks
of a river that falls in a cascade among rich meadows, hills and woods:
it belongs to Lord Cardigan: his father[29] pulled down a large house
here, lest it should interfere with the family seat, Deane.[30] We returned through Wakefield, where is a pretty Gothic chapel on a
bridge, erected by Edward IV in memory of his father,[31] who lived
at Sandal Castle just by, and perished in the battle here. There is
scarce anything of the castle extant, but it commanded a rich prospect.

By permission from their Graces of Norfolk,[32] who are at Tunbridge, Lord Strafford carried us to Worksop,[33] where we passed two
days. The house is huge, and one of the magnificent works of old
Bess of Hardwicke,[34] who guarded the Queen of Scots[35] here for some
time in a wretched little bedchamber within her own lofty one: there
is a tolerable little picture of Mary's needlework. The great apartment is vast and trist, the whole leanly furnished: the great gallery,
of above two hundred feet, at the top of the house, is divided into a
library, and into nothing. The chapel is decent. There is no prospect,
and the barren face of the country is richly furred with evergreen
plantations, under the direction of the late Lord Petre.[36]

On our way we saw Kiveton, an ugly neglected seat of the Duke
of Leeds, with noble apartments and several good portraits—Oh!
portraits!—I went to Welbeck—It is impossible to describe the
bales of Cavendishes, Harleys, Holleses, Veres, and Ogles: every
chamber is tapestried with them; nay, and with ten thousand other
fat morsels; all their histories inscribed; all their arms, crests, devices,
sculptured on chimneys of various English marbles in ancient forms

29. George Brudenell (d. 1732), 3d E.
of Cardigan, 1703.

30. In Northants near Wansford.

31. Richard (1411–60), 3d D. of York,
died in the battle of Wakefield.

32. The 9th D. of Norfolk had m. (1727)
Mary Blount (ca 1702–73).

33. Built between 1568 and 1590 at
least in part by Robert Smythson (ca
1536–1614), for George Talbot, 6th E. of
Shrewsbury; it burned down in 1761
(John Summerson, *Architecture in Britain
1530 to 1830*, 1954, pp. 31, 35; HW to

Montagu 24 Oct. 1761, Montagu i. 397).
An 18th-century drawing of it by Samuel
Birch is reproduced in Summerson, op.
cit. plate 17.

34. Elizabeth Hardwick (ca 1521–1608),
m. 1 (1532) Robert Barley; m. 2 (1549)
Sir William Cavendish; m. 3 Sir William
St Loe; m. 4 (1568) George Talbot, 6th
E. of Shrewsbury.

35. It was Bess's husband, the E. of
Shrewsbury, who was Mary's keeper.

36. Robert James Petre (1713–42), 8th
Bn Petre, 1713, an amateur botanist.

(and, to say truth, most of them ugly). Then such a Gothic hall, with pendent fretwork in imitation of the old, and with a chimney-piece extremely like mine in the library! Such water-colour pictures! such historic fragments! In short, such and so much of everything I like, that my party thought they should never get me away again. There is Prior's portrait, and the column and Varelst's flower on which he wrote;[37] and the authoress Duchess of Newcastle[38] in a theatric habit, which she generally wore, and, consequently, looking as mad as the present Duchess; and dukes of the same name, looking as foolish as the present Duke; and Lady Mary Wortley, drawn as an authoress,[39] with rather better pretensions; and cabinets and glasses wainscoted with the Greendale oak, which was so large, that an old steward wisely cut a way through it to make a triumphal passage for his lord and lady on their wedding, and only killed it!—But it is impossible to tell you half what there is. The poor woman who is just dead,[40] passed her whole widowhood, except in doing ten thousand right and just things, in collecting and monumenting the portraits and reliques of all the great families from which she descended, and which centred in her. The Duke and Duchess of Portland[41] are expected there to-morrow, and we saw dozens of cabinets and coffers with the seals not yet taken off. What treasurers to revel over! The horseman Duke's[42] *manège* is converted into a lofty stable, and there is still a grove or two of magnificent oaks that have escaped all these great families, though the last Lord Oxford[43] cut down above an hundred thousand

37. Alluding to two poems by Prior: 'To the Lady Elizabeth Harley, since Marchioness of Carmarthen, on a Column of her Drawing,' and 'On a Flower Painted by Simon Verelst [1644–1721].'

38. Margaret Lucas (1617–73), m. (ca 1645) William Cavendish, D. of Newcastle. She wrote plays, and a life of her husband.

39. Almost certainly the portrait by Carlo Francesco Rusca (1696–1769), reproduced in Robert Halsband, *Life of Lady Mary Wortley Montagu*, Oxford, 1956, facing p. 160, from the painting in the possession of the Earl of Wharncliffe, which is inscribed on the back 'done from life by Carolus de Rusca London 1739. Given by her Ladyship to Lady Oxford.' After Lady Oxford's death it presumably went to her daughter the Duchess of Portland who was a great friend of Lady

Mary's daughter Lady Bute and may have given it to her, and she in turn may have left it to her second son's family (information supplied by Professor Halsband).

40. Lady Oxford [Henrietta Cavendish 1694–9 Dec. 1755, m. 1713 Edward Harley, 2d E. of Oxford], widow of the second Earl of Oxford, and mother to the Duchess of Portland (HW).

41. William Bentinck (1709–62), 2d D. of Portland, 1726; m. (1734) Margaret Cavendish Harley (1715–85).

42. William Cavendish (1593–1676), cr. (1665) Duke of Newcastle. He was the author of *La Methode et invention nouvelle de dresser les chevaux*, 1657, and *A New Method and Extraordinary Invention to Dress Horses*, 1667 (not a translation of the former).

43. Edward Harley (ca 1699–1755), 3d E. of Oxford, 1741.

pounds' worth. The place has little pretty, distinct from all these reverend circumstances.

From BENTLEY, October 1756

Missing; mentioned by HW to Montagu 14 Oct. 1756.

From BENTLEY, ca Tuesday 13 February 1759

Missing; mentioned by HW to Gray 15 Feb. 1759.

From BENTLEY, Wednesday 7 March 1781

Printed from Toynbee *Supp.* ii. 162. The MS was among those which passed from HW to Mrs Damer, who bequeathed it to Sir Wathen Waller, 1st Bt; sold Sotheby's 5 Dec. 1921 lot 8 to an unknown purchaser.

March 7, 1781.

Sir,

I JUST now receive from a friend at Oxford the enclosed critique of Dr Johnson upon Gray.[1] Excuse me if from the impulse of sudden indignation, I take a liberty with you, which, most probably, if ever I cool, I shall repent of. This work is to make its appearance within these two months, to *the making,* my correspondent adds *all Oxford too happy.* Such is University rivalry.

I am,
Sir,
Your most humble servant,

R. BENTLEY

From BENTLEY, November 1781

Missing; mentioned by HW to Mason 2 April 1782 (MASON ii. 218–19).

1. In Johnson's life of Gray, published ?May 1781 in vol. 10 of the *Lives of the* *Poets* (Johnson's *Letters,* ed. R. W. Chapman, Oxford, 1952, iii. 468).

Heath Sculp.

William Wentworth, Earl of Strafford, &c.

Pub.^d as the Act directs May 1st 1798. by G.G. & J. Robinson Paternoster Row London.

THE CORRESPONDENCE
WITH THE EARL
OF STRAFFORD

To Strafford, Sunday 6 June 1756

Printed from *Works* v. 431–3; reprinted, Wright iii. 220–2, Cunningham iii. 15–17, Toynbee iii. 428–30.

Strawberry Hill, June 6, 1756.

My dear Lord,

I AM not sorry to be paving my way to Wentworth Castle[1] by a letter, where I suppose you are by this time,[2] and for which I waited: it is not that I stayed so long before I executed my embassy *auprès de milord* Tylney.[3] He has but one pair of gold pheasants[4] at present, but promises my Lady Strafford[5] the first fruits of their loves. He gave me hopes of some pied peacocks sooner, for which I asked directly, as one must wait for the lying-in of the pheasants. If I go on *negotiating* so successfully, I may hope to arrive at a peerage a little sooner than my uncle has.[6]

As your Lordship, I know, is so good as to interest yourself in the calamities of your friends, I will, as shortly as I can, describe and grieve your heart with a catastrophe that has happened to two of them. My Lady A[ilesbury], Mr Conway, and Miss Rich passed two days last week at Strawberry Hill. We were returning from Mrs Clive's through the long field, and had got over the high stile that comes into the road,[7] that is, three of us. It had rained, and the stile was wet. I could not let Miss Rich straddle across so damp a palfrey; but took her in my arms to lift her over. At that instant I saw a coach and six come thundering down the hill from my house; and hurrying to set down my charge, and stepping backwards, I missed the first step, came down headlong with the nymph in my arms: but

1. The Yorkshire seat of William Wentworth (1722–91), 4th E. of Strafford, 1739, three miles southwest of Barnsley. For HW's visit, see *post* 28 Aug. 1756.
2. The Straffords seem to have been still at Boughton, their seat in Northants, on 8 June (Coke, *Journals* i. 1–2).
3. Of Wanstead House, Essex.
4. Lady Strafford's interest in birds, animals, and children is noticed by Lady Louisa Stuart: 'Lady Strafford delighted in animals of every sort and species, had favourite horses, dogs, cats, squirrels, parroquets, and singing birds . . .' ('Some

Account of John Duke Argyll and His Family,' written 1827, privately printed 1863, reprinted in Coke, *Journals* i. p. xlviii).
5. Lady Anne Campbell (ca 1720–85), m. (1741) William Wentworth, 2d E. of Strafford, 1739.
6. 'Old Horace' Walpole had been created Bn Walpole of Wolterton 4 June.
7. The scene of this accident is shown on the plan of SH in 1797, in *SH Accounts*, ed. Toynbee, Oxford, 1927, between pp. 192 and 193.

turning quite round as we rushed to the ground, the first thing that touched the earth was Miss Rich's head. You must guess in how improper a situation we fell; and you must not tell my Lady Strafford before anybody, that every petticoat, etc. in the world were canted— high enough indeed! The coach came on, and never stopped. The apprehension that it would run over my Chloe, made me lie where I was, holding out my arm to keep off the horses, which narrowly missed trampling us to death. The ladies, who were Lady Holderness, Miss Pelham,[8] and your sister Lady M[ary] C[oke], stared with astonishment at the theatre which they thought I had chosen to celebrate our loves; the footmen laughed; and you may imagine the astonishment of Mr Conway and Lady A[ilesbury], who did not see the fall, but turned and saw our attitude. It was these spectators that amazed Miss Pelham, who described the adventure to Mrs Pitt, and said, 'What was most amazing, there was Mr Conway and Lady A[ilesbury] looking on!' I shall be vexed to have told you this long story, if Lady Mary has writ it already;[9] only tell me honestly if she has described it as decently as I have.

If you have not got the new letters and mémoires of Madame Maintenon,[10] I beg I may recommend them for your summer reading. As far as I have got, which is but into the fifth volume[11] of the letters, I think you will find them very curious, and some very entertaining. The fourth volume[12] has persuaded me of the sincerity of her devotion; and two or three letters at the beginning of my present tome[13] have made me even a little jealous for my adored Madame de Sévigné. I am quite glad to find that they do *not* continue equally agreeable. —The extreme misery to which France was reduced at the end of Queen Anne's war,[14] is more striking than one could conceive. I hope it is a debt that they are not going to pay, though the news that ar-

8. Frances Pelham (1728–1804), dau. of Henry Pelham (Montagu i. 53, n. 7).

9. She had probably told the story to the Straffords, her brother-in-law and sister, at Boughton, where she was visiting on the date of this letter (Coke, *Journals* i. 1–5).

10. *Lettres de Mme de Maintenon*, 9 vols 12mo, 1755–6, ed. Laurent Angliviel de la Beaumelle (1726–73), and *Mémoires pour servir à l'histoire de Mme de Maintenon et à celle du siècle passé*, 6 vols 12mo, compiled by him, published in Amsterdam, Feb. 1756. HW's annotated sets of both are now wsl (Hazen, *Cat. of HW's Lib.*, Nos 1255, 1280).

11. Containing letters to the Duc de Noailles, the husband of Mme de Maintenon's niece, pp. [1]–255, and to and from various persons, pp. 255–88.

12. Chiefly her letters to the Cardinal de Noailles, with a few from him.

13. The fifth volume.

14. Or War of the Spanish Succession, 1701–14, ended by the treaties of Utrecht, 1713, Rostatt, and Beden, 1714.

rived on Wednesday[15] have but a black aspect.—The consternation on the behaviour of Byng,[16] and on the amazing council of war at Gibraltar,[17] is extreme: many think both next to impossibilities. In the meantime we fear the loss of Minorca![18] I could not help smiling t'other day at two passages in Madame Maintenon's letters relating to the Duc de Richelieu, when he first came into the world:[19] 'Jamais homme n'a mieux réussi à la cour, la première fois qu'il y a paru: c'est réellement une très jolie créature!' Again:—'C'est la plus aimable poupée qu'on puisse voir.'[20] How mortifying, that this *jolie poupée* should be the avenger of the Valoises![21]

Adieu, my Lord!—I don't believe that a daughter of the Duke of Argyle[22] will think that the present I have announced in the first part of my letter balances the inglorious article in the end. I wish you would both renew the breed of heroes,[23] which seems scarcer than that of gold pheasants!

Your most faithful servant,

Hor. Walpole

15. 2 June, when a Spanish courier arrived from France with reports that the English and French fleets had engaged off Port Mahon, 20 May, 'that ours though they had it in their power, did not choose to come very near, and that after a fight of about three hours . . . ours retired without having received or done the French any considerable damage . . . that our fleet was the superior, Admiral Byng having 13 ships of the line and Monsieur de la Galissonière but 12' (Digby to Sir Charles Hanbury Williams 29 May 1756, Williams's MSS, now WSL, lxiii. f. 34). See also HW to Mann 14 June 1756, MANN iv. 559–62.

16. In retiring without forcing a battle. Byng was court-martialled and executed 14 March 1757 for neglect of duty, having fought on 20 May 1756 an unsuccessful battle with the French fleet that was besieging Port Mahon, Minorca, and not attempting to relieve Minorca. See also *ante* HW to Chute 27 Feb. 1757.

17. 4 May, when it was determined not to give Byng a battalion from the garrison to reinforce Minorca. The news had reached London 31 May; see *ante* HW to Chute 8 June 1756; MANN iv. 559–62.

18. Port Mahon surrendered to the French, 28 June.

19. In 1710.

20. The quotations are from letters to the Duc de Noailles 12 Jan. and 22 May 1711 (Maintenon, op. cit. v. 192, 216).

21. Richelieu commanded the French forces at Minorca. HW is referring to the Hundred Years' War, one cause of which was the accession of the Valois line to the throne of France despite the claim of Edward III of England.

22. Lady Strafford was the youngest daughter of John [2d] Duke of Argyle (HW). HW is mistaken; Lady Strafford was the Duke's second daughter; Lady Mary Coke and Lady Elizabeth Mackenzie were both younger. Lady Greenwich was older.

23. The Straffords 'both . . . bitterly deplored their ill fate in being childless' (Lady Louisa Stuart in Coke, *Journals* i. p. xlviii).

To Strafford, Saturday 28 August 1756

Printed from photostat of the MS which in 1936 was owned by Dr James Strachey, London; left by Mrs Damer to Sir Wathen Waller; sold at the first Waller sale, 5 Dec. 1921, lot 44, to Dobell for £3.

First printed Toynbee *Supp.* i. 142–3.

Arlington Street, Aug. 28, 1756.

My dear Lord:

AFTER such civilities, such kindnesses, as you honoured me with at Wentworth Castle,[1] it is impossible not to trouble you with my thanks and gratitude. I cannot, nor for your sake, would try to make them in proportion, but I shall always remember with the utmost satisfaction the agreeable fortnight I have passed in Yorkshire, and must reproach myself for having so long deferred indulging myself in such pleasure. However, my Lord, as much as I think myself obliged to you, I must be allowed to own how much my Lady Strafford contributed too to make me think this the most agreeable fortnight of my life—don't you think, my Lord, you are a little to be envied who have a wife whose chief pleasure is to distinguish your friends?

Had I not regretted leaving Wentworth Castle, the disagreeableness of my journey would have made me sigh after it: deluges of rain, execrable roads, fractures of my chaise and tumbles of postilions[2] were all I had in change for the prospects, the buildings, the amusements I had left. At Nottingham I could not stir about the town; I did not even see the Castle, which like its master,[3] promises so much and, they say, contains so little; nor did I visit the hole where the *Lord Mortimer*[4] was, *or is to be* caught, I forget which. I

1. HW had reached SH on the night of 25 Aug. on his return from a fortnight's visit in Yorkshire (HW to Montagu 28 Aug. 1756, MONTAGU i. 195). For this and HW's later visits to Strafford, see HW to Bentley *ante* Aug. 1756; *Country Seats* 27–8 (1760), 65 (1768), 71 (1772).

2. 'Besides floods the whole day, I had twenty accidents with my chaise, and once saw one of the postilions with the wheel upon his body; he came off with making his nose bleed' (MONTAGU loc. cit).

3. The Duke of Newcastle (HW).

4. Roger de Mortimer (1287–1330), 8th Bn Mortimer, 1304, cr. (1328) E. of March. 'Mortimer's Hole' is the cavern where he was supposedly captured by Edward III's agents after the governor of Nottingham Castle had revealed to them a secret underground passage leading into the castle (Robert Thoroton, *History of Nottinghamshire*, ed. John Throsby, Nottingham, 1790, ii. 27–9); or more plausibly, the underground passage itself. See also MANN vi. 53 and n. 7.

did go to Clifton,[5] that is I swam thither, and as one can't swim post, I lost half a day in that expedition. The prospect has all the extent and magnificence of Wentworth Castle, with all the beauty of our poor little Thames: no spot ever wanted so little to be made enchantment. I was disappointed in the church;[6] though there are many monuments, their ruins are ruined, and their place no more. In the house, there are about three pictures standing on the ground, of which one is a very fine Vandyke.[7] I passed Newstead[8] and Wollaton[9] literally in the dark and another place where, though quite night, I started at the vision of one of my own towers. I was sure it did not appear to me to tell me there was money buried under it, and I hoped it had not been murdered—I soon recollected that it must be Boughton.[10]

The Thames is more overflowed than in the depth of winter: a coach full of ladies were overturned into it t'other day just at your Lordship's door at Twickenham:[11] if these floods continue, one shall be forced to travel in post-arks. Mr Bentley has got the ground-plan,[12] and is most proud to be employed for Wentworth Castle;[13] though I have frightened him with the accounts of the good taste that pre-

5. Clifton Hall, built on an escarpment overlooking the Trent; 4 m. SW of Nottingham; seat of Sir Robert Clifton, 5th Bt, in whose family it had been since the Conquest; described and illustrated in *Country Life*, 1923, liv. 246–54.

6. St Mary's Church, Clifton. It contains monuments and brasses of the Clifton family (Thoroton, op. cit. i. 109–13). See also Harry Gill, 'The Church of St Mary, Clifton,' *Transactions of the Thoroton Society*, 1919, xxiii. 23–32.

7. Not identified but possibly the 'Descent from the Cross' illustrated in *Country Life*, op. cit. 247.

8. Newstead Abbey, the seat of Lord Byron, about 10 miles north of Nottingham. HW visited it in 1760 (*post* HW to Strafford 4 Sept. 1760).

9. Wollaton Hall, across the Trent from Clifton Hall; the seat of Bn Middleton; now in the western suburbs of Nottingham.

10. Seat of Lord Strafford where he had copied a tower of Strawberry Hill (HW). Boughton Park, near Northampton, purchased by Strafford's father from Lord

Ashburnham, 1717. In 1889 it was the property of Mr Howard Vyse, who inherited it through Lady Lucy Howard, Strafford's sister (Coke, *Journals* i. 1, n. 2).

11. Strafford's house, on the river at Twickenham, had originally belonged to the Pepys's friend Dr William Fuller; Strafford's father bought it in 1701. On Strafford's death it went to his sister Lady Anne Conolly, who pulled it down and built a house known as Mount Lebanon (R. S. Cobbett, *Memorials of Twickenham*, 1872, p. 249; Daniel Lysons, *Environs of London*, 1892–6, iii. 576).

12. For a Gothic building in a wood, modelled on a market-cross; see *ante* HW to Bentley Aug. 1756, and n. 10. It was completed by 1760, when HW saw it standing 'on a high bank in the menagerie'; Arthur Young also praised it (MONTAGU i. 295 and n. 15).

13. Bentley in 1755 had designed a chimney-piece for Lord Strafford, who considered it 'old fashioned' (*ante* HW to Bentley 27 March 1755). Later plans had also been rejected (*ante* HW to Bentley Aug. 1756).

dominates there. If he produces an ugly design, I have threatened that it shall be pounded in a paddock with half a dozen colts and temples at Wentworth House.[14]

I called yesterday at Chiswick and found the Duke of Norfolk, but the Duchess was at Tunbridge; I thanked abundantly for myself,[15] and as much as was proper for my friends. I commended all I could remember, but found I did not make my court about the new menagerie;[16] he cut me short with, 'I think the old one was pretty enough.'—I immediately thought so too.

The enclosed cards[17] are the newest productions of this new-producing season; the two portraits[18] are droll, and undoubtedly G. Townshend's;[19] the other card[20] is dull and obscure. Adieu! my dear good Lord, I hope your seeds of kindness will always fall in as thankful ground as they have with

Your most obliged
and most devoted humble servant

HOR. WALPOLE

From STRAFFORD, ca Saturday 2 July 1757

Missing; mentioned *post* 4 July 1757.

14. See HW's comments on Wentworth Woodhouse, Lord Rockingham's seat, *ante* HW to Bentley Aug. 1756.
15. And General Conway had been two days at Worksop with Lord and Lady Strafford with the Duke's permission (HW).
16. Presumably at Worksop.
17. Missing.
18. Perhaps 'The Pillars of the State,' an engraving published in August, representing half-length portraits in profile of Fox and Newcastle. Newcastle is examin-ing Fox through his glass (BM, *Satiric Prints* iii pt ii. 997–8, No. 3371).
19. George Townshend (1724–1807), 4th Vct Townshend, 1764; cr. (1787) M. Townshend; soldier and politician. For his caricatures, see *Mem. Geo. II* ii. 228; *Mem. Geo. III* i. 18; Herbert M. Atherton, 'George Townshend, Caricaturist' in *Eighteenth-Century Studies*, Berkeley, Cal., 1971, iv. 437–46.
20. Not identified. HW sent the two prints to Montagu the same day (MONTAGU i. 195).

To Strafford, Monday 4 July 1757

Printed from *Works* v. 433–5; reprinted, Wright iii. 301–4, Cunningham iii. 87–9, Toynbee iv. 70–3.

Strawberry Hill, July 4, 1757.

My dear Lord,

IT IS well I have not obeyed you sooner, as I have often been going to do: what a heap of lies and contradictions I should have sent you! What joint ministries and sole ministries! What acceptances and resignations!—Viziers and bowstrings never succeeded one another quicker. Luckily I have stayed till we have got an administration that will last a little more than for ever.[1] There is such content and harmony in it, that I don't know whether it is not as perfect as a plan which I formed for Charles Stanhope,[2] after he had plagued me for two days for news. I told him the Duke of Newcastle was to take orders, and have the reversion of the bishopric of Winchester;[3] that Mr Pitt was to have a regiment, and go over to the Duke;[4] and Mr Fox to be chamberlain to the Princess,[5] in the room of Sir William Irby.[6] Of all the new system I believe the happiest is O[ffley];[7] though in great humility he says he only takes the Bedchamber *to accommodate*.[8] Next to him in joy is the Earl of Holderness[9]—who

1. The coalition ministry of Pitt and Newcastle. Pitt accepted the appointment 18 June and the new ministry kissed hands 29 June. For further details of this extended government crisis, see Mann 20 June 1757, MANN v. 103–5.

2. See *ante* HW to Chute 30 April 1754.

3. Benjamin Hoadly was Bishop of Winchester from 1734 until his death in 1761.

4. Of Cumberland, who was commanding the army in Germany.

5. Of Wales. Fox was particularly unpopular with the Princess.

6. (1707–75), 2d Bt, 1718, cr. (1761) Bn Boston; lord chamberlain to the Ps of Wales 1751–72; M.P. Launceston 1735–47.

7. John Offley had been appointed groom of the Bedchamber (*ante* HW to Bentley 9 Jan. 1755).

8. The post Offley lost in July 1757, surveyor of the King's private roads, paid £1018 a year; his new post paid £500 a year, to which was added in 1758 a secret service pension of £400 a year. He was a supporter of Newcastle when he held both offices (Sir Lewis Namier and John Brooke, *House of Commons 1754–1790*, 1964, iii. 223).

9. Secretary of State for the North 1754 – March 1761. He had resigned in June but had been reappointed; see HW to Mann 9, 14, 20 June 1757, MANN v. 98, 100, 103.

has not got the Garter.[10] My Lord Waldegrave[11] has; and the Garter by this time I believe has got fifty spots.[12]

Had I written sooner, I should have told your Lordship too of the King of Prussia's triumphs—but they are addled too![13] I hoped to have had a few bricks from Prague to send you towards building Mr Bentley's design,[14] but I fear none will come from thence this summer. Thank God, the happiness of the menagerie does not depend upon administrations or victories! The happiest of beings in this part of the world is my Lady Suffolk: I really think her acquisition and conclusion of her lawsuit[15] will lengthen her life ten years. You may be sure I am not so satisfied, as Lady Mary[16] has left Sudbroke.[17]

Are your charming lawns burnt up like our humble hills? Is your sweet river[18] as low as our deserted Thames?—I am wishing for a handful or two of those floods that drowned me last year all the way from Wentworth Castle. I beg my best compliments to my Lady, and my best wishes that every pheasant egg and peacock egg may produce as many colours as a harlequin-jacket.

I am hers and your Lordship's most devoted humble servant,

HOR. WALPOLE

Tuesday, July 5.

Luckily, my good Lord, my conscience had saved its distance. I had writ the above last night, when I received the honour of your kind letter[19] this morning. You had, as I did not doubt, received

10. Holdernesse, 'to whom the King had long promised a Garter, . . . died without receiving it' (*Last Journals* ii. 175).

11. James Waldegrave (1715–63), 2d E. Waldegrave, 1741; named as first lord of the Treasury 8–12 June 1757, but did not form a ministry; elected and invested K. G. 30 June, installed 30 Aug. 1757.

12. He was apt to be dirty (HW). Cf. MANN v. 98, n. 5.

13. Frederick II had been besieging Prague, but the siege was raised 20 June. News of this and of Frederick's defeat at Kolin arrived in London 1 July (MANN v. 95, n. 1, 109 and nn. 4–7).

14. See *ante* HW to Bentley Aug. 1756, n. 10.

15. Perhaps concerned with her family affairs; her brother, Lord Buckinghamshire, had died in the preceding year.

16. Lady Mary Coke, daughter of John Campbell, Duke of Argyle, and sister to Lady Strafford (HW).

17. Sudbrooke, near Richmond; built ca 1726–8 by John, 2d D. of Argyll; seat of his widow 1743–67, Lady Mary's mother, then of Lady Mary's sister, Lady Greenwich, 1767–94, then of the Dukes of Buccleuch 1794–1825; sold 1825 to Robert Wilmot Horton, sold 1842 to Crown; later leased to the Richmond Golf Club. See H. M. Cundall, *Sudbrook and Its Occupants*, 1912.

18. The Dearne.

19. Missing.

accounts of all our strange histories. For that of the pretty Countess,[20] I fear there is too much truth in all you have heard: but you don't seem to know that Lord Corydon[21] and Captain Corydon his brother[22] have been most abominable. I don't care to write scandal; but when I see you, I will tell you how much the chits deserve to be whipped.[23] Our favourite general[24] is at his camp:[25] Lady A[ilesbury] don't go to him these three weeks. I expect the pleasure of seeing her and Miss Rich and Fred. Campbell[26] here soon for a few days.[27] I don't wonder your Lordship likes St Philippe[28] better than Torcy:[29] except a few passages interesting to Englishmen, there cannot be a more dry narration than the latter. There is an addition of seven volumes of Universal History[30] to Voltaire's Works, which I think will charm you: I almost like it the best of his works.[31] It is what you have seen extended,[32] and the mémoires of Louis XIV[33] *refondues* in it. He is a little tiresome with contradicting La Beaumelle[34] out of pique—and

20. Lady Coventry; see *ante* HW to Bentley 2 March 1754.

21. Lord Bolingbroke (ibid.).

22. Hon. Henry St John (1738–1818), Ensign 2d Foot Guards, 1754; Capt. 18 Foot, 1758; became General, 1797; M.P. Wootton Bassett 1761–84, July–Dec. 1802.

23. Presumably HW is referring to the St John brothers, who were gamblers and rakes. Bolingbroke was to marry Lady Diana Spencer in September.

24. General Conway (HW).

25. At Bradford, near Dorchester (Conway to HW 5 July).

26. Frederick (from 15 April 1761, Lord Frederick) Campbell (1729–1816), brother of Lady Ailesbury; HW's friend and executor; lord clerk register of Scotland 1768–1816; M.P. Glasgow Burghs 1761–80, Argyllshire 1780–99.

27. See *ante* HW to Chute 12 July 1757.

28. Vicente Bacallar y Saña (ca 1669–1726), Marqués de San Felipe, author of *Comentarios de la guerra de España, e historia de su rey Phelipe V*, Genoa, ?1725 (DALRYMPLE 137; BM Cat.). Strafford had probably been reading the French translation (hence 'St Philippe'), Amsterdam, 1756, which HW also owned (Hazen, *Cat. of HW's Lib.*, No. 1266).

29. Jean-Baptiste Colbert (1665–1746), Marquis de Torcy, author of *Mémoires . . . pour servir à l'histoire des négocia-*

tions depuis le traité de Riswick jusqu'à la paix d'Utrecht*, The Hague, 1707 and later editions (NBG; BM Cat.). HW's copy, London [i.e., Paris?], 1757, is Hazen, *Cat. of HW's Lib.*, No. 1272.

30. *Essai sur l'histoire générale et sur les mœurs et l'esprit des nations*, the first complete edition of which was published 1756, 7 vols. (Georges Bengesco, *Voltaire: bibliographie de ses œuvres*, 1882–5, i. 327–31). HW's copy is Hazen, *Cat of HW's Lib.*, No. 1172.

31. A view HW reaffirmed to Lady Ossory 8 Nov. 1789, OSSORY iii. 79.

32. Portions of this work had appeared in the *Mercure de France*, beginning in 1745, and in various separate publications. HW may refer, however, to Jean Néaulme's edition, *Abrégé de l'histoire universelle depuis Charlemagne jusqu'à Charlequint*, The Hague, 1753, which Voltaire disavowed (Bengesco, op. cit. i. 329).

33. *Le Siècle de Louis XIV*, originally published in two volumes, Berlin, 1751, was incorporated into the 1756 edition of *Essai sur l'histoire générale*, comprising chapters cxlv–ccxv (Bengesco, op. cit. i. 331; Voltaire, *Œuvres*, ed. Moland, 1877–85, xi. p. iii).

34. Laurent Angliviel de la Beaumelle (1726–73), Voltaire's life-long enemy who attacked *Le Siècle de Louis XIV* in an

there is too much about Rousseau.[35] Between La Beaumelle and Voltaire, one remains with scarce a fixed idea about that time. I wish
they would produce their authorities and proofs; without which,
I am grown to believe neither. From mistakes in the English part, I
suppose there are great ones in the more distant histories; yet altogether it is a fine work. He is, as one might believe, worst informed
on the present times.—He says eight hundred persons were put to
death for the last rebellion[36]—I don't believe a quarter of the number
were: and he makes the first Lord Derwentwater[37]—who, poor man!
was in no such high-spirited mood—bring his son,[38] who by the way
was not above a year and a half old,[39] upon the scaffold to be sprin-
kled with his blood.[40]—However, he is in the right to expect to be
believed: for he believes all the romances in Lord Anson's *Voyage*,[41]
and how Admiral Almanzor[42] made one man of war box the ears of
the whole empire of China![43]—I know nothing else new but a new
edition of Doctor Young's works.[44] If your Lordship thinks like me,

edition of the work 'augmentée d'un très
grand nombre de remarques,' Frankfurt,
1753. Voltaire replied in *Supplément au
siècle de Louis XIV*, Dresden, 1753, eventually incorporated into *Essai sur l'histoire générale* (NBG; Voltaire, op. cit. xiv.
pp. iv–v; xv. 87–8). See also *ante* HW to
Strafford 6 June 1756, n. 10.

35. Jean-Baptiste Rousseau (1670–1741),
poet (NBG). See 'Catalogue de la plupart
des écrivains français' in *Le Siècle de
Louis XIV*, sub Lamotte, Rousseau, and
Saurin (Voltaire, op. cit. xiv. 87–94, 124–5,
133–5).

36. Voltaire enumerates only about two
hundred executions in the 1745 rebellion
in *Précis du siècle de Louis XV* (Voltaire,
op. cit. xv. 301–306).

37. James Radclyffe (1689–1716), 3d (not
1st) E. of Derwentwater, 1705, beheaded
for his part in the insurrection of 1715.
Toynbee iv. 72, n. 10 suggests that HW
calls the 3d Earl the 'first' to distinguish
him from his brother Charles, four years
younger, who in 1731 became titular 5th
E. of Derwentwater and in 1746 was beheaded on Tower Hill under sentence
imposed thirty years earlier for his part
in the 1715 rebellion.

38. John Radclyffe (d. 1731), styled Vct
Radclyffe, titular 4th E. of Derwentwater.

39. The date of his birth has not been
traced. His parents were married 10 July
1712 and his father was executed 24 Feb.
1716.

40. 'Ce fut qui voulut que son fils,
encore enfant, montât sur l'échaufaud, et
qui lui dit: "Soyez couvert de mon sang,
et apprenez à mourir pour vos rois"'
(*Précis du siècle du Louis XV*, Voltaire,
op. cit. xv. 303).

41. *A Voyage round the World 1740–44
. . .* compiled by Richard Walter, 1748.
HW's copy (now WSL) is Hazen, *Cat. of
HW's Lib.*, No. 458.

42. Anson. The nickname, a favourite
of HW's, is from Dryden's *Conquest of
Granada, or Almanzor and Almahide*,
1670.

43. Anson refused to pay at Canton
harbour the duties required by the Emperor of all ships entering his ports (Walter, op. cit. Book III, chap. IX, 'Transactions in the River of Canton,' pp. 387,
390–1; *Précis du siècle de Louis XV*,
Voltaire op. cit. xv. 318–19; MONTAGU i.
55, 90).

44. Edward Young (1683–1765), poet.
*The Works of the Author of Night
Thoughts*, 1757, 'revised and corrected by
himself,' was published 10 June (*Daily
Adv.* 9, 10 June), 4 vols 12mo; Vol. V,
1767; Vol. VI, 1778. HW's copy is Hazen,
Cat. of HW's Lib., No. 1885.

who hold that even in his most frantic rhapsodies there are innumerable fine things, you will like to have this edition. Adieu, once more, my best Lord!

To Strafford, Tuesday 11 October 1757

Printed from *Works* v. 435–6; reprinted, Wright iii. 325–6, Cunningham iii. 110, Toynbee iv. 101–2.

Strawberry Hill, October 11, 1757.

My dear Lord,

YOU will have seen or heard that the fleet is returned.[1] They have brought home nothing but one little island,[2] which is a great deal more than I expected,[3] having neither thought so despicably of France, or so considerably of ourselves, as to believe they were exposed to much damage. My joy for Mr Conway's return[4] is not at all lessened by the clamour on this disappointment. Had he been chief commander,[5] I should be very sure the nothing he had done was all he could do. As he was under orders, I wait with patience to hear his General's vindication.[6]

I hope the Yorkists[7] have not knocked out your brains for living in a county.[8] In my neighbourhood they have insulted the Parliament

1. From the expedition against Rochfort (HW). 'Yesterday [7 Oct.] an express arrived at the Admiralty Office with advice of the safe arrival of Sir Edward Hawke's fleet at Spithead' (*Daily Adv.* 8 Oct.). See also MANN v. 117, 143–4; SELWYN 138–44.

2. The Isle of Aix.

3. See HW to Mann 25 July, MANN v. 118.

4. See HW to Conway [8 Oct.].

5. Conway was second in command to Lt-Gen. Sir John Mordaunt (*ante* HW to Bentley 18 Sept. 1755; MANN v. 118 and *passim*).

6. Following an inquiry 12–17 Nov., Mordaunt was tried by court martial (14–18 and 20 Dec.) and acquitted. George II, however, 'expressed great indignation against the court martial; and said he should look upon . . . the officers, who composed it, in the same light, that he did those, who went upon the expedition' (Newcastle to Hardwicke 3 Jan. 1758, BM Add. MSS 32877, f. 8). The controversy over the failure of the expedition continued for several months (MANN v. 143–4, 154–5, 164–5, 177–8).

7. Riots over the Militia Bill of 1757 (see n. 12 below) 'began in Bedfordshire, and . . . has been . . . communicated. . . . [to] Cambridgeshire . . . Hertfordshire, and so on' (Hardwicke to Newcastle 11 Sept., BM Add. MSS 32874, f. 3). Disorder was particularly violent in Lincolnshire, Northamptonshire, and Yorkshire (GM 1757, xxvii. 430–1; MANN v. 137, nn. 10, 11).

8. Wentworth Castle, Strafford's seat, was in Yorkshire.

in person.[9] He called in the Blues,[10] instead of piquing himself on dying in his curule chair in the stable-yard at Ember Court.[11]—So entirely have we lost our spirit, that the standing army is forced to defend us against the people, when we endeavour to give them a militia,[12] to save them from a standing army; and that the representative of the Parliament had rather owe his life to the Guards than die in the cause of a militia. Sure Lenthall's[13] ghost will come and pull him by the nose![14]

I hope you begin to cast a southward look,[15] and that my Lady's chickens and ducklings are old enough to go to a day-school, and will not want her any longer.

My Lord Townshend[16] and George[17] are engaged in a paper-war against one another, about the militia.[18] That bill, the suspension at Stade,[19] and the late expedition which has cost millions,[20] will find us in amusements this winter. It is lucky, for I despair of the opera. The Mattei[21] has sent certificates to prove that she is stopped by an inun-

9. Mr Onslow, the Speaker (HW). 'The Speaker himself was insulted at Guildford, and menaced in his own house at Ember Court, and could not disperse the insurrection but by promising no further steps should be taken till the next session of Parliament' (*Mem. Geo. II* iii. 41).

10. The Royal Horse Guards.

11. Onslow's house at Guildford. HW parallels Onslow with the Romans who 'had held curule magistracies . . . [who] put on the stately robes . . . and, thus habited, seated themselves on ivory chairs in the middle of their houses,' which were in the Forum, to await the coming of the Gauls (Livy V. xli. 2–8; MANN iv. 469; OSSORY ii. 327).

12. The Militia Bill of 28 June (30 Geo. II c. 25) was bitterly opposed (MANN v. 137, nn. 10, 11).

13. William Lenthall, speaker of the Long Parliament; see *ante* HW to Bentley Sept. 1753.

14. Lenthall as Speaker several times accepted the dictation of the populace and supported the Parliament's authority against the King's army.

15. To his house in St James's Square, London. HW is paraphrasing Shakespeare's 'threw many a northward look' (2 *Henry IV* II. iii. 13).

16. Charles Townshend (1700–64), 3d Vct Townshend, 1738.

17. The present Marquis Townshend (HW).

18. George Townshend had been one of the Militia Bill's principal supporters while his father raised a mob against it in Norfolk; for their quarrel see MANN v. 137–8; SELWYN 142; Sir Lewis Namier and John Brooke, *House of Commons 1754–1790*, 1964, iii. 549–51.

19. The Convention of Kloster-Zeven, concluded 8 Sept. by the Duke of Cumberland and Maréchal de Richelieu. It provided, among other things, for cessation of hostilities, withdrawal of a portion of the Duke of Cumberland's army to Stade in Hanover, and the occupation of Bremen and Verden by the French (MANN v. 136, n. 1, *et passim*). For the uproar it caused, see ibid.; SELWYN 142.

20. Estimates of the cost of the Rochefort expedition varied from £500,000 to £2,000,000 (SELWYN 140–1 and n. 5).

21. Colomba Mattei (fl. 1751–66) had sung at Venice in 1751 (Taddeo Wiel, *I Teatri musicali Veneziani del settecento*, 1897, p. 186); she first sang at the Opera House in London for the season of 1754–5. At the end of the 1756–7 season

dation.[22] The certificates I suppose can swim. Adieu, my dear Lord!

My Lady's and your most faithful humble servant,

HOR. WALPOLE

To Strafford, Friday 16 June 1758

Printed from *Works* v. 436–7; reprinted, Wright iii. 362–3, Cunningham iii. 142–3, Toynbee iv. 146–8.

Arlington Street, June 16, 1758.

My dear Lord,

I STAYED[1] to write to you, in obedience to your commands, till I had something worth telling you. St Maloes is taken by storm.[2] The governor[3] leaped into the sea at the very name of the Duke of Marlborough.[4] Sir James Lowther[5] put his hand into his pocket, and gave the soldiers two hundred and fifty thousand pounds[6] to drink

she and her husband, Trombetta, had assumed the management of the Theatre Royal, Haymarket, which they retained until the end of the 1762–3 season, when they left England, but she returned for the season of 1765–6. She had arrived in England by 10 Oct., and assumed the dignity of first woman singer when the season opened 8 Nov. (*Daily Adv.* 11 Oct.; Charles Burney, *General History of Music,* ed. Mercer, 1935, ii. 855–6; *London Stage 1660–1800,* pt 4, ed. G. W. Stone, Carbondale, Ill., 1962, i. lix, lxix, 437, 450).

22. Great floods, occasioned by melting snows of the Tyrol and the resultant swelling of the Adige River, are reported in the *Whitehall Evening Post,* 1–4 Oct.

———

1. In London, instead of going to SH.

2. HW is here satirizing the paltry achievements of the British force, which merely landed at Cancale Bay near St-Malo 5 June at night, and re-embarked 12 June after burning 'upwards of 100 ships' on 9 June (*London Gazette* No. 9800, 13–17 June, *sub* 'Whitehall June 17'; see also MANN v. 210–14 and C. Hippeau, *Gouvernement de Normandie,* Caen, 1863–

9, i. 165–289). For an account of the expedition to St-Malo and to Cherbourg by 'an Officer,' see GM 1758, xxviii. 297–300.

3. 'M. le Marquis de la Châtre, qui est chargé de défendre cette place' (Belle-Isle to the Duc d'Harcourt 9 June 1758, Hippeau, op. cit. i. 176). Actually, he was made maréchal de camp 'en considération de ses services à l'affaire de S.-Cast en Bretagne' (*Répertoire . . . de la Gazette de France,* ed. de Granges de Surgères, 1902–6, iii. 44), and perished in the Revolution: Charles de la Châtre (1724–after 1792), Marquis de la Châtre; Lt-Gen., 1762 (A. Reverend, *Titres de la Restauration,* 1901–6, iv. 120).

4. The Duke of Marlborough, who had distinguished himself at Dettingen in 1743, was in command of the expedition.

5. (1736–1802), 5th Bt, 1751; cr. (1784) E. of Lonsdale; M.P. 1757–84. He was a volunteer in the expedition (*London Chronicle,* 27–30 May, iii. 505; Robert Beatson, *Naval and Military Memoirs of Great Britain,* 1804, ii. 166).

6. Before Lowther came of age he was reckoned the richest commoner in Eng-

the King's health on the top of the Great Church.[7] Norborne Berke-ley[8] begged the favour of the Bishop[9] to go back with him and see his house in Gloucestershire.[10] Delaval[11] is turned Capuchin, with re-morse, for having killed four thousand French with his own hand. Commodore Howe[12] does nothing but *talk*[13] of what he has done. Lord Downe,[14] who has killed the intendant,[15] has sent for Dupré[16] to put in his place; and my Lord A[nson][17] has ravished three ab-besses, the youngest of whom was eighty-five.[18] Sure, my Lord, this account is glorious enough! Don't you think one might 'bate a little of it? How much will you give up? Will you compound for the town capitulating, and for threescore men of war and two hundred priva-teers burned in the harbour? I would fain beat you down as low as I could.—What, if we should not have taken the town? Shall you be very much shocked, if, after burning two ships of fifty-four and thirty-six guns, and a bushel of privateers and small-ware,[19] we had thought it prudent to leave the town where we found it, and had re-embarked last Monday[20] (in seven hours,[21] the dispatch of which implies at least

land (Sir Lewis Namier and John Brooke, *House of Commons 1754–1790*, 1964, iii. 56). In 1751 he had succeeded to estates of the Lowther branch of the family, in 1755 to those of the Whitehaven branch, and in 1756 to the Marske estates. Cf. Montagu i. 184–5; Mann iv. 550; HW to Conway 16 April 1756.

7. The cathedral, presumably.

8. Also a volunteer; see *ante* HW to Chute 29 June 1758.

9. The Bishop of St-Malo, 1740, was Jean-Joseph Fougasse d'Entrechaux de la Bastie (1704–67) (*Almanach royal*, 1758, p. 50; Granges de Surgères, op. cit. iii. 8).

10. Berkeley was of Stoke Gifford, Glos, and was lord lieutenant of Gloucestershire 1762–6.

11. Francis Blake Delaval, another vol-unteer, and a notorious rake; see *ante* HW to Bentley 17 March 1754.

12. The present Earl Howe (HW). Richard Howe (1726–99), 4th Vct Howe (Ireland), 6 July 1758; cr. (1782) Vct, (1788) E. Howe; entered the Navy, 1739, becoming Capt., 1746, and Adm., 1782; M.P. Dartmouth 1757–82. He took part in the Rochefort, St-Malo, and Cherbourg expeditions; in the St-Malo expedition, under Anson, he was commodore com-manding the frigates and transports.

13. 'Howe, with the expedition of harlequin as well as the taciturnity . . .' (HW to Conway 16 June 1758; Ossory i. 321).

14. Henry Pleydell Dawnay (1727–80), 3d Vct Downe, 1741; M.P. Yorkshire 1750–60; a volunteer on the expedition to St-Malo; died of wounds received in battle at Campen. See Mann v. 466 for HW's generous estimate of him.

15. The Marquis de Landal (GM loc. cit.).

16. A French master (HW).

17. Anson was in command of an escort fleet lying off Brest.

18. The familiar joke about his alleged impotence.

19. 'One man of war of 50 guns on the stocks, two . . . of 36 guns each, 24 privateers from 30–40 guns each, 70 mer-chant ships and 40 small craft, in all 137 besides all the naval stores and magazines' (*London Chronicle* 15–17 June, iii. 574). This estimate was later revised to 86 ships burned ('An exact list of the ship-ping burned at St Maloes,' ibid. 4–6 July, iv. 15).

20. 12 June.

21. 'Commodore Howe had made so good a disposition of the boats and trans-ports that four brigades, and the com-

as much precipitation as conduct), and that of all the large bill of fare above, nothing should be true but Downe's killing the intendant; who coming out to reconnoitre, and not surrendering, Downe at the head of some grenadiers shot him dead. In truth, this is all the truth, as it came in the middle of the night;[22] and if your Lordship is obstinately bent on the conquest of France, you must wait till we have found another loophole into it, which it seems our fleet is gone to look for.[23] I fear it is not even true that we have beat them in the Mediterranean![24] nor have I any hopes, but in Admiral Forbes,[25] who must sail up the Rhône, burn Lyons, and force them to a peace at once.

I hope you have had as favourable succession of sun and rain as we have. I go to Park Place next week, where I fancy I shall find our little Duchess[26] quite content with the prospect of recovering her Duke,[27] without his being loaded with laurels like a boar's head. Adieu, my dear Lord! My best compliments to my Lady and her whole menagerie.

Yours ever,

Hor. Walpole

panies of grenadiers, were re-embarked in less than seven hours, the enemy not having attempted to attack him' (*London Chronicle* 17–20 June, iii. 577).

22. 'Late on Thursday night [15 June] . . . Captain Fraine of the *Speedwell* sloop' brought 'letters from the Duke of Marlborough, dated at Cancalle the 12th,' which reported the troops were 'on board, waiting to take advantage of the first wind' (*London Gazette* No. 9800, 3–17 June, *sub* 'Whitehall, 17 June').

23. After leaving Cancale Bay the fleet made feints at Havre, Caen, Harfleur, and Cherbourg, returning to England in July (MANN v. 214, n. 12).

24. 'A report was current on the Royal-Exchange that an engagement had happened in the Mediterranean between the English fleet and a squadron lately come

out of Toulon, wherein six of the French ships were taken and five sunk; so that not one of the enemy's vessels escaped' (*London Chronicle* 15–17 June, iii. 569, *sub* 16 June). This rumour was unfounded.

25. John Forbes (1714–96), Rear-Adm., 1747; Vice-Adm. 1755; Adm. 1758; Adm. of the fleet 1781–96; lord of the Admiralty 1756–63. Much of his service had been in the Mediterranean, but ill health kept him from sea duty 1755–96.

26. Of Richmond (HW). Lady Mary Bruce (1740–96), m. (1757) Charles Lennox, 3d D. of Richmond, 1750.

27. The Duke of Richmond was a volunteer on the expedition to St Maloes (HW). As Colonel of the 72nd Foot, he took part in this attack (Beatson, op. cit., 175).

From Strafford, ca May 1759

Missing; mentioned by HW to Strafford *post* 12 June 1759.

To Strafford, Tuesday 12 June 1759

Printed from *Works* v. 438; reprinted, Wright iii. 456–7; Cunningham iii. 231; Toynbee iv. 273–4.

Strawberry Hill, June 12, 1759.

My dear Lord,

AFTER so kind a note[1] as you left for me at your going out of town, you cannot wonder that I was determined to thank you the moment I knew you settled in Yorkshire. At least I am not ungrateful, if I deserve your goodness by no other title. I was willing to stay till I could amuse you; but I have not a battle big enough even to send in a letter. A war that reaches from Muscovy to Alsace, and from Madras to California, don't produce an article half so long as Mr Johnson's riding three horses at once.[2] The King of Prussia's campaign is still in its papillotes;[3] Prince Ferdinand is laid up[4] like the rest of the pensioners on Ireland;[5] Guadaloupe has taken a sleeping draught;[6] and our heroes in America seem to be planting suckers of

1. Missing.

2. 'Mr Johnson, who had the honour to exhibit his surprising and wonderful feat of activity of horsemanship before his Royal Highness Prince Edward, and other royal personages . . . will this day . . . at the Star and Garter Tavern . . . perform several more wonderful and surprising feats on horseback than were ever attempted by any other person' (advertisement in *Daily Adv.* 12 June, May–June, *passim*). See also Boswell, *Life of . . . Johnson,* ed. G. B. Hill and L. F. Powell, i. 399, iii. 231; Boswell, *Private Papers,* ed. G. Scott and F. A. Pottle, i. 149, xi. 149.

3. Curling papers. For other comments by HW on the lack of news from Frederick II's army, see MANN v. 294–5. HW to Conway 6 Oct. 1748 is cited in OED *sub* papillote.

4. 'Hanover, Mar 28. The last letters from our army say that Prince Ferdinand had transferred his headquarters to Dorsten, from whence he proposed to advance to give the enemy battle' (*London Chronicle* 7–9 June, v. 448). 'Hague, June 5. Prince Ferdinand keeps his former position upon the Lippe and Roer' (ibid. 9–12 June, v. 451).

5. Ferdinand had been awarded a pension of Ireland of £2,000 per annum 31 Aug. 1758, for his victory at Crevelt 23 June 1758 (Rowley Lascelles, *Liber munerum publicorum Hiberniæ,* 1852, II pt vii. 86; see also *Mem. Geo. II* iii. 238; MANN v. 491, n. 44).

6. News of the capitulation of Guadaloupe did not arrive until the day after this letter was written (MANN v. 301, n. 15).

laurels that will not make any figure these three years.⁷ All the war that is in fashion lies between those two ridiculous things, an invasion⁸ and the militia. Prince Edward is going to sea,⁹ to inquire after the invasion from France; and all the old pot-bellied country colonels are preparing to march and make it drunk¹⁰ when it comes. I don't know, as it is an event in Mr Pitt's administration, whether the Jacobite corporations,¹¹ who are converted by his eloquence which they never heard,¹² do not propose to bestow their freedom on the first corps of French that shall land.

Adieu, my Lord, and my Lady! I hope you are all beauty and verdure. We are drowned with obtaining ours.

Yours most faithfully,

Hor. Walpole

7. For similar observations on the Guadeloupe capitulation see Mann v. 289–90, 297.

8. Rumours of invasion had been reported as early as 1 Feb., but had been more frequent since May, beginning with the news of the building of a 'great number of flat-bottomed boats at Havre-de-Grâce' (Daily Adv. 16 May, sub 'Paris, May 4'; Mann v. 293 and n. 2, 296 and n. 4).

9. 'The baggage of . . . Prince Edward was ordered to be sent from Saville House yesterday from Plymouth, and his Royal Highness will soon follow, to go on board in an expedition that is fitting out' (Daily Adv. 12 June).

10. 'The regiment of the militia of the county of Wilts . . . went through their exercise to the administration of thousands of spectators. . . . The Right Hon. Lord Bruce their colonel, and all the other officers . . . expressed great satisfaction and delight at their behaviour; and when they left Devizes, the mayor of the town ordered ale to be given to the private men at every house where they were quartered, as a testi-

mony of their good and orderly behaviour. They were told there was a probability that his Majesty might call them out on some important service; and being asked if they were willing to go, they testified their approbation by cheerful huzza's' (London Chronicle 12–14 June, v. 564, sub Devizes, 10 June; see also Mann v. 300).

11. On the 'affair of the Hanoverian soldier' (William Schroeder) of Nov. 1756, the counties of York and Chester, and Ipswich, and the Corporation of London had issued instructions which HW said were 'in the style of 1641, and really in the spirit of 1715 and 1745' (Mann v. 12–13 and n. 14).

12. In 1756 Pitt had brought in a Militia Bill which passed the Commons but was rejected by the Lords. He had also sponsored George Townshend's Militia Bill (30 Geo. II [28 June 1757] c. 25). The militia was needed as part of the war, which required the use of regular troops abroad. In June–July 1759 the first of the militia, in eleven counties, were embodied.

To Strafford, Thursday 9 August 1759

Printed from *Works* v. 438–9; reprinted, Wright iii. 471–2, Cunningham iii. 244, Toynbee iv. 290–1.

Strawberry Hill, Thursday 3 o'clock, August 9, 1759.

My dear Lord,

LORD Granby[1] has entirely defeated the French![2]—The foreign gazettes, I suppose, will give this victory to Prince Ferdinand;[3] but the mob of London,[4] whom I have this minute left, and who must know best, assure me that it is all their own Marquis's doing. Mr Yorke[5] was the first to send this news,[6] *to be laid with himself and all humility at his Majesty's feet,*[7] about eleven o'clock yesterday morning. At five this morning came Captain Ligonier,[8] who was dispatched in such a hurry that he had not time to pack up any particulars[9] in his portmanteau: those we are expecting with our own army, who we conclude are now at Paris, and will lie tomorrow night at Amiens. All we know is, that not one Englishman is killed,[10] nor

1. John Manners (1721–70), styled M. of Granby; army officer; M.P. Grantham 1741–54, Cambridgeshire 1754–70.

2. At Minden (HW). 1 Aug.

3. He was in command. Granby headed the second line of cavalry on the right wing, and was specially thanked by the Prince in his order of the day 2 Aug. (*London Chronicle* 14–16 Aug., vi. 153).

4. 'On the arrival of the news of the glorious victory . . . the guns at the Park and Tower were fired, houses illuminated, and all other demonstrations of joy were exhibited' (*Daily Adv.* 10 Aug.).

5. The late Lord Dover, then minister at The Hague (HW). Joseph Yorke (1724–92), K.B., 1761; cr. (1788) Bn Dover; M.P. East Grinstead 1751–61, Dover 1761–74, Grampound 1774–80; army officer; minister 1751–61 and ambassador 1761–80 at The Hague.

6. His dispatch, dated 6 Aug., reached London the morning of 8 Aug., and was printed in a *London Gazette Extraordinary* the same day. It was reprinted in *London Chronicle* 7–9 Aug., vi. 134.

7. The words of his dispatch (HW). 'May I presume in all humility, to lay myself at the King's feet with my most

dutiful congratulations upon this glorious news' (ibid.).

8. Edward Ligonier (1740–82), 2d Vct Ligonier, 1770; cr. (1776) E. Ligonier; army officer and one of Prince Ferdinand's aides-de-camp (MANN v. 314 and n. 2; *Mem. Geo. II* iii. 190–1).

9. 'Adjutant General Estorf and Capt. Ligonier arrived here Thursday morning. They having been dispatched . . . immediately from the field of battle . . . could not bring an account of the particulars of the glorious victory' (*London Chronicle* 9–11 Aug., vi. 142). 'They have brought nothing in writing with them and their verbal account not appearing sufficient to draw out a narrative of the victory . . . it has been thought most advisable by Mr Pitt and myself only to publish the enclosed paragraph in the ordinary papers, and to wait the arrival of Col. Fitzroy whom the Prince intends to dispatch with *une relation détaillée*' (Holdernesse to Newcastle 9 Aug., BM Add. MSS 32894, f. 69).

10. 'Our loss is very small, considering the whole first line was engaged' (Ligonier's letter to Yorke, *London Gazette Extraordinary* 8 Aug.). According to Fitz-

one Frenchman left alive.[11] If you should chance to meet a bloody wagon-load of heads, you will be sure that it is the part of the spoils that came to Downe's share,[12] and going to be hung up in the great hall at Cowick.[13]

We have a vast deal of other good news; but as not one word of it is true, I thought you would be content with this victory. His Majesty is *in high spirits,*[14] and is to make a triumphal entry into Hanover on Tuesday fortnight.[15] I envy you the illuminations and rejoicings that will be made at Worksop[16] on this occasion.

Four days ago we had a great victory over the Russians;[17] but in the hurry of this triumph it has somehow or other been mislaid, and nobody can tell where to find it:—however, it is not given over for lost.

Adieu, my dear Lord! As I have been so circumstantial in the account of this battle, I will not tire you with anything else. My compliments to the lady of the menagerie.—I see your new offices[18] rise every day in a very respectable manner.

Yours most faithfully,

Hor. Walpole

roy's more circumstantial account 'Prince Ferdinand had about *1000* killed, in the *whole*' (dispatch, 11 Aug., BM Add. MSS 32894, f. 115).

11. 'The loss of the French in the battle . . . consists of 5,000 killed, 3,000 drowned, 8,000 made prisoners' (*London Chronicle* 7–9 Aug., vi. 136). This agrees with Col. Fitzroy's later estimate (Holdernesse to Newcastle 11 Aug., BM Add. MSS 32894, f. 118).

12. Downe, appointed Lt-Col. (brevet) 9 Dec. 1758, was attached to the 25th Regiment of Foot, which he commanded at the Battle of Minden (*Army Lists* 1759, p. 9; 1760, p. 9; R. T. Higgins, *The Records of the King's Own Borderers*, 1873, p. 116).

13. Lord Downe's seat in Yorkshire (HW).

14. 'Nothing can surpass the joy this important news gave his Majesty' (Holder-

nesse to Newcastle 8 Aug., BM Add. MSS 32894, f. 37).

15. 28 Aug. A facetious remark: George II last visited Hanover in 1755.

16. Worksop Manor, Notts, seat of the 9th D. of Norfolk, 1732, who had been tried for high treason in 1715, and arrested again in 1722 for suspected Jacobite activities.

17. As reported by Mitchell's letter to Holdernesse 24 July (in the *London Gazette* No. 9919, 4–7 Aug.), the Prussians under Lt-Gen. Karl Heinrich Wedell had defeated the Russians at Palzig and had 'killed 7,000 on the spot.' The *London Chronicle* 9–11 Aug., vi. 144, more correctly reported the battle as a Russian victory: 'the Prussians retired in the greatest disorder.' See also Mann v. 315 and n. 7; Selwyn 156 and n. 5.

18. At Lord Strafford's house at Twickenham (HW).

To Strafford, Thursday 13 September 1759

Printed from *Works* v. 440–1; reprinted, Wright iii. 478–80, Cunningham iii. 250–1, Toynbee iv. 301–3.

Arlington Street, September 13, 1759.

My dear Lord,

YOU are very good to say you would accept of my letters, though I should have no particular news to tell you; but at present, it would be treating heroes and conquerors with great superciliousness, if I made use of your indulgence and said nothing of them. We have taken more places and ships in a week than would have set up such pedant nations as Greece and Rome to all futurity. If we did but call Sir William Johnson, Gulielmus Johnsonus Niagaricus;[1] and Amherst,[2] Galfridus Amhersta Ticonderogicus,[3] we should be quoted a thousand years hence as the patterns of valour, virtue, and disinterestedness; for posterity always ascribes all manner of modesty and self-denial to those that take the most pains to perpetuate their own glory. Then Admiral Boscawen has, in a very Roman style, made free with the coast of Portugal,[4] and used it to make a bonfire of the French fleet. When Mr Pitt was told of this infraction of a neutral territory, he replied, 'It is very true, but they are burned.'—In short, we want but a little more insolence and a worse cause to make us a very classic nation.

My Lady T[ownshend] who has not learning enough to copy a Spartan mother, has lost her youngest son.[5] I saw her this morning—

1. For having been second, and, after the death of his superior officer, first in command at the capture of Niagara, 25 July (*London Chronicle* 6–8 Sept., vi. 238). His letters and papers connected with the siege and capture are in BM Add. MSS 21678.

2. Jeffrey Amherst (1717–97), K.B., 1761; cr. (1776, 1778) Bn Amherst; commander-in-chief in North America 1758–64; governor of Virginia 1759–68; commander-in-chief 1778–82, 1793–5; field marshal, 1796.

3. Ticonderoga was taken 27 July by the British under Amherst (*London Chronicle*, loc. cit.; see also L. H. Gipson, *British Empire before the American Revolution*, New York, 1936–70, vii. 363).

4. Boscawen to Clevland 20 Aug. re-

counts the engagement 18 Aug. off Lagos, near Fort Almadana, in which three French ships were taken and two burnt, including La Clue's flagship (*London Gazette Extraordinary* 7 Sept.; reprinted in *London Chronicle* 6–8 Sept., vi. 237; Frederick Hervey, *The Naval History of Great Britain*, 1779, v. 180–3). A fuller account is in the *London Chronicle* 11–13 Sept., vi. 253–4; see also *Mem. Geo. II* iii. 211.

5. Hon. Roger Townshend (ca 1732–25 July 1759); Lt-Col., 1758; deputy adjutant-general; killed at Ticonderoga, 'in reconnoitring the fort, by a cannon ball' (*Army Lists*, 1759, p. 8; Collins, *Peerage*, 1812, ii. 477; *London Chronicle* 6–8 Sept., vi. 238; see also Montagu i. 32, 248).

her affectation is on t'other side; she affects grief—but not so much for the son she has lost, as for t'other[6] that she may lose.

Lord George[7] is come,[8] has asked for a court martial, was put off,[9] and is turned out of everything.[10] Waldegrave[11] has his regiment,[12] for what he did;[13] and Lord Granby the ordnance[14]—for what he would have done.[15]

Lord Northampton[16] is to be married[17] tonight in full *Compton-hood*.[18]

I am indeed happy that Mr Campbell[19] is a general; but how will his father[20] like being the *Dowager General* Campbell?

6. Her eldest son, George, in command (after the death of Gen. Wolfe) at the siege of Quebec.

7. Lord George Sackville (HW). As commander-in-chief of the British forces in Germany, he had failed to obey Prince Ferdinand's repeated orders to advance with the British cavalry at the Battle of Minden, 1 Aug., and had been dismissed the service 10 Sept.

8. 6 Sept. (*London Chronicle* 6–8 Sept., vi. 233) or 7 Sept. (*Daily Adv.* 10 Sept.; MANN v. 328 and n. 10).

9. In a letter written to Holdernesse 'on his arrival,' Sackville applied to the King for a court martial (*London Chronicle* 18–20 Sept., vi. 273). He 'was told it was impossible now, as the officers necessary are in Germany' (HW to Mann 13 Sept., MANN v. 328). He was tried 3 Feb.–5 Apr. 1760, was found guilty of having disobeyed the orders of his superior, and was judged unfit to serve in any military capacity.

10. 'He remains with a patent place [deputy ranger of Phoenix Park] in Ireland of £1,200, and about £2,000 a year of his own and wife's' (MANN v. 328). He was deprived of appointments worth £5,000 or more (ibid.; Sir Lewis Namier and John Brooke, *House of Commons 1754–1790*, 1964, iii. 391).

11. John Waldegrave (1718–84), 3d E. Waldegrave, 1763; Lt-Gen., 1759; Gen., 1772; M.P. Orford 1747–54, Newcastle-under-Lyme 1754–63.

12. 2d Dragoon Guards 1759–73 (MANN, loc. cit.).

13. Waldegrave and Kingsley were cited in Prince Ferdinand's orders of 2 Aug. for 'their great courage and good order in which they conducted their brigades' (printed in *London Chronicle* 14–16 Aug.,

vi. 153; see also MANN v. 316 and n. 16).

14. Granby was Lt-Gen. 1759–63 and master-gen. 1763–70 of the Ordnance. His and Waldegrave's appointments were announced in the *London Chronicle* 11–13 Sept., vi. 249. In August, Granby had succeeded Sackville as commander-in-chief of the British forces in Germany. See also MANN v. 328 and n. 14; Namier and Brooke, loc. cit.

15. 'His Serene Highness further orders it to be declared to . . . the Marquis of Granby, that he is persuaded, that if he had had the good fortune to have had him at the head of the cavalry of the right wing, his presence would have greatly contributed to make the decision of that day more complete and more brilliant' (Prince Ferdinand's Orders of 2 Aug., loc. cit.).

16. Charles Compton (1737–63), 7th E. of Northampton, 1758; ambassador to Venice 1761–3.

17. To Lady Anne Somerset (HW). (1741–63), 1st dau. of Charles Noel Somerset, 4th D. of Beaufort. The wedding was at Audley Chapel, St George's, Hanover Square.

18. HW announced the engagement to Mann 1 June 1759; 'He seems to have too much of the coldness and dignity of the Comptons' (MANN v. 294). See also MANN v. 313.

19. The present Duke of Argyle (HW). John, 5th D. of Argyll, 1770; Maj.-Gen., 25 June 1759 (*Army Lists*, 1761, p. 4; *ante* HW to Chute 1 Feb. 1759).

20. John Campbell (ca 1693–1770), 4th D. of Argyll, 1761; Lt-Gen., 1747; Gen., 1765; first cousin to the 2d and 3d Dukes of Argyll and first cousin once removed to Lady Strafford.

You are very kind, my Lord (but that is not new), in interesting yourself about Strawberry Hill. I have just finished a Holbein Chamber,[21] that I flatter myself you will not dislike; and I have begun to build a new printing-house,[22] that the old one may make room for the Gallery and Round Tower.[23] This noble summer is not yet over with us—it seems to have cut a colt's *week*.[24] I never write without talking of it, and should be glad to know in how many letters *this summer* has been mentioned.

I have lately been at Wilton,[25] and was astonished at the heaps of rubbish. The house is grand, and the place glorious; but I should shovel three parts of the marbles and pictures[26] into the river. Adieu, my Lord and Lady!

Your faithful servant,

Hor. Walpole

To Strafford, Tuesday 30 October 1759

Printed from *Works* v. 441–2; reprinted, Wright iii. 489–91, Cunningham iii. 259–60, Toynbee iv. 315–47.

Arlington Street, October 30, 1759.

My dear Lord,

IT WOULD be very extraordinary indeed if I was not glad to see one whose friendship does me so much honour as your Lordship's, and who always expresses so much kindness to me. I have an

21. On 27 Sept. HW paid £673.11.0. 'for the Holbein Chamber, pantry, and garrets etc. and doorway, and balconies to that building' (*SH Accounts*, ed. Toynbee, Oxford, 1927, pp. 8, 102–3).

22. Begun 28 Aug., it was completed by 30 Oct., and in use 1 May 1760 (ibid. 104; *post* HW to Strafford 30 Oct. 1759).

23. Work on both had been begun by late May 1760 (Mann v. 410). The Gallery was completed by 20 Aug. 1768 (Cole i. 151) and the Round Tower, after suspension of work from 1764–1769, was completed in June 1771 (Mann v. 410 and n. 25; vii. 128, 311; *SH Accounts* 8–9, 11, 106–7).

24. Nonce phrase, analogue of 'colt's

tooth,' which HW frequently uses; cf. OED *sub* colt 8.

25. Lord Pembroke's seat near Salisbury. HW had probably visited Wilton during his recent visit to Chute at the Vyne, about twenty miles from Wilton (HW to Conway 13 Sept. 1759).

26. In HW's library at this time were C. Gambarini, *A Description of the Earl of Pembroke's Pictures*, Westminster, 1731, formerly Vertue's, now wsl (HW owned another copy also); James Kennedy, *A Description of the Antiquities and Curiosities in Wilton-House*, Salisbury, 1769 (an earlier edition, perhaps 1758, is cited in *Anecdotes of Painting*). He also owned a seventeenth century book on Wilton

additional reason for thanking you now, when you are erecting a building after the design of the Strawberry committee.[1] It will look, I fear, very selfish, if I pay it a visit next year;[2] and yet it answers so many selfish purposes that I certainly shall.

My ignorance of all the circumstances relating to Quebec[3] is prodigious; I have contented myself with the rays of glory that reached hither, without going to London to bask in them. I have not even seen the conqueror's mother,[4] though I hear she has covered herself with more laurel-leaves than were heaped on the children in the wood.[5] Seriously it is very great; and as I am too inconsiderable to envy Mr Pitt, I give him all the honour he deserves.

I passed all the last week at Park Place,[6] where one of the bravest men in the world, who is not permitted to contribute to our conquests,[7] was indulged in being the happiest by being with one of the most deserving women—for Campbell-goodness no more wears out than Campbell-beauty[8]—all their good qualities are *huckaback*.[9] You see the Duchess[10] has imbibed so much of their durableness, that she is good-humoured enough to dine at a tavern at seventy-six.[11]

and a guide book, 1774, now WSL. See Hazen, *Cat. of HW's Lib.*, Nos. 297, 1072, 2378, 2387:6, 3667.

——————

1. Bentley's design for 'a little gothic building' (*ante* HW to Bentley Aug. 1756, and illustration; MONTAGU i. 295).
2. In Sept. 1760 (*post* 4 Sept. 1760).
3. The news of Quebec's surrender 13 Sept. (articles of capitulation signed 18 Sept.) reached London 16 Oct. (MANN v. 337, n. 1).
4. Lady Townshend. On the death of General Wolfe, Colonel now Marquis Townshend received the surrender (Mary Berry). She had written to HW 17 Oct.: 'Lady Townshend . . . is very sure he will now share in her joy when she acquaints him that Mr Townshend is safe and well and has most miraculously been preserved in the midst of the most desperate enterprise in the taking of Quebec in which he has made a glorious figure.'
5. From the ballad 'The Children in the Wood: or The Norfolk Gentleman's Last Will and Testament':

'No burial these pretty babes [or 'this
    pretty pair'],
Of any man receives,

Till Robin-red-breast piously,
Did cover them with leaves.'

(Thomas Percy, *Reliques of Ancient English Poetry*, 2d edn, 1767, HW's copy now WSL, iii. 176, 171–7; praised in the *Spectator* No. 85, 7 June 1711).
6. HW arrived ca 22 Oct. (HW to Conway 18 Oct.).
7. Henry Seymour Conway, who had been in semi-disgrace since the fiasco of the Rochefort expedition in Sept.–Oct. 1757.
8. Lady Strafford and Lady Ailesbury were first cousins twice removed, the latter being dau. of John Campbell, 4th D. of Argyll, 1761, Lady Strafford's first cousin once removed.
9. Lady A[ilesbury], and Lady Strafford, both Campbells, preserved their beauty so long, that Mr Walpole called them *huckaback beauties*, that never wear out (HW).
10. The Duchess of Argyle, widow of John Campbell [2d] Duke of Argyle, and mother to Lady Strafford (HW). Jane Warburton (ca 1683–1767), m. (1717) John Campbell, 2d D. of Argyll, 1703. Cf. OED *sub* huckaback, where this passage is quoted.
11. This age agrees with the record in GEC that she died 16 April 1767, 'aged 84.'

Sir William Stanhope[12] wrote to Mrs Ellis,[13] that he had pleased himself, having seen much of Mr Nugent and Lady Berkeley,[14] this summer, and having been so charmed with the felicity of their menage, that he could not resist marrying again.[15] His daughter replied, that it had always been her opinion, that people should please themselves,[16] and that she was glad he had; but as to taking the precedent of my Lady Berkeley, she hoped it would answer in nothing but in my Lady Stanhope having three children the first year.[17] You see, my Lord, Mrs Ellis has bottled up her words,[18] till they sparkle at last!

I long to have your approbation of my Holbein Chamber; it has a comely sobriety that I think answers very well to the tone it should have. My new printing-house is finished, in order to pull down the old one, and lay the foundations next summer of my round tower. Then follows the gallery and chapel-cabinet.[19]—I hear your Lordship has tapped your magnificent front[20] too. Well, when all your

12. Hon. Sir William Stanhope (1702–72) K.B., 1725; 2d son of 3d E. of Chesterfield; M.P. Lostwithiel, 1727, Buckinghamshire 1727–41, 1747–68. He had bought Pope's home in Twickenham, near SH (Montagu i. 72).

13. His daughter (HW). Elizabeth Stanhope (d. 1761), m. (1747) Welbore Ellis (1713–1802), cr. (1794) Bn Mendip.

14. Elizabeth Drax (ca 1720–92), m. 1 (1744) Augustus Berkeley (1716–55), 4th E. of Berkeley, 1736; m. 2 (1757) as 3d wife, Robert Nugent. She is the 'charming Berkeley' of 'The Beauties' (MS Poems 155) but HW was to change his opinion: 'There is nothing so black of which she is not capable. Her gallantries are the whitest specks about her' (HW to Mann 16 Nov. 1778, Mann viii. 422). Nugent did not recognize her second daughter born during their marriage (ibid. viii. 422, n. 5).

15. His first wife had died in 1740, his second in 1746; he m. (6 Oct. 1759) Anne Hussey Delaval (1737–1812), sister of John Hussey Delaval, cr. (1761) Bt, (1783, 1786) Bn Delaval; the Stanhopes separated in 1763, and she m. 2 (1773) Charles Morris, army officer and songwriter (Mann v. 550, vi. 164, 170, 521; Francis Askham, The Gay Delavals, New York, [1955], pp. [2], 106–110; GM March 1812, lxxxii pt i. 298–9; Notes and Queries 10 May 1910, 11th ser. i. 392; Montagu i. 260, n. 10,

with 1811 incorrectly given as the date of her death).

16. She had pleased herself and displeased her father when she married Ellis in 1747; see HW to Mann 7 June 1748 OS, Mann iii. 485.

17. By her first husband Lady Berkeley had four sons and four daughters born 24 May 1745–10 Aug. 1753, including, the fifth year of the marriage, Ladies Louisa, Elizabeth and Frances, born 22 July 1748, all three of whom died shortly after they were christened (Collins, Peerage, 1812, iii. 625; GM 1748, xviii. 332).

18. She was very silent (HW).

19. Also projected in 1758 and begun in 1760, the chapel-cabinet (eventually to be known as the Tribune) was 'finished, except for the carpet' by April 1763 (SH Accounts, ed. Toynbee, Oxford, 1927, pp. 114–15).

20. Strafford had evidently completed his plans for the east and south fronts of Wentworth Castle, which were eventually to become 'heavier and more severely classical' (M. E. Macartney, English Houses and Gardens in the Seventeenth and Eighteenth Centuries, 1908, p. 30; Country Life, lviii. 634–42). HW reported that the work was 'very little advanced' by August 1760 (to Countess of Ailesbury, 23 Aug. 1760) but he admired the completed work (see post HW to Strafford 31 August 1781).

magnificences and my *minimificences*²¹ are finished, then, we—won't sit down and drink, as Pyrrhus said,²²—no, I trust we shall never conclude our plans so filthily; then—I fear we shall begin others.— Indeed, I don't know what the Countess²³ may do: if she imitates her mother, she will go to a tavern at fourscore, and then she and Pyrrhus may take a bottle together—I hope she will live to try at least whether she likes it. Adieu, both!

Yours most faithfully,

HOR. WALPOLE

To STRAFFORD, Saturday 7 June 1760

Printed from *Works* v. 443–4; reprinted, Wright iv. 59–61, Cunningham iii. 315–17, Toynbee iv. 393–5.

Strawberry Hill, June 7, 1760.

My dear Lord,

WHEN at my time of day one can think a ball worth going to London for on purpose, you will not wonder that I am childish enough to write an account of it. I could give a better reason, your bidding me send you any news; but I scorn a good reason when I am idle enough to do anything for a bad one.

You had heard, before you left London, of Miss Chudleigh's intended loyalty on the Prince's birthday.¹ Poor thing, I fear she has thrown away above a quarter's salary!² It was magnificent and well-understood³—no crowd—and though a sultry night, one was not a

21. A nonce word not recorded in OED.

22. Cineas asked Pyrrhus (ca 318–272 B.C.), King of Epirus, 'But when we have conquered all, what is the next thing we are to do?' Pyrrhus replied, 'Why, we will live at our ease. We will spend whole days in banquetting and entertaining ourselves with agreeable conversation. We will think of nothing but our pleasures' (Plutarch, 'Life of Pyrrhus,' in *Lives*, Dryden translation, with notes by Dacier, iv. 30; Hazen, *Cat. of HW's Lib.*, No. 1718, HW's copy now WSL). See also HW to Lady Ailesbury 13 June 1761; to Lady Mary Coke ?ca Nov. 1771, MORE 160–1.

23. Lady Strafford.

———

1. 'Yesterday [4 June] being the birthday of . . . the Prince of Wales, who then entered into the twenty-third year of his age, there was a very splendid court at Savile and Leicester Houses, to compliment his Royal Highness and the Royal Family on the occasion; and at Leicester House there was a ball at night' (*London Chronicle* 3–5 June, vii. 541).

2. £50; her salary was £200 a year (*Court and City Register*, 1760, p. 100).

3. A literal translation of *bien entendu*.

moment incommoded. The court was illuminated on the whole summit of the wall with a battlement of lamps; smaller ones on every step, and a figure of lanthorns on the outside of the house.[4] The virgin-mistress[5] began the ball with the Duke of York, who was dressed in a pale blue watered tabby, which, as I told him, if he danced much, would soon be *tabby all over,* like the man's advertisement;[6] but nobody did dance much. There was a new Miss Bishop from Sir Cecil's[7] endless hoard of beauty daughters,[8] who is still prettier than her sisters. The new Spanish embassy[9] was there—alas! Sir Cecil Bishop has never been in Spain! Monsieur de Fuentes[10] is a halfpenny print of my Lord H——.[11] His wife[12] homely, but seems good-humoured and civil. The son[13] does not degenerate from such high-born ugliness—the daughter-in-law[14] was sick, and they say is not ugly, and has as good a set of teeth as one can have, when one has but two and those black. They seem to have no curiosity, sit where they are placed, and ask no questions about so strange a

4. Miss Chudleigh's ball was at her newly completed house in Hill Street, Berkeley Square (Elizabeth Mavor, *Virgin Mistress,* 1964, pp. 66, 71, 78, 79).

5. See the title of Elizabeth Mavor's book, n. 4 above.

6. A stay-maker of the time, who advertised in the newspapers making stays at such a price; 'tabby all over' (Mary Berry).

7. Sir Cecil Bishopp, later Bisshopp (d. 1778), 6th Bt, 1725, of Parham Park, Sussex; M.P. Penryn 1727–34, Boroughbridge 1755–68; owner of the house in Berkeley Square which HW purchased from Bisshopp's heirs in 1779.

8. Three had died young; five (two of whom were already married) were living: 1. Anne (ca 1729–1803), m. (1759) Hon. Robert Brudenell; 2. Charlotte (ca 1731–62), m. (1751) Sir William Maynard, 4th Bt, 1738; 3. Frances (d. 1804), maid of honour to Queen Charlotte 1761–4, m. (1764) Sir George Warren, K.B.; 4. Harriet (d. before July 1825), m. 1 (1766) Thomas Dummer; m. 2 (1790) Nathaniel Dance (from 4 July 1800, Holland), cr. (1800) Bt; 5. Catherine (1744–1827), m. 1 (1767) Sir Charles Cope; m. 2 (1782) Charles Jenkinson, cr. (1786) Bn Hawkesbury, (1796) E. of Liverpool. HW probably refers to Frances Bishopp, whose beauty he

subsequently mentions (Montagu i. 82, 140, 269, 377; Burke, *Peerage,* 1867, p. 95; Berry i. 242, n. 9; Mason i. 453, n. 1; William Betham, *Baronetage of England,* 1801–5, i. 195; Sir Lewis Namier and John Brooke, *House of Commons, 1754–1790,* 1964, ii. 351).

9. The ambassador had presented his credentials 27 May (Mann v. 417, n. 12).

10. Juan Joaquín Atanasio Pignatelli de Aragón (1724–76), Conde de Fuentes, was Spanish ambassador to Sardinia 1754–8; to England 1760; and later to France (Du Deffand ii. 367, n. 18, iii. 406, n. 13; Mann v. 417, n. 12).

11. 'Huntingdon' in Wright, Cunningham, Toynbee. Huntingdon had asked to be appointed ambassador to Spain (HW to Mann 11 Jan. 1758, Mann v. 166).

12. María Luisa Gonzaga (1726–73), Duquesa di Solferino, m. (1741) the Conde de Fuentes (Du Deffand iii. 406, n. 13; Mann v. 417, n. 12).

13. The elder son, José Pignatelli y Gonzaga (1744–74), Marqués de Mora (Du Deffand iii. 158). He later became the lover of Julie de Lespinasse.

14. María Ignacia del Pilar (ca 1745–64), dau. of the Conde d'Aranda, m. (1760) the Marqués de Mora (Pierre-Marie-Maurice-Henri, Marquis de Ségur, *Julie de Lespinasse,* [1905], pp. 303–5, 309–10).

country. Indeed the ambassadress could see nothing; for Dodding-ton[15] stood before her the whole time,[16] sweating Spanish at her, of which it was evident by her civil nods without answers she did not understand a word. She speaks bad French, danced a bad minuet, and went away—though there was a miraculous draught of fishes for their supper, as it was a fast[17]—but being the octave of their *fête-dieu*,[18] they dared not even fast plentifully. Miss Chudleigh desired the gamblers would go up into the garrets—'Nay, they are not gar-rets—it is only the roof of the house hollowed for upper servants[19]— but I have no upper servants.' Everybody ran up: there is a low gallery with bookcases, and four chambers practised[20] under the pent of the roof,[21] each hung with the finest Indian pictures on different colours, and with Chinese chairs of the same colours. Vases of flowers in each for nosegays, and in one retired nook a most critical couch!

The lord of the festival[22] was there, and seemed neither ashamed nor vain of the expense of his pleasures. At supper she offered him tokay, and told him she believed he would find it good. The supper was in two rooms and very fine, and on all the sideboards, and even on the chairs, were pyramids and troughs of strawberries and cher-ries; you would have thought she was kept by Vertumnus.[23] Last night my Lady Northumberland[24] lighted up her garden for the Spaniards:[25] I was not there, having excused myself for a headache, which I had not, but *ought* to have caught the night before. Mr Doddington entertained these Fuenteses at Hammersmith;[26] and to

15. Afterwards Lord Melcombe. He had been minister in Spain (HW). He was en-voy extraordinary and plenipotentiary 1715–17 (Horn, *Diplomatic Representa-tives* 131–2).

16. He was very fat; see, for example, George Townshend's 'The Recruiting Ser-jeant,' April 1757, illustrated in MANN v. facing p. 77.

17. June 4, 1760 was the eve of Corpus Christi Day.

18. Corpus Christi.

19. Upper menservants included land or house steward, clerk of the stables or kitchen, cook, bailiff, valet, butler, gar-dener, groom of the chambers; upper womenservants included lady's maid, and cook. See J. Jean Hecht, *The Domestic Servant Class in Eighteenth-Century Eng-land*, [1956], pp. 35–70.

20. Executed, built; cf. OED.

21. Quoted in OED, *sub* 'pent.'

22. The Duke of Kingston (HW). See *ante* HW to Chute 30 April 1754.

23. In Roman myth, the husband of Pomona, the god of the changing seasons who presided over gardens and orchards. His festival was celebrated 12 Aug.

24. Elizabeth Seymour (1716–76), m. (1740) Hugh Smithson (from 1750, Percy), 2d E. of Northumberland, 1750, cr. (1766) D. of Northumberland.

25. 'Great preparations are making at Northumberland House for the entertain-ment of the Spanish ambassador' (*Lloyd's Evening Post* 2–4 June, vi. 534).

26. At his villa, La Trappe, demolished 1822–3 (Thomas Faulkner, *History and Antiquities of . . . Hammersmith*, 1839, pp. 278–9; C. J. Fèret, *Fulham Old and*

the shame of our nation, while they were drinking tea in the summer-house, some gentlemen, aye, my Lord, gentlemen, went into the river and showed the ambassadress and her daughter[27] more than ever they expected to see of England.

    I dare say you are sorry for poor Lady Anson.[28] She was exceedingly good-humoured, and did a thousand good-natured and generous actions. I tell you nothing of the rupture of Lord Halifax's[29] match, of which you must have heard so much; but you will like a bon mot upon it—They say, the *hundreds of Drury* have got the better of the *thousands of Drury*.[30]

    The pretty Countess[31] is still alive, was thought actually dying on Tuesday night,[32] and I think will go off very soon.[33]

    I think there will soon be a peace: my only reason is, that everybody seems so backward at making war. Adieu, my dear Lord!

I am your most affectionate servant,

Hor. Walpole

New, 1800; *The Beautiful Lady Craven*, ed. A. M. Broadley and Lewis Melville, 1914, i. pp. lxxviii–lxxix; Mann vi. 76).

27. Daughter-in-law; see above.

28. Elizabeth Yorke (1725 – 1 June 1760), eldest dau. of Philip, 1st E. of Hardwicke, m. (1748) George Anson, cr. (1747) Bn Anson. She died of 'an epidemic fever and sore throat' (HW to Mann 20 June, 1760, Mann v. 416).

29. George Montagu (from 2 July 1741 Montagu Dunk), (1716–71), 2d E. of Halifax, 1739.

30. Lord Halifax kept an actress belonging to Drury Lane theatre. And the marriage broken off was with a daughter of Sir Thomas Drury, an heiress (HW). Mary Anne Drury (1740–69), heiress to £50,000, m. (14 July 1761) John Hobart, 2d E. of Buckinghamshire, 1756. Anna Maria

Faulkner (Falkner), a singer, m. (1748) William Donaldson. She was for many years Lord Halifax's mistress and had two children by him (Montagu i. 278–9 and n. 2, ii. 335, and *passim*; information kindly supplied by Dr C. Beecher Hogan; *London Stage 1660–1800*, pt 4, ed. G. W. Stone, Carbondale, Ill., 1962, i. *passim*). For a circumstantial, fictionalized account of her career, see *The Genuine Memoirs of Miss Faulkner; Otherwise Mrs D * * * l * * * n; or Countess of H * * * *, in Expectancy . . .*, 1770.

31. Of Coventry (HW).

32. 'The account of the death of the Countess of Coventry, inserted in one of yesterday's daily papers, is without foundation' (*London Chronicle* 31 May–3 June, vii. 535).

33. She died of tuberculosis, 30 Sept.

To Strafford, Thursday 7 August 1760

Printed from *Works* v. 445; reprinted, Wright iv. 76–7, Cunningham iii. 330, Toynbee iv. 413–14.

Strawberry Hill, August 7, 1760.

My dear Lord,

YOU will laugh, but I am ready to cry, when I tell you that I have no notion when I shall be able to wait on you.—Such a calamity!—My tower[1] is not fallen down, nor Lady Fanny Shirley[2] run away with another printer;[3] nor has my Lady D——[4] insisted on living with me as half way to Weybridge. Something more disgraceful than all these, and woefully mortifying for a young creature, who is at the same time in love with Lady M[ary] C[oke], and following the Duchess of G[rafton][5] and loo all over the kingdom. In short, my Lord, I have got the gout—yes, the gout in earnest. I was seized on Monday morning, suffered dismally all night, am now wrapped in flannels like the picture of a Morocco ambassador, and am carried to bed by two servants. You see virtue and leanness are no preservatives. I write this now to your Lordship, because I think it totally impossible that I should be able to set out the day after tomorrow, as I intended. The moment I can, I will; but this is a tyrant that will not let one name a day. All I know is, that it may abridge my other parties,[6] but shall not my stay at Wentworth Castle.[7] The Duke of Devonshire was so good as to ask me to be at

---

1. The new Round Tower, begun ca May 1760 (see *ante* HW to Strafford 30 Oct. 1759).

2. Lady Frances Shirley (ca 1706–78), dau. of Robert, 1st E. Ferrers, was HW's neighbour at Twickenham.

3. An allusion to HW's own difficulty with printers. William Robinson, his first printer, worked from June 1757 until March 1759, when he 'went away.' Benjamin Williams came 29 March and 'went away' 25 May 1759. James Lister came 19 June 1759, 'stayed but a week.' Thomas Farmer arrived 16 July 1759; on 2 Dec. he 'ran away for debt.' See HW's *Journal of the Printing Office* 3–10 and notes.

4. Perhaps Lady Denbigh who lived next to Lord Strafford at Twickenham.

She was presumably an admirer of Lord Lincoln, whose seat, Oatlands, was at Weybridge.

5. Anne Liddell (ca 1738–1804), m. 1 (1756) Augustus Henry Fitzroy, 3d D. of Grafton, 1757; divorced 1769; m. 2 (1769) John Fitzpatrick, 2d E. of Upper Ossory, 1758; HW's correspondent.

6. As part of his visit to the Straffords, HW also saw: Ragley, Whichnor, Lichfield, Wentworth Castle, Chatsworth, Haddon, Hardwicke, Newstead, and Althorp, Aug. 1760; see *Country Seats* 26–33. HW had already made, and continued to make, a number of similar tours.

7. Where he arrived the night of 23 Aug., and left for Chatsworth 25 Aug. (HW to Lady Ailesbury 23 Aug. 1760).

Chatsworth[8] yesterday, but I did not know it time enough. As it happens, I must have disappointed him. At present I look like Pam's[9] father more than one of his subjects; only one of my legs appears:

The rest my parti-colour'd robe conceals.[10]

Adieu, my dear Lord!

Yours most faithfully,

Hor. Walpole

To Strafford, Thursday 4 September 1760

Printed from *Works* v. 445–7; reprinted, Wright iv. 88–90, Cunningham iii. 340–2, Toynbee iv. 426–8.

Strawberry Hill, September 4, 1760.

My dear Lord,

YOU ordered me to tell you how I liked Hardwicke.[1] To say the truth, not exceedingly. The bank of oaks over the ponds is fine, and the vast lawn behind the house: I saw nothing else that is superior to the common run of parks. For the house, it did not please me at all; there is no grace, no ornament, no Gothic in it. I was glad to see the style of furniture of that age; and my imagination helped me to like the apartment of the Queen of Scots.[2] Had it been the château of a Duchess of Brunswic,[3] on which they had exhausted the

8. The Duke's seat in Derbyshire.

9. Pam: 'The knave of clubs, esp[ecially] in . . . five-card loo in which this card is the highest trump' (OED).

10. After Pope's description of the King of Spades:

The hoary majesty of Spades appears
Puts forth one manly leg, to sight reveal'd;
The rest his many colour'd robe conceal'd.
(*Rape of the Lock*, iii. 56–8.)

1. Hardwick Hall, completed in 1599; seat of D. of Devonshire, in Derbyshire, 8 m. SE of Chesterfield. HW's more detailed descriptions are in Montagu i. 296–8. HW had planned to be at Ragley 20 Aug., was at Whichnor 23 Aug., Wentworth Castle 24 Aug., Chatsworth

28 Aug., and had returned to Arlington Street 1 Sept.; see his correspondence 12 Aug.–1 Sept.

2. As Hardwick Hall was only half-built when she died, she probably did not stay there (Montagu i. 297, n. 27).

3. That is, Hardwick Hall was of interest to HW because of its supposed connections with Mary Queen of Scots and with the Cavendishes and their ancestress, 'Bess of Hardwick,' the builder of Hardwick Hall: Elizabeth Hardwick by the second of her four marriages, (1549) to Sir William Cavendish, became the ancestress of the Dukes of Devonshire (*ante* HW to Bentley Aug. 1756, n. 34). A 'Duchess of Brunswic,' possibly an ancestress of the royal family, even with as colourful a

revenues of some centuries, I don't think I should have admired it at all. In short, Hardwicke disappointed me as much as Chatsworth[4] surpassed my expectation. There is a richness and vivacity of prospect in the latter; in the former, nothing but trist grandeur.

Newsteade[5] delighted me. There is grace and Gothic indeed—good chambers and a comfortable house. The monks formerly were the only sensible people that had really good mansions. I saw Althorpe[6] too, and liked it very well: the pictures are fine. In the gallery I found myself quite at home; and surprised the housekeeper by my familiarity with the portraits.[7]

I hope you have read Prince Ferdinand's Thanksgiving,[8] where he has made out a victory by the excess of his praises.[9] I supped at Mr Conway's[10] t'other night with Miss West,[11] and we diverted ourselves with the encomiums on her Colonel Johnston.[12] Lady A[ilesbury] told her, that to be sure next winter she would burn nothing but laurel-faggots. Don't you like Prince Ferdinand's being so tired with thanking, that at last he is forced to turn God over to be thanked by the officers?[13]

background as Bess of Hardwick's, would not have interested HW.

4. See Montagu i. 296–7; *Country Seats* 28–9.

5. See *ante* HW to Strafford 28 Aug. 1756.

6. Seat of Lord Spencer, 6 miles NW of Northampton. See *Country Seats* 31–3.

7. At Althorp HW found 'a gallery of all one's acquaintance by Vandyke and Lely' (Montagu i. 299) and a 'Virgin and Child by Guido, one of the most capital pictures I ever saw; I have a copy of it by Sasso Ferrati [sold SH xiii. 42 to Norton for £10.10.0] but which gives little idea of the divine beauty of the original: the child's head has uncommon dignity and expression' (*Country Seats* 31).

8. For the victory at Warburg, 31 July. Ferdinand's orders for 1 Aug., *London Chronicle* 28–30 Aug., viii. 216, contain the thanksgiving, in which five military units and eighteen individuals receive public thanks.

9. HW admitted that at Warburg 'the French were again worsted by Prince Ferdinand . . . yet so little advantage was reaped by that achievement that the French soon overcame Hesse, seized Göt-

tingen and Munden, and were at the eve of possessing Hanover' (*Mem. Geo. II* iii. 298; see also HW to Conway 19 Sept. 1760).

10. In Warwick Street (*Court and City Register*, 1760, p. 58).

11. Eldest daughter of John (afterwards) Earl of [*sic*] De la Warre (HW). Hon. (from 1761, Lady) Henrietta Cecilia West (1727–1817), dau. of John, 7th Bn, cr. (1761) E. de la Warr, m. (1762) Col. (afterwards Gen.) James Johnston (Montagu i. 269).

12. The late General James Johnston (Mary Berry). James Johnston (ca 1721–97), at this time Lt-Col. in command of the 1st (Royal) Dragoons; Gen., 1793; Lt-Gov. of Minorca 1763–74 (Montagu i. 28; Berry i. 48). He should be distinguished from his kinsman and namesake (Montagu i. 245).

13. 'His Serene Highness desires that on the first occasion the army will return thanks to the Almighty for the success of yesterday, and flatters himself that by His assistance and the bravery showed yesterday, we shall in the end overcome every obstacle that offers' (Prince Ferdinand's orders for 1 Aug., loc. cit.).

In London there is a more cruel campaign than that waged by the Russians:[14] the streets are a very picture of the murder of the innocents—one drives over nothing but poor dead dogs![15] The dear, good-natured, honest, sensible creatures! Christ! how can anybody hurt them? Nobody could but those Cherokees the English, who desire no better than to be halloo'd to blood:—one day Admiral Byng, the next Lord George Sackville, and today the poor dogs!

I cannot help telling your Lordship how I was diverted the night I returned hither. I was sitting with Mrs Clive, her sister[16] and brother,[17] in the bench near the road at the end of her long walk. We heard a violent scolding; and looking out, saw a pretty woman standing by a high chaise, in which was a young fellow, and a coachman riding by. The damsel had lost her hat, her cap, her cloak, her temper, and her senses; and was more drunk and more angry than you can conceive. Whatever the young man had or had not done to her, she would not ride in the chaise with him, but stood cursing and swearing in the most outrageous style: and when she had vented all the oaths she could think of, she at last wished *Perfidion* might seize him. You may imagine how we laughed.—The fair intoxicate turned round, and cried, 'I am laughed at!—Who is it?—What, Mrs Clive? Kitty Clive?—No: Kitty Clive would never behave so!'—I wish you could have seen my neighbour's confusion.—She certainly did not grow paler than ordinary.—I laugh now while I repeat it to you.

I have told Mr Bentley the great honour you have done him, my Lord. He is happy the temple[18] succeeds to please you.

I am your Lordship's most faithful friend and servant,

HOR. WALPOLE

---

14. HW to Mann 20 Oct. refers to the Russians' 'horrid custom' of sacking and burning captured towns (MANN v. 441).

15. In July–Sept. a large number of deaths was attributed to the bites of mad dogs. On 26 Aug., the Common Council of London issued 'an order . . . for the constables, beadles of the several wards, watchmen, and other ward-officers, to kill *all* dogs that shall be found in the streets or highways of . . . London . . . and a reward of 2s. . . . paid for each dog that shall be so killed and buried in the skin,

being first several times slashed in the body. . . . No less than the bodies of 30 dead dogs were told in one day in Tower ditch, by a person of undoubted veracity' (GM 1760, xxx. 392, *sub* 26 Aug.; see also *London Chronicle*, viii. *passim*).

16. —— Raftor, m. —— Mestivyer; living in 1783. She lived with Mrs Clive (OSSORY ii. 57, n. 28).

17. James Raftor.

18. See *ante* HW to Strafford 28 Aug. 1756, n. 12.

To Strafford, Saturday 25 October 1760

Printed from *Works* v. 447–8; reprinted, Wright iv. 102, Cunningham iii. 351–2, Toynbee iv. 441–2.

Misdated by HW, who also misdated his letter to Montagu on the same subject (Montagu i. 312).

Arlington Street, Oct. 26 [25], 1760.

My dear Lord,

I BEG your pardon for so long a silence in the late reign; I knew nothing worth telling you; and the great event of this morning you will certainly hear before it comes to you by so sober and regular a personage as the postman. The few circumstances known yet are, that the King went well to bed last night; rose well at six this morning; went to the water-closet a little after seven; had a fit, fell against a bureau, and gashed his right temple: the valet-de-chambre heard a noise and a groan, and ran in: the King tried to speak, but died instantly.[1] I should hope this would draw you southward: such scenes are worth looking at, even by people who regard them with such indifference as your Lordship or I. I say no more, for what will mix in a letter with the death of a king?

I am my Lady's and your Lordship's most faithful servant,

Hor. Walpole

To Strafford, Sunday 5 July 1761

Printed from *Works* v. 448–9; reprinted, Wright iv. 150–1, Cunningham iii. 409–10, Toynbee v. 71–2.

Strawberry Hill, July 5, 1761.

My dear Lord,

I CANNOT live at Twickenham and not think of you: I have long wanted to write, and had nothing to tell you. My Lady D.[1] seems to have lost her sting; she has neither blown up a house nor a quarrel since you departed. Her wall, contiguous to you, is built, but so

1. For HW's more detailed account of the King's death see Mann v. 442–4.

———

1. Apparently Isabella de Jong (ca 1693–1769), m. (ca 1718) William Feilding (1697–

1755), 5th E. of Denbigh, 1717. She lived for a time at Riverside, between Orleans House and Strafford's Mount Lebanon (R. S. Cobbett, *Memorials of Twickenham*, 1872, pp. 248–9).

precipitate and slanting, that it seems hurrying to take water. I hear she grows sick of her undertakings. We have been ruined by deluges; all the country was under water. Lord Holderness's new *fossé*[2] was beaten in for several yards: this tempest was a little beyond the dew of Hermon, that fell on the *hill of Sion*.[3] I have been in still more danger by water: my perroquet[4] was on my shoulder as I was feeding my gold-fish, and flew into the middle of the pond: I was very near being the Nouvelle Eloise,[5] and tumbling in after him;[6] but with much ado I ferried him out with my hat.

Lord E[gremont][7] has had a fit of apoplexy; your brother Charles[8] a bad return of his old complaint;[9] and Lord Melcombe[10] has tumbled down the kitchen stairs, and—waked himself.

London is a desert; no soul in it but the King. Bussy has taken a temporary house.[11] The world talks of peace—would I could believe it! every newspaper frightens me: Mr Conway would be very angry if he knew how I dread the very name of the Prince de Soubise.[12]

We begin to perceive the Tower of Kew[13] from Montpellier Row;[14] in a fortnight you will see it in Yorkshire.

2. At Sion Hill, near Brentford (HW). Syon Hill, Isleworth, was built by Robert Darcy, 4th E. of Holdernesse (Ossory i. 160, n. 17).

3. Psalms 133.3; HW's play on *Zion* and *Syon Hill*.

4. Parakeet.

5. Jean-Jacques Rousseau's *Julie, ou la Nouvelle Héloïse*, HW's copy, Amsterdam, 1761, 6 vols 12mo, is Hazen, *Cat. of HW's Lib.*, No. 819.

6. Julie saves her son Marcellin by jumping into the lake, but she catches cold and dies; see the final letters Nos. clix–clxii.

7. Expanded to 'Edgcumbe' by Wright, Cunningham, and Toynbee, but 'Egremont' is more likely: Sir Charles Wyndham (1710–63), 4th Bt, 1740, 2d E. of Egremont, 1750, had a stroke of apoplexy in 1762 (HW to Mann 22 March 1762, Mann vi. 17), and died of apoplexy 21 Aug. 1763. No record has been found that Edgcumbe, about 9½ years younger than Egremont, had a stroke of apoplexy about this time.

8. Charles Townshend, married to Lady Greenwich, eldest sister to Lady Strafford (HW).

9. Epilepsy, attacks of which had set in after puberty; in Dec. 1761 he apparently had another severe fit (Sir Lewis Namier and John Brooke, *Charles Townshend*, 1964, pp. 2–3, 69).

10. George Bubb Dodington, cr. (6 April 1761) Bn Melcombe. He was notoriously somnolent (HW to Montagu 28 July 1761, Montagu i. 382).

11. As French minister plenipotentiary, he took a house in Suffolk Street, 31 May to 26 Sept. (Mann v. 514, n. 5).

12. News of a battle between Soubise and the Hereditary Prince was expected. Conway was with the latter, whose forces defeated Soubise. See Montagu i. 377–8, Mann v. 515–16; *post* HW to Strafford 22 July 1761.

13. The Pagoda in the Royal Garden at Kew (HW). Sir William Chambers, the architect, wrote that the tower was 'begun . . . in the autumn of 1761 and covered in the spring of the year 1762,' but his account was designed to emphasize the speed with which the structure was completed (Sir William Chambers, *Plans, Elevations, Sections, . . . Views of the . . . Buildings at Kew*, 1763, pp. 5–6). If the framework had not been almost completed, probably HW could not have seen it from Twickenham.

14. On the eastern side of Twickenham.

The apostle Whitfield[15] is come to some shame: he went to Lady Huntingdon[16] lately, and asked for forty pounds for some distressed saint or other. She said she had not so much money in the house, but would give it him the first time she had. He was very pressing, but in vain. At last he said, 'There's your watch and trinkets, you don't want such vanities; I will have that.' She would have put him off; but he persisting, she said, 'Well, if you must have it, you must.' About a fortnight afterwards, going to his house, and being carried into his wife's[17] chamber, among the paraphernalia of the latter the Countess found her own offering. This has made a terrible schism: she tells the story herself—I had not it from Saint Frances,[18] but I hope it is true.

Adieu, my dear Lord!

Yours ever,

Hor. Walpole

PS. My gallery sends its humble duty to your new front, and all my creatures beg their respects to my Lady.

To Strafford, Wednesday 22 July 1761

Printed from *Works* v. 449–50; reprinted, Wright iv. 157–8, Cunningham iii. 418–19, Toynbee v. 83–5.

Strawberry Hill, July 22, 1761.

My dear Lord,

I LOVE to be able to contribute to your satisfaction, and I think few things would make you happier than to hear that we have totally defeated the French combined armies,[1] and that Mr Conway

15. George Whitefield (1714–70), evangelist, leader of the Calvinist Methodists.

16. Lady Selina Shirley (1707–91), m. (1728) Theophilus Hastings (1696–1746), 9th E. of Huntingdon. A prominent Methodist, she in 1748 had appointed Whitefield her chaplain and was his patron for many years (*ante* HW to Chute 10 Oct. 1766, n. 4; Montagu i. 73–4; [A. C. H. Seymour] *The Life and Times of Selina Countess of Huntingdon*, 1844, i. 87–94).

17. Elizabeth Burnell (ca 1704–1768), m. 1 —— James; m. 2 (1741) George White-

field, at Caerphilly, Glamorganshire, Wales (*Dictionary of American Biography*).

18. Lady Frances Shirley (HW). An enthusiastic Methodist, half-sister of Lady Huntingdon's father, she bequeathed £1618 to Lady Huntingdon's Connexion ([A. C. H. Seymour], op. cit. ii. 496).

1. Prince Ferdinand's victory over the French forces commanded by Broglie and Soubise at Kirch Denkern, commonly called the Battle of Villinghausen, 16 July (Mann v. 515–16).

is safe.[2] The account came this morning:[3] I had a short note[4] from poor Lady A[ilesbury], who was waked with the good news, before she had heard there had been a battle. I don't pretend to send you circumstances, no more than I do of the wedding and coronation,[5] because you have relations and friends in town nearer and better informed. Indeed, only the blossom of victory is come yet.—Fitzroy[6] is expected, and another fuller courier after him.[7] Lord Granby, to the mob's heart's content, has the chief honour of the day—rather, of the two days.[8] The French behaved to the mob's content too, that is, shamefully. And all this glory cheaply bought on our side. Lieutenant-Colonel Keith[9] killed; and Colonel Marlay[10] and Harry Townshend[11] wounded. If it produces a peace, I shall be happy for mankind—if not, shall content myself with the single but pure joy of Mr Conway's being safe.

Well! my Lord, when do you come? You don't like the question, but kings will be married and must be crowned—and if people will be earls, they must now and then give up castles and new fronts, for processions and ermine. By the way, the number of peeresses that propose to excuse themselves makes great noise; especially as so many are breeding, or trying to breed, by commoners, that they cannot walk.[12] I hear that my Lord D[e la Warr], concluding all women

2. He was not engaged in the battle (MANN v. 516, n. 5).

3. At noon (MANN v. 515, n. 3).

4. Missing.

5. Of George III, who had announced 8 July his intention to marry Princess Charlotte Sophia (1744–1818), dau. of the Duke of Mecklenburg-Strelitz. They were married 8 Sept. and crowned 22 Sept. 1761.

6. Charles Fitzroy (1737–97), cr. (1780) Bn Southampton; M.P.; brother of 3d D. of Grafton; entered the army, 1752; Lt-Col., 1758; Gen., 1793; aide-de-camp to Prince Ferdinand at the Battle of Minden, 1759, and at that of Kirch Denkern. He arrived 23 July, with a letter of Prince Ferdinand and Lord Granby, dated 17 July (MANN v. 516, n. 9).

7. Later reports proved the victory not 'so total as it was' at first said to be; see MANN v. 518–19.

8. 'The French attacked the light troops in the front of Lord Granby's corps, which was encamped on the heights of Kirch

Denkern. His Lordship ordered the regiments . . . to support the posts. There was an uninterrupted fire of cannon and small arms till nine, when the enemy gave way, in great disorder' (Maj. Wedderbourn's account, London Chronicle 21–23 July, x. 78).

9. Sir Robert Murray Keith (1730–95), K.B., 1772; Lt-Col., 1760; M.P. The report of his death was a mistake for that of his Major, Campbell (London Chronicle 4–6 Aug. 1761, x. 121; MONTAGU i. 379, n. 8; MANN v. 516, n. 6).

10. Lt-Col. Thomas Marlay (d. 1784), of the 5th Foot (MONTAGU i. 379, n. 9).

11. Lt-Col. Henry Townshend (1736–62), 3d son of Hon. Thomas Townshend; M.P. Eye 1758–60, 1761–2; Ensign 2d Foot Guards, 1755; Capt. 5th Foot, 1758; Capt.-Lt 1st Foot Guards and Lt-Col., 1762; killed at Wilhelmstal (MONTAGU i. 379, n. 10).

12. Leake, the Garter King of Arms, gave warning that dowager peeresses 'who have married again since the death of

would not dislike the ceremony, is negotiating his peerage[13] in the City, and trying if any great fortune will give fifty thousand pounds for one day, as they often do for one night. I saw Miss ——[14] this evening at my Lady Suffolk's, and fancy she does not think my Lord —— quite so ugly as she did two months ago.[15]

Adieu, my Lord! This is a splendid year!

Yours ever,

HOR. WALPOLE

To STRAFFORD, Tuesday 8 September 1761

Printed from *Works* v. 450–2; reprinted, Wright iv. 167–9, Cunningham iii. 430–1, Toynbee v. 101–3.

Arlington Street, Tuesday morning.

My dear Lord,

NOTHING was ever equal to the bustle and uncertainty of the town for these three days. The Queen was seen off the coast of Sussex [Suffolk] on Saturday last,[1] and is not arrived yet—nay, last night at ten o'clock it was neither certain when she landed, nor when she would be in town. I forgive history for knowing nothing, when so public an event as the arrival of a new Queen is a mystery even at the very moment in St James's Street.[2] The messenger that brought the letter yesterday morning, said, she *arrived* at half an hour after four at Harwich.[3] This was immediately translated into *landing,* and notified in those words to the ministers. Six hours afterwards it proved no such thing, and that she was only in Harwich Road; and they recollected that *half an hour after four* happens twice

---

their lords' could not walk in the Coronation procession as dowagers (MANN v. 535, n. 10).

13. John West, 7th Bn de la Warr, 1723, had been cr. (18 March 1761) E. de la Warr. His first wife had died in 1735, his second in 1748; he did not remarry.

14. On 6 Aug. 1761, Miss Emma Gilbert (1729–1807), dau. of John Gilbert, Abp of York, m. George Edgcumbe (1721–95), 3d Bn Edgcumbe. The marriage took place 'at her father's house at Twicken-

ham.' Her husband was cr. (1781) Vct Mount Edgcumbe, and (1789) E. of Mount Edgcumbe.

15. Edgcumbe had inherited his peerage on 10 May.

————

1. 5 Sept.

2. At St James's Palace.

3. 'The Queen landed on Monday last at three in the afternoon at Harwich in Essex' (*London Chronicle* 8–10 Sept., x. 241).

in twenty-four hours, and the letter did not specify which of the *twices* it was. Well! the bridesmaids⁴ whipped on their virginity; the New Roads⁵ and the parks⁶ were thronged; the guns were choking with impatience to go off; and Sir James Lowther, who was to pledge his Majesty,⁷ was actually married to Lady Mary Stuart.⁸ Five, six, seven, eight o'clock came, and no Queen⁹—She lay at Witham¹⁰ at Lord Abercorn's,¹¹ who was most tranquilly in town; and it is not certain even whether she will be composed enough to be in town tonight. She has been sick but half an hour; sung and played on the harpsichord all the voyage, and been cheerful the whole time. The coronation will now certainly not be put off¹²—so I shall have the pleasure of seeing you on the 15th. The weather is close and sultry; and if the wedding is tonight, we shall all die.

They have made an admirable speech for the Tripoline ambassador¹³—that he said he heard the King had sent his *first eunuch* to fetch the Princess. I should think he meaned Lord [Anson].¹⁴

4. All ten are named in HW to Mann 10 Sept. 1761, MANN v. 529–30.

5. The 'main thoroughfare or continuation of the City Road from the Angel at Islington to the Regents' Park, St John's Wood, and the Edgware Road' (*London Past and Present*). It was laid out and built 1754–7 (ibid).

6. Princess Charlotte Sophia came by 'the City Road, across Islington, along the New Road into Hyde Park, down Constitution Hill into St James's Park, and then to the garden gate of the Palace' (GM 1761, xxxi. 416; *London Chronicle* 8–10 Sept., x. 241–2).

7. Mr John Brooke suggests that HW is using 'pledge' in the sense of 'guarantee, or assure the performance of' (OED, *sub* 'Pledge' 4a)—in other words, Lowther's marriage may have been timed to come immediately before the King's so that one wedding was a guarantee of the other one. There was no proxy wedding, and no public banquet at which there would be a toast pledging George III.

8. (1740–1824), eldest dau. of Lord Bute, m. (7 Sept.) Sir James Lowther, 5th Bt, 1751, cr. (1748) E. of Lonsdale. They were married in the morning, at Bute's house in South Audley Street (MANN v. 527, n. 17; 531, n. 29). 'After the marriage . . . the . . . couple set out for Lord Bute's

house at Kew in Surrey' (*London Chronicle* 5–8 Sept., x. 239).

9. 'Last night [7 Sept.] about eight o'clock a messenger arrived at St James's from Harwich. . . . Till this messenger arrived she was expected in town last night, and orders were given for proper persons to attend the celebration of the nuptials' (*London Chronicle*, loc. cit.).

10. Near Chelmsford, Essex (MANN v. 528, n. 6).

11. James Hamilton (1712–89), styled Bn Paisley 1734–44, 8th E. of Abercorn, 1744.

12. 'His Majesty . . . expressed his impatience [at the delay, caused by contrary winds, in the arrival of Princess Charlotte], and fresh instructions, it is said, were dispatched to . . . [Anson] to sail at all events, . . . that the ceremony of the nuptials might precede that of the coronation' (GM 1761, xxxi. 415). Anson had received 'a paper of instructions a—full sheet—all writ with his [the King's] own hand' (Hardwicke to his son Lord Royston 8 Aug., quoted in J. H. Jesse, *Memoirs of . . . King George the Third*, 2d edn, 1867, i. 94).

13. Hüsejn (or Hasan or Hussem) Bej, Tripolitan ambassador to England 1759–61 (MANN v. 528, n. 3).

14. He 'was suspected of being im-

You will find the town over head and ears in disputes about rank, precedence, processions, entrées, etc. One point, that of the Irish peers, has been excellently liquidated:[15] Lord Halifax[16] has stuck up a paper in the coffee-room at Arthur's,[17] importing, 'that his Majesty, not having leisure to determine a point of such great consequence, permits for this time such Irish peers as shall be at the marriage to walk in the procession.' Everybody concludes those personages will understand this order, as it is drawn up in their *own* language; otherwise it is not very clear how they are to walk *to* the marriage, if they are *at* it before they come *to* it.

Strawberry returns its duty and thanks for all your Lordship's goodness to it, and, though it has not got its wedding-clothes yet, will be happy to see you. Lady B[etty] M[ackenzie][18] is the individual woman she was—she seems to have been gone three years, like the sultan in the Persian tales,[19] who popped his head into a tub of water, pulled it up again, and fancied he had been a dozen years in bondage in the interim. She is not altered in a tittle. Adieu, my dear Lord!

Your most faithful servant,

HOR. WALPOLE

Twenty minutes past three in the afternoon,
not in the middle of the night.

Madame Charlotte is this instant arrived. The noise of coaches,

potent' (HW's note, HW to Mann 10 Sept. 1761, MANN v. 528, n. 4, where this anecdote is repeated). Anson, Commander-in-Chief of the Fleet since 30 July 1761, commanded at sea for the last time in convoying the Princess to England; Lord Harcourt, ambassador to Mecklenburg-Strelitz on the occasion of the marriage, served jointly with Anson.

15. 'To make clear or plain (something obscure or confused); to render, unambiguous; to settle differences, disputes' (OED, which marks the word in this sense obsolete, and quotes HW twice).

16. Lord lieutenant of Ireland.

17. White's Club, called 'Arthur's' for Robert Arthur (d. 6 June 1761) who managed the Club's rooms from its founding in 1736 until his retirement in 1755; see MONTAGU i. 202, n. 1; W. B. Boulton,

History of White's, 1892, i. 117, 121–2, and *passim.*

18. Lady Elizabeth Campbell (ca 1722–99), Lady Strafford's sister, m. (1749) Hon. James Stuart Mackenzie, Bute's brother, who had been M.P. and envoy extraordinary 1758–60 and envoy extraordinary and plenipotentiary 1760–1 at Turin. They had left England in Oct. 1758. On 6 Aug. 1768 they had 'landed, and we expected them in town [London] tomorrow' (Horn, *Diplomatic Representatives* 125; *Letters to and from Henrietta, Countess of Suffolk . . . from 1712 to 1767,* ed. J. W. Croker, 1824, ii. 260).

19. HW had two sets of François Pétis de la Croix (1653–1713), *The Persian and Turkish Tales,* 1729, 2 vols 12mo (Hazen, *Cat. of HW's Lib.,* No. 2742).

chaises, horsemen, mob, that have been to see her pass through the parks, is so prodigious that I cannot distinguish the guns.[20] I am going to be dressed, and before seven shall launch into the crowd. Pray for me!

To Strafford, Thursday 5 August 1762

Printed from *Works* v. 452–3; reprinted, Wright iv. 231–2, Cunningham iv. 10–11, Toynbee v. 228–9.

Strawberry Hill, August 5, 1762.

My dear Lord,

AS YOU have correspondents of better authority in town, I don't pretend to send you great events, and I know no small ones. Nobody talks of anything under a revolution. That in Russia[1] alarms me, lest Lady [Mary Coke] should fall in love with the Czarina,[2] who has deposed *her* Lord ——,[3] and set out for Petersburgh.[4] We throw away a whole summer in writing *Britons*[5] and *North Britons*;[6] the Russians change sovereigns faster than Mr Wilkes can choose a motto for a paper.[7] What years were spent here in controversy on the abdication of King James, and the legitimacy of the Pretender! Commend me to the Czarina. They doubted, that is, her husband did, whether her children[8] were of genuine blood-royal. She appealed to

20. Her 'arrival at the Palace was immediately proclaimed by the firing of the guns in St James's Park and at the Tower' (*London Chronicle* 8–10 Sept., x. 242).

———

1. Catherine II's dethronement on 9 July of her husband, Peter III (1728–17 July 1762). She was also implicated in his murder at Ropsha.

2. Lady Mary Coke 17 Nov. 1749 swore the peace against her husband. She brought suit for divorce, but the proceedings broke down, and they were separated in 1750.

3. Peter III, as Lady Mary had 'deposed' her husband.

4. Lady Mary had set out for France on 15 June 1762 (More 25, n. 4).

5. *The Briton*, a weekly periodical supporting Bute, in 38 numbers, 29 May

1762–12 Feb. 1763, ed. Tobias Smollett (*Cambridge Bibliography of English Literature*, 1941, ii. 664).

6. *The North Briton*, a weekly periodical edited and largely written by John Wilkes (1721–97) in opposition to Lord Bute. Numbers 1–45 were published 5 June 1762–23 April 1763, with No. 46 variously dated. Under different direction *The North Briton* continued until 1 May 1771 (*Cambridge Bibliography*, op. cit. ii. 664). HW's copy, 1763, 2 vols 8vo, is Hazen, *Cat. of HW's Lib.*, No. 1576.

7. In the eight numbers of *The North Briton* published 5 June–31 July 1762, two mottoes or epigraphs were in English, one in Greek, and five in Latin.

8. Paul I, and Anna (1757–9) (Mann vi. 57).

the Preobazinsky Guards,[9] excellent casuists, and, to prove Duke Paul heir to the crown, assumed it herself.[10] The proof was compendious and unanswerable.

I trust you know that Mr Conway has made a figure by taking the Castle of Waldeck.[11] There has been another action[12] to Prince Ferdinand's advantage, but no English were engaged.

You tantalize me by talking of the verdure of Yorkshire; we have not had a tea-cup full of rain till today for these six weeks. Corn has been reaped that never wet its lips; not a blade of grass; the leaves yellow and falling as in the end of October. In short, Twickenham is rueful; I don't believe Westphalia looks more barren. Nay, we are forced to fortify ourselves too. Hanworth[13] was broken open last night, though the family was all there. Lord Vere[14] lost a silver standish, an old watch, and his writing-box with fifty pounds in it. They broke it open in the park,[15] but missed a diamond ring, which was found, and the telescope, which by the weight of the case they had fancied full of money. Another house in the middle of Sunbury[16] has had the same fate. I am mounting cannon on my battlements.

Your château, I hope, proceeds faster than mine. The carpenters are all associated for increase of wages;[17] I have had but two men at work these five weeks. You know, to be sure, that Lady Mary Wortley[18] cannot live. Adieu, my dear Lord!

Your most faithful servant,

Hor. Walpole

9. The Ismaelovsky, Semenovsky, and Preobrazhensky Guards declared Catherine 'their Empress and Sovereign' 9 July NS (Mann vi. 61, n. 3).

10. 'Petersburg, July 10. Yesterday her Imperial Majesty . . . [Catherine II] was proclaimed sole and reigning Empress, and Sovereign of this Empire . . . [and] the several orders . . . took the oath of fidelity to her . . . and to her son the Great Duke Paul as her lawful heir' (London Gazette No. 10231 31 July – 3 Aug., reprinted in London Chronicle 3–5 Aug., xii. 121).

11. Which surrendered, 11 July (Mann vi. 56, n. 31).

12. At Lutternberg, 23 July (ibid. vi. 60, n. 65).

13. Hanworth House, seat of Lord Vere; formerly a palace of Henry VIII; destroyed by fire, 1797 (Ossory ii. 294, n. 4).

14. Vere Beauclerk (1699–1781), cr. (1750) Bn Vere of Hanworth.

15. Presumably Richmond Park.

16. In Middlesex.

17. One of the earliest journeymen's associations, the 'Journeymen Taylors,' had been founded in 1720. The associated carpenters had left SH 26 June (Mann vi. 49, n. 22; SH Accounts, ed. Toynbee, Oxford, 1927, pp. 109–10). By March 1763 work on the Gallery was proceeding (Montagu ii. 53).

18. Lady Mary Wortley Montagu d. 21 Aug.; she had cancer of the breast (Mann vi. 56).

To Strafford, Wednesday 10 August 1763

Printed from *Works* v. 453–4; reprinted, Wright iv. 294–5, Cunningham iv. 104, Toynbee v. 358–9.

Strawberry Hill, August 10, 1763.

My dear Lord,

I HAVE waited in hopes that the world would do something worth telling you: it will not, and I cannot stay any longer without asking you how you do, and hoping you have not quite forgot me. It has rained such deluges, that I had some thoughts of turning my gallery into an ark, and began to pack up a pair of bantams, a pair of cats, in short, a pair of every living creature about my house: but it is grown fine at last, and the workmen quit my gallery today without hoisting a sail in it. I know nothing upon earth but what the ancient ladies in my neighbourhood knew threescore years ago; I write merely to pay you my peppercorn of affection,[1] and to inquire after my Lady, who I hope is perfectly well. A longer letter would not have half the merit: a line in return will however repay all the merit I can possibly have to one to whom I am so much obliged.

I am, my dear Lord, your most faithful servant,

Hor. Walpole

To Strafford, Tuesday 3 September 1765

Printed from *Works* v. 454–5. Printed also in Wright v. 61–2, Cunningham iv. 397–8, Toynbee vi. 285–6.

Arlington Street, September 3, 1765.

My dear Lord,

I CANNOT quit a country where I leave anything that I honour so much as your Lordship and Lady Strafford, without taking a sort of leave of you. I shall set out for Paris on Monday next the 9th,[1]

---

1. Cf. OED, *sub* peppercorn: 'Formerly often, and still sometimes, stipulated as a quit-rent or nominal rent.' See also Ossory i. 302.

1. When HW left London at 8:30 A.M., reached Dover at 7:30 P.M., and sailed 10 Sept. ('Paris Journals,' du Deffand v. 258).

and shall be happy if I can execute any commission for you there.[2]

A journey to Paris sounds youthful and healthy. I have certainly mended much this last week,[3] though with no pretensions to a recovery of youth. Half the view of my journey is to re-establish my health—the other half, to wash my hands of politics, which I have long determined to do whenever a change should happen. I would not abandon my friends while they were martyrs; but now they have gained their crown of glory,[4] they are well able to shift for themselves; and it was no part of my compact to go to that heaven, St James's, with them. Unless I dislike Paris very much, I shall stay some time;[5] but I make no declarations, lest I should be soon tired of it, and come back again. At first I must like it, for Lady Mary Coke will be there, as if by assignation.[6] The Countesses of Carlisle[7] and Berkeley too, I hear, will set up their staves[8] there for some time;[9] but as my heart is faithful to Lady Mary, they would not charm me if they were forty times more disposed to it.

The Emperor is dead[10]—but so are all the Maximilians[11] and Leopolds[12] his predecessors, and with no more influence on the present state of things. The Empress Dowager Queen[13] will still be master—unless she marries an Irishman,[14] as I wish with all my soul she may.

The Duke[15] and Duchess of Richmond will follow me in about a fortnight: Lord and Lady George Lenox[16] go with them; and

2. In 1767, HW sent Lady Strafford 'a box of colours' from Paris (ibid. v. 406) but no earlier commission is recorded.

3. HW had been ill with gout in his feet and stomach since late June (MANN vi. 309, and *passim*).

4. The change of ministry in late June, in which the chief figures were Rockingham, and Henry Seymour Conway, who became secretary of state for the southern department. The changes are discussed in MANN vi. 309–12, 315–16.

5. He returned to London 22 April 1766 ('Paris Journals,' DU DEFFAND v. 314).

6. On his way to Paris, 11 Sept. HW 'Met Lady Mary Coke coming out of Amiens on her way to England' (ibid. v. 259).

7. Hon. Isabella Byron (1721–95), m. 1 (1743) Henry Howard, 4th E. of Carlisle, 1738; m. 2 (1759) Sir William Musgrave, 6th Bt, 1755.

8. Plural of *staff*. 'To set up . . . one's staff*: to settle down in a place, take up

one's abode' (OED, *sub* staff, I. 5. d).

9. Lady Berkeley is frequently mentioned in HW's 'Paris Journals,' 1765–6, but HW does not mention Lady Carlisle.

10. Francis I d. 18 Aug. The news reached London 30 Aug. (MANN vi. 328 and n. 2).

11. Maximilian I (1459–1519), Holy Roman Emperor 1493–1519; and Maximilian II (1527–76), Emperor 1564–76.

12. Leopold I (1640–1705), Holy Roman Emperor 1658–1705.

13. Maria Theresa.

14. HW often ridiculed the rich widows who married handsome Irish adventurers.

15. Appointed ambassador to Paris (HW). Envoy extraordinary and plenipotentiary, appointed 9 Aug., he arrived in Paris 6 Nov.; HW arrived there 13 Sept. (Horn, *Diplomatic Representatives* 22; MANN vi. 323, n. 8; 'Paris Journals,' DU DEFFAND v. 260, 270).

16. Lord George Henry Lennox (1737–1805), the Duke of Richmond's brother;

Sir Charles Bunbury and Lady Sarah[17] are to be at Paris too for some time:[18] so the English court there will be very juvenile and blooming. This set is rather younger than the dowagers with whom I pass so much of my summers and autumns; but this is to be my last sally into the world; and when I return, I intend to be as sober as my cat,[19] and purr quietly in my own chimney corner.

Adieu, my dear Lord! May every happiness attend you both, and may I pass some agreeable days next summer with you at Wentworth Castle![20]

Your most devoted and faithful servant,

Hor. Walpole

To Strafford, Tuesday 29 October 1765

Missing: 'Lord Strafford. by Comte Lauraguais's English coachman. Written 29, went 31' ('Paris Journals,' du Deffand v. 377).

To Strafford, Thursday 23 January 1766

Missing: 'Lord Strafford. 23 [Jan. 1766]. by Marmora's courier' ('Paris Journals,' du Deffand v. 379).

M.P. Chichester 1761–7, Sussex 1767–90; m. (1759) Lady Louisa Ker (1739–1830), HW's correspondent. They arrived with the Richmonds, 6 Nov. Lord George was commissioned secretary of embassy 16 Aug. 1765, served until 1 July 1766, when he became minister plenipotentiary (Ossory i. 16, n. 32, 23, n. 18).

17. Sir Thomas Charles Bunbury (1740–1821), 6th Bt., 1764, m. (1762) Lady Sarah Lennox (1745–1826), Lord George's sister.

18. Lady Sarah, without Sir Charles, had been in Paris 29 April – 2 June 1765,

and after HW's visit both went there for about two months, Dec. 1766 – Jan. 1767 (*Life and Letters of Lady Sarah Lennox*, ed. Lady Ilchester and Lord Stavordale, 1901–2, i. 161, 167, 207; du Deffand i. 199–234).

19. 'Harold, my venerable cat . . . found on the Goodwin Sands fifteen years ago or more, died last night' (HW to Lady Ossory 6 July 1779, Ossory ii. 108).

20. He did not go until 1768; see *post* 16 Aug. 1768.

To Strafford, Saturday 4 October 1766

Printed from MS now wsl; left by Mrs Damer to Sir Wathen Waller; sold at first Waller Sale, 5 Dec. 1921, lot 45, to Harper; sold at the second Waller Sale, 15 Dec. 1947, lot 38 to Maggs for wsl.
First printed Toynbee *Supp.* i. 142–3.

Bath, Oct. 4, 1766.

My dear Lord,

I GIVE you ten thousand thanks for your goodness, of which I had heard before from Lady Mary[1] and Mr Conway, and which for so many years has never failed me. I have been indeed extremely ill, with a violent disorder in my stomach, but I think it was not the gout, though I do not love to haggle with physicians about names: I have my feelings and they have their words. All I know, is, that I recovered very fast from the moment I refused to take any more medicines, and am now much better than I could have expected to be in the time.[2]

We have all the great ones of the earth here, Chancellor,[3] President,[4] and Privy Seal.[5] I saw Lady Rockingham[6] for a moment in the street, but have not begun my visits yet, nor been at the rooms,[7] which only cure those who have no complaint.

Lord and Lady Powis[8] and Lord and Lady Spencer[9] are here, but

1. Coke.
2. On Sunday 28 Sept. Lady Mary Coke and Lady Betty Mackenzie called on Lady Suffolk. 'She was just gone to Strawberry Hill, and her servant told us Mr Walpole was to set out for Bath tomorrow morning, upon which I proposed to Lady Betty to return to our boat, and as the day was fine to go by water to Mr Walpole. She consented, and we found it very pleasant, and, what was better, such an extraordinary alteration in him that I should not have found out he had been ill. We stayed till half an hour after two' (Coke, *Journals* i. 62).
3. Charles Pratt (1714–94), cr. (1765) Bn, (1786) E. Camden; lord chancellor July 1766 – Jan. 1770. The arrival of 'Lord and Lady Camden' is announced in the *London Chronicle* 23–5 Sept., xx. 302, *sub* 'Bath, Sept. 22.'
4. Robert Henley (ca 1708–72), cr. (1760) Bn Henley, (1764) E. of Northington;

M.P. Bath 1747–57; lord chancellor Jan. 1761 – July 1766; lord president of the Council July 1766 – Dec. 1767.
5. William Pitt, cr. (4 Aug. 1766) E. of Chatham, lord privy seal July 1766 – Oct. 1768. In *Mem. Geo. III* ii. 261–2 HW reports a conversation of two hours he had with Chatham at Bath at this time.
6. Mary Bright (1735–1804), m. (1752) Charles Watson Wentworth, 2d M. of Rockingham, 1750 (*Correspondence of Edmund Burke*, ed. Copeland, i. 267, n. 2).
7. HW stayed in Chapel Court, near Cross Bath, not so much frequented as the Pump Room or King's Bath (Montagu ii. 228 and n. 2).
8. Henry Arthur Herbert (ca 1703–72), cr. (1743, 1749) Bn Herbert of Chirbury, (1748) E. of Powis; M.P. Bletchingley 1724–7, Ludlow 1727–43; m. (1751) Barbara Herbert (1735–86).
9. John Spencer (1734–83), cr. (1761) Bn and Vct Spencer, (1765) E. Spencer, m.

I believe it is by no means a full season yet. Their Graces of Bedford are expected, and so I hear is the mob, to settle some little differences with my Lord Chatham about the price of corn and butter.[10] As they are not quieted by the embargo,[11] I suppose they take it for a new tax. If the people should not happen to understand the language of Demosthenes,[12] here is my Lord President in the *purloins*[13] ready to translate it into the *vulgar* tongue.[14]

I beg a thousand compliments to my Lady Strafford; I rejoice she is so well, and that the exportation[15] is prohibited, that her pea-fowls and guinea-fowls may have their rolls and household bread in their usual plenty. Adieu! my dear Lord,

Yours with the utmost warmth and friendship,

HOR. WALPOLE

To STRAFFORD, Wednesday 29 July 1767

Printed from *Works* v. 455–6; reprinted, Wright v. 178–9, Cunningham v. 57–7, Toynbee vii. 120–2.

Strawberry Hill, July 29, 1767.

My dear Lord,

I AM very sorry that I must speak of a loss that will give you and Lady Strafford concern; an essential loss to me, who am deprived of a most agreeable friend, with whom I passed here many hours. I need not say I mean poor Lady Suffolk.[1] I was with her[2] two hours

(1755) Margaret Georgiana Poyntz (1737–1814), dau. of Stephen Poyntz the diplomatist.

10. There had been uprisings in 21 localities because exports of wheat had resulted in high food prices (MANN vi. 455, n. 3).

11. Because of scarcity, high prices, and a poor wheat crop in 1766, the Privy Council in a special meeting 24 Sept. recommended and the King ordered 26 Sept. 'that an embargo be forthwith laid upon all ships and vessels laden or to be laden, in the ports of Great Britain, with wheat or wheat flour, to be exported to foreign parts,' the embargo to continue until 14

Nov., when Parliament, then prorogued was to meet (*London Gazette* No. 10662, 23–7 Sept.; *London Chronicle* 23–29 Sept., passim; *Mem. Geo. III* ii. 259–60).

12. George III, in whose name the embargo was proclaimed.

13. Northington's supposed mistake for *purlieus*.

14. Northington was said to be fond of low company and was notorious for hard swearing.

15. Of wheat.

___

1. Who died on Sunday 26 July at Marble Hill, her house at Twickenham.
2. At Marble Hill.

on Saturday night; and indeed found her much changed, though I did not apprehend her in danger. I was going to say she complained —but you know she never did complain—of the gout and rheumatism all over her, particularly in her face. It was a cold night, and she sat below stairs when she should have been in bed; and I doubt this want of care was prejudicial. I sent next morning. She had a bad night; but grew much better in the evening. Lady Dalkeith[3] came to her; and when she was gone, Lady Suffolk said to Lord Chetwynd,[4] she would eat her supper in her bedchamber. He went up with her, and thought the appearances promised a good night: but she was scarce sat down in her chair, before she pressed her hand to her side, and died in half an hour.

I believe both your Lordship and Lady Strafford will be surprised to hear that she was by no means in the situation that most people thought. Lord Chetwynd and myself were the only persons at all acquainted with her affairs, and they were far from being even easy to her.[5] It is due to her memory to say, that I never saw more strict honour and justice. She bore *knowingly* the imputation of being covetous, at a time that the strictest economy could by no means prevent her exceeding her income considerably. The anguish of the last years of her life, though concealed, flowed from the apprehension of not satisfying her few wishes, which were, not to be in debt, and to make a provision for Miss H[otham].[6] I can give your Lordship strong instances of the sacrifices she tried to make to her principles. I have not yet heard if her will is opened;[7] but it will surprise those

3. Lady Strafford's sister, cr. (19 Aug. 1767) Bns Greenwich. Lady Mary Coke in Frankfort, Germany on 12 Aug. 'received a letter from Lady Dalkeith with the sad news of the death of poor Lady Suffolk . . . I never had a better friend, and many are the obligations I had to her. Lady Dalkeith says she died in two hours after she had been with her. 'Twas dreadfully sudden' (Coke, *Journals* ii. 91).

4. William Richard Chetwynd (?1683–1770), 3d Vct Chetwynd, 21 June 1767; M.P. Strafford 1715–22, 1734–70, Plymouth 1722–7; Lady Suffolk's 'dearest friend to her death' (HW, *Reminiscences*, ed. Paget Toynbee, Oxford, 1924, p. 20n).

5. Her fortune 'had never been near so great as it was believed,' and 'of late years was so diminished, as to have brought her

into great difficulties' (HW to Mann 31 July, MANN vi. 544).

6. Her great-niece (HW). Henrietta Gertrude Hotham (1753–1816), Lady Suffolk's companion (MONTAGU ii. 93, n. 1). HW wrote the *Magpie and Her Brood*, SH, 1764, for her. Her portrait by Romney is reproduced in A. M. W. Stirling, *The Hothams*, 1918, ii. facing 94.

7. Except for one legacy of £500, to a goddaughter and 'a few minor legacies, all else was bequeathed to Henrietta [Hotham] though Marble Hill was to belong to Lord Buckinghamshire [d. 1793] for his lifetime, and to come to her only at his decease' (ibid. ii. 109; MANN vi. 543–4). In 1771, Henrietta Hotham's father, Sir Charles Hotham, became 8th Bt and succeeded to the family estate.

who thought her rich. Lord Chetwynd's friendship to her has been unalterably kind and zealous, and is not ceased. He stays in the house with Miss H[otham] till some of her family come to take her away. I have perhaps dwelt too long on this subject; but as it was not permitted me to do her justice when alive, I own I cannot help wishing that those who had a regard for her, may now at least know how much more she deserved it than even they suspected. In truth, I never knew a woman more respectable for her honour and principles, and have lost few persons in my life whom I shall miss so much.

I am, my dear Lord, yours most sincerely,

HOR. WALPOLE

To STRAFFORD, Saturday 25 June 1768

Printed from *Works* v. 457–8. Reprinted, Wright v. 210–1, Cunningham v. 111–12, Toynbee vii. 204–6.

Strawberry Hill, June 25, 1768.

YOU ordered me, my dear Lord, to write to you, and I am always ready to obey you, and to give you every proof of attachment in my power: but it is a very barren season for all but cabalists, who can compound, divide, multiply No. 45[1] forty-five thousand different ways. I saw in the papers today, that somehow or other this famous number and the number of the beast in the Revelations[2] is the same—an observation from which different persons will draw various conclusions. For my part, who have no ill wishes to Wilkes, I wish he was in Patmos or the New Jerusalem, for I am exceedingly

1. For No. 45 of the *North Briton,* an alleged libel on George III, John Wilkes had been arrested and outlawed. He had returned from the Continent to London 6 Feb. 1768, had failed to carry the City of London but had been returned for Parliament by the County of Middlesex 28 March (when No. 45 had been used as a slogan), had surrendered to his outlawry and had been committed to King's Bench Prison 27 April. On 18 June his outlawry was reversed but he was sentenced to one year and ten months in prison and fined £1000; he was in the King's Bench prison at the date of this letter. Riots and disturbances had accompanied Wilkes's recent activities, and, in the election, 'papers inscribed "No. 45, Wilkes and Liberty"' were carried by his followers (HW to Mann 31 March, 22 June 1768, MANN vii. 5–8, 33–4; *Mem. Geo. III* iii. 128–32 and *passim*).

2. See Revelation 13. 17, 18; 15. 2. According to 13.18, the 'number of the beast' was 666.

tired of his name. The only good thing I have heard in all this controversy was of a man who began his letter thus: 'I take the Wilkes-and-liberty to assure you, etc.'

I peeped at London last week, and found a tolerably full opera.[3] But now the Birthday[4] is over, I suppose everybody will go to waters and races till his Majesty of Denmark arrives.[5] He is extremely amorous; but stays so short a time, that the ladies who intend to be undone must not haggle. They must do their business in the twinkling of an allemande, or he will be flown. Don't you think he will be a little surprised, when he inquires for the seraglio in Buckingham House,[6] to find, in full of all accounts, two old *Mecklenburgheresses?*[7]

Is it true that [Lady Rockingham] is turned Methodist?[8] It will be a great acquisition to the sect to have their hymns set by Giardini.[9] Pope Joan[10] Huntingdon will be deposed, if the husband becomes first minister.[11] I doubt too the saints will like to call at Can-

3. HW to Conway 16 June: 'I go to town tomorrow to see [Samuel Foote's] *The Devil upon Two Sticks,*' a satirical comedy, not an opera, at the Little Theatre in the Haymarket, with Foote as the Devil. Operas were performed at the King's Theatre in the Haymarket on 14 (when HW was not in London) and 18 June; on the 18th, Pietro Guglielmi's *I viaggiatori ridicoli* was performed (*London Stage 1660–1800*, pt 4, ed. G. W. Stone, Carbondale, Ill., 1962, iii. 1339).

4. 23 June, observed as George III's birthday.

5. George III's first cousin, Christian VII (1749–1808), K. of Denmark 1766–1808, who in 1766 had married George III's youngest sister. He arrived at St James's Palace 11 Aug. and left 13 Oct. for Dover to embark for Calais (*London Chronicle* 13–16 Aug., 11–18 Oct., xxiv. 153, 360, 363, 370). He travelled under the title of 'Comte de Travendahl' (HW to Mann 13 Aug. 1768, MANN vii. 43, n. 13).

6. In St James's Park; purchased for Queen Charlotte shortly after her marriage; sometimes known as the Queen's House; first occupied by the King and Queen 22 May 1762 (OSSORY i. 8, n. 31).

7. The Queen's German keepers of the Robes: Elizabeth Juliana Schwellenberg

(Schwellenbergen) (ca 1728–97), 'the first of the Queen's two German ladies' (*Last Journals* i. 86; OSSORY i. 168, n. 14) and Mrs Hagerdorn (fl. 1761–86). Both accompanied Queen Charlotte to England; in 1786 Mrs Hagerdorn retired to Mecklenburg-Strelitz (MASON ii. 35, n. 31).

8. This is not confirmed; HW's correspondent, the Rev. Henry Zouch, an Anglican clergyman, was her chaplain (DNB *sub* Zouch).

9. Felice de' Giardini (1716–96), violinist, composer; in England ca 1750–84, 1790. HW thought Giardini's compositions lacked force and simplicity, but Burney admired his performance and composition. Giardini 'taught many ladies of the first rank to sing' (MONTAGU ii. 73, n. 22; MASON i. 343, 345; Charles Burney, *General History of Music,* 1776–89, ii. 849 and *passim*).

10. The legendary figure supposed to have lived in the 9th century and to have reigned as Pope John for more than two years; here applied to the Methodist leader, Lady Huntingdon.

11. Rockingham had been first lord of the Treasury (prime minister) 13 July 1765 – July 1766; he refused the post in 1767 (*Mem. Geo. III* iii. 56–61) but held it again from 27 March 1782 until his death 1 July 1782.

terbury and Winchester in their way to heaven.[12] My charity is so small, that I do not think their virtue a jot more obdurate than that of patriots.

We have had some severe rain; but the season is now beautiful, though scarce hot. The hay and the corn promise that we shall have no riots on their account. Those black dogs the Whiteboys[13] or coal-heavers are dispersed or taken;[14] and I really see no reason to think we shall have another rebellion this fortnight. The most comfortable event to me is, that we shall have no civil war all the summer at Brentford.[15] I dreaded two kings there;[16] but the writ for Middlesex will not be issued till the Parliament meets[17]; so there will be no pretender against King Glynn.[18] As I love peace, and have done with politics, I quietly acknowledge the King *de facto;*[19] and hope to pass and repass unmolested through his Majesty's *long, lazy, lousy* capital.[20]

My humble duty to my Lady Strafford and all her pheasants. I have just made two cascades;[21] but my naiads are fools to Mrs

12. That is, if Rockingham were prime minister, his wife might rule the Methodists through the chief Anglican sees, which the Methodists would dislike.

13. Members of a secret agrarian association in Ireland.

14. Some of the coalheavers were Irish Whiteboys. For details of the riots, in which several people were killed, see HW to Mann 22 June, 4 Aug. 1768; *Mem. Geo. III* iii. 148–50.

15. Riots and disturbances had occurred at the poll for the Middlesex election at Brentford 28 March; see *Mem. Geo. III* iii. 128–31.

16. As in Buckingham's *The Rehearsal,* first acted 7 Dec. 1671, printed 1672; cf. Ossory i. 143 and n. 23. The 'two kings' are 'The King and Wilkes' (HW to Mann 22 June 1768, Mann vii. 34, n. 9), but another implication is possible: 'We hear that an offer was made to Mr Wilkes by his friends, that if he chose anyone to be joint candidate with him, they would vote for them jointly; . . . Mr Wilkes replied that he was infinitely obliged to them for the offer, but as the public had interested itself so much in his favour, he thought himself sufficiently honoured if they chose him without presuming to dictate their choice of anyone else, and

very politely declined the offer' (*London Chronicle* 29–31 March 1768, xxiii. 310). According to HW, Wilkes on the second day of the poll, threw some of his votes to George Cooke, who was elected, although on the first day he had been third in the poll (*Mem. Geo. III* iii. 129).

17. After the general election of 1768, the Parliament met on 10 May, took no action on Wilkes, adjourned on 21 May to 2 June, was prorogued to 21 June and then to 8 Nov., when it met. Wilkes was expelled the House of Commons 3 Feb. 1769 on which day a writ for a new election was issued, and Wilkes was re-elected 16 Feb. 1769. See Cobbett, *Parl. Hist.* xvi. 423–75.

18. Serjeant Glynn, Member of Parliament for Middlesex (HW). John Glynn (1722–79), sergeant-at-law, 1763; counsel for the printers of the *North Briton,* 1764, and for Wilkes, 1768; M.P. Middlesex from 14 Dec. 1768 (following the death of George Cooke, who had been elected with Wilkes 28 March) until his death; 'a man of unexceptional character' (*Mem. Geo. III* iii. 190).

19. Wilkes.

20. Brentford (HW).

21. In the Cottage Garden *(SH Accounts,* ed. Toynbee, Oxford, 1927, p. 54).

C[hetwynd][22] or my Lady S[ondes], and don't give me a gallon of water in a week.[23]—Well, this is a very silly letter! But you must take the will for the deed. Adieu, my dear Lord!

Your most faithful servant,

Hor. Walpole

To Strafford, Tuesday 16 August 1768

Printed from *Works* v. 458–60. Reprinted, Wright v. 217–20, Cunningham v. 121–3, Toynbee vii. 217–21.

Strawberry Hill, August 16, 1768.

AS YOU have been so good, my dear Lord, as twice to take notice of my letter, I am bound in conscience and gratitude to try to amuse you with anything new. A royal visitor,[1] quite fresh, is a real curiosity—by the reception of him, I do not think many more of the breed will come hither. He came from Dover[2] in hackney-chaises; for somehow or other the Master of the Horse[3] happened to be in Lincolnshire;[4] and the King's coaches having received no orders, were too good subjects to go and fetch a stranger king of their own heads.[5] However, as his Danish Majesty travels to improve himself

---

'My cascades give themselves the air of cataracts' (HW to H. S. Conway 25 Dec. 1770).

22. Hon. Deborah Chetwynd (d. 1788), dau. of William Richard, 3d Vct Chetwynd; sempstress and laundress to George II ca 1755–60, to Q. Charlotte 1761–88. She is called *Miss* in the court calendars 1756–60 and Mrs 1762–88. (*Court and City Register; European Magazine,* 1788, xiv. 312; Coke, *Journals, passim; Letters to and from Henrietta, Countess of Suffolk . . . from 1712 to 1767,* ed. J. W. Croker, 1824, ii. 256–62).

23. Lady Sondes's tearfulness is mentioned by HW to Bentley *ante* 17 March 1754.

---

1. Christian VII of Denmark, whose visit HW describes in *Mem. Geo. III* iii. 159–61.

2. Where he had landed 10 Aug. (*London Chronicle* 13–16 Aug., xxiv. 153–4).

3. Peregrine Bertie (1714–78), 3d D. of Ancaster, 1742; Master of the Horse 1766–78.

4. His chief seat was at Grimsthorpe, Lincs, and he was lord lieutenant of the county 1742–78. He entertained Christian VII at Grimsthorpe 30 Aug. (*London Chronicle* 1–3 Sept., xxiv. 218, 224).

5. 'The coaches of the [King's] Household which had been sent down to Dover were all left behind, and his Majesty travelled in hired chaises, with a design, as is imagined, of keeping more incog.' (*London Chronicle* 11–13 Aug., xxiv. 146) or 'for the sake of expedition, and to avoid ceremony' (*Annual Register,* 1768, xi. 152).

for the good of his people, he will go back extremely enlightened in the arts of government and morality, by having learned that crowned heads may be reduced to ride in a hired chaise.

By another mistake, King George happened to go to Richmond[6] about an hour before King Christiern arrived in London.[7] An hour is exceedingly long; and the distance to Richmond still longer: so with all the dispatch that could possibly be made, King George could not get back to his capital till next day at noon. Then, as the road from his closet at St James's to the King of Denmark's apartment on t'other side of the palace[8] is about thirty miles, which posterity, having no conception of the prodigious extent and magnificence of St James's, will never believe, it was half an hour after three before his Danish Majesty's courier could go, and return to let him know that his good brother and ally was leaving the palace in which they both were, in order to receive him at the Queen's palace,[9] which you know is about a million of snail's paces from St James's. Notwithstanding these difficulties and unavoidable delays, Woden, Thor, Friga, and all the gods that watch over the Kings of the North, did bring these two invincible monarchs to each other's embraces about half an hour after five that same evening. They passed an hour in projecting a family compact that will regulate the destiny of Europe to latest posterity: and then, the Fates so willing it, the British Prince departed for Richmond, and the Danish potentate repaired to the widowed mansion[10] of his royal mother-in-law,[11] where he poured forth the fullness of his heart in praises on the lovely bride[12]

6. Richmond Lodge, the lodge built temp. Henry VIII in Richmond Park at West Sheen; see MONTAGU ii. 131, n. 15.

7. HW is ironic; George III's absence was intentional. He had tried to prevent Christian VII's visit (*Mem. Geo. III* iii. 159), of which he wrote Lord Weymouth 8 June, after the visit had become definite: 'you know very well that the whole of it *is very disagreeable to me*' (J. H. Jesse, *Memoirs of . . . George the Third*, 2d edn, 1867, i. 450). 'Their Majesties were not at St James's . . . , having set out that afternoon for Richmond.' 'As soon as the King of Denmark came to St James's, he was immediately waited on by the Earl of Hertford [Lord Chamberlain] and Falmouth, to compliment him on his arrival' (*London Chronicle* 11–13 Aug., xxiv. 146, 152).

8. Christian VII was assigned 'The Prince of Wales's apartments 5 rooms and a closet for the King.' For the housing arrangements as they had been planned on 15 July, see Geo. III's *Corr.* ed. Fortescue, ii. 33–5.

9. Buckingham House, now Buckingham Palace.

10. Carlton House.

11. Augusta, Ps Dowager of Wales.

12. Caroline Matilda (1751–75), posthumous dau. of Frederick Louis, P. of Wales, m. (1766) Christian VII. Divorced in 1772 after her disgrace in the affair with Struensee, she retired to the Castle at Celle (Zell) in Hanover. Christian VII 'had taken an early dislike to' her (*Mem. Geo. III* iii. 160).

she had bestowed on him, from whom nothing but the benefit of his subjects could ever have torn him.[13]—And here let calumny blush, who has aspersed so chaste and faithful a monarch with low amours; pretending that he has raised to the honour of a seat in his sublime council, an artisan of Hamburgh, known only by repairing the soles of buskins,[14] because that mechanic would, on no other terms, consent to his fair daughter's[15] being honoured with majestic embraces. So victorious over his passions is this young Scipio from the Pole, that though on Shooter's Hill[16] he fell into an ambush laid for him by an illustrious Countess, of blood-royal herself,[17] his Majesty, after descending from his car, and courteously greeting her, again mounted his vehicle, without being one moment eclipsed from the eyes of the surrounding multitude.[18]—Oh! mercy on me! I am out of breath—Pray let me descend from my stilts, or I shall send you as fustian and tedious a history as that of Henry II.[19]—Well then, this great King is a very little one; not ugly, nor ill-made. He has the sublime strut of his grandfather,[20] or of a cock-sparrow; and the divine white eyes of all his family by the mother's side.[21] His curi-

13. He was unfaithful to his wife, and had left her behind when on his travels.

14. Gaiters (W. H. Wilkins, *A Queen of Tears*, 1904, i. 156).

15. His step-daughter, Anna Catherina Benthagen (or Benthacken or Benthaken) also known as Frau Maes (ibid. i. 136–7; *Kabinetsstyrelsen i Denmark 1768–1772*, ed. Holger Hansen, Copenhagen, 1916–23, iii. 380, 397, 536, 537). She was called 'Støvlet-Katrine' because she had sewed the gaiters at her stepfather's tailor shop. Later she became an opera dancer (Wilkins, loc. cit.), and Christian VII's mistress; payments to her are recorded (ibid.; Hansen, op. cit. iii. 536, 537, 589 and *passim*).

16. 'At the northeast extremity of . . . [Eltham, co. of London] lies Shooter's Hill, over which is the high road from London to Dover. . . . Shooter's Hill was formerly a place much dreaded by travellers, the steepness and narrowness of the roads, and the harbour which the neighbouring coppices afforded to the robbers rendering it a very fit place for their depredations. Shakespeare makes it the scene of Falstaff's and his companions' robberies in Henry IV' (Daniel Lysons, *Environs of London*, Vol. IV, 1796, p. 418).

17. Lady Caroline Fitzroy, great-grand-daughter of Charles I, and wife of the 2d E. of Harrington.

18. 'Lady Harrington, it is remarked, pays him particular attentions. She met him upon the road, and followed him to Ranelagh from Lady Hertford's, where I think I was told he danced with Lady Bell,' Lady Harrington's daughter, Lady Isabella Stanhope, mentioned *post* HW to Hamilton 22 Sept. 1768 (Coke, *Journals* ii. 336, *sub* 13 Aug.). 'Lady Betty [Mackenzie] . . . . wants to find out what can be Lady Harrington's view in taking such pains to make up to the King of Denmark. I think I have guessed it: he is said to be very generous and to like making presents, and you well know she has been suspected of inclining to receive them' (ibid. ii. 337, *sub* 14 Aug.).

19. By George Lyttelton, 1st Bn Lyttelton: *The History of the Life of King Henry the Second*, of which Vols I–II and an unnumbered volume of notes had been published 16 June 1767; the work was not completed until 1771 (Ossory i. 30, n. 7).

20. George II; cf. HW to Montagu 13 Aug., Montagu ii. 265.

21. Louisa (1724–51) 5th dau. of George II, m. (1743) Frederik V, K. of Denmark 1746–66.

osity seems to have consisted in the original plan of travelling, for I cannot say he takes notice of anything in particular. His manner is cold and dignified, but very civil and gracious and proper. The mob adore him and huzza him; and so they did the first instant. At present they begin to know why—for he flings money to them out of his windows;[22] and by the end of the week I do not doubt but they will want to choose him for Middlesex.[23] His court is extremely well ordered; for they bow as low to him at every word as if his name was Sultan Amurat.[24] You would take his first minister[25] for only the first of his slaves.—I hope this example, which they have been so good as to exhibit at the opera,[26] will contribute to civilize us.[27] There is indeed a pert young gentleman, who a little discomposes this august ceremonial. His name is Count Holke,[28] his age three-and-twenty; and his post answers to one that we had formerly in England, many ages ago, and which in our tongue was called the Lord High Favourite. Before the Danish monarchs became absolute, the most refractory of that country used to write libels, called *North Danes*,[29] against this great officer; but that practice has long since ceased. Count Holke seems rather proud of his favour, than shy of displaying it.

End of Volume the first.[30]

I hope, my dear Lord, you will be content with my Danish politics, for I trouble myself with no other. There is a long history about the Baron de Bottetourt, and Sir Jeffery Amherst, who has resigned

22. The newspapers record numerous instances of such generosity throughout his visit. See also *Delany Corr.* iv. 188.

23. As they had chosen Wilkes.

24. Or Amurath, an alternate form of Murad: Murad I, II, III, IV, Sultans of Turkey 1359–89, 1421–51, 1574–95, 1623–40.

25. Johan Hartvig Ernst von Bernstorff (1712–72), Greve; born in Hanover; ambassador from Denmark to Paris, 1744; minister of foreign affairs 1751 until his dismissal was effected by Struensee in 1770 (DU DEFFAND ii. 128, n. 5).

26. Christian VII and his suite attended [*Cecchina, ossia] La buona figliuola maritata*, popular comic opera composed by Niccolò Piccini (1728–1800), at the King's Theatre in the Haymarket 13 Aug., one of the special performances of opera

during his visit (HW to Mann 13 Aug. 1768, MANN vi. 473, n. 26, vii. 42; *London Chronicle* 13–16 Aug., xxiv. 154).

27. At the Opera, 'His Court behaved to him with Eastern submission. What would I have taken to be Bernsdorffe, bowing and cringing to him at every word in the face of a new and free nation!' (MANN, vii. 43).

28. Frederik Vilhelm Conrad Holck (1745–1800), Count (Greve) Holck, 'Grand Master of the Wardrobe,' who fell from favour in 1770 on the rise of Struensee (MONTAGU ii. 265, n. 5; *London Gazette* No. 10858, Aug. 9–13, 1768).

29. Cf. *North Britons*. Bute, who was called George III's favourite, was attacked in it (MANN vi. 136, n. 20).

30. This line is omitted in Wright, Cunningham, Toynbee.

his regiment;[31] but it is nothing to me, nor do I care a straw about it.[32] I am deep in the anecdotes of the new Court; and if you want to know more of Count Holke or Count Molke,[33] or the Grand Vizier Bernsdorff, or Mynheer Schimmelman,[34] apply to me and you shall be satisfied—But what do I talk of? You will see them yourself. Minerva, in the shape of Count Bernsdorff, or out of all shape in the person of the Duchess of [Northumberland] is to conduct Telemachus to York races;[35] for can a monarch be perfectly accomplished in the mysteries of kingcraft, as our Solomon James I[36] called it,[37] unless he is initiated in the arts of jockeyship? When this northern star travels towards its own sphere, Lord Hertford will go to Ragley.[38] I shall go with him;[39] and if I can avoid running foul of the magi that will be thronging from all parts to worship that star, I will endeavour to call at Wentworth Castle for a day or two, if it will not be inconvenient. I should think it would be about the sec-

31. The 60th Foot. For details, see HW to Mann 13 Aug.; Geo. III's *Corr.* ed. Fortescue, ii. 38–41; *Army Lists*.

32. Inasmuch as Conway was drawn into the affair, HW took a greater interest than he here indicates. See *Mem. Geo. III* iii. 161–4; HW to Mann 13 Aug. 1768. Amherst had been governor of Virginia since 1759 but was unwilling to reside there. Botetourt had kissed hands 29 July; he sailed 29 Aug. from Spithead for Virginia, in the '*Rippon* man of war' (*London Chronicle* 28–30 July, 30 Aug.– 1 Sept., xxiv. 102, 216; MANN vii. 44, n. 22). Some of the numerous paragraphs and letters printed in the newspapers are reprinted in GM 1768, Aug.–Oct.

33. Count Moltke, called 'grand marshal' in *Annual Register*, 1768, xi. 152 and in *London Gazette* No. 10850, 12–16 July. Anton Henrik Moltke (1734–92), had become Marshal to Christian VII (as Crown Prince) in 1763 (*Dansk Biografisk Lexikon*, ed. C. F. Bricka, Copenhagen, 1887–1905, xi. 399–400).

34. 'Baron de Schimmelmann, treasurer' to Christian VII (*London Gazette*, loc. cit.). He was Heinrich Carl Schimmelmann (1724–82), Greve (Bricka, op. cit. xv. 122–31).

35. A 'belly-ache' or 'the gripes' prevented his attending the races 22–27 Aug. (HW to Mann 24 Aug., to Conway 25 Aug.). He arrived at York at 3 P.M., 31

Aug., and left before noon 1 Sept. (*London Chronicle* 3–6 Sept., xxiv. 230).

36. 'That pedant King James' (HW, *Works* iv. 371).

37. 'Nor must I forget to let you know how perfect the King was in the art of dissimulation, or to give it his own phrase (*Kingcraft*),' quoted in OED from Sir Anthony Weldon, *The Court and Character of King James*, 1651, p. 102; the earliest use of *kingcraft* cited in OED is 1643. HW's copy of Weldon's book is Hazen, *Cat. of HW's Lib.*, No. 1767.

38. As Lord Chamberlain to George III, Hertford had to be in London as long as Christian VII was at St James's Palace. 'The evening before . . . [Christian VII] set out for Cambridge [and other places in his tour], he honoured . . . Hertford with a visit to take leave of him, a compliment paid to no other nobleman, on account of the great pains taken by his Lordship to render that monarch's stay at this Court as agreeable as possible' (*London Chronicle* 30 Aug.– 1 Sept., xxiv. 214).

39. Hertford 'sets out for Ragley on Wednesday next [31 Aug.], and that day I intend to be at Park Place, and from thence shall go to Ragley on Friday [2 Sept.]. I shall stay there three or four days and then go to Lord Strafford's for about as many' (HW to Conway 25 Aug.).

ond week in September; but your Lordship shall hear again, unless you should forbid me,[40] who am ever

> Lady Strafford's and your Lordship's
> most faithful humble servant,
>
> HOR. WALPOLE

To STRAFFORD, ca Wednesday 21 September 1768

Missing. HW's letter *post* 10 Oct. 1768 contains no reference to his visit at Wentworth Castle in September. He must have written a letter of thanks before or shortly after his return to SH.

To STRAFFORD, Monday 10 October 1768

Printed from *Works* v. 461–2. Reprinted, Wright v. 223–4, Cunningham v. 129–30, Toynbee vii. 231–2.

Strawberry Hill, Monday, October 10, 1768.

I GIVE you a thousand thanks, my dear Lord, for the account of the ball at Welbeck. I shall not be able to repay it with a relation of the masquerade tonight;[1] for I have been confined here this week with the gout in my foot, and have not stirred off my bed or couch since Tuesday.[2] I was to have gone to the great ball at Sion[3]

40. On 'Sept. 2d 1768' HW (presumably leaving from Park Place) began his 'journey to Weston, Ragley, Warwick Castle, Combe Abbey, Newnham Padox, Kenelworth, Guy's Cliff, Donnington, Kedleston, Matlocke, Wentworth Castle, etc.' (*Country Seats* 62–7). He returned to Arlington Street 18 Sept. and to SH 19 Sept. (HW to Thomas Warton 20 Sept.; to Mann 22 Sept.). No record of letters HW wrote 2–19 Sept. has been found.

1. Given by Christian VII at the Opera House; see *ante* 16 Aug. 1768, n. 27. He left London for Dover 13 Oct. and embarked for Calais 14 Oct.

2. 4 Oct. 'I have been laid up with a fit of gout in both feet and a knee . . . I took the air for the first time the day before yesterday' (HW to Montagu 10 Nov. 1768, MONTAGU ii. 266).

3. The villa of the Duke of Northumberland near Brentford (HW).

on Friday,[4] for which a new road, paddock and bridge were made,[5] as other folks make a dessert. I conclude Lady Mary[6] has and will tell you of all these pomps,[7] which health thinks so serious, and sickness with her grave face tells one are so idle. Sickness may make me moralize, but I assure you she does not want humour. She has diverted me extremely with drawing a comparison between the repose (to call neglect by its dignified name) which I have enjoyed in this fit, and the great anxiety in which the whole world was when I had the last gout three years ago—You remember my friends were then coming into power.[8] Lord W[eymouth][9] was so good as to call at least once every day, and inquire after me; and the foreign ministers insisted that I should give them the satisfaction of seeing me, that they might tranquillize their sovereigns with the certainty of my not being in any danger. The Duke and Duchess of Newcastle were so kind, though very nervous themselves, as to send messengers and long messages every day from Claremont.[10] I cannot say this fit has alarmed Europe quite so much. I heard the bell ring at the gate, and asked with much majesty if it was the Duke of Newcastle had sent? No, Sir, it was only the butcher's boy. The butcher's boy is indeed the only courier I have had. Neither the King of France nor King of Spain appears to be under the least concern about me.

My dear Lord, I have had so many of these transitions in my life, that you will not wonder they divert me more than a masquerade.

4. 7 Oct. At the 'grand ball' the 'supper consisted of five courses of 35 dishes each; and the house and garden were illuminated with 4000 lamps' (*London Chronicle* 6–8 Oct., xxiv. 342).

5. Robert Adam's design for a bridge at Sion House is dated 1768; his gateway was put up later (Mason i. 102, 108; A. T. Bolton, *Architecture of Robert and James Adam*, New York, 1922, i. 278). 'Capability' Brown worked on the grounds between 1767 and 1772 (Dorothy Stroud, *Capability Brown*, 1950, p. 142).

6. Lady Mary Coke, sister to Lady Strafford (HW).

7. Her detailed account is in her *Journals* ii. 379–80. She supped at Christian VII's table; she thought the entertainment 'finer than anything I ever saw . . . I really believe nothing ever exceeded it

in any country' (ibid. ii. 379). Although she would not 'persuade myself to go' to the masquerade, she gives a brief account of it as reported to her (ibid. ii. 382–3).

8. In July 1765 (and the following months), the first Rockingham ministry, when H. S. Conway became secretary of state for the southern department and leader of the House of Commons.

9. Thomas Thynne (1734–96), 3d Vct Weymouth, 1751, cr. (1789) M. of Bath; then lord lieutenant of Ireland, later secretary of state for the northern department (succeeding H. S. Conway) Jan.–Oct. 1768 and for the southern 1768–70, 1775–9.

10. These letters of 1765 have not survived, but HW's correspondence with the Duke of Newcastle in 1766 shows the concern of the Duke over HW's later attack of gout.

I am ready to say to most people, 'Mask, I know you.'—I wish I might choose their dresses!

When I have the honour of seeing Lady Strafford, I shall beseech her to tell me all the news; for I am too nigh and too far to know any. Adieu, my dear Lord!

Yours most sincerely,

HOR. WALPOLE

From STRAFFORD, June 1769.

Missing. See *post* 3 July 1769.

To Strafford, Monday 3 July 1769

Printed from *Works* v. 462–3. Reprinted, Wright v. 240–2, Cunningham v. 173–5, Toynbee vii. 291–3.

Arlington Street, July 3, 1769.

WHEN you have been so constantly good to me, my dear Lord, without changing, do you wonder that our friendship has lasted so long?[1] Can I be insensible to the honour or pleasure of your acquaintance? When the advantage lies so much on my side, am I likely to alter the first? Oh, but it will last now! We have seen friendships without number born and die. Ours was not formed on interest, nor alliance; and politics, the poison of all English connections, never entered into ours.[2] You have given me a new proof by remembering the Chapel of Luton.[3] I hear it is to be preserved; and

1. HW first mentions Strafford in a letter to Mann 4 Feb. 1742: 'I am invited to dinner today by Lord Strafford, Argyle's son-in-law' (MANN i. 320). The identifying phrase suggests that HW's acquaintance with Strafford was then recent, dating

possibly from Strafford's marriage in 1741.
2. Strafford, like his father, was a 'Tory in politics,' HW a Whig.
3. Luton Hoo, Beds, the seat of the Earl of Bute who bought it in 1763. Gray had written HW ca April 1769 that the

am glad of it, though I might have been the better for its ruins.⁴

I should have answered your Lordship's last post,⁵ but was at Park Place.⁶ I think Lady Ailesbury quite recovered; though her illness has made such an impression that she does not yet believe it.⁷

It is so settled that we are never to have tolerable weather in June,⁸ that the first hot day was on Saturday—hot by comparison; for I think it is three years since we have really felt the feel of summer. I was, however, concerned to be forced to come to town yesterday on some business;⁹ for, however the country feels, it looks divine, and the verdure we buy so dear is delicious. I shall not be able, I fear, to profit of it this summer in the loveliest of all places, as I am to go to Paris in August.¹⁰ But next year I trust I shall accompany Mr Conway and Lady Ailesbury to Wentworth Castle.¹¹ I shall be glad to visit Castle Howard¹² and Beverley;¹³ but neither would carry me so far, if Wentworth Castle was not in the way.

The Châtelets¹⁴ are gone,¹⁵ without any more battles with the Rus-

chapel was going to be demolished and that HW might purchase the Gothic woodwork inside the chapel 'for a song.' The chapel, built in the reign of Henry VI, contained embellishments dated 1475–1546, probably taken from Luton church and installed in the chapel in the late 17th century; they were transferred shortly before 1830 to a new chapel built by Lord Bute at Luton Park. For these and other details, see GRAY ii. 184, nn. 4–6.

4. HW asked to see the chapel in 1772 but 'admittance was denied' (OSSORY i. 84).

5. Saturday, 1 July; the post left London for York every day except Sunday (New Complete Guide to All Persons Who Have Any Trade or Concern with the City of London, 1777, p. 103).

6. HW went there 27 June (COLE i. 177); apparently he did not return to SH until Sunday, 2 July.

7. On 9 June Lady Ailesbury and others were at SH; Lady Mary Coke, who was there mentioned no illness (Coke, Journals iii. 87). On 6 July, 'Lady Ailesbury, I'm told, still continues very indifferent' (ibid. iii. 105). When Lady Mary arrived at Park Place 27 July 'Lady Ailesbury [was] tolerably well' (ibid. iii. 122). The nature of the illness is not mentioned.

8. 'Mr Walpole says we have had but

one warm day, and that we scolded away' (ibid. iii. 87, sub 10 June).

9. Perhaps in connection with HW's imminent trip to Paris (see n. 10 below).

10. He left for Paris 16 Aug. and returned to London 11 Oct. ('Paris Journals,' DU DEFFAND v. 324–33).

11. They did not go; see post 9 July 1770; HW to Conway 12 July 1770.

12. The seat of Lord Carlisle in Yorkshire, near Malton. While on a visit to Strafford, HW visited it 12 Aug. 1772. For his detailed description, see Country Seats 72–3 and HW to Selwyn 12 Aug. 1772, SELWYN 256–9.

13. Beverley, Yorks, near Scarborough. HW planned to go there in 1772 (MASON i. 37) but he did not, and the journey of 1772 was his last into Yorkshire.

14. Louis-Marie-Florent (1727–93) Comte (Duc, 1777) du Châtelet; son of Voltaire's mistress; ambassador to England 1767–70; m. (1751) Diane-Adélaïde de Rochechouart (d. 1794), who was guillotined (OSSORY i. 39–40, nn. 18, 21–2).

15. They were to leave on 'Friday next,' 16 June (Coke, Journals iii. 86, sub 8 June). The London Chronicle reported that he 'set out from his house in Great George Street, Westminster, for France' 16 June.

sians.[16] The papers say the latter have been beaten by the Turks;[17] which rejoices me, though against all rules of politics: but I detest that murderess,[18] and like to have her humbled. I don't know that this piece of news is true: it is enough to me that it is agreeable. I had rather take it for granted, than be at the trouble of inquiring about what I have so little to do with. I am just the same about the City and Surrey petitions.[19] Since I have *dismembered*[20] myself, it is incredible how cool I am to all politics.

London is the abomination of desolation; and I rejoice to leave it again this evening. Even Pam has not a levee above once or twice a week. Next winter I suppose it will begin to be a fashion to remove into the City; for, since it is the mode to choose aldermen at this end of the town,[21] the macaronies will certainly adjourn to Bishopsgate Street,[22] for fear of being fined for sheriffs.[23] Mr J[ames][24]

16. At the ball at St James's on the King's birthday, du Châtelet made a scene about precedence. He had jostled the Russian ambassador in order to push himself ahead of the Russian and next to the ambassador from the Holy Roman Empire. The Russian ambassador was Ivan Chernyshev. The affair created a considerable stir; see HW to Mann 14 June, MANN vii. 125–6; *Mem. Geo. III* iii. 245–7; Coke, *Journals* iii. 84, 86, 152: 'Mr Walpole was in the right to say the French ambassador was the person blamed in the quarrel between him and the Russian' (Coke, op. cit. iii. 86).

17. The *Daily Advertiser*, 1 July, reported, *sub* Transylvania, 31 May, that 'the defeat of the Russians near Choczim is no longer a matter of doubt,' and (*sub* Warsaw, 3 June) that 'it is said the loss his [Golitsyn's] army sustained on the attack of Choczim, and in his retreat, has been very great.'

18. Catherine II.

19. The petition of the Livery of the City of London was presented to George III 5 July, that of the freeholders of the County of Surrey 24 Aug. (*London Chronicle* 4–6 July, 24–26 Aug., xxvi. 22, 194, with the text of the Surrey petition); the text of both is in GM 1769, xxxix. 329–30, 373–4. The first enumerates nine charges against the King's ministers; the ninth charge is: 'they have at length completed their designs by violently wresting from the people *the last sacred right we have left*, the right of election, by the unprece-

dented seating of a candidate notoriously set up and only chosen by themselves,' and by refusing to seat Wilkes. The Surrey petition deals only with the right of election.

20. Mr Walpole means, since he quitted Parliament (HW). On 11 March 1768, his last Parliament had been dissolved. Cf. OED, 'dismember,' 4, where the first use quoted in this sense is dated 1649. The word had also been used 1749–68 in prints dealing with the dismembering of the British empire; see BM, *Satiric Prints* Nos. 3069, 3547, 4183, iii pt i. 767, iii pt ii. 1105, iv. 421.

21. Outside the City; an allusion to the political emphasis in recent City affairs. In George III's reign, opposition to Bute was followed by support of Wilkes, and the conflicts between Court and Opposition were reflected in the City. The three aldermen recently elected were in the Opposition: Wilkes (27 Jan.), James Townsend (23 June), and John Sawbridge (1 July). See A. B. Beaven, *Aldermen of the City of London*, 1908–13, ii. pp. lviii, 134.

22. Bishopsgate Street Within and Bishopsgate Without, so called from being within or without the walls of the City. An alderman was elected from Bishopsgate ward, which included both sections of the street.

23. As those nominated or elected sheriffs of London were fined for refusing to accept nomination or the duties of office.

24. Haughton James (ca 1738–1813), son

and Mr B[oothby][25] will die of the thought of being aldermen of Grosvenor Ward and Berkeley Square Ward. Adam and Eve[26] in their paradise laugh at all these tumults, and have not tasted of the tree that forfeits paradise; which I take to have been the tree of politics, not of knowledge. How happy you are not to have your son Abel knocked on the head by his brother Cain at the Brentford election! You do not hunt the poor deer and hares that gambol around you.—If Eve has a sin, I doubt it is angling; but as she makes all other creatures happy, I beg she would not impale worms nor whisk carp out of one element into another. If she repents of that guilt, I hope she will live as long as her grandson Methuselah. There is a commentator that says *his* life was protracted for never having boiled a lobster alive. Adieu, dear couple, that I honour as much as I could honour my first grandfather and grandmother!

Your most dutiful

HOR. JAPHET

To STRAFFORD, Friday 8 September 1769

Printed from *Works* v. 464–6; in HW's list of 'Letters written to England 1769,' DU DEFFAND v. 389: 'to Lord Strafford, ditto,' i.e., 'by the post 9 [Sept.].' Reprinted, Wright v. 253–5, Cunningham v. 187–9, Toynbee vii. 312–15.

Paris, September 8, 1769.

T'OTHER night at the Duchess of Choiseul's at supper[1] the Intendant of Rouen[2] asked me, if we have roads of communication all over England and Scotland?—I suppose he thinks that in general we inhabit trackless forests and wild mountains, and that once a year a few legislators come to Paris to learn the arts of civil life, as to

of Haughton James of Jamaica; bibliophile and man of fashion; friend of Selwyn and his circle (OSSORY i. 313, n. 12).

25. HW's third cousin, Charles Boothby Skrymsher (Clopton after 1792) (ca 1740–1800), known as 'Prince Boothby' (BERRY ii. 201, n. 16; MANN v. 431, n. 14).

26. Lord and Lady Strafford.

———

1. HW had supped at her country house, Gennevilliers, 28 Aug., 1 Sept., and at her house in Paris 5 Sept. ('Paris Journals,' DU DEFFAND v. 326, 328; on 5 Sept. 'Duchesse de Choiseul's,' but 'Gennevilliers' for 28 Aug., 1 Sept.).

2. Louis Thiroux de Crosne (1736–93), *intendant des finances* of Rouen 1767–ca 1785; last *intendant de police* in Paris, 1785–9; guillotined (BERRY i. 40, n. 11; *Almanach royal*, 1769, p. 189, 1785, p. 258, 1786, p. 262).

sow corn, plant vines, and make operas. If this letter should contrive to scramble through that *desert* Yorkshire, where your Lordship has *attempted* to improve a dreary hill and uncultivated vale, you will find I remember your commands of writing from this capital of the world, whither I am come for the benefit of my country, and where I am intensely studying those laws and that beautiful frame of government, which can alone render a nation happy, great and flourishing; where *lettres de cachet* soften manners, and a proper distribution of luxury and beggary insures a common felicity. As we have a prodigious number of students in legislature of both sexes here at present, I will not anticipate their discoveries; but, as your particular friend, will communicate a rare improvement on nature, which these great philosophers have made, and which would add considerable beauties to those parts which your Lordship has already recovered from the waste, and taught to look a little like a Christian country. The secret is very simple, and yet demanded the effort of a mighty genius to strike it out. It is nothing but this: Trees ought to be educated as much as men, and are strange awkward productions when not taught to hold themselves upright or bow on proper occasions. The academy *de belles-lettres*[3] have even offered a prize for the man that shall recover the long-lost art of an ancient Greek, called *le sieur Orphée,* who instituted a dancing school for plants, and gave a magnificent ball on the birth of the Dauphin of Thrace, which was performed entirely by forest trees. In this whole kingdom there is no such thing as seeing a tree that is not well behaved. They are first stripped up[4] and then cut down; and you would as soon meet a man with his hair about his ears as an oak or ash. As the weather is very hot now, and the soil chalk, and the dust white, I assure you it is very difficult, powdered as both are all over, to distinguish a tree from a hairdresser. Lest this should sound like a travelling hyperbole, I must advertise your Lordship, that there is little difference in their heights; for a tree of thirty years' growth being liable to be marked as royal timber,[5] the proprietors take care not to let their trees live to the age of being enlisted, but burn them, and plant others as often almost as they change their fashions. This gives an

3. Académie des Inscriptions et Belles-Lettres, one of the five academies of the Institut de France.

4. HW writes, of walnut trees: 'They strip up the latter for firing' ('Paris Journals,' DU DEFFAND v. 259).

5. Probably for use in ship-building.

air of perpetual youth to the face of the country, and if adopted by us would realize Mr Addison's visions, and

> Make our bleak rocks and barren mountains smile.[6]

What other remarks I have made in my indefatigable search after knowledge must be reserved to a future opportunity; but as your Lordship is my friend, I may venture to say without vanity to you, that Solon nor any of the ancient philosophers who travelled to Egypt in quest of religions, mysteries, laws and fables, ever sat up so late with the ladies and priests and *présidents de parlement* at Memphis, as I do here—and consequently were not half so well qualified as I am to new-model a commonwealth. I have learned how to make remonstrances,[7] and how to answer them. The latter, it seems, is a science much wanted in my own country[8]—and yet is as easy and obvious as their treatment of trees, and not very unlike it. It was delivered many years ago in an oracular sentence of my namesake—

> *Odi profanum vulgus, et arceo.*[9]

You must drive away the vulgar, and you must have an hundred and fifty thousand men to drive them away with—that is all. I do not wonder the Intendant of Rouen thinks we are still in a state of barbarism, when we are ignorant of the very rudiments of government.

The Duke and Duchess of Richmond have been here a few days,[10] and are gone to Aubigné.[11] I do not think him at all well, and am exceedingly concerned for it, as I know no man who has more estimable qualities. They return by the end of the month.[12] I am fluc-

6. 'Tis Liberty that crowns Britania's isle
And makes her barren rocks and her bleak mountains smile'
(Addison, 'A Letter from Italy, to . . . Charles Lord Halifax. In the year MCCDI' in Addison's *Miscellaneous Works*, 1726, i. 55; HW's copies, now WSL, are Hazen, *Cat. of HW's Lib.*, Nos. 1844, 1860).

7. Alluding to the number of remonstrances under the name of petitions which were presented this year from the Livery of London and many other corporate bodies on the subject of the Middlesex election (Mary Berry).

8. George III had received the petitions ungraciously, and had taken no steps to have Wilkes seated.

9. Horace, *Carm.* III i. 1: 'I hate the vulgar crowd and keep them far away.'

10. They arrived 31 Aug.; HW last mentions them in 'Paris Journals' on 6 Sept. (DU DEFFAND v. 327–8 and n. 17).

11. Aubigny in northern France, NW of Arras. Richmond had been there in 1765 (HW to Conway 5 Dec. 1765). In 1776 Louis XVI recognized him as Duke of Aubigny and the Parliament of Paris registered the peerage (GEC x. 841 n. *b*).

12. Richmond called on HW, 1 Oct. ('Paris Journals,' DU DEFFAND v. 332).

tuating whether I shall not return with them, as they have pressed me to do, through Holland.[13] I never was there, and could never go so agreeably; but then it would protract my absence three weeks,[14] and I am impatient to be in my own cave, notwithstanding the wisdom I imbibe every day. But one cannot sacrifice one's self wholly to the public: Titus and Wilkes have now and then lost a day.[15] Adieu, my dear Lord! Be assured that I shall not disdain yours and Lady Strafford's conversation, though you have nothing but the goodness of your hearts, and the simplicity of your manners, to recommend you to the more enlightened understanding of

Your old friend,

Hor. Walpole

To Strafford, Monday 9 July 1770

Printed from *Works* v. 466–7. Reprinted, Wright v. 280–1, Cunningham v. 248–9, Toynbee vii. 394–5.

Strawberry Hill, July 9, 1770.

I AM not going to tell you, my dear Lord, of the diversions or honours[1] of Stowe, which I conclude Lady Mary has writ to Lady Strafford.[2] Though the week passed cheerfully enough, it was more glory than I should have sought of my own head.[3] The journeys to Stowe and Park Place[4] have deranged my projects so that I don't know where I am, and I wish they have not given me the gout into the bargain; for I am come back very lame, and not at all with

13. HW did not go with them.

14. 'On Tuesday [28 Nov.] . . . the Duchess of Richmond arrived at her house in Privy Garden from France [*sic*]. His Grace is daily expected' (*London Chronicle* 28–30 Nov. 1769, xxvi. 528; *Leinster Corr.* iii. 30, 32).

15. Titus Flavius Sabinus Vespasianus (40–81), Roman emperor 79–81. He is quoted by Suetonius, *Titus*, Ch. 8. 1, as saying, *Amici, diem perdidi* ('Friends, I have lost a day').

———

1. Princess Amelia was there (HW). The other guests were Lady Mary Coke, Lady Anne Howard, Lord Bessborough, Catharine Middleton, and HW.

2. See Coke, *Journals* iii. 252–4; parts of her account are quoted in the notes to Montagu ii. 313–16.

3. Princess Amelia 'insisted,' 'commanded' that he meet her at Stowe (HW to Montagu 29 June 1770, Montagu ii. 310).

4. HW was at Park Place when Princess Amelia, Lady Mary Coke, Lady Anne Howard, and Catharine Middleton arrived, 26 June.

the bloom that one ought to have imported from the Elysian Fields.[5] Such jaunts when one is growing old is playing with edged tools, as my Lord Chesterfield, in one of his *Worlds,* makes the husband say to his wife, when she pretends that grey powder does not become her.[6] It is charming at twenty to play at Elysian Fields, but it is no joke at fifty; or too great a joke. It made me laugh as we were descending the great flight of steps from the house to go and sup in the grotto on the banks of Helicon: we were so cloaked up, for the evening was very cold, and so many of us were limping and hobbling, that Charon would have easily believed we were going to ferry over in earnest. It is with much more comfort that I am writing to your Lordship in the great bow window of my new round room,[7] which collects all the rays of the southwest sun, and composes a sort of summer; a feel I have not known this year, except last Thursday. If the rains should ever cease, and the weather settle to fine, I shall pay you my visit at Wentworth Castle; but hitherto the damps have affected me so much, that I am more disposed to return to London and light my fire, than brave the humours of a climate so capricious and uncertain, in the country. I cannot help thinking it grows worse: I certainly remember such a thing as dust; nay, I still have a clear idea of it, though I have seen none for some years, and should put some grains in a bottle for a curiosity, if it should ever fly again.

News I know none. You may be sure it was a subject carefully avoided at Stowe; and Beckford's death had not raised the glass or spirits of the master of the house.[8] The papers make one sick with talking of that noisy vapouring fool, as they would of Algernon Sidney.[9]

5. At Stowe (HW); a section of the gardens entered by a shell bridge over a serpentine river (*Pocket Companion for Oxford . . . Blenheim, Ditchly, and Stow,* new edn [1772], p. 142; MONTAGU ii. 314, n. 10).

6. In Chesterfield's first contribution to *The World* No. 18, 3 May 1753, he writes a letter in the character of a country gentleman whose wife and daughter adopt French fashions and extravagances. His daughter uses grey powder on her 'dark-coloured hair' to give it a 'bluish cast,' but his wife says grey powder 'does not suit with' her complexion, 'and I never use it.' The husband replies, 'You are much in the right, my dear . . . not to play with edge-tools. Leave it to the girl.'

7. Or Round Tower; see *SH Accounts* ed. Toynbee, Oxford, 1927, *passim.*

8. Temple and Beckford had supported Wilkes in opposition to the King. In 1763 Temple had been displaced as lord lieutenant of Buckinghamshire for his patronage of Wilkes. Beckford, in his second term as Lord Mayor of London at the time of his death, 21 June 1770, had been opposed by a Court candidate in 1769.

9. (1622–83), patriot admired and defended by HW; see OSSORY i. 105.

I have not happened to see your future nephew,[10] though we have exchanged visits. It was the first time I had been at Marble Hill, since poor Lady Suffolk's death; and the impression was so uneasy, that I was not sorry not to find him at home. Adieu, my good Lord! Except seeing you both, nothing can be more agreeable than to hear of yours and Lady Strafford's health, who, I hope, continues perfectly well.

Your most faithful humble servant,

HOR. WALPOLE

To Strafford, Tuesday 16 October 1770

Printed from *Works* v. 467–8. Reprinted, Wright v. 286–7, Cunningham v. 262–3, Toynbee vii. 416.

Arlington Street, October 16, 1770.

THOUGH I have so very little to say, it is but my duty, my dear Lord, to thank you for your extreme goodness to me and your inquiring after me.[1] I was very bad again last week, but have mended so much since Friday night, that I really now believe the fit is over. I came to town on Sunday, and can creep about my room even without a stick, which is more felicity to me than if I had got a white one.[2] I do not aim yet at such preferment as walking up stairs; but having moulted my stick, I flatter myself I shall come forth again without being lame.

The few I have seen tell me there is nobody else in town. That is no grievance to me, when I should be at the mercy of all that should please to bestow their idle time upon me. I know nothing of the war-egg,[3] but that sometimes it is to be hatched, and sometimes to

10. John, second Earl of Buckingham, married to his second wife a daughter of Lady Anne Conolly, sister of Lord Strafford (HW). John Hobart (1723–93), 2d E. of Buckinghamshire, 1756, m. (24 Sept. 1770) Caroline Conolly (d. 1817), 3rd dau. of William and Lady Anne Conolly.

1. HW's fit of gout had lasted for 'seven long weeks' (HW to Montagu 16 Oct., MONTAGU ii. 322).

2. A white stick (rod, staff, wand) used by some Court and other officials as a symbol of office; see OED *sub* 'White stick,' 'White staff.'

3. Alluding to the dispute with Spain about the affair of Falkland Island (Mary Berry). The news reached England in September that a small Spanish fleet from Buenos Aires had captured the English settlement at Port Egmont on Saunders Island in the Falkland Islands (*London*

be addled. Many folks get into the nest and sit as hard upon it as they can, concluding it will produce a golden chick. As I shall not be a feather the better for it, I hate that game-breed, and prefer the old hen Peace and her dunghill brood. My compliments to my Lady and all her poultry.

I am, my dear Lord,

Your infinitely obliged and faithful humble servant,

HOR. WALPOLE

To STRAFFORD, Thursday 20 June 1771

Printed from *Works* v. 468–9. Reprinted, Wright v. 300–1, Cunningham v. 306–7, Toynbee viii. 46–7.

Strawberry Hill, June 20, 1771.

I HAVE waited impatiently, my dear Lord, for something worth putting into a letter; but trees do not speak in Parliament, nor flowers write in the newspapers; and they are almost the only beings I have seen. I dined on Tuesday at Notting Hill[1] with the Countesses of Powis and Holderness, Lord and Lady Pelham,[2] and Lord Frederic Cavendish[3]—and Pam; and shall go to town on Friday to meet the same company at Lady Holderness's;[4] and this short journal comprises almost my whole history and knowledge.

I must now ask your Lordship's and Lady Strafford's commands for Paris. I shall set out on the seventh of next month.[5] You will think, though you will not tell me so, that these are very juvenile jaunts at my age. Indeed I should be ashamed if I went for any

Chronicle 25–7 Sept., xxviii. 298). Early in 1771, Spain yielded the islands to Great Britain (MANN vii. 268).

1. The villa of Lady Mary Coke near Kensington (HW).
2. Thomas Pelham (1728–1805), 2d Bn Pelham, 1768; cr. (1801) E. of Chichester; M.P. Rye 1749–54, Sussex 1754–68; m. (1754) Anne Frankland (ca 1734–1813), dau. of Frederick Meinhart Frankland.

3. (1729–1803), M.P. Derbyshire 1751–4, Derby 1754–80; field marshal, 1756; 'by far the most agreeable and possessed the most useful sense of the whole family' (*Mem. Geo. III* ii. 17).
4. In Hertford Street, Park Lane (*Royal Kalendar*, 1771, p. 19).
5. See 'Paris Journals,' DU DEFFAND v. 333.

other pleasure but that of once more seeing my dear blind friend,[6] whose much greater age forbids my depending on seeing her often. It will indeed be amusing to change the scene of politics; for though I have done with our own, one cannot help hearing them—nay reading them; for, like flies, they come to breakfast with one's bread and butter. I wish there was any other vehicle for them but a news- paper; a place into which, considering how they are exhausted, I am sure they have no pretensions. The Duc d'Aiguillon I hear is min- ister.[7] Their politics, some way or other, must end seriously, either in despotism, a civil war, or assassination. Methinks it is playing deep for the power of tyranny. Charles Fox is more moderate: he only games for an hundred thousand pounds that he has not.[8]

Have you read the *Life of Benvenuto Cellini,*[9] my Lord? I am angry with him for being more distracted and wrong-headed than my Lord Herbert.[10] Till the revival of these two, I thought the pres- ent age had borne the palm of absurdity from all its predecessors. But I find our cotemporaries are quiet good folks, that only game till they hang themselves, and do not kill everybody they meet in the street. Who would have thought we were so reasonable?

Ranelagh, they tell me, is full of foreign dukes. There is a Duc de la Trémouille,[11] a Duc d'Aremberg,[12] and other grandees. I know the former,[13] and am not sorry to be out of his way.

It is not pleasant to leave groves and lawns and rivers for a dirty town with a dirtier ditch, calling itself the Seine; but I dare not en- counter the sea and bad inns in cold weather. This consideration will bring me back by the end of August.[14] I should be happy to

6. Madame du Deffand (HW).

7. The appointment of Emmanuel-Ar- mand Vignerot du Plessis-Richelieu (1720– 88), Duc d'Aiguillon, to succeed the Duc de Choiseul as secretary of state for foreign affairs was announced 10 June at Paris, but strong opposition to him de- layed the appointment for six months. See DU DEFFAND iii. 5–82; OSSORY i. 49, 195–6.

8. For discussion of Fox's debts, vari- ously estimated at between £100,000 and £147,000, see OSSORY i. 162–6, especially p. 164, n. 5 and the references there cited.

9. The first English edition: *The Life of Benvenuto Cellini, a Florentine Artist,* 'Written by himself and translated by Thomas Nugent,' 1771, 2 vols, 8vo (Hazen, *Cat. of HW's Lib.,* No. 3181).

10. Edward Herbert (1583–1648), cr. (1629) Bn Herbert of Chirbury, whose autobiography, *The Life of Lord Herbert of Cherbury,* HW printed at SH in 1764; see Hazen, *SH Bibl.* 68–72.

11. Jean - Bretagne - Charles - Godefroy (1737–92), Duc de la Trémoïlle (DU DEF- FAND ii. 54, n. 21).

12. Charles-Marie-Raymond (1721–78), Duc d'Arenburg d'Arschot and de Croÿ; field marshal, 1766, in the service of Maria Theresa (OSSORY i. 264, n. 9, where fur- ther details are given).

13. HW and he had supped in the same company in 1765 and 1766 (DU DEF- FAND v. 290, 312).

14. 6 Sept. ('Paris Journals,' DU DEF- FAND v. 342).

execute any commission for your Lordship. You know how earnestly I wish always to show myself

Your Lordship's most faithful humble servant,

Hor. Walpole

To Strafford, Sunday 25 August 1771

Printed from *Works* v. 468–9. Reprinted, Wright v. 314–16, Cunningham v. 327–8, Toynbee viii. 75–7.

Paris, August 25, 1771.

I HAVE passed my biennial six weeks here, my dear Lord, and am preparing to return as soon as the weather will allow me. It is some comfort to the patriot-virtue, envy, to find this climate worse than our own. There were four very hot days at the end of last month, which you know with us northern people compose a summer: it has rained half this, and for these three days there has been a deluge, a storm, and extreme cold. Yet these folks shiver in silk, and sit with their windows open till suppertime.—Indeed, firing is very dear, and nabobs very scarce. Economy and retrenchment are the words in fashion, and are founded in a little more than caprice. I have heard no instance of luxury but in Mademoiselle Guimard,[1] a favourite dancer, who is building a palace:[2] round the *salle à manger* there are windows that open upon hothouses, that are to produce flowers all winter.—That is worthy of —— ——. There is a finer dancer whom Mr H[obart][3] is to transplant to London; a Mademoiselle Heinel[4] or Ingle, a Fleming. She is tall, perfectly made, very handsome, and has a set of attitudes copied from the classics. She moves as gracefully slow as Pygmalion's statue[5] when it

1. Marie-Madeleine Guimard (1743–1816), m. (1787) Jean-Étienne Despréaux (Mann vii. 322–3, n. 16).
2. The 'Temple de Terpsychore' in the Rue de la Chausée d'Antin, designed by Ledoux, sold by lottery in 1786 (Mann vii. 323, n. 18).
3. George Hobart (1731–1804), 3d E. of Buckinghamshire, 1793. For some of his difficulties in management of the operas, see Mann vii. 271.
4. Anne-Frédérique Heinel (1753–1808), born in Bayreuth; made her début at Stuttgart, 1767, and at Paris, 1768; in London for the opera season 1771–2, 1772–3, 1774, 1776; m. (1792) Gaetano Appolino Baldassare Vestris, the famous dancer (Ossory i. 66, n. 15).
5. Galatea.

was coming to life, and moves her leg round as imperceptibly as if she was dancing in the zodiac.—But she is not Virgo.

They make no more of breaking parliaments here than an English mob does of breaking windows. It is pity people are so ill-sorted. If this king and ours could cross over and figure in, Louis XV would dissolve our Parliament if Polly Jones[6] did but say a word to him. They have got into such a habit of it here, that you would think a parliament was a polypus: they cut it in two, and by next morning half of it becomes a whole assembly. This has literally been the case at Besançon.[7] Lord and Lady Barrymore,[8] who are in the highest favour at Compiègne,[9] will be able to carry over the receipt.[10]

Everybody feels in their own way. My grief is to see the ruinous condition of the palaces and pictures. I was yesterday at the Louvre. Le Brun's[11] noble gallery, where the battles of Alexander are, and of which he designed the ceiling, and even the shutters, bolts and locks, is in a worse condition than the old gallery at Somerset House.[12] It rains in upon the pictures,[13] though there are stores of much more valuable pieces than those of Le Brun. Heaps of glorious works by Raphael and all the great masters are piled up and equally neglected at Versailles. Their care is not less destructive in private houses. The Duke of Orléans's[14] pictures and the Prince of Monaco's[15] have been cleaned, and varnished so thick that you may see your face

6. Former mistress of Henry, D. of Cumberland (H. Bleackley, *Ladies Fair and Frail*, 1925, p. 152).

7. The parliament of Besançon was suppressed, 5 Aug., and then reconstituted (Mann vii. 320, n. 1). Fourteen of the old members reappeared in the new parliament (*Mercure historique*, 1771, clxxi. 374).

8. Richard Barry (1745–73), 6th E. of Barrymore, 1751, m. (1767) Lady Emily Stanhope (1749–80).

9. During the summer the Court often removed to Louis XV's château at Compiègne, about 45 miles NE of Paris.

10. Perhaps a reference to the financial grants which the officers of the new parliament received. One of the old members was promoted to be first president, with 12,000 livres' salary and 3,000 livres' allowance for lodging (*Mercure historique*, loc. cit.).

11. Charles Le Brun (1619–90).

12. The old Somerset House, not yet replaced by Chambers's new structure. 'It was so far neglected as to be permitted to fall to ruin in some of the back parts' (*Encyclopedia of London*, ed. W. Kent, 1937, p. 587, citing Noorthouck's *History of London*, 1773). The Royal Academy's schools of design were moved there in 1771 (Kent, loc. cit.). HW's old friend Mrs Grosvenor had been housekeeper there (Gray i. 220, n. 17).

13. 24 Aug.: 'Saw the great gallery of Le Brun with battles of Alexander, all the ornaments, ceiling, shutters, and even locks and bolts designed by Le Brun, but so abominably neglected that it rained in' ('Paris Journals,' du Deffand v. 339).

14. Louis-Philippe de Bourbon (1725–85), Duc d'Orléans, 1752.

15. Honoré-Camille-Léonor Goyon-de-Matignon de Grimaldi (1720–95), P. of Monaco.

in them; and some of them have been transported from board to cloth, bit by bit, and the seams filled up with colour; so that in ten years they will not be worth sixpence. It makes me as peevish as if I was posterity! I hope your Lordship's works will last longer than these of Louis XIV. The glories of his *siècle* hasten fast to their end, and little will remain but those of his authors.

I am, my dear Lord,

Your most faithful humble servant,

Hor. Walpole

To Strafford, Friday 24 September 1773

Printed from *Works* v. 471–2. Reprinted, Wright v. 350–1, Cunningham v. 503–5, Toynbee viii. 337–8.

Strawberry Hill, Sept. 24, 1773.

THE multiplicity of business which I found chalked out to me by my journey to Houghton,[1] has engaged me so much, my dear Lord, and the unpleasant scene opened to me there struck me so deeply, that I have neither had time nor cheerfulness enough to flatter myself I could amuse my friends by my letters. Except the pictures, I found everything worse than I expected, and the prospect almost too bad to give me courage to pursue what I am doing. I am totally ignorant in most of the branches of business that are fallen to my lot, and not young enough to learn any new lesson well. All I can hope is to clear the worst part of the way; for in undertaking to retrieve an estate, the beginning is certainly the most difficult of the work. It is fathoming a chaos. But I will not unfold a confusion to your Lordship which your good sense will always keep you from experiencing—very unfashionably; for the first geniuses of this age hold, that the best method of governing the world is to throw it into disorder. The experiment is not yet complete, as the rearrangement is still to come.

I am very seriously glad of the birth of your nephew,[2] my Lord.

1. Where HW had been for several days attending to the affairs of his nephew, who was intermittently insane.

2. A son of John Earl of Buckingham's, who died young (HW): John Hobart (30 Aug. 1773 – Dec. 1775), styled Lord Hobart. The child's mother was Strafford's niece (*ante* HW to Strafford 9 July 1770).

I am going this evening with my gratulations;[3] but have been so much absent, and so hurried, that I have not yet had the pleasure of seeing Lady Anne,[4] though I have called twice.[5] To Gunnersbury I have had no summons this summer: I receive such honours, or the want of them, with proper respect. Lady [Mary Coke], I fear, is in chase of a *Dulcineus*[6] that she will never meet. When the ardour of peregrination is a little abated, will not she probably give in to a more comfortable pursuit; and, like a print I have seen of the blessed martyr Charles I abandon the hunt of *a corruptible* for that of *an incorruptible crown?*[7] There is another beatific print just published in that style: it is of Lady Huntingdon. With much pompous humility, she looks like an old basket-woman trampling on her coronet at the mouth of a cavern.[8]—Poor Whitfield! If he was forced to do the honours of the *spelunca!*[9]—Saint Fanny Shirley[10] is nearer consecration. I was told two days ago that she had written a letter to Lady Selina[11] that was not intelligible. Her Grace of Kingston's glory ap-

3. To Buckinghamshire's villa, Marble Hill, in Twickenham, near SH. Lord Hobart's christening on 20 Sept. 1773 is recorded in the registers of Twickenham Church (Edward Ironside, *History and Antiquities of Twickenham*, in *Bibliotheca Topographica Britannica*, Vol. X, No. 6, p. 20).

4. Lady Anne Conolly (HW). Strafford's sister and Lord Hobart's grandmother: Lady Anne Wentworth (1713–97), m. (1733) William Conolly (BERRY i. 56, n. 8).

5. At Copt Hall, her villa in Twickenham; a 'very ancient' house with 'good gardens.' Lady Anne paid the rates on it from 1771 until her death. Earlier tenants and owners included Sir Thomas Skipwith; John Erskine, 6th E. of Mar; Admiral Fox; Nicholas Tuite; and Mrs Douglas (Ironside, op. cit. 85, 142; R. S. Cobbett, *Memorials of Twickenham*, 1872, pp. 356–8; MORE, back endpaper; OSSORY iii. 260).

6. Frederick II of Prussia, who, in July and Aug. 1773, refused to meet 'Mme Coucou' (MANN vii. 539, n. 4).

7. A print by William Faithorne the younger (copied by the younger Faber) of Charles I, half-length, looking upwards; at upper left a hand holds a crown; at the top of the print is the inscription 'Corruptibilem pro incorruptibile' (John C. Smith, *British Mezzotinto Portraits*,

1884, i. 326–7, ii. 462; Freeman O'Donoghue [British Museum, Department of Prints and Drawings], *Catalogue of Engraved British Portraits*, 1908–25, i. 390, sub Charles I, Nos 137–8; BM, *Satiric Prints* i. 410–11, No. 745).

8. 'Selina Countess Dowager of Huntington, Carrington Bowles *excudit*. From the Original Picture, painted by J. Russel. Published . . . 10 June 1773 . . .' (Smith, op. cit. iv. 1733–4; O'Donoghue, op. cit. ii. 593, Nos 2, 3). There is a smaller version of the original print. Smith calls the 'cavern' a 'sepulchre,' quotes HW's comment, and observes: 'Walpole's correct taste thus seems to have detected the really blasphemous assumption underlying such treatment of so sacred a subject, attempted to be cloaked by a mask of religion.'

9. 'Speluncam Dido dux et Troianus eandem/devenient' (*Æneid* iv. 124–5). 'To the same cave shall come Dido and the Trojan chief.' Cf. OSSORY iii. 7.

10. Lady Frances Shirley, who lived until 1778.

11. Lady Selina Shirley (ca 1701–77), sister of Lady Frances, and aunt of Lady Huntingdon, m. (1720) Peter Bathurst of Clarendon Park, Wilts, brother of Allen, 1st E. Bathurst (GM 1777, lxvii. 612; Collins, *Peerage*, 1812, v. 87–8; Burke, *Peerage*, 1928, p. 224).

proaches to consummation in a more worldly style. The Duke is dying,[12] and has given her the whole estate, £17,000 a year.[13] I am told she has already notified the contents of the will,[14] and made offers of the sale of Thoresby.[15] Pious matrons have various ways of expressing decency.

Your Lordship's new bow-window thrives.—I do not want it to remind me of its master and mistress, to whom

I am ever the most devoted humble servant,

HOR. WALPOLE

To STRAFFORD, Monday 15 November 1773

Printed from *Works* v. 472–3. Reprinted, Wright v. 351–3, Cunningham vi. 4–5, Toynbee viii. 356–8.

Arlington Street, Nov. 15, 1773.

I AM very sorry, my dear Lord, that you are coming towards us so slowly and unwillingly.[1] I cannot quite wonder at the latter. The world is an old acquaintance that does not improve upon one's hands:—however, one must not give way to the disgusts it creates. My maxim, and practice too, is to laugh, because I do not like to cry. I could shed a pailful of tears over all I have seen and learnt since my poor nephew's misfortune[2]—the more one has to do with men the worse one finds them.—But can one mend them?—No.—Shall we shut ourselves up from them?—No.—We should grow humourists—and of all animals an Englishman is least made to live alone. For my part, I am conscious of so many faults, that I think I grow better the more bad I see in my neighbours; and there are so many I would not resemble, that it makes me watchful over myself.

12. He died 23 or 24 Sept. (Ossory i. 145, n. 1).

13. While she 'continues my widow and unmarried' (Mann vii. 520, n. 9).

14. Dated 5 July 1770 (ibid. n. 8).

15. Thoresby Park, near Ollerton, Notts. The Duchess could not have sold Thoresby, because the Duke bequeathed his landed estates to her for her life only, and then to his nephew, Charles Pierre-pont Medows, cr. (1806) E. Manvers, in the possession of whose family it remains. HW to Mann 4 Oct. 1773, Mann vii. 520, notes the limited inheritance of the Duchess. See also Ossory i. 149 and n. 33; GEC *sub* Manvers.

———

1. Presumably from Wentworth Castle.

2. The insanity of George Earl of Orford (HW).

You, my Lord, who have forty more good qualities than I have, should not seclude yourself. I do not wonder you despise knaves and fools; but remember, they want better examples. They will never grow ashamed by conversing but with one another.

I came to settle here on Friday,[3] being drowned out of Twickenham. I find the town desolate, and no news in it, but that the ministry give up the Irish tax[4]—some say, because it will not pass even in Ireland;[5] others, because the City of London would have petitioned against it;[6] and some, because there were factions in the Council[7]—which is not the most incredible of all.[8] I am glad, for the sake of some of my friends who would have suffered by it,[9] that it is over. In other respects, I have too much private business of my own to think about the public, which is big enough to take care of itself.

I have heard of some of Lady [Mary Coke]'s mortifications.[10] I have regard and esteem for her good qualities, which are many—but I doubt her genius will never suffer her to be quite happy. As she will not take the psalmist's advice of not putting trust,[11] I am sure she would not follow mine; for, with all her piety, King David is the only royal person she will not listen to, and therefore I forbear my sweet counsel. When she and Lord H[untingdon] meet,[12] will not

3. 12 Nov.

4. A proposal, not adopted, to tax absentee landlords in Ireland from one to four shillings in the pound. See Ossory i. 159 and n. 11, 161–2, 164. Because of strong opposition to the plan in London, 'It is no wonder that on the 13th of November, before the tax could even be known to have been proposed in Ireland, so far from passed (which it was now thought it would not be), it was declared here that the Court relinquished the plan, and would not confirm it even if sent over' (Last Journals i. 259).

5. Nov. '30th. An express arrived from Dublin that the tax on absentees had been rejected [25 Nov.] by a majority of 14' (Last Journals i. 260); the vote was 120 to 106 (Mann vii. 524, n. 5, 530, n. 4).

6. Because the absentee tax, if passed, would decrease the 'influx of money from Ireland' to be spent in London, 'the City of London soon took the alarm and intended to call a Council that they might petition against it' (Last Journals i. 258).

7. 'Lord North . . . had promised Lord Harcourt [lord lieutenant of Ireland] that

if the bill should be sent from Ireland he would use all his power to have it confirmed by the King and Council here' (Last Journals i. 252).

8. HW attributed the defeat of the tax to the 'immediate self-interest' of those voting (Last Journals i. 261).

9. Lord Hertford and Lord Ossory, for example.

10. She was repulsed by Frederick II and Maria Theresa (HW to Mann 30 Dec. 1773, Mann vii. 538–9).

11. 'Put not your trust in princes' (Psalms 146.3).

12. 'About one o'clock [20 Nov. 1773] I arrived at Parma . . . I found Lord Huntingdon and his two nephews in the same house where I am lodged' (Coke, Journals iv. 263). Lady Mary mentions him frequently in the journals written in Parma and Florence. Her preoccupation with royalty and nobility would be a suitable complement to Huntingdon's descent from Edward III. For her approaching quarrel with Huntingdon, see Mann vii. 543, 553.

they put you in mind of Count Gage[13] and Lady Mary Herbert,[14] who met in the mines of Asturias[15] after they had failed of the crown of Poland?[16]—Adieu, my dear Lord! Come you and my Lady among us. You have some friends that are not odious, and who will be rejoiced to see you both—witness, for one,

Yours most faithfully,

HOR. WALPOLE

To STRAFFORD, Friday 11 November 1774

Printed from *Works* v. 474. Reprinted, Wright v. 387–8, Cunningham vi. 144–5, Toynbee ix. 87–8.

Strawberry Hill, Nov. 11, 1774.

I AM sorry there is still time, my dear Lord, to write to you again; and that though there is, I have so little to amuse you with. One is not much nearer news for being within ten miles of London than if in Yorkshire; and besides, whatever reaches us, Lady Greenwich catches at the rebound before me, and sends you before I can. Our own circle furnishes very little. Dowagers are good for propagating news when planted, but have done with sending forth suckers. Lady Blandford's[1] coffee-house is removed to town, and the Duchess of Newcastle's[2] is little frequented, but by your sister Anne,[3] Lady

13. Joseph Edward Gage (ca 1678–1766), Count Gage, brother of Thomas, 1st Vct Gage (SELWYN 215, n. 29). Huntingdon had been dismissed by George III, and was therefore somewhat an exile, as Gage was after his fiasco in the Mississippi Bubble.

14. (d. 1775), dau. of William, 2nd M. of Powis; see n. 16 below.

15. Ancient province in NW Spain, now officially called Oviedo.

16. After winning and losing fortunes in the Mississippi speculation, both Gage and Lady Mary Herbert operated mining concessions in Asturias. Gage in 1719 had offered £3,000,000 for the crown of Poland; Lady Mary had aspired to a royal marriage. See DU DEFFAND v. 288–9 and n. 201, 398; SELWYN 215 and n. 31; and

OSSORY ii. 280 and n. 10 for HW's account of them, and Pope's references to Poland and the Asturian mines in *Moral Essays*, (Ep. iii, to Bathurst) ll. 129–34.

1. Maria Catherina de Jong (ca 1697–1779), m. 1 (1729) William Godolphin, styled M. of Blandford, 1722; m. 2 (1734) as 2d wife, Sir William Wyndham, 3d Bt, 1695. Her house was at East Sheen (OSSORY i. 48, n. 21).

2. Twickenham Park, the life use of which she had from the death of her husband in 1768, under the will of Diana, Cts of Mountrath (d. 1766). See Daniel Lysons, *Environs of London*, iii (1795). 566; MORE 123.

3. Lady Anne Conolly.

Browne[4] and me. This morning indeed I was at a very fine concert at old Franks's[5] at Isleworth, and heard Leoni,[6] who pleased me more than anything I have heard these hundred years. There is a full melancholy melody in his voice, though a falsetta, that nothing but a natural voice almost ever compasses. Then he sung songs of Handel in the genuine simple style, and did not put one in pain like rope-dancers. Of the opera I hear a dismal account;[7] for I did not go to it to sit in our box[8] like an old king dowager by myself. Garrick is treating the town, as it deserves and likes to be treated, with scenes, fireworks, and his own writing.[9] A good new play I never expect to see more, nor have seen since *The Provoked Husband,*[10] which came out when I was at school.

Bradshaw[11] is dead, they say by his own hand: I don't know wherefore.[12] I was told it was a great political event.[13] If it is, our politics run as low as our plays. From town I heard that Lord Bristol[14] was

4. Frances Sheldon (1714–90), m. 1 (1736) Henry Fermor; m. 2 Sir George Browne (d. 1754), 3d Bt; HW's correspondent (MORE 49, n. 4). Her cottage at Twickenham was called Riverside (MORE 287, n. 7).

5. Aaron Franks (ca 1685 or 1692–1777), jeweller and money-lender of London, who had a house in Isleworth, where he died 21 Sept. 1777, aged 92 (GM 1777, xlvii. 460) or 85 (Hilda F. Finberg, 'Jewish Residents of Eighteenth-Century Twickenham,' Jewish Historical Society of England, *Transactions Sessions 1945–1951*, xvi. 129–30). See also MANN i. 343 and n. 3.

6. The stage name of Myer Lyon (d. 1796), Jewish opera singer and cantor; uncle and teacher of John Braham (whose daughter was Frances, Lady Waldegrave); bankrupt ca 1788; died in Jamaica, where he was cantor to the English and German synagogue (OSSORY i. 217, n. 17).

7. The only performance of the season had been Sacchini's *Armida* on 8 Nov. The mediocrity of the singers and dancers is suggested in *London Stage 1660–1800* pt 4, ed. G. W. Stone, Carbondale, Ill., 1962, iii. 1831–2, 1847–8 ff.

8. Box No. 3 on the ground tier, which HW shared with Conway, Lady Ailesbury, Lady Strafford, and Lord Hertford, according to a ground plan owned in 1859 by Dr John Doran (HW's *Journal of the Reign of King George the Third . . . 1771 to 1783*, ed. Doran, 1859, ii. 277n). A silver subscription ticket owned in 1936 by Frederick Charles Neville identifies HW's box as No. 21.

9. Probably a reference to Garrick's epilogue to the *Maid of the Oaks* (*Letters of David Garrick*, ed. Little and Kahrl, Cambridge, Mass., 1963, iii. 967).

10. *The Provok'd Husband; or, A Journey to London* by Cibber and Vanbrugh, first acted at Drury Lane 10 Jan. 1728 and published in 1728. For HW's copies, see Hazen *Cat. of HW's Lib.*, No. 936.

11. Thomas Bradshaw (1733–6 Nov. 1774), of Hampton Court, Middlesex; M.P. Harwich 1767–8, Saltash 1768–May 1772, 8 June 1772–6 Nov. 1774; secretary of the Treasury 1767–70; a lord of the Admiralty 1772–4.

12. Bradshaw, 'overwhelmed with debts . . . shot himself' (*Last Journals* i. 407). See also OSSORY i. 214, n. 2; HW to Mann 11 Nov. 1774, MANN viii. 56.

13. A supporter of the administration, patronized by Lord Barrington and the Duke of Grafton, Bradshaw received a pension of £1500 a year; after his death his widow and two younger sons and a daughter received pensions (Sir Lewis Namier and John Brooke, *House of Commons 1754–1790*, 1964, ii. 111).

14. George William Hervey (1721–75), 2d E. of Bristol, 1751.

taken speechless with a stroke of the palsy.[15] If he dies, Madam Chudeigh must be tried by her peers, as she is certainly either Duchess or Countess.[16]

Mr Conway and his company[17] are so pleased with Paris, that they talk of staying till Christmas.[18] I am glad; for they will certainly be better diverted there than here.

Your Lordship's most faithful servant,

HOR. WALPOLE

To STRAFFORD, Saturday 2 November 1776

Printed from *Works* v. 475–6. Reprinted, Wright v. 458–9, Cunningham vi. 390–1, Toynbee ix. 434–5.

Strawberry Hill, November 2, 1776.

THOUGH inclination, and consciousness that a man of my age, who is neither in Parliament nor in business, has little to do in the world, keep me a good deal out of it, yet I will not, my dear Lord, encourage you in retirement, to which for the interest of your friends you have but too much propensity. The manners of the age cannot be agreeable to those who have lived in something soberer times; nor do I think, except in France, where old people are never out of fashion, that it is reasonable to tire those whose youth and spirits may excuse some dissipation. Above all things it is my resolution never to profess retirement, lest, when I have lost all my real teeth, the imaginary one, called a colt's, should hurry me back and make me ridiculous. But one never outlives all one's cotemporaries; one may assort with them. Few Englishmen, too, I have observed, can bear solitude without being hurt by it. Our climate

---

15. He died 18 March 1775 'of a palsy from a repelled gout' (*Last Journals* i. 449; cf. HW to Mann 20 March 1775, MANN viii. 86–7).

16. The trial of the Duchess of Kingston for bigamy did not begin until 15 April 1776; see OSSORY i. 285 and n. 31.

17. His wife and daughter, Lady Ailes-

bury and Mrs Damer; see ibid. i. 200, n.

16. The latter was Anne Seymour Conway (1748–1828), m. (1767) Hon. John Damer.

18. Lady Ailesbury and Mrs Damer left London 4 Oct. 1774 to meet Conway in Paris; all three returned to London 21 Feb. 1775 (ibid.).

makes us capricious, and we must rub off our roughnesses and humours against one another. We have too an always increasing resource, which is, that though we go not to the young, they must come to us: younger usurpers tread on their heels, as they did on ours, and revenge us that have been deposed. They may retain their titles, like Queen Christina,[1] Sir M—— N——,[2] and Lord R——;[3] but they find they have no subjects. If we could but live long enough, we should hear Lord C[arlisle], Mr S[torer],[4] etc. complain of the airs and abominable hours of the youth of the age. You see, my dear Lord, my easy philosophy can divert itself with anything, even with visions; which perhaps is the best way of treating the great vision itself, life. For half one's time one should laugh *with* the world; the other half, *at* it—and then it is hard if we want amusement.

I am heartily glad, for your Lordship's and Lady Anne Conolly's sakes, that General Howe[5] is safe.[6] I sincerely interest myself for everybody you are concerned for. I will say no more on a subject on which I fear I am so unlucky as to differ very much with your Lordship, having always fundamentally disapproved our conduct with America. Indeed the present prospect of war with France, when we have so much disabled ourselves, and are exposed in so many quarters, is a topic for general lamentation, rather than for canvassing of opinions,[7] which every man must form for himself: and I doubt the

1. (1626–89), Q. of Sweden 1644–54; abdicated, 1654.

2. Perhaps merely the 'M' and 'N' of the catechism in the Book of Common Prayer.

3. Perhaps Lord Rockingham, former prime minister and now nominal leader of the Opposition.

4. HW presumably refers to Frederick Howard (1748–1825), 5th E. of Carlisle, and to Carlisle's friend and contemporary, Anthony Morris Storer (1746–99), M.P. Carlisle 1774–80, Morpeth 1780–4; collector; benefactor of the Eton Library, to which he left his collection of SH books; famous for his dancing.

5. Hon. Sir William Howe (1729–1814), K.B., 1776; 5th Vct Howe, 1799; brother of Admiral Lord Howe; M.P. Nottingham 1758–80; Maj.-Gen., 1772, and now commanding the British troops at New York.

He had m. (1765) Frances Conolly (ca 1742–1817), the dau. of Lord Strafford's sister Lady Anne Conolly.

6. Nov. '2d. At night General Howe's second aide-de-camp arrived with an account of his being in possession of New York from the 15th of September' (*Last Journals* i. 587). Howe's letter to Germain 21 Sept. 1776 is in the *London Gazette Extraordinary* 4 Nov. Conflicting reports of his failure or success against the Americans had been current in October; see *Last Journals* i. 574–86 *passim*.

7. As illustrated in the exchanges between Opposition and Ministry at the opening of Parliament 31 Oct. HW's account of the debate on moving the Address to the King (*Last Journals* i. 580–6) is a commentary on some of the implications of this paragraph.

moment is advancing when we shall be forced to think alike at least on the present.

I have not been yet above a night at a time in town—but shall be glad to give your Lordship and Lady Strafford a meeting there whenever you please.

Your most faithful humble servant,

HOR. WALPOLE

To STRAFFORD, Wednesday 4 February 1778

Printed from photostat of Add. MSS 22130, f. 27. First printed Toynbee, x. 184.

February the 4th 1778.

My dear Lord,

I AM always as proud as happy in having the honour of waiting on your Lordship, as I will on Saturday, and as I should much oftener in a morning if I went out—but I may tell you the truth, as you will not laugh at me. I am not young enough to have spirits for the whole day, and if I did not stay at home in a morning, I should not be able to go through the evening with any satisfaction, and sup out as I must do, if I will live with some of those I am most connected with. When one grows so old as I do, one must be an economist of one's spirits as well as money, or go off like the fashionable people of the age.

Your Lordship's most truly devoted

H. WALPOLE

To STRAFFORD, Thursday 2 July 1778

Missing. 'I wrote the Earl [of Strafford] a letter two days ago that will not please him, but can one always contain one's chagrin when one's country is ruined by infatuation?' (HW to Mason 4 July 1778, MASON i. 411). Like the letter to Mason, this missing letter probably contained observations on the American war.

To Strafford, Monday 12 June 1780

Printed from *Works* v. 476–7. Reprinted, Wright vi. 87–9, Cunningham vii. 398–400, Toynbee xi. 219–21.

Strawberry Hill, June 12, 1780.

My dear Lord,

IF THE late events[1] had been within the common proportion of news, I would have tried to entertain your Lordship with an account of them; but they were far beyond that size, and could only create horror and indignation. Religion has often been the cloak of injustice, outrage and villainy: in our late tumults, it scarce kept on its mask a moment; its persecution was downright robbery; and it was so drunk, that it killed its banditti faster than they could plunder. The tumults have been carried on in so violent and scandalous a manner, that I trust they will have no copies. When prisons are levelled to the ground,[2] when the bank is aimed at,[3] and reformation is attempted by conflagrations, the savages of Canada are the only fit allies of Lord George Gordon and his crew.[4] The Tower is much too dignified a prison for him—but he had left no other.[5]

I came out of town on Friday, having seen a good deal of the shocking transactions of Wednesday night—in fact, it was difficult to be in London and not see, or think some part of it in flames—I saw those of the King's Bench, New Prison, and those on the three sides of the Fleet Market, which united into one blaze.[6] The town and parks are now one camp[7]—the next disagreeable sight to the capital

1. The Gordon riots which had begun 2 June. See J. P. De Castro, *The Gordon Riots*, 1926, and HW to Mann 5, 14 June 1780, MANN ix. 52–7, 61–4.

2. Newgate, New Prison, Fleet Prison, and King's Bench Prison had been burnt; Clerkenwell Bridewell had been damaged by the rioters but had not been fired by the rioters because of the houses that might be destroyed with it. See De Castro, op. cit. *passim*.

3. The Bank of England was twice attacked during the night of 7–8 June; see MASON ii. 56–7, n. 17.

4. The Protestant Association, of which Gordon was president, and its sympathizers who had participated in the riot.

5. Taken into custody 9 June at his house in Welbeck Street, Gordon was examined at the Horse Guards in the War Office and was sent to the Tower; on 5 Feb. 1781 he was tried and acquitted on a charge of high treason.

6. HW describes it to Lady Ossory 8 June 1780, OSSORY ii. 186–90.

7. An official list 'of troops stationed in and passing near London' shows on 4 June a total of 6,287, a number which gradually increased to 12,367 on 12 June. Another official list of 'docketed posts' on June 12 shows the disposition of 1,455 foot guards, 2,142 infantry, and 607 cavalry stationed in and near London. For details, see De Castro, op. cit., pp. 263–5.

being in ashes. It will still not have been a fatal tragedy, if it brings the nation *one*[8] and all to their senses. It will still be not quite an unhappy country, if we reflect that the old constitution, exactly as it was in the last reign, was the most desirable of any in the universe. It made us *then* the first people in Europe—we have a vast deal of ground to recover—but can we take a better path than that which King William pointed out to us? I mean the system he left us at the Revolution. I am averse to *all* changes of it—it fitted us just as it was.

For some time even individuals must be upon their guard. Our new and now imprisoned apostle[9] has delivered so many congenial Saint Peters from jail, that one hears of nothing but robberies on the highway. Your Lordship's sister,[10] Lady Browne and I have been at Twickenham Park this evening, and kept together and had a horseman at our return. Baron d'Aguilar[11] was shot at in that very lane[12] on Thursday night. A troop of the fugitives[13] had rendezvoused in Combe Wood,[14] and were dislodged thence yesterday by the Light Horse.

I do not know a syllable but what relates to these disturbances. The newspapers have neglected few truths. Lies, without their natural propensity to falsehoods, they could not avoid, for every minute produces some, at least exaggerations. We were threatened with swarms of good Protestants *à brûler* from all quarters, and report sent various detachments from the metropolis on similar errands; but thank God they have been but reports!—Oh! when shall we have peace and tranquillity? I hope your Lordship and Lady Strafford will at least enjoy the latter in your charming woods. I have long doubted which of our passions is the strongest—perhaps every one

8. George III.

9. Lord George Gordon.

10. Lady Anne Conolly.

11. Ephraim Lopez-Pereira (1739–1802), Baron d'Aquilar (of Portugal), 1759; wealthy and eccentric Portuguese Jew, born in Vienna and naturalized in England in 1757 (MASON ii. 59, n. 35; Alfred Rubens, *Anglo-Jewish Portraits*, 1935, pp. 4–5 and references there cited). He had 'a large house at Twickenham (formerly his country retreat), which was . . . shut up' in the later part of his life (William Granger and James Caulfield, *Wonderful Museum*, 1803, i. 147, with full account,

and two prints of him at pp. 141–55); no payments by him, however, are recorded in the extant Twickenham Rate Books 1748–97.

12. His 'coach was shot here last night close to the Crown' (HW to Mason 9 June 1780, MASON ii. 59).

13. Prisoners released by the rioters when Newgate and other prisons were fired or plundered.

14. Near Kingston-upon-Thames, Surrey. One of the 'Docketed Posts' in an official list of 12 June is for twelve cavalrymen at 'Comb Wood, near Kingston' (De Castro, op. cit., pp. 193, 265).

of them is equally strong in some person or other—but I have no doubt but ambition is the most detestable, and the most inexcusable; for its mischiefs are by far the most extensive, and its enjoyments by no means proportioned to its anxieties. The latter, I believe, is the case of most passions—but then all but ambition cost little pain to any but the possessor. An ambitious man must be divested of all feeling but for himself. The torment of others is his high road to happiness. Were the transmigration of souls true, and accompanied by consciousness, how delighted would Alexander or Crœsus be to find themselves on four legs, and divested of a wish to conquer new worlds, or to heap up all the wealth of this! Adieu, my dear Lord!

I am most gratefully your Lordship's obedient humble servant,

HOR. WALPOLE

To STRAFFORD, ca Tuesday 1 August 1780

Missing; mentioned in Lady Mary Coke, 'MS Journals,' 9 Aug. 1780: 'You mention in your letter Lord Strafford having had a letter from Mr Walpole, but are you not both acquainted with him? Do you not know how artful he is in dressing up everything to the advantage of those relations [the Gloucesters and Waldegraves], and though I shall not say that what he has wrote to Lord Strafford is not true, yet I will affirm that he has suppressed a great many truths that lead to an explanation of the dislike showed by Lord Egremont to the marriage, first the mother's behaviour upon Lord Egremont's making those noble offers I mentioned and which she told him were not so great as some others, and that her daughter had equal pretentions . . .'

To STRAFFORD, Saturday 9 September 1780

Printed from *Works* v. 478–9. Reprinted, Wright vi. 91–3, Cunningham vii. 437–8, Toynbee xi. 273–4.

Strawberry Hill, September 9, 1780.

I AM very happy at receiving a letter from your Lordship this moment, as I thought it very long since we had corresponded, but am afraid of being troublesome, when I have not the excuse of thanking you, or something worth telling you, which in truth is not the case at present. No soul, whether interested or not, but deafens one about elections. I always detested them, even when in Parliament;[1] and when I lived a good deal at White's, preferred hearing of Newmarket to elections; for the former, being uttered in a language I did not understand, did not engage my attention; but as they talked of elections in *English,* I could not help knowing what they said. It does surprise me, I own, that people can choose to stuff their heads with details and circumstances, of which in six weeks they will never hear or think more. The weather till now has been the chief topic of conversation. Of late it has been the third very hot summer; but refreshed by so little rain, that the banks of the Thames have been and are, I believe, like those of the Manzanares.[2] The night before last we had some good showers, and today a thick fog has dissolved in some as thin as gauze. Still I am not quite sorry to enjoy the weather of adust climates without their tempests and insects.—Lady Cowper[3] I lately visited, and but lately: if what I hear is true, I shall be a gainer, for they talk of Lord D[uncannon][4] having her house at Richmond:[5] like your Lordship, I confess I was surprised at his choice. I know nothing to the prejudice of the young lady[6]—but I should not have selected, for so gentle and very amiable a man, a sister of the empress of fashion,[7] nor a daughter of the goddess of wisdom.[8]

They talk of great dissatisfactions in the fleet. Geary[9] and Barring-

1. For HW's aversion to elections, see Mann iv. 337, ix. 297, 483. On 26 March 1784, he wrote 'I hated elections forty years ago,' and he then repeated this passage about White's (ibid. ix. 483).

2. A town in Spain, on the banks of the river Azuer in the province of Ciudad Real; one of the towns of La Mancha, in the centre of the district described by Cervantes in *Don Quixote.*

3. Georgiana Caroline Carteret (d. 21 Aug. 1780), dau. of John, 1st E. Granville; m. 1 (1734) Hon. John Spencer; m. 2 (1750) William Cowper, 2d E. Cowper, 1723 (Ossory i. 318, n. 12, ii. 211, 217, n. 12).

4. Frederick Ponsonby (1758–1844), styled Vct Duncannon, 3d E. of Bessborough, 1793.

5. Cholmondeley House, built by HW's brother-in-law, was later purchased for

Lady Cowper by her son, John, 1st E. Spencer. After her death the house was bought by the D. of Queensbury and in 1828 was torn down (Ossory i. 318, n. 12). The Duncannons did not live there.

6. Lady Henrietta Frances Spencer (1761–1821), granddaughter of Lady Cowper, m. (27 Nov. 1780) Lord Duncannon.

7. The Duchess of Devonshire.

8. Margaret Georgiana Poyntz (1737–1814) m. (1755) Hon. John Spencer, cr. (1761) Bn and (1765) E. Spencer.

9. Francis Geary (1709–96), cr. (1782) Bt; entered the navy, 1727, and became Admiral of the White, 1778. In May 1780, on Hardy's death, Geary had accepted the command of the Channel fleet. When he resigned, 'It was said he was disgusted at not having had frigates enough to watch the Brest fleet, and that the Admiralty had not answered his demands of

ton[10] are certainly retired.[11] It looks, if this deplorable war should continue, as if all our commanders by sea and land were to be disgraced or disgusted.

The people here have christened Mr Shirley's[12] new house,[13] *Spite Hall*.[14] It is dismal to think that one may live to seventy-seven,[15] and go out of the world doing as ill-natured an act as possible! When I am reduced to detail the gazette of Twickenham, I had better release your Lordship—but either way it is from the utmost attention and respect for your Lordship and Lady Strafford, as I am ever

Most devotedly and gratefully yours,

HOR. WALPOLE

To Strafford, Wednesday 13 June 1781

Printed from *Works* v. 479–80. Reprinted, Wright vi. 128–9, Cunningham viii. 51–2, Toynbee xii. 10–11.

Strawberry Hill, June 13, 1781.

IT WAS very kind, my dear Lord, to recollect me so soon: I wish I could return it by amusing you; but here I know nothing, and suppose it is owing to age that even in town I do not find the transactions of the world very entertaining. One must sit up all night to

many articles. The command was offered to Admiral Barrington; he said he would take it, with full powers—that is, he would not be dependent on Lord Sandwich; or he would serve under any other Admiral; neither being granted, he struck his flag and retired' (*Last Journals* ii. 329).

10. Hon. Samuel Barrington (1729–1800), son of John, 1st Vct Barrington; Rear-Adm., 1778, Vice-Adm., 1782, Adm., 1787.

11. Barrington's retirement was temporary. After the fall of North's ministry he accepted an appointment to the Channel fleet under Howe. See also n. 9 above; MASON ii. 47 and n. 31.

12. Hon. George Shirley (1705–22 Oct. 1787), son of Robert 1st E. Ferrers, by

his second marriage; brother of Lady Frances Shirley; of Ettington, Warw., where he died (Collins, *Peerage*, 1812, iv. 99; GM 1787, lvii. 1024; Burke, *Peerage*, 1953, p. 790, *sub* Ferrers).

13. The Twickenham Rate Books record his payment of the rates on his old house 1762–77 and on the new 1783–7.

14. Because built (it was said) on purpose to intercept a view of the Thames from his opposite neighbour (Mary Berry). The neighbour, according to the map based on an actual survey of Twickenham in 1784 (see back end-paper in MORE), was John Blake, an attorney at law mentioned in BERRY ii. 237–40 and in the Twickenham Rate Books.

15. Born 23 Oct. 1705, Shirley was almost seventy-five.

see or hear anything—and if the town intends to do anything, they never begin to do it till next day.

Mr Conway will certainly be here the end of this month,[1] having thoroughly secured his island[2] from surprise, and it is not liable to be taken any other way. I wish he was governor of this bigger one too, which does not seem quite so well guaranteed.

Your Lordship will wonder at a visit I had yesterday: it was from Mr [Storer], who has passed a day and night here. It was not from my being a fellow-scholar of Vestris,[3] but from his being turned antiquary;[4] the last patina I should have thought a Macaroni would have taken. I am as proud of such a disciple as of having converted Dicky Bateman[5] from a Chinese to a Goth. Though he was the founder of the Sharawadgi[6] taste in England, I preached so effectually that his every pagoda took the veil.[7] The Methodists say, one must have been very wicked before one can be of the elect—yet is that extreme more distant from *the ton,* which avows knowing and liking nothing but the fashion of the instant, to studying what were the modes of five hundred years ago? I hope this conversion will not ruin Mr [Storer]'s fortune under the Lord Lieutenant of Ireland.[8] How his Irish Majesty will be shocked, when he asks how large Prince B[oothby]'s shoe-buckles are grown, to be answered, he does not know, but that Charles Brandon's[9] codpiece at the last Birthday had

1. He did not return until Sunday 26 Aug., when he called on HW at SH, on his way to Park Place (*post* 31 Aug. 1781).

2. 'General Conway is gone to Jersey with strong additional force' (HW to Hon. Thomas Walpole 25 March 1781).

3. The elder Vestris, Gaetano Appollino Baldassare Vestris (1729–1808), ballet dancer who was teaching dancing in London at this time; see Ossory ii. 268 and n. 7.

4. See Ossory ii. 273 and n. 4.

5. Richard Bateman (ca 1705–73), collector. For an account of his house and collection, see Thomas E. Harwood, *Windsor Old and New*, 1929, pp. 313–34.

6. See Mann iv. 127, n. 54. Miles Hadfield, *A History of British Gardening*, 1969, p. 177n, says that the word is 'probably . . . of Japanese origin, from *souro*, of which the negative participle is *soro-wa-ji*, "not being symmetrical." ' See also *Journal of Æsthetics and Art Criticism*, 1963, xxii. No. 2, p. 128.

7. 'I converted it [Bateman's house] from Chinese to Gothic' (HW to Montagu 24 Sept. 1762, Montagu ii. 43, opposite Müntz's Gothic design, 1761, for a room at Bateman's house).

8. Storer's intimate friend, Frederick Howard, 5th E. of Carlisle, was lord lieutenant of Ireland 1780–2. On Carlisle's interest, Storer was elected M.P. Carlisle 1774–80 and Morpeth 1780–4; in 1778 he went to America as Carlisle's assistant on the conciliation commission to the colonies; but Storer received no appointment in Ireland, and their friendship was severed in 1783 when Storer accepted an appointment for which he was indebted to Fox. See Sir Lewis Namier and John Brooke, *House of Commons 1754–1790*, 1964, iii. 485–7.

9. Henry VIII's brother-in-law, Charles Brandon (ca 1484–1545), cr. (1514) D. of Suffolk. He and those mentioned later in this paragraph were prominent at the court of Henry VIII.

three yards of velvet in it! and that the Duchess of Buckingham[10] thrust out her chin two inches farther than ever, in admiration of it! and that the Marchioness of Dorset[11] had put out her jaw by endeavouring to imitate her!

We have at last had some rains, which I hope extended to Yorkshire, and that your Lordship has found Wentworth Castle in the bloom of verdure. I always, as in duty bound, wish prosperity to everybody and everything there, and am

Your Lordship's ever devoted and grateful humble servant,

HOR. WALPOLE

To STRAFFORD, Friday 31 August 1781

Printed from *Works* v. 480–1. Reprinted, Wright vi. 135–6, Cunningham viii. 73–4, Toynbee xii. 42–4.

Strawberry Hill, August 31, 1781.

YOUR Lordship's too friendly partiality sees talents in me, which I am sure I do not possess. With all my desire of amusing you, and with all my sense of gratitude for your long and unalterable goodness, it is quite impossible to send you an entertaining letter from hence. The insipidity of my life, that is passed with a few old people that are wearing out like myself, after surviving so many of my acquaintance, can furnish no matter of correspondence. What few novelties I hear, come stale, and not till they have been hashed in the newspapers; and though we are engaged in such big and wide wars, they produce no striking events, nor furnish anything but regrets for the lives and millions we fling away to no purpose! One cannot divert when one can only compute; nor extract entertainment from prophecies that there is no reason to colour favourably. We

---

10. Eleanor Percy (d. 1530), dau. of Henry, 4th E. of Northumberland, m. (1490) Edward Stafford, 3d D. of Buckingham, 1483, although his titles were not formally restored until 1485.

11. Katherine Fitzalan (living 1552), dau. of William, E. of Arundel, by his second wife, Anne Percy, dau. of Henry, E. of Northumberland; m. (before 1530) Henry Grey, 3d M. of Dorset, 1530, who repudiated (divorced) her and remarried in 1533.

have indeed foretold success for seven years together, but debts and taxes have been the sole completion.

If one turns to private life, what is there to furnish pleasing topics? Dissipation without object, pleasure, or genius, is the only colour of the times. One hears every day of somebody undone, but can we or they tell how, except when it is by the most expeditious of all means, gaming? And now, even the loss of an hundred thousand pounds is not rare enough to be surprising. One may stare or growl, but cannot relate anything that is worth hearing. I do not love to censure a younger age; but in good truth they neither amuse me nor enable me to amuse others.

The pleasantest event I know, happened to myself last Sunday[1] morning, when General Conway, very unexpectedly, walked in as I was at breakfast, in his way to Park Place. He looks as well in health and spirits as ever I saw him; and though he stayed but half an hour, I was perfectly content, as he is at home.

I am glad your Lordship likes the fourth book of *The Garden*,[2] which is admirably coloured. The version of Fresnoy[3] I think the finest translation I ever saw. It is a most beautiful poem extracted from as dry and prosaic a parcel of verses as could be put together: Mr Mason has gilded lead, and burnished it highly. Lord and Lady Harcourt[4] I should think would make him a visit, and I hope for their sakes will visit Wentworth Castle. As they both have taste, I should be sorry they did not see the perfectest specimen of architecture I know.

Mrs Damer certainly goes abroad this winter. I am glad of it for every reason but her absence. I am certain it will be essential to her health; and she has so eminently a classic genius, and is herself so superior an artist, that I enjoy the pleasure she will have in visiting Italy.

1. 26 Aug.

2. William Mason's *The English Garden: A Poem. Book the Fourth*, York and London, 1781; published in London 1 Sept. (MASON ii. 152, n. 11). See also MASON, *passim;* Hazen, *Cat. of HW's Lib.*, No. 3222:12.

3. Charles-Alphonse Dufresnoy (1611–65), whose Latin poem, *De arte graphica* was published posthumously at Paris, 1668. Mason's English translation, on which he had worked sporadically from his Cambridge years, was not published until 1783: *The Art of Painting . . . of Du Fresnoy With Annotations by Sir Joshua Reynolds*, York and London 1783. See MASON, *passim;* Hazen, *Cat. of HW's Lib.*, No. 3890.

4. George Simon Harcourt (1736–1809), styled Vct Nuneham 1749–77; 2d E. Harcourt, 1777, m. (1765) Elizabeth Venables Vernon (1746–1826); HW's friends and correspondents.

As your Lordship has honoured all the productions of my press with your acceptance,[5] I venture to enclose the last,[6] which I printed to oblige the Lucans.[7] There are many beautiful and poetic expressions in it. A wedding to be sure is neither a new nor a promising subject, nor will outlast the favours: still I think Mr Jones's ode is uncommonly good for the occasion;[8] at least, if it does not much charm Lady Strafford and your Lordship, I know you will receive it kindly as a tribute from Strawberry Hill, as every homage is due to you both from its master.

Your devoted humble servant,

HOR. WALPOLE

To STRAFFORD, Tuesday 27 November 1781

Printed from *Works* v. 482–3. Reprinted, Wright vi. 148–50, Cunningham viii. 116–18, Toynbee xii. 105–7.

Berkeley Square, November 27, 1781.

EACH fresh mark of your Lordship's kindness and friendship calls on me for thanks and an answer: every other reason would enjoin me silence. I not only grow so old, but the symptoms of age increase so fast, that, as they advise me to keep out of the world, that retirement makes me less fit to be informing or entertaining. The philosophers who have sported on the verge of the tomb, or they who have *affected* to sport in the same situation, both tacitly implied that it was not out of their thoughts—and however dear what we are going to leave may be, all that is not particularly dear must cease

5. His presentation copy of the first edition of *Anecdotes of Painting*, five volumes bound in four, was in 1942 in the possession of Major-General Sir John Hanbury-Williams (Hazen, *SH Bibl.* 68); his editions of Hentzner and Lucan are now WSL.

6. *The Muse Recalled, an Ode Occasioned by the Nuptials of Lord Viscount Althorp and Miss Lavinia Bingham, Elder Daughter of Charles Lord Lucan, March VI, MDCCLXXXI*, by William Jones (1746–94), Kt, 1783, the Oriental scholar.

The printing of 250 copies was finished 11 Aug. (Hazen, *SH Bibl.* 119–21).

7. Sir Charles Bingham (1735–99), 7th Bt, 1752, cr. (1776) Bn Lucan and (1795) E. of Lucan; M.P.; m. (1760) Margaret Smith (d. 1814), whose painting and drawing HW admired.

8. The marriage of Lord Althorp with Miss Bingham (HW). George John Spencer (1758–1834), styled Vct Althorp 1765–83, 2d E. Spencer, 1783, m. (6 March 1781) Lavinia Bingham (1762–1831), daughter of Lord and Lady Lucan.

to interest us much. If those reflections blend themselves with our gayest thoughts, must not their hue grow more dusty when public misfortunes and disgraces cast a general shade? The age, it is true, soon emerges out of every gloom, and wantons as before.—But does not that levity imprint a still deeper melancholy on those who do think? Have any of our calamities corrected us? Are we not revelling on the brink of the precipice? Does administration grow more sage, or desire that we should grow more sober? Are these themes for letters, my dear Lord? Can one repeat common news with indifference, while our shame is writing for future history by the pens of all our numerous enemies? When did England see two whole armies lay down their arms and surrender themselves prisoners?[1] Can venal addresses[2] efface such stigmas, that will be recorded in every country in Europe? Or will such disgraces have no consequences? Is not America lost to us? Shall we offer up more human victims to the demon of obstinacy—and shall we tax ourselves deeper to furnish out the sacrifice? These are thoughts I cannot stifle at the moment that enforces them; and though I do not doubt but the same spirit of dissipation that has swallowed up all our principles, will reign again in three days with its wonted sovereignty, I had rather be silent than vent my indignation.—Yet I cannot talk, for I cannot think, on any other subject. It was not six days ago, that in the height of four raging wars I saw in the papers[3] an account of the opera and of the dresses of the company;[4] and thence the town, and thence of course the whole nation, were informed that Mr Fitzpatrick[5] had very little powder in his hair. Would not one think that our newspapers were

1. Burgoyne's army surrendered at Saratoga in 1777; Cornwallis's army at Yorktown, 19 Oct. 1781. The news of the latter reached London 25 Nov. (MANN ix. 208, n. 1).

2. Lord Feilding 'who was to have moved the Address in the Commons, and had prepared his speech, avoided being as ridiculous as the Royal Speech, by excusing himself.' Lord Southampton 'had probably been selected for moving the Address to insinuate that the Prince [of Wales] approved of his father's measures' (Last Journals ii. 378–9).

3. 'The *ton* at the Opera, in respect to gentlemen, has abated in the article of *dress*—almost every head was in queue,

not many *bien poudré;* and a few, among whom was Mr Fitzpatrick, were with scarce any powder at all' (*Public Advertiser* 23 Nov. 1781).

4. *Ezio*, a pasticcio composed by Ferdinando Giuseppe Bertoni (1725–1813), opened at the Haymarket 17 Nov. with a company led by Pacchierotti; Noverre's ballet, *Les Amants réunis*, was performed by dancers. It was repeated on 20 and 24 Nov. (*London Stage 1660–1800*, pt 5, Carbondale, Ill., 1968, i. 476–8; Sir George Grove, *Dictionary of Music*, 5th edn, ed. Blom, 1954, i. 689–90).

5. Hon. Richard Fitzpatrick (1748–1813), M.P.

penned by boys just come from school for the information of their sisters and cousins? Had we had *Gazettes* and *Morning Posts* in those days, would they have been filled with such tittle-tattle after the Battle of Agincourt, or in the more resembling weeks after the Battle of Naseby? Did the French trifle equally even during the ridiculous War of the Fronde? If they were as impertinent then, at least they had wit in their levity. We are monkeys in conduct, and as clumsy as bears when we try to gambol. Oh! my Lord! I have no patience with my country! and shall leave it without regret!—Can we be proud when all Europe scorns us? It was wont to envy us, sometimes to hate us, but never despised us before. James I was contemptible, but he did not lose an America! His eldest grandson[6] sold us, his younger[7] lost us—but we kept ourselves. Now we have run to meet the ruin—and it is coming!

I beg your Lordship's pardon, if I have said too much—but I do not believe I have. You have never sold yourself, and, therefore, have not been accessary to our destruction. You must be happy *now* not to have a son,[8] who would live to grovel in the dregs of England. Your Lordship has long been so wise as to secede from the follies of your countrymen. May you and Lady Strafford long enjoy the tranquillity that has been your option even in better days!—and may you amuse yourself without giving loose to such reflections as have overflowed in this letter from

Your devoted humble servant,

Hor. Walpole!

6. Charles II, who in 1675 agreed to accept £100,000 a year from France if he dissolved Parliament when it showed hostility to France. He dissolved Parliament; payment of the pension was begun. See Mann ii. 247 and n. 24.

7. James II.

8. 'The truth was this: both [Lord and Lady Strafford] . . . bitterly deplored their ill-fate in being childless; both (she more especially) felt the want of objects deeply interesting the heart' (Lady Louisa Stuart, 'Some Account of John Duke of Argyle and His Family,' written 1827, privately printed 1863, reprinted in Coke, *Journals* i. p. xlviii). He 'longed for heirs' and she 'pined for playthings' (ibid.).

To STRAFFORD, Friday 16 August 1782

Printed from *Works* v. 483–4. Reprinted, Wright vi. 177–9, Cunningham viii. 266–7, Toynbee xii. 312–13.

Strawberry Hill, August 16, 1782.

IF THIS letter reaches your Lordship, I believe it must be conveyed by a dove; for we are all under water, and a postman has not where to set the sole of his foot. They tell me, that in the north you have not been so drowned: which will be very fortunate; for in these parts everything is to be apprehended for the corn, the sheep, and the camps—but, in truth, all kinds of prospects are most gloomy, and even in lesser lights uncomfortable. Here we cannot stir, but armed for battle. Mr Potts,[1] who lives at Mr Hindley's, was attacked and robbed last week[2] at the end of Gunnersbury Lane, by five footpads who had two blunderbusses. Lady Browne and I do continue going to Twickenham Park;[3] but I don't know how long it will be prudent, nor whether it is so now.

I have not been at Park Place, for Mr Conway is never there, at least only for a night or two. His regiment was reviewed yesterday at Ashford Common,[4] but I did not go to see it.—In truth, I have so little taste for common sights, that I never did see a review in my life. I was in town last week,[5] yet saw not Monsieur de Grasse;[6] nor have seen the giant[7] or the dwarf.[8]

1. Samuel Potts of London was nephew and heir-at-law of Frederick Atherton Hindley at Radnor House, Twickenham, who died in 1781 after selling the house in 1780 to Nathaniel Webb. Potts was a pew-holder at Twickenham Church until 1783, and perhaps had remained in his uncle's former house temporarily (R. S. Cobbett, *Memorials of Twickenham*, 1872, pp. 28, 293; OSSORY i. 75, ii. 105, 180, 183).

2. 'On Tuesday night [6 Aug.] Samuel Potts, Esq., Comptroller of the General Post Office, with two other gentlemen, were stopped in Gunnersbury Lane by seven footpads, who robbed Mr Potts of about £19 and the other two of what money they had' (*Daily Adv.* 10 Aug.).

3. The Duchess of Montrose's house (OSSORY ii. 234; Cobbett, op. cit. 224). HW and Lady Browne had been robbed on their way to it in 1781 (OSSORY ii. 295).

4. 'Yesterday morning General Conway reviewed the Oxford Blues on Ashforth Heath, and on Thursday the same regiment is to be reviewed by the King at the same place' (*Daily Adv.* 13 Aug.). See also HW to Conway 20 Aug. 1782.

5. 5–6 Aug. (MASON ii. 270–2).

6. François-Joseph-Paul de Grasse (1722–88), Comte de Grasse, Marquis de Grasse-Tilly, captured by the British in the West Indies; he was in London, 3–12 Aug. (OSSORY ii. 351, n. 13).

7. 'The Irish giant respectfully begs leave to acquaint the nobility and the public in general, that he still continues to be seen . . . at the Caneshop, in Spring Garden Gate . . . only 21 years of age [he] measures eight feet two inches high' (*Daily Adv.* 23 July; also ibid. 18 and 30 July).

8. Perhaps the 'surprising gigantic infant' advertised ibid. 6 Aug.

Poor Mrs Clive is certainly very declining,[9] but has been better of late, and, which I am glad of, thinks herself better. All visions that comfort one are desirable—the conditions of mortality do not bear being pried into; nor am I an admirer of that philosophy that scrutinizes into them: the philosophy of deceiving one's self is vastly preferable. What signifies anticipating what we cannot prevent?

I do not pretend to send your Lordship any news, for I do not know a tittle, nor inquire. Peace is the sole event of which I wish to hear. For private news I have outlived almost all the world with which I was acquainted, and have no curiosity about the next generation, scarce more than about the 20th century. I wish I was less indifferent for the sake of the few with whom I correspond, your Lordship in particular, who are always so good and partial to me, and on whom I should indubitably wait, were I fit to take a long journey; but as I walk no better than a tortoise, I make a conscience of not incommodating my friends, whom I should only confine at home. Indeed both my feet and hands are so lame, that I now scarce ever dine abroad. Being so antiquated and insipid, I will release your Lordship, and am, with my unalterable respects to Lady Strafford,

Your Lordship's most devoted humble servant,

HOR. WALPOLE

To STRAFFORD, Thursday 3 October 1782

Printed from *Works* v. 485–6; reprinted, Wright vi. 182–3, Cunningham viii. 287–8, Toynbee xii. 341–3.

Strawberry Hill, October 3, 1782.

I DID think it long since I had the honour of hearing from your Lordship; but conscious how little I could repay you with any entertainment, I waited with patience. In fact, I believe summer-correspondences often turn on complaints of want of news. It is unlucky that that is generally the season of correspondence as it is of separation. People assembled in a capital contrive to furnish mat-

9. She had 'fits of the jaundice' (HW to Mason 4 Aug. 1782, MASON ii. 271 and n. 10).

ter, but then they have not occasion to write it. Summer being the season of campaigns ought to be more fertile—I am glad when that is not the case, for what is an account of a battle but a list of burials? Vultures and birds of prey might write with pleasure to their correspondents in the Alps of such events—but they ought to be melancholy topics to those who have no beaks or talons. At this moment if I was an epicure among the sharks, I should rejoice that General Elliot[1] has just sent the carcasses of 1500 Spaniards down to market under Gibraltar[2]—but I am more pleased that he dispatched boats and saved some of those whom he had overset.[3] What must a man of so much feeling have suffered at being forced to do his duty so well as he has done! I remember hearing such another humane being, that brave old admiral Sir Charles Wager,[4] say, that in his life he had never killed a fly.

This demolition of the Spanish armada is a great event—a very good one, if it prevents a battle between Lord Howe and the combined fleets,[5] as I should hope; and yet better if it produces peace; the only political crisis to which I look with eagerness. Were that happy moment arrived, there is ample matter to employ our great men, if we have any, in retrieving the affairs of this country, if they are to be retrieved.—But though our sedentary politicians write abundance of letters in the newspapers, full of plans of public spirit, I doubt the nation is not sober enough to set about its own work in earnest. When none reform themselves, little good is to be expected. We see by the excess of highwaymen how far evils will go before any attempt is made to cure them. I am sure, from the magnitude of this inconvenience, that I am not talking merely like an old man. I have lived here above thirty years, and used to go every where round at all hours of the night without any precaution. I cannot now stir a mile from my own house after sunset without one or two servants with blunderbusses. I am not surprised your Lordship's pheasants were stolen: a woman was taken last Saturday night loaded with nine geese, and they say has impeached a gang of fourteen

1. Gen. Sir George Augustus Eliott (1717–90), K.B., 1783; cr. (1787) Bn Heathfield; Gov. of Gibraltar 1776–90.

2. HW heard this news from Conway before 1 Oct. 1782, see OSSORY ii. 358, also MANN ix. 326–7 and nn. 2–7.

3. HW heard this from Conway (Ossory, loc. cit.). 'Governor Elliot made

every exertion which his humanity dictated to him to save as many of them as possible' (Daily Adv. 2 Oct.).

4. Adm. Sir Charles Wager (ca 1666–1743), Kt, 1709; M.P.

5. Howe arrived safely at Gibraltar, 11 Oct., without being intercepted (MANN ix. 330, n. 10, 336, n. 2).

house-breakers—but these are undergraduates—when they should have taken their doctor's degrees, they would not have piddled in such little game. Those Regius Professors the nabobs have taught men not to plunder for farthings.

I am very sensible of your Lordship's kindness to my nephew Mr C——.[6] He is a sensible, well-behaved young man, and, I trust, would not have abused your goodness.

Mr Mason writes to me,[7] that he shall be at York[8] at the end of this month. I was to have gone to Nuneham; but the house is so little advanced, that it is a question whether they can receive me.[9] Mason, I doubt, has been idle there. I am sure, if he found no muses there, he could pick up none at Oxford, where there is not so much as a bed-maker that ever lived in a muse's family.

Tonton[10] begs his duty to all the lambs, and trusts that Lady Strafford will not reject his homage.

I am ever her Ladyship's and your Lordship's

Most devoted humble servant,

Hor. Walpole

To Strafford, Tuesday 24 June 1783

Printed from *Works* v. 486–9; reprinted, Wright vi. 190–3, Cunningham viii. 381–3, Toynbee xiii. 14–17.

Strawberry Hill, June 24, 1783.

THOUGH your Lordship's partiality extends even to my letters, you must perceive that they grow as antiquated as the writer. News are the soul of letters: when we give them a body of our own in-

6. Perhaps George James Cholmondeley (1752–1830), son of HW's nephew the Rev. Hon. Robert Cholmondeley. HW recommended him to Mann in the following year (MANN ix. 418).

7. Mason to HW 26 Sept. 1782 (MASON ii. 274), written from Nuneham.

8. 'On the 30th I must be at York' (ibid.).

9. 'Our *lambris-doré* and all our other Frencheries go on so slowly that I have my doubts whether we shall be able to receive the party that you were to have come with this next month' (ibid.).

10. The dog bequeathed to HW by Mme du Deffand.

vention, it is as unlike to life as a statue. I have withdrawn so much from the world, that the newspapers know everything before me, especially since they have usurped the province of telling everything, private as well as public; and consequently a great deal more than I should wish to know, or like to report. When I do hear the transactions of much younger people, they do not pass from my ears into my memory; nor does your Lordship interest yourself more about them than I do. Yet still, when one reduces one's department to such narrow limits, one's correspondence suffers by it. However, as I desire to show only my gratitude and attachment, not my wit, I shall certainly obey your Lordship as long as you are content to read my letters, after I have told you fairly how little they can entertain you.

For imports of French, I believe we shall have few more. They have not ruined us so totally by the war, much less enriched themselves so much by it, but that they[1] who have been here, complained so piteously of the expensiveness of England, that probably they will deter others from a similar jaunt—nor, such is their fickleness, are the French constant to anything but admiration of themselves. Their *anglomanie* I hear has mounted—or descended—from our customs to our persons. English people are in fashion at Versailles. A Mr ——,[2] who wrote some pretty verses at Bath two or three years ago, is a favourite there. One who was so, or may be still, the *beau Dillon*,[3] came upon a very different errand—in short, to purchase at any price a book written by Linguet,[4] which was just coming out, called *Antoinette*.[5] That will tell your Lordship why the *beau Dillon* was the messenger.

Monsieur de Guignes[6] and his daughters[7] came hither—but it was

1. HW mentions some of these French visitors in his letter to Mann, 29 May 1783 (MANN ix. 408–9, and nn. 16–21).

2. George Ellis (1753–1815), author of *Poetical Tales by Sir Gregory Gander*, 1778; M.P.

3. Édouard (1750–1839), Comte Dillon, an Englishman who became an army officer and diplomatist in the French service. He was a member of Marie-Antoinette's circle at the Petit Trianon (*Dictionnaire de biographie française*, 1933– , xi. 359–60).

4. Simon-Nicolas-Henri Linguet (1736–94), lawyer and writer, who had been re-

leased from the Bastille in 1782, and had gone to England (NBG).

5. Presumably an attack upon Marie-Antoinette, but no book of this title is listed in Linguet's works.

6. Adrien-Louis de Bonnières (1735–1806), Comte and (1776) Duc de Guines; French ambassador to England, 1770–6 (MANN vii. 256, n. 16; DU DEFFAND *passim*). The visit to SH was presumably on 16 June (OSSORY ii. 402–3).

7. Marie-Louise-Philippine de Bonnières de Guines (d. 1796), m. (1778) Armand-Charles-Augustin de La Croix, Comte de Charlus, later Marquis and Duc de

at eight o'clock at night in the height of the deluge. You may be sure I was much flattered by such a visit! I was forced to light candles to show them anything; and must have lighted the moon to show them the views. If this is their way of seeing England, they might as well look at it with an opera glass from the shore of Calais.[8]

Mr Mason is to come to me on Sunday, and will find me mighty busy in making my lock of hay, which is not yet cut. I don't know why, but people are always more anxious about their hay than their corn, or twenty other things that cost them more. I suppose my Lord Chesterfield, or some such dictator, made it fashionable to care about one's hay.—Nobody betrays solicitude about getting in his rents.

We have exchanged spring and summer for autumn and winter, as well as day for night. If religion or law enjoined people to love light and prospects and verdure, I should not wonder if perverseness made us hate them—no, nor if society made us prefer living always in town to solitude and beauty.—But that is not the case. The most fashionable hurry into the country at Christmas and Easter, let the weather be ever so bad—and the finest ladies, who will go no whither till eleven at night, certainly pass more tiresome hours in London alone than they would in the country.—But all this is no business of mine: they do what they like, and so do I—And I am exceedingly tolerant about people who are perfectly indifferent to me. The sun and the seasons were not gone out of fashion when I was young—and I may do what I will with them now I am old: for fashion is fortunately no law but to its devotees. Were I five-and-twenty, I dare to say, I should think every whim of my cotemporaries very wise, as I did then. In one light I am always on the side of the young; for they only silently despise those who do not conform to their ordinances; but age is very apt to be angry at the change of customs, and partial to others no better founded. It is happy when we are occupied by nothing more serious. It is happy for a nation, when mere fashions are a topic that can employ its attention; for though dissipation may lead to graver moments, it commences with ease and tranquillity; and they at least who live before the scene shifts are fortunate, considering and comparing themselves with the various regions who enjoy

Castries, and Marie-Louise-Charlotte de Bonnières de Guines (d. 1792), m. (1782) Charles-Philibert-Gabriel Le Clerc, Comte, later (1807) Marquis de Juigné (OSSORY ii. 403, n. 10).

8. HW describes this visit more fully to Lady Ossory 20 June 1783 (OSSORY ii. 402–4).

no parallel felicity. I confess my reflections are *couleur de rose* at present. I did not much expect to live to see peace, without far more extensive ruin than has fallen on us. I will not probe futurity in search of less agreeable conjectures. Prognosticators may see many seeds of dusky hue—but I am too old to look forwards. Without any omens, common sense tells one, that in the revolution of ages nations must have unprosperous periods.—But why should I torment myself for what may happen in twenty years after my death, more than for what may happen in two hundred? Nor shall I be more interested in the one than in the other. This is no indifference for my country.—I wish it could always be happy—But so I do to all other countries. Yet who could ever pass a tranquil moment, if such future speculations vexed him?

Adieu, my good Lord!—I doubt this letter has more marks of senility than the one I announced at the beginning. When I had no news to send you, it was no reason for tiring you with commonplaces. —But your Lordship's indulgence spoils me. Does not it look as if I thought, that, because you commend my letters, you would like whatever I say? Will not Lady Strafford think that I abuse your patience? —I ask both your pardons—and am to both

A most devoted humble servant,

HOR. WALPOLE

To STRAFFORD, Friday 1 August 1783

Printed from *Works* v. 489–91; reprinted, Wright vi. 193–6, Cunningham viii. 391–3; Toynbee xiii. 33–6.

Strawberry Hill, August 1, 1783.

IT would be great happiness indeed to me, my dear Lord, if such nothings as my letters could contribute to any part of your Lordship's; but as your own partiality bestows their chief merit on them, you see they owe more to your friendship than to the writer. It is not my interest to depreciate them; much less to undermine the foundation of their sole worth. Yet it would be dishonest not to warn your Lordship, that if my letters have had any intrinsic recommendation, they must lose of it every day. Years and frequent returns of gout have made a ruin of me. Dullness, in the form of indolence, grows upon me. I am inactive, lifeless, and so indifferent to most things, that I neither inquire after nor remember any topics that might enliven my letters. Nothing is so insipid as my way of passing my time. But I need not specify what my letters speak.—They can have no spirit left—and would be perfectly inanimate, if attachment and gratitude to your Lordship were as liable to be extinguished by old age as our more amusing qualities. I make no new connections; but cherish those that remain with all the warmth of youth and the piety of grey hairs.

The weather here has been, and is, with very few intervals, sultry to this moment. I think it has been of service to me; though by over-heating myself I had a few days of lameness. The harvest is half over already all round us, and so pure, that not a poppy or cornflower is to be seen. Every field seems to have been weeded like B——'s[1] bowling-green. If Ceres, who is at least as old as many of our fashionable ladies, loves tricking herself out in flowers as they do, she must be mortified; and with more reason; for she looks well always with top-knots of ultramarine and vermilion, which modern goddesses do not for half so long as they think they do. As providence showers so many blessings on us, I wish the peace may confirm them! Necessary I am sure it was—and when it cannot restore us, where should we have been, had the war continued! Of our situation and prospect I confess my opinion is melancholy—not from present politics, but from past. We flung away the most brilliant position—I doubt, for a long season! With politics I have totally done. I wish the present ministers may last; for I think better of their principles than of those of their opponents (with a few salvos on both sides), and so I do of their abilities.—But it would be folly in me to concern myself about new generations.—How little a way can I see of their progress!

I am rather surprised at the new Countess of Denbigh.[2] How could a woman be ambitious of resembling Prometheus, to be pawed and clawed and gnawed by a vulture?[3] I beg your Earldom's pardon; but I could not conceive that a coronet was so very tempting!

1. Expanded by Toynbee to 'Brisco.' Stafford Briscoe (ca 1713–89) was a silver-smith living at Twickenham (Mason i. 447, n. 23).

2. Sarah Farnham (1741–1814), m. 1 (1769) Sir Charles Haldford, 7th Bt; m.

2 (21 July 1783) Basil Feilding, 6th E. of Denbigh, 1755. HW had mentioned her marriage to Lady Ossory 4 Aug. 1783 (Ossory ii. 412).

3. HW describes Denbigh as 'a disagree-able suitor' (ibid.).

Lady Browne is quite recovered—unless she relapses from what we suffer at Twickenham Park from a Lord Northesk,[4] an old seaman, who is come to Richmond on a visit to the Duke of Montrose.[5] I think the poor man must be out of his senses—at least he talks us out of ours. It is the most incessant and incoherent rhapsody that ever was heard. He sits by the card-table, and pours on Mrs Noel[6] all that ever happened in his voyages or his memory. He details the ship's allowance, and talks to her as if she was his first mate. Then in the mornings he carries his daughter[7] to town to see St Paul's, and the Tower, and Westminster Abbey; and at night disgorges all he has seen; till we don't know the ace of spades from Queen Elizabeth's pocket-pistol in the armoury.[8] Mercy on us!—And mercy on your Lordship too! Why should you be stunned with that alarum? Have you had your earthquake, my Lord? Many have had theirs. I assure you I have had mine. Above a week ago, when broad awake, the doors of the cabinet by my bedside rattled, without a breath of wind.[9] I imagined somebody was walking on the leads, or had broken into the room under me. It was between four and five in the morning. I rang my bell. Before my servant[10] could come it happened again; and was exactly like the horizontal tremor I felt from the earthquake some years ago.[11] As I had rung once, it is plain I was awake. I rang again; but heard nothing more. I am quite persuaded there was some commotion; nor is it surprising that the dreadful eruptions of fire on the coasts of Italy and Sicily[12] should have occasioned some alteration that has extended faintly hither, and contributed to the heats and mists that have been so extraordinary.[13] George Montagu said of our last earthquake, that it was so tame you might have stroked it.[14] It is comfortable to live where one can reason on them without

---

4. George Carnegie (1716–92), 6th E. of Northesk; Adm., 1770 (John Charnock, *Biographia navalis*, 1794–8, v. 109–11).

5. William Graham (1712–90), 2d D. of Montrose, 1742.

6. Mrs Noel, a 'near relation' of the Manners family, was a member of the Duchess of Montrose's circle (Mann ix. 187, n. 11).

7. Presumably his youngest (and only unmarried) daughter, Lady Mary Anne Carnegie (1764–98), m. (1797) Rev. John Kemp (*Scots Peerage*, vi. 504).

8. Contemporary guide-books to the Tower do not mention this pistol in the Armoury.

9. HW also mentions this earthquake to Lady Ossory 4 Aug. 1783 (Ossory ii. 409). Slight earthquakes in England in August were reported (ibid. n. 1).

10. Presumably HW's valet, Philip Colomb (d. 1799) (Mann viii. 211, n. 5).

11. Probably in 1750 (HW to Mann 11 March 1750 OS, Mann iv. 130).

12. The earthquake and volcanic eruption of 5–7 Feb. in Calabria and Sicily, when many 'perished in the flames of the volcano' (Mann ix. 374–6).

13. HW and others often spoke of hot weather as 'earthquake weather' (Mann iv. 119, v. 268, viii. 442, ix. 392).

14. For HW's other mentions, 1765–79,

dreading them! What satisfaction should you have in having erected such a monument of your taste, my Lord, as Wentworth Castle, if you did not know but it might be overturned in a moment and crush you? Sir William Hamilton[15] is expected: he has been groping in all those devastations.—Of all vocations I would not be a professor of earthquakes! I prefer studies that are *couleur de rose*—nor would ever think of calamities, if I can do nothing to relieve them. Yet this is a weakness of mind that I do not defend. They are more respectable who can behold philosophically the great theatre of events —or rather this little theatre of ours! In some ampler sphere, they may look on the catastrophe of Messina[16] as we do on kicking to pieces an ant-hill.

Bless me! what a farrago is my letter! It is like the extracts of books in a monthly magazine—I had no right to censure poor Lord Northesk's ramblings! Lady Strafford will think he has infected me. Goodnight, my dear Lord and Lady!

Your ever devoted

Hor. Walpole

To Strafford, Friday 12 September 1783

Printed from *Works* v. 491–3; reprinted, Wright vi. 199–201, Cunningham viii. 408–9, Toynbee xiii. 54–6.

Strawberry Hill, Sept. 12, 1783.

YOUR Lordship tells me you hope my summer has glided pleasantly, like our Thames. I cannot say it has passed very pleasantly to me, though, like the Thames, dry and low; for somehow or other I caught a rheumatic fever in the great heats, and cannot get rid of it. I have just been at Park Place and Nuneham,[1] in hopes change of air would cure me; but to no purpose. Indeed, as want of sleep is my chief complaint, I doubt I must make use of a very differ-

of this witticism, see Ossory ii. 93, n. 9.

15. (1730–1803), K.B., 1772; M.P.; English envoy to Naples; HW's correspondent. He was at Court on 13 Aug. (Mann ix. 427, n. 3).

16. Where the chief devastation oc-

curred in the Calabrian earthquake of 5–7 Feb. (n. 12 above).

———

1. HW went to Park Place 2 Sept. and from there to Nuneham, returning to SH by 9 Sept. (Mann ix. 428; Ossory ii. 415, 417).

ent and more disagreeable remedy, the air of London, the only place that I ever find agree[s] with me when I am out of order. I was there for two nights a fortnight ago, and slept perfectly well. In vain has my predilection for Strawberry made me try to persuade myself that this was all fancy; but I fear, reasons that appear strong, though contrary to our inclinations, must be good ones. London at this time of year is as nauseous a drug as any in an apothecary's shop. I could find nothing at all to do, and so went to Astley's,[2] which indeed was much beyond my expectation. I do not wonder any longer that Darius was chosen king by the instructions he gave to his horse; nor that Caligula made his consul. Astley can make his dance minuets and hornpipes;[3] which is more extraordinary than to make them vote at an election, or act the part of a magistrate, which animals of less capacities can perform as dextrously as a returning officer or a master in chancery. —But I shall not have even Astley now. Her Majesty the Queen of France, who has as much taste as Caligula, has sent for the whole dramatis personas to Paris.[4]

Sir William Hamilton was at Park Place, and gave us dreadful accounts of Calabria: he looks much older, and has the patina of a bronze.

At Nuneham I was much pleased with the improvements both within doors and without. Mr Mason was there; and, as he shines in every art, was assisting Mrs Harcourt[5] with his new discoveries in painting, by which he will unite miniature and oil.[6] Indeed, she is a very apt and extraordinary scholar. Since our professors seem to have lost the art of colouring, I am glad at least that they have ungraduated assessors.

We have plenty and peace at last![7] consequently leisure for repairing some of our losses, if we have sense enough to set about the task. On what will happen I shall make no conjectures, as it is not likely I should see much of what is to come. Our enemies have humbled us

2. Philip Astley (ca 1742–1814) kept an 'Amphitheatre Riding House' in Lambeth (OSSORY ii. 317, n. 9).

3. John Astley (ca 1767–1821), son of Philip, danced minuets on running horses (ibid. ii. 418, n. 24).

4. For Astley's amphitheatre at Paris, see ibid. ii. 515, n. 16. John Astley's departure for Paris is mentioned in MANN ix. 451.

5. Mary Danby (1749–1833), m. 1 (1772)

Thomas Lockhart; m. 2 (1778) Hon. William Harcourt, 3d E. Harcourt, 1809.

6. Mason's 'marriage of oil and watercolours' (HW to Mason 22 Sept. 1783, MASON ii. 311 and n. 3).

7. The preliminary treaty with Holland had been signed 2 Sept. (MANN ix. 437, n. 6); the preliminaries with France and Spain had been signed in January (ibid. ix. 356, n. 1) and those with the United States in Nov. 1782 (ibid. ix. 347, n. 4).

enough to content them; and we have succeeded so ill in innovations, that surely we shall not tempt new storms in haste.

From this place I can send your Lordship nothing new or entertaining, nor expect more game in town, whither nothing but search of health should carry me. Perhaps it is a vain chase at my age—but at my age one cannot trust to nature's operating cures without aiding her—it is always time enough to abandon one's self, when no care will palliate our decays. I hope your Lordship and Lady Strafford will long be in no want of such attentions: nor should I have talked so much of my own cracks, had I had anything else to tell you. It would be silly to aim at vivacity when it is gone: and though a lively old man is sometimes an agreeable being, a pretending old man is ridiculous. Aches and an apothecary cannot give one genuine spirits. 'Tis sufficient if they do not make one peevish. Your Lordship is so kind as to accept of me as I am, and you shall find nothing more counterfeit in me than the sincere respect and gratitude with which I have the honour to be

> Your Lordship's most devoted humble servant,
>
> Hor. Walpole

To Strafford, Saturday 11 October 1783

Printed from *Works* v. 493–5; reprinted, Wright vi. 201–3, Cunningham viii. 417–18, Toynbee xiii. 69–71.

> Strawberry Hill, October 11, 1783.

MY RHEUMATISM, I thank your Lordship, is certainly better, though not quite gone. It was very troublesome at night till I took the bark; but that medicine makes me sleep like opium—But I will say no more about it, nothing is so troublesome as to talk of chronical complaints: has one any right to draw on the compassion of others, when one must renew the address daily and for months?

The aspect of Ireland is very tempestuous. I doubt they will hurt us materially without benefiting themselves. If they obtain very short parliaments, they will hurt themselves more than us, by introducing a confusion that will prevent their improvements.[1]—Whatever country does adopt short parliaments, will, I am entirely persuaded, be forced to recur to their former practice—I mean, if the disorders introduced do not produce despotism of some sort or other. I am very sorry Mr Mason concurs in trying to revive the Associations.[2] Methinks our state is so deplorable, that every healing measure ought to be attempted instead of innovations. For my own part, I expect nothing but distractions, and am not concerned to be so old. I *am* so old, that, were I disposed to novelties, I should think they little became my age. I should be ashamed, when my hour shall come, to be caught in a riot of country squires and parsons, and haranguing a mob with a shaking head. A leader of faction ought to be young and vigorous. If an aged gentleman does get an ascendant, he may be sure that younger men are counting on his exit, and only flatter him to succeed to his influence, while they are laughing at his misplaced activity. At least, these would be my thoughts, who of all things dread being a jest to the juvenile, if they find me out of my sphere.

I have seen Lord Carlisle's play,[3] and it has a great deal of merit—perhaps more than your Lordship would expect. The language and images are the best part, after the two principal scenes, which are really fine.

I did, as your Lordship knows and says, always like and esteem Lady F——.[4] I scarce know my Lord; but, from what I have heard of him in the House of Lords, have conceived a good opinion of his sense: of his character I never heard any ill—which is a great testimonial in his favour, when there are so many horrid characters, and when all that are conspicuous have their minutest actions tortured to depose against them.

You may be sure, my dear Lord, that I heartily pity Lady Strafford's and your loss of four-legged friends. Sense and fidelity are wonderful recommendations; and when one meets with them, and can

1. 'If an army of Volunteers carry a reform of Parliament will an army stop there? A popish army, fine reformers of a Protestant constitution!' ('Mem. 1783–91' sub Oct. 1783). See also *post* HW to Strafford 10 Nov. 1783, nn. 5–6; MASON ii. 314, n. 10. Annual or triennial parliaments were suggested (R. B. McDowell, *Irish Public Opinion 1750–1800*, 1944, p. 90).

2. On 1 Oct., Mason had attended at York a meeting of the Committee of Association (MASON ii. 313, n. 2).

3. *The Father's Revenge*, 1783, privately printed, by Lord Carlisle; HW's copy is Hazen, *Cat. of HW's Lib.*, No. 3222:20:2.

4. Expanded by Toynbee to 'Fitzwilliam.' Lady Charlotte Ponsonby (1747–1822), m. (1770) William Fitzwilliam (1748–1833), 2d E. Fitzwilliam, 1756; Lord Rockingham's nephew and heir.

be confident that one is not imposed upon, I cannot think that the two additional legs are any drawback. At least I know that I have had friends who would never have vexed or betrayed me, if they had walked on all fours.

I have no news to send your Lordship—indeed I inquire for none, nor wish to hear any. Whence is any good to come? I am every day surprised at hearing people eager for news. If there is any, they are sure of hearing it.—How can one be curious to know one does not know what—and perpetually curious to know? Has one nothing to do but to hear and relate something new?—And why can one care about nothing but what one does not know?—And why is every event worth hearing, only because one has not heard it? Have not there been changes enough? divorces enough? bankruptcies and robberies enough?—and, above all, lies enough?—No; or people would not be every day impatient for the newspaper. I own, I am glad on Sunday when there is no paper, and no fresh lies circulating. Adieu, my good Lord and Lady! May you long enjoy your tranquillity, undisturbed by villainy, folly and madness!

Your most faithful servant,

Hor. Walpole

To Strafford, Monday 10 November 1783

Printed from *Works* v. 495–6; reprinted, Wright vi. 209–10, Cunningham viii. 429–31, Toynbee xiii. 85–7.

Berkeley Square, November 10, 1783.

IF I consulted my reputation as a writer, which your Lordship's partiality is so kind as to allot me, I should wait a few days till my granary is fuller of stock, which probably it would be by the end of next week—but in truth, I had rather be a grateful, and consequently a punctual correspondent, than an ingenious one; as I value the honour of your Lordship's friendship more than such tinsel bits of fame as can fall to my share, and of which I am particularly sick at present, as the *Public Advertiser* dressed me out t'other day[1] with a

1. By printing bits of HW's *Mysterious Mother* (Ossory ii. 429, n. 8; HW to Woodfall 8 Nov. 1783).

heap of that dross, which he had pillaged from some other strolling playwrights, who I did not desire should be plundered for me.

Indeed, when the Parliament does meet,[2] I doubt, nay hope it will make less sensation than usual. The orators of Dublin have brought the flowers of Billingsgate to so high perfection, that ours comparatively will have no more scent than a dead dandelion. If your Lordship has not seen the speeches of Mr Flood[3] and Mr Grattan,[4] you may perhaps still think that our oyster-women can be more abusive than members of Parliament.

Since I began my letter, I hear that the meeting of the delegates from the Volunteers is adjourned to the first of February.[5] This seems a very favourable circumstance. I don't like a reformation begun by a popish army! Indeed I did hope that peace would bring us peace, at least not more than the discords incidental to a free government: but we seem not to have attained that era yet! I hope it will arrive, though I may not see it. I shall not easily believe that any radical alteration of a constitution that preserved us so long and carried us to so great a height, will recover our affairs. There is a wide difference between correcting abuses, and removing landmarks. Nobody disliked more than I the strides that were attempted towards increasing the prerogative; but as the excellence of our constitution above all others, consists in the balance established between the three powers of King, Lords, and Commons, I wish to see that equilibrium preserved. No single man, nor any private junto, has a right to dictate laws to all three. In Ireland, truly, a still worse spirit I apprehend to be at bottom—in short, it is frenzy or folly to suppose that an army composed of three parts of Catholics[6] can be intended for any good purposes.

2. 11 Nov. (MANN ix. 437, and n. 1).

3. Henry Flood (1732–91), Irish and British M.P. (ibid. ix. 438, n. 8).

4. Henry Grattan (1746–1820), Irish M.P.; later M.P. in the United Kingdom (ibid. ix. 438, n. 7). After he accepted a Parliamentary grant in 1782, he had been denounced by other Irish leaders, especially Flood with whom he had an altercation in the Irish House of Commons on 28 Oct. (ibid. ix. 438, n. 9).

5. The grand national convention of the Volunteer delegates met 10 Nov.– 2 Dec. 1783. They agreed upon resolutions for Parliamentary reform which Flood proposed in the Irish House of Commons but which were defeated. They then voted a 'most loyal, decent modest Address to the King,' and closed their session (ibid. ix. 438, n. 12 and HW to Mann ca 6 Dec. 1783, ibid. ix. 453 and nn. 3–5).

6. 'For at least the first three years of their existence, the Irish Volunteers were essentially a non-Catholic body, and . . . [the] Volunteer corps closed their existence as Protestant in personnel and sentiment as they had begun' (Patrick Rogers, *The Irish Volunteers and Catholic Emancipation*, 1934, p. 57).

These are my sentiments, my dear Lord, and, you know, very disinterested. For myself, I have nothing to wish but ease and tranquillity for the rest of my time. I have no enmities to avenge. I do hope the present administration[7] will last, as I believe there are *more* honest men in it, than in any set that could replace them, though I have not a grain of partiality more than I had for their associates. Mr Fox I think by far the ablest and soundest head in England, and am persuaded that the more he is tried the greater man he will appear.

Perhaps it is impertinent to trouble your Lordship with my creed —it is certainly of no consequence to anybody—but I have nothing else that could entertain you—and at so serious a crisis, can one think of trifles? In general I am not sorry that the nation is most disposed to trifle—the less it takes part, the more leisure will the ministers have to attend to the most urgent points. When so many individuals assume to be legislators, it is lucky that very few obey their institutes.

I rejoice to hear of Lady Strafford's good health, and am her and your Lordship's

Most faithful humble servant,

Hor. Walpole

To Strafford, Thursday 11 December 1783

Printed from *Works* v. 497–8; reprinted, Wright vi. 211–13, Cunningham viii. 443–5, Toynbee xiii. 100–2.

Berkeley Square, Dec. 11, 1783.

YOUR Lordship is so partial to me and my idle letters, that I am afraid of writing them—not lest they should sink below the standard you have pleased to affix to them in your own mind, but from fear of being intoxicated into attempting to keep them up to it, which would destroy their only merit, their being written naturally and without pretensions. Gratitude and good breeding compel me to make due answers; but I entreat your Lordship to be assured, that however vain I am of your favour, my only aim is to preserve the honour of your friendship; that it is all the praise I ask or wish; and that, with regard to letter-writing, I am firmly persuaded that it is a province in which women will always shine superiorly; for our sex is

---

7. The Duke of Portland was first lord of the Treasury, but resigned, with North and Fox, in December (Mann ix. 460, nn. 1, 2).

too jealous of the reputation of good sense, to condescend to hazard a thousand trifles and negligences, which give grace, ease and familiarity to correspondence.—I will say no more on that subject, for I feel that I am on the brink of a dissertation—and though that fault would prove the truth of my proposition, I will not punish your Lordship only to convince you that I am in the right.

The winter is not dull or disagreeable: on the contrary, it is pleasing, as the town is occupied on general subjects, and not, as is too common, on private scandal, private vices and follies. The India Bill,[1] air-balloons,[2] Vestris[3] and the automaton,[4] share all attention. Mrs Siddons,[5] as less a novelty, does not engross all conversation. If abuse still keeps above par, it confines itself to its prescriptive province, the ministerial line. In that walk it has tumbled a little into the kennel—The low buffoonery of Lord ——,[6] in laying the caricatura of the Coalition[7] on the table of your Lordship's house, has levelled it to Sadler's Wells;[8] and Mr Flood,[9] the pillar of invective, does not promise to re-erect it—not, I conclude, from want of having imported a stock of ingredients, but his presumptuous début on the very night of his entry was so wretched, and delivered in so barbarous a brogue, that I question whether he will ever recover the blow Mr Courtenay[10] gave him. A young man may correct and improve, and rise from a first fall; but an elderly formed speaker has not an equal chance. Mr H——,[11] Lord A——'s[12] heir, but by no means so laconic, had more

1. Charles Fox's first and second India Bills, both ordered on 18 Nov. (MANN ix. 448, n. 4).

2. For the popularity of balloon flights in England and France, see ibid. ix. 449, nn. 7–11.

3. See ante HW to Strafford 13 June 1781.

4. Not explained.

5. Sarah Kemble (1755–1831), m. (1773) William Siddons; actress. For HW's opinion of her, see OSSORY ii. 359–60, iii. 2.

6. Expanded to 'Thurlow' by Toynbee, but HW must have written 'Abingdon.' 'Lord Abingdon's buffoon speech, offering the print of the Coalition to the Lords' is mentioned in HW's 'Mem. 1783–91' sub [2] Dec. He was Willoughby Bertie (1740–99), 4th E. of Abingdon, 1760. His speech and the print were published as a broadside, 15 Dec. (Debrett's Parliamentary Register, 1783, xiv. 12–16).

7. 'The Coalition Dissected,' published 12 Aug. (Satiric Prints v. 727).

8. A theatre for tumbling, rope-dancing, etc. at Sadler's Wells, Islington' (London Adviser and Guide, 1790, p. 175, cited in London Past and Present iii. 200).

9. He had come over from Ireland 8 Dec. and entered Parliament that night as M.P. for Winchester, attacking the India Bill (Sir Lewis Namier and John Brooke, House of Commons 1754–1790, 1964, ii. 441).

10. John Courtenay (1738–1816), M.P. Tamworth 1780–96, Appleby 1796–1807, 1812, who 'turned him into complete ridicule,' 8 Dec. ('Mem. 1783–91').

11. Expanded by Toynbee to 'Hamilton.' John James Hamilton (1756–1818), who in 1789 succeeded his uncle as 9th E. of Abercorn. He was M.P. East Looe 1 Dec. 1783–1784, St Germans 1784–9.

12. See ante HW to Strafford 8 Sept. 1761.

success.[13] Though his first essay, it was not at all dashed by bashful-ness—and though he might have blushed for discovering so much personal rancour to Mr Fox, he rather seemed to be impatient to dis-charge it.

Your Lordship sees in the papers,[14] that the two houses of Ireland have firmly resisted the innovations of the Volunteers.[15] Indeed it was time for the Protestant proprietors to make their stand; for though the Catholics behave decently, it would be into their hands that the prize would fall. The delegates, it is true, have sent over a most loyal Address[16]—but I wish their actions may not contradict their words! Mr Flood's discomfiture here will, I suppose, carry him back to a field wherein his wicked spirit may have more effect. It is a very serious moment!—I am in pain lest your county, my dear Lord (you know what I mean), should countenance such pernicious de-signs.

I am impatient for next month, for the pleasure of seeing your Lordship and Lady Strafford, and am of both

The devoted humble servant,

Hor. Walpole

To Strafford, Friday 6 August 1784

Printed from *Works* v. 498–9; reprinted, Wright vi. 222–3, Cunningham viii. 490–1, Toynbee xiii. 172–3.

Strawberry Hill, August 6, 1784.

I AM very sorry, my dear Lord, that I must answer your Lordship's letter by a condolence. I had not the honour of being acquainted with Mrs Vyse,[1] but have heard so much good of her, that it is im-possible not to lament her.

13. His maiden speech, 8 Dec., attack-ing Fox's East India Bill (Namier and Brooke, op. cit. ii. 571).

14. *London Chronicle* 9–11 Dec., liv. 567.

15. On 29 Nov., Flood's reform pro-posals were turned down by the Irish Parliament (Mann ix. 453, n. 3).

16. Of 2 Dec., brought over to England by Flood and Brownlow (ibid. ix. 453, n. 5).

———

1. Anne Howard (d. 2 Aug. 1784), who m. Gen. Richard Vyse, was the dau. of Sir George Howard by Lord Strafford's sister, Lady Lucy Wentworth (GM 1784,

Since this month began, we have had fine weather, and 'twere great pity if we had not, when the earth is covered with such abundant harvests! They talk of an earthquake having been felt in London.[2] Had Sir W. Hamilton been there, he would think the town gave itself great airs. He I believe is *putting up* volcanoes in his own country. In my youth, philosophers were eager to ascribe every uncommon discovery to the deluge—now it is the fashion to solve every appearance by conflagrations. If there was such an inundation upon the earth, and such a furnace under it, I am amazed that Noah and company were not boiled to death. Indeed I am a great sceptic about human reasonings. They predominate only for a time, like other mortal fashions, and are so often exploded after the mode is passed, that I hold them little more serious, though they call themselves wisdom. How many have I lived to see established and confuted! For instance, the necessity of a southern continent as a balance was supposed to be unanswerable—and so it was, till Captain Cook[3] found there was no such thing. We are poor silly animals: we live for an instant upon a particle of a boundless universe, and are much like a butterfly that should argue about the nature of the seasons and what creates their vicissitudes, and does not exist itself to see one annual revolution of them!

Adieu, my dear Lord!—If my reveries are foolish, remember, I give them for no better. If I depreciate human wisdom, I am sure I do not assume a grain to myself, nor have anything to value myself upon more than being

Your Lordship's most obliged humble servant,

HOR. WALPOLE

liv. 637; DNB *sub* Vyse, Richard William Howard).

2. No earthquakes in London between 1758 and 1864 are recorded in Charles Davison, *History of British Earthquakes*, Cambridge, 1924, p. 336; Davison's 'Cata-

logue' (ibid. 16) lists no earthquakes anywhere in Britain in 1784.

3. *A Voyage to the Pacific Ocean* by Capt. James Cook (1728–79) had been published 4 June (Ossory ii. 436, n. 6).

To Strafford, Tuesday 7 September 1784

Printed from *Works* v. 499–500; reprinted, Wright vi. 225–7, Cunningham viii. 502–3, Toynbee xiii. 186–8.

Strawberry Hill, September 7, 1784.

THE summer is come at last, my Lord, dressed as fine as a Birthday, though not with so many flowers on its head. In truth, the sun is an old fool, who apes the modern people of fashion by arriving too late: the day is going to bed before he makes his appearance; and one has scarce time to admire his embroidery of green and gold. It was cruel to behold such expanse of corn everywhere, and yet see it all turned to a water-souchy.[1] If I could admire Dante, which, asking Mr Hayley's pardon,[2] I do not,[3] I would have written an olio of Jews and Pagans, and sent Ceres to reproach Master Noah with breaking his promise of the world never being drowned again.—But this last week has restored matters to their old channel; and I trust we shall have bread to eat next winter, or I think we must have lived on apples, of which to be sure there is enough to prevent a famine. This is all I know, my Lord; and I hope no news to your Lordship. I have exhausted the themes of air-balloons and highwaymen;[4] and if you *will* have my letters, you must be content with my commonplace chat on the seasons. I do nothing worth repeating, nor hear that others do: and though I am content to rust myself, I should be glad to tell your Lordship anything that would amuse you. I dined two days ago at Mrs Garrick's with Sir William Hamilton, who is returning to the kingdom of cinders.[5] Mrs Walsingham[6] was there with her son[7] and

1. 'Fish (properly perch) boiled and served in its own liquor' (OED, which remarks that HW used the term to denote 'a sodden mass'). HW wrote to Conway, 30 June 1784, about his hay crop becoming 'nothing but a water-souchy.'

2. William Hayley (1745–1820), whose *Essay on Epic Poetry*, 1782, was addressed to William Mason. HW's annotated copy is Hazen, *Cat. of HW's Lib.*, No. 3222:18:4.

3. HW called Dante a 'Methodist parson in Bedlam' (MASON ii. 256). Dr A. T. Hazen suggests that HW had been reading Charles Rogers's translation, 1782, of the *Inferno*, dedicated to Sir Edward

Walpole (Hazen, *Cat. of HW's Lib.*, No. 3222:18:3).

4. HW had described balloons to Mann 9 Aug. 1784 (MANN ix. 517), and robberies to Conway 14 Aug. 1784; similar accounts had probably been sent to Lord Strafford.

5. He started out before 30 Sept. (HW to Mann 30 Sept. 1784, MANN ix. 530).

6. Charlotte Hanbury Williams (1738–90), m. (1759) Hon. Robert Boyle, later Walsingham.

7. Richard Boyle (1762–88) (Sir Bernard Burke and A. P. Burke, *Peerage*, 1928, p. 2085).

daughter.[8] He is a very pleasing young man; a fine figure; his face like hers, with something of his grandfather Sir Charles Williams, without his vanity; very sensible, and uncommonly well bred. The daughter is an imitatress of Mrs Damer, and has modelled a bust of her brother. Mrs Damer herself is modelling two masks for the keystones of the new bridge at Henley.[9] Sir William, who has seen them, says they are in her true antique style. I am in possession of her sleeping dogs in terra cotta.[10] She asked me if I would consent to her executing them in marble for the Duke of Richmond?[11]—I said, 'Gladly; I should like they should exist in a more durable material'— but I would not part with the original, which is sharper and more alive. Mr Wyat[12] the architect saw them here lately; and said, he was sure that if the idea was given to the best statuary in Europe, he would not produce so perfect a group. Indeed, with these dogs and the riches I possess by Lady Di,[13] poor Strawberry may vie with much prouder collections.

Adieu, my good Lord! When I fold up a letter I am ashamed of it—but it is your own fault. The last thing I should think of would be troubling your Lordship with such insipid stuff, if you did not command it. Lady Strafford will bear me testimony how often I have protested against it.

I am her Ladyship's and your Lordship's obedient humble servant,

HOR. WALPOLE

8. Charlotte Boyle (1769–1831), m. (1791) Lord Henry Fitzgerald; she was Bns Ros or Roos, s.j., 1806.

9. 'Thame' and 'Isis' (HW to Mann 7 May 1785, MANN ix. 576 and nn. 3–7).

10. In the Little Parlour at SH ('Des. of SH,' Works ii. 418).

11. Her half-sister's husband.

12. James Wyatt (1746–1813), who later designed the Offices at SH.

13. The number of original drawings by Lady Diana Beauclerc, at Strawberry Hill (HW). Lady Diana Spencer (1734–1808) m. 1 (1757) Frederick St John, 2d Vct Bolingbroke; m. 2 (1768) Topham Beauclerk. Her drawings, illustrating HW's Mysterious Mother, were placed in the Beauclerk Closet at SH, and all but one are now WSL (OSSORY i. 289, 294–5).

To Strafford, Tuesday 29 August 1786

Printed from *Works* v. 501–2; reprinted, Wright vi. 271–2, Cunningham ix. 64–5, Toynbee xiii. 401–4.

Strawberry Hill, August 29, 1786.

SINCE I received the honour of your Lordship's last, I have been at Park Place for a few days. Lord and Lady Frederick Campbell[1] and Mrs Damer were there. We went on the Thames to see the new bridge at Henley, and Mrs Damer's colossal masks. There is not a sight in the island more worthy of being visited. The bridge is as perfect as if bridges were natural productions, and as beautiful as if it had been built for Wentworth Castle; and the masks, as if the Romans had left them here. We saw them in a fortunate moment; for the rest of the time was very cold and uncomfortable, and the evenings as chill as many we have had lately. In short, I am come to think that the beginning of an old ditty which passes for a collection of blunders, was really an old English pastoral, it is so descriptive of our climate:

> Three children sliding on the ice
> All on a summer's day—

I have been overwhelmed more than ever by visitants to my house. Yesterday I had Count Oghinski,[2] who was a pretender to the crown of Poland at the last election,[3] and has been stripped of most of a vast estate.[4] He had on a ring of the new King of Prussia[5]—or I should have wished him joy on the death of one of the plunderers of his country.[6]

It has long been my opinion that the out-pensioners of Bedlam are so numerous, that the shortest and cheapest way would be to confine in Moorfields[7] the few that remain in their senses, who would

1. Mary Meredith (ca 1738–1807), m. 1 (1752) Laurence Shirley, 4th E. Ferrers; m. 2 (1769) Lord Frederick Campbell.
2. Michal Kasimierz (1731–1800) Prince Oginski, hetman of Lithuania (Ossory ii. 511, n. 10). He visited SH on 27 Aug. according to HW's 'Book of Visitors,' Berry ii. 226.
3. In 1764 (Ossory ii. 511, n. 13).
4. In 1771, he had joined the Confedera-

tion of Bar against Stanislas II of Poland, but fled to France after his defeat by Suvorov (ibid. ii. 511, n. 12).
5. Frederick William II (1744–97), who had inherited the Prussian throne on the death of his uncle, Frederick II, 17 Aug. (Isenburg, *Stammtafeln* i. taf. 63).
6. Frederick II was one of the partitioners of Poland in 1772.
7. Bethlehem Royal Hospital, for the

then be safe; and let the rest go at large. They are the out-pensioners who are for destroying poor dogs! The whole canine race never did half so much mischief as Lord George Gordon; nor even worry hares, but when hallooed on by men. As it is a persecution of animals, I do not love hunting; and what old writers mention as a commendation, makes me hate it the more, its being an image of war. Mercy on us! that destruction of any species should be a sport or a merit! What cruel unreflecting imps we are! Everybody is unwilling to die, yet sacrifices the lives of others to momentary pastime, or to the still emptier vapour, fame! A hero or a sportsman who wishes for longer life, is desirous of prolonging devastation. We shall be crammed, I suppose, with panegyrics and epitaphs on the King of Prussia—I am content that he can now have an epitaph. But, alas! the Emperor will write one for him probably in blood! and, while he shuts up convents for the sake of population,[8] will be stuffing hospitals with maimed soldiers, besides making thousands of widows!—I have just been reading a new published history of the colleges in Oxford by Anthony Wood,[9] and there found a feature in a character that always offended me, that of Archbishop Chicheley,[10] who prompted Henry V to the invasion of France, to divert him from squeezing the overgrown clergy. When that priest meditated founding All Souls, and 'consulted his friends' (who seem to have been honest men) 'what great matter of piety he had best perform to God in his old age, he was advised by them to build an hospital for the[11] wounded and sick soldiers, that daily returned from the wars then had in France'—I doubt his Grace's friends thought as I do of his artifice—'But,' continues the historian, '*disliking those motions,*[12] and valuing the welfare of the deceased more than the wounded and diseased, he resolved with himself to promote his design'—which was, to have masses, said for the King, Queen, and himself, etc. while living, and for their

insane, generally known as Bedlam, was then situated in Moorfields, north of the City of London (*London Past and Present,* i. 171–3, ii. 560–1).

8. For Joseph II's suppression of convents in 1782, see MANN ix. 236, n. 7. HW wrote, 18 May 1782, 'I doubt he calculates, that the more copulation is encouraged, the more soldiers he shall have' (ibid. ix. 280).

9. Anthony à Wood (1632–95), *The History and Antiquities of the Colleges and* *Halls in the University of Oxford,* ed. John Gutch, Oxford, 1786. HW's copy is Hazen, *Cat. of HW's Lib.,* No. 3219.

10. Henry Chichele or Chicheley (ca 1362–1443), Abp of Canterbury, 1414, who in 1437–9 founded All Souls' College, Oxford.

11. Wood's text reads: 'for the entertainment of the wounded and sick soldiers' (p. 254).

12. The italics are HW's.

souls when dead.¹³—And that mummery the old foolish rogue thought more efficacious than ointments and medicines for the wretches he had made! And of the chaplains and clerks he instituted in that dormitory, one was to teach grammar, and another, prick-song¹⁴—How history makes one shudder and laugh by turns!—But I fear I have wearied your Lordship with my idle declamation, and you will repent having commanded me to send you more letters; and I can only plead that I am

Your (perhaps too) obedient humble servant,

Hor. Walpole

To Strafford, Saturday 28 July 1787

Printed from *Works* v. 502–4; reprinted, Wright vi. 283–5, Cunningham ix. 101–3, Toynbee xiv. 10–12.

Strawberry Hill, July 28, 1787.

ST SWITHIN¹ is no friend to correspondence, my dear Lord. There is not only a great sameness in his own proceedings, but he makes everybody else dull—I mean, in the country, where one frets at its raining every day and all day. In town he is no more minded than the proclamation against vice and immorality.² Still, though he has all the honours of the quarantaine, I believe it often rained for forty days³ long before St Swithin was born, if ever born he was;⁴ and the proverb was coined and put under his patronage, because people observed that it frequently does rain for forty days together at this season. I remember Lady Suffolk telling me, that Lord Dysart's⁵ great meadow had never been mowed but once in

13. 'To daily pray for the souls of the King, Queen, and of the said Archbishop, while they lived, and after their decease' (Wood, op. cit. 254–5).

14. There were to be eight chaplains, four clerks, and six choristers. 'Of which number of chaplains, or clerks, one was to teach grammar, and another pricksong' (ibid.).

———

1. St Swithin's Day was 15 July.

2. A proclamation, 1 June 1787, 'for the encouragement of piety and virtue, and the preventing and punishing of vice,

profaneness, and immorality' (*Handlist of Proclamations*, Wigan, 1913, p. 164, *Bibliotheca Lindesiana* Vol. VIII).

3. 'St Swithin's Day, if thou dost rain
    For forty days it will remain'
(William Hone, *Every-Day* Book, 1826–7, i. 955 cited in DNB *sub* Swithun).

4. The date of his birth is unknown, but he was consecrated Bishop of Winchester in 852, and died 2 July 862.

5. Lionel Tollemache (1708–70), 4th E. of Dysart, the father of the Lionel Tollemache (1734–99) who was husband of HW's niece, Charlotte Walpole. He lived

forty years without rain. I said, 'all that that proved was, that rain was good for hay,' as I am persuaded the climate of a country and its productions are suited to each other. Nay, rain is good for haymakers too, who get more employment the oftener the hay is made over again. I do not know who is the saint that presides over thunder; but he has made an unusual quantity in this chill summer, and done a great deal of serious mischief,[6] though not a fiftieth part of what Lord George Gordon did seven years ago—and happily he is fled.

Our little part of the world has been quiet as usual. The Duke of Queensberry[7] has given a sumptuous dinner to the Princesse de Lam-balle[8]—*et voilà tout*. I never saw her, not even in France.[9] I have no particular penchant for sterling princes and princesses, much less for those of French plate.

The only entertaining thing I can tell your Lordship from our district is, that old Madam French,[10] who lives close by the bridge at Hampton Court, where, between her and the Thames, she had nothing but one grass-plot of the width of her house, has paved that whole plot with black and white marble in diamonds, exactly like the floor of a church; and this curious metamorphosis of a garden into a pavement has cost her three hundred and forty pounds:—a tarpaulin she might have had for some shillings, which would have looked as well, and might easily have been removed. To be sure this exploit, and Lord Dudley's[11] obelisk *below* a hedge, with his canal at right angles with the Thames, and a sham bridge no broader than that of a violin, and *parallel* to the river,[12] are not preferable to the monsters in clipt yews of our ancestors;

Bad taste *expellas furcâ, tamen usque recurret.*[13]

at Ham House, Surrey, across the Thames from SH.

6. Violent storms in Somersetshire and at Birmingham, 24 May, were reported in GM 1787, lvii pt i. 541.

7. William Douglas (1725–1810), 3d E. of March; 4th D. of Queensberry, 1778.

8. Marie-Thérèse-Louise de Savoie-Ca-rignan (1749–92), m. (1767) Louis-Alex-andre-Joseph-Stanislas de Bourbon, Prince de Lamballe; she was a friend of Marie-Antoinette, and was killed in the French Revolution (DU DEFFAND i. 225, n. 9). She arrived in London 10 July (*London Chronicle* 24–6 July, lxii. 82).

9. HW mentions seeing her at the bal

paré at Versailles, 17 Aug. 1775 (HW to Lady Ossory 18 Aug. 1775, OSSORY i. 255).

10. Katherine Lloyd (d. 1791), m. (before 1743) Jeffry French (BERRY i. 57, n. 17; OSSORY ii. 285, n. 3).

11. John Ward (1725–88), 2d Vct Dudley and Ward, 1774; M.P.

12. All these circumstances actually existed till within these five years, at the villa of the late Viscount Dudley and Ward at Teddington (Mary Berry).

13. HW substitutes 'bad taste' for 'naturam' in 'Naturam expelles furcas tamen usque recurret' ('If you drive out Nature with a pitchfork; yet she will

On the contrary, Mrs Walsingham is making her house at Ditton[14] (now baptized Boyle Farm) very orthodox. Her daughter Miss Boyle,[15] who has real genius, has carved three tablets in marble with boys designed by herself.[16] Those sculptures are for a chimney-piece; and she is painting panels in grotesque for the library, with pilasters of glass in black and gold. Miss Crewe,[17] who has taste too, has decorated a room for her mother's[18] house at Richmond, which was Lady Margaret Compton's,[19] in a very pretty manner. How much more amiable the old women of the next age will be, than most of those we remember, who used to tumble at once from gallantry to devout scandal and cards! and revenge on the young of their own sex the desertion of ours. Now they are ingenious, they will not want amusement.

Adieu, my dear Lord! I am most gratefully

Your Lordship's very faithful humble servant,

HOR. WALPOLE

To STRAFFORD, Tuesday 17 June 1788

Printed from *Works* v. 504–6; reprinted, Wright vi. 291–3, Toynbee xiv. 48–50.

Strawberry Hill, Tuesday night, June 17, 1788.

I GUESS, my dear Lord, and only guess that you are arrived at Wentworth Castle. If you are not, my letter will lose none of its bloom by waiting for you; for I have nothing fresh to tell you, and only write because you enjoined it. I settled in my Lilliputian towers but this morning. I wish people would come into the country on May Day, and fix in town the first of November. But as they will not, I

soon come back,' Horace's Epistles I. x. 24).

14. Thames Ditton, Surrey (OSSORY ii. 573, n. 28).

15. Since married to Lord Henry Fitzgerald (HW).

16. See HW to the Hon. Mrs Boyle Walsingham 26 July 1787, and to Lady

Ossory 6 Sept. 1787 (OSSORY ii. 572 and n. 27).

17. Elizabeth Emma Crewe (d. 1850), m. (1809) Foster Cunliffe-Offley (MORE 287, n. 14).

18. Frances Anne Greville (d. 1818), m. (1766) John Crewe, cr. (1806) Bn Crewe.

19. (ca 1703–86) (MORE 199, n. 5).

have made up my mind; and having so little time left, I prefer London when my friends and society are in it, to living here alone, or with the weird sisters of Richmond and Hampton. I had additional reason now, for the streets are as green as the fields: we are burnt to the bone, and have not a lock of hay to cover our nakedness: oats are so dear, that I suppose they will soon be eaten at Brooks's and fashionable tables as a rarity. The drought has lasted so long, that for this fortnight I have been foretelling hay-making and winter, which June generally produces; but today is sultry, and I am not a prophet worth a straw. Though not resident till now, I have flitted backwards and forwards, and last Friday came hither to look for a minute at a ball at Mrs Walsingham's at Ditton; which would have been very pretty, for she had stuck coloured lamps in the hair of all her trees and bushes, if the east wind had not danced a reel all the time by the side of the river.

Mr Conway's play,[1] of which your Lordship has seen some account in the papers,[2] has succeeded delightfully both in representation and applause. The language is most genteel, though translated from verse; and both prologue and epilogue are charming. The former was delivered most justly and admirably by Lord Derby,[3] and the latter with inimitable spirit and grace by Mrs Damer. Mr Merry[4] and Mrs Bruce[5] played excellently too.—But General Conway, Mrs Damer, and everybody else are drowned by Mr Sheridan,[6] whose renown has engrossed all fame's tongues and trumpets.[7] Lord Townshend said he should be sorry were he forced to give a vote directly on Hastings, before he had time to cool; and one of the peers saying the speech

1. A comedy translated from *L'homme du jour* of Boissy. It was first acted at the private theatre at Richmond House, and afterwards at Drury Lane (HW). The play, called *False Appearances*, was translated from Louis de Boissy's *Les Dehors Trompeurs;* the first performance, 23 May, is described in *Passages from the Diaries of Mrs Philip Lybbe Powys,* ed. Climenson, 1899, p. 232; the last performance at Richmond House had been given on 14 June (MORE 263 and n. 1). HW's copy is Hazen, *Cat. of HW's Lib.,* No. 1810:47:9.

2. *The World,* 2 June 1788; *London Chronicle* 31 May–3 June, lxiii. 532.

3. Edward Smith Stanley (1752–1834), 12th E. of Derby, 1776, M.P.

4. Charles Merry (ca 1759–after 1789), Capt. (OSSORY ii. 586, n. 14).

5. Perhaps the Mrs Bruce who may have visited SH in the previous year (BERRY ii. 229).

6. Richard Brinsley Sheridan (1751–1816), the dramatist.

7. From the speech he made in Westminster Hall, on bringing the charge of cruelty to the Begums of the province of Benares in the trial of Mr Hastings (HW). Mrs Philip Lybbe Powys, *sub* 6 June, gives an account of the speech, which lasted four and a quarter hours (*Passages from the Diaries,* ed. Climenson, 1899, pp. 232–3).

had not made the same impression on him, the Marquis replied, a seal might be finely cut, and yet not be in fault for making a bad impression.

I have, you see, been forced to send your Lordship what scraps I brought from town: the next four months, I doubt, will reduce me to my old sterility; for I cannot retail French gazettes, though as a good Englishman bound to hope they will contain a civil war.[8] I care still less about the double imperial campaign,[9] only hoping that the poor dear Turks will heartily beat both Emperor and Empress. If the first Ottomans could be punished, they deserve it—but the present possessors have as good prescription on their side as any people in Europe. We ourselves are Saxons, Danes, Normans—our neighbours are Franks, not Gauls—who the rest are, Goths, Gepidæ, Heruli, Mr Gibbon knows—and the Dutch usurped the estates of herrings, turbots, and other marine indigenæ.—Still, though I do not wish the hair of a Turk's beard hurt, I do not say that it would not be amusing to have Constantinople taken—merely as a lusty event—for neither could I live to see Athens revive, nor have I much faith in two such bloody-minded vultures, cock and hen, as Catherine and Joseph, conquering for the benefit of humanity; nor does my Christianity admire the propagation of the gospel by the mouth of cannon. What desolation of peasants and their families by the episodes of forage and quarters!—Oh! I wish Catherine and Joseph were brought to Westminster Hall and worried by Sheridan! I hope too, that the poor Begums are alive to hear of his speech—it will be some comfort, though I doubt nobody thinks of restoring them a quarter of a lac!

Adieu, my dear Lord!

Yours most faithfully,

Hor. Walpole

8. 'Wednesday 11 [June]. The Duke of Orléans is said to have received an express, that the tumults in Brittany had arrived at such a height, that two regiments, of one of which he is colonel, were on their march to quell them; and that there were serious apprehensions for the dock-yard of Brest, lest it should be set on fire by the populace' (GM 1788, lviii pt i. 559).

9. The Imperial army, which was advancing towards Belgrade, suffered a defeat at Dubicza, and, by the end of May, the army was fortifying a camp on the Save. The Russians were inactive, being threatened by plague, and by the Swedes (GM 1788, lviii pt i. 550–1).

To Strafford, Saturday 2 August 1788

Printed from *Works* v. 506–7; reprinted, Wright vi. 297–9, Cunningham ix. 136–7, Toynbee xiv. 64–6.

Strawberry Hill, August 2, 1788.

MATTER for a letter, alas! my dear Lord, I have none—but *about* letters I have great news to tell your Lordship, only may the goddess of post offices grant it be true! A Miss Sayer[1] of Richmond, who is at Paris, writes to Mrs Boscawen,[2] that a Baron de la Garde[3] (I am sorry there are so many *a*'s in the genealogy of my story) has found in a *vieille armoire* five hundred more letters of Madame de Sévigny,[4] and that they will be printed, if the expense is not too great. I am in a taking lest they should not appear before I set out for the Elysian Fields;[5] for though the writer is one of the first personages I should inquire after on my arrival, I question whether St Peter has taste enough to know where she lodges: he is more likely to be acquainted with St Catherine of Sienna and St Undecimillia;[6] and therefore I had rather see the letters themselves. It is true I have no small doubt of the authenticity of the legend; and nothing will persuade me of its truth so much as the non-appearance of the letters—a melancholy kind of conviction. But I vehemently suspect some new coinage, like the letters of Ninon de l'Enclos,[7] Pope

1. Frances Julia Sayer (1757–1850) of Marsh House, Marsh Gate, Richmond, a cousin of Mrs Boscawen (see n. 2 below). She m. (1805) Marie-Charles-Joseph de Pougens (Berry i. 45, n. 30).

2. Frances Glanville (1719–1805), m. (1742) Hon. Edward Boscawen (Ossory i. 335, n. 13; HW to Mary Berry 29 July 1789, Berry i. 45).

3. Jean-Baptiste de Castellane (d. 1790), Marquis d'Esparron et de la Garde, had married Mme de Sévigné's great-grand-daughter (Ossory iii. 81, n. 12), but Lady Eleanor Butler wrote in her diary *sub* 23 Oct. and 4 Dec. 1788 that the letters were in the Château de la Garde, apparently in the possession of a Président de la Garde (*Hamwood Papers*, ed. E. M. Bell, 1930, pp. 142, 154).

4. Supposedly her letters to M. de la Grange (HW to Lady Ossory 26 Nov. 1789, Ossory iii. 81). No such cache of letters appeared at that time (ibid. n. 6).

5. Mme du Deffand's letter to HW, under the name of Mme de Sévigné, was headed 'Des Champs Elysées, point de succession de temps, point de date' (Du Deffand i. 51; the letter is reproduced in W. S. Lewis, *Horace Walpole's Letter from Madame de Sévigné*, Farmington, Conn., 1933, after p. iii).

6. St Ursula, so called because of the 11,000 virgins who were alleged to be her companions.

7. The *Lettres de Ninon de Lenclos au Marquis de Sévigné*, 1750, were by Louis Damours (d. 1788) (More 278, n. 11; *Dictionnaire de biographie française*, 1933– , x. 62). HW's copy is Hazen, *Cat. of HW's Lib.*, No. 1185.

Ganganelli,[8] and the Princess Palatine.[9] I have lately been reading some fragments of letters of the Duchess of Orléans, which are certainly genuine, and contain some curious circumstances; for though she was a simple gossiping old gentlewoman, yet many little facts she could not help learning: and to give her her due, she was ready to tell all she knew. To our late Queen[10] she certainly did write often; and her Majesty, then only Princess, was full as ready to pay her in her own coin: and a pretty considerable treaty of commerce for the exchange of scandal was faithfully executed between them; insomuch that I remember to have heard forty years ago, that our gracious sovereign entrusted her Royal Highness of Orléans with an intrigue of one of her women of the Bedchamber, Mrs S.[11] to wit; and the good Duchess entrusted it to so many other dear friends, that at last it got into the Utrecht Gazette,[12] and came over hither, to the signal edification of the court of Leicester Fields.[13] This is an additional reason, besides the internal evidence, for my believing the letters genuine. This old dame was mother of the Regent: and when she died, somebody wrote on her tomb, *Cy gist l'Oisiveté*. This came over too; and nobody could expound it, till our then third Princess, Caroline,[14] unravelled it—'Idleness is the mother of all vice.'

I wish well enough to posterity to hope that dowager highnesses will imitate the practice, and write all the trifles that occupy their royal brains; for the world so at least learns some true history, which their husbands never divulge; especially if they are privy to their own history, which their ministers keep from them as much as possible. I do not believe the present King of France knows much more of what

8. *Lettres intéressantes du Pape Clément XIV*, 1775, was a mixture of genuine and fictitious elements written by Louis-Antoine (1719–1803), Marquis de Caraccioli (*Dictionnaire de biographie française*, 1933– , vii. 1093–4; Bibliothèque Nationale Catalogue). English translations appeared in England and Ireland as *Interesting Letters of Pope Clement XIV (Ganganelli)*; see BM Cat.; More 278. Clement XIV (Giovanni Vincenzo Antonio Ganganelli 1705–74) was pope 1769–74.

9. Élisabeth-Charlotte (or Charlotte-Élisabeth) (1652–1722), m. (1671) Philippe, Duc d'Orléans; she was called 'La Princesse Palatine,' being the daughter of an Elector Palatine, but HW, below, refers to her as the Duchess of Orléans. Perhaps, as suggested in More 278, n. 13, HW had

read a criticism of the letters, without connecting them with the *Fragmens de lettres originales*, Hamburg and Paris, 1788, which he seems to regard as genuine (his copy is Hazen, *Cat. of HW's Lib.*, No. 3298).

10. Caroline, wife of George II.

11. Toynbee suggests Mrs Selwyn. Mary Farrington (ca 1690–1777), m. (ca 1708–9) Col. John Selwyn. She was mother of HW's correspondent, George Selwyn, and had been Bedchamber woman to Queen Caroline (Ossory iii. 12, n. 12; Mann i. 339, n. 33).

12. This letter has not been found.

13. Where Queen Caroline had lived when she was Princess of Wales.

14. Caroline Elizabeth (1713–57).

he, or rather his Queen, is actually doing, than I do. I rather pity him; for I believe he means well, which is not a common article of my faith.

I shall go about the end of this week to Park Place, where I expect to find the Druidic temple[15] from Jersey erected. How dull will the world be, if constant pilgrimages are not made thither! where, besides the delight of the scenes, that temple, the rude great arch,[16] Lady Ailesbury's needle-works,[17] and Mrs Damer's Thame and Isis on Henley Bridge,[18] with other of her sculptures, make it one of the most curious spots in the island, and unique. I want to have Mr Conway's comedy acted there; and then the father, mother and daughter would exhibit a theatre of arts as uncommon. How I regret that your Lordship did not hear Mrs Damer speak the epilogue!

I am, my dear Lord, your Lordship's most faithful humble servant,

HOR. WALPOLE

To Strafford, Friday 12 September 1788

Printed from *Works* v. 508–9; reprinted, Wright vi. 301–3, Cunningham ix. 145–6, Toynbee xiv. 77–80.

Strawberry Hill, September 12, 1788.

MY LATE fit of gout,[1] though very short, was a very authentic one, my dear Lord, and the third[2] I have had since Christmas. Still, of late years I have suffered so little pain, that I can justly complain of nothing but the confinement and the debility of my hands and feet, which however I can still use to a certain degree; and as I enjoy such good spirits and health in the intervals, I look upon the gout as no enemy: yet I know it is like the compacts said to be made

15. A prehistoric dolmen, uncovered in 1785 on the hill at St Helier, and presented to Conway. See OSSORY iii. 15, n. 3, and HW to Conway 11 Nov. 1787.

16. The 'rocky bridge' or 'rustic bridge' of which 'every stone' was placed by Conway's 'own direction' (OSSORY iii. 15, n. 4).

17. Her worsted-work pictures (ibid. iii. 15, n. 5).

18. See *ante* HW to Strafford 7 Sept. 1784, n. 9.

———

1. HW wrote to Lady Ossory, 16 Aug., that he had 'been confined a fortnight by the gout' (OSSORY iii. 12).

2. HW had the gout in February (to Lady Ossory 14 Feb., OSSORY iii. 4) and his letter to Mrs Dickenson, 13 April (MORE 261) may be a reply to condolences on another attack of gout.

with the devil (no kind comparison to a friend!), who showers his favours on the contractors, but is sure to seize and carry them off at last.

I would not say so much of myself, but in return to your Lordship's obliging concern for me—yet, insignificant as the subject, I have no better in bank—and if I plume myself on the tolerable state of my outward man, I doubt your Lordship finds that age does not treat my interior so mildly as the gout does the other. If my letters, as you are pleased to say, used to amuse you, you must perceive how insipid they are grown, both from my decays, and from the little intercourse I have with the world. Nay, I take care not to aim at false vivacity: what do the attempts of age at liveliness prove, but its weakness? What the *Spectator* said wittily, ought to be practised in sober sadness by old folks: when he was dull, he declared it was by design.[3] So far, to be sure, we ought to observe it, as not to affect more spirits than we possess. To be purposely stupid, would be forbidding our correspondents to continue the intercourse; and I am so happy in enjoying the honour of your Lordship's friendship, that I will be content (if you can be so) with my natural inanity, without studying to increase it.

I have been at Park Place, and assure your Lordship that the Druidic temple vastly more than answers my expectation. Small it is, no doubt, when you are within the enclosure, and but a chapel of ease to Stonehenge; but Mr Conway has placed it with so much judgment, that it has a lofty effect, and infinitely more than it could have had, if he had yielded to Mrs Damer's and my opinion, who earnestly begged to have it placed within the enclosure of the home grounds. It now stands on the ridge of the high hill without, backed by the horizon, and with a grove on each side at a little distance; and being exalted beyond and above the range of firs that climb up the sides of the hill from the valley, wears all the appearance of an ancient castle, whose towers are only shattered, not destroyed; and devout as I am to old castles, and small taste as I have for the ruins of ages absolutely barbarous, it is impossible not to be pleased with so very rare an antiquity so absolutely perfect, and it is difficult to prevent visionary ideas from improving a prospect.

If, as Lady Anne Conolly told your Lordship, I have had a great

3. 'Authors have established it as a kind of rule, that a man ought to be dull sometimes; as the most severe reader makes allowances for many rests and nodding-places in a voluminous writer' (*Spectator* No. 124).

deal of company, you must understand it of my house,[4] not of me; for I have very little. Indeed, last Monday both my house and I were included. The Duke of York[5] sent me word the night before, that he would come and see it, and of course I had the honour of showing it myself. He said, and indeed it seemed so, that he was much pleased; at least, I had every reason to be satisfied; for I never saw any prince more gracious and obliging, nor heard one utter more personally kind speeches.

I do not find that *her Grace* the Countess of Bristol's[6] will is really known yet. They talk of two wills[7]—to be sure, in her double capacity; and they say she has made three coheiresses to her jewels,[8] the Empress of Russia,[9] Lady Salisbury,[10] and the whore of Babylon.[11] The first of those legatees, I am not sorry, is in a piteous scrape: I like the King of Sweden[12] no better than I do her and the Emperor: but it is good that two destroyers should be punished by a third,[13] and that two crocodiles should be gnawed by an insect. Thank God! *we* are not only at peace, but in full plenty—nay, and in full beauty too. Still better; though we have had rivers of rain, it has not, contrary to all precedent, washed away our warm weather. September, a month I generally dislike for its irresolute mixture of warm and cold, has hitherto been peremptorily fine. The apple and walnut trees bend down with fruit as in a poetic description of Paradise.

I am with great gratitude, my dear Lord,

Your Lordship's devoted humble servant,

HOR. WALPOLE

4. HW's 'Book of Visitors' lists 57 visitors in August 1788, and 17 in the first twelve days of September (BERRY ii. 231).

5. George III's second son, Frederick Augustus (1763–1827), styled Bp of Osnabrück 1764–84; cr. (1784) D. of York and Albany, who came to SH with five companions on 8 Sept. (ibid.).

6. The Duchess of Kingston (HW). She d. 28 Aug. at the Château de Saint-Assise near Fontainebleau.

7. Her will was probated in Dec. 1789 (GEC *sub* Kingston); it is described by C. E. Pearce, *The Amazing Duchess,* [1914], ii. 347–51.

8. Her jewels presumably were carried off by her husband's nephew, Evelyn Medows, who was in Paris then (Elizabeth Mavor, *Virgin Mistress,* 1964, pp. 192, 195); they were sold at Christie's in 1792 for £7,400 (Pearce, op. cit. ii. 351).

9. Whom she had visited, in Russia.

10. Mary Amelia Hill (1750–1835), m. (1773) James Cecil, styled Vct Cranborne to 1780; 7th E. of Salisbury, 1780; cr. (1789) M. of Salisbury.

11. The Duchess had entrusted her 'treasure' to Pius VI in Rome when she had to leave for England (MANN viii. 83–4, 167, 234).

12. Gustav III (1746–92), K. of Sweden 1771–92.

13. Who was threatening Russia (GM 1788, lviii pt ii. 644–5).

To Strafford, Saturday 26 June 1790

Printed from *Works* v. 510; reprinted, Wright vi. 359, Cunningham ix. 245–6, Toynbee xiv. 253–4.

Strawberry Hill, June 26, 1790.

My dear Lord,

I DO not forget your Lordship's commands, though I do recollect my own inability to divert you. Every year at my advanced time of life would make more reasonable my plea of knowing nothing worth repeating, especially at this season. The general topic of elections is the last subject to which I could listen: there is not one about which I care a straw: and I believe your Lordship quite as indifferent. I am not much more *au fait* of war or peace; I hope for the latter, nay and expect it, because it is not yet war. Pride and anger do not deliberate to the middle of the campaign; and I believe even the great incendiaries are more intent on making a good bargain than on saving their honour. If they save lives, I care not who is the better politician: and as I am not to be their judge, I do not inquire what false weights they fling into the scales. Two-thirds of France, who are not so humble as I, seem to think they can entirely new-model the world with metaphysical compasses, and hold that no injustice, no barbarity need to be counted in making the experiment. Such legislators are sublime empirics, and in their universal benevolence have very little individual sensibility.—In short, the result of my reflections on what has passed in Europe for these latter centuries is, that tyrants have no consciences, and reformers no feeling—and the world suffers both by the plague and by the cure.—What oceans of blood were Luther and Calvin the authors of being spilt! The late French government was detestable—yet I still doubt whether a civil war will not be the consequence of the revolution—and then what may be the upshot? Brabant[1] was grievously provoked—is it sure that it will be emancipated?[2] For how short a time do people who set out on the most just

1. By Austria, which controlled it, and had recently changed its government. The États of Brabant went into exile in Sept. 1789, alleging 'the wanton and oppressive infractions, the lawless and shameless subversion of their constitution' (GM 1789, lix pt ii. 948–9). Armed revolt

followed, and the rebellious États appealed to England (under threat of overtures to France) for aid (*Mercure de France* 26 June 1790, pp. 253–7, *sub* 'Bruxelles, le 19 juin').

2. It was not. Prussia agreed to aid Austria, and by December, the Austrian

principles, advert to their first springs of motion, and retain consistency? Nay, how long can promoters of revolutions be sure of maintaining their own ascendant? They are like projectors, who are commonly ruined, while others make fortunes on the foundation laid by the inventors.

I am always your Lordship's very devoted humble servant,

Hor. Walpole

To Strafford, Thursday 12 August 1790

Printed from *Works* v. 511–12; reprinted, Wright vi. 365–6, Cunningham ix. 250–1, Toynbee xiv. 282–3.

Strawberry Hill, Aug. 12, 1790.

I MUST not pretend any longer, my dear Lord, that this region is void of news and diversions. Oh! we can innovate as well as neighbouring nations. If an Earl Stanhope,[1] though he cannot be a tribune,[2] is ambitious of being a plebeian, he may without a law be as vulgar as heart can wish;[3] and though we have not a National Assembly to lay the axe to the root of nobility, the peerage have got a precedent for laying themselves in the kennel. Last night the Earl of Barrymore[4] was so humble as to perform a buffoon dance and act Scaramouch in a pantomime at Richmond for the benefit of Edwin, Junior the comedian:[5] and I, like an old fool, but calling myself a philosopher that loves to study human nature in all its disguises, went to see the performance.

Mr Gray thinks that some Milton or some Cromwell may be lost

forces again controlled the area (*London Gazette* No. 13228, 14–17 Aug.; GM 1790, lx pt ii. 1135–6; Ossory iii. 102, n. 13).

1. Charles Stanhope (1753–1816), styled Vct Mahon 1763–86, 3d E. Stanhope, 1786; M.P. HW called him 'a savage, a republican, a royalist, I don't know what' (to Mann 30 March 1784, Mann ix. 490).

2. That is, a member of the House of Commons.

3. '14 [July] Lord Stanhope, Price and Sawbridge celebrated the French jubilee at the Crown and Anchor. Horne there and was hissed; and Sheridan. Much riot and drunkenness' ('Mem. 1783–91'). An account is in Ghita Stanhope and G. P. Gooch, *Life of Charles, Third Earl Stanhope*, 1914, pp. 93–5.

4. Richard Barry (1769–93), 7th E. of Barrymore, 1773, a patron of the theatre (Berry i. 95, 101, 207).

5. John Edwin (1768–1805), actor and a protégé of Lord Barrymore.

to the world under the garb of a ploughman.[6] Others may suppose that some excellent Jack-pudding[7] may lie hidden under red velvet and ermine. I cannot say that by the experiment of last night the latter hypothesis has been demonstrated, any more than the inverse proposition in France, where, though there seem to be many as bloody-minded rascals as Cromwell, I can discover none of his abilities. They have settled nothing like a constitution; on the contrary, they seem to protract everything but violence, as much as they can, in order to keep their louis a day,[8] which is more than two-thirds of the Assembly perhaps ever saw in a month—I do not love legislators that pay themselves so amply! They might have had as good a constitution as twenty-four millions of people could comport. As they have voted an army of an hundred and fifty thousand men,[9] I know what their constitution will be, after passing through a civil war—in short, I detest them; they have done irreparable injury to liberty, for no monarch will ever summon *États* again; and all the real service that will result from their fury will be, that every king in Europe, for these twenty or perhaps thirty years to come, will be content with the prerogative he has, without venturing to augment it.

    The Empress of Russia has thrashed the King of Sweden; and the King of Sweden has thrashed the Empress of Russia.[10] I am more glad that both are beaten than that either is victorious; for I do not, like our newspapers, and such admirers, fall in love with heroes and heroines who make war without a glimpse of provocation. I do like *our* making peace, whether we had provocation or not.

6. 'Some mute inglorious Milton here
        may rest,
    Some Cromwell guiltless of his country's blood.'

7. 'Buffoon' or 'mountebank' (OED, *sub* Jack-pudding).

8. Eighteen livres a day, according to BERRY i. 86, n. 15; a louis d'or was twenty-four livres (*Gentleman's Guide in his Tour through France*, 10th edn, 1788, p. 8). See also OSSORY iii. 109, 117, 119, 120; DALRYMPLE 207–8.

9. On 29 July, 'M. Alexandre de Lameth a fait lecture du plan militaire du ministre de la guerre, qui demande une armée active en temps de paix de 150 mille hommes, et de 100 mille auxiliaires.

Le rapporteur a ensuite comparé ce plan avec celui du comité qui s'en écarte peu, mais qui reduit à 50 mille en temps de paix, le nombre des auxiliaires' (*Mercure de France*, 7 Aug. 1790, pp. 65–6).

10. 'Russia, who had just beaten, and immediately been beaten by, the Swedes' ('Mem. 1783–91' *sub* Aug. 1790). HW refers to two sea battles off Swensk Sound in the Baltic on 3–4 and 9–11 July, in the first of which the Russians seemed victorious, but they were defeated by the Swedes in the second (*Cambridge Modern History*, Cambridge, 1909, vi. 782; *Annual Register* 1791, xxxiii. 68–70; *London Gazette* Nos. 13222, 13225, 27–31 July and 3–7 Aug.).

I am forced to deal in European news, my dear Lord, for I have no homespun.

I don't think my whole inkhorn could invent another paragraph, and therefore I will take my leave with (your Lordship knows) every kind wish for your health and happiness.

Your most devoted humble servant,

HOR. WALPOLE

ETCHING BY SIR JOHN FENN

THE CORRESPONDENCE
WITH SIR WILLIAM
HAMILTON

From Hamilton, ca Tuesday 15 October 1765

Missing. 'I have taken the liberty of enclosing a letter for Mr Walpole, which I will beg the favour of you to forward to him. Lady Aylesbury tells Mrs Hamilton that he is in France, but does not say where. . . . I have told him the charming effect this climate has had upon Mrs Hamilton, and I wish I could tempt him here, as I verily believe it might do him great service, for the winter is delightful here' (Hamilton to Mann, Naples, 15 Oct. 1765, cited in MANN vi. 354, n. 5). 'Mr. Hamilton at Naples has sent me the enclosed' (Mann to HW 25 Oct. 1765, MANN vi. 354). This may be one of the five letters from Hamilton to HW sold, Sotheby's, 24 April 1879, John B. C. Healt Sale, lot 150, to Waller.

To Hamilton, ca Friday 15 November 1765

Missing, 'I trouble you to forward the enclosed to Hamilton, and direct it' (HW to Mann, Paris, 13–15 Nov. 1765, MANN vi. 366). HW's letters to Mann and Hamilton were sent 24 Nov. 'by post,' and HW noted that Mann's was 'writ a week sooner' ('Paris Journals,' DU DEFFAND v. 378). This letter to Hamilton was presumably the one 'from Mr Walpole,' which Mann sent to Hamilton 10 Dec., and which is acknowledged by Hamilton to Mann 21 Dec. (MANN vi. 366, n. 12).

To Hamilton, ca August 1768

Missing. 'I am not sure that he [Hamilton] received one that I wrote to him some time ago by the post' (HW to Mann 22 Sept. 1768, MANN vii. 59). 'Mr Walpole . . . was dubious about the fate of a letter which he wrote to you some time ago' (Mann to Hamilton 11 Oct. 1768, BM Egerton MSS 2641). 'I had a letter lately from our friend Hor. Walpole, and am pleased to hear that he is in good health and spirits' (Hamilton to Mann, Naples, 30 Aug. 1768, MANN vii. 59, n. 13).

To Hamilton, Thursday 22 September 1768

Printed from the MS now WSL; previously printed Toynbee *Supp.* iii. 13, when it was owned (ca 1925) by Francis Edwards. Sold Sotheby's 3 March 1886, Hamilton sale, lot 108 to Thibaudeau. (?)Pettigrew sale, July 1887. Sold Sotheby's 7 May 1919, Alfred Morrison sale, Part IV, lot 3127 to Maggs Bros. Sold by Maggs Bros, Sept. 1942 to WSL.

'I must beg you to transmit the enclosed to Mr Hamilton our minister at Naples' (HW to Mann 22 Sept. 1768, MANN vii. 59).

Endorsed by Hamilton: Horace Walpole August 1768. Mentions fêtes on acct of the King of Denmark. The proposal of his favourite young Count Holke to Lady Bel Stanhope—Her refusal—

Warwick Castle mentioned as the first place in the world.

Strawberry Hill, Sept. 22, 1768.

Dear Sir,

I HAVE just been a progress with Mr Conway to Lord Hertford's,[1] Lord Strafford's[2] and other places,[3] and at my return three days ago found the cases arrived. I tore them open with the utmost impatience, and cannot describe how agreeably I was surprised to find the contents[4] so much beyond my expectation. They are not only beautiful in themselves and well preserved, but the individual things I should have wished for, if I had known they existed. For this year past I have been projecting a chimney in imitation of the tomb of Edward the Confessor,[5] and had partly given it up, on finding how

1. Ragley Hall. For HW's itinerary, see *ante* HW to Strafford 16 Aug. 1768, n. 40.

2. Wentworth Castle.

3. See *Country Seats* 62–7 for HW's 'Journey to Weston, Ragley, Warwick Castle, Combe Abbey, Newnham Padox, Kenilworth, Guy's Cliff, Donnington, Kedleston, Matlocke, Wentworth Castle, etc. Sept. 2d 1768.'

4. Parts of 'a magnificent shrine of mosaic, three stories high,' which HW had repaired, altered ('parts supplied'), and re-erected by Richter in the Chapel in the 'southwest corner of the wood' at SH: 'The shrine . . . was brought in . . . 1768 from the Church of Santa Maria Maggiore in Rome, when the new pavement was laid there. This shrine was erected in . . . 1256 over the bodies of the holy martyrs Simplicius, Faustina, and

Beatrix, by James Capoccio and Vinia his wife; and was the work of Peter Cavalini, who made the tomb of Edward the Confessor in Westminster Abbey. See *The Anecdotes of Painting*, [*Works* iii.] p. 24' ('Des. of SH,' *Works* ii. 507–8). An engraving of the shrine, by W. Bawtree, 1798, is reproduced in *SH Accounts*, ed. Toynbee, Oxford, 1927, Plate XVII, facing p. 128. The shrine was purchased SH xxiv. 85 on behalf of Sidney Herbert, who used 'some of the columns in the church at Wilton' (*SH Accounts* 159).

5. The tomb or shrine of Edward (ca 1004–66), the Confessor, King of the English 1042–66, canonized 1163, is in the middle of the Chapel of St. Edward the Confessor in Westminster Abbey. For an illustration of the shrine as it appeared in 1723, see John Dart, *Westmonasterium*, [1742], ii. facing p. 23.

enormously expensive it would be. Mr Adam[6] had drawn me a design[7] a little in that style, prettier it is true, and at half the price. I had actually agreed to have it executed in scagliola, but have just heard that the man[8] complained he could not perform his compact for the money settled.[9] Your obliging present is I am certain executed by the very person who made the Confessor's monument;[10] and if the scagliola-man wishes to be off his bargain, I shall be glad; if not, still these materials will make me a beautiful chimney-piece for another room. I again give you ten thousand thanks for them, dear Sir. I value them for themselves, and much more for the person they come from.

If you could like to be a moment out of Italy, you would be charmed with Lord Strafford's new front, which for grace, proportion, lightness, and every beauty in architecture I sincerely think the most perfect building I ever saw in any country.[11]

We are here all triumphs, balls and masquerades. The King of Denmark is to give one of the latter at Ranelagh,[12] to which the whole earth is invited and as the whole earth will make something too great a crowd, I shall dispense with myself from attending it. He has a jackanapes of a favourite, a young Count Holke, who had chosen to be in love with Lady Bel Stanhope,[13] and his master wrote

6. Robert Adam (1728–92), the architect; see HW's letter to him, Sept. 1766.
7. Two drawings by Adam, dated 1766 and 1767, are in the Soane Museum (Toynbee *Supp.* iii. 12, n. 6). In 1769 the chimney-piece in the Round Room was executed from Adam's design; see below.
8. Probably John Augustus Richter (fl. 1772–1800), born in Dresden, senior partner in the firm of Richter and Bartoli, of Newport Street, 'who supplied scagliola work for table tops, columns, chimney-pieces, etc.' (*SH Accounts* 159). Richter executed the chimney-piece and hearth in the Round Room in 1769 and repaired the Capoccio shrine in 1774 (*SH Accounts* 15, 134 *et passim*).
9. The amount of the estimate is not known. On 20 July 1769 HW paid £288.13.7½ for 'the Chimney-piece [including the hearth] in the Round Room' (*SH Accounts* 11).
10. Henry III had the shrine of Edward the Confessor erected in 1268 by Peter of Rome ('Hoc opus est factum, quod Petrus duxit in actum Romanus civis'), identified

by HW, following Vertue's conjecture, as Pietro Cavallini (ca 1259–1344), whose conjectural birth-date appears to rule out the ascription of Edward's shrine and the Capoccio shrine to him (COLE ii. 370; Thieme and Becker; *Anecdotes of Painting, Works* iii. 25; *Anecdotes of Painting*, ed. Wornum, 1876, i. 17, n. 1).
11. 'I had been . . . [to Wentworth Castle] before, but had not seen the new front, entirely designed by the present Earl himself. Nothing ever came up to the beauty of it. The grace, proportion, lightness and magnificence of it are exquisite' (HW's account, Sept. 1768, in *Country Seats* 65).
12. Christian VII gave his masquerade ball at the Opera House (King's Theatre in the Haymarket) 10 Oct. The guests were said to number between 2000 and 3000. For accounts, see *London Chronicle* 8–15 Oct., xxiv. 352, 359, 366; GM 1768, xxxviii. 450, 491, with illustration facing p. 450, 'A View of the Dresses . . .'
13. Isabella Stanhope (1748–1819), Lady Harrington's 2d dau., m. (3 Dec. 1768)

to Lady Harrington with every kind of offer to obtain her for him, but Lady Bel had too much sense to trust the caprices of such boys.[14] The Duke of Portland[15] gives a great masquerade at Welbeck,[16] on the birth of his son.[17] Two masquerades are such crying sins, that our bishops would be as much obliged to you, as I am, if you would send them over five cases of earthquake from Vesuvius. I forgot to tell you that we called at Warwick Castle, which to my taste is the first place in the world. The new eating-room will be magnificent.[18] Lady Ailesbury is not quite well and could not go with us;[19] but designs to go to Bath. Adieu! dear Sir, I am Mrs Hamilton's[20] and

Your most obliged and obedient humble servant

Hor. Walpole

From Hamilton, Tuesday 5 March 1771

Here first printed from MS now wsl; purchased from G. Michelmore and Co., June 1936.

Naples, March 5th 1771.

Dear Sir,

EXCUSE the liberty I take in sending you a table made out of a fragment of Gothic Saracen mosaic[1] that I got from a church

Charles William Molyneux, 8th Vct Molyneux, 1759, cr. (1771) E. of Sefton.

14. Lady Isabella's husband was a little over three months older than Christian VII and three years younger than Holck.

15. William Henry Cavendish Bentinck (1738–1809) styled M. of Titchfield till 1762, 3d D. of Portland, 1762; lord chamberlain of the King's Household 1765–6; prime minister April – Dec. 1783, 1807–9.

16. On 28 Sept. the Duchess of Portland gave a masquerade ball to about 200 guests (*London Chronicle* 6–8 Oct. xxiv. 344).

17. William Henry Cavendish Cavendish-Scott-Bentinck (24 June 1768 – 1854), styled M. of Titchfield till 1809, 4th D. of Portland, 1809; M.P. Petersfield 1790–1, Bucks 1791–1809.

18. In *Country Seats* 63, HW mentions 'a large dining-room new built' at Warwick Castle.

19. 'I wish I could cure my Lady Ailesbury' (HW to Conway 9 Aug. 1768).

20. Catherine Barlow (d. 1782), m. (1758) Sir William Hamilton, K.B., 1772.

———

1. The table 'supported by a finely carved antique ebony frame, with beautiful borders of carved open scroll work, representing masques, fruits, and flowers, on 4 twisted legs, the . . . top 38 inches square,' sold SH xvi. 11 to Charles Kean, Esq., for £42. HW placed it on the 'window side' of the Great North Bedchamber (*Des. of SH*, SH, 1774, p. 105; 'Des. of SH,' *Works* ii. 497).

at Salerno,[2] and which accompanies the mosaic I had the pleasure of sending you from Rome.[3] The stars in the middle were repaired at Naples with pieces of antique marble whose colours I thought would suit the rest, formerly I believe the circles were only of porphyry. Don't be scrupulous of accepting this trifle as I do assure you it cost me little. I have added a *basso-relievo*, the portrait of the Lady Eleonora of the family d'Este[4] and who was Tasso's mistress,[5] and which I thought might be acceptable to you. Believe me I have more pleasure in sending you these small tokens of my remembrance of your goodness to me than you can possibly have in receiving them. When I was in Sicily at Girgenti[6] in a Capucins' convent, round the cloister I saw Gothic paintings much decayed by time. I thought the Italian explanation of the figures curious so had them transcribed for you. They are all Scripture subjects, or as an Italian drolly expressed it, *della favola sacra*,[7] and were executed (as is plain by a globe painted) before the discovery of America. I am in great hopes of receiving soon the King's[8] permission to return home for a few months.[9] You shall then see that I have not been idle since I have been here[10] and the lovers of antiquity will I think be obliged to me for enriching our country with a most singular collection,[11] and the lovers of painting for a picture of Corregio, excelled I believe by none.[12] If you ever attend the R[oyal] Society you may perhaps have heard read a

2. 30 miles SE of Naples.

3. The Capoccio shrine (*ante* HW to Hamilton 22 Sept. 1768).

4. Leonora d'Este (1537–81), sister of Alphonso II, D. of Ferrara 1559–97, the patron of Tasso and Guarini. In the little cloister at SH was 'a bas-relief head in marble, inscribed *Dia Helianora* [Helionora] . . . the portrait of Princess Eleanora d'Este, with whom Tasso was in love, and who was the cause of his misfortunes . . . sent . . . from Italy by Sir William Hamilton . . .' (*Des. of SH*, SH, 1774, p. 3n.). It was sold SH xix. 33 to Thorne of Richmond for £6.16.6.

5. Tasso addressed to her some verses in the conventional poetic language of the time, but the view that she was his mistress in any sense is no longer held.

6. Formerly Agrigento.

7. 'Of sacred fable.' Hamilton's transcripts are missing.

8. George III's.

9. Rev. William Preston was in charge of affairs at Naples for Hamilton, June 1771 – Jan. 1773 (Horn, *Diplomatic Representatives* 77).

10. Hamilton had arrived in Naples 17 Nov. 1764. He was envoy extraordinary and plenipotentiary 1767–1800 (ibid. 76).

11. Which arrived in London in November 1771 and was purchased in March 1772 for the British Museum with a grant of £8410 voted by Parliament. See HW to Lady Ossory 14 Dec. 1771, Ossory i. 70–1 and nn. 22–3.

12. 'Venus, Cupid, and Satyr,' sometimes called 'Venus Disarming Cupid' now attributed to Luca Cambiaso (1527–85); later in the collection of the Earl of Radnor. For details see Ossory loc. cit.; HW to Mann 18 Nov. 1771, when HW had seen the 'divine' picture; Oliver Warner, *Emma Hamilton and Sir William*, 1960, pp. 45–6.

late paper of mine upon the subject of volcanoes.[13] I expect you printers will make your court to us authors soon. Mrs H.[14] desires her kind compliments to you. Lady O——d[15] prefers the young men of Aix[16] to those of Naples, but her houses, horses, etc., are to be kept here. Excuse this vile scrawl, but really I was worn out with writing before I began this letter. Be so good as to remember me kindly to Conway, Lady Ailesbury and Lady Waldegrave.[17]

Dear Sir,
Your most obedient and obliged humble servant

WM HAMILTON

To HAMILTON, ca Sunday 8 September 1771

Missing; see *post* 15 Sept. 1771.

13. Since June 1766 Hamilton had been writing letters which had been read at the Royal Society beginning in March 1767 and continuing to the date of this letter; see the Society's *Philosophical Transactions*, lvii (1768). 192–200; lviii (1769). 1–14; lix (1770). 18–22; lx (1771). 1–19; lxi (1772). 1–50. HW did not own these volumes of *Philosophical Transactions* (Hazen, *Cat. of HW's Lib.*, No. 1628), and there is no record that he attended meetings, although he had become a Fellow of the Royal Society 19 Feb. 1747. All of these letters with 'explanatory notes' added were reprinted in Hamilton's *Observations on Mount Vesuvius, Mount Etna and Other Volcanoes,* 1772; 2d edn, 1773; and in his *Campi*

Phlegræi, Naples, 1776–9. HW later acquired a first edition (Hazen, *Cat. of HW's Lib.*, No. 2865).
14. Hamilton's wife (*ante* HW to Hamilton 22 Sept. 1768, n. 20).
15. HW's sister-in-law (*ante* Chute to HW 17 April 1742 NS). She was widow of the 2d E. of Orford.
16. Aix-les-Bains, where she had been in 1769 (Mann to HW 28 Nov., 18 Dec. 1769, MANN vii. 155).
17. Maria Walpole (1736–1807), dau. of Sir Edward Walpole, m. 1 (1759) James Waldegrave, 2d E. Waldegrave, 1741; m. 2 (1766, privately, the marriage not being declared until 1772) William Henry, cr. (1764) D. of Gloucester.

From HAMILTON, Sunday 15 September 1771

Printed from MS now WSL; previously printed Toynbee *Supp.* iii. 224–5. Bequeathed by Mrs Damer to Sir Wathen Waller. Sold Sotheby's 5 Dec. 1921 (first Waller sale), lot 138 (bought in); sold Christie's 15 Dec. 1947 (second Waller sale) lot 53 to Maggs Bros for WSL.

Warwick Castle, September 15th 1771.

Dear Sir,

I WAS in great hopes that you would have returned from Paris[1] before I went upon my tour to Warwick Castle, Drayton[2] and Burgligh;[3] as it is I cannot hope for the pleasure of seeing you till the beginning of October, when if you should happen to be at Strawberry Hill Mrs Hamilton and I will surely have the great satisfaction of passing a few days with you.[4] Immediately upon the receipt of your very kind letter[5] I asked about the pictures you mention. That of Lady Catherine Gray[6] and her son[7] has been given to the Duchess of Northumberland.[8] There are two original pictures of the heroic Lord Brooke[9] at the Castle; the best in armour is now well situated

1. For HW's journey to Paris 7 July – 6 Sept., see 'Paris Journals,' DU DEFFAND v. 333–42.
2. Drayton House, Northants, near Thrapston; built in the reigns of Edward III, Elizabeth and William III. It was the seat of Lady Elizabeth Germain when HW and Cole were there in 1763 (*Country Seats* 55–8; MONTAGU ii. 84–90, 341–3).
3. Burghley House, near Stamford, Northants; seat of the Cecils, Earls (from 1801, Marquesses) of Exeter. HW visited it in 1763 (*Country Seats* 59–60).
4. The Hamiltons 'passed one day last week here [SH], and I left them this morning at Park Place' (HW to Mann 22 Oct., MANN vii. 339).
5. ca 8 Sept. 1771, missing.
6. Lady Catherine Grey (1540–68), sister of Lady Jane Grey and great-granddaughter of Henry VII, m. 1 (1553, dissolved in 1554) Henry Herbert, styled Lord Herbert, later (1570) 2d E. of Pembroke; m. 2 (1560) secretly, Edward Seymour, cr. (1559) E. of Hertford.
7. She had two sons, both born in the Tower of London: Edward Seymour

(1561–1612), styled Lord Beauchamp, and Hon. Thomas Seymour (1563–1600). HW's description of the picture in 1768 is in *Country Seats* 63: 'Lady Catherine Grey and her son, in a round, companion to the Jane Grey, engraved by Vertue. I believe they were part of the moveables divided between Lord Warwick and Frances Duchess of Somerset,' mother of the Ds of Northumberland, mentioned below: Frances Thynne (ca 1699–1754), dau. of Hon. Henry Thynne, only son of Thomas, 1st Vct Weymouth, m. (1715) Algernon, 7th D. of Somerset.
8. Who was descended from Lady Catherine Grey. See GEC, *sub* Somerset and Hertford, xii. 69–82, vi. 504–8. Lord Warwick's mother was the Ds of Somerset's only sister: Mary Thynne (ca 1701–20) m. (1716) William Greville; 7th Bn Brooke of Beauchamps Court.
9. Robert Greville (1607–43), 2d Bn Brooke, 1628; a republican; appointed Col. of a Regiment of Foot, 1642, and Maj.-Gen. 7 Jan. 1643 for the counties of Warwick and Stafford for the Parliament; killed at Lichfield by a musket ball when he was directing the siege of St Chad's Church;

in the new great dining-room; the other is in a black dress; it is not so good nor well placed. Lord Greville[10] has promised to bring the book of designs of the old English architect[11] to London and will send it for your inspection and advice. The marble profile I took the liberty of sending you is of Diana d'Este[12] who had an amour with Tasso. I once heard a long story of this affair which ended unhappily for both, but I have forgot it. The profile is admirably executed but I would advise your taking it out of the abominable heavy frame.[13] I shall be most happy to communicate to you some curious observations I have made relative to the formation of mountains by mere explosion from volcanoes, which I think will place this subject in a different point of view than has been hitherto considered and I am convinced that my observations may lead to many curious discoveries and account for various phenomena hitherto little understood with respect to whimsical stratas [sic] that are met with in the bowels of the earth.

Mrs Hamilton desires her kind compliments to you. Till the beginning of October, adieu, my dear Sir.

Ever with true regard and esteem

Your most obedient and obliged humble servant

WM HAMILTON

HW's 'hero' (Ossory i. 353 and n. 16). HW in 1768 mentioned only one picture of him: 'In a passage, *Lord Brooke* shot at Litchfield' (*Country Seats* 63). This portrait and the one in armour mentioned later by Hamilton have been attributed to William Dobson (1610–46); see Ossory i. 353, n. 16.

10. George Greville (1746–1816), styled Lord Greville, 2d E. Brooke and E. of Warwick, 1773; M.P. Warwick 1768–73; F. R. S., 1767; F. S. A., 1768.

11. John Thorpe (ca 1563–1655), a sur-

veyor and architect. HW was the first to draw attention to his significant folio of drawings, now in the Soane Museum. See Ossory ii. 248–9 and n. 18, 256.

12. Leonora d'Este; see *ante* Hamilton to HW 5 March 1771, n. 4.

13. The frame is not mentioned in *Des. of SH*, SH, 1774, p. 3n.; *Des. of SH*, 1784, p. 2n; 'Des. of SH,' *Works* ii. 400n; SH sale catalogue xix. 33, but the drawing in Richard Bull's extra-illustrated *Des. of SH*, 1784, now WSL, shows the bas-relief in a heavy frame.

From HAMILTON, ca July 1773

Missing. Sold Sotheby's 31 March 1853, lot 10. In this letter, Hamilton enclosed a copy, now in the Bibliothèque Nationale, of a letter to him from Voltaire 17 June 1773, of which a photostat was presented to WSL by Dr Theodore
Besterman, 25 July 1959. For the text and provenance of Voltaire's letter, see
Voltaire's Correspondence, ed. Besterman, Geneva, 1953–65, lxxxv. 135–6.

To HAMILTON, Friday 13 August 1773

Printed from photostat of MS in the possession of Mr Morris Wolf, Philadelphia. Previously printed, Toynbee *Supp.* iii. 15–18. The first and last paragraphs
were printed in *Voltaire's Correspondence,* ed. Besterman, Geneva, 1953–65,
lxxxv. 216–17.
Sold Sotheby's 31 March 1853, lot 10; Sotheby's 22 April 1912, 'Autograph
letters' lot 57 to Sabin; offered by Maggs Bros in Cat. 291, June 1912, lot 2841
(and again offered in their catalogues 309, 326, 346, 365, 394, 433 and 473, in
the years 1913–26); sold American Art Association–Anderson Galleries 13 Oct.
1929, John M. Geddes sale, lot 216, to Rosenbach.
Endorsed by Hamilton: Walpole August 13th 1773.

Strawberry Hill, Aug. 13, 1773.

I AM always glad to see Voltaire's letters; but much more when
they procure me one from you, whom I love much better, and
without a drawback. There is spirit in his letter, it is true, but while
he is contesting volcanoes, his thoughts seem to have been blown up
by the explosion of one. It looks as if his head had fallen to pieces
on a sheet of paper, and that his ideas had tumbled out higgledy-
piggledy—Cyclops, St Januarius, ants, Archimedes, Trajan, Anto-
nine, Mont Taurus, comets, oysterwomen, St Luke and St Paul, did
ever mortal make such a salmagundi?—but I will not dispute with
him or you, though I have a little difficulty in believing that volcanoes produce regular columns like those in the giant's causey[1]—
I should as soon suppose that the Gunpowder Plot, if it had taken
place, would have caused a methodical debate in both Houses of

1. Or causeway, in Co. Antrim, near Ballycastle, Northern Ireland. The rocky promontory of basalt, perfectly formed into polygonal columns, is itself of vol- canic origin and is one of the most per- fectly formed examples of its kind in the world.

Parliament. We folks of old-fashioned understandings look on burning mountains as very petulant ovens, and a little destructive—The modern French philosophers seem to have a mind to make them parents of order, and a kind of providence, as far as they will admit any. They put me in mind of George Montagu, who said of the last earthquake, 'I protest, it was so tame one might have stroked it.'[2] Methinks, dear Sir, I wish you was not quite so fond of these outrageous monsters—they sometimes put out their claws to a horrible degree, and when Voltaire quoted Pliny to you, he had better have put you in mind of his catastrophe;[3] or have invited you to his own icy domains that never furnish bonfires.

We have had ten days of weather that Vesuvius would not disown. *Les dames de la cour et les dames de la halle* say that Sir Isaac Newton foretold that, beginning with last summer, we are to have eighteen noble summers running.[4] I like any vulgar belief when it is agreeable to my wishes, and therefore trust Sir Isaac upon the faith of such illiterate commentators. Eighteen summers would be such an eternity to me, that I will reckon upon them, since I am too old to accept your kind invitation to Naples. I have always thought that great solicitude about health in the latter end of life is only taking care to be well against one dies. The pleasure of seeing you and Lady Hamilton and Italy once more would be a greater inducement, but five months and half of pain since you left England,[5] have terrified me from journeying. Comforts at home are the most I dare propose. This was the year of my biennial tour to Paris—but I cannot venture being confined in an inn or a *hôtel garni*. I have some patience, a good deal of resignation, but no adventurous blood. I think I shall live to see you again—I should not be so sure of returning. You can shorten the time, by letting me sometimes have the pleasure of a letter, and it will not want Voltaire's introduction.

I am just come from Park Place, where I left everybody well. I have been uneasy many months about Mrs Damer, who has seemed consumptive, and is not very tractable; but she is better. Her friend

2. HW uses this witticism in letters to Hertford 10 Jan. 1765, to Montagu 26 May 1765, to Lady Ossory 17 Feb. 1779, and to Strafford *ante* 1 Aug. 1783.
3. Pliny's, killed by the volcano.
4. For a similar reference to Newton's

predictions, see MANN iv. 119–20 and n. 3.
5. Hamilton left England for Naples about 10 Sept. 1772 and passed through Florence, leaving there on 18 Dec. for Rome and Naples (MANN vii. 431, n. 1, 448).

Lady Barrymore has lost her Lord by a fever,[6] and I suppose will get another the same way.

The Duke[7] and Duchess of Gloucester are gone a tour into the North.[8] You may depend on my remembering your compliment to the Duchess. The Duke and Duchess of Cumberland[9] are sailed to Italy;[10] but as they propose, I hear, to fix their residence at Milan,[11] you will not see them soon, unless they change their minds, which may happen. You are still more likely I think to see the posthumous Duchess of York.[12]

I will now bid you adieu! Ransack Herculaneum, sift Pompeii, give us charming vases, bring us Corregios and all Etruria, but do not dive into the caverns of Ætna and Vesuvius. You are a knight of water[13] not of the opposite element; and it is better to be an antiquary of taste, than a salamander that had passed a thousand ordeals —I am sure Lady Hamilton is on my side—I am most sincerely her, and dear Sir

Your most faithful humble servant

HOR. WALPOLE

From HAMILTON, ca Monday 31 January 1774

Missing. See *post* 22 Feb. 1774.

6. He died 1 Aug. at Dromana, Co. Waterford.

7. William Henry (1743–1805), cr. (1764) D. of Gloucester; brother of George III; m. (1766) Maria Walpole, HW's niece, widow of Lord Waldegrave (*ante* Hamilton to HW 5 March 1771, n. 17).

8. The Duchess wrote to Jane Clement, 23 Aug., that the Duke's asthma had abated (MS now WSL).

9. Anne Luttrell (1743–1808), dau. of Simon, 1st E. of Carhampton, m. 1 (1765) Christopher Horton; m. 2 (1771) Henry Frederick (1745–90), cr. (1766) D. of Cumberland; brother of George III.

10. They left, 17 Sept., for Dover to embark for Calais (MANN vii. 505, n. 1).

11. Where they arrived the evening of 1 Nov., and left for Rome in Feb. 1774 (ibid. vii. 543, 559, n. 4).

12. 'Lady Mary Coke had hoped to marry Edward Duke of York. . . . On the death of the Duke of York, she tried ridiculously to make it believed that she had been married to him' (HW's note, MANN viii. 179, n. 17; see also ibid. vii. 530–1, viii. 14). When HW wrote this letter to Hamilton she was in Berlin. She later visited Vienna, Venice, Parma, Florence, Turin, etc., but 'I determined not to go to Naples before I left England' (Coke, *Journals* iv. 217, 260, *passim*).

13. Hamilton had been nominated K.B. 15 Jan. 1772 and installed 15 June 1772 (W. A. Shaw, *Knights of England*, 1906, i. 171).

To Hamilton, Tuesday 22 February 1774

Printed from the MS now wsl. Previously printed Toynbee *Supp.* i. 232, ii. 244. Sold Sotheby's 22 April 1912, 'Autograph Letters' lot 54 to Maggs Bros; offered by Maggs Bros 1912–19 in Catalogues No. 293, 314, 329, 353, and 376; sold Hodgson's 3 May 1951, Cornelius C. Paine lot 224, to Maggs Bros for wsl. *Endorsed by Hamilton:* H. Walpole A. Feb. 1774.

Arlington Street, Feb. 22, 1774.

I AM much obliged to you, dear Sir, for your own[1] and Lady Orford's letters which I received last night. I will have the honour of answering her Ladyship's very soon.[2]

As Lord Orford is perfectly recovered, has taken into his own hands the management of his affairs, and is in the country,[3] I have no longer the least to do with his boroughs,[4] which you, who know my aversion to Parliament,[5] will be sure delivers me from the most irksome of all my trouble. While his Lordship's affairs were in my hands, they necessarily obliged me to trouble Lady Orford with some discussion on her Ladyship's boroughs, in order to save her son's places.[6] In that view I thought it very fortunate that Mr Skrine[7] declined Callington for fear of the expense, and that Mr Charles Boone,[8] in consideration of his obligations to my Lord, offered to

1. Missing.

2. HW's correspondence with Lady Orford is missing.

3. Orford '*will* go into the country on Monday [7 Feb.] though a week sooner than the physicians had fixed' (HW to Mann 2 Feb. 1774, Mann vii. 551–2). His insanity had lasted from April through Dec. 1773. See, for example, Ossory i. 97, 118–9, 175.

4. He had the nomination of one seat for Castle Rising and he recommended for one seat at Ashburton, his mother's borough. Lady Orford recommended for both seats at her other borough, Callington, but her influence was declining (L. B. Namier, *Structure of Politics at the Accession of George III*, 1961, pp. 145, 170, 302; Sir Lewis Namier and John Brooke, *House of Commons 1754–1790*, 1964, i. 225–7, 249–50, 339–40).

5. HW had been M.P. Callington 1741–54, Castle Rising 1754–7, King's Lynn 1757–68. Thereafter he refused to stand for election.

6. The Parliamentary boroughs.

7. William Skrine (?1721–83), of Arlington Street, London; M.P. Callington 1771–80; a friend of Lord Orford, he later agreed to stand and was returned unopposed on the Orford interest, 13 Oct. 1774 with John Dyke Acland, M.P. Callington 1774–8. Cf. HW to Mann 6 Oct. 1774, Mann viii. 46–7; Namier and Brooke, op. cit. i. 225–7, ii. 4–5, iii. 443.

8. (? 1729–1819), of Barking Hall, Suffolk, and Lee Place, Kent; M.P. Castle Rising 1757–68, 1784–96, Ashburton 1768–84, as nominee of Lord Orford, with whom Boone had been at Eton; 'the single friend' of Orford 'that had shown gratitude to him, when he was deemed no

stand there and go as far as spending two thousand pounds, as part of the expense.⁹ The moment my Lord began to recover, I advertised her Ladyship of it, and desired she would not send me any answer about the boroughs, as I was not likely to have anything to do with them, and did not think it right to pry into her Ladyship's dispositions. I even told Mr Sharpe¹⁰ that if the letter came, I would deliver it unopened into his hands. A letter¹¹ did come, but it was to Mr Sharpe, who in great anxiety sent me an extract¹² relating to you, dear Sir, and telling me that the nomination of a person abroad would risk the loss of the borough, and invite greater opposition, which was before apprehended.¹³ He informed me that he had explained the case to Mr Ross,¹⁴ and had convinced him that you could not be chosen there without great expense, and probably not with. You may be certain that I should be very glad if you came into Parliament without expense, as I flatter myself it would bring you and Lady Hamilton to England—but a western borough would undoubtedly not tempt you;¹⁵ and I have known ever since April or May last by Mr Boone's offer that Callington is in great danger; and indeed I doubt whether two members will be chosen there on the family interest, unless Lady Orford and her son join.¹⁶ It does not become me to meddle there any longer; but you are welcome to show

longer capable of serving anybody' because of insanity (HW to Mann 28 April 1777, MANN viii. 292; Namier and Brooke op. cit. ii. 101).

9. He would not have needed £2000, even though, with Lady Orford abroad but wishing to retain control of Callington, her interest was declining. In 1768, two candidates without the Orford interest, it was estimated, could have been elected for £2000, and in 1771 Skrine had been elected by a narrow margin which included doubtful or illegal votes. In 1774, however, the Orford candidates were unopposed (Namier and Brooke, op. cit. i. 225–7).

10. Joshua Sharpe (d. 1786), Lady Orford's attorney (MANN iv. 547, n. 5).

11. Missing.

12. Missing.

13. As the result of the opposition in the elections of 1768 and 1771. It appears from HW to Mann 2 Feb. 1774 that Hamilton had first approached Lady Or- ford about standing for Callington and she had agreed; the plan was not HW's. 'There is an end I believe of the promise to your brother at Naples, who finds it would have proved a very expensive affair. I have good wishes for him, though I own I was piqued at his interfering in an affair so important to my nephew' (HW to Mann 23 Feb. 1774, MANN vii. 557).

14. Presumably Hamilton's English agent.

15. Hamilton would hardly return to England to stand in an expensive and doubtful election. In HW's view, Hamilton should have, in addition to a seat in Parliament, a government place of the same value as his appointment at Naples; see following paragraphs.

16. Two members were elected at Callington in October on the Orford family interest, but no evidence has been found that Lord Orford supported his mother's interest.

her Ladyship this letter if you please, as it is for her interest to know her danger.

As your friend I will take the liberty of saying that I hope you will be sure of an equivalent at home, before you give up Naples.[17] The market is greatly overstocked at present, and a seat in Parliament gives little chance of a place. The Opposition gives up the game,[18] and half of them, I conclude, are trying to make a bargain—you may judge therefore whether this is a proper moment for quitting a certainty for a great improbability. Forgive my freedom, but a person on the spot can see the situation of things better than those at a distance.

I am heartily glad you have escaped both the real[19] and posthumous[20] Duchess. For the Duchess[21] who was long a virgin after being married and a mother,[22] and who became a second wife before she ceased to be a first,[23] I think she will only entertain you.[24] We have such plenty of wonderful characters, that we do not miss those that are absent. They are even in the right to search new theatres, where they will strike more than at home. We can spare a heaven-born general,[25] or a peeress that does not date her patent from quite so high.[26] If you were to come over, you would find us a general mas-

17. The 'emoluments and allowances' were 'something like £3000 a year' (Oliver Warner, *Emma Hamilton and Sir William*, 1960, p. 22).

18. In *Last Journals* i. 287, *sub* 11 Feb. 1774, HW noted that 'Opposition had in a manner given up the contest in Parliament.' See also HW to Lady Ossory 19 Jan. 1774, OSSORY i. 184 and n. 15.

19. The Duchess of Cumberland, who had gone from Milan to Rome without going to Naples, and was about to return to England (MANN vii. 559).

20. Lady Mary Coke (*ante* HW to Hamilton 13 Aug. 1773), who had left Florence on her return to England via Turin and Paris (Coke, *Journals* iv. 294, *et passim*).

21. Of Kingston.

22. Privately married, 1744, to the Hon. Augustus Hervey, who became 3d E. of Bristol in 1775, she retained her post as 'Miss Chudleigh,' maid of honour to Augusta, Ps of Wales, until 1769, when she married illegally, the Duke of Kingston. By her first husband she had one or

possibly two children (OSSORY i. 145, n. 4).

23. The suit of jactitation which she obtained in the Ecclesiastical Court 10 Feb. 1769, did not legally free her to marry the Duke of Kingston 8 March 1769 (Elizabeth Mavor, *Virgin Mistress*, 1964, pp. 87–95; MANN vii. 93, n. 9).

24. She was then at Rome (MANN vii. 559).

25. Clive, so called by Pitt in a speech on the army estimates in the House of Commons 14 Dec. 1757 (*Mem. Geo. II* iii. 90; MANN vi. 176 and n. 13, 243, vii. 381, 387). 'Yesterday Lord Clive set out from his house in Berkeley Square for Italy, for the recovery of his health' (*Public Adv.* 27 Nov. 1773; *Last Journals* i. 266). 'Lord Clive is arrived [at France] in his way to Naples: he stays here till Wednesday [Jan. 1774]. He passed two days at Milan' (Coke, *Journals* iv. 287, written at Florence 2 Jan. 1774).

26. Lady Orford, who had returned to Naples (HW to Mann 28 Nov. 1773, MANN vii. 529).

querade. The Macaronies,[26a] not content with producing new fashions every day—and who are great reformers, are going to restore the Vandyck dress, in concert with the Macaronesses—As my thighs would not make a figure in breeches from my navel to my instep, I shall wait till the dress of the Druids is revived, which will be more suitable to my age. In the meantime your Gothic shields[27] will be extremely welcome. As both duels[28] and change of raiment are in fashion, I will wear one at the first tournament in defence of the next maid of honour that is accused of bigamy.[29]

I have been just reading Pliny on ancient music;[30] pray have you found any silver flutes in Herculaneum or Pompeii?[31] As the edition of the former seems at a stand,[32] would not it be worth your while to send over and publish a mere list of all the utensils etc. that have been discovered at either? My press is at your service. I should be particularly glad of an account of any new musical instruments or singularities in old ones. A friend of mine[33] is actually employed on

26a. For the Macaroni Club, see Montagu ii. 139, n. 11.

27. 'Two shields, of leather, for tournaments, painted by Polidore. One has a head of a Medusa, the other of Perseus. On the inside are battles in gold; they came out of the collection of Commendatore Vittoria at Naples, and were sent to Mr Walpole by Sir W. Hamilton, together with a third, which hangs on the opposite side of the staircase; it is of iron and seems to have been gilt. It represents the story of Curtius; but by an embattled tower in the background, ['it's probably not Roman,' struck by HW] and a cannon on the border, is certainly not antique' HW's MS note in his *Des. of SH*, SH, 1774, now WSL, p. 41; printed with slight changes, ibid., SH, 1784, pp. 31–2; *Works* ii. 439). HW did not receive them until 17 June 1774; see *post* 19 June 1774. The Medusa shield was sold SH xix. 87 to the Earl of Charleville for £5.5.0; the Perseus shield was sold SH xix. 86 to Samuel Pratt of New Bond Street for £10.10.0. The third shield had not been identified in the SH sale.

28. One of the most recent, between Temple and Whately, had been fought on 11 Dec. 1773 (Ossory i. 167).

29. In 1776 the Duchess of Kingston was found guilty of bigamy.

30. HW had just acquired the *Histoire naturelle de Pline, traduit en français avec le texte latin*, Paris, 1771, a translation by Louis Poinsinet de Sivry in 6 vols (Hazen, *Cat. of HW's Lib.*, No. 3140). He discusses it with Mason (Mason i. 159–61) and Mme du Deffand (du Deffand iv. 47).

31. Hamilton's collection of vases had come 'chiefly from Herculaneum' (Mann x. 46), and his antiquities purchased for the British Museum included objects 'from Herculaneum, Pompeii and Sicily' (Ossory i. 70). The 'instruments' in it, catalogued in GM 1778, xlviii. 505 include no musical ones.

32. *Le antichità di Ercolano exposte*, Naples, 1757–92, 8 vols folio, published by the Reale Accademia Ercolanese di Archeologia. Six volumes had been published. VII and VIII appeared in 1779 and 1792. HW owned these volumes and O. A. Baiardi's *Catalogo degli antichi monumenti*, Naples, 1754. See Hazen, *Cat. of HW's Lib.*, No. 3590; Mann v. 131, 363.

33. Sir John Hawkins (1719–89), Kt, 1772; editor and biographer of Samuel Johnson.

such a work³⁴—and Lady Hamilton is better qualified than anybody to assist you.³⁵ My best compliments to her—

Yours most sincerely

Hor. Walpole

PS. Don't forget your promised history of the great lady and *her médecin malgré lui.*³⁶

To Hamilton, Sunday 19 June 1774

Printed from a photostat of the original in the Harvard College Library, the gift of Mrs Harold Murdock. It was sold Sotheby's 3 March 1886, Hamilton sale lot 109; sold 5 May 1904, John W. Ford sale lot 205 to B. F. Stevens; sold 1904 to Mr Harold Murdock, Boston. First printed, Toynbee ix. 10.
Endorsed by Hamilton: Mr Walpole June 19th 1774.

Strawberry Hill, June 19, 1774.

FOR fear of troubling you, dear Sir, with two letters instead of one, I waited for the arrival of the shields¹ before I thanked you for them—but it put my gratitude to pain, for I did not receive them till the day before yesterday. Now they are come, it will, which is very selfish, double my gratitude, for they are fine and most charming—nay, almost in too good taste, not to put my Gothic house to shame—I wish the Medusas could turn it to stone! In short I am exceedingly obliged to you; but though I have spared you one letter of my own, it will cost you another of yours, for you must tell me more about them. The two that are painted,² are in the great style of the best age; and by the Earl of Surry's shield in the Duke of Norfolk's possession,³ which is in the same manner as to the form and

---

34. *General History of the Science and Practice of Music,* 1776, 5 vols 4to, the writing of which HW had suggested to Hawkins; see Hazen, *Cat. of HW's Lib.,* No. 34.

35. She was described in 1779 as 'the finest pianoforte player in Italy' (Oliver Warner, op. cit. 44).

36. The title of Molière's comedy, but the allusion here is unexplained. The 'great lady' might be Maria Carolina,

Queen of Naples, or her mother, the Empress Maria Theresa.

———

1. See *ante* HW to Hamilton 22 Feb. 1774.

2. One with the head of Medusa, one with the head of Perseus.

3. Probably at Worksop, Notts, where HW in 1768 had seen portraits of Henry Howard, styled E. of Surrey (*Country Seats* 65).

disposition, though not so bold, I should conclude they are by Polidore,[4] or of that school. Pray satisfy me, and of the pedigree of the
other too, which by the battlements on the buildings my house pretends is of its own family. I am going to hang them by the beautiful
armour of Francis I[5] and they will certainly make me dream of another Castle of Otranto, or at least of a tournament more superb than
Lord Stanley's *fête-champêtre*,[6] though the latter cost half a million.[7]
Indeed if gratitude was apt to colour one's dreams, I have so many
monuments of your kindness and friendship, that my house and garden would make my sleep as agreeable as my waking hours. I should
write another *Gierusalemme*[8] for Eleonora d'Este, and pray for you
in my new chapel, which is just finished,[9] and where the shrine[10] appears more gorgeous than the spoils

—of Ormus and of Ind—[11]

I do not mean new Claremont,[12] which is not half so magnificent.
You will not expect English news at this time of year. We have

4. Polidoro Caldara (ca 1495–1500 – ca
1543), known as Polidoro da Caravaggio, a
pupil of Raphael. HW attributed one of
the pictures at Houghton Hall to Polidoro, although it had been assigned to
Giulio Romano (*Ædes Walpolianæ, Works*
ii. 271; E. Bénézit, *Dictionnaire . . .
des peintures, sculpteurs . . .*, 1956–62;
Thieme and Becker; *Grande dizionario
enciclopedico Utet*, Turin, 1966–72, iii.
644).
5. On the staircase at SH, where Hamilton had seen it. For the alleged armour
of François I (1494–1547), which HW had
purchased in 1771, see OSSORY i. 66 and n.
16, iii. 235–6.
6. On 9 June at The Oaks, in Surrey,
for about 300 guests, on his engagement
to Lady Elizabeth Hamilton; see below.
For a detailed description of the festival, which began at 6:30 p.m. with rural
sports and continued with theatrical
diversions, supper and a ball until 4 a.m.,
see *London Chronicle* 9–16 June, xxxv.
560, 569–70; GM 1774, xliv. 263–5, there
called 'the first diversion of the kind
given in England.'
7. 'It will cost five thousand pounds'
(HW to Mann 8 June 1774, MANN viii. 14,
and n. 13). Special rooms were constructed

on the grounds for the supper and the
evening entertainment. 'He has bought
all the orange trees round London' (ibid.).
8. *Gerusalemme liberata*, by Tasso.
9. For the cost and description of the
Chapel in the Garden, begun in 1772, see
SH Accounts, ed. Toynbee, Oxford, 1927,
pp. 13–15, 151–60; 'Des. of SH,' *Works*
ii. 507, with a view by Pars engraved by
Godfrey, COLE i. 244 and n. 3.
10. By Capoccio (*ante* HW to Hamilton 22 Sept. 1768).
11. *Paradise Lost* ii. 2.
12. In Esher, Surrey, formerly the Duke
of Newcastle's seat, afterwards that of
Robert Clive (1725–22 Nov. 1774), cr.
(1762) Bn Clive of Plassy, who bought it
for £25,000 (estimated), pulled down the
house, and had a new one (sold after
Clive's death) built from plans by Brown
'at the cost of £100,000' (GEC iii. 326 n. *a*;
London Chronicle 6–11 July 1769, xxvi. 30,
38; Dorothy Stroud, *Capability Brown*,
[1950], pp. 130, 138–9, 151, 154–8). HW
thought the new house 'most admirable . . . ; it has more good rooms than
ever I saw in so small a compass, and
is very convenient too' (HW's 'Book of
Materials' 1771, p. 84; Toynbee *Supp.* ii.
164).

none but what we import from France, where the new King[13] and his brothers[14] were to be inoculated yesterday.[15] His Majesty is so economic that he will not give *fêtes-champêtres*. The French, who did not intend to like, adore him; and the Queen, who is too much the *Virgin* Mary,[16] has quite dethroned the latter in their idolatry. The Duc d'Aiguillon is removed,[17] which delights almost everybody, and the Duc de Choiseul has been at Versailles, which pleases almost as many[18]—though not us, for we have no mind to a war.

General Conway is gone a tour of armies,[19] because he has not seen enough of them. Lady Ailesbury and Mrs Damer are to fetch him from Paris in October.[20]

The Duke of Devonshire is married;[21] Lord Stanley and Lady Betty Hamilton[22] are to be in July.[23] Some wedlocks are breaking too: Lord Valentia[24] has preferred Dr Elliot's[25] pretty wife[26] to his

13. Louis XVI had become King 10 May 1774.

14. The Comte de Provence, Louis XVIII in 1814; and the Comte d'Artois, Charles X in 1824.

15. 'The King . . . having resolved to be inoculated for the smallpox, together with . . . his brothers and the Countess d'Artois, they set out . . . for Marly . . . to undergo the operation the 18th instant' (*London Chronicle* 18–21 June, xxxv. 582). Mme du Deffand wrote HW 19 June that they had been inoculated 'hier à neuf heures du matin' (DU DEFFAND iv. 62; cf. *London Chronicle* 23–25 June, xxxv. 606, the time given as 'eight o'clock').

16. Marie-Antoinette and Louis XVI, married in 1770, had no child until 19 Dec. 1778. See OSSORY i. 387 and n. 10.

17. As secretary of state for foreign affairs since 1771 (*ante* HW to Strafford 20 June 1771) and as secretary at war since Jan. 1774. See OSSORY i. 196 and n. 5.

18. Choiseul, d'Aiguillon's predecessor as foreign (principal) secretary, did not return to power.

19. 'To see armies, Prussian, Austrian, and French' (HW to Mann 18 Sept. 1774, MANN viii. 38; for Conway's itinerary see HW to Conway 23 June 1774, *et passim*, and especially Appendix 8, compiled from the journal of his tour).

20. They left for Paris 4 Oct. and returned with Conway, who arrived in London 21 Feb. 1775 (OSSORY, i. 200, n. 16).

21. The 5th Duke of Devonshire m. (5 June 1774) Lady Georgiana Spencer.

22. Elizabeth Hamilton (1753–97), dau. of James, 6th D. of Hamilton, m. (23 June 1774) Lord Stanley, from whom she separated in 1778 because of her affair with the D. of Dorset. Sir William Hamilton was grandson and she was great-great-granddaughter of William Douglas, 3d D. of Hamilton.

23. 'The report of . . . [their] marriage . . . is premature, their nuptials being deferred till the beginning of next week' (*London Chronicle* 16–18 June, xxxv. 578).

24. Arthur Annesley (1744–1816), 8th Vct Valentia, 1761, cr. (1793) E. of Mountnorris.

25. Sir John Elliott (1736–86), Kt. 1776, cr. (1778) Bt; M.D. St Andrews, 1759; later the physician to the P. of Wales.

26. Grace Dalrymple (ca 1754–1823), dau. of an advocate of Edinburgh, m. (1771) John Elliot. She had eloped with Valentia, with whom she lived until early in 1775. As a fashionable demi-rep, she was known as 'Dally (or Dolly) the Tall.' See also HW to Mann 8 June 1774, MANN viii. 15; BM, *Satiric Prints* for 1774–5; H. W. Bleackley, *Ladies Fair and Frail*, 1925, pp. 191–244.

own plain one;[27] but I do not find that there was much preference on her side, but rather on the Doctor's, for he has selected Lord Valentia from several other lords and gentlemen who have been equally kind to the fair one.[28]

We have the most delightful of all summers—fruits, flowers, corn, grass, leaves—in short though Judæa flowed with milk and honey, I do not believe it was much richer than the present face of England. I know but one richer spot, which is Almack's,[28a] where a thousand meadows and cornfields are staked at every throw, and as many villages lost as in the earthquake that overwhelmed Herculaneum and Pompeii.[29]

Pray tell Lady Hamilton I heard a new instrument yesterday, which transported me, though I have not the most musical ears in the world. It is a copulation of a harpsichord and a violin; one hand strikes the keys and the other draws the bow; the sounds are prolonged, and it is the softest and most touching melody I ever heard. The instrument is so small, it stands on a table,[30] and is called[31] a celestinette.[32] St Cecilia or Lady Hamilton would draw all the angels out of heaven with it, or immediately be appointed organists there.

Adieu! dear Sir—*shield* me from any more presents. Consider how you have loaded me,[33] and though gratitude is seldom mortal, I cannot bear so many obligations. I do not know how to be enough

Your very thankful humble servant

Hor. Walpole

27. Lucy Fortescue Lyttelton (1743–83), sister of Thomas, 2d Bn Lyttelton, m. (1767) Lord Valentia.

28. Elliott obtained a divorce, and Valentia was sentenced to pay £12,000 damages to him.

28a. The club noted for gambling; see Ossory i. 67, n. 3.

29. In A.D. 79.

30. 'It is not above two feet long and one foot and a half in the broadest part, where the keys are, which are placed on the top of the instrument' (*Delany Corr.*

11 Jan. 1775, v. 91, with a rough sketch).

31. MS reads 'calls.'

32. Invented by Mason; for details, see Mason *passim*, especially i. 178 and n. 17; J. W. Draper, *William Mason*, New York, 1924, p. 289.

33. In addition to the gifts mentioned earlier, Hamilton had given HW 'A silver gilt plate in relievo, the meeting of Charles V and Francis I' (*Des. of SH*, SH, 1774, p. 108; *Works* ii. 499), sold SH xvi. 53 to Zimmerman for £13.15.6.

To Hamilton, Monday 23 October 1775

Here first printed from MS now WSL; purchased from Hamill and Barker, April 1951. Sold Sotheby's 3 March 1886, Hamilton sale lot 110 to Ellis; sold American Art Galleries 22 March 1900, Augustin Daly sale lot 762 to J. O. Wright, a dealer who sold it to C. S. Bement at whose sale, American Art Association 2 March 1923, lot 1171, it was sold; obtained shortly afterwards by an anonymous gentleman.

Endorsed by Hamilton: Mr Walpole Arlington Street, October 23, 1775.

Arlington Street, Oct. 23d 1775.

My dear Sir,

I AM doing you a greater favour than I am asking, by recommending Mr Pars,[1] the bearer, to you. He has executed several views of Strawberry Hill for me delightfully,[2] and a glorious volume of Swisserland and other views for Lord Palmerston,[3] for he is excellent at washed drawings.[4] He will draw views of Pompeii in perfection. He has taken to oil, because We have no idea but of portraits of ourselves;[5] but as he is going to Italy to improve,[6] I flatter myself he

1. William Pars (1742–82), draughtsman and painter regarded as one of the founders of the English school of water-colourists, died in Rome of fever. HW also recommended him to Mann at Florence (to Mann 23 Oct., 14 Nov. 1775, MANN viii. 134–5, 144). When Pars sent or delivered this letter is not clear; he was in Naples 27 Oct.–15 Nov. 1780 and 30 May–12 August 1781 (Thomas Jones, 'Memoirs,' *Walpole Society 1946–1948*, 1951, xxxii. 100–02, 103–6) and probably at other times.

2. Five of the engravings in *Des. of SH* are after drawings by Pars; one drawing (illustrated, MANN viii. 135) is now WSL. Hamilton had met Pars in 1772: 'Soon after my first collection of vases was placed in the British Museum, Mr Paars [*sic*], a landscape painter, looking over that collection in my presence, assured me . . .' (Hamilton, *Collection of Engravings from Ancient Vases*, Vol. I, Naples, 1791, p. 20).

3. Henry Temple (1739–1802), 2d Vct Palmerston, 1757; M.P. for various boroughs 1762–1802; a lord of Trade 1765–6, of the Admiralty 1766–77, and of the Treasury 1777–82; member of the Society of Dilettanti, 1765. In 1767 Pars had ac-

companied him to the Continent and had made drawings for him in Switzerland, the Tyrol, and Rome. In 1771 he exhibited at the Royal Academy 8 of these views, chiefly of Switzerland (Algernon Graves, *Royal Academy of Arts*, 1905–6, vi. 63–4).

4. In 1772 he had exhibited two 'stained drawings' at the Royal Academy: 'Part of the lake of Sligo in Ireland' and 'Part of the lake of Keswick, Cumberland' (ibid. vi. 64); in 1761 he had exhibited 'A lady; in water colours' (Algernon Graves, *The Society of Artists . . . The Free Society of Artists*, 1907, p. 190).

5. At the Royal Academy 1769–76 Pars exhibited 27 works, of which 8 were portraits; in 1760–4 he had exhibited 11 portraits and two 'miniatures' but no views (Graves, works cited in preceding note).

6. In March the Society of Dilettanti had named Pars a 'student' to 'go into Italy' under the protection of the Society, his annual stipend for three years to be half of the interest from £4,000 'three per cent,' or £60 a year, the stipend to begin after he reached Rome 21 Dec. 1775 (Lionel Cust, *History of the Society of Dilettanti*, ed. Sidney Colvin, 1898, pp. 57–8).

finds he cannot improve by drawing our faces. He is so modest you will like him, and the Italian ladies will not; but he looks as if it was worth their while to cure him.[7]

I cannot content myself with only sending you Mr Pars, but though you will not receive this the Lord knows when, I must take the opportunity of adding a few words. What are you doing? Have you exhausted all the towns above ground and under? Are we to have no more volcanoes or the ruins they make? What flight have you taken? you cannot be idle. Has Lady Hamilton cured all the persons bitten by tarantulas?[8] Have you been underground quite to Elysium? and has Eurydice fetched you back again? give some account of yourself.

I am just returned from Paris, where I have been two months.[9] They are reviving architecture[10] and effacing painting. They have varnished all the pictures at Versailles[11] and the Palais-Royal,[12] till you can see no face in them but your own; and they were going to serve the Chartreuse[13] so, but Monsieur d'Anchevilliers,[14] Intendant des Bâtiments, saved them.[15]

Your old passion Lady Di Beauclerc has lately turned to modelling in wax, and has executed some bas-reliefs that have infinitely more grace, yes, yes, than the antique, and ten times more nature and expression. Come and believe your eyes: I have two of them.[16]

7. Pars was accompanied to Rome by 'Mrs Pars,' who lived with him until her death at Rome 6 June 1778. She was the estranged wife of John Smart (1741–1811), the miniaturist. See Thomas Jones, op. cit. xxxii. 73–4.

8. The bite of the tarantula, a 'large wolf-spider of Southern Europe (Lycossa tarantula), named from the town' Taranto, southeast of Naples, 'was formerly supposed to be cured by nothing but music; though it occasions a great deal of pain, it is almost never fatal' (OED; Encyclopædia Britannica, Edinburgh, 1810, viii. 222). For the symptoms thought to accompany its bite, which is only slightly poisonous, and the effect of music in promoting a cure, see A New and Complete Dictionary of Arts and Sciences, 1754–5, sub Tarantula.

9. 18 Aug. – 17 Oct., HW's last visit to Paris ('Paris Journals,' DU DEFFAND v. 342–53).

10. See post HW to Hamilton 18 Feb. 1776.

11. HW had been there 22, 26 Sept. 1775 ('Paris Journals,' DU DEFFAND v. 343–4).

12. HW records a visit there 24 July 1771 but none in 1775 (ibid. v. 336).

13. HW had been there 6 Aug. 1771 but did not record a visit in 1775 (ibid. v. 337; ante HW to Strafford 25 Aug. 1771).

14. Charles-Claude Flahaut (1730–1809), Comte de la Billarderie d'Angiviller, had been appointed directeur général des bâtiments on the accession of Louis XVI, emigrated in 1791 and lived thereafter in Russia and Germany. See Jacques Silvestre de Sacy, Le Comte d'Angiviller, dernier directeur général des bâtiments, [1953]. HW had met him in Paris 11 Sept., 3 Oct. ('Paris Journals,' DU DEFFAND v. 348, 352).

15. See post HW to Hamilton 18 Feb. 1776.

16. In the Great North Bedchamber

She has since taken to drawing children in bistre.[17] I will only tell you that Sir Joshua Reynolds[18]—yes, I will tell you on my own authority, that I never saw anything like them. Albano's boys are fools to them—dull jolter-headed[19] cubs, and all alike, as if they were the Countess of Haynault's three hundred and sixty-five children.[20] She has promised me one a day as long as I live, and did three the first day—I mean, Lady Di did, not the Countess of Haynault. As I don't expect an answer these two years, I will add no more news—but I should be very happy to see you before you receive my letter.

Yours most affectionately

Hor. Walpole

were 'Two bas-reliefs of boys in wax on glass, designed and modelled in the most graceful and perfect Roman taste by Lady Diana Beauclerk sister of George Spencer Duke of Marlborough 1775,' followed by eight lines of HW's verse (HW's MS note in his copy, now WSL, of *Des. of SH*, 1774, p. 103). The phrase 'in the most perfect Roman taste' was omitted in the 1784 edn pp. 72–3, and in *Works* ii. 495; see also HW's *Fugitive Verses*, p. 182. In HW's MS copy, the last line reads '. . . bright lightning's dart,' instead of 'keen lightning's dart' of the printed versions. These two bas-reliefs were sold SH xviii. 116 to Thorne of Richmond for £2. Later HW had in the Breakfast Room at SH: 'Two beautiful bas-reliefs in wax of boys by Lady Diana Beauclerk, set in frames with her arms and cameos by Wedgwood and Tassie in festoons' (HW's MS note in his copy, now WSL, of *Des. of SH*, 1774, p. 25; slightly rephrased in the 1784 edn, p. 19, and *Works* ii. 423); sold SH xxii. 51 (one frame said to be of satinwood, the other of ebony) to Town and Emanuel for £11.0.6. In HW's extra-illustrated *Des. of SH*, 1784, now WSL, p. 19, is 'Lady Di's sketch for the frames of her bas-reliefs' 'by Lady Di Beauclerc 1776' (HW's MS notes). The wax medallion is round, the frame square.

17. 'In 1774 she took to modelling in

wax, and did several bas-reliefs of boys as finely and with more grace than the antique. In 1775 she did a great many most charming drawings of children in soot water, tinging the faces with carmine; nothing could be superior to them' (*Anecdotes of Painting*, v. ed. Hilles and Daghlian, New Haven, 1927, p. 234). None of these drawings can be identified in the *Des. of SH* or the SH sale catalogue. Many of her drawings of children are illustrated in Beatrice Erskine, *Lady Diana Beauclerk*, 1903.

18. No specific comment by him on her drawings has been found.

19. 'Clumsy-, dull-, heavy-headed' (OED).

20. Margaretha, wife of Herman, Count of Hennenberg, and dau. of Floris, Count of Holland and Zeeland, was supposed to have given birth in 1276 to 365 children, as the result of a curse. See HW to Mann 30 April 1762, MANN vi. 32 and n. 15, and to Mason 17 Jan. 1780, MASON ii. 4 and n. 4, where HW calls her 'Countess of Holland'; to Hannah More 20 Feb. 1790, MORE 338 and n. 2. 'Countess of Hainault'; to the Cts of Mount Edgcumbe 29 Nov. 1794, 'the Flemish Countess.' She was sometimes styled 'Countess of Holland' and 'Countess of Zeeland' but not, in the sources other than HW, 'Countess of Hainault.'

To Hamilton, Sunday 18 February 1776

Printed from Toynbee *Supp.* iii. 22–5; there printed from MS in the possession of Mr Francis Edwards, 83 High Street, Marylebone, W., London. Sold
Sotheby's 3 March 1886, Hamilton sale lot 111 to Thibaudeau; sold Sotheby's
7 May 1919, Alfred Morrison sale lot 3127 to Maggs Bros.

Arlington Street, Feb. 18, 1776.

I HASTE to answer your kind letter, dear Sir, lest I should not
find you at Naples. Yourself and Lady Hamilton are as much as
I desire thence, and I shall not trouble you with any commission but
to bring them safe.[1] The mountains of Swisserland are, I am persuaded, a fine sight, and I shall desire to be a subscriber to your
Vesuvius:[2] but I wish you had not exchanged your taste in painting
and antiquity for phenomena. A turn for natural history possesses
people enough; so do the arts, but not many who have your taste.
Perhaps my own inclinations bias me, for I own I have no curiosity
about the anatomy of Nature. I admire and revere, but am not more
struck, probably less, with the dissection than with the superficies.

Thank you for the inscription[3] on the Duke of Matalone's[4] villa.
It is a prudent precaution, and would prevent many people from
being left quite alone. But inscriptions are like mottoes of families,
which seldom suit two generations. I believe the Pretender thought
so, when the present royal family adopted *Dieu et mon Droit.*[5] *Ich
dien*[6] has not been always applicable, but I believe the late Prince[7]

1. The Hamiltons arrived in England
in September (HW to Mann 20 Sept.
1776, MANN viii. 241).
2. *Campi Phlegræi. Observations* [text
in English and French] *on the Volcanos
of the Two Sicilies . . . Map . . . Annexed, with 54 Plates Illuminated from
Drawings Taken and Colour'd after Nature . . . by . . . Peter Fabris*, Naples,
1776, 2 vols folio, with *Supplement*, Naples,
1779. Apparently HW did not own the work,
in which no list of subscribers is printed.
The first two volumes sold, 'half-bound,'
for '60 Neapolitan ducats' (i. 90; Cadell
advertised 'some copies . . . on sale at the
price of *Twelve Guineas*' [*Monthly Review*, May 1777, lvi. 381 n.]), and the text
was a reprint, with slight additions, of
Hamilton's letters to the Royal Society
1766–71. See Hazen, *Cat of HW's Lib.*,
No. 2865; *ante* HW to Hamilton 5 March

1771; and especially Oliver Warner, *Emma
Hamilton and Sir William*, 1960, pp. 48–
50, for comment on *Campi Phlegræi* as a
fine example of printing and illustration.
3. Missing.
4. Marzio Domenico Carafa V (1758–
1829), last Duke of Matalona, whose family's palace on the Via Toledo is described by Casanova (Giacomo Casanova
di Seingalt, *Storia della mia vita*, ed.
Chiara, 1965, iv. 285, 316, vii. 471).
5. A phrase used by Richard I at the
battle of Gisors, 1198; the motto of the
sovereigns of England since the time of
Henry VI.
6. The motto of the P. of Wales, 'I
serve.'
7. Frederick Louis (1707–51), P. of
Wales, whose father, George II, lived
until 1760.

thought that maxim of our law was too literally true, that *the King never dies.*

I have no new anecdotes for you of painters or architects. It is nothing new that pictures keep up at high-water mark; and yet Mr Pearson[8] has been greatly disappointed. He brought over a Madonna and Child, by Vandyck as he said, which I doubt, though a very fine picture. He said too that he had refused two thousand pounds for it, and asked four. It was put up to auction yesterday at Christie's at one thousand. Not one shilling was bidden.[9]

I hear of little brought over from Mariette's[10] glorious sale[11] of drawings and prints, which sold enormously, though not for near what the King of France offered for the whole four days before the sale.[12] I have got a few trifles that I wished for.[13]

You will find Park Place still augmented in beauty. Mr Conway is gone thither on an alarm of a crack by the late terrible frost[14] in his *own* bridge,[15] but I do not doubt but his skill will repair it. I advise Lady Hamilton to beg, buy, or steal all the plumes from all the theatres on her road: she will want them for a single fashionable head-dress, nay, and gourds and melons into the bargain.[16] You will

8. James Bradshaw Pierson (1741 – ca 1818), of Stokesley, Yorks; son of Victor Repinder, an Italian who took the name of Pierson; born in Italy; admitted as a fellow-commoner at Peterhouse, Cambridge, 1762; admitted to London's Lincoln Inn, 1762 (MANN vii. 569, n. 13 and sources there cited; OSSORY i. 289, n. 22).

9. For this sale, see Frits Lugt, *Répertoire des catalogues des ventes*, The Hague, 1938–64, No. 2490; see also HW to Lady Ossory 27 Dec. 1775, OSSORY i. 289. No further history of the picture has been found.

10. Pierre-Jean Mariette (1694–1774), engraver and collector (Barbara Scott, 'Pierre-Jean Mariette,' *Apollo*, 1973, xcvii. 54–9).

11. 15 Nov. 1775 – 30 Jan. 1776 (Lugt, op. cit. No. 2453). HW had seen some of the contents before the sale, 20 Sept., 6 Oct. ('Paris Journals,' DU DEFFAND v. 350, 352; HW to Lady Ossory 3 Oct. 1775, OSSORY i. 265–6).

12. See OSSORY i. 282–3. To purchase Mariette's drawings and prints for the King's collection, d'Angiviller offered, before the auction, 160,000 then 250,000, and

finally 300,000 livres, but the heirs refused; the auction fetched 297,000 livres (Jacques Silvestre de Sacy, *Le Comte d'Angivillers, dernier directeur général des bâtiments*, [1953], pp. 127–8; NBG).

13. In addition to the items mentioned to Lady Ossory 20 Dec. 1775, OSSORY i. 281–3, HW purchased an original drawing of a clock, by Holbein, sold SH xx. 72 to Lord Waldegrave for £735.0.0, and two architectural drawings by Giovanni Paolo Pannini, sold SH xvii. 36 to 'Hon. Col. D. Damer, M.P.,' for £7.7.0.

14. See MASON i. 240.

15. The 'rocky bridge' (still in use) designed by and constructed under the supervision of Conway; described in MONTAGU ii. 104–5 and n. 8, *sub* 1763; OSSORY iii. 15 and n. 4.

16. 'The heads are higher than ever, with feathers *en rayons de soleil* and *le jardin anglais*—fruit, turnips, and potatoes; the gowns trimmed the same way . . . my gown for the Birthday was trimmed with grapes, acorns, and roses, so that I looked like a walking hothouse' (*Life and Letters of Sir Gilbert Elliot*, ed. Lady Minto, 1874, i. 49). See BM, *Satiric*

think like William the Conqueror that you meet marching forests.[17]

The hard frost, as I choose to suppose, has given me an eccentric fit of the gout,[18] which has confined me to my chamber, and almost to my bed these three weeks. I hope to be quite well to receive you and Lady Hamilton at Strawberry Hill, where you will find Diva Eleanora and particularly your shrine of Capoccio worthily consecrated. I wish I could find engravers as reasonable as you do:[19] but here one must have plundered Bengal to afford their prices;[20] and I plunder nobody but myself.

As you pass through Paris, look at the new front of Ste-Geneviève,[21] at the École de Chirurgie[22] (which by the by you cannot stand far enough from to see) and at some of the new *hôtels*.[23] Don't look at any of the finest pictures, for they have all been so varnished, that you can see nothing but yourself in them. Some of those at the Palais-Royal and those of the Prince of Monaco, have been transported to new canvases, inch by inch, and the junctures filled up, and the whole repainted. They had begun on the glorious Chartreuse, but Monsieur d'Anchevilliers, Intendant des Bâtiments, had

Prints v. 237–48, Nos 5370–96, for caricatures of extravagant head-dresses in 1776, showing the use of ostrich feathers, fruit, vegetables, corn, flowers, etc.

17. In Holinshed's *Chronicles*, 1587 (HW's copy is Hazen, *Cat. of HW's Lib.*, No. 597), iii. 2, is the familiar legend of the men of Kent marching to meet the Conqueror with green boughs for concealment. See Thomas Deloney's ballad in *Strange Histories*, 1607 for another version of the Birnam Wood story: '. . . So that unto the Conqueror's sight, amazed as he stood,/They seemed to be a walking grove, or else a moving Wood.' See also HW to Montagu 14 Oct. 1756, Montagu i. 198 and n. 8.

18. 'Eccentric' because, according to HW's theory about his gout, he had an attack every two years, and 1776 was supposed to be his odd year. See HW to Mason 6 Feb. 1776, Mason i. 240.

19. The engravers most employed by Hamilton on his *Collection of Etruscan, Greek and Roman Antiquities* were Antoine Cardon, Carmine Pignatoro, Giuseppe Bracci, and Carlo Nolli (Brian Fothergill, *Sir William Hamilton*, New York, 1969, p. 66).

20. Three payments to Charles Grignion (1717–1810) in 1757 are recorded in the *Journal of the Printing Office at Strawberry Hill*, ed. Paget Toynbee, 1923, pp. 23, 30, 77: for 'the fleuron' (approximately 3 1/8 inches), £2.12.6; Queen Elizabeth's coin (5/8 x 1 inch), £1.1.0; the 'lesser fleuron' (2 x 2 3/4 inches), £2.2.0.

21. Which HW had seen 12 Sept. 1775. It was being replaced by the new church, now the Panthéon (du Deffand v. 348; Ossory i. 260).

22. Which HW had also seen 12 Sept. 1775. Here, in Ossory i. 260, and in 'Paris Journals' he seems to have written *École de Chirurgie* when he should have written *Académie Royale de Chirurgie*. Under the latter, the surgical departments were just completing a magnificent new building in the Rue des Cordeliers, where the École de Médecine now is (du Deffand v. 348 and n. 26).

23. See HW to Lady Ossory 9 Sept. 1775, Ossory i. 260–1; 'Paris Journals,' 12, 19 Sept., 10 Oct. 1775, du Deffand v. 348, 349, 353.

the sense to stop them, will transplant the originals to Versailles, and give copies to the Convent.[24] He must make haste, or they will perish, or he be displaced; and taste is not hereditary in places more than in families. Adieu! dear Sir,

Yours most cordially,

Hor. Walpole

From Hamilton, ca Monday 19 May 1777

Missing. See *post* 23 May 1777.

To Hamilton, Friday 23 May 1777

Printed from photostat (gift of Mr Robert H. Taylor, Yonkers, N. Y., 20 Oct. 1950) of the MS bought 30 Jan. 1950 by Mr Taylor from Mr Charles S. Boesen acting for the estate of Gabriel Wells. Previously printed Toynbee x. 54. Sold Sotheby's 3 March 1886 Hamilton sale lot 112 to Ellis; sold Sotheby's 21 Jan. 1899 lot 278 to Ellis; in 1900 in the possession of Ellis and Elvey booksellers, 29 New Bond Street, London; sold Sotheby's 28 Oct. 1902, Gilbert J. Ellis sale lot 212 to W. Browne.

Address: To Sir William Hamilton.
Endorsed by Hamilton: Note from Mr Walpole 1777.

Arlington Street, May 23d 1777.

LAST Monday I found on my table a curious case of tortoise-shell studded with silver,[1] with an anonymous note,[2] telling me it

---

24. At d'Angiviller's suggestion, the Carthusians gave twenty-two pictures (now in the Louvre) of *The Life of St Bruno*, by Eustache Lesueur. In return, the King gave the Chartreuse his portrait, and the royal treasury paid 30,000 livres towards the cost of repairs. D'Angiviller had the paintings transferred from wood to canvas, but despite the care of the restorer, Hacquin, the pictures 'ne retrouvèrent jamais le fraîcheur de leurs tons primitifs' (Jacques Silvestre de Sacy, op. cit. 130, with details, including letters of negotiation, at pp. 128–30).

1. In the Great North Bedchamber: 'A tortoise-shell case studded with silver, in which Van Trump used to carry his pipes to sea to prevent their being broken. A present from . . . [*sic*] Hamilton Esq.' (HW's MS note in his copy, now wsl, of *Des. of SH*, 1774, p. 110, printed in the Appendix to that work, ca 1781, p. 139, with *Trump* printed *Tromp, to prevent . . . broken* omitted and *Mr Hamilton* named as donor; 1784 edn, p. 77; *Works* ii. 502); sold SH xvi. 87 to Thomas Garle for £5.15.6.
2. Missing.

had belonged to Van Trump.[3] My stupid footboy[4] could not recollect the name of the sender. I was going to advertise for my benefactor, and have made such a rout with my gratitude, that at last the house-maid[5] recollected the footman[6] had told her it was Sir William Hamilton: you know, dear Sir, how many reasons I have for believing her; Strawberry Hill is filled with your presents, and if they could speak, would be with my gratitude. Your name is in every page of my catalogue,[7] which is some proof of what I say—but as gratitude without shame, is but an honest whore that owns she will take money, I beg that if you deserve to sit for Liberality, I may have some claim to be drawn for Modesty, and therefore I do beg you will never give me anything more, as I could not be more ashamed, nor more than I am

Your most obliged humble servant

HOR. WALPOLE

From Lady Hamilton, ca Tuesday 10 June 1777

Missing. HW wrote to H. S. Conway 10 July 1777: 'This is more to Lady Hamilton than to you. Pray tell her I have seen *Monsieur la Bataille d'Agincourt*. He brought me her letter yesterday: and I . . . flatter myself he was, and she will be, content with the regard I paid to her letter.'

To Hamilton, ca Thursday 6 December 1781

Missing. 'Pray convey the enclosed to Sir W. Hamilton as soon as you can, and safely' (HW to Mann, PS, 6 Dec., to letter of 4 Dec. 1781, Mann ix. 218). 'I sent you a long letter by your servant, with another enclosed for Sir William Hamilton' (HW to Mann 21 Dec. 1781, ibid. ix. 219).

3. Martin Harpertzoon Tromp (1597–1653), killed in action against the English; or his son Cornelius van Tromp (1629–91), both Dutch admirals.

4. Probably James Sibley, the second footman named in HW to Charles Bedford 18 June 1781. HW's will, dated 15 May 1793, lists a legacy of £100 to 'Ann Sibley of Teddington, widow of my late footman James Sibley' (SELWYN 362).

5. Presumably Mary, mentioned in HW to Lady Ossory 13 Nov. 1776, Ossory i. 330.

6. David Monnerat (d. 1785), HW's Swiss footman.

7. The *Des. of SH*, 1774.

To HAMILTON, ca April 1782.

Missing. See first sentence, *post* 28 May 1782.

From HAMILTON, Tuesday 28 May 1782

Here first printed from photostat of MS in the possession of the Edinburgh University Library.

Address: To the Honourable Hor. Walpole, Berkeley Square, London, *Inghilterra, via Mantua.*

Postmark: IU 17.

Naples, May 28, 1782.

My dear Sir,

THOUGH I cannot yet answer as fully as I could wish to every part of your last letter, I will not defer answering as far as I am able. Though I expected much from what you had told me of Mrs Damer's talents, I was astonished at what she did here;[1] from an idea she took from a profile on a Sicilian medal of a Ceres she made a bust[2] considerably bigger than life, and in my opinion there is not an artist now in Italy that could have done it with so much of the true sublime, and which none but the first artists of Greece seem to have understood perfectly. They might perhaps have made the model more correct, from the great habit of daily modelling, but it would have wanted, I am certain, that true simplicity and dignity which Mrs Damer has given it. She copied also a medallion of a head of Jupiter most admirably—but that is not so surprising as the bust, which may be said to be a creation of her own. When we have peace I will send you a cast from it. At present we have no ships that go directly from hence to England. If Mrs Damer should be with you, pray kiss the fair hand for me that is capable of such wonder-working. As to your idea of giving forms to masses of lava,[3] to be sure

1. HW had written to Mann, 7 Sept. 1781: 'Mrs Damer . . . is going abroad to confirm a very delicate constitution, I believe at Naples' (MANN ix. 183–4).

2. This, and the copied medallion which is mentioned below, are not iden-tified by HW and the others who list or discuss her works.

3. When at Warwick Castle in 1768, HW had seen a 'table of lava inlaid with marbles' (*Country Seats* 63).

something of the kind might be done, and there are rocks of it in this Sicilian Majesty's[4] garden at Portici[5] ready for the chisel, but by looking at the VIIIth plate of my book, *Campi Phlegræi*, and reading (No. 6) of the references to that plate,[6] you will understand why nothing very colossal can be made out of the lava. It would admit of fine large vases, and from your idea I will endeavour at persuading the King of Naples to have some executed in the Portici garden, but alas! the sublime of art at this Court consists in shooting flying.[7] I have done all in my power to excite a little love of the arts in the King of Naples and by having directed some pictures of different *chasses* to be painted by some of the best painters and shown to his Majesty, he bought them and ordered others, and now he begins to think himself a judge of painting; in time this may be of service to the poor artists who are famished—for you know how far the example of the Court is followed in such countries as these—at present there is not one of the nobility that can distinguish between the worst daub and the finest picture, but they can all shoot flying.

Madame de Genlis[8] has been ill-informed as to the story of the Duchess of *Cirifalco*.[9] Lady Hamilton[10] intends to send you the whole story,[11] which is a cruel one and which she is to get from a

---

4. Ferdinand IV (1751–1825), K. of Naples (Ferdinand III of Sicily), who in 1817 became Ferdinand I of the Two Sicilies. He is frequently mentioned in MANN.

5. About 4 miles SE of Naples, on the Bay at the foot of Vesuvius. The Palazzo Reale stood there.

6. '(6) Hollows formed in the lava by the air which was confined therein, and are distinctive marks of lavas in general, as are likewise the horizontal, and perpendicular cracks which are formed at the time of the lava's cooling, and shrinking' (*Campi Phlegræi*, Naples, 1776–9, ii. letter-press accompanying Plate VIII).

7. During Ferdinand IV's minority, Bernardo Tanucci, who was influential in the regency, encouraged the King's tendencies to pleasure, idleness, sports (especially shooting and fishing), and non-intellectual interests. Tanucci had been dismissed in 1776, but the King did not change. An account from Naples 13 Dec. 1785 indicates that the King was 'willing as much as possible' to encourage exca-

vation for the discovery of ancient monuments, which he was to have the option of purchasing 'at a fair price, in order to enrich his museum' (*London Chronicle* 14–17 Jan. 1786, lix. 54).

8. Stéphanie-Félicité Ducrest de Saint-Aubin (1746–1830), m. (1763) Charles-Alexis Brulart, Comte de Genlis, later Marquis de Sillery; dramatist and educational writer, mistress of the Duc de Chartres (Duc d'Orléans, 1785), and 'governor' to his children. According to Litta (see below) she wrote a novelette about the Duchessa di Girifalco.

9. Olimpia Maria Maddalena Colonna (1731–1800) m. (1748) Gennaro Maria Caracciolo, Duca di Girifalco (or Cirifalco) and Stella (Pompeo Litta, *Famiglie celebri italiane*, 1st ser. *sub* Colonna, tavola x; 2d ser. i, Naples, 1902, tavola xxxvii; *Fortgesetzte neue genealogisch-historiche Nachrichten*, viii, Leipzig, 1768–9, pp. 133–4).

10. In failing health in the spring, she died 25 Aug. 1782.

11. The Duchess's husband, finding

lady[12] who was well acquainted with her—but it could not be pro-cured for this post. The Duchess of Cirifalco was a daughter of the Princess Barberini,[13] and I saw her at Rome[14] with her mother after she got her liberty. The Duke Cirifalco[15] died in prison at Naples, supposed to have been poisoned—for the Duchess could never be brought to accuse her husband.[16] His Cast[ilian] Majesty (then King of Naples) ⟨was⟩[17] very desirous to bring him to an exemplary pun-ishment.

I rejoice at our friend Mr Conway's possessing at last the place in the world that I know suits his inclination best.[18] His capacity is fit for any post. Give us peace that we may have the pleasure of mak-ing you another visit. I have no other request to the new ministry[19] but to leave me where I have been above 17 years.[20] Adieu, my dear Sir,

Yours ever

W. HAMILTON

her with a young man, imprisoned her in the castle of Girifalco, and declared her dead, but her cries were heard by passing monks whose superior warned her family and she was liberated by the president of the province (Litta, 1st ser., loc. cit.).

12. Not identified.

13. Cornelia Barberini (ca 1711–97), Principessa di Palestrina, m. (1728) Giulio Cesare Colonna, Principe di Carbognano and Duca di Bassanello; she was heiress of the Barberini family (Litta, 1st ser., loc. cit.).

14. The Duchessa di Girifalco retired to a convent at Rome, and died in a monastery there in 1800 (Litta, 1st ser. loc. cit., 2d ser. loc. cit.).

15. Gennaro Maria Caracciolo (1720–66), Duca di Girifalco (or Cirifalco) and Stella, Marchese (*Fortgesetzte neue Genea-*

logisch-historiche Nachrichten, loc. cit.).

16. According to Litta, 1st ser., loc. cit., his wife would never discuss her hus-band's ill-treatment of her.

17. MS torn.

18. In March, Conway had come in with the Rockingham ministry as com-mander-in-chief of the Army and a mem-ber of the cabinet. After Rockingham's death 1 July 1782 Conway continued as commander-in-chief, but not as a member of the cabinet, until Dec. 1783.

19. Rockingham's, 27 March – 1 July 1782.

20. Hamilton had arrived in Naples 17 Nov. 1764, his credentials and instruc-tions were dated 31 Aug. 1764 (Horn, *British Diplomatic Representatives, 1689–1789,* p. 76).

To Hamilton, Thursday 17 January 1788

Here first printed from MS now wsl; purchased from the Brick Row Book Shop, Nov. 1942; sold Sotheby's 3 March 1886, Hamilton sale, lot 113, to Pearson.

Address: À Monsieur Monsieur le Chevalier Hamilton, envoyé extraordinaire de sa Majesté Britannique à la Cour de Naples.

Berkeley Square, Jan. 17th 1788.

Dear Sir,

I AM ashamed to write to you, when it is only to trouble you with a trifling commission that interests nobody but myself—but indeed it will cost you no more trouble than that of writing a couple of short letters. In a word, a person[1] not long ago brought me from Italy a drawing of the real Castle of Otranto, and said it had been actually taken on the spot in 1785.[2]

When I wrote my fantastic tale,[3] I did not know that there existed, or ever had existed, a castle at that place, but looked into the map of Naples[4] for a name, and adopted Otranto as well-sounding. Still,

1. Lady Elizabeth Berkeley (1750–1828), m. 1 (1767) William Craven, 6th Bn Craven, 1769, from whom she was separated ca 1783; m. 2 (1791) Christian Friedrich Karl Alexander, Margrave of Brandenburg-Ansbach and Bayreuth. Hamilton 'had been attentive to Lady Craven . . . [and] as Hamilton soon revealed [to his nephew Charles Greville], it was a close thing with Lady Craven, though it could only have been a liaison for at least some years' (Oliver Warner, *Emma Hamilton and Sir William,* 1960, p. 79). See also HW to Lady Craven 27 Nov. 1786, in which he thanks her for sending him the drawing.

2. 'A view of the real Castle of Otranto on the eastern coast of the kingdom of Naples, a washed drawing taken on the spot in March 1785, by Mr Revely, and given to Mr Walpole by Eliz. Lady Craven' (HW's MS note in his copy, now wsl, of *Des. of SH,* 1774, p. 158; MS note, altered, ibid. 1784, p. 92, printed ibid., p. 94, and in *Works* ii. 494, with omission of 'on the eastern . . . Naples' and 'taken . . . Revely' and with other changes). Willey Reveley (d. 1799) accompanied Sir Richard Worsley (1751–1805), 7th Bt, 1768, as 'architect and draughtsman' to Italy, Greece, Turkey, and Egypt. In Constantinople, April–May 1786, Worsley told Lady Craven he planned to give the drawing to HW, but she offered to present it, Worsley being unacquainted with HW (HW to Lady Ossory 6 Feb. 1789, Ossory iii. 36 and n. 15; *Beautiful Lady Craven,* ed. A. M. Broadley and Lewis Melville, 1914, i. p. xxxix *et passim*). No reference to the drawing as the gift of Worsley has been found in the SH records; it was sold SH xvi. 117, with another drawing to Forster for £1.13.0.

3. 'June [1764], I began *The Castle of Otranto,* a Gothic story, and finished it August 6th . . . Dec. 24 . . . published,' but dated 1765 ('Short Notes,' Gray i. 41).

4. HW owned the *Atlas nouveau* of Guillaume and Nicolas Sanson, n.d. and Nicolas Châtelain's *Atlas historique,* Amsterdam, 1705–8 (Hazen, *Cat. of HW's Lib.,* Nos 533, 425), as well as several historical works about Naples, which may have contained maps.

the drawing corresponds so very well with the circumstances of the narrative, that I cannot help suspecting the idea was conceived, or at least adapted to flatter the vanity of the author; and I do wish you would be so kind as to inform yourself, and then me, whether there is in fact such an actual castle—I will tell you why I wish to know, from more than personal curiosity.

Mr Edwards,[5] a very ingenious bookseller, and of much taste, has been this summer in Italy in the pursuit of curiosities in his profession. He formed an intimacy at Parma with the renowned printer of that city (whose name, though a kind of printer myself, I have shamefully forgotten)[6] the Parmesan Elzevir promised Edwards to print some English book for him;[7] and Edwards (I suppose from partiality for me as a printer) wished it might be one of my productions. I named (though never printed at my own press) my *Otranto*, as the only one of my writings which is ever likely to be much known out of our island—indeed the Duchess of Gloucester tells me it has been translated into Italian[8]—when or where I had never heard, nor know yet—though should it ever come into your hands, dear Sir, I should be obliged to you for a sight of it—it was early translated in France, but very imperfectly.[9]

To be short, should the drawing not be imaginary, I would have it engraved for a frontispiece to the edition of Parma[10]—I have done about myself.

The papers tell us that *your* school, Mount Vesuvius, is going to

5. James Edwards (1757–1816), bookseller in Pall Mall, bibliographer, bibliophile, and HW's occasional correspondent (Berry i. 150 and n. 24).

6. Giambattista Bodoni (1740–1813), type-designer and printer (Berry i. 150 and nn. 22–3).

7. Although Bodoni printed a few English books and occasional poems 1788–1800, *The Castle of Otranto* was the only one said on the title-page to be printed for Edwards; see H. C. Brooks, *Compendiosa bibliografia di edizione Bodoniane*, Florence, 1927, pp. 65–141.

8. The earliest printed Italian translation that has been found is *Il castello di Otranto. Storia gotica*, tr. Giovanni [Jean] Sivrac, and 'Stampato da T. Bensley, sotto l'ispezione di Giovanni Sivrac,' London, 1795, 'Presso Molini, Polidori, Molini e Co. Hay-Market; ed I. [James]

Edwards, Pall-Mall,' the only Italian edition recorded in Hazen, op. cit., No. 3728; now wsl.

9. *Le Château d'Otrante*, tr. Marc-Antoine Eidous, Amsterdam and Paris, 1767, 2 vols 12mo. In 'Short Notes,' *sub* March 1767, HW called it a 'bad translation' (Hazen, op. cit., No. 3908).

10. Barlow's engraving of Reveley's drawing (Reveley is not named on the plate) exists in three different states in *The Castle of Otranto*, 'The Sixth Edition,' Parma, 'Printed by Bodoni, for I. [James] Edwards, Bookseller, of London. MDCCXCI.' For a discussion of the states of the plate and the edition, the difficulties and delays in printing, see Hazen, *Bibl. of HW* 56–63. HW's copy of the book, now wsl, is Hazen, *Cat. of HW's Lib.*, No. 3729.

give you another lecture on conflagration.[11] Your more practical brother professor, Lord George Gordon, is in Newgate,[12] as has happened to other Jewish[13] prophets and incendiaries. You, who only expound, not preach, have all the merit he wants, that of communicating knowledge, but I always fear lest like some heathen philosophers of old,[14] you should probe too far into those blazing abysses of Nature.

Mrs Damer has finished a bust of an infant Atys or Paris in marble,[15] that not only surpasses any Grecian flesh, but comes up to the softness and delicacy of Correggio. Yet while her mornings are so Athenian, in the evenings she is a capital actress in comedy;[16] and as I conclude she possesses every talent she pleases, I am teasing her to appear in tragedy. She has a pathetic harmony in her voice that Mrs Siddons wants.

While you deal in fire, our friend General Conway is as indefatigable in improving smoke[17]—but I am too ignorant to talk on that subject—and having in my first page stated my business, and

11. References to the eruption of Vesuvius which began at the end of November are in the *London Chronicle* 29 Dec. 1787–2 Feb. 1788, lxiii. 3, 9, 24, 38, 120; at pp. 9, 38, Hamilton's expected account of the eruption for the Royal Society is mentioned, and at p. 9 it is reported that Hamilton 'has written to England respecting the late violent eruption.'

12. Gordon, having been convicted 6 and 13 June 1787 on two charges of libel (attacks on British justice and on Marie-Antoinette), fled to Holland but was returned by the magistrates. He was arrested at Birmingham 7 Dec., brought to London 8 Dec., placed in the custody of the Marshal of the King's Bench Prison and on 12 Dec. was committed to Newgate Prison, where he remained until 28 Jan. 1788, when he was sentenced to five years in Newgate and then to pay a fine of £500 and find two securities for £2,500 each for his good behaviour (*London Chronicle* 8–18 Dec. 1787, lxii. 560, 569, 579).

13. Gordon had become interested in Judaism and had 'entered the Jewish faith [in Birmingham], one month after his arrest there' (Alfred Rubens, *Anglo-Jewish Portraits*, 1935, p. 48, No. 136).

14. Pliny the Elder, for example.

15. 'The Rossi's [Mlle Rossi (d. 1799), dancer] boy as a young Paris or Atys with a Phrygian cap. She had modelled it in terra-cotta in 1784. In 1787 executed it in marble incomparably; no antique bust I ever saw approached so nearly to the softness of flesh' (HW's 'List of Mrs Damer's works,' BERRY ii. 273). This bust appears in Cosway's drawing of Mrs Damer, illustrated in BERRY i. facing 122, and in Percy Noble, *Anne Seymour Damer*, 1908, facing p. 98.

16. HW had seen her in Centlivre's *The Wonder*, in which she was rehearsing the part of Violante which she played at the Richmond House theatricals, early in February, when HW saw her again (HW to Lady Ossory 15 Dec. 1787, 15 Jan., 14 Feb. 1788, OSSORY ii. 585, 586, 588, iii. 1, 5). She had acted at Richmond House in 1787 and she continued to take an interest in amateur theatricals (Noble, op. cit. 95–106).

17. 'If I am not quite credulous about your turning smoke into gold, it is perhaps because I am very ignorant' (HW to Conway 17 Sept. 1782, with HW's note 'Alluding to the coke ovens, for which Mr Conway afterwards obtained a patent'). This furnace was designed for brewers and distillers. Conway apparently

rambled in the second, I will not tap a third without occasion, but, begging your pardon, bid you adieu!

Yours, dear Sir, most sincerely

HOR. WALPOLE

From HAMILTON, Tuesday 19 February 1788

Here first printed from MS now WSL. Sold Sotheby's 14 June 1869, John Dillon sale, lot 725; sold Sotheby's 25 April 1876, Addington sale, lot 257, to Naylor; sold Sotheby's 29 April 1937, Arthur Potts sale, lot 834 to Maggs Bros for WSL.

Address: To the Honourable Hor. Walpole, Berkeley Square, *London, Inghilterra, via Mantua.*

Postmark: [Illegible, the MS being torn at this place].

Caserta, February 19th 1788.

Dear Sir,

YOU may be very sure that the Castle of Otranto does exist and is not a castle in the air, for since I have been here some of the nobility of my acquaintance have been confined in it, and others of an inferior class are lately gone there. If there is an Italian translation of your fantastic tale it is unknown here, but I have given a commission to my bookseller to get it for me, which he will certainly do very soon if it has been translated and published, and you may be assured that I shall send it to you by the first opportunity.

I can believe everything you say of Mrs Damer whom [*sic*] I always thought was the cleverest creature in the world next to Lady Di.[1] I hope General Conway will be more lucky in his present pursuit than his first on fire, which I believed only produced smoke.[2]

was continuing his experiments to reduce smoke by increasing the efficiency of combustion (see CONWAY Appendix 15)

1. Mrs Damer 'had had continued civilities at his [Hamilton's] hands' (Oliver Warner, *Emma Hamilton and Sir William*, 1960, p. 79).

2. Hamilton, aide-de-camp to Conway, told HW: 'While they were on the Isle of Aix [in 1757], Mr Conway was so careless and so fearless as to be trying a burning-glass on a bomb—yes a bomb, the match of which had been cut short to prevent its being fired by any accidental spark of tobacco—Hamilton snatched the glass out of Conway's hand before he had at all thought what he was about' (HW to Mann 20 Nov. 1757, MANN V. 155).

My occupation here when his Sicilian Majesty[3] does not take me on his shooting parties, is to superintend the Queen's English garden,[4] but it is an ungrateful business, as not one of the Court have the least taste and have not the least idea of the simplicity of our gardens, but ask if we do not mean to cut figures upon our turf, which as we have command of water, is really as fine as that in England, and the money we have spent in making the ground lie well they imagine the gardener[5] has put in his pocket, for they see no difference, and even the King when he eat [sic] melons from the Queen's garden in March said very quietly that if he had waited three months he mi⟨ght⟩ have had them as good with⟨out⟩ expense. I assure you it will be very complete soon and we shall exhibit a specimen of English pleasure ground—an excellent kitchen garden and perhaps the richest botanic garden in Europe[6]—if they have not taste to enjoy it, it is not my fault.

Adieu, my dear Sir,

Yours most sincerely,

W. Hamilton

From Hamilton, 1791

Missing. See *post* 30 Sept. 1792.

3. King Ferdinand.
4. This garden of fifty acres adjoining the Royal Caserta Garden had been started in 1786; it was planned to include a kitchen garden, a botanic garden, and a bowling green. Hamilton wrote Sir Joseph Banks 19 Aug. 1788 that 'the King has taken the garden under his protection as it was too expensive for the Queen's purse.' For details, see Warner, op. cit. *passim;* British Museum (Natural History), *The Banks Letters,* ed. W. R. Dawson, 1958, pp. 384–92.

5. John Graefer (d. 1803), botanist, nurseryman, gardener to the Queen and King of Naples 1786–99; left Naples because of the war upheavals; steward at Brontë in Italy, Lord Nelson's estate, 1799–1803. Sir Joseph Banks, at Hamilton's request, arranged for Graefer's position as the Queen's gardener (British Museum, op. cit. 364–5, 384–92; Warner, op. cit. *passim*).
6. For the luxuriant growth of plants and trees in the garden, see the works cited in the two preceding notes.

TO HAMILTON, 1792

Missing. See *post* 30 Sept. 1792.

From HAMILTON, Tuesday 17 April 1792

Here first printed from MS now WSL. Sold Sotheby's 7 May 1919, Alfred Morrison sale, Part IV, lot 3127, to Maggs Bros (in whose catalogue some extracts were printed); sold Sotheby's 16 Dec. 1941, Mrs F. M. Guedalla sale, lot 311, to Maggs Bros for WSL.

Address: Earl of Orford, Berkeley Square, *London, Inghilterra, via Mantua.*
Postmark: 9 MA.
Endorsed: Sir William Hamilton.

Naples, April 17th 1792.

My dear Lord,

SINCE my return here[1] I have been in one perpetual hurry, and the Holy Week[2] having carried off most of the foreign travellers to Rome, it is now only that I begin to breathe. Having resided at Naples upwards of 27 years, foreigners of every denomination contrive to bring letters of recommendation and as our countrymen can without much difficulty, *paying 2 guineas at the Secretary's Office,*[3] get a letter they now all bring me such letters and think themselves entitled to get that penny's worth out of me, and after all it is most difficult to content them. It appears to me that education in England does not improve, for of upwards of 100 British travellers that have been here this winter[4] I can scarcely name three who can have reaped the least profit, for they have lived together and led exactly the same life they would have done in London. I respect Magna Charta but wish there had been in it some little restraint upon

1. Hamilton and Lady Hamilton (see below) left Naples via Paris to return to London 8 Sept. 1791 (BERRY i. 350, n. 14; below, n. 6).

2. 1–7 April.

3. The office, in Whitehall, of the secretary of state for the Foreign Department; he was William Wyndham Grenville (1759–1834), cr. (1790) Bn Grenville (*London Calendar,* 1792, p. 104).

4. Hamilton had written to Sir Joseph Banks 27 March 1792 that 'there are swarms of visitors from every country but France, and he has presented 99 English to the King and Queen.' See British Museum (Natural History), *The Banks Letters,* ed. W. R. Dawson, 1958, p. 389.

emigrants. Lady H.,[5] who has had also a difficult part to act and has succeeded wonderfully, having gained, by having no pretensions the thorough approbation of all the English ladies. The Queen of Naples as you may have heard was very kind to her on our return[6]— and treats her like any other travelling lady of distinction—in short we are very comfortably situated here. I have often thought of you, my dear Lord, and the infinite trouble you must have had upon coming to a title[7] which would have made the happiness of most people, but I should imagine must rather disturb your philosophic retirement. But in this world one must do one's duty and fulfill every obligation in the best manner one can—without which no thinking man can be happy. You cannot imagine how delighted Lady H. was in having gained your approbation in England.[8] She desires to be kindly remembered to you. She goes on improving daily, particularly in music and in the French and Italian languages. She is really an extraordinary being and most grateful to me for having saved her from the precipice into which she had good sense enough to see she must without me have inevitably fallen, and she sees that nothing but a constant good conduct can maintain the respect that is now shown her by everybody.[9] It has often been remarked that a reformed rake makes a good husband.[10] Why not *vice versa?* The barbarous assassination of the King of Sweden[11]

5. Amy Lyon (Emma Hart) (ca 1765–1815), mistress of (among others) Charles Greville, Hamilton's nephew, 1782–6 (and probably from 1781); mistress of Hamilton from late in 1786 until he married her in London 6 Sept. 1791; later Nelson's mistress. See Oliver Warner, *Emma Hamilton and Sir William*, 1960; Brian Fothergill, *Sir William Hamilton*, 1969, pp. 225–57 *et passim.*

6. The *Times* 13 Dec. 1791 'with much pleasure' reported that Lady Hamilton 'was introduced to their Neapolitan Majesties on the 16th of November, and received in a very gracious manner. The Queen of Naples had always spoken of her with great esteem while she was Miss Hart, and was glad that her matrimonial alliance . . . afforded an opportunity of her being introduced to her Majesty.' See also Oliver Warner, *Emma Hamilton and Sir William*, 1960, pp. 116–7; BERRY i. 340, n. 5.

7. On the death of his nephew 5 Dec.

1791 HW had become 4th Earl of Orford.

8. HW had met her and Sir William Hamilton at the Duke of Queensberry's at Richmond 20 Aug. 1791 (BERRY i. 340).

9. Lady Hamilton to Romney, Caserta, 20 Dec. 1791: '. . . I am the happiest woman in the world. Sir William is fonder of me every day, and I hope he will have no corse [cause] to repent of what he has done, for I feel so grateful to him that I think I shall never be able to make him amends for his goodness to me' (sold Sotheby's 13 Dec. 1917, Alfred Morrison sale, lot 475).

10. A proverb recorded in Sir William Gurney Benham, *Book of Quotations*, [1948], p. 775).

11. Jacob Johan Anckarström shot Gustav III at a masked ball 16 March 1792; the King died 29 March 1792. The assassin was tortured, beheaded, and quartered (BERRY ii. 117, n. 20; OSSORY iii. 175, n. 7).

makes a strong impression at this Court. It is really terrible to reflect what disasters have afflicted crowned heads in our time. The Neapolitans, provided they can get their bellies filled at a cheap rate, will not I am sure trouble their heads with what passes in other countries and great pains are taken to prevent any of the democratic propaganda or their writings finding their way into this kingdom.[12]

Now that I have a little leisure I shall endeavour that the first volume of my new collection of vases,[13] all of which were under ground three years ago, shall be published within two months,[14] and I flatter myself that this publication will be of infinite use to the arts and will lay open a noble field for antiquaries to display their erudition, but my object is principally as it always has been, to assist and promote the arts.[15]

Prince Augustus[16] is still here and has really been very ill,[17] but is now perfectly recovered and will probably go to Rome next week.[18]

12. For the effects of the French Revolution on the Neapolitan government at this time and after the death of Marie-Antoinette, the Queen's sister, and for some of the repressive measures taken, see Harold Acton, *The Bourbons of Naples (1734–1825)*, [1956], chapters XIII–XIV.

13. *Collection of Engravings from Ancient Vases Mostly of Pure Greek Workmanship Discovered in Sepulchres in the Kingdom of the Two Sicilies but Chiefly in the Neighbourhood of Naples . . . MDCCLXXXIX and MDCCLXXXX Now in the Possession of Sir Wm Hamilton*, ed. W. Tischbein, 5 vols folio, text in English and French. No list of subscribers is printed in the volumes. HW had only Vol. I, 1791 and Vol. II, 1795 (Hazen, *Cat. of HW's Lib.*, No. 3498), the only volumes published before HW's death—Vol. III, dated 1795 on the title-page, contains Hamilton's dedicatory letter to the E. of Leicester 1 Jan. 1797 preceding p. 2. Vol. I 'has only in the present year been imported for sale' by Cadell at three guineas (*Monthly Review . . . Enlarged*, [Aug.], 1794, xiv. Appendix, 555).

14. Hamilton's dedicatory letter to the Earl of Leicester, P.S.A., is dated 10 March 1791; his postscript, undated, on pp. 156–9, suggests a date of publication later than June 1792, and probably as

late as 1794 when Hamilton sent a copy to Sir Joseph Banks and one to the Royal Society; see British Museum (Natural History), *The Banks Letters*, ed. W. R. Dawson, 1958, p. 390; see also n. 13 above.

15. In the dedicatory letter Hamilton explains that the four volumes of his first collection of vases were too expensive for young artists; 'I have now confined this new publication to the simple outline of the figures on the vases, which is the essential, and no unnecessary ornament, or colouring have been introduced; by this means the purchase becoming easy, it will be in the power of lovers of antiquity, and artists to reap the desired profit from such excellent models as are now offered to them' (p. [4]). Hamilton alludes to this basic view on p. 8 (and later) in his letter 'To the Reader.'

16. Augustus Frederick (1773–1843), cr. (1801) D. of Sussex; 6th son of George III. His friendship with Lady Hamilton continued until her death, see Oliver Warner, *Emma Hamilton and Sir William*, 1960, pp. 115–16, 123, 126, 203–4.

17. Of asthma; he had been sent to Italy to get relief from it.

18. Where he married 4 April 1793 (and again at St. George's, Hanover Square, London, 5 Dec. 1793) Lady Augusta Murray, a marriage invalid under the Royal Marriage Act, 1772 (12 Geo. III c. 11).

You may well imagine that H.R.H.'s illness has also given me some employment. He is most amiable but I fear will never enjoy perfect health. Adieu, my dear Lord.

Ever yours most sincerely

WM HAMILTON

To HAMILTON, Sunday 30 September 1792

Printed from MS now WSL; previously printed in part, Toynbee *Supp.* ii. 62–4. Sold Sotheby's 21 May 1890, 'Important Collection of Autograph Letters,' lot 127, to Pearson; sold Sotheby's 19 Oct. 1953, Lord Derby sale, lot 71, to WSL. *Endorsed by Hamilton:* Lord Orford Sept. 30th 1792.

Strawberry Hill, Sept. 30, 1792.

I DID receive your letter,[1] dear Sir, early last winter, but when I was much too ill to answer it, and so continued long;[2] but as soon as I was able, I do assure you, I did write to you, and perfectly remember the contents of my letter,[3] which I shall repeat now, at least the topics. I told you that I did not doubt that the good sense of Lady Hamilton, of which I had witnessed proofs in her acting,[4] would make her conduct as grateful as you have a right to expect, and as I hope you will always find.

I begged you, which I now repeat, to order your bookseller, to send me the volume of your vases,[5] as soon as it shall appear, for I love the forms of antique vases; and I believe I added something of indifference for the mythologic parts; for though the ancients had some ingenious and beautiful allusions in their mythology, they mixed or engrafted on it a great deal of fantastic and contradiction, and parts so far-fetched, that they have left to the moderns a vast deal to guess, and little determinate, and that obscurity is much increased by the bad address of the ancients in telling their stories, which flowed chiefly from the little art they had or exerted in ex-

---

1. Missing.
2. The illness and death of Lord Orford, HW's nephew, in November and December 1791, and the business transactions his accession to the Norfolk estates required, had tired and distressed HW, who had then suffered intermittent attacks of gout.
3. Missing.
4. HW praised her singing and acting at the Duke of Richmond's 20 Aug. 1791 (BERRY i. 340).
5. See *ante* 17 April 1792.

pressing the passions. The drawing of their single figures was perfection—but how ill did they put any number together! In the four
former volumes of your Etruscan Vases,[6] can anything be more insipid or uninteresting than the arrangement of the figures? Even in
your famous Barbarini vase,[7] the finest large cameo extant,[8] the story
is so wretchedly told, and the personages have so little relation to or
connection with each other, that no mortal can tell what they mean;
and so many explanations, totally different from each other, have
been given, that it is plain the artist, or the person who gave him
the design, was as unfit to unfold the subject, as the former was incomparable in executing it.[9] I admire, nobody more, the productions
of the ancients (especially of the Grecians the inventors and standards of all works of genius) in all the works in which they remain
superior or at least equal to later ages; but where they were extremely defective, I cannot applaud. In nothing do they appear to
fall so short of perfection as in their sculpture and painting, from
that capital merit, expression of the passions: except in the La-

6. *Collection of Etruscan, Greek and Roman Antiquities from the Cabinet of the Hon[oura]ble W. Hamilton,* Naples, 1766–7, 4 vols folio, the text by Pierre-François Hugues (1719–1805), called D'Hancarville (Hazen, *Cat. of HW's Lib.,* No. 3536). Many of the vases and other antiquities were in the collection Hamilton sold to the British Museum in 1772.

7. The Portland vase: purchased about 1780 in Rome by James Byres for £500 (according to some reports) from the Principessa di Palestrina (*ante* Hamilton to HW 28 May 1782, n. 13) of the Barberini family in whose possession it had been for over 100 years; sold by Byres for £1,000 to Hamilton, who brought it to England and sold it to the Duchess of Portland in 1785 for £1,800 guineas; bought in by the Duke of Portland at the Duchess's sale, 1786; shattered (and later repaired) while on loan to the British Museum, 1845; now in the British Museum, having been purchased for the nation, 1945 (Ossory ii. 485–6 and n. 6; Oliver Warner, *Emma Hamilton and Sir William,* 1960, pp. 63–6; Wolf Mankowitz, *Portland Vase and the Wedgwood Copies,* 1952).

8. The vase, made of two layers of glass, white on blue, has the white cut away as in a cameo to reveal the designs in relief.

9. For some of these explanations, about which there is little agreement, see Neil McKendrick, 'Story of the Portland Vase,' *The Listener* 14 Jan. 1960, pp. 69, 71. D'Hancarville had been criticized for some of his far-fetched interpretations in the 1766–7 volumes, and Hamilton was later criticized, as in the *Monthly Review,* (Aug.), 1794, xiv. Appendix, 558–9, for the same weakness in the 1791 volume: 'Indeed, on perusing the explanations and comparing them with the plates, we are obliged to acknowledge that a great part of them appear to us mere vague guesses, scarcely supported by a gleam of probability, and which no two persons would be likely to form of their own accord.' Two illustrations follow, 'Surely it would be better to avoid *ignorance* (or, if that be too harsh a word, let us write *uncertainty*), than to explain in this manner.' **The rest of this paragraph is here first printed.**

ocoön,[10] the Niobe,[11] the Apollo Belvedere,[12] and a very few more, where do we see them attempted? I conclude from the multitudes of statues and busts which remain, that the ancients were as fond of portraits as we are, and portraits at most exhibit character, not passions —but the frescoes that have been found are as inexpressive as Etruscan or Greek vases and their bas-reliefs are still worse, and have no assistance from perspective: nor do they seem to have conceived that distance could be represented by lessening objects in the upper part of a delineated tablet. You see figures in the upper line as large as those on the foreground;[13] as on Indian screens a man is often spearing a tiger that appears to be up in the air from being as big as the lowest figures. I am not angry at everything not being brought to perfection in any mortal works—but you must allow me to proportion my applause to the degree of merit—and if a story-teller does not tell his story well or very obscurely, the difficulty of understanding him destroys or abates my curiosity.

I do not wonder that the Queen of Naples was so much shocked at the outrageous treatment of her heroic sister.[14] No Christian martyr was ever tortured so inhumanly for three years together—nor is there on record any memorial of such over-savage barbarities as have been committed by that atrocious and detestable nation!—a nation as contemptible as it is odious—and when La Fayette after the affair of Lisle, called them *cowardly cannibals,* he gave but a faint idea of half their detestable qualities;[15] nor can the dictionaries of all nations

10. See MANN ii. 326, vi. 67–8, nn. 1, 3, vi. 71, n. 17.

11. For the Niobe Group (incomplete), copies of originals attributed to Scopas, in the Uffizi at Florence, see Mann to HW 24 July 1781, HW to Mann 23 Aug. 1781, MANN ix. 170–1, 177.

12. Marble figure of the period of the early Roman empire; a copy of a Greek original in bronze; now in the Belvedere, Vatican, Rome.

13. HW here accepts the system of single-point perspective which developed in western Europe during the Renaissance and denies the validity of earlier systems of multipoint perspective.

14. Marie-Antoinette. The outbreak of war between France and Austria in April had led to the storming of the Tuileries by the mob in June and August, and in August the royal family had been removed to the Temple.

15. In his letter to the Minister of War 2 May 1792, apropos of the murder 29 April by French soldiers at Lille of their commanding officer Gen. Theobald Dillon, an engineer, and several Austrian soldiers captured at Tournai. See HW to Lady Ossory 29 May 1792, OSSORY iii. 141, n. 2; *London Chronicle,* 3–15 May, lxxi. 432, 438, 451, 455, 461. The rest of the paragraph is previously unpublished except for the two clauses ending 'friends of the survivors'; the following paragraph, too, is here printed for the first time save for 'France must be abhorred to latest posterity.'

furnish words enough to paint them in the colours they deserve. If Macbeth murdered sleep,[16] they have murdered hyperbole, for it is impossible to exaggerate in relating their horrible crimes! The butchery of the Princesse de Lamballe with every refinement of cruelty,[17] the murdering four thousand untried prisoners at once,[18] and above a hundred poor confined conscientious priests,[19] who had committed no crimes but preferring starving to poverty,[20] dragging fifty-four other prisoners from Orléans to Paris to hew them in pieces[21]—but oh! who can enumerate a quarter of the massacres those horrible monsters have committed? or can calculate or guess at the agonies they have occasioned in the friends of the survivors? What must the Duchesse d'Anville[22] have felt at being forced to stand and behold her son[23] hacked piecemeal—that Duc de la Rochfoucault, who had been one of the first apostles of the new system, and who had no crime, to them, but of having been shocked at their excesses, and of having retired from their diabolic league?[24] To publish in the face of day rewards for assassination of their enemies,[25] was almost making the enormous lies they forge daily and

16. *Macbeth* II. ii. 35.

17. Imprisoned with the royal family in the Temple 10 Aug., she was transferred to La Force 19 Aug., and was delivered to (and killed by) the Paris mob 3 Sept. Her head on a pike was paraded in front of the windows at the Temple for Louis XVI and Marie-Antoinette to see. Cf. Dalrymple 219–20.

18. 'On a moderate computation . . . not less than 4,000 victims have been offered up to the fury of the Jacobine [*sic*] mob' (*London Chronicle* 6–8 Sept. lxxii. 239). Later estimates in the same newspaper raised the number to as high as 12,000 massacred 2–5 Sept., a number more conservatively estimated today at 1,400 (Ossory iii. 160 and n. 2).

19. See Ossory iii. 163, where estimates ranging from 130 to 220 are given.

20. HW also referred to the 'option of perjury or starving' faced by 'all the conscientious clergy' because of the decree to take the clerical oath (27 Nov. 1790) and the civic oath (29 Nov. 1791) or be deported (27 May 1792, a decree Louis XVI refused to approve); see HW to Lady Ossory 4 Sept. 1792, Ossory iii. 158 and n. 12.

21. The *London Chronicle* 8–15 Sept., lxxii. 248, 264, reported that the prisoners being brought from Orléans to Paris for protection were intercepted at Versailles 8 Sept. by the mob who, 'abandoning themselves to the frenzy of their political enthusiasm, butchered the whole [fifty-four] of them except two.'

22. Marie-Louise-Nicole-Élisabeth de la Rochefoucauld (1716–94), m. (1732) Jean-Baptiste-Louis-Frédéric de la Rochefoucauld de Roye, Duc d'Anville.

23. Louis-Alexandre de la Rochefoucauld d'Anville (1743–92), Duc de la Rochefoucauld, murdered at Gisors while being conducted from Forges to Paris. See Dalrymple 220; Ossory iii. 174. HW wrote Nares 12 Sept. 1792 that both mother and wife witnessed La Rochefoucauld's murder (Dalrymple 220); no evidence that either was present has been found.

24. HW wrote Nares that the Duc had left Paris and retired to his mother's estate 'last July' (ibid.).

25. HW wrote this to Conway also, 31 Aug. 1792. Jean Debry had proposed to the National Assembly, 26 Aug., the organization 'd'un corps de 1,200 hommes,

hourly but petty crimes; and repetitions of perjury but sins unstained with blood, and thence the most harmless of their acts.

It would be falling into the bathos if after such a catalogue of horrors I should descend to their laying waste so many beautiful or valuable monuments of the arts[26]—and yet you, dear Sir, and I too, must now and then steal a sigh for them!—but I will say no more—France must be abhorred to latest posterity—I only hope that such an accumulation of crimes will never be renewed, while the frame of our globe exists—it certainly never was precedented!

I shall endeavour to get this conveyed to you in the Prince of Castelcicalo's[27] packet, as I should be mortified at your thinking that, old as I am, I am forgetful of so old a friend, and no longer

Sincerely yours

ORFORD

From HAMILTON, n.d.

Missing. Sold Sotheby's 24 April 1879, John B. C. Healt sale, lot 150, to Waller. Described in Sotheby's catalogue: 'Dilating on natural history and antiquities, and speaking in high terms of the salubrity and beauty of the climate.'

qui seraient appellés les *Douze-cents*, et dont la mission sera principalement de s'attacher corps-à-corps aux chefs des armées ennemies, des rois qui les dirigent, et de les poignarder.' Debry's proposal was attacked by Vergniaux, and was set aside (*Journal de Paris*, [? 1 Oct.] 1792, p. 934).

26. Such as the later destruction of the royal tombs in the church at St-Denis, the levelling of the Bastille, the looting of palaces and châteaux.

27. Fabrizio Ruffo (1763–1832), Principe di Castelcicala, Neapolitan minister plenipotentiary to England 1790–3, to France 1815–32 (except for short periods in 1816 and 1820) (BERRY i. 341, n. 9; *Times* 9 Sept. 1790).

THE CORRESPONDENCE
WITH VISCOUNT
NUNEHAM LATER 2D
EARL HARCOURT AND
WITH THE COUNTESS
HARCOURT

A View of the RUINS of the CHAPPEL at STANTON-HARCOURT in the COUNTY of OXFORD

The Mannor of Stanton came into the Family of HARCOURT
by the marriage of Robe de Harcourt Knt (temp. Hen. I) with Isabella
daughter and heir of Rich᷎d de Camuill, by Milicent his wife
Cozen of the said K. Hen. I᷎t.

to R Milicent had a royal Grant of the same
It has now remained in the possession of the HARCOURTS above 600 years.
and from them assumed the name of STANTON-HARCOURT

Drawn after Nature 1760 and Etched 1763 by Nuneham.

ETCHING BY LORD NUNEHAM

To Nuneham,[1] Wednesday 16 March 1763

Printed from a photostat of the MS in Lord Harcourt's possession at Stanton Harcourt, Oxon. First printed, *Harcourt Papers* viii. 91–2, reprinted Toynbee v. 293.

Arlington Street, March 16, 1763.

My Lord,

I WISH all words had not been so prostituted in compliments, that some at least might be left to express real admiration. Your Lordship's etchings[2] deserve such sincere praises, that I cannot bear you should think that mere civility or gratitude dictate what I would say of them, though I assure you the latter is what I feel to a great degree. I will even trust your Lordship with my vanity; I think I understand your prints, and that mine is not random praise. If it has any worth, it will encourage you to proceed, and yet you have already gone beyond what I have ever seen in etching.[3] I must beg for the white paper edition too, as I shall frame the brown, and bind the rest of your Lordship's works together.[4]

I am my Lord your Lordship's most obliged humble servant,

H. WALPOLE

1. George Simon Harcourt (1736–1809), styled Vct Nuneham 1749–77; 2d E. Harcourt, 1777; M.P.

2. [*A Series of four views of the*] *Ruins at Stanton-Harcourt in the County of Oxford,* 1763. 'Three views of the kitchen, offices, and chapel *at Stanton Harcourt,* the seat of the Earl of Harcourt, in whose family it has been 600 years, were drawn and etched by Lord Newnham, 1760. 1763. One of them drawn by P[aul] Sandby' (Richard Gough, *British Topography,* 1780, ii. 90; BM Cat.).

3. 'Lord Nuneham's etchings are superior in boldness and freedom of stroke to anything we have seen from established artists' (HW's 'On Modern Gardening,' *Anecdotes of Painting,* 1771, iv. 150).

4. HW's etchings by Lord Nuneham, 'bound in red morocco,' with etchings by other noble amateurs were sold SH viii. 56 to Pickering for £16.10.0, and are now wsl. Nuneham's etchings are on white paper.

To NUNEHAM, Tuesday 21 August 1764

Printed from a photostat of the MS in Lord Harcourt's possession. First printed, *Harcourt Papers* viii. 92–3, reprinted, Toynbee vi. 110.

Endorsed by Nuneham: Honourable Horace Walpole August 21st 1764.

Strawberry Hill, Aug. 21st 1764.

My Lord,

WHEN you talk of obligations, what does your Lordship leave to me to say? and when you make apologies, what can I make but excuses for having given you the trouble of writing at all, which I assuredly did not expect?

I rejoice Lord Herbert[1] has diverted you. I own, it appears to me the most singular book that ever was written. I am overpaid if it has answered my purpose in amusing you.

As your Lordship is not particularly fond of the country, I would condole with you on its being more disagreeable than common by the continual rains, but I am so selfish as to hope that your having been detained much in the House has contributed to the employment of your graver. Your friends gain so much by that, that you must forgive their wishing you constantly engaged.

I am my Lord your Lordship's most obedient and most obliged humble servant,

HOR. WALPOLE

1. *The Life of Edward Lord Herbert of Cherbury*, printed by HW at the SH Press, 27 Jan. 1764, but not distributed until July (Hazen, *SH Bibl.* 68–70); the copy presented to Lord Nuneham is at Stanton Harcourt.

To Nuneham ?May 1771

Printed from a photostat of the MS in Lord Harcourt's possession. First printed in *Harcourt Papers* viii. 93; reprinted, Toynbee xv. 445–6. Dated by the reference to Lady Ligonier's affair with John Harding (n. 2 below).

Address: To the Right Honourable Lord Nuneham, at Leicester House.[1]
Endorsed by Nuneham: The Honourable Horace Walpole.

LORD Nuneham is very cross. The first of all rules is to do as we would be done by. I wish the second was as well established, that we should do as others would do by us—and then as Mr Walpole would disengage himself to wait on Lord N. Lord Nuneham *would ought* to disengage himself to dine at Strawberry Hill next Saturday. All one knows, is, that Lady Nuneham is goodness itself and has a wicked husband who does not deserve her. However I trust some day or other she will return time enough (not on Saturday) to find him with Countess Alfieri,[2] and to learn that he had passed the morning with the postilion's wife.

So prays your Honour's poor Beadsman,

H. W.

1. Leicester House, occupied at this time by Lord Nuneham, stood on the northeast corner of Leicester Square (*London Past and Present* ii. 380; *Harcourt Papers* iii. 119n).

2. Penelope Pitt (1749–?1827), m. 1 (1766) Edward Ligonier, 2d Vct Ligonier who divorced her by Act of Parliament (7 Nov. 1771) for adultery with Vittorio Amadeo (1749–1803), Count Alfieri; she m. 2 (1784) Capt. Smith. Following Alfieri's duel with Ligonier in May 1771, her next affair with John Harding (Lord Ligonier's groom, sometimes called 'postilion') became common knowledge (SELWYN 255, nn. 4, 6; Marquis of Ruvigny and Raineval, *Plantagenet Roll . . . Exeter Vol.,* 1907, pp. 39, 458).

To Nuneham, Thursday 14 May 1772

Printed from a photostat of the MS in Lord Harcourt's possession. First printed Cunningham v. 387, reprinted, Toynbee viii. 165–6.

Address: To the Right Honourable Lord Nuneham at Leicester House.

Endorsed by Nuneham: Honourable Horace Walpole May 14th 1772.

Thursday May 14th.

My dear Lord,

I WAITED on you this morning, to learn your motions. There is an evil report of your thinking of the country[1]—but sure you remember that I have a mortgage on you, and that you must pay it off before you can stir. I beg to know your plan, that I may obtain a day from you at Strawberry Hill before you go: and I cannot have the conscience, even for your sake and Strawberry's, to ask it before the east wind is rained away. As there is no *wind-bow* to *insure* us that the world is not to be blown away, as there is to defend us against being drowned, it is impossible to tell when the weathercock will change its mind; but wet or dry, I must insist on your promise, and flatter myself that Lord and Lady Jersey[2] will do me the same honour.

Your most faithful humble servant,

Hor. Walpole

1. Nuneham left London before 10 June, when he wrote to his father from Nuneham Courtenay (*Harcourt Papers* iii. 113).

2. George Bussy Villiers (1735–1805), 4th E. of Jersey, 1769, m. (1770) Frances Twysden (1753–1821). The Nunehams dined at SH with 'the Duke and Duchess of Queensberry, Lord and Lady Jersey, Lord and Lady Temple, Miss Vernon, Miss Fanquier [*sic*], and Mrs Clive' (Lord Nuneham to his father, 'Monday night, 1772,' *Harcourt Papers* iii. 112–13).

D. Gardiner pinxit   Published June 26th 1772   V. Green fecit.
by V. Green Salisbury Street
Strand.

1736   George Simon Harcourt   1809
Viscount Nuneham
Eldest Son
of
Simon Earl of Harcourt.

To Nuneham, ?May 1772

Printed from a photostat of the MS in Lord Harcourt's possession. First printed, Cunningham v. 388, reprinted, Toynbee viii. 166. Since the MS of this letter had been numbered to follow the preceding one, it was presumably written after 14 May.

Address: To the Right Honourable Lord Nuneham at Leicester House.
Endorsed by Nuneham: Mr Walpole 1772.

I AM in such confusion, my dear Lord, that I do not know what to say, but the truth. I had read *Tuesday* on your Lordship's card instead of *Monday* and never knew my mistake till this instant. My servant asked me what I would have for dinner. I replied, I dine at Lord Nuneham's. He said, I beg your pardon, Lord Nuneham's card was for yesterday; I thought your Honour had disengaged yourself. I dined at home alone yesterday, and am shocked to think that I probably made your Lordship, Lady Nuneham and your company wait. You will possibly forgive me, but I can never see my own face again—nor will ever read a card again without spectacles. Consider what pleasure I have lost, and pity

Your mortified humble servant,

Hor. Walpole

To Nuneham, ?January 1773

Printed from a photostat of the MS in Lord Harcourt's possession. First printed, *Harcourt Papers* viii. 95; reprinted, Toynbee viii. 223 where it is placed before the letter of 8 Jan. to Cole.

Address: To Lord Nuneham.
Endorsed: Mr Walpole 1773.

DON'T think you shall be kind to me every day, my dear Lord, and that I will never be grateful. I must thank you in detail, for the debt would otherwise be enormous. The print[1] is valuable, your own etchings are more, your company[2] most so. I have another little

1. Perhaps of Nuneham himself (see illustration).
2. Mason wrote HW, 23 Feb. 1773, that 'Lord Nuneham told me that you were a convalescent,' and that 'notwithstanding so long an illness he never saw you in better spirits or look more healthy' (Mason i. 62).

pain in one foot, so you see even my gratitude is interested—but if you corrupt me, is my venality quite criminal?

Yours most faithfully,

H. Walpole

To Nuneham, April 1773

Printed from a photostat of the MS in Lord Harcourt's possession. First printed Cunningham v. 456, reprinted, Toynbee viii. 266.
Address: To the Right Honourable Lord Nuneham.
Endorsed by Nuneham: Mr Walpole April 1773.

I WILL certainly wait on your Lordship and Lady Nuneham on Wednesday, and endeavour to prepare Mrs Clive's spirits to hazard even a *vole sans prendre,*[1] which is the thing she dreads the most in the world next to a crowd. I am going to Princess Amelie, my greatest earthly joy next to going to St James's.

To Nuneham, Saturday 17 July 1773

Printed from a photostat of the MS in Lord Harcourt's possession. First printed, Cunningham v. 486, reprinted, Toynbee viii. 309.
Endorsed by Nuneham: Honourable Horace Walpole July 17th 1773.

Strawberry Hill, July 17, 1773.

I HAVE had two reasons, my dear Lord, for not offering myself to Nuneham till now. The first was, that I could not;[1] the second that I would not, no, not till you should be free from your royal guests.[2] As I hear they are to be with you next week, I am humble

1. 'The winning of all the tricks in certain card-games, such as écarté, quadrille, or ombre' (OED).

———

1. HW was occupied with the health and affairs of his nephew, the 3d E. of Orford, who was temporarily insane (see HW to Mann 13 July 1773, Mann vii. 495).

2. The Duke and Duchess of Gloucester were to reach Nuneham 23 July (see the Duke's letters to Lord Nuneham 18, 21 July 1773, *Harcourt Papers* iii. 181–2). HW's refusal to meet them at this time was due to a coolness between him and the Duke, occasioned by HW's disapproval of the marriage; he had refused to attend their daughter's baptism (Ossory i. 132).

enough to be content to succeed them; AND SO, as Bishop Burnet[3] says, if you will accept of me any day after Monday sevennight the 26th, I am at your commands, provided it is not too near your embarkation,[4] and that I shall not interrupt your packing up. Do not make any ceremony with me, but tell me freely if so late a visit will be inconvenient. I can come you know next summer, as I suppose the King of Ireland[5] will not make an interregnum, and your Royal Highness probably does not intend to make the inhabitants of your principality quite so happy. If you should not have leisure to receive me, I most cordially wish Lady Nuneham and your Lordship a good voyage, as tolerable a sojourn as possible, a quick return, and that you may soon, like Roderick O'Connor,[6]

Turn your harp into a harpsichord;

So prays your faithful Beadsman,

Hor. Walpole

From Nuneham, July 1773

Two missing letters, acknowledged *post* 27 July 1773.

3. Gilbert Burnet (1643–1715), Bp of Salisbury, grandfather of HW's friend Richard West, from whom HW may have heard this saying.

4. Lord and Lady Nuneham were planning to spend the winter in Ireland with Nuneham's father, Simon Harcourt (1714–77), 1st E. Harcourt, who had become lord lieutenant of Ireland in October 1772; they reached Dublin 7 Oct. 1773

and stayed till May 1774 (*Harcourt Papers* iii. 128, 140–1).

5. Lord Harcourt.

6. Roderic O'Connor (1116?–1198), King of Ireland (1166); in 1175, O'Connor acknowledged Henry II as his liege lord. HW probably alludes to this transference of fealty from Ireland to England in this figure, which he repeated to Mason, 18 Sept. 1779 (Mason i. 467, n. 1).

To NUNEHAM, Tuesday 27 July 1773

Printed from a photostat of the MS in Lord Harcourt's possession. First printed (incompletely) in Cunningham v. 486, completely printed, *Harcourt Papers* viii. 94–5, reprinted Toynbee viii. 309–10.
Endorsed by Nuneham: Honourable Hor. Walpole July 27th 1773.

Strawberry Hill, July 27, 1773.

I RECEIVED your Lordship's two kind letters with the gratitude they deserved: and will thank you for them on Monday evening next, the 2d, trusting you will harbour me till Thursday morning; which is long enough to trespass on you, when you have so many state affairs[1] in your mind.

Lady Nuneham is very good to bestow a thought on me, and it brings forth an hundredfold.

I was in London yesterday, where there is scarce a soul, but Maccaronis lolling out of windows at Almack's like carpets to be dusted; and not a syllable of news. Foote's new play,[2] they say, is very dull; and so is

Your Lordship's faithful humble servant,

HOR. WALPOLE

To NUNEHAM, Tuesday 10 August 1773

Printed from a photostat of the MS in Lord Harcourt's possession. First printed, Cunningham v. 491–2, reprinted Toynbee viii. 315–17.
Endorsed by Nuneham: Honourable Hor. Walpole August 10th 1773.

Strawberry Hill, Aug. 10, 1773.

YOU must forgive my troubling you with my gratitude my dear Lord. It is impossible to be silent after experiencing so much kindness and receiving so much pleasure at Nuneham. The scenes

1. HW probably refers to Nuneham's preparations for his extended visit in Ireland.
2. *The Bankrupt*, a satire on contemporary dramatists by Samuel Foote, was produced at the Little Theatre in the Haymarket 21 July 1773 (Allardyce Nicoll, *A History of Late Eighteenth Century Drama,* Cambridge, 1927, p. 260), and repeated 20 times, that season (*London Stage 1660–1800,* pt 4, ed. G. W. Stone, Carbondale, Ill. 1962, iii. 1735–9). HW's copy is Hazen, *Cat. of HW's Lib.,* No. 1810:26.

and prospect made great impression upon me, but your Lordship's and Lady Nuneham's goodness much more. Can neither you nor she guess, my Lord, what made the strongest impression of all? Not the showing me what your park may be—not, that it may be Paradise, but that it is Parnassus; that one of the Muses[1] resides there, and is so bashful as to pretend to be only one of the graces. I hope her eight sisters, who are seldom modest, will be provoked at her possessing a virtue they want, and will expose her stark to the eyes of the whole world. A Vice-Queen[2] blushing in a brazen age, and in a brazen kingdom!—well, well, she will return intrepid—it is incredible how many awkward virtues a crown can cure people of. Such talents were not given to be locked up in a little flower-garden, though it is enamelled, and fit for the loves of Vertumnus and Pomona.[3] They must be transplanted. Oh! that ever I might be honoured so far, as to be allowed to join certain lines to those of Lady Temple.[4] The editions of Strawberry would be immortal, and Cipriani[5] should design a frontispiece in which Friendship should present the sister-poetesses to Apollo—and the best engraver in England should etch it—no, my Lord, not Bartolozzi,[6] but an idle creature,[7] as humble as his wife, who is able to do justice by his landscapes to the rich vale that is bounded by Abingdon[8] and Oxford, and who leaves a thousand venerable oaks, that stand before his nose, unengraved, as his father leaves their site unimproved. Oh! I pray to all the Dryads to do justice on such a family—and that justice I hope will be poetical!

Well! ye are however a tender-hearted set of people—some of ye—

1. Lady Nuneham, whose verses HW was eager to publish; see below.

2. Lady Nuneham acted as Lord Harcourt's hostess (his wife had died in 1765) in Dublin during the winter of 1773–4 (*Harcourt Papers* iii. 140–1).

3. Vertumnus, the Italian god of the changing year and giver of fruits, fell in love with Pomona, the goddess of gardens; having pursued her in various shapes, he won her in the guise of a handsome boy; cf. Pope, 'Vertumnus and Pomona,' translated from Ovid, *Metamorphoses* xiv.

4. HW printed *Poems by Anna Chamber Countess Temple*, as well as her 'Verses Sent to Lady Charles Spencer' at

SH in 1764 (Hazen, *SH Bibl.* 72–7, 181–6).

5. Giovanni Battista Cipriani (1727–85), Florentine painter and engraver; moved to London, 1755; R. A., 1768; he was a prolific book-illustrator.

6. Francesco Bartolozzi (1727–1815), Florentine engraver; moved to England as engraver to the King, 1764; original member of the Royal Academy.

7. Lord Nuneham himself.

8. Abingdon, Berks, on the Thames six miles south of Oxford. Nuneham's estate, 'a park of six miles and an half in circumference, well wooded, and containing near twelve hundred acres' (*Nuneham-Courtenay*, 1783, p. 2), lay between Abingdon and Oxford.

you will pity me, I am sure. Rosette[9] has suffered dreadfully ever since she was seized at Nuneham; it seems a mixture of complaint, paralytic and in her bowels—I dare scarce flatter myself with a glimpse of hope!—but it is a bad return, to give you concern—pray, my Lord, tell Mr Jerningham,[10] that the next pair of true lovers he kills, I insist on their being buried in your church,[11] which is so unlike a parish, and worthy of entombing Abelard and Heloisa—nay, I beg the whole plan may lie at Nuneham; the swain shall talk to the nymph through the grate of your flower-garden;[12] they shall wander in the wood over the lock—I hope Corydon[13] will not be too pressing—the spot is savage, and tempting—and then think what a gloomy evening walk for the funeral procession along the terrace to the church! There is no resisting such a subject.

Before I take my leave, I must beg you would not be too impatient to embark.[14] I have heard a whisper, as if the King of Poland[15] would not be the first monarch in Europe that may resign his crown rather than meet a refractory *Diet*.[16] I should not congratulate any

9. HW's dog, which died in October (see *post* HW to Nuneham 6 Nov. 1773).

10. Edward Jerningham (1737–1812), poet and dramatist; his poem, *Faldoni and Teresa*, 1773, was 'founded on a very singular event that happened near Lyons in . . . June 1770. Two lovers (Faldoni and Teresa Meunier) meeting with an invincible obstacle [parental objections] to their union, determined to put an end to their existence. . . . The place they chose for . . . their terrible project was a chapel. . . . They even decorated the altar for the occasion: they also paid a particular attention to their own dress. . . . Each held the ribband that was fastened to the other's trigger, which they draw at a signal agreed upon' (Advertisement in 1773 edn).

11. 'The church is a beautiful building of the Ionic order, in the style of an antique temple: it was erected in the year 1764 at the sole expense of Simon Earl of [sic] Harcourt, who gave the original design, which afterwards received a small alteration from Mr [James, "Athenian"] Stuart [1713–88]' (*Nuneham-Courtenay*, 1783, p. 18; *The New Oxford Guide*, 1785, p. 136).

12. For a detailed description of the flower-garden at Nuneham, see *Harcourt Papers* iii. 206–14; see also *Nuneham-Courtenay*, 1783, pp. 12–13, or *The New Oxford Guide*, 1785, pp. 131–3, which contains the account given in *Nuneham-Courtenay*. William Mason later revised the landscaping at Nuneham (*Country Life*, 1913, xxxiv. 746–55).

13. The name of a shepherd in the eclogues of Theocritus and Virgil, later used conventionally in pastorals.

14. See *ante* HW to Nuneham 17 July 1773, n. 4.

15. Henri III (1551–89), K. of France, 1574, was crowned King of Poland 21 Feb. 1573, but, fearing to convoke a diet, fled from the kingdom 18 June.

16. Lord Harcourt, who was to meet his first Irish Parliament 12 October of this year, rightly anticipated a stormy session. In a 'Review of Earl Harcourt's Administration in Ireland,' John Lees, Harcourt's private secretary, wrote: 'To expect good humour from an exasperated Parliament; to call for money from an exhausted treasury; to prescribe economy to a corrupt community, to impose taxes upon a bankrupt nation; to demand forces from a defenceless people were difficulties peculiar to Lord Harcourt's administration' (*Harcourt Papers* x. 245–6).

other prince on being reprieved from a throne, but your Lordship;
not your Lordship, unless I was entirely

Your devoted humble servant,

Hor. Walpole

To Nuneham, Tuesday 17 August 1773

Printed from a photostat of the MS in Lord Harcourt's possession. First
printed, Cunningham v. 493–4, reprinted, Toynbee viii. 320–2.
Endorsed by Nuneham: Honourable Hor. Walpole August 17th 1773.

Strawberry Hill, Aug. 17, 1773.

> Your Pinks, your Tulips live an hour:
> A fortnight bounds your utmost pow'r.
> Flora,[1] the niggard Goddess, pays
> With short-liv'd joys the toil of days.
> But, Walter Clark,[2] your happy lot
> Is fallen in a fairer spot:
> A Muse has deign'd to view your bow'r,
> And stamp'd immortal ev'ry flow'r.
> Her breath new perfumes can disclose,
> Her touch improve the damask rose:
> And ages hence the buds you raise
> Shall bloom in Nuneham's living lays.
> The lilies of the field that shone
> With brighter blaze than Solomon
> Shall beg to quit their rural stations,
> And mix with Walter Clark's carnations—

had Lady Nuneham condescended to let me see the other lines[3] you
tell me of, my dear Lord, they would, I trust, have inspired me with
a better return. Those I have scribbled are however more disin-

1. In the flower-garden at Nuneham
were 'a bust of Flora on a term' and a
'Temple of Flora.' The latter was of a 'design taken from a Doric portico at
Athens: in the centre of the back wall is
a medallion of Flora, from the antique,
in white marble' (*Nuneham-Courtenay*,
1783, pp. 13–14; *The New Oxford Guide*,
1785, pp. 131, 133).

2. (d. 1784), gardener at Nuneham; an
inscription to his memory by William
Whitehead (1715–85) was carved on a
stone in the garden (see *Harcourt Papers*
iii. 208).

3. Lady Nuneham's verses have not
been found.

terested, though not worthy of the subject, which, *without a flower,* would make *St Paul run mad.*[4] Well, you are a fortunate husband! I do not wonder you despise crowns and sceptres. If you had those of an Emperor, you should not make me destroy the lines you have sent me, though I give you and Lady Nuneham my honour that they shall never go out of my hands.

I have neither read the *Ode*[5] nor the *Spiritual Quixote:*[6] but you are too hard on their panegyrist.[7] Would not it be cruel on bad authors, if nobody was found to like their writings? For my own part I am persuaded that foolish writers and readers are created for each other; and that Fortune provides readers, as she does mates for ugly women.

I shall be proud to appear in the Oxford Guide.[8] One's works are sure to live and pass through many editions, when one labours in such vineyards. I submit to Bassan[9] with an *O,* but Titiano[10] I doubt will sound too formal and in the style of General Guise.[11]

4. When St Paul asserted his belief in the resurrection, 'Festus said with a loud voice, "Paul, thou art beside thyself; much learning doth make thee mad"' (Acts 26. 24).

5. Perhaps *An Ode Addressed to the Sçavoir Vivre Club,* the only ode reviewed in the *Monthly Review* of 1773 (April, xlviii. 317) which is the magazine to which Nuneham apparently refers; see following note.

6. *The Spiritual Quixote, or the Summer's Ramble of Mr Geoffrey Wildgoose,* a comic romance published anonymously in three volumes, is favourably reviewed in the *Monthly Review,* May, 1773, xlviii. 384–8. The reviewer states that the tale, which deals with 'the adventures of a frantic enthusiast (a Methodist preacher) . . . deserves to be distinguished from the common trash of modern novels.' The author of the work was the Rev. Richard Graves (1715–1804), poet and novelist; rector of Claverton, 1749–1804.

7. The reviewer, in the *Monthly Review,* of the *Spiritual Quixote* was William Woodfall (1746–1803), actor and journalist (B. C. Nangle, *The Monthly Review . . . Indexes,* Oxford, 1934, pp. 47, 202). The reviewer of the *Ode* has not been identified.

8. HW does not 'appear' in the *New*

Oxford Guide, 1775 (6th edn), but he is mentioned five times in the description of Nuneham in the next edition, 1785, as also in *Nuneham-Courtenay,* 1783, the text of which is the same as that in the 1785 *Guide.* In these two books, *Anecdotes of Painting* is quoted at page 120 and page 2, respectively; and gifts of paintings by HW to Nuneham are acknowledged at pages 123, 124, 129, and 5, 6, 11, respectively.

9. Jacopo da Ponte (1510–92), like the other artists of his family, took his name, 'Il Bassano,' from their place of origin (*Enciclopedia italiana*). His name is spelled with an *o* in the *New Oxford Guide,* 1775, p. 128, where his 'Christ driving the Money-Changers out of the Temple, on marble,' is listed among the pictures at Nuneham. The *o* was left off in *Nuneham-Courtenay,* 1783, p. 4, and in the *New Oxford Guide,* 1785, p. 122.

10. Tiziano Vecellio (1477–1576), better known as Titian; his name is spelled Titiano in the 1775 *Guide,* p. 128, but the *o* is left off in *Nuneham-Courtenay,* p. 8, and in the 1785 *Guide,* p. 126. Nuneham owned 'Saint Margeret, whole-length,' by Titian.

11. Gen. John Guise (1682 or 3–1765), army officer and art collector. HW speaks

Mrs Clive is gone to Marlow[12] on a visit for a week. If she does not meet with a harvest of cards, she will not think there was any prospect. My poor Rosette[13] is better, though I still fear not likely to recover. I shall set out for my Viceroyalty on Thursday;[14] a shorter indeed, but not a pleasanter journey than your Lordship's. May we meet in Leicester Fields[15] sooner than you expect! and as a prosperous reign would only prolong your calamities, I shall not be sorry if your Highness's father is speedily dethroned,[16] which is the hearty prayer of

My dear Lord
Your most faithful humble servant,

HOR. WALPOLE

To Nuneham, Saturday 6 November 1773

Printed from a photostat of the MS in Lord Harcourt's possession. First printed Cunningham vi. 3–4, reprinted, Toynbee viii. 355–6.

Endorsed by Nuneham: Honourable Horace Walpole 9ᵇʳ [November] 6th 1773.

Strawberry Hill, Nov. 6, 1773.

My dear Lord,

I HAVE once or twice begun to write to you, and commenced my epistle with *May it please your O-royal Highness,*[1] but as I concluded you are as weary of royalty by this time, as I am of my portion of it, I will use the freedom you have long allowed me, and only tell you how happy I shall be to hear you and Lady Nuneham are well. When you get into your closet and have locked your door and

of his 'hyperboles at the mouth of a cannon' (MANN iv. 450). HW printed the catalogue of Guise's collection at SH, 1760, 'taken from [Lysons's] *London and its Environs*' (Hazen, *SH Bibl.* 52). Guise left his collection to Christ Church, Oxford. For HW's unflattering opinion of it, see OSSORY ii. 55.

12. Marlow, Bucks, is five miles northwest of Maidenhead on the Thames.

13. See HW to Nuneham, *ante* 10 Aug. 1773, n. 9 and *post* 6 Nov. 1773.

14. HW went to Houghton during the

illness of his nephew, the 3d E. of Orford, to assist in managing his affairs (see HW to Conway 30 Aug. 1773).

15. That is, at Leicester House, at this time occupied by Nuneham; see *ante* ?May 1771, n. 1.

16. See *ante* HW to Nuneham 10 Aug. 1773, n. 16.

1. Nuneham was at this time visiting his father, the lord lieutenant of Ireland, having reached Dublin 7 Oct. (*Harcourt Papers* iii. 140).

have washed off pounds of snuff that you have taken against every-body that has approached you, pray, before you double yourself up, take a pen and write me a line; 'tis all the tax I will lay on your Absenteeship.² Mrs Clive has long threatened to write before me, but the campaign is not yet finished, nor all the Kings, Queens and Knaves retired into winter-quarters, so at most she can tell you but of a miraculous draught of fishes that she won in a *vole sans prendre*.³ In truth I have no better materials. London is a desert, and nobody asks but if there is any mail from Ireland? There is not a new book, play, wedding or funeral. Duchess Hervey⁴ is already forgotten. My life is passed alone here, or in going to London to talk with lawyers and stewards, and writing letters to Norfolk about farms⁵— So that your Lordship is not singular in being out of your element. The rest of my time has been employed in nursing Rosette—alas! to no purpose. After suffering dreadfully for a fortnight from the time she was seized at Nuneham, she has only languished till about ten days ago. As I have nothing to fill my letter, I will send you her epitaph—it has no merit, for it is an imitation, but in coming from the heart, if ever epitaph did, and therefore your Dogmanity⁶ will not dislike it.

> Sweetest roses of the year
> Strew around my Rose's bier.
> Calmly may the dust repose
> Of my pretty faithful Rose!
> And if yon cloud-topt hill⁷ behind,
> This frame dissolv'd, this breath resign'd,
> Some happier Isle, some humbler Heav'n
> Be to my trembling Wishes giv'n,

2. HW refers to the tax of two shillings per pound on the rents of absentee landlords, proposed by Lord Harcourt as a means of improving the condition of Ireland. The tax met with such strenuous opposition in England that it was defeated; see *Harcourt Papers* ix. 108 *et passim;* MANN vii. 524, 531.

3. For Mrs Clive's fondness for cards, see *ante* HW to Nuneham April, 1773 and 17 Aug. 1773.

4. The Duchess of Kingston, still legally married to her first husband, Augustus John Hervey. 'All tongues are busy with

her Grace of Kingston; the Duke is dead' (HW to Mann 4 Oct. 1773, MANN vii. 520).

5. HW was busy with the Norfolk estates of his nephew Lord Orford (see *ante* HW to Nuneham 17 Aug. 1773, n. 14); he made two trips to Houghton during the winter (HW to Cole 4 May 1774, COLE i. 324).

6. For another instance of his use of this word, see HW to Lady Ossory 13 Aug. 1773, OSSORY i. 139.

7. Richmond, (HW).

Admitted to that equal sky
May sweet Rose bear me company!

Lady Nuneham should not see these lines, if she had time to write any herself—but Clio hates crowds and drawing-rooms, and I am persuaded took leave when her Ladyship embarked. I hope they will meet again in Wales, and that we shall all meet again in Leicester Fields. So prays

Your Lordship's most faithful humble servant,

HOR. WALPOLE

From NUNEHAM, December 1773

Missing. Answered in the following letter.

To NUNEHAM, Monday 6 December 1773

Printed from a photostat of the MS, now in Lord Harcourt's possession. First printed Cunningham vi. 23–5, reprinted, Toynbee viii. 373–6.

Endorsed by Nuneham: Honourable Horace Walpole 10ᵗ [December] 6th 1773.

Strawberry Hill, Dec. 6, 1773.

I WANTED an excuse for writing to you, my dear Lord, and your letter gives me an opportunity of thanking you—yet that is not all I wanted to say. I would, if I had dared, have addressed myself to Lady Nuneham, but I had not confidence enough, especially on so unworthy a subject as myself. Lady Temple,[1] my friend, as well as that of human nature, has shown me some verses—but alas! how came such charming poetry to be thrown away on so unmeritorious a topic?[2] I don't know whether I ought to praise the lines most, or censure the object most. Voltaire makes the excellence of French

1. See *ante* HW to Nuneham 10 Aug. 1773, n. 4.
2. Lady Nuneham's verses were addressed to HW 'August, 1773, occasioned

by his approbation of' her verses to Lady Temple (*Harcourt Papers* xi. 140). See Appendix 3.

poetry consist in the number of difficulties it vanquishes.³ Pope who celebrated Lord Bolinbroke,⁴ could not have succeeded, did not succeed better; and yet I hope that, though a meaner subject, I am not so bad an one—well! with all my humility, I cannot but be greatly flattered. Madame de Sévigné spread her leaf-gold over all her acquaintance, and made them shine. I should not doubt of the same glory, when Lady Nuneham's poetry shall come to light, if my own works were but burnt at the same time—but alas! Coulange's⁵ verses were preserved, and so may my writings too. Apropos, my Lord, I have got a new volume⁶ of that divine woman's letters. Two are entertaining; the rest, not very divine. But there is an application, the happiest, the most exquisite, that even she herself ever made. She is joking with a Président de Provence,⁷ who was hurt at becoming a grandfather. She assures him there is no such great misfortune in it; I have experienced the case, says she, and believe me, *Pæte, non dolet.*⁸ If you are not both transported with this, ye are not the Lord and Lady Nuneham I take ye to be. There are besides some twenty letters of Madame de Simiane,⁹ who shows she would not have degenerated totally, if she had not lived in the country or had had anything to say;¹⁰ and at the end are reprinted Madame de Sévigné's letters on Fouquet's trial,¹¹ which are very interesting.

3. 'La difficulté surmontée, dans quelque genre que ce puisse être, fait une grande partie du mérite. Point de grandes choses sans de grandes peines: et il n'y a point de nation au monde chez laquelle il soit plus difficile que chez la nôtre de rendre une véritable vie à la poésie ancienne' (Voltaire, 'Discours à l'Académie française, prononcé le lundi 9 mai 1746,' *Œuvres*, ed. Moland, 1877–85, xxiii. 208). Voltaire expressed this idea frequently; see ibid. ii. 56; vii. 333, 437, xxii. 194; xxv. 176.

4. Pope addressed 'Epistle I, Book I' and the opening lines of his *Essay on Man* to Henry St John (1678–1751), 1st Vct Bolingbroke.

5. Mme de Sévigné's cousin and correspondent (*ante* HW to Chute 4 Aug. 1753, n. 20). His verses, *Recueil de chansons*, were printed in 1694 apparently without his permission (Édouard de Barthélemy, *La Marquise d'Huxelles et ses amis*, 1881, p. 157).

6. *Lettres nouvelles ou nouvellement recouvrées de la marquise de Sévigné et de la marquise de Simiane, sa petite-fille*, 1773. The volume was carelessly edited (see Mme du Deffand to HW 13 Nov. 1773, DU DEFFAND iii. 419–20; HW to Lady Ossory 25 Dec. 1773, OSSORY i. 172). HW's copy is Hazen, *Cat. of HW's Lib.*, No. 952.

7. Président de Moulceau (or Monceaux) was 'président de la chambre des comptes de Montpellier' (*Lettres de Madame de Sévigné*, ed. Monmerqué, 1862–6, i. 156). The letter to which HW refers is dated 27 Jan. 1687 (ibid. viii. 13).

8. 'Pætus, it doesn't hurt.' See DU DEFFAND iii. 424, n. 8 for the origin of this anecdote.

9. Françoise-Pauline d'Adhémar de Monteil de Grignan (1674–1737), granddaughter of Mme de Sévigné, m. (1695) Louis de Simiane du Claret, Marquis de Truchenu et d'Esparron (OSSORY i. 172).

10. For a similar criticism of the letters of Mme de Simiane, see HW to Mme du Deffand ca 18 Nov. 1773, DU DEFFAND iii. 423–4.

11. Nicolas Fouquet (1615–80), superin-

I do not know how you like your new subjects,[12] but I hear they are extremely content with their Prince and Princess. I ought to wish your Lordship joy of all your prosperities, and of Mr Fludd's[13] baptism into the Catholic or universal faith[14]—but I reserve public felicities for your old *Drawing-Room* in Leicester Fields. Private news we have little but Lord Carmarthen's[15] and Lord Cranborn's[16] marriages, and the approaching one of Lady Bridget Lane and Mr Tall-Match.[17] Lord Holland has given Charles Fox a draught of an hundred thousand pounds, and it pays all his debts, but a trifle of thirty thousand pounds, and those of Lord Carlisle, Crewe[18] and Foley,[19] who being only friends, not Jews, may wait. So now any younger son may justify losing his father's and elder brother's[20] estate on precedent.

Neither Lord nor Lady Temple are well, and yet they are both gone to Lord Clare's[21] in Essex for a week. Lord Temple had a very bad fall in the park, and lost his senses for an hour. Yet though the horse is a vicious one, he has been upon it again—In short, there are no right-headed people but the Irish.

As it is ancient good breeding not to conclude a letter without troubling the reader with compliments, and as I have none to send, I must beg your Lordship not to forget to present my respects to the

tendent of finances (1653) under Louis XIV, was arrested for embezzlement (1661); his trial, which lasted three years, led to his conviction and banishment. Louis commuted his sentence to life imprisonment and he died in prison (DU DEFFAND i. 187–8; NBG). For Mme de Sévigné's letters on the trial, see her letters to M. de Pomponne, 17 Nov – 30 Dec. 1664 (*Lettres de Madame de Sévigné*, ed. Monmerqué, 1862–6, i. 435–83).

12. That is, the Irish.

13. Henry Flood (1732–91) (*ante* HW to Strafford 10 Nov. 1783, n. 3), who supported Lord Harcourt's proposed absentee tax (see *Harcourt Papers* ix. 117 and *ante* HW to Nuneham 6 Nov. 1773, n. 2).

14. HW apparently refers to Flood's withdrawal from the Opposition, to which he had belonged since his entry into the Irish Parliament; he had been particularly opposed to Townshend's administration (1767–72), and supported the government only after Lord Harcourt's appointment as viceroy.

15. Francis Godolphin Osborne (1751–

99), styled M. of Carmarthen; 5th D. of Leeds, 1789; m. (29 Nov. 1773) Lady Amelia Darcy (1754–84).

16. James Cecil (1748–1823), styled Vct Cranborne, 7th E. of Salisbury, 1780; cr. (1789) M. of Salisbury; m. (2 Dec. 1773), at Lambeth Palace, Lady Mary Amelia Hill (1750–1835).

17. Lady Bridget Henley (d. 1796), m. 1 (1761) Hon. Robert Fox Lane; 2 (1773) Hon. John Tollemache (1750–77) (OSSORY i. 124, 164).

18. John Crewe (1742–1829), cr. (1806) Bn Crewe.

19. Hon. Thomas Foley (1742–93), 2d Bn Foley, 1777.

20. Stephen Fox (1745–74), 2d Bn Holland, 1774, Lord Holland's eldest son, and a gambler like his brother Charles James Fox.

21. Robert Nugent, who was cr. Vct Clare, 1767 and (1776) E. Nugent; his seat was Gosfield Hall, in eastern Essex; for HW's description of it, see HW to Montagu 25 July 1748, MONTAGU i. 64–5.

Countesses of Barrymore[22] and Massareene[23] my dear sisters in loo. You may be sure I am charged with a large parcel from Cliveden,[24] where I was last night. Except being extremely ill, Mrs Clive is extremely well; but the tax-gatherer is gone off, and she must pay her window-lights[25] over again; and the road before her door is very bad, and the parish won't mend it, and there is some suspicion that Garrick is at the bottom of it;[26] so if you please to send a shipload of the giant's causey[27] by next Monday, we shall be able to go to Mr Rofey's[28] rout at Kingston. The papers said she was to act at Covent Garden, and she has printed a very proper answer in the *Evening Post*.[29] Mr Raftor[30] told me that formerly when he played Luna in *The Rehearsal*, he never could learn to dance the hays,[31] and at last he went to the man that teaches grown gentlemen.[31a]

Miss Davies[32] is the admiration of all London, but of me, who do not love the perfection of what anybody can do, and wish she had less top to her voice and more bottom. However she will break Millico's[33] heart, which will not break mine. Fierville[34] has sprained his leg, and there is another man[35] who sprains his mouth with smiling

22. Margaret Davys (d. 1788), m. (1738) James Barry (d. 1751), 5th E. of Barrymore.

23. Anne Eyre (ca 1716–1805), m. 1741), as his 2d wife, Clotworthy Skeffington (d. 1757), 5th Vct Massereene; cr. (1756) E. of Massereene.

24. Mrs Clive's house.

25. 'The window-tax, as it stands at present (January 1775) . . . lays a duty upon every window, which in England augments gradually from two-pence, the lowest rate upon houses with not more than seven windows, to two shillings, the highest rate upon houses with twenty-five windows and upwards' (Adam Smith, *Wealth of Nations*, 1904, ii. 330–1).

26. He lived at Hampton Court, nearby.

27. See *ante* HW to Hamilton 13 Aug. 1773, n. 1.

28. Probably William Roffey (1713–85), who died at 'Surbiton House, near Kingston' (GM Sept. 1785, lv pt i. 750).

29. Dated 'Twickenham, Nov. 17,' and entitled 'Part of a Letter from Mrs Clive to a Lady in London' (*Lloyd's Evening Post* 19–22 Nov. 1773).

30. Her brother (*ante* HW to Bentley 15 Aug. 1755, n. 17).

31. The 'hay' or 'hays' was a country dance with serpentine figures; see *The Rehearsal* V. i.

31a. This sentence is quoted in the BM *Satiric Prints* iv. 493 to annotate the caricature *Grown Gentlemen Taught to Dance*. The dancing-master was one Le Roque.

32. Cecilia Davies, 'l'Inglesina' (ca 1750–1836), sang Italian opera at the King's Theatre in the Haymarket in 1773. She sang the part of Berenice, Queen of Armenia, in Sacchini's *Lucio Vero*, with text by Apostolo Zeno, which opened 20 Nov. (MANN vii. 547, n. 10).

33. Giuseppe Millico (b. 1739), Italian castrato singer and composer, sang the part of Berenice's husband, Vologesus, in *Lucio Vero* (MANN vii. 403, n. 21; *London Stage 1660–1800*, pt 4, ed. G. W. Stone, Carbondale, Ill., 1962, iii. 1764–6).

34. One of the 'Principal Dancers' in *Lucio Vero* ('Dramatis Personæ' of 1773 edn).

35. Evidently a dancer, perhaps Pitrot who danced as 'Orfeo' with the Faviers (*London Stage*, pt 4, iii. 1766).

on himself—as I have heard, for I have not seen him yet, nor a fat old woman and her lean daughter[36] who dance with him. London is very dull, so pray come back as soon as you can. Mason is up to the ears in Gray's life;[37] you will like it exceedingly, which is more than you will do this long letter—well! you have but to go into Lady Nuneham's dressing-room and you may read something ten thousand times more pleasing. No, no, you are not the most to be pitied of any human being, though in the midst of Dublin Castle.[38]

From NUNEHAM, June 1775

Missing. Answered *post* 14 June 1775.

To NUNEHAM, Wednesday 14 June 1775

Printed from a photostat of the MS in Lord Harcourt's possession. First printed, Cunningham vi. 222, reprinted, Toynbee ix. 210.
Endorsed by Nuneham: Honourable Horace Walpole June 14th 1775.

Strawberry Hill, June 14, 1775.

HAVING been absent hence a few days,[1] I have but just now received your Lordship's most kind note[2] with the direction, or should certainly have thanked you sooner, as I do most gratefully. I shall as gladly obey your commands before you go to Ireland,[3]

36. Probably 'Mme Mimi Faviere' and 'Mlle Nina Faviere,' dancers in the ballet (accompanying *Lucio Vero*) which first appeared on 30 Nov. (*London Stage* pt 4, iii. 1766). The name is spelled Favier ibid. pt 4, iii. 1744 and in the 'Dramatis Personæ.'
37. At Gray's death in 1771, Mason was made his literary executor, and he published in 1775 Gray's *Poems. To which are prefixed Memoirs of his life and writings by William Mason.* HW's copy is Hazen *Cat. of HW's Lib.,* No. 3841.
38. Where Nuneham's father, Lord Harcourt, lived, as lord lieutenant of Ireland.

1. HW had apparently been in town, since he wrote to Mason from Arlington Street on 12 June.
2. Missing.
3. It is not clear when the Nunehams went to Ireland in 1775—indeed, whether Lady Nuneham went at all; she was in ill health at this time (see Earl Harcourt to Lady Vernon 1 July 1775, *Harcourt Papers* iii. 137) and was at Harcourt House, Cavendish Square in Feb. 1775 (Earl Harcourt to Lady Nuneham 13 Feb. 1775, ibid.).

and will take the liberty of writing to know if my visit will not be unseasonable.4

I am exceedingly concerned to hear of Lady Nuneham's loss,5 and when it is proper, will entreat your Lordship to say how very much I interest myself in whatever touches her Ladyship.

Mr Fitzpatrick6 has written a *Town Eclogue*,7 and has let me print it. The subject is not new, but as the versification is very good, I thought it might divert a melancholy quarter of an hour at Nuneham, and therefore enclose it. I know it is not just the moment for mentioning it, or I would say how very preferably my press might be employed, if I could have my earnest wish. How sincerely do I say, what is reduced to a common ceremony, that I am

With the greatest regard

Your Lordship's most obedient humble servant,

HOR. WALPOLE

To Nuneham, Tuesday 18 July 1775

Printed from a photostat of the MS in Lord Harcourt's possession. First printed, Cunningham vi. 230–1, reprinted, Toynbee ix. 219.
Endorsed by Nuneham: Honourable Horace Walpole July 18th 1775.

Strawberry Hill, July 18th 1775.

I SHALL be at Park Place next week, my dear Lord, and if you assure me that I shall not be troublesome either to Lady Nuneham or yourself, I will have the honour of passing a night at Nuneham, and asking your commands to Paris,1 whither I am going next month—with great satisfaction in one respect, the certainty of find-

4. HW visited Nuneham in late July (HW to Lady Ossory 23 July, 3 Aug. 1773, OSSORY i. 242, 247).

5. Her sister, the Hon. Catherine Vernon (1749–75), had died 8 June (GM 1775, xlv. 304; Debrett, *Peerage*, 1806, i. 312; the date of her death as given in Collins, *Peerage*, 1812, vii. 408, is incorrect).

6. Hon. Richard Fitzpatrick (*ante* HW to Strafford 27 Nov. 1781, n. 5).

7. Fitzpatrick's *Dorinda, a Town Eclogue*, was printed at SH in June 1775 (Hazen, *SH Bibl.* 112–14).

1. HW set out for Paris 16 Aug. 1775 ('Paris Journals,' DU DEFFAND v. 342).

ing the Hôtel d'Harcourt² open next winter. I should be ashamed
of such a trip at my age, if it was not to see an older person; yet I
shall not go *incog.*³ and call myself *Dr* W., but what I always am

Your Lordship's most faithful humble servant,

H. W.

To Nuneham, ca Tuesday 28 May 1776

Printed from a photostat of the MS in Lord Harcourt's possession. First
printed, Cunningham vi. 344, reprinted, Toynbee ix. 370–1.

Dated approximately by the reference to the 'revolution in the Penetralia,'
which became known, 28 May (see n. 2 below).

Address: To the Right Honourable Lord Nuneham.

Endorsed by Nuneham: Honourable Horace Walpole May 1776.

I AM very sorry, my dear Lord, to have missed seeing you both
yesterday and today; and so I always am, as your goodness to me
is excessive and most gratefully felt. I wished particularly to ask a
favour, which is that your Lordship will do me the honour of dining
at Strawberry Hill some day before you go out of town, and I flatter
myself Lady Nuneham will do so too, though she ought to be
ashamed to come so near my printing-house, when she is so cruel as
to refuse to do it the honour it is so ambitious of. Any day after the
Birthday¹ will be equal to me, and if you both condescend, I will
beg Lord and Lady Jersey to be so good as to meet you.

Are you thunderstruck or laughterstruck with the revolution in

2. Harcourt House, Cavendish Square, which HW is comparing to the Paris residence of Anne-Pierre (1701–83), Duc d'Harcourt, head of the French branch of the Harcourt family. HW is also indulging Lord Nuneham's 'decided preference to French manners and fashions,' see the character of him in Collins, *Peerage,* 1812, iv. 450. The Nunehams were at Harcourt House by Feb. 1776 (*Harcourt Papers* viii. 177).

3. 'In allusion to the Earl of Bute's having travelled (in imitation of princes) *incognito,* under an assumed title' (note on MS in Nuneham's hand). When Bute

was in Italy in 1769 'he received very few visits anywhere, never wore his Garter, and left cards under the name of Mr Stuart' (Mann to HW 25 March 1769). HW later refers to his incognito as Sir John Stewart (HW to Mason 28 March 1777, Mason i. 294). The allusion is more likely to be to Lord Mansfield, who had attempted to travel as 'Dr Murray' on his visit to France in the summer of 1774 (*Last Journals* i. 373).

1. Probably the King's birthday, June 4.

the Penetralia?[2] Whither shall we go, if Lord Solon, and Bishop Plato are not perfect enough to form young Montezuma,[3] the future Emperor of America? I hear even Mlle *Crumb*[4] is no longer our *Mie.*

Yours most devotedly,

H. W.

To Nuneham, Monday 7 July 1777

Printed from a photostat of the MS in Lord Harcourt's possession. First printed, Cunningham vi. 454–5, reprinted, Toynbee x. 76–7.

Endorsed by Nuneham: July 7, 1777. Honourable Horace Walpole.

Strawberry Hill, July 7, 1777.

My good Lord,

AS I know your Lordship and Lady Nuneham are so good as to interest yourselves about the Duke and Duchess of Gloucester, I cannot deny myself the satisfaction of telling you that, though the express on Saturday was as bad as possible, yet another letter yesterday from the Duke's surgeon[1] dated three days later brought a more favourable account.[2] His R. Highness had been taken out of bed and

---

2. Changes in the royal household: it was declared 28 May that Lord Holdernesse and Leonard Smelt (ca 1719–1800) had resigned their posts as governor and sub-governor to the Prince of Wales; and that William Markham (1719–1807), Bp of Chester, 1771; Abp of York, 1777; and Cyril Jackson (d. 1819), Dean of Christ Church 1783–1809, had been dismissed as preceptor and sub-preceptor to the Prince. HW gives an account of the affair and the disputes leading up to it in *Last Journals,* i. 554–8; see also *The Correspondence of King George the Third with Lord North,* ed. W. Bodham Donne, 1867, ii. 24–9, 31–3.

3. The Prince of Wales, later George IV, is 'Montezuma,' and Holdernesse and Bishop Markham are 'Lord Solon' and 'Bishop Plato.'

4. Mlle Krohme (d. 1777), French teacher in the royal nursery 1768–77 (GM 1777, xlvii. 195; *Court and City Registers*).

'Mie' is presumably the familiar form of 'm'amie,' which might be used by a child to a nurse.

---

1. Robert Bryant (d. 1788), 'surgeonpage' and 'page of the presence' to the Duke 1777–88 (OSSORY i. 362, n. 3).

2. '5th [August]. An express arrived from the Duchess of Gloucester for Dr Jebbe and Mr Adair, the Duke of Gloucester being dangerously ill at Verona. . . . At Padua he was seized with a dysentery, but it stopped; yet at Verona he grew so weak and unable to bear the heat, that Bryant, his surgeon, advised his returning to England; and his danger increased so fast, that he was taken out of his bed and put into his post-chaise. He got to Trent, seemed to mend by the journey and by the coolness of the air from the mountains; but his flux returned, and he was again confined to his bed for some days' (*Last Journals* ii. 38–

put into a post-chaise, as it was thought nothing but change of air and motion could save him. He bore the travelling for two days very well, and got eight hours of sleep. The third day he was less well from fatigue, but the surgeon did not think him otherwise worse. I hope in God this alarm will pass off like the former!³—but nothing, except her own words, could paint the agonies of the Duchess. She is alarmed too for the little Prince.⁴ They are coming to England, but not to stay, as Italian winters agree with the Duke, though the summers are so prejudicial.

Now I have taken this liberty, my dear Lord, I must take a little more. You know my admiration and envy are your garden. I don't grudge Pomona or Sir James Cockburn⁵ their hothouses, nor intend to ruin myself by raising sugar and water in tanner's bark and peach skins. The Flora Nunehamica is the height of my ambition: and if your Linnæus⁶ should have any disciple that would condescend to look after my little flower garden, it would be the delight of my eyes and nose, provided the cataracts of heaven are ever shut again!⁷ Not one proviso do I make, but that the pupil be not a Scot.⁸ We had peace and warm weather before the inundation of that northern people, and therefore I beg to have no Attila for my gardener.

Apropos, don't your Lordship think that another set of legislators, the Maccaronis and Maccaronesses, are very wise? People abuse them for turning days, nights, hours and seasons topsyturvy? but surely it was upon mature reflection. We had a set of customs and ideas borrowed from the continent, that by no means suited our

9). See also ibid. ii. 51–3, and HW to Lady Ossory 6 July 1777, Ossory i. 362–3. Lady Mary Coke in her 'MS Journals' for 6 July 1777 mentions that HW was not at Lady Blandford's that evening 'the news of the Duke of Gloucester's illness had I suppose put him into low spirits, though it was followed very soon, according to custom, with an account of his being better, and that he was set out on his return to England, but proposed going back before winter to Rome.'

3. The Duke of Gloucester had been thought to be dying in Jan. 1775; see HW to Conway 22–24 Jan., to Lord Ossory 24 Jan., and to Mann 25–27 Jan. 1775. His life had also been despaired of when he

was at Leghorn in Oct. 1771; see Mann to HW, 15, 18, 21, 29 Oct. 1771.

4. William Frederick (1776–1834), 2d D. of Gloucester, 1805. He also was ill; see Last Journals, ii. 52, and HW to Lady Ossory 6 July 1777, Ossory i. 362–3.

5. Sir James Cockburn (1729–1804), 8th Bt, M.P. Linlithgow 1772–84.

6. Walter Clark (ante HW to Nuneham 17 Aug. 1773).

7. 'The weather is really dreadful. I never remember such a continuance of rain in all my life' (Lady Mary Coke, 'MS Journals,' 5 July 1777).

8. HW's present gardener was a Scot; see post HW to Harcourt 18 Oct. 1777.

climate. Reformers bring back things to their natural course. Notwithstanding what I said in spite in the paragraph above, we are in truth but Greenlanders, and ought to conform to our climate. We should lay in store of provisions and candles and masquerades and coloured lamps for ten months in the year, and shut out our twilight and enjoy ourselves. In September and October we may venture out of our ark, and make our hay and gather in our corn, and go to horse-races and kill pheasants and partridges for stock for our winter's supper. I sailed in a skiff and pair this morning to Lady Cecilia Johnsone,[9] and found her like a good huswife sitting over her fire with her cats and dogs and birds and children.[10] She brought out a dram to warm me and my servants, and we were very merry and comfortable. As Lady Nuneham has neither so many two-footed or four-footed cares upon her hands, I hope her hands have been better employed. I wish I could peep over her shoulder one of these wet mornings!

Adieu! my dear Lord; forgive all my babble. Yesterday's letter raised my spirits, and I love to impart my satisfaction to those I love, which with all due respect I must take leave to say I feel for you, and am most sincerely

Your Lordship's most obedient humble servant,

HOR. WALPOLE

To Nuneham, Sunday 24 August 1777

Printed from a photostat of the MS in Lord Harcourt's possession. First printed, Cunningham vi. 468, reprinted, Toynbee x. 96–7.

Endorsed by Nuneham: August 24th 1777. Honourable Horace Walpole.

Strawberry Hill, Aug. 24, 1777.

AS I am sure the Duke and Duchess of Gloucester have no well-wishers more sincere than your Lordship and Lady Nuneham, I flatter myself I shall give both pleasure by taking the liberty of

9. See *ante* HW to Strafford 4 Sept. 1760, n. 11. She was a friend and frequent correspondent of Nuneham; **selections** from her letters to him are printed in *Harcourt Papers* viii. 11–29. She lived at Petersham (OSSORY ii. 299, n. 9).

10. Henry George Johnston (1766–1809),

army officer (BERRY ii. 55, n. 20); and Caroline Georgina Johnston (ca 1764–1823), m. (1780) Francis Evelyn Anderson (BERRY i. 23, n. 38). Her third child Hester Maria Johnston died in infancy (GM 1817, lxxxvii pt i. 281).

letting you know that all the letters of the 12th[1] are in a new style and speak of his Royal Highness as much mended. Those of the eighth were full of despair. He had set up an hour, and the Duchess had been out to take the air, after not quitting one floor for seven weeks, nor writing for three,[2] so immediate had been her apprehensions. The physicians[3] flattered her that the Duke would be able to begin his journey in a fortnight. I shall be overjoyed to hear he has, as constant change of air, and motion, will restore his strength faster than anything. They hope to be in England in October.

I dined today at Lady Cecilia's. She tells me the French Ambassador[4] and Ambassadress[5] are going to Nuneham. The poor Prince of Masserano[6] I doubt is on the point of a longer journey.[7] I will not, under pretence of a duty, be tiresome, though so great a pleasure to converse with you.

Your Lordship's most assured humble servant,

HOR. WALPOLE

1. The report had presumably reached London at the same time as a letter from the Duchess of Gloucester to HW 10–11 Aug. 1777, which is postmarked 22 Aug. All the details HW mentions in this paragraph, except the Duke's sitting up, are from the Duchess's letter.

2. Her last letter (missing) to HW had been written 21 July (Ds of Gloucester to HW 10–11 Aug. 1777).

3. Drs Robert Adair (d. 1790) and Richard Jebb (1729–87), cr. (1778) Bt (MANN vii. 356–7, nn. 1, 2, viii. 322–3, et passim).

4. Emmanuel-Marie-Louis (1743–1822), Marquis de Noailles; ambassador to England 1776–8 (DU DEFFAND, passim; Court and City Registers).

5. Charlotte-Françoise de Hallencourt de Dromesnil (b. 1745), m. (1762) Emmanuel-Marie-Louis, Marquis de Noailles (DU DEFFAND iv. 461, n. 3). The visit was made in early Sept.; for details see the extract from Mrs Montagu's letters (who was at Nuneham at the same time) in Reginald Blunt, Mrs Montagu, [1923], ii. 33–5.

6. Vittorio Filippo Ferrero di Biella (1713–77), Principe di Masserano; Spanish ambassador to England 1763–72, ca 1775–7 (MANN vi. 441, n. 11).

7. He was seriously ill, and died 14 Oct. (see HW to Mann 18 Sept. 1777, MANN viii. 328, n. 16).

To Harcourt, Sunday 28 September 1777

Printed from a photostat of the MS in Lord Harcourt's possession. First printed, Cunningham vi. 488–9, reprinted, *Harcourt Papers* viii. 96, Toynbee x. 121.

Endorsed by Harcourt: 7ᵇʳ [September] 28th 1777. Honourable Horace Walpole.

Strawberry Hill, Sept. 28, 1777.

I FLATTER myself my zeal will not appear too prompt in assuring your Lordship and Lady Harcourt of the part I take in your late terrible shock.[1] I wished to express it the first moment, but trusted you both know me too well to doubt of what I felt for you. I still write in pain lest I should be importunate, and beg you will not trouble yourself to answer me, as all I mean is to show that I never can be insensible to anything that affects you.

It may be some satisfaction to your Lordship to know that every letter brings better accounts of the Duke of Gloucester.[2] I will answer for the Duchess that she is too sensible of your Lordship's friendship not to share with me in all I have felt for you. I have the honour to be with the greatest regard

My dear Lord

Your Lordship's most obedient humble servant,

Hor. Walpole

From Harcourt, Sunday 5 October 1777

Missing. Dated in the postscript to the following letter.

---

1. Lord Harcourt was drowned 16 September while attempting to rescue his dog from a well; see *Harcourt Papers* iii. 146–8; HW to Mann 19 Sept., to Mason 18 Sept., and to Lady Ossory 20 Sept. 1777 (MANN viii. 328, MASON i. 327, OSSORY i. 380–1).

2. See Ds of Gloucester to HW 4 Sept., 14 Sept. 1777.

To Harcourt, Wednesday 8 October 1777

Printed from a photostat of the MS in Lord Harcourt's possession. First printed, Cunningham vi. 495–6, reprinted, Toynbee x. 130–1.
Endorsed by Harcourt: 8ᵇʳ [October] 8, 1777. Honourable Horace Walpole.

Strawberry Hill, Oct. 8, 1777.

I WILL never believe in impulses more—no, for I tore open the sacred box with as much impatience and as little reverence, as Lady Barrymore¹ could have done if she expected a new coiffure from Paris. No holy frisson, no involuntary tear warned me that there was but a piece of paper between my sacrilegious fingers, and the most precious relics in the world.² Alas! why am not I a Gregory or a Boniface, and possess treasures enough to found a Casa Santa over the invaluable offering your Lordship has sent me? You enriched my museum before;³ you have now enriched me, for who is not rich, who possesses what the world cannot buy? You have done more, my Lord; you have given me a talisman that will forever keep off Macphersons⁴ and evil spirits from entering my dwelling. You have shown generosity too in the highest sense, for you have given me what I know you value so much. I have seriously kissed each spur devoutly, and think them more lovely than Cellini's bell.⁵ You

1. Probably the dowager Countess, Lady Emily Stanhope (1749–80), widow of the 6th E. of Barrymore.

2. 'The spurs worn by King William at the Battle of the Boyne, preserved in an Irish family, and given to the late Earl of Harcourt when Lord Lieutenant, and by the present Earl to Mr W., in a red leather box lined with green velvet (*Des. of SH,* 1784, p. 77). The spurs were kept in the glass cabinet in the Great North Bedchamber. They were sold SH xvi. 86 to a dealer and passed into the possession of the Earls of Enniskillen.

3. With his etchings (see *ante* HW to Harcourt 16 March 1763), 'a large old white china teapot, that was the Duke of Monmouth's ('Des. of SH,' *Works* ii. 415), 'James Brydges, first Duke of Chandos, in enamel, by Zincke' (ibid. ii. 477). HW also had a portrait of Harcourt 'in Wedgwood's ware, the only one executed in that manner' (ibid. ii. 416); it was sold SH xviii. 8.

4. James Macpherson (1736–96), author of *Ossian*, had aroused HW's wrath by his *History of Great Britain*, 1775, in which he espoused the Jacobite cause. For HW's opinion of Macpherson's political writings, see *Last Journals* i. 444–5; HW to Mason 14 April 1775, MASON i. 191–2.

5. One of the most admired objects at SH. '*A truly magnificent and matchless specimen of art,* which *may unquestionably be denominated the* GEM *of this extraordinary assemblage of all that is rare and valuable,* THE RENOWNED SILVER BELL, made expressly for Pope CLEMENT VII, by that unrivalled artist BENVENUTO CELLINI. . . . This extraordinary bijou was for a long period in the collection of the Marquis Leonati of Parma, and was purchased by the Marquis of Rockingham, who exchanged it with Horace Walpole for some very scarce Roman coins and medals . . .' (sold SH xv. 83; 'Des. of SH,' *Works* ii. 487; DAL-

could have bestowed your bounty on no man living who could worship it more; nor is there any man living whom I should not envy the possession—except General Washington. If he *gains his spurs,* I think I could cede them. Thanks are poor, words could ill express my gratitude. The Muse of the *Dispensary* would alone be capable of doing justice to your Lordship as she did to the hero who wore these inestimable trophies.[6]

One grief mixes with my transports. How could Ireland suffer the removal of her Palladium?[7] Does she not expect a host of toads, locusts, Scots and every venomous insect in swarms on her coast? or is it not a mark of her degeneracy?

> To some new clime or far more distant sky,
> O friendless and forsaken virtue, fly![8]

Do not expect, my Lord, that I should talk but poetry and enthusiasm. What day ever secured so much felicity, prevented so much mischief as that festival on which these spurs were worn?[9] Allowing credibility to legends, and sanctity to relics, what was the merit of martyrs but to themselves? What obligation was it to the world that they did not like to go to the Devil? and why should we hoard up their teeth or their bones against the resurrection, when they would know where to find them wherever they were? In short, Saint William is my patron, his spurs are the dearest treasure of my museum, and your Lordship's letter shall never, while I have breath, be separated from them. Yet obliged as I am, I shall think your Lordship and Lady Harcourt heretics, if you do not both at least once a year make a pilgrimage to kiss the spurs. How can I say how much I am your Lordship's

> Devoted humble servant,
>
> Hor. Walpole

PS. Your Lordship's letter is dated on Sunday, yet I received it only tonight Wednesday.

RYMPLE 316, n. 4). The bell, no longer considered Cellini's, is now in the British Museum (DALRYMPLE, loc. cit.)

6. Sir Samuel Garth praises King William in his mock-epic, *The Dispensary;* see end of Canto VI.

7. That is, King William's spurs.

8. Adapted from ll. 13–14 of Pope's 'Chorus of Athenians,' written to follow Act I of Buckingham's *Marcus Brutus,* 1722.

9. The Battle of the Boyne, 1 July 1690, in which William III defeated James II.

From Harcourt, ca Thursday 16 October 1777

Missing. Answered in the next letter.

To Harcourt, Saturday 18 October 1777

Printed from a photostat of the MS in Lord Harcourt's possession. First printed, Cunningham vi. 501–2, reprinted Toynbee x. 140–2.

Endorsed by Harcourt: 8ᵇʳ [October] 18th 1777. Honourable Horace Walpole.

Strawberry Hill, Oct. 18, 1777.

I AM sensibly obliged, my dear Lord, by your great goodness, and am most disposed to take the gardener you recommend, if I can. You are so good-natured, that you will not blame my suspense. I have a gardener[1] that has lived with me above five and twenty years; he is incredibly ignorant and a mule. When I wrote to your Lordship, my patience was worn out, and I resolved at least to have a gardener for flowers. On your not being able to give me one, I half consented to keep my own; not on his amendment, but because he will not leave me, presuming on my long suffering. I have offered him fifteen pounds a year to leave me; and when he pleads that he is old and that nobody else will take him, I plead that I am old too, and that it is hard I am not to have a few flowers or a little fruit as long as I live. I shall now try if I can make any compromise with him, for I own I cannot bear to turn him adrift, nor will starve an old servant, though never a good one, to please my nose and mouth. Besides, he is a Scot, and I will not be unjust even to that odious nation: and the more I dislike him, the less will I allow my partiality to persuade me I am in the right. Everybody would not understand this, and the Scotch none of them—but I am sure your Lordship will, and will not be angry that I dally with you. I know how strong my prejudices are, and am always afraid of them. As long as they only hate, they are welcome—but prejudices are themselves so much Scots, that I must not let them be my *friends*[2] and govern me. I will

---

1. John Cowie (d. 1795), HW's gardener from about 1749 until after 1781 (Berry ii. 179, n. 7, 183).

2. Alluding to the 'King's friends,' some of whom, such as Bute, were Scots.

take the liberty of letting you know, if I can persuade the serpent that has reduced my little Eden to be as nasty and barren as the Highlands, to take a pension³ or a yellow ribband.⁴

Lady Harcourt or your Lordship may frisk and vagary anywhere separately, I shall not be alarmed, nor think it by choice. Nay, if it were, where could either mend yourself? I have so high an opinion of Miss Fauquiere,⁵ that, with all her regard for your Lordship, I believe you are the last man from whom she would bear to hear a gallantry—so you see, my Lord, how awkwardly you set about mischief! It is plain you are a novice, and have no talent for it, and therefore I advise you as a friend not to attempt what would not become you. You are like a young tragic author, that meaning to draw a politic villain, makes him so very wicked and lay such gross traps, that they would not catch an elephant. One laughs at his tragedy, but loves his heart. I am sure Miss Fauquiere agrees with me in desiring to remain the confidants of the two perfect characters of the drama.

Your Lordship's most devoted,

Hor. Walpole

From Harcourt, ca Monday 24 November 1777

Missing. Answered in the following letter.

---

3. HW had not succeeded in doing so by 1781, but does speak of Cowie as 'superannuated' in 1795 in a way that suggests he had been retired before the beginning of HW's friendship with the Berrys. In his will dated 15 May 1793 HW left him an annuity of twenty pounds for Cowie's life and after Cowie's death a like sum to his wife Catherine (HW to Charles Bedford 18 June 1781; Berry ii. 179, n. 7).

4. Ribbons worn by naval captains who retired as rear-admirals (see OED sub Yellow 1.e).

5. Jane Georgiana Fauquier (d. 1823), dau. of William Fauquier of Hanover Square; m. (1786), as his second wife, George Venables Vernon, 2d Bn Vernon, Lady Harcourt's half-brother. She lived with the Harcourts before her marriage.

To Harcourt, Wednesday 26 November 1777

Printed from a photostat of the MS in Lord Harcourt's possession. First printed, Cunningham vi. 504–5, reprinted, Toynbee x. 159.
Endorsed by Harcourt: Honourable Horace Walpole 9ᵇʳ [November] 26, 1777.

Nov. 26, 1777.

I AM quite ashamed, my dear Lord, to receive such a mark of your Lordship's too kind partiality, in consulting my judgment rather than your own: nor have I any other way of answering it, than by preferring your honour to my own prejudices, as I did, when I presumed to think that, had *they* sent, you ought to have gone to Court.[1] It is very vexatious to pay 80 guineas for a daub ‹and *for a* chimpanzee›,[2] but as I know your scrupulous punctuality in performing your duties, permit me to say that I think your regard for the person that bespoke the picture should preponderate; and that even paying for it and then giving it away, distinguishes between your respect for your father, and your sensibility to the neglect shown to his memory.

May I add that there may even be in two or three years *two* reasons to *one* for your keeping the picture? Your Lordship must have heard a saying of your great-grandfather[3] that had much wit in it— that grandfathers should love their grandsons, as the latter revenge

---

1. 'When Lord Harcourt died, his son, Lord Nuneham, imagined that the King did not pay sufficient respect to his father's memory; and this, he being of a sensitive nature, led to his absenting himself from the Court for a period of six years' (*Harcourt Papers* iii. 166). One of his grievances seems to have been the failure of the King to give his father the Garter.

2. These words are scratched out, but are legible. They probably allude to a portrait of Harcourt's father requested by the Corporation of Dublin, to be 'placed in the Mansion House of their city, to testify to posterity our affectionate regard for the memory of so faithful and sincere a friend to this kingdom' (*Har-* court Papers iii. 153). The portrait was of 'Simon, first Earl Harcourt, in royal robes, as Lord-Lieutenant of Ireland; the head by [Robert] Hunter of Dublin, the figure by [William] Doughty' (ibid. iii. 243). Harcourt promised to 'put the original portrait into the hands of the best copyist' he could find and to send the copy to Dublin (ibid. iii. 154). HW implies, however, that Harcourt was paying for a picture which his late father had previously ordered. In writing to Hertford 8 June 1764, HW uses 'chimpanzee' as a term for an ugly and ill-bred person.

3. Simon Harcourt (1661–1727), cr. (1711) Bn and (1721) Vct Harcourt; D. C. L.; lord chancellor 1713–4; friend of Bolingbroke, Pope and Swift.

their quarrel by wishing their fathers dead.[4] Do not *sons* then pun-ish parents?[5]

I wish you as rich as Crœsus, my dear Lord, but impatient as I am to see you call out all the beauties of Nuneham, I had rather see you dig in your own garden, than not have you a *Harcourt sans re-proche,* I mean, that even Dr Hunter[6] should not be able to invent a blemish that would stick. The poor lady[7] you couple with him can only repeat, not invent. My greatest ambition is to admire you, and prove myself, my good Lord

Your Lordship's most sincere friend and devoted servant,

HOR. WALPOLE

To Harcourt, Saturday 27 December 1777

Printed from a photostat of the MS in Lord Harcourt's possession. First printed, Cunningham vii. 137–8, reprinted, Toynbee x. 170–1.

Dated by the death of Bishop Keppel, and HW's letter to Lady Ossory 27 Dec. 1777.

Address: To the Earl of Harcourt.

Endorsed by Harcourt: Honourable Horace Walpole 1778.

Saturday morning.

IT is so impossible for me, my dear Lord, to know what I shall have it in my power to do on Friday, that I believe the most re-spectful to your Lordship, which I certainly always mean to be, is to excuse myself for Friday next, though waiting on you and Lady Harcourt would be the most agreeable. The case is, that I have been going to Ampthill[1] these three days, but have been delayed by the

---

4. 'Lord Chancellor Harcourt was par-ticularly fond of his grandson; for, says he, this child will revenge me; he will wish his father dead, as his father wishes me' (HW's *MS Commonplace Book of Verses,* now WSL, p. 11).

5. HW is hoping that in two or three years, Harcourt may have a son (or sons) who will cherish the picture of their grandfather which their father despises.

6. John Hunter (1728–93) or William Hunter (1718–83), Scots physicians prac-tising in London. Perhaps they were re-lated to the Hunter who painted the por-trait, and would reproach Harcourt if he did not pay for it.

7. Not identified.

———

1. Lord Ossory's seat, seven miles south-west of Bedford.

danger of the poor Bishop of Exeter,[2] of whom I every minute expect the worst news. Should I fortunately hear anything good, I shall go on Monday to Lord Ossory's[3] for a week as I have promised. If the Bishop should linger, his death may make it improper for me to dine abroad on Friday. Forgive my troubling your Lordship with so many circumstances, since it proves how much I wish to be always at your command, and how much I am afraid of laying you [under] any difficulty by my unavoidable uncertainty. If I am at liberty, I hope at least Lady Harcourt will allow me to pay my duty to her in the evening.

Your Lordship's most devoted,

HOR. WALPOLE

From HARCOURT, 1778

Missing. A request for treillage paper, answered in the next letter.

To HARCOURT, 1778

Printed from a photostat of the MS in Lord Harcourt's possession. First printed, Cunningham vii. 137, reprinted, Toynbee x. 331.

Address: To the Earl of Harcourt.

Endorsed by Harcourt: Honourable Horace Walpole 1778.

I TRUST I need not say how happy and honoured I am whenever your Lordship is so good as to give me any commands. I must then be as unhappy when I cannot obey them immediately. I have kept your servant while I hunted for the treillage paper, but I cannot find it. I flatter myself I carried it to Strawberry, whither I go tomorrow and shall search for it—but I fear? It had laid here in an empty room two years: I have an imperfect notion of having lent a bit or the whole piece to somebody whom I cannot recollect cer-

2. Frederick Keppel (1729–77); canon of Windsor 1754–62; Bp of Exeter, 1762, Dean of Windsor, 1765. He was married to HW's niece, Laura Walpole. The Bishop died on the morning this letter was written (HW to Lady Ossory 27 Dec. 1777, Ossory i. 410).

3. John Fitzpatrick (1745–1818), 2d E. of Upper Ossory, 1758.

tainly, but think it was Lady Ailesbury, whom I will ask about it.
In short, your Lordship may depend upon my recovering it if possible. I only know it was ill done, for the roses were not interlaced
among the *bâtons,* but seemed tacked against them, which, had I had
it executed here, I intended should be corrected—however, I shall
be exceedingly vexed, if I do not find the original.

Your Lordship's most devoted,

H. Walpole

To Harcourt, 1778 *bis*

Printed from a photostat of the MS in Lord Harcourt's possession. First
printed, Cunningham vii. 137, reprinted, Toynbee x. 331.
Address: To Lord Harcourt.
Endorsed by Harcourt: Honourable Horace Walpole 1778.

My dear Lord,

I HAVE hunted in vain at Strawberry for the treillage paper, and
cannot find it. I must have lent it to somebody, that has forgotten
it as well as I. I am vexed, though I hope the bower[1] will not suffer
by it—and that it will give jealousy to Queen Eleanor still—or to
King Eleanor.[2]

1. In the flower garden at Nuneham. 'From the temple of Flora the path bends to the right, between large elms, and makes a gentle descent before it reaches the bower, which is a square building with a covered ceiling and painted green. The front is an arched treillage of the same colour, interwoven with jessamine, woodbine, and other creeping plants. On either side of it are busts of Venus and Apollo. . . . Within is a cast of Cupid and Psyche, from the antique. . . . There is something in the inside form of this bower, which gives it a peculiar and most pleasing quietness: while the view through the arches across the centre of the garden is gay with "shrubs and flow'rets of a thousand dies," backed by a plantation of very high elms beyond its boundary' (*Description of Nuneham Courtenay,* 1797, pp. 17–18). The 1806 edn of the *Description* adds that it 'was designed by Mr Mason for that particular spot' (p. 57). Mason and Harcourt were discussing the advisability of building it in June 1778 (*Harcourt Papers* vii. 57). It no longer exists (M. L. Batey, *Nuneham Courtenay,* Abingdon, 1970, p. 27).

2. Henry II's mistress, 'Fair Rosamond' (Rosamond Clifford, d. ?1176), was allegedly traced to her secret bower and slain there by his jealous Queen Eleanor. The Harcourts' bower is to be beautiful enough to make any sovereign jealous.

From Harcourt, ca Saturday 31 January 1778

A missing note of invitation, answered in the next letter.

To Harcourt, ca Saturday 31 January 1778

Printed from a photostat of the MS in Lord Harcourt's possession. First printed, Cunningham vii. 138, reprinted, Toynbee x. 180–1.

Dated by the apparent reference to Lord Pigot's death.

Endorsed by Harcourt: Honourable Horace Walpole 1778.

I RETURN your Lordship Mrs Macaulay's[1] letter with many thanks. I need not say how much I agree with her in most topics; but I smiled at her account of the provisions in France and their *bad* cookery.[2]

I accept always with great pleasure your Lordship's invitations; and certainly have no exceptions to the company specified. Though you are so very good as to name them, I think I may trust to never meeting at Harcourt House[3] anybody that would be very disagreeable to me, much less that could balance the honour and pleasure of waiting on your Lordship and Lady Harcourt. I remember that Lady Townshend in 1746 said she did not dare to dine anywhere for fear of meeting with rebel pies. Thank God we are in no danger *now* of such dishes. Indeed your Lordship and I have been more likely

---

1. Catherine Sawbridge (1731–91), m. 1 (1760) George Macaulay, M.D.; m. 2 (1778) William Graham; historian. She had recently returned from Paris. Her letter to Harcourt, dated Bath, 17 January 1778, is in *Harcourt Papers* viii. 105–13. She was at this time on good terms with HW, who had recommended her to Mme du Deffand and to a physician at Paris, but their relations cooled after the publication of her *History of England from the Revolution to the Present Time*, 3 March 1778, containing abuse of Sir Robert Walpole. See DU DEFFAND iv. 486–95 *passim;* HW to Mason 16 March 1778, MASON i. 371–2; and *Harcourt Papers* viii. 106, 115.

2. '. . . As my stomach was always very unfortunately delicate, I nauseated from the first, though I was prejudiced in its favour, at all the food I met with in France; their meat is carrion, their poultry and even their game insipid, and their cookery most detestable. They have no good spices to season their meats with, and they use them too sparingly; their made dishes are a collection of gravy drawn from bad meat, fat, etc. without other flavour but what a little onion gives' (*Harcourt Papers* viii. 110).

3. In Cavendish Square.

to be the ingredients than the guests at such banquets!—poor Lord Pigot![4] He *has dined* with a Scotchman![5]

To Harcourt, Thursday 16 April 1778

Printed from a photostat of the MS in Lord Harcourt's possession. First printed, Cunningham vii. 52, reprinted, Toynbee x. 220.
Address: To the Earl of Harcourt.
Endorsed by Harcourt: Honourable Horace Walpole April 16 1778.

April 16, 1778.

IT is at the bottom of the first column of the notes to p. 346 of Warton's 2d volume, that your Lordship will find how the Erle of Harcourt served the Kyng of his spyce-plate.[1] That Kyng was the real[2] not nominal Kyng of France.[3] Will not this piece of intelligence entitle me at least to the post of Harcourt-Pursuivant? I am very ambitious of serving that most ancient and noble House, to which I am bounden by inclination, zeal and gratitude; and though I am not thought worthy of being *Printer* to it, I will never miss any occasion of showing myself Lord and Lady Harcourt's

Most devoted humble servant,

H. Walpole

4. George Pigot (1719–77), cr. (1766) Bn Pigot of Patshull; governor of Madras 1755–63, 1775–6. Confirmation of his death at Madras reached the India House 31 Jan. (*Public Advertiser* 2 Feb. 1778).
5. Col. (later Major-Gen.) James Stuart (d. 1793), second in command of the troops at Madras, 1775; commander-in-chief at Madras 1776–7, 1781–2. 'On the 24th of August, 1776, the Colonel passed the greater part of the day in company or in business with Lord Pigot; he both breakfasted and dined with him as his familiar friend, and was driving in the carriage with him when, according to the Colonel's previous orders, the carriage was surrounded and stopped by troops. His Lordship was then informed that he was their prisoner' (P. H. Stanhope, *History of England*, Boston, 1854, vii. 269).

1. In *The History of English Poetry*, 1774–81, by Thomas Warton (1728–90): ' "Than wine and spyces was brought. The Erle of Harcourt served the Kyng of his spyce-plate. And Sir Gerard de la Pyen served the Duke of Burbone. And Sir Moraunt of Noailles served the Erle of Foiz, etc." ' (ii. 346). The reference is to Froissart. The 'Erle of Harcourt' was Jean VII (d. 1452), Comte d'Harcourt et d'Aumale, son of Jean VI and Catherine de Bourbon, who in 1389 accompanied Charles VI to Toulouse (*Œuvres de Froissart*, ed. Baron Kervyn de Lettenhove, Brussels, 1867–77, xiv. 75, xxi. 514). HW's copy of Warton is Hazen, *Cat of HW's Lib.*, No. 3214.
2. Charles VI (1368–1422).
3. I.e., not the King of England, though the latter, and his successors, styled themselves kings of France.

From Harcourt, ca Wednesday 6 May 1778

Missing. Answered in the following letter.

To Harcourt, Wednesday 6 May 1778

Printed from a photostat of the MS in Lord Harcourt's possession. First printed, Cunningham vii. 58, reprinted Toynbee x. 230.
Address: To the Earl of Harcourt.
Endorsed by Harcourt: Honourable Horace Walpole May 6 1778.

May 6, 1778.

THE space for the inscription, on which your Lordship does me the honour of consulting me, I do not remember to have seen, and yet I am far from objecting to it, as it is quite in the *esprit du gothique*. The person however who drew it, is not correct, especially in his trefoils. He ought to copy the pattern exactly, of which there are many in Dart's *Westminster* or *Canterbury*. If the figures are painted, the arms must be so too; and then I should like to have the whole tomb[1] enlivened with gold and azure. Mr. T. Pitt[2] would sketch the Gothic part for your Lordship better than anybody—or so would Sandby[3] next.

Pray do not give yourself the trouble, my dear Lord, this week of calling, unless you have a moment tomorrow, for I go to Strawberry on Friday. I would not take the liberty of naming tomorrow, if I had not something to show you, that I cannot bring to you, and that would pay your pains.

Your Lordship's most devoted,

H. Walpole

1. Presumably a tomb proposed for the first Earl Harcourt, who was buried in 1777 in the family chapel in the church at Stanton Harcourt. If such a tomb was built, it was soon removed because now the only monument to him is a classical tablet on the wall, erected after his sons had died. The tomb of the second Earl, HW's correspondent, fits HW's description, since it is Gothic, with trefoils, and is painted and gilded.

2. Thomas Pitt (1737–93), cr. (1784) Bn Camelford; M.P. he aided HW in designs for SH (Mann vi. 25, n. 15).
3. Thomas Sandby (1721–98), draughtsman and architect, who made some drawings of SH. One of Harcourt's etchings is from a drawing by Sandby (HW's *Collection of Prints Engraved by Various Persons of Quality*, now wsl).

To Harcourt, Tuesday 26 May 1778

Printed from a photostat of the MS in Lord Harcourt's possession. First printed, Cunningham vii. 71, reprinted, Toynbee x. 252.

Address: To the Earl of Harcourt.

Endorsed by Harcourt: Honourable Hor. Walpole, May 29 [*sic*] 1778.

May 26, 1778.

My dear Lord,

AS the weather is as fine as it is likely to be till the summer is gone, and as you have flattered me with the honour of a visit, may I ask if Sunday or Monday next will be agreeable to your Lordship and Lady Harcourt, or what other day before you go out of town to pull[1] your own house.

Your Lordship's most devoted,

H. WALPOLE

PS. If you did not give yourself inland airs, you would wait to rebuild your house, till the French had burnt it down. I trust to the talisman of King William's spurs.

From Harcourt, September 1778

A missing note of invitation answered in the next letter.

---

1. I.e., to pull down (OED *sub* pull, II. 13, where the last example of the expression given is from 1655). As the postscript shows, the Harcourts were in the process of rebuilding Nuneham.

To Harcourt, Thursday 17 September 1778

Printed, introducing a letter to Mason, in *Correspondence of Horace Walpole . . . and the Rev. William Mason*, ed. John Mitford, 1851, ii. 18–20. Reprinted, Cunningham vii. 124–5, Toynbee, x. 317–18. The last paragraph is printed, *Harcourt Papers* iii. 237.

Strawberry Hill, Sept. 17, 1778.

I SHOULD not for one moment have delayed thanking your Lordship for the honour of your very kind invitation if I had not been absent, and did not receive it till last night when I returned from Park Place after the post was gone. I had gone thither to keep Mr Conway and Lady Ailesbury company on the death of Lord William Campbell,[1] and was frightened home by an attack of the gout in my knee, which prevents me, my dear Lord, from daring to name a day for having the great pleasure of waiting on your Lordship and Lady Harcourt. I do hope to execute my wish on Monday next, for the motion of the chaise has removed the pain into my foot, and when it flutters about I have seldom found it to end in a fit; yet vexatious as it would be to lose my visit to Nuneham, it would mortify me still more to trouble your Lordship with my decrepitude, and therefore be assured I will not venture if I am not quite well, and as *Herculean* as ever. My best friends shall not be troubled with my moans, nor my enemies neither, though the last sooner; and yet I abhor Lady Mary Wortley, who said, 'People wish their enemies dead—but I do not; I say give them the gout, give them the stone!' indeed I would not give them a bodily pang—a little twitch in their minds, that would make them feel for others, would be rather wholesome.

I must not omit my compliments on Colonel Harcourt's[2] marriage,[3] and yet it is not with perfect cordiality. It is not thence I wish

1. Lord William Campbell (ca 1732–4 Sept. 1778), naval officer; M.P. Argyllshire 1764–6; Gov. of Nova Scotia, 1766; of South Carolina, 1773; Lady Ailesbury's brother.

2. Col. William Harcourt (1743–1830), 2d son of Simon, 1st E. Harcourt; succeeded his brother as 3d E. Harcourt, 1809; field marshal, 1821.

3. Col. Harcourt m. (3 Sept. 1778) Mrs

Lockhart (*ante* HW to Strafford 12 Sept. 1783, n. 6). 'Col. Harcourt seems to have married in a hurry, for it is not above two months ago that the lady knew nothing of his intentions. She had at that time greater views. She thought of the Duke of Northumberland and declared (perhaps with the intention of its coming to his Grace's ears) that if he would offer she should accept of him.

for a Lord Nuneham. Pray forgive me; in friendship I am a Tory, and love the right line, though I desire the house of Harcourt may reach to the end of the world, as it has reached from the beginning.[4]

I beg your Lordship's prayers for those that are to travel by land or water, or rather that they may travel, and pray do it as sincerely and fervently as he does for whom your prayers are desired.

Your Lordship's most faithful and obedient humble servant,

HOR. WALPOLE

PS. Your Lordship authorizes me and therefore I presume to add the following words to an Israelite indeed.[5]

To Harcourt, Sunday 27 September 1778

Printed from a photostat of the MS in Lord Harcourt's possession. First printed, Cunningham vii. 131–2, reprinted Toynbee x. 323–5.

Endorsed by Harcourt: Honourable Horace Walpole 7[br] [September] 27th 1778.

Strawberry Hill, Sunday evening Sept. 27, 1778.

I CANNOT let the first evening of my return home pass, my dear Lord, without telling you how happy I was, and am, with the four days I enjoyed at Nuneham.[1] The sensation was more than pleasure, for the reflection is as dear as the reality. To experience

She has however done very well, married a very pretty young man who if he outlives his brother will prove a very great marriage' (Lady Mary Coke, 'MS Journals,' 10 Sept. 1778).

4. 'This ancient and illustrious family [Harcourt] is descended from Bernard, a nobleman of the blood royal of Saxony, who, being born in Denmark, was surnamed the Dane. This Bernard was chief counsellor, and second in command to the famous Rollo, progenitor to the Kings of England of the Norman line, in his descent upon Normandy, A.D. 876, and obtained the lordships of Harcourt, Caileville, and Beauficel, in recompence for his eminent services, when Rollo, who was also a Dane, made himself master of that province' (Collins, *Peerage,*

1812, iv. 428, following the first entry in a pedigree compiled by Joseph Edmondson, and printed *Harcourt Papers* i. 233). The editor of the *Harcourt Papers* accepts the descent from Bernard the Dane, whom he calls a kinsman of Rollo, but seems to reject the Saxon connection (*Harcourt Papers* i. 3, 5). Other mythical accounts, to which HW may be alluding, trace the ancestry to Antenor the Trojan, and Danus, the mythical first prince of Denmark (ibid. i. 2–3).

5. Here follows the letter to Mason of 17 Sept. 1778 (MASON i. 442–3).

———

1. HW describes this visit in his letter to Lady Ossory 27 Sept. 1778, OSSORY ii. 54–5.

so much goodness and friendship from those one most esteems, contents every feeling and flatters every vanity—nay, would force vanity upon one, if one were ever so humble. Pray allow my gratitude to say thus much. Shall impudent adulation give what doses it will, shall power swallow them and be ready for more, and shall I not thank your Lordship for honouring me with the select distinction of your friendship, because you have no post to bestow, and I ambition none? It would be hard indeed if sincere professions were to be abolished, because falsehood chooses to profess. When I go to seats of power, or when your Lordship shall blush to receive my homage from the conscience of not deserving it,—why, then I shall have no call to offer it, for there will be no room for me at Nuneham.

Were I to fulfill all the duties I contracted this last week, I should write to Lady Harcourt too—but she is too bashful to hear what I would say, and I know will receive it with more pleasure from your Lordship;

> Her husband the relater, she prefers
> Before an angel—[2]

in one word, though not the most beautiful of Lady Harcourt's compositions, not one pleased me so much as her lines on your Lordship's birthday.[3] They contain such a picture of virtue and felicity, that they deserve a *Spectator* by Mr Addison—not that he could do justice to them, but having the talent of preaching and of yet being fashionable, the verses with his commentary would have been an immortal memorial of an union, that deserves to be an immortal model. These above all I beg to print, that I in my generation may do some good. The poem occasioned by the censures on the Duchess of Kingston[4] is of higher class, and another lecture of morality and good nature united. I know they will lose in the impression, I mean as I heard them, for after Lady H. had conquered her timidity and amiable modesty, I never heard anybody read so well—In short, my Lord, you will not deserve such a wife, if once in your life you do not command. No man has a right to marry a Muse and engross her. You must order her to appoint me her printer, nor will I be Harcourt-Pursuivant, if I am not their typographer too—but I have not

2. *Paradise Lost* viii. 52–3.
3. Which was 1 Aug. The verses are
not in *Harcourt Papers* and have disappeared.
4. These also have disappeared.

said a word of my gratitude to Lady Harcourt—yes, I hope all this page has breathed it. To suppress a vast deal is the best proof of the rest.

I cannot quit such a society without begging a thousand compliments to Miss Fauquier, who merits such friends, and who does as much honour to their choice, as they do to her—but in truth I am come back in such raptures, that I doubt whether I am not rather drunk with self-love, than an enthusiast to the virtues and good sense resident at Nuneham—well! We shall see—when you are all three given up for fools etc. etc. etc., I will allow that I was an old idiot to be so blind—till then allow me to be passionately (a fig for high regard and perfect esteem!) your Lordship's and Lady Harcourt's, ay and Miss Fauquier's

Most devoted

Hor. Walpole

Mem. The letter to myself when I shall be fifty[5] is not finished. Till that is perfect, Lady H. will not be.

From Harcourt, ca Thursday 8 October 1778

Missing. Answered in the following letter.

To Harcourt, Friday 9 October 1778

Printed from a photostat of the MS in Lord Harcourt's possession. First printed, Cunningham vii. 135–6, reprinted, Toynbee x. 329–31.
Endorsed by Harcourt: Honourable Horace Walpole 8ᵇʳ [October] 9th 1778.

Arlington Street, Oct. 9, 1778.

THOUGH I received so very kind a letter from your Lordship this morning, I should have been too modest to answer it, if Lady Laura[1] had not told me last night of Lady Harcourt's obliging

5. Not found. It was presumably another of Lady Harcourt's verses; she would be fifty in 1796.

1. Lady Elizabeth Laura Waldegrave (1760–1816), m. (1782) George Waldegrave, styled Vct Chewton; 4th E. Waldegrave, 1784; HW's great-niece.

commands to her to make me escort her.[2] I should gladly obey that and your Lordship's friendly hint, were it in my power, but I am come to town this morning on disagreeable business with my brother,[3] and which will cost me some hundreds of pounds,[4] a clerk[5] in our joint-office[6] having chosen to dispose of some money entrusted to him, à la Maccaroni; and it will tax my time for some days, as well as my purse; but you shall hear no more of it, for I do not take the loss of money enough to heart to draw on my friends for their pity. If I could wait on you at Nuneham, you would not find I have much occasion for consolation.

You do not think, I trust, my dear Lord, that I took the opportunity of your asking for my 4th volume,[7] to thrust another old thing upon you. Lady Harcourt ordered me to send her the tragedy,[8] and I suppose I forgot to say so. All I have to say of the play, is, that Mr Mason could write a much better, if he would. I can prove what I say, for with the alteration of a few words and with the addition of as few lines, he made my tragedy fit for the stage,[9] if the rest of it is so. It was one of the most masterly feats ever performed—but I need not do *him* justice to your Lordship. I only mention it, that you may not hesitate to set him to work on any little corrections that Lady

2. To Nuneham; see HW to Mason 11 Oct. 1778 (MASON i. 445).

3. Sir Edward Walpole (1706–84), K.B.; M.P.

4. £700 (HW to Mason 11 Oct. 1778, MASON i. 445; HW to Lady Ossory 21 Oct. 1778, OSSORY ii. 63).

5. Possibly Henry Wootton, receiver of plantation duties, whose name disappears from Customs Inwards after the 1779 issue of the *Court and City Register*, p. 116 (John Mann, who died in 1778, disappears at the same time, see MANN viii. 358, n. 2). In the *Royal Kalendar*, 1779, the office is vacant.

6. The collectorship of the customs, inwards, the proceeds of which HW shared with his brother Sir Edward.

7. Of the *Anecdotes of Painting*, printed at the SH Press in 1771, but not published until 1780 (Hazen, *SH Bibl.* 63–5). HW apparently did not give Harcourt a copy of the volume at this time; see *post* HW to Harcourt 3 Oct. 1780.

8. The *Mysterious Mother*, printed at SH in 1768 (Hazen, op. cit. 79–85). The request is somewhat mysterious, since the Harcourts seem to have already possessed a copy that they lent to Mrs Montagu in the winter of 1777 (*Harcourt Papers* viii. 124, where Mrs Montagu's letter returning the copy is undated, but clearly written ca Feb. 1777). The only copy of the *Mysterious Mother* now owned by Lord Harcourt is a presentation copy of the London edition, 1781.

9. Mason's proposed alterations, sent to HW in 1769, are printed, MASON i. 11–16. They differ considerably from those in a copy of the 1768 edition of the play (now WSL) inscribed by HW 'with MS alterations by Mr Mason,' the copy returned by Mason to HW in 1781 in which he had entered his alterations (ibid. ii. 141–2). These later alterations are printed in *The Castle of Otranto and The Mysterious Mother*, ed. Montague Summers, 1924, pp. 268–71. HW praised the proposed alterations in similar terms to those above in his letter to their author, 11 Oct. 1778, and again when he was preparing the 1781 edition of the tragedy, though his real opinion of them was highly unfavourable; see MASON i. 9, 445; ii. 140, 144, 148.

Harcourt's poems may want, the faults of which are evidence of the facility with which she writes. Your Lordship is so tender of her honour, that I see you promote her bashfulness instead of giving her courage; but I hope Mr Mason's judgment will encourage you both. He is no flatterer, I will swear; and when you have the imprimatur of Apollo's own Licenser of the Press, shall I not flatter myself that my office of printer to Nuneham will no longer be a sinecure?

Lady Laura will give your Lordship an account of a fête I gave her and my other nieces last night.[10] Strawberry really looked very pretty, though neither the prospect nor the painted glass had their share—but forgive me if I say that my nieces supplied those deficiencies. Lady Laura I doubt will miss the prospect still less, when she comes from Nuneham. The Duchess[11] is charmed with your Lordship's and Lady Harcourt's goodness to her daughter, which, you find, I was eager to trumpet, for after the very agreeable days I passed at Nuneham myself, it was natural to wish that my niece should [be] as happy—so your Lordship should be upon your guard, and not to be too indulgent to me, since I cannot help on all occasions being

Your most grateful and obedient humble servant,

HOR. WALPOLE

To HARCOURT, Monday 1 February 1779

Printed from a photostat of the MS in Lord Harcourt's possession. First printed, Cunningham vii. 168–9, reprinted, Toynbee x. 368–9.
Address: To the Earl of Harcourt, Cavendish Square.
Endorsed by Harcourt: Honourable Horace Walpole February 1st 1779.

Feb. 1, 1779.

My dear Lord,

MRS Damer has consulted me on a case of heraldic conscience, on which I am not competent. You must forgive me for troubling your Lordship, for whither can I recur but to an oracle?

10. For a description of the fête, see   11. Of Gloucester.
HW to Mason 11 Oct. 1778 (MASON i.
445–8).

She has been told that she has no right to use crest[1] and motto[2]—is that so? Ought not she too, as an only child, to bear her arms in an escutcheon of pretence?[3]

I was at the Vesey-Chaos[4] last night, and wish Lady Harcourt and your Lordship had been behind a cloud. I must do Mrs Montagu[5] the justice to say that I never heard more warm encomiums on both; and the Irish bore equal testimonies.

I hope you are all perfectly easy about Mrs Harcourt, of whom I heard a very good account yesterday.

Your Lordship's most dutiful

H. WALPOLE

To Harcourt, October 1779

Printed from a photostat of the MS in Lord Harcourt's possession. First printed, Cunningham vii. 255–7, reprinted, Toynbee xi. 29–32.

Endorsed by Harcourt: Honourable H. Walpole 8ᵇʳ [October] 1779.

October 1779.

MORTIFICATIONS never come single. Pain not only makes its *prerogative* felt, but deprives one of collateral satisfactions that might compensate. It annuls promises, and like other imperial tyrants, roots out both wishes and virtues. I had set the remains of my heart on passing part of September at Nuneham,[1] my dear Lord; but, after a very uncomfortable summer, in which I had scarce a day

1. The crest has never been officially used by a woman (A. C. Fox-Davies, *A Complete Guide to Heraldry*, rev. edn, n.d., p. 326).

2. No control has been exercised over the use of the motto as such, but it is often attached to the crest (ibid. 448, 452).

3. The escutcheon of pretence is usually used by a husband with reference to his wife's family (ibid. 536).

4. The 'salon' of Elizabeth Vesey (ca 1715–91), m. 1 William Handcock; m. 2 (before 1746) Agmondesham Vesey; bluestocking. HW frequently attended her assemblies, which reflected the confusion and absent-mindedness of their hostess.

5. Elizabeth Robinson, widow of Edward Montagu; bluestocking (*ante* HW to Chute 7 Jan. 1766, n. 10). Harcourt had made 'a very pretty plan' for the garden of her new house in Portman Square the preceding autumn (Reginald Blunt, *Mrs Montagu*, [1923], ii. 61). Letters from her to the Harcourts between 1771 and 1778 are printed *Harcourt Papers* viii. 119–34.

—————

1. HW to Mason 14 Sept. 1779 (MASON i. 463–4) mentions that he has given up his projected visit to Nuneham.

of health, I was confined to my couch the whole month with the gout, and have now the use but of one hand. Constitutional evils one learns to bear; but when the *Constitution* is undermined, the breach lets in any enemy. In one word, my nerves are so shattered, that at last my spirits are affected, and I am less fit to wait on your Lordship and Lady Harcourt from the feebleness of my mind, than of my poor person. I have not slept one night out of my own houses since I had the honour of seeing you, not even at Park Place, which I had settled for my first stage to Nuneham. I can comfort myself only by your Lordship's and Lady Harcourt's overflowing goodness to my nieces;[2] and as they are of an age to taste the fullness of joy, they will be better company, than one who even in so favourite an Elysium, could not stifle many melancholy reflections—for Indignation itself must sour into Despondence, when it sees no prospect of any kind of redress. Shame and disgrace correct neither the million nor the master, and both seem to hope from defeat what success alone used to delude fools into bestowing on knaves—but then indeed the latter had parts. Now they put me in mind of what Charles II said of a silly preacher that was much admired in his parish; 'I suppose,' said his Majesty, 'that his nonsense suits their nonsense.'[3]

My sole hope at present is peace. Victory would rivet our chains— and, next to the insolence of Tories, I abhor the insolence of the French. A peace would be so bad an one, that at least it would complete the ignominy of the last five years, and yet leave us some foundation to recommence our career, should the nation ever awaken from its lethargy—in short, my dear Lord, decaying as I am, and bastardized as my country is, I cannot part with the darling visions

2. HW's four great-nieces were still at Nuneham on 21 Oct. (Mason i. 470).

3. 'He [Charles II] told me, he had a chaplain, that was a very honest man, but a very great blockhead, to whom he had given a living in Suffolk, that was full of that sort of people: he had gone about among them from house to house, though he could not imagine what he could say to them; for he said he was a very silly fellow: but that, he believed, his nonsense suited their nonsense, for he had brought them all to church: and, in reward of his diligence, he had given him a bishopric in Ireland' (Gilbert Burnet, *History of His Own Time*, 1724–34,

i. 258–9). The chaplain is identified by Swift in his notes on Burnet as Edward Wolley (ca 1604–84) D.D., 1642; chaplain to Charles I and Charles II; rector of Toppesfield, Essex, 1662; Bp of Clonfert 1665–84; the later editors of Burnet and the author of the article on Wolley in DNB accept the identification. HW uses the same illustration in his letters to Mann 31 July 1762 and 22 Oct. 1774, Mann vi. 57, viii. 52, and to Lady Ossory 18 Oct. 1783, Ossory ii. 426. He gives a somewhat different account of the occasion that provoked the King's remark in an anecdote in *Walpoliana*, 1799, i. 57.

of the liberty and glory of England—Is not it grievous too to feel ourselves in as bad a plight as before the Union? Then Scotland and France were allies and harassed us—now they are foes, and yet we are in still greater peril!—Paul Jones[4] to be sure has been agreeable; and were Oxford not so near Nuneham, I should not have sighed if he could have sailed up the Isis and committed sacrilege on some college plate, though good Dr Johnson holds sacrilege the sin against the Holy Ghost,[5] who, I suppose, he thinks has a particular fondness for silver basins and ewers—so I dare to say does Bishop Butler,[6] and of all sterling utensils thinks the consecrated plate at Lambeth the holiest of holies. Did you hear, my Lord, that that renegade priest wrote to Sir Edward,[7] that *if* there were any toleration allowable to opponents, your Lordship would deserve to be saved from the flames (he hopes to see) in Smithfield?[8]

If my cousin[9] Miss Fauquier is with you, ten thousand compliments to her. Tell her that the most pious of Princes,[10] who in the tumult of civil affairs never neglects religion, has lately taken on him the dispensation of cathedral fees at Windsor,[11] and endeavoured to put them on a new footing; but as hornets love honey, though they do not make it, one of the canons withstands the head of the church, and defends the property of faith against its defender.

Adieu! my best Lord; excuse and pity me. You will be charmed,

4. John Paul Jones (1747–92), American naval officer, had been in the Firth of Forth the middle of September, threatening Edinburgh, but had been driven off by bad weather.

5. 'Sacrilege. . . . The crime of appropriating to himself what is devoted to religion; the crime of robbing heaven; the crime of violating or profaning things sacred' (Johnson's *Dictionary*, 1755 edn). See also DALRYMPLE 149.

6. John Butler (1717–1802), D.C.L.; Bp of Oxford 1777–88, of Hereford 1788–1802.

7. HW's brother, Sir Edward Walpole.

8. Where heretics and others were at one time burned. 'The Bishop of Oxford, once a writer in patriot opposition, wrote t'other day to his friend and patron my brother, that Lord Harcourt had invited him to dinner, treated him with benignity, and not mentioned a word of politics; "surely," added the meek apostle, "if there were a toleration of patriots, Lord Harcourt would be entitled to the benefit of it"' (HW to Mason 18 Aug. 1779, MASON i. 458).

9. HW's cousin, Charlotte Townshend, widow of John Norris, had m. (7 May 1779) Thomas Fauquier of London, presumably a relative of Jane Georgiana Fauquier (*East Anglian*, 1903–4, n.s. x. 348–50; GM 1779, xlix. 326).

10. George III.

11. St George's Chapel at Windsor is a collegiate church with a dean and chapter, not a cathedral. The fees may have been those in connection with the installation of Knights of the Garter. There was no installation between 1771 and 1801, when the installation of those knights made since 1771 was dispensed with, but the fees were paid (E. H. Fellowes, *The Vicars or Minor Canons of His Majesty's Free Chapel of St George, Windsor*, [1945], p. 49).

I flatter myself with poor Horatia,[12] who is not at all well, but has behaved with a gentleness, sweetness, modesty that are lovely. She has had no romantic conduct, concealed all she could, and discovered nothing she felt but by her looks. She is now more pleasing, though she looks ill, by her silent softness, than before by her youthful vivacity. Maria,[13] almost as much wounded and to be pitied, carries off another kind of misfortune with a noble spirit—I will say no more, but that Mr F.[14] has had the confidence to make me a visit with his father-in-law.[15] Luckily the Duke arrived the moment after. F. said, 'Do not let us keep you'—'No, Sir,' said I, 'that you cannot do'—and left them. Your Lordship is such a father to these poor girls, that I am sure you will forgive my troubling you with my anxieties about them. I ought to make an apology for my whole letter—but alas! my Lord, there are few to whom men of our sentiments can talk freely; and then it is no wonder that one's heart flows through one's pen. Mine you know is devoted to your Lordship.

12. Lady Anna Horatia Waldegrave (1762–1801), m. (1786) Hon. Hugh Seymour Conway (later Lord Hugh Seymour). She had been engaged to Robert, Duke of Ancaster, who died 8 July 1779; see Violet Biddulph, *The Three Ladies Waldegrave*, 1938, pp. 146–9.

13. Lady Charlotte Maria Waldegrave (1761–1808), m. (1784) George Henry Fitzroy, styled E. of Euston. She became engaged to the Earl of Egremont, but it was broken off. See *post* HW to Harcourt 2 Sept. 1780.

14. Probably William Augustus Fawkener (1747–1811), who was not welcomed as a possible son-in-law by the Duchess of Gloucester (BERRY i. 95, n. 24; John H. Jesse, *George Selwyn and His Contemporaries*, 1882, iv. 141).

15. Fawkener's stepfather was Thomas Pownall (1722–1805).

To Harcourt, ca Monday 29 November 1779

Printed from a photostat of the MS in Lord Harcourt's possession. First printed Cunningham vii. 250, reprinted, *Harcourt Papers* viii. 97–8, Toynbee xi. 69.

Dated conjecturally by HW's reference to the gout returning and forcing him to dictate. This attack (his 15th) began 18 Nov. 1779 (Ossory ii. 141) and lasted two months. The present note was probably written close to 29 Nov. 1779 when, according to HW's letter to Mason of 11 Dec., 'the gout seized my right hand' (Mason i. 485).

Endorsed by Harcourt: Honourable Horace Walpole 1780.

EXCUSE me, my dear Lord, from not writing with my own hand,[1] but I am just got into bed with a little return of pain.

I hate to avoid any opportunity of being good-natured, but when your Lordship puts the question to me I must speak truth. I do know Mr Hammond,[2] for I was at school with him. I know that he is a gentleman, and has children, and that he had a very good estate at Teddington, which his extravagance obliged him to sell above twenty years ago. He has existed ever since by genteel begging of all his cotemporaries and schoolfellows, whom he wore out, and he is now, I suppose, taking a new lease of the generosity of their grandchildren. In short, my dear Lord, I can say no good of him; and if your Lordship will be so noble as to send him a guinea or two, and tell him it is upon condition that he never troubles you any more, it will be beyond what he has any reason to expect.

I am grieved to hear your Lordship is out of order, and do hope you will not stir out till you are quite recovered: you will do more service to any part of your country that deserves it by taking care of yourself, than you could do even if you were a member of the convocation, by sitting amongst them.

Your Lordship's
Most faithful humble servant,

H. W.

1. The letter is in Kirgate's hand.
2. Probably Leonard Hammond (ca 1714–?1787) of Teddington; at Eton, 1728; matriculated at Oxford, 1731 (R. A. Austen-Leigh, *Eton College Register 1698–1752*, Eton, 1927, p. 156).

To Harcourt, ?Friday 7 January 1780

Printed from a photostat of the MS in Lord Harcourt's possession. First printed, Cunningham vii. 249, reprinted, *Harcourt Papers* viii. 96–7; Toynbee xi. 86.

Dated conjecturally by the reference to HW's 15th attack of gout. When he wrote this letter he spoke of it lasting 'long enough to wear out anybody's patience,' and the letter was therefore written towards the end of the attack. On Jan. 4, 1780 he wrote Mason, 'I have not seen Lord Harcourt these ten days' (Mason ii. 3).

Address: To the Earl of Harcourt.

Endorsed by Harcourt: Honourable Horace Walpole 1780.

Friday night.

My dear Lord,

YOU have used me so much to your goodness, that I catch cold, when I am long without feeling it. I have not had the honour of seeing you this age, and cannot yet *go* to see anything. My gout, I own, lasts long enough to wear out anybody's patience, and has reduced me to solitude—nor dare I complain but to the very good, for who else would mind me—but pray do not think *that* is my only reason for petitioning your Lordship;

> Blest be the Gout for those it took away,
> And those it left me—if you are one of them![1]

However, do not be frightened; I trust that next week I shall be able to crawl about again—and then you will have as much reason to be alarmed with my gratitude, for I have already received obligations—ay, and presents enough to be always

Your Lordship's most bounden servant,

Hor. Walpole

---

1. A parody of Pope's 'Epistle to Dr Arbuthnot,' ll. 255–6:

> 'Bless'd be the great! for those they take away,
> And those they left me—for they left me Gay'

To Harcourt, February 1780

Printed from the MS of HW's copy, now WSL. First printed, Cunningham vii. 411–13 (as June or July 1780), reprinted, Toynbee xi. 236–9 (as the end of June 1780).

This copy by HW, headed by him 'To Lord Harcourt 1780,' was acquired by WSL from the estate of Richard Bentley, 1937. See heading, *ante* HW to Chute 20 Aug. 1743 OS.

The letter must have been written between the voting of the Westminster petition for economic reform at a public meeting, 2 Feb. 1780 (*Last Journals* ii. 268), and the presentation of the petition to the House of Commons, 13 March (*Journals of the House of Commons* xxxvii. 716), presumably shortly after it was first discussed.

My Lord,

THOUGH I think myself so inconsiderable a man, that it would be impertinent to give an account of my conduct to the public;[1] yet as I should be most unhappy to lie under any suspicion in the eyes of my friends of acting or being silent from mercenary views in the present most serious moment; I declare that my reasons for not appearing in Westminster Hall and signing a petition to Parliament *for a necessary and effectual reform of the expenditure of public money,*[2] are not from disapprobation of the measure, or from a wish that so salutary a measure should miscarry, or from the least disposition to court favour anywhere or with any party; the last of which mean and interested views would be inconsistent with the whole tenor of my life, and shall never stain the small remaining part of it.

But the reason of my not signing such petition, is, that possessing nothing but sinecure places, I must consider myself rather as a remote object of the reformation, than as a proper person to demand it. To petition for the abolition of sinecure places, and to hope not to be included in the reduction, would be unworthy of a man. To

1. Two years later HW wrote, but did not publish, an *Account of My Conduct Relative to the Places I Hold under Government, and towards Ministers.* It is printed in *Works* ii. 363–70.

2. 'Your petitioners . . . appealing to the justice of this honourable House, do most earnestly request, that, before any new burthens are laid upon this country, effectual measures may be taken, by this House, to inquire into and correct the gross abuses in the expenditure of public money, to reduce all exorbitant emoluments; to rescind and abolish all sinecure places and unmerited pensions; and to appropriate the produce to the necessities of the state, in such manner as to the wisdom of Parliament shall seem meet' (*Journals of the House of Commons* xxxvii. 716).

say I was ready to resign mine, would be hypocritic ostentation (for no man, I believe, is ready to part with his whole income) and would be a hardship on others in the same predicament, who should be unwilling to offer the same sacrifice, and would be honester men, as more sincere.

The line of conduct therefore that I think the most decent for me to take, is to be totally silent, and submit myself to the determination of the legislature of my country, and to be content with what in its wisdom it shall decide for the benefit of the nation. I hold nothing from personal merit or services, and must not complain if my ease and comforts are diminished for the public good. But I cannot in conscience sign a request for the abolition of the places of others, who hold them by law, as I do mine, and who are more worthy of them than I am of mine. Neither can I demand the abolition of places, not held for life, but the possessors of which are more useful members of society, have smaller incomes than mine, and execute more business than I do, who execute none—for I must speak the truth and the whole truth. It would be a great want of feeling and of generosity in me, to desire that any man should be discarded, who is removable at pleasure, because nothing but a new law can remove me from my place.

Upon the whole, my Lord, it is no selfishness or change in my principles that makes me decline signing the petition. I shall die in the principles I have ever invariably professed. My fortune may be decreased or taken away; but it never shall be augmented by any employment, pension or favour, beyond what I now enjoy by the gift of my father alone. I have more than I can pretend to deserve; and I beg your Lordship, in whose incorruptible integrity I have the firmest confidence, to produce this testimony under my own hand, if ever I deviate from what I have here professed. And I will flatter myself, that if your Lordship should hear me suspected, from not signing any petition, of having swerved from my principles, you will do me the justice to defend me from that imputation. My character cannot be safer than in your Lordship's hands, and in them I beg leave to deposit it—for as next to the imputation of being mercenary, I dread the charge of vanity, I entreat that this letter may not be made public. I am of too little consequence to give myself airs of clearing my conduct before it is censured; and am so obscure a man, that I may never be mentioned; and therefore I will cer-

tainly not thrust myself upon the public eye from self-conceit and
with an unnecessary parade, which I despise. Allow me the honour
of choosing your Lordship for my confessor, and with leaving my
conscience in your trust. I am ready, with the utmost submission to
the laws of my country, to take my fate with others in whatever shall
be decided. I ask no favour or partiality; I am entitled to none; I
have no merits to plead—but I cannot think it would become me to
be at once a petitioner, and a party petitioned against. I have the
honour to be with the highest esteem, my Lord,

Your Lordship's most obedient humble servant,

HORACE WALPOLE

From HARCOURT, ca Friday 2 June 1780

A missing invitation, answered in the next letter.

To HARCOURT, Saturday 10 June 1780

Printed from a photostat of the MS in Lord Harcourt's possession. First
printed, Cunningham vii. 396–7, reprinted, Toynbee xi. 216–18.
Endorsed by Harcourt: Honourable Horace Walpole June 10th 1780.

Strawberry Hill, June 10, 1780.

My dear Lord,

IF confusion and every horror are excuses, your Lordship will forgive my not thanking you sooner, as I intended, for the very kind
message and invitation you was so good as to leave at my house. I did
drive to yours, in total ignorance of what was passing, at the very
instant that you was in such danger at the House of Lords![1] Thank
God, your Lordship and all my friends escaped massacre!

1. 2 June, when Lord George Gordon, at the head of a mob, presented Parliament with the petition of the Protestant Association against the repeal in 1778 of certain Roman Catholic disabilities. This was the beginning of the Gordon Riots; several peers were personally assaulted and the House of Lords laid under virtual siege for several hours. For details, see MASON ii. 51–3 and notes and references there given, HW to Lady Ossory 3 June 1780, and HW to Mann 5 June 1780. HW says he did not learn of the tumult until 'past eight at night' (MASON ii. 51).

It was my plan a week ago to go to Malvern, the beginning of July, and to wait [on] your Lordship and Lady Harcourt going or coming, as should be least inconvenient to you.[2]

One must have the confidence of a true enthusiast—or of a false one, to say what one will do three weeks hence! *I will* is no longer a phrase in the now narrow vocabulary of an Englishman. Two days ago the mob,[3] today the army,[4] tomorrow who, were, are, will be our masters?

Exhausted with fatigue and watching, I came from town yesterday at two o'clock to seek a little repose, leaving a fierce calm. Since the early part of Thursday evening I have not heard of any disturbance[5]—and whether terrified like a brat that has set his frock on fire—or to evoke new legions, Scoticè clans, of infernals, the Gordon[6] is fled.

Wednesday[7] no mortal pen can describe that has not seen a city taken by storm. Yet whoever saw even a capital of the size of London in flames in more than a dozen places,[8] and its own inhabitants rioting in every barbarity? How it escaped a wide conflagration is incomprehensible; and that not threescore lives were lost that night,[9]

2. HW told Mason, 2 June, that he intended to go 'to Malvern in July for a month or six weeks, and visit Nuneham in autumn' (MASON ii. 49). He subsequently postponed and eventually abandoned his trip to Malvern, but did visit Nuneham in mid-October (*post* HW to Harcourt 2 Sept. 1780; HW to Lady Ossory 29 June 1780, OSSORY ii. 203, n. 10; HW to Mason 13 Oct. 1780, MASON ii. 83–4).

3. The Gordon Riots were at their worst during the night of 7–8 June.

4. London was filled with troops of the regular army and of the militia who had been empowered by the Privy Council, 7 June, to act at their own discretion, though martial law was not proclaimed; see MASON ii. 58 and notes 27 and 30. In addition, the House of Commons had adjourned on the 8th to 19 June, leaving the military forces in control.

5. There was no further rioting in London.

6. Lord George Gordon (1751–93), president of the Protestant Association and instigator of the riots. The report of his

flight, which HW had heard on the evening of the 8th, was false; see below, n. 21.

7. 7 June. For HW's description of the events of that day and night, see *Last Journals* ii. 310–11, and his letters to Mason 9 June (MASON ii. 55–7) and to Lady Ossory 7–8 June (OSSORY ii. 183–92).

8. 'Wednesday night there were no less than fourteen places on fire at one time, in different parts of the town' (*Public Advertiser* 9 June 1780).

9. Principally in two clashes between the mob and the troops guarding the Bank of England; see MASON ii. 56, n. 17. There are no accurate figures for the dead and wounded that night; HW himself mentions two conflicting reports, an early one (2 A.M. on the 8th) that sixty or seventy had been shot before the Bank alone, and one a few hours later that **'not above a dozen'** had been killed at the Bank and 'some few elsewhere' (HW to Lady Ossory 8–9 June 1780, OSSORY ii. 187–8, 190).

is equally amazing. Treble that number or more were dead by morning by wallowing in the casks of spirits they had staved.[10] I do not exaggerate, my Lord; they sucked them as they flowed about the streets.

Yesterday was more bloody[11]—yet not excessively, though the army was let loose, and it was merciful to the frantic wretches themselves, who seem to be awed. As men recover from their consternation they begin to arm for common safety.[12] Zeal soon threw away the mask, and like Spanish missionaries in Mexico aimed at nothing but gold. Lady Albemarle[13] was robbed by a horseman on that identic Wednesday night at Mrs Keppel's[14] door.[15] *The Duke,*[16] wrapped in a greatcoat and in a hackney coach, was surrounded by the mob in the Fleet Market and obliged to give them his purse.[17]

How poor a sketch have I given your Lordship of what Guicciardin[18] would have formed a folio! yet he would forget the wretched wives and mothers that will rue that night, and expatiate on the precious manuscripts burnt in Bloomsbury.[19] Yet already can I look with more tranquillity backward, than to what is to come. However one may foresee too much, as one could not foresee what has happened. Conjectures are idle—and I will release your Lordship.

Mrs Mestivyer[20] is a good deal better, and I think not immediately going. If there is any such thing as gratitude I am most truly your Lordship's and Lady Harcourt's

Devoted humble servant,

HOR. WALPOLE

10. In destroying Thomas Langdale's distillery. See MASON ii. 56 and n. 16, 59 and n. 31, and HW to Lady Ossory 9 June 1780, OSSORY ii. 193.

11. In encounters between the mob and the Horse Guards in Fleet Street and in skirmishes in Southwark; see MASON ii. 57 and notes 21 and 22, and HW to Lady Ossory 9 June 1780, OSSORY ii. 192.

12. Both as individuals and in volunteer associations. For one such parish association, see *Harcourt Papers* viii. 296–7; and for another, formed by the Middle Templars, see J. Paul de Castro, *The Gordon Riots,* 1926, pp. 167–70.

13. Lady Anne Lennox (1703–89), m. (1723) William Anne Van Keppel, 2d E. of Albemarle.

14. HW's niece, Laura Walpole (ca 1734–1813), m. (1758) Hon. Frederick Keppel, Bp of Exeter.

15. In Pall Mall (HW to Lady Ossory 8–9 June 1780, OSSORY ii. 191).

16. Of Gloucester.

17. HW also mentions this incident in *Last Journals* ii. 310.

18. Francesco Guicciardini (1483–1540), Florentine historian.

19. In Lord Mansfield's house, burnt 6 June; see MASON ii. 57, n. 20.

20. See *ante* HW to Strafford 4 Sept. 1760, n. 17. She was still living in 1785 (Lady Mary Coke, 'MS Journals,' 27 Dec. 1785).

One o'clock at noon.

The post is just come in; I have two letters to confirm what I heard half an hour ago, that Lord George Gordon was overtaken in his flight to Scotland by a party of light horse and brought prisoner to the Horse Guards.[21] This is all I will warrant, for there are twenty different reports already, which there must be at least where one is twenty miles from town. I will still less conjecture or reason, for I do not often guess rightly, and one argues yet worse but on the most certain grounds.

To Harcourt, Saturday 2 September 1780

Printed from a photostat of the MS in Lord Harcourt's possession. First printed, Cunningham vii. 436, reprinted, Toynbee xi. 269–70.

Endorsed by Harcourt: Honourable Hor. Walpole 7ʙʳ [September] 12th [*sic*] 1780.

Strawberry Hill, Sept. 2d 1780.

YOUR Lordship I am sure will forgive my troubling you so soon to inquire how Lady Harcourt does since her late loss.[1] I have seen such charming instances of her Ladyship's filial tenderness, that I cannot but be anxious for her on this melancholy occasion.

I have been unfortunately disappointed of the great pleasure of waiting on your Lordship, as you gave me leave to do. My journey to Malvern was prevented by the strange story of Lady Maria;[2] and when that and its consequences were quite over, and I was literally setting out in two days to Park Place, and intended to proceed to Nuneham, Lady Jersey, whom I met at Lady Di Beauclerc's at Richmond,[3] and told so, said, 'You will not find them, for they go on the

21. Gordon was imprisoned in the Tower on 9 June. He had not fled, but was taken into custody at his house in Welbeck Street (De Castro, op. cit. 180).

1. Her father, George Venables Vernon (1710–80), cr. (1762) Bn Vernon, died 21 August.
2. The breaking of her engagement to Lord Egremont, which HW attributed to the influence of Egremont's mistress, Lady Melbourne, assisted by the Duchess of

Devonshire (*Last Journals* ii. 351). HW tells the story of Lady Maria in his letters to Mann 6, 24 July 1780, Mann ix. 68, 74–5, and to Lady Ossory ca 12–18 July, 1 Aug. 1780, Ossory ii. 205, 209–10. See also Mason ii. 74, n. 2.
3. At about this time Lady Diana Beauclerk removed from Twickenham to Devonshire Cottage at Richmond (Mrs Stuart Erskine, *Lady Diana Beauclerk*, 1903, p. 190).

10th to Lord Vernon's'4—this was on the 8th,5 and as soon as I was at liberty to stir. As I have not been willingly neglectful of the honour your Lordship and Lady Harcourt did me, I shall be very happy if you will still allow me to pay my duty to you, when the elections are a little subsided6—I do not mean that I am engaged in any, but on the contrary, dread falling foul of them. Do not imagine, my dear Lord, that I suppose you fling open your cellars to Doctors of Divinity, or give gin to Alma Mater, or cram Bishop Butler till he is still more willing to strangle you before you are half roasted in Smithfield. You neither expect to cleanse Augeas's stable, nor to drench his grooms—but I had rather stay quietly here, till the drunken riots are over even on the road; and if any part of October will not be inconvenient to you, I shall be happy to look once more at Nuneham; though I beseech you not to accept my homage, if it will in the least interfere with any of your engagements, as I never can be less than I am

Your Lordship's most devoted humble servant,

Hor. Walpole

To Harcourt, Tuesday 3 October 1780

Printed from a photostat of the MS in Lord Harcourt's possession. First printed, Cunningham vii. 446–7, reprinted, Toynbee xi. 289–90.

Endorsed by Harcourt: Honourable Horace Walpole 8ᵇʳ [October] 3d 1780.

Berkeley Square, Oct. 3d 1780.

I HAVE had but too melancholy excuses, my dear Lord, for not having yet paid my duty to you. For these three weeks I have been alarmed and been expecting the death of my dear old friend, Madame du Deffand.1 I have had no letter from Paris this week, and fear it is over. In the midst of this distress, I was shocked with

4. Sudbury Hall, Derbyshire.
5. The conversation actually took place over tea at SH on 7 Aug. (HW to Mason 8 Aug. 1780, Mason ii. 72–3).
6. Parliament had been suddenly dissolved 1 Sept., necessitating a general election (*Journals of the House of Commons* xxxviii. 3; *Last Journals* ii. 329).

1. She died 23 Sept., but HW did not receive the news until 7 Oct. (HW to T. Walpole 8 Oct. 1780).

an account of General Conway having broken his arm[2]—too true, though he is in the fairest way possible. Before these misfortunes I had settled with my bookseller[3] to publish my last volume of the *Anecdotes of Painting*, and had calculated that I should be returned from Nuneham before the publication, which having been advertised for the ninth,[4] I must perform. This will make it impossible for me to wait on your Lordship before the beginning of next week, when I shall make Mr Conway another visit, whom I had time to stay with but one night since his accident. I flatter myself that I shall not interfere with any of your Lordship's or Lady Harcourt's plans, in which case you would forbid the homage of

Your Lordship's most devoted humble servant,

Hor. Walpole

PS. I will bring the volume with me, that you may not have the trouble of sending for it.

To Harcourt, May 1781

Printed from a photostat of the MS in Lord Harcourt's possession. First printed, Cunningham viii. 43, reprinted, *Harcourt Papers* iii. 242, Toynbee xi. 454.
Dated by the endorsement, and with reference to the following letter.
Address: To the Earl of Harcourt.
Endorsed by Harcourt: The Honourable Horace Walpole 1781.

I HAVE such numberless obligations to your Lordship, and so little power of returning them, that you must allow me to take the first moment of showing that at least I wish to prove my gratitude—and you will not I am sure reject the testimonial, as you know it is of no other worth. You liked the picture[1] I take the liberty

2. HW learned of Conway's accident on 27 Sept. (HW to Lady Ossory 27 Sept., Ossory ii. 231, to T. Walpole 28 Sept. 1780).
3. John Bell (1745–1831), publisher.
4. 'On Monday, October 9, will be published, *Anecdotes of Painting in England. Volume the Fourth and last.* Printed at Strawberry Hill; and sold by John Bell, British Library, in the Strand' (*London Chronicle* 26–28 Sept., 30 Sept.–3 Oct. 1780, xlviii. 304, 319; Hazen, *SH Bibl.* 63).

1. 'Philip, Duke de Vendôme (Grand Prieur in 1710) a very fine portrait, by Mignard; a present from the Hon. Horace Walpole' (*Nuneham-Courtenay*, 1783, p.

of sending; yet it is so indifferent, that I could not presume to offer it, if I did not like it too, which proves that I have more pleasure in pleasing your Lordship than myself, and *that* I hope will give it a little value, though it has none else.

To Harcourt, Friday 18 May 1781

Printed from a photostat of the MS in Lord Harcourt's possession. First printed, Cunningham viii. 42–3, reprinted, *Harcourt Papers* iii. 242 (in part), Toynbee xi. 453.
Endorsed by Harcourt: The Honourable Horace Walpole May 18th 1781.

May 18th 1781.

My dear Lord,

I DID not see the Clive last night, as she was gone to Mr Franks's,[1] but I left your Lordship's invitation with Mrs Mestivyer, who told me her sister was very weak and out of order, and so I find by the enclosed, which I received this morning. Indeed poor women! they are both in a bad way!

I am delighted to find that Philip de Vendôme[2] was the famous Grand Prieur, who had so much wit and spirit, as the enclosed note from Anderson[3] proves. How lucky that a Prince who had so interesting a countenance when a boy, should have had common sense afterwards! I cannot say his beauty remained; Lord Dacre has a whole length of him at last, in a *habit de chasse*.[4] It looks like one of those drunken red-faced old women, who follow a camp, and half of whose clothes are scoured regimentals.[5]

6). The painting then hung in the eating-room at Nuneham. See also *Harcourt Papers* iii. 241–2 and the following letter.

———

1. Probably Moses Franks (1718–89), who had houses at Richmond and Isleworth (Cole ii. 373, n. 23).

2. Philippe (1655–1727), Chevalier de Vendôme; great-grandson of Henri IV and Gabrielle d'Estrées; grand prieur de France in the Knights of Malta, 1679–1719 (F. W. Ryan, *House of the Temple*, 1930, p. 58).

3. Missing; possibly the brief notice of Philippe in James Anderson (? 1680–1739), *Royal Genealogies*, 2d edn, 1735, p. 634, which contains the erroneous date

of his appointment as grand prieur given in Harcourt's description of the portrait, though it says nothing of his wit and spirit, and it seems unlikely that HW would make a separate enclosure of so brief an identification.

4. HW describes the portrait in his journal of his visit to Belhus, Lord Dacre's seat in Essex, in 1761: 'The grand Prior de Vendosme, whole length *en habit de chasse*, with nymphs dancing and the temple of Janus shut, a large odd picture but good, by Trevisani' (*Country Seats* 34).

5. 'Il avait eu dans sa jeunesse un visage singulièrement beau et une tournure parfaite; les débauches altérèrent ses

To Harcourt, ?February–March 1782

Printed from a photostat of the MS in Lord Harcourt's possession. First printed, Cunningham viii. 147, reprinted, Toynbee xii. 152.

Dated by the endorsement and by the possibility that it refers to the events mentioned in n. 1.

Address: To the Earl of Harcourt.

Endorsed by Harcourt: Mr Walpole 1782.

Friday night late.

THOUGH I am infinitely obliged to your Lordship for so readily undertaking to make peace,¹ I shall have no occasion to trouble you, unless you should by mere accident have an opportunity of softening the reception, for Mr C. and Lady A.² have taken the matter with the utmost good humour and good sense, and neither of them care a straw whether they are received a little better or a little worse: all the difference will be, that the latter will make them go the seldomer. He is not aiming to be Prime Minister by the House of Commons, and still less by Cumb[erland] House. It would be well if everybody had as little pride, and had had as little ambition.

Your Lordship's most devoted

H. WALPOLE

traits et détruisirent peu à peu tous ses avantages extérieurs' (NBG).

———

1. This letter suggests a coolness between Conway and the Duke of Gloucester, but HW does not mention it elsewhere. It may have occurred at the time of Conway's motion for ending the American war, 27 Feb. 1782. As Gloucester was then on good terms with the King, he might have expressed disapproval of Conway's taking the lead in Opposition by neglecting him at one of his levees. The latter part of the letter seems to say that, despite Conway's prominence in the debate, he does not seek power either through taking the lead in the House or through an intrigue with the Duke of Cumberland, then much courted by the Opposition, on bad terms with Gloucester, and, according to HW, possessing great influence over Rockingham (HW to T. Walpole 14 May 1781). Harcourt, as an intimate of the Duke and Duchess of Gloucester, would be well qualified to mediate any such misunderstanding.

2. Conway and Lady Ailesbury.

To Harcourt, Sunday 17 March 1782

Printed from a photostat of the MS in Lord Harcourt's possession. First printed, Cunningham viii. 181, reprinted, Toynbee xii. 200.

Address: To the Earl of Harcourt.

Endorsed by Harcourt: Mr Walpole March 17th 1782.

March 17, 1782.

My best Lord,

I AM such a courtier and trimmer, that if I beg you to intercede with Lady Harcourt to excuse me from waiting on her this evening, you will suspect it is, that I may meet the Prince of Wales at Lady Hertford's.[1] *That* would be like me, but for once it is a contrary reason—in short, I do not mean to go to Lady Hertford's, and as I promised I would, she might take it ill, if I should be at Lady Harcourt's and not go to her afterwards. Four days in a week, royally thrown away, content my appetite for courts[2]—and I will embark no farther—till the Chancellor is sent to fetch me. *Then* all my ambition may break out, and I may cease to be Lady Harcourt's and your Lordship's

Most devoted

Hor. Walpole

From Lady Harcourt, March 1782

Two missing notes, acknowledged in the next letter.

To Lady Harcourt, Wednesday 27 March 1782

Printed from a photostat of the MS in Lord Harcourt's possession. First printed, *Harcourt Papers* iii. 171–3 (misdated).

Endorsed by Harcourt: Honourable H. Walpole March 27 1782.

Wednesday night late.

I THINK it impossible, Madam, that something should not be offered to Lord Harcourt, though they who do *not* ask will be

1. Probably the 'grand route [*sic*] at the Earl of Hertford's at which the Prince of Wales and a great number of the nobility were present' mentioned in the *St James's Chronicle* 19–21 March, though that dates it Monday 18 March.

2. Doubtless waiting on Princess Amelia and the Duke and Duchess of Gloucester.

thought on the last.[1] They who have lost places will be very clamorous, and some who deserve none will not be less vociferous. Though I had got Mr Conway already to name the Jewel Office to the Duke of Richmond,[2] the moment I received the honour of your Ladyship's first note this morning, I wrote to his Grace myself,[3] and begged something proper might be offered to Lord Harcourt, and that it might not be the Bedchamber. I told him I asked nothing for myself; on the contrary, I begged no favour should be shown to me about my places, if they found it necessary to make any reformation.[4] The Duke was not at home, nor have I heard from him—but I am as satisfied, as if I had had the most favourable answer, that he will do all in his power to please Lord Harcourt, though I know enough of Lord Rockingham by what I saw in his former administration, to foresee that he will engross all the power he can to himself,[5] and communicate as little as possible to the Duke and Mr Conway, though so much greater men than himself. I am sorry on this occasion that they are the only two, of whom, insignificant as I am myself, I would condescend to ask a favour. It is, I feel, Madam, presumptuous in me to talk of asking a favour for Lord Harcourt—but I knew he would not ask one himself, nor have allowed one to be asked for him. Being sensible of these two points, and knowing that in such a scramble, a Minister cannot refuse many who are pressing

1. Lady Harcourt wrote on the letter: 'At the time the ministry was changed, Mr Walpole, who was much attached to Lord Harcourt, wished to have some compliment paid to him, and hoped that the offer of some honourable situation (whether he accepted it, or not) might be the means of drawing him a little out of the retirement he was too much inclined to indulge in. Mr Walpole spoke to me upon the subject, desired me to consider it, and write my opinion to him; finding that it agreed with his, he took the step mentioned in this letter. No offer was then made to Lord Harcourt, but when Mr Pitt came into the ministry in the year 1783 he (unsolicited) proposed to him the embassy to Spain. Lord H. declined it, but thinking the King had been ill treated by the old ministry, and that the new one ought to be supported, he returned to Court, from whence he had absented himself for six years.' HW, in

one of his accounts of his quarrel with Harcourt and Mason on their return to Court at the end of 1783, gives a somewhat different account of his incentives at the time: 'Lady Harcourt . . . during Lord Rockingham's short administration had overwhelmed Mr W. with letters, two or three in a day, to get her Lord a place, which he had tried in vain' (Mason ii. 332; see also ibid. ii. 328).

2. I.e. HW had asked Conway to ask Richmond to suggest Harcourt for the Jewel Office.

3. HW's letter to Richmond is missing.

4. HW refers obliquely to these instructions in his 'Account of My Conduct Relative to the Places I Hold Under Government' (Works ii. 370). See also ante HW to Harcourt Feb. 1780.

5. HW makes similar complaint about Rockingham's conduct towards Grafton and Conway in 1765–6 in Mem. Geo. III ii. 219.

for one who does not intimate a wish (which I must in fair justice conclude is Lord Rockingham's case) I did take on me to remind the Duke of Richmond, though perhaps Lord Harcourt might think I had taken an impertinent liberty with his name, though I shall certainly not be arrogant or vain enough to ascribe any share to my-self, should my idea succeed, as Lord Harcourt's virtues, rank, and zeal in the cause, entitle him to every distinction, while I am no-body, nor can claim any interest but with my relation and oldest friend Mr Conway, and in the goodness the Duke of Richmond has long had for me. Indeed so far from pretending interest with the party, I shall, as I did in their former administration, have as little as possible to do with any one of them, but with my two most vir-tuous friends, of whom I am indeed proud—but who I am sure will have no power beyond their own provinces. The Marquis and Lord Shelburne[6] will have a constant struggle for power and favour, and will probably aid the King to recover the ground he has lost, either by their flattery or their quarrels. Something I hope will be done for the nation before this happens—but whatever is not done soon, will not be done at all.

I am so apprehensive of having gone too far in my zeal for Lord Harcourt that I wish him not to know it, though your Ladyship may be assured, that I am too conscious of my indiscretion, not to keep it an absolute secret, nor shall a soul know it, but your Ladyship and the two persons I mentioned.

I have the honour to be with the utmost respect

> Your Ladyship's most devoted and most obedient
> humble servant,

> HOR. WALPOLE

Berkeley Square
March 27th 1782.

---

6. William Petty (1737–1805), 2d E. of Shelburne, 1761; cr. (1784) M. of Lans-downe, who succeeded Rockingham as prime minister in July (*post* HW to Har-court 5 July 1782, n. 1).

To Harcourt, Monday 3 June 1782

Printed from a photostat of the MS in Lord Harcourt's possession. First printed, Cunningham viii. 227, reprinted, Toynbee xii. 259–60.
Endorsed by Harcourt: Mr Walpole June 3d 1782.

June 3d.

I AM much obliged, my dear Lord, for the sight of the Dictionary[1] as much as I understand. The two articles you pointed out are fine indeed! and how excellent to make the sublime one of *Génie* end in a bitter epigram;[2] it is giving the Leviathan a sting that does more execution than his strength. All he says on operas is just—and yet I am so English, such a modern Englishman, that I had rather *see* an opera than *hear* it.[3] I am sorry for it, yet the longer one's ears are, and the more like *King* Midas's ears, the worse they hear.

Dr Maty[4] is very pert and foolish[5]—I must confess it, for I cannot be grateful at the expense of my understanding. Bishop Newton[6] is a greater fool—and as Lord Mansfield was his hero, or made himself so (for he had the MS some time in his custody) I hope he inserted

1. From the articles mentioned below, this was apparently Rousseau's *Dictionnaire de musique,* first published in 1767, and subsequently included in the various editions of Rousseau's *Works,* of which several were appearing at this time.

2. In the brief article on *génie,* Rousseau advises the young artist to go to Naples to hear masterpieces by Leo, Durante, Jommelli, Pergolesi, and Metastasio. If he is moved, he will follow them. 'Mais si les charmes de ce grand art te laissent tranquille, si tu n'as ni délire ni ravissement, si tu ne trouves que beau ce qui transporte, oses-tu demander ce qu'est le *génie?* Homme vulgaire, ne profane point ce nom sublime. Que t'importeroit de le connôitre? tu ne saurais le sentir: fais de la musique françoise' (*Œuvres complètes de J. J. Rousseau,* 3d edn, 1827–30, xiii. 423–4).

3. Rousseau's long article on opera concentrates on the music, discussing poetry and scenery only in relation to it (ibid. xiv. 118–42).

4. Paul Henry Maty (1744–87), F.R.S.; assistant librarian at the British Museum. HW is referring to his *New Review,* which began publication in Feb. 1782.

5. HW may be referring to a brief notice of the *Anecdotes of Painting* in the *New Review's* 'Literary Intelligence' in the May number: '*Volvenda dies en attulit!* Long looked for come at last. This will likewise make a precious extract for the next number. Why must we complain so long of this great writer, *Haud hominum curare triumphos?* that he cares not to receive his laurels from contemporaries, and will leave them to be bestowed by posterity. Where, in short, is the *Mysterious Mother,* those *graves Camoenæ* so long promised, so long expected, and so sure of not missing the bosoms at which they are directed' (*New Review* i. 334). An enthusiastic review followed in the *Review* for June (ibid. i. 355–64).

6. Thomas Newton (1704–82), D.D.; Bp of Bristol 1761–82. His *Works* in three volumes were reviewed in the *New Review* for May 1782; see MASON ii. 254.

the panegyric himself.[7] If he did not, he cannot be sick of the smell of paint as I am.

Your Lordship's ever devoted

H. Walpole

To Harcourt, Monday 1 July 1782

Printed from a photostat of the MS in Lord Harcourt's possession. First printed, Cunningham viii. 238–40, reprinted, Toynbee xii. 276–7.
Endorsed by Harcourt: Honourable Horace Walpole July 1st 1782.

Berkeley Square, July 1st 1782.

I WISH, my dear Lord, I had told you how very much I admire Lady Harcourt! I am sure you would have left her at my house. I did but mention the head of Addison[1]—and I found it on my table. I must have Aladdin's lanthorn, without knowing it, and you are certainly one of the *génies* subservient to it, that obey in a twinkling whatever—but no, for once, Mr Génie, you are mistaken. I not only did not order you to send Addison, but you must transport it back, or I will. It is very hard if one cannot make a visit to a gentleman, and ask whose that picture is, but one must have an officious lanthorn at one's tail, like Io, Mio, and Rio,[2] that fancies one *longs,* and that one's next child will be marked with what one longed for, if one has not it that instant. Good Génie, take notice I am not breeding, nor do I wish for everything I see. You have filled

---

7. 'He always regarded Lord Mansfield as the best and ablest speaker that ever he had heard in Parliament. . . . His language was more natural and easy [than Chatham's], his speeches were more in a continued chain of reasoning, and sometimes with regular divisions, so that you easily accompanied him. . . . Persuasion flowed from his lips, conviction was wrought in all unprejudiced minds, and for many years the House of Lords paid greater deference to his authority than to

that of any man living' (quoted in the *New Review* i. 280–2).

1. Probably the portrait of Addison in the Library at Nuneham 'after Kneller, by old Vandergucht' *(Description of Nuneham-Courtenay,* 1806, p. 17), since HW says he is going to return the picture. It is not mentioned in *Nuneham-Courtenay,* 1783.

2. Unexplained.

my house and every cranny of it already, and it will hold nothing
more. Do you think because I am old, that I covet more and more?
and that I am as rapacious as you are bountiful and magnificent?

Seriously, my dear Lord, you shall allow me next winter to return
you the Addison. I truly have no room for it: you have a collection
of English poets;[3] I have not; and over and above all these reasons,
pray believe that I am as interested in Nuneham as in Strawberry,
and have as much pleasure in its being ornamented. I have little
time left to enjoy anything, and who knows what will become of
Strawberry, and how soon it may be put up to auction? I am infinitely sensible of all your goodness to me, and much prouder of it
than of a collection, were it the Tribune of Florence.[4] I cannot pay
a thousandth part of my debts to you, nor mark as I would my attachment and respect to your Lordship and Lady Harcourt; and
when you heap new favours on me, you add to my distress. I meant
to quarrel with you ironically, but my heart overflowed: gratitude is
a simple awkward creature that cannot disguise its feelings; and
though it has the shortest memory of all the virtues, it cannot help
saying what it thinks, when taken by surprise. This time my gratitude shall be perfectly pure, for though it shall restore your present,
it shall never forget it.

I came to town yesterday for *our* last Drawing-Room;[5] but heard
nothing new. The suspense about Lord Rockingham continues:[6]
Dr Warren[7] thought him likely to recover on Saturday, but the night
was bad. The message today is, that his days are good, but the nights
bad. By what I can collect, his friends, if Lord R. fails, are little disposed to submit to the probable successor.[8] I shall take the liberty
of writing, should the event happen. You know I have little connection, but my accounts may be a little more authentic than the news-

3. In the Library at Nuneham; see
Description of Nuneham-Courtenay, 1806,
pp. 14–17. Several of them are visible in
a photograph of the Library in *Country
Life*, 1913, xxxiv. 754. The copy by Gogain
of Allan Ramsay's portrait of HW hung
there.

4. In the Uffizi.

5. I.e., the Duke and Duchess of
Gloucester's. They left London for the
continent 4 July (Lady Mary Coke, 'MS
Journals,' 4 July 1782).

6. He had been seriously ill since 23
June (*Memorials and Correspondence of
Charles James Fox*, ed. Lord John Russell,
1853, i. 435), and had, in fact, died shortly
before HW began this letter.

7. Richard Warren (1731–97), M.D.;
practiced in London 1756–97.

8. Lord Shelburne. HW's prediction
that the ministry would collapse was correct.

papers. I must finish abruptly, for, my dear Lord, you have made it impossible for words to tell you how much I am

Yours,

H. Walpole

4 o'clock. I wrote this but two hours ago. Lord Cholmondeley[9] has this moment been here and told me that Lord Rockingham died three hours ago. Your Lordship shall hear again the moment I know anything that can be depended upon.

To Harcourt, Friday 5 July 1782

Printed from a photostat of the MS in Lord Harcourt's possession. First printed, Cunningham viii. 244–5, reprinted, Toynbee xii. 282–3.
Endorsed by Harcourt: Honourable Horace Walpole July 5th 1782.

July 5, 1782.

I WISH, my dear Lord, that I had not promised to send you farther accounts, as I can tell you nothing that is agreeable. At present, though the humours are come to a *head*, they break faster than they gather. To speak intelligibly, the death of Lord Rockingham, whom I cannot admire more than I did, on the mere merit of being dead, has already produced great dissension. What has happened, I can tell you, that is, what had happened before last night. I begin this letter at noon, not answering for anything that may have passed this morning. Lord Shelburne is named, I don't say appointed, to the Treasury.[1] Charles Fox[2] and Lord John Cavendish[3]

9. George James Cholmondeley (1749–1827), 4th E. of Cholmondeley; cr. (1815) M. of Cholmondeley; HW's great-nephew.

1. The King had offered him the post, 1 July, immediately on learning of Rockingham's death. The Rockinghamites in the Cabinet countered, 2 July, by insisting on the appointment of a friend of Rockingham's, preferably the Duke of Portland; but the King refused to consider it and confirmed his offer to Shelburne on the 3rd (*The Correspondence of King George the Third,* ed. Sir John Fortescue,

1927–8, vi. 71–3; *Memorials and Correspondence of Charles James Fox,* ed. Lord John Russell, 1853, i. 435–6). The distinction HW draws is that Shelburne had been nominated to the Treasury but had not yet been formally invested with the office.

2. Fox resigned precipitately as Foreign Secretary, 4 July; see HW to Mann 7 July for an account of his behaviour, confirmed by Lady Mary Coke, 'MS Journals,' 5 July 1782.

3. Lord John Cavendish (1732–96), chancellor of the Exchequer under Rock-

have resigned. The Duke of Richmond,[4] General Conway,[5] T. Townshend,[6] the Duke of Manchester,[7] Lord Effingham,[8] are for going on; Lord Keppel[9] will stay a little while. Of others I know only flying reports—Mr William Pitt is to be secretary of state or chancellor of the Exchequer[10]—but these are individuals—What is to become of England? what, of the peace with America? what, of the favourable dispositions there may be in Europe? here are the Whigs divided almost as soon as triumphant!—what a moment gave, a moment has destroyed!—

2 o'clock.

I was interrupted by several persons calling in. The report is, that

ingham, had declared his intention of resigning immediately upon the Marquis's death, but was unable to execute his decision until his successor had been formally appointed (Lord John Russell, op. cit. i. 435–7, 463; *Last Journals* ii. 446–9, 453–4). HW's charges that he resigned partly because, as a Cavendish, he was not allowed to name the First Minister, are severely questioned in Lord John Russell, op. cit. i. 440–1, notes.

4. Master-General of the Ordnance under Rockingham, and continued in the office, except for the period of the Fox-North coalition, until 1795. Shelburne told the King on the evening of the 4th that 'The Duke of Richmond condemns in very strong terms Mr Fox's precipitate and unadvised conduct; he promises support upon condition that he is allowed to consult with those friends who remain about the persons who may be to fill up the vacant offices' (Fortescue, op. cit. vi. 75). He took the lead in attempting to persuade the rest of the Rockinghams to remain in office; see *Last Journals* ii. 449–51; Lord John Russell, op. cit. i. 435–7.

5. Commander-in-chief with a seat in the Cabinet under Rockingham and continued under Shelburne; for his opinions at this time, see *Last Journals* ii. 451–2.

6. Thomas Townshend (1733–1800), cr. (1783) Bn and (1789) Vct Sydney; secretary at war under Rockingham and Home Secretary under Shelburne. The King

told Shelburne on the 4th that 'Mr Townshend reprobates the idea of him [Fox] quitting if measures are right because they cannot fill offices to their wish' (Fortescue, op. cit. vi. 75).

7. George Montagu (1737–88), 4th D. of Manchester; lord chamberlain under Rockingham and continued under Shelburne.

8. Thomas Howard (1747–91), 3d E. of Effingham; deputy earl marshal 1777–82; treasurer of the Household under Rockingham and Shelburne.

9. First Lord of the Admiralty March 1782 – Jan. 1783, April – Dec. 1783. Shelburne told the King, 4 July, that 'Lord Keppel does not seem ill-disposed' and Keppel himself informed the King that Richmond had 'dissuaded him' from thinking of retiring (Fortescue, op. cit. vi. 75).

10. William Pitt (1759–1806) became chancellor of the Exchequer in Shelburne's administration. At the moment his post was still undetermined; he wrote to his mother on the 5th: 'My lot will be either at the Treasury as chancellor of the Exchequer, or in the Home Department as secretary of state. The arrangement cannot be finally settled until to-day or tomorrow [it was not settled until 9 July], but everything promises as well as possible in such circumstances' (Earl Stanhope, *Life of . . . William Pitt*, new edn, 1879, i. 66).

Burke resigns,[11] and it is concluded, the Duke of Portland[12] will. Mr Pitt has returned his briefs to his clients, and within this hour the first battle will be fought in the House of Commons between him and Mr Fox, the former declaring loudly against the factious resignation of the latter.[13] This is Mr Pitt's language, not mine— the motives of both are the same. The Duke of Richmond and Mr Conway have laboured to prevent disunion in the administration, and implored harmony, at least till pacification with America should be accomplished; but in vain!—in short, on every side there is nothing to comfort—a vast deal to lament! Mr Stonhewer[14] and I have been sighing together. Is Mr Mason at Nuneham? I wrote a line to him on Monday,[15] which probably has not reached him—when it does, he will know what I chiefly lament,[16] yet I did not foresee all that I do now.

I can tell your Lordship nothing you will be glad to hear, but that the parting of two persons you love[17] was much better than I expected.

6 o'clock.

I have just received a letter from Mr Mason of the 2d,[18] and find that he will not be with your Lordship before tomorrow at soonest.

11. Edmund Burke (1729–97), resigned as paymaster of the forces, officially vacating his office on 17 July (*Correspondence of Edmund Burke*, Vol. V, ed. Furber, 1965, p. 21, n. 2), though he did not wholly approve Fox's precipitate resignation; see Lord John Russell, op. cit. i. 457–8.

12. Lord lieutenant of Ireland Apr.–Aug. 1783.

13. 'Yesterday 5 July there was one of the greatest appearances of members in the House of Commons, as well as the most crowded gallery, perhaps ever known at this time of year, under the idea of Mr Fox's stating his reasons for resigning his office of secretary of state. Mr Fox came into the House about four o'clock quite undressed, and gave the signal of his resignation, by taking his place on the opposite side of the treasury bench; but as soon as the ordinary business of the day was over, and everybody was on the tip-toe of expectation for hearing the reason of so sudden and extraordinary a change,

they were disappointed by General Conway moving for an adjournment' (*London Chronicle* 4–6 July 1782, lii. 24). 'It was expected last Friday [5 July] that Mr Fox would have told his story to the House of Commons but though he took his seat on the opposition side of the House he said nothing but put on the appearance of great gaiety laughing very much with Mr Burke' (Lady Mary Coke, 'MS Journals,' 6 July 1782). The expected debate took place 9 July when both Pitt and Conway attacked Fox (Cobbett, *Parl. Hist.* xxiii. 165–8, 185–6).

14. Richard Stonhewer (ca 1728–1809), auditor of excise 1772–89; close friend of Gray (Mason i. 11, n. 4).

15. Printed Mason ii. 258.

16. That the American war would revive and that many of its 'authors' would return to office. HW expresses the same sentiments in *Last Journals* ii. 449.

17. Unexplained.

18. Printed Mason ii. 258–60.

The Prince of Wales dined with Mr Fox yesterday by previous engagement.[19] They drank royally. Charles went thence to Brooks's, stayed till four in the morning, and it being so early, finished the evening at White's with Lord Weymouth—'and the evening and the morning and the next day, were the first day.' Amen—and so be it!

From HARCOURT, ca Saturday 6 July 1782

Missing; mentioned by HW to Mason, 8 July 1782, as saying that Mason had arrived at Nuneham and was 'sitting on a rafter and dining out of a hod of mortar' (MASON ii. 262–3).

To HARCOURT, Saturday 7 September 1782

Printed from a photostat of the MS in Lord Harcourt's possession. First printed, Cunningham viii. 275–7, reprinted, Toynbee xii. 327–8.
Endorsed by Harcourt: Honourable Horace Walpole Sept. 7th 1782.

Strawberry Hill, Sept. 7, 1782.

I AM most impatient, my dear Lord, for an account of the conclusion of all the various and great works carrying on at Nuneham. I am earnest to hear that the house is finished,[1] that the tower designed by Mr Mason is ready to receive my painted glass,[2] that he

19. 'The Prince of Wales dined with Mr Fox on the day of his resignation, and expressed much kindness towards him, assuring him that he should ever consider Lord Rockingham's friends as the persons the most to be depended upon, and as the best friends of the country' ('General Fitzpatrick's Journal,' quoted in Lord John Russell, op. cit. i. 437). 'After Mr Fox resigned on Thursday the Prince of Wales dined with him, and H.R.H. hearing in the Drawing-Room that Lord Shelburne was to be the Minister swore a great oath and said he was sorry for it' (Lady Mary Coke, 'MS Journals,' 6 July 1782).

1. Extensive reconstruction and redecoration was in progress at Nuneham;

see *Harcourt Papers* vii. 352, 354, 357–9; MASON ii. 268, 274.

2. Harcourt wrote to Mason, probably in 1782 'Mr Walpole's rage being to make me presents, he insists on giving me painted glass for the upper part of a window which is to be put together and ?united ?by a mosaic ground by Mr Peckit' (John Mitford's extracts from the Harcourt-Mason correspondence, Add. MSS 32563, f. 111). The tower was a projected Gothic structure to be built at Nuneham, much discussed in Mason's letters to Harcourt in the winter of 1782; but, as it was never undertaken, the letters and passages relating to it are omitted from the *Harcourt Papers* (microfilms of MSS in possession of Lord Harcourt). See also MASON ii. 263, 268, 270, 310.

has written several novelties, and is coming to make me a visit as he promised,[3] and that Lady Harcourt has settled and had transcribed the MS that I am to print.[4] These things, and perhaps a great many more, I conclude have been pursued with unremitting diligence, as no soul has had a moment's time to send me a line, though Mr Mason is so punctual a correspondent, that I know he would not have been so long silent, if he had not been so occupied by the works at Nuneham, which he knows I prefer to my own satisfaction. However, as all must be terminated in two or three days, I beg that on the first holiday after the masons, bricklayers, upholsters, Muses, and amanuenses are paid off, that somebody or other will tell me the society are well and have not broken their necks off a scaffold, nor their bones by a fall from Pegasus.

By my little specimen in Strawberry I guess that Nuneham is in the highest beauty, as a whole summer has been spent on decorating autumn with verdure, leaves and rivers. Your Lordship's Thames must be brimfull. I never saw it such a Ganges at this time of year: it is none of your home-brewed rivers,[5] that people make with a drain, half a bridge, and a clump of evergreens, and then overlay with the model of a ship.

I know nothing, for I live as if I were just arrived from Syria and were performing quarantine. Nobody dares stir out of their own house. We are robbed and murdered if we do but step over the threshold to the chandler's shop for a pennyworth of plums.[6] Lady Mary Mordaunt[7] is at Petersham with Lady Cecilia, and they are to dine here next week, if Admiral Milbank[8] is returned from the Baltic[9] and they can obtain a convoy. Dame Clivden is the only

---

3. In his letter to HW 2 July 1782 (MASON ii. 260); he finally made the visit in mid-October (*post* HW to Harcourt 23 Oct. 1782).

4. Lady Harcourt had finally agreed in Feb. 1782 to allow HW to print a selection of her verses and even sent some by Sept. 1783; see Mason ii. 183, 263, 312; *Harcourt Papers* vii. 78. The project was given up in the subsequent coolness between HW and the Harcourts.

5. HW uses the same expression and a similar image in his letter to Lady Ossory 31 Aug. 1782 (OSSORY ii. 355 and n. 25).

6. HW's other letters, Lady Mary

Coke's 'MS Journals,' and the newspapers contain many accounts of violent robberies by gangs of highwaymen during the late summer of 1782.

7. Lady Mary Anastasia Grace Mordaunt (1738–1819), Bns Mordaunt, s.j., 1814; died unmarried.

8. Mark Milbanke (ca 1725–1805), naval officer; Rear-Adm., 1779; Vice-Adm., 1780; Adm., 1793.

9. 'On Thursday [5 Sept.] in the afternoon Admiral Milbanke, with 17 sail of men of war, passed by the back of Goodwin Sands for the North Sea to convoy home the Baltic fleet' (*London Chronicle* 5–7 Sept. 1782. lii. 240). Such

heroine amongst all us old dowagers; she is so much recovered,[10] that she ventures to go out cruising on all the neighbours, and has made a miraculous draught of fishes.

My nieces are gone to Hackwood,[11] and thence are to meet their sister and Lord Chewton[12] at Weymouth— I have heard a whisper of a little miscarriage—it must have been a very small one. The Duchess,[13] when I heard last, was at Lausanne but going to Geneva, and intended a visit to Madame de Virri,[14] who is within three hours of the former. I do not know whither bound next.

Has your Lordship seen Mr Tyrwhit's book[15] in answer to Mr Bryant[16] and Dr Archimage?[17] It is as good as argument and proofs

reports somewhat distort Milbanke's objective; he had indeed sailed from Spithead, 28 Aug., in command of a fleet sent into the North Sea to frighten the Dutch from attempting to intercept the Baltic fleet of merchantmen, but his orders were to return to Spithead as soon as the wind changed after his demonstration off the Texel. He did so, 6 Sept., and on the 11th sailed as third in command under Lord Howe with the fleet for the relief of Gibraltar (W. M. James, *The British Navy in Adversity*, 1926, p. 370; Augustus Henry, 3d Duke of Grafton, *Autobiography*, ed. Anson, 1898, pp. 342–4; John Charnock, *Biographia navalis*, 1794–8, vi. 82; *London Chronicle* 29–31 Aug. 1782, lii. 214). Other details of the movement of his ships and conflicting reports of the probable object of his fleet are in the *London Chronicle* 31 Aug.– 3 Sept., 5–7 Sept. 1782, lii. 221, 234, 236.

10. She had been so seriously ill of jaundice in July that HW doubted of her recovery (MASON ii. 271).

11. Seat of the Duke of Bolton, near Basingstoke.

12. George Waldegrave (1751–89), styled Vct Chewton 1763–84; 4th E. Waldegrave, 1784; m. (5 May 1782) his cousin, Lady Elizabeth Laura Waldegrave.

13. Of Gloucester.

14. Henrietta Jane Speed (1728–83), m. (1761) Francesco Maria Giuseppe Giustino, Barone di la Perrière, Conte di Viry, 1766 (GRAY ii. 123). HW's account of them, printed in *Harcourt Papers* iii. 274–5, is as follows: 'The Count de Viry was son of one of the same title, who had

been the Sardinian minister in England, and was himself ambassador in France. While in England, in 1760 [1761] he married Miss Speed, niece of Lady Cobham. The Countess de Viry was supposed to be the cause of the disgrace her husband suffered, She was a very intriguing woman, and instigated him to keep up a secret correspondence at Turin, with the object of making himself prime minister. This was discovered, and the minister dismissed. Lord Shelburne, who was a friend of the Countess, prevailed on the King to obtain their pardon of the King of Sardinia in 1783; about which time she died suddenly. She was one of the heroines of Mr Gray's "Long Story," and had a great deal of wit.' A longer account of her, probably by Lord Harcourt, is in *Harcourt Papers* viii. 1–3. See also HW's notes on a copy of his letter to the Contessa di Viry, April 1776, in Mme du Deffand's *Recueil de lettres*, now WSL.

15. *Vindication of the Appendix to the Poems Called Rowley's*, 1782, by Thomas Tyrwhitt (1730–86), classical commentator.

16. Jacob Bryant (1715–1804), Fellow of King's College, Cambridge, was the author of *Observations upon the Poems of Thomas Rowley*, 1781.

17. The enchanter in *The Faerie Queene*, symbolizing Hypocrisy. HW is alluding to Jeremiah Milles (1714–84), Dean of Exeter and President of the Society of Antiquaries, editor of *Poems, Supposed to Have Been Written . . . by Thomas Rowley . . . With a Commentary*, 1782.

can be after what is much better, wit and ridicule.[18] As Mr Mason is absorbed in Fresnoy,[19] and Associations,[20] I conclude he does not condescend to look at such trifles as *Archæologic Epistles* and dissertations on the language of Chaucer.[21]

Charles Fox is languishing at the feet of Mrs Robinson.[22] George Selwyn says, 'Who should the *man of the people* live with, but with the *woman of the people?*' Tonton sends his archæocompliments to Druid,[23] and I am the whole sacred grove's devoted

H. W.

From HARCOURT, October 1782

A missing invitation, answered in the next letter.

18. HW is alluding to Mason's *Archæological Epistle to . . . Jeremiah Milles,* published the preceding March (MASON ii. 199, n. 1).

19. Mason was engaged in translating *De Arte graphica,* by Charles-Alphonse Dufresnoy (1611–65). It was published early in 1783 (MASON ii. 284).

20. The Yorkshire Association; Mason was a member of its Committee. See MASON, *passim.*

21. Probably another allusion to Tyrwhitt's *Vindication,* which contains many references to Chaucer.

22. Mary Darby (1758–1800), 'Perdita'; m. (1774) Thomas Robinson; actress and author; first mistress of the Prince of Wales. 'I hear Charles saunters about the streets, and brags that he has not taken a pen in hand since he was out of place.

Pour se désennuyer he *lives* with Mrs Robinson, goes to Sadler's Wells with her, and is all day figuring away with her. I long to tell him he does it to show that he is superior to Alcibiades, for *his* courtesan forsook him when he was unfortunate, and Mrs Robinson takes *him* up' (Lady Sarah Napier to Lady Susan O'Brien 11 Sept. 1782, in *The Life and Letters of Lady Sarah Lennox,* ed. Lady Ilchester and Lord Stavordale, 1902, ii. 25–6). For Fox's liaison with Mrs Robinson, which came to an end in a few months, and was said to be 'perfectly political on the part of the lady,' see Christopher Hobhouse, *Fox,* 1934, pp. 153–4, 166, 197; Robert Bass, *Green Dragoon,* New York, 1957, pp. 199–203.

23. The Harcourts' dog.

To Harcourt, Wednesday 23 October 1782

Printed from a photostat of the MS in Lord Harcourt's possession. First printed, Cunningham viii. 289–91, reprinted, Toynbee xii. 346–8.
Endorsed by Harcourt: Honourable H. Walpole 8ᵇʳ [October] 23d 1782.

Strawberry Hill, Oct. 23d 1782.

MR Mason (who by the by is grown too plump for a poet and patriot on whom the constitutional as well as *the whole Castalian state*[1] depends) has been here, and brought me your Lordship's most kind invitation.[2] I am afraid, my dear Lord, I dare not accept it so late in the season and in such wet weather. The spirit is willing, but the bones, I must not say the flesh,[3] are weak. I am going to settle in town, not daring to stay even here in my own house, for fear of the damps bringing on the gout. I should not be able to resist walking out at Nuneham, or going into your new rooms, and the consequence would be, encumbering you with an invalid for two months—So that I have still passions to conquer at sixty-five; and though I might not have resolution enough to subdue them on my own account, I can for your Lordship's and Lady Harcourt's sakes. If I have a next summer, I shall hope to enjoy all your improvements within doors and without.

Mrs Clivden, I flatter myself, is really recovered, having had no relapse since I mentioned her last. She even partakes of the diversions of the carnival, which at Twickenham commences at Michaelmas, and lasts as long as there are four persons to make a pool. I am to go to her this evening to what she calls *only two tables.* I have preached against hot rooms, but the Devil who can conceal himself in a black ace as well as in an apple or a guinea, has been too mighty for me—and so, like other divines, when I cannot root out vice, I join in it.

1. Castalia was a spring on Mount Parnassus sacred to the Muses; this quotation is from Pope, 'Epistle to Dr Arbuthnot,' l. 230.

2. 'I have been at Strawberry, where I found its owner in good health and despairing political spirits, which seemed the higher for that very reason; full of old anecdote, but as barren of news as London itself, which does not seem to know anything. . . . But to revert to the Master of Strawberry. I delivered all your messages, so kind and so civil, but he seems to be afraid of the gout at so late a season, but at the same time does not bid me plead this as an excuse for not coming, but says he'll write himself' (Mason to Harcourt 22 Oct. 1782, *Harcourt Papers* vii. 75–6).

3. Because of his excessive thinness.

Lady Cecilia I have not seen this age. The highwaymen have cut off all communication between the nearest villages: it is as dangerous to go to Petersham as into Gibraltar.⁴ I comfort myself with the Gothicity of the times. Is not it delightful not to dare stir out of one's own castle but armed for battle? However, I am so scrupulous an adherent to good old customs, that I intend to be knighted, and shall appoint Mr Raftor my esquire, who is as great a coward as Sanco Panca, and has more humour. As it is right too, according to Cervantes, to mistake the objects of one's fury, I know whom I intend to attack as a highwayman, whom as a footpad, housebreaker or assassin; and should I repeat the same ideas fifty times, I can justify myself by the same authority; and shall not want subjects.

Still as even in this ferocious age I do not abandon all literary pursuits, I presume to send your Lordship a composition of my own, in that ingenious way that was last in vogue, before martial glory quite expelled the Muses. I mean *a charade*. The word is a French name—*la voici,*

The first part is thine; the second part belongs only to the most fashionable people; and the whole belongs only to me.⁵

Your Lordship's most devoted

Hor. Walpole

PS. If your Lordship nor Lady Harcourt, nor Miss Fauquier nor Mr Whithed⁶ can guess the charade, as I conclude; I will lay a wager Druid⁷ can.

4. Which Lord Howe had sailed to relieve on 11 Sept. Reports were current in London by 15 Oct. that he had succeeded in lifting the siege, though he had been unable even to land supplies there before 16 Oct. and failed completely to lift the siege. Reports of the limited relief reached London 28 Oct., but were not confirmed until 7 Nov. (HW to Mann 12 Oct., 23 Oct., 2–4 Nov. 1782, Mann ix. 326–7, 331, 335–6; *St James's Chronicle* 5–7 Nov. 1782).
5. The answer is Tonton, the dog bequeathed to HW by Mme du Deffand.
6. William Whitehead (1715–85), the poet laureate, who was a close friend of the Harcourts.
7. The Harcourts' dog.

To Harcourt, Tuesday 29 October 1782

Printed from a photostat of the MS in Lord Harcourt's possession. First partly printed, Cunningham viii. 292–3, partly reprinted, Toynbee xii. 351–2. The passage between angular brackets is first printed here.

Endorsed by Harcourt: The Honourable Horace Walpole October 29, 1782.

Berkeley Square, Oct. 29, 1782.

I MUST trouble your Lordship with one word more to say how infinitely obliged I am by your goodness, and how ashamed at your putting yourself to any inconvenience on my account—I could not pardon myself, were I not sure that I should be a greater encumbrance to you. I should either be confined, or running away for fear of being so—and I know there is nothing so troublesome as tormenting others with whims about one's health.

I had heard with concern the reports that Mrs Mac.[1] gave your Lordship: and almost wish I could shut my ears on that chapter. That ugly monkey Lord Gr.[2] was one of the most impertinent. We have had a sprig from the same bough lately in my neighbourhood, which I expect to see in the papers, though I believe a mere accident; but *Mrs Coaxer*[3] (you will probably think I mean *Mrs Vixen*) was in such *a consternation* that she published it wherever she went, though it was nothing but a chance firing of a pistol.

I believe I did not do complete justice to my own charade. After I had sealed my letter, I recollected that I had omitted these words, 'and my whole, *though doubly thine,* belongs' etc. I think it very important to set this right, as whatever relates to Tonton is the law and the prophets to me. I can prove it is not from self-vanity, for with equal scrupulousness I must reject your Lordship's compliment on my courage. I assure you I am no hero, but

A puny insect shiv'ring at a breeze.[4]

1. Possibly Mrs Macaulay, though she had become Mrs Graham in 1778.
2. Possibly George Mason Villiers (1751–1800), 2d E. Grandison, 29 May 1782, whom HW describes as 'homely' and as not adding 'to the decoration' (Ossory i. 48).
3. This seems to be Mrs Keppel, with whom HW connects this story in his letter of 10 Nov. to Lady Ossory (Ossory

ii. 370). He related that some gentlemen were cleaning their pistols at the window of the Toy, a tavern at Hampton Court, and discharged them as his nieces were going by. 'Mrs Keppel took an alarm; and much less falling on such a soil as Hampton Court will bring forth lies an hundredfold.'
4. Pope, *Moral Essays* iv. 108.

I shall delight in Mason's altar-piece⁵—is the Levite who passed by, at all like my Lord of York?⁶ ⟨I frightened him with a comment that I wonder has never been made on a certain line

Lull'd on his *St John*'s philosophic breast⁷—

If anybody reads *Saint John*'s, it will look like what one has seen on other altar-pieces.⟩ Adieu! my best Lord; forgive me, and be assured how very grateful I am for all your goodness to

Your most devoted

H. Walpole

From Harcourt, ca Monday 11 November 1782

Missing. Answered in the next letter.

To Harcourt, Tuesday 12 November 1782

Printed from a photostat of the MS in Lord Harcourt's possession. First printed, Cunningham viii. 306–7, reprinted, Toynbee xii. 370–1.
Endorsed by Harcourt: The Honourable Horace Walpole 9ᵇʳ [November] 12th 1782.

Berkeley Square, Nov. 12, 1782.

I AM certainly little worthy of the great honour you do me, my best Lord, but I should be utterly unworthy of it, were I to give myself airs of intelligence, or presume to give you advice when I am totally in the dark. I have not the least idea what is to be the subject of the opening.¹ My ignorance of what is passing is extreme, for

---

5. Mason painted an altar-piece for the church at Nuneham, on the subject of the Good Samaritan (*Harcourt Papers* iii. 201).
6. William Markham (*ante* HW to Harcourt ca 28 May 1776). Mason's dislike of him is apparent throughout the HW-Mason correspondence.
7. 'Sunk in his St John's philosophic breast' (Mason, *Heroic Epistle to Sir*

William Chambers, l. 32). The line refers to David Mallet and Henry St John, 1st Vct Bolingbroke.

———

1. At this time Parliament was scheduled to open 26 Nov., but on the 23d was prorogued to 5 Dec. The subject of the King's speech was chiefly negotiations for peace and the economies that had been

I do not even ask a question. By the violence with which the old ministers[2] or their dependants rave against the independence of America, Lord Shelburne perhaps expects great opposition.[3] If he does, he cannot have concluded a treaty with them:[4] and unless they oppose him, who is there to be apprehended in the House of Lords? The promotion of Jenkinson[5] I have only seen in the newspapers, or from those who saw it there.

Should I, which is not likely, hear what the specific business is, I will undoubtedly acquaint your Lordship. At this moment, I own, my head, which has entirely forsworn politics, is not very capable of attending to them. I have lost, and very suddenly, poor Lady Hertford,[6] whom I sincerely loved and valued, and who has in all times treated me most kindly for forty years. Her loss to her husband and family is irreparable—I feel for them, but I confess, I feel the loss to myself too, heavily. I knew all her great and good qualities, and time and accidents have reduced my friends to so very small a number, that I neither seek nor am likely to find a succedaneum of equal merit.

I beg pardon for talking of my own griefs, when I ought only to reply to your Lordship—why should not you come for a day and judge for yourself? Nobody has authority to retain you—surely your Lordship is independent and unhampered, if any man is! Should the business be to approve American independence, I think you would be sorry not to give your vote for it. Excuse my saying no more, for my heart is full—yet though of the dead, I can never forget how much I ought to be and am

Your Lordship's devoted humble servant,

HOR. WALPOLE

instituted (Cobbett, *Parl. Hist.* xxiii. 203–10).

2. Both North and his friends and Fox and his friends were criticizing the handling of American independence, but for different reasons.

3. The King's speech received very little opposition in either House.

4. Shelburne seems to have made no attempts at a treaty with either group of Opposition before Parliament opened; attempts made later failed.

5. Charles Jenkinson (1729–1808), cr. (1786) Bn Hawkesbury and (1796) E. of Liverpool; M.P.; secretary at war 1778–82. A false report that he had kissed hands as secretary of state, 8 Nov. was printed in the *St. James's Chronicle* 7–9 Nov. 1782 and in the *London Chronicle* 7–9 Nov., lii. 456, but denied in the latter paper, 9–12 Nov.: 'Mr Jenkinson was certainly at Court on Friday last, but he neither had a private audience with the King, which is the invariable custom on receiving the seals of so high an employment as secretary of state, nor did he kiss hands at all. His attendance was a mere visit of ceremony' (lii. 459).

6. Isabella, Countess of Hertford, died 10 Nov. 1782.

From Harcourt, ca Wednesday 27 November 1782

Missing. Answered in the next letter.

To Harcourt, Thursday 28 November 1782

Printed from a photostat of the MS in Lord Harcourt's possession. First printed, Cunningham viii. 312, reprinted, *Harcourt Papers* viii. 98–9, Toynbee xii. 376–7.

In Kirgate's hand.

Endorsed by Harcourt: Honourable Horace Walpole 9^{br} [November] 28, 1782.

Berkeley Square, November 28, 1782.

My best Lord,

YOU are so very kind that I must obey you though I hold it very idle to trouble anybody with the details of my decay. I have indeed for a little while been extremely ill,[1] and much worse with its fever than with the gout itself, though I have that in five places: but this last was a very good night, and I think the fever very much abated.[2] Philip[3] told before dinner that he saw I was better, for I had taken up a book, which I had not done for six days. Thus, my dear Lord, I have complied with your injunction, but I don't intend to make a practice of it, for the gout is such a tiresome old story, that it is not fit anybody should be plagued with it but those who must endure it—never those who have so much sensibility as your Lordship.

I have just received a most kind and pleasing letter from Lady Maria, who is so charmed with the improvements at Nuneham, though it snowed all day, that she seems to think

That Paradise was open'd in the wild.[4]

I beg your Lordship to tell her that I will write to her as soon as I am able, but I cannot even dictate now for any time. I hear poor

---

1. HW had been seized with the gout accompanied by a 'higher fever than usual' about 23 Nov. (HW to Mann 26 Nov. 1782, Mann ix. 343; HW to Mason 27 Nov. 1782, Mason ii. 276).

2. HW made a similar report to Mason on the 28th (Mason ii. 277).

3. Philip Colomb (d. 1799), HW's Swiss valet (du Deffand iii. 89, n. 2; Berry i. 19, n. 9).

4. Pope, *Eloisa to Abelard*, l. 134.

Lady Waldegrave[5] is extremely ill, which is all I know, not having been able to see anybody till today. Adieu! my good Lord, and be assured that while I have breath, I shall be your Lordship's

Most devoted

H. W.

To Harcourt, ? Saturday 1 March ?1783

Printed for the first time from the MS now WSL, who acquired it from Walter T. Spencer in 1932.

The year date is conjectural. A somewhat similar request for Lady Diana Beauclerk is found in HW to Mason 22 Sept. 1783, MASON ii. 311.

Note in unidentified hand: Addressed to Earl Harcourt.

Berkeley Square, March 1st.

I BEG your Lordship's pardon for giving you this trouble, but Lady Di Beauclerc desired me to ask if you have not a receipt for a beautiful green for house-painting, and if I thought you would be so good as to let [her] have a copy. I said, I did not doubt of your Lordship's complaisance, if it is no secret, yet that I concluded you would be still more ready to oblige *her* with it, if it were to paint anything rather than a house. I have the honour to be

Your Lordship's most obedient humble servant,

Hor. Walpole

5. Lady Elizabeth Leveson Gower (d. 1784), m. (1751) John Waldegrave, 3d E. Waldegrave. The report of her illness at this time seems to have been somewhat exaggerated; Lady Mary Coke mentions, 30 Nov., that she had 'come to town from Bath and not well, great dejection of spirits as she had last year' ('MS Journals,' 30 Nov. 1782).

To Harcourt, Tuesday 5 August 1783

Printed from a photostat of the MS in Lord Harcourt's possession. First printed, Cunningham viii. 396–8, reprinted, Toynbee xiii. 40–3.
Endorsed by Harcourt: Honourable Hor. Walpole August 5th 1783.

Strawberry Hill, Aug. 5, 1783.

DO not think, my best Lord, that I forget or neglect the very kind and favourite invitations from Nuneham: but I weigh my own incapacities, and how likely I am to be an encumbrance. The result of my meditations is, that as I can neither entirely resign my own satisfaction, nor purchase it with clogging you and Lady Harcourt, nor abstain from visiting the additional beauties of Nuneham before they are *in the sere and yellow leaf,* I have determined to offer myself in the beginning of September. In the morning I can drive out with you; and as the days will then be short, I shall not be the cause of your being in the house, and consequently can enjoy your company without having it on my conscience to have shortened your walks, in which I am not able to join. If this scheme will interfere with none of your Lordship's, you will be so good as to let me know your commands at your leisure.

By your note to Mrs Clive, I learn that Miss Fauquier is with you, and Mr Whitehed—and so I hope they will be in September, if you admit me. Where Mr Mason is I am ignorant, which is pretty much the state of my intelligence about everybody and everything, except my own calamities, which consist in having had a little gout, and in having a little more rheumatism, from having been able to bear not so much clothing as our ancestor's old jacket a fig leaf in the excessive heats, and from being overrun with all the languages of Babel who come to see my house from morning to night—

Ev'n Sunday shines no Sabbath-day to me.[1]

The Duc de Chartres[2] was in my hall before I knew he was to come; Monsieur de Guines and *sa tribu* by candlelight,[3] and the Chev. de

1. Pope, 'Epistle to Dr Arbuthnot,' l. 12.

2. Louis-Philippe-Joseph de Bourbon (1747–93), Duc de Chartres; Duc d'Orléans, 1785; 'Philippe-Égalité' of the French Revolution. He visited SH some-

time between 1 and 5 June (HW to Lady Ossory 20 June 1783, OSSORY ii. 402–3, and n. 9).

3. HW gives an account of their visit, 16 June, in his letters to Lady Ossory 20 June 1783 and *ante* to Strafford 24 June

Jerningham[4] brought a host of Luxembourgs and Lusignans[5] while I was at dinner, as Mr Mason may have told you.[6] Madame de Cambis[7] dined with me last week—and who do you think came with her? *Diane* de Poitiers[8] of the next reign. You will guess who I mean when I tell you she was a little embarrassed with sitting over against a picture that cost me more than three hundred *shillings.*[9] Madame de Cambis, who is not yet deep in the *chronique scandaleuse,* telling me what and whom she had already seen, said, 'Et j'ai vu le _____ de _____.'[10] I replied, without looking up, 'Il est fort beau'—but let us change the subject; my niece Maria is extremely recovered, and Lady Chewton perfectly well. She has a fine little girl,[11] and suckles it herself, and not at the commerce table.[12]

At Lady Cecilia's last week I saw Mr and *Mrs* Majendie.[13] I hope your Lordship will be pleased to hear, if you do not know, that a friend of the husband, had the good sense to pass eldest,[14] and attend them to church, and now is reckoned to have made the match—to change the subject again; the Duke and Duchess are gone to Strasbourg, the Margravine[15] being dying.

1783. The party consisted of the Duc, his two daughters, the French ambassador, Lady Pembroke, Lord Herbert, and Lord Robert Spencer.

4. Charles Jerningham (d. 1814), general officer in the French service; Knight of Malta and St Louis (Sir Bernard Burke and A. P. Burke, *Peerage,* 1928, p. 1301).

5. HW describes their visit, 29 June, in his letter to Lady Ossory 15 July 1783. See also *ante* HW to Strafford 24 June 1783.

6. Mason was spending the day at SH when they made their visit (HW to Lady Ossory 15 July 1783, OSSORY ii. 406–7).

7. Gabrielle-Françoise-Charlotte d'Alsace-Hénin-Liétard (1729–1809), m. (1755) Jacques-François-Xavier-Régis-Ignace, Vicomte de Cambis (OSSORY iii. 77, n. 8). She and Lady Melbourne planned to dine with HW 29 July (HW to Conway 27–28 July 1783).

8. Diane de Poitiers (1499–1566), Duchesse de Valentinois; mistress of Henri II of France, though twenty years his senior. HW is alluding to Elizabeth Milbanke (d. 1818), m. (1769) Peniston Lamb, cr. (1770) Bn and (1781) Vct Mel-

bourne. She was mistress of the Prince of Wales.

9. Reynolds's portrait of the three Ladies Waldegrave, for which HW paid 300 guineas, according to the receipt, now WSL. HW attributed the broken engagement, between Lady Maria and Lord Egremont, to Lady Melbourne (*ante* HW to Harcourt 2 Sept. 1780, n. 2).

10. 'Le Prince de Galles.'

11. Lady Maria Wilhelmina Waldegrave (ca 15 July 1783–1805), m. (1804) Nathaniel Micklethwait of Taverham, Norfolk (BERRY ii. 50, n. 9; HW to Lady Ossory 23 July 1783, OSSORY ii. 408).

12. As did the Duchess of Devonshire; see HW to Lady Ossory 23 July 1783, OSSORY ii. 408, n. 6.

13. Lewis Majendie (ca 1756–1833), captain-lieutenant in the 15th Dragoons; m. (15 July 1783) Elizabeth Hoghton (ca 1761–1807), only dau. of Sir Henry Hoghton, 6th Bt (GM 1833, ciii. pt ii. 281).

14. A 'loo phrase'; see MONTAGU i. 181, n. 20.

15. Friederike Luise (1714–84), of Prussia, m. (1729) Karl Wilhelm, Margrave of Ansbach 1723–57. According to Lady Mary Coke, the Duke and all his family

The Prince of Wales dined lately at Gunnersbury.[16] Before they rose from table Lady Clermont[17] said, 'I am sure the Duke of Portland is dying for a pinch of snuff,' and pushed her box to him cross the Princess, who said to her, 'Pray, Madam, where did you learn that breeding? did the Queen of France teach it to you?'[18]—these are the gossiping anecdotes our village affords—but they are better than news of burning towns and sinking ships!

I hope the Isis makes a little water in your Thames. Ours who is an old bachelor and has no such conveniencies, is as dry as a stick. We have no more verdure than there is in the Thuilleries—but the evenings are delicious—but the nights are insupportable—in short one is never contented—however, one is very happy, when one has no more terrible miseries!—and one has very little [to] say when one talks of the weather and princes and princesses. Your Lordship probably thinks that I might have found that out two pages ago. I am to eat your Lordship's health at Clivden in your own venison at the end of the week,[19] and to drink Miss *Pope's*[20] *eye,* who is with

had been 'living ever since they left England at the expense of the Margrave of Anspach' ('MS Journals,' 11 July 1783).

16. 'The Prince of Wales dines at Gunnesbury with the Princess Amelia on Monday [28 July]. He had signified to her some time ago he wished to have that pleasure but she declined it saying it would be a very dull party for him and she was sure he would not like it. Upon this he made her a visit and desired she would allow him to come so she has invited the Duke and Duchess of Portland, Lord and Lady Southampton, Mrs Howe and Mr Walpole; there are others I suppose but I've not heard who they are' (Lady Mary Coke, 'MS Journals,' 26 July 1783). 'Lord Duncannon and Lady Clermont were of the party at Gunnesbury which Mrs Howe says went off extremely well, they played two pools at commerce in the evening and the Prince of Wales took his leave at ten o'clock. Perhaps he would turn them all into ridicule the next day' (ibid. 29 July 1783). HW apparently did not go; see HW to Ps Amelia 2 April 1786.

17. Frances Cairnes Murray (ca 1733–1820), m. (1752) William Henry Fortescue, cr. (1770) Bn, (1776) Vct, and (1777) E. of Clermont.

18. Lady Clermont was a friend of Marie-Antoinette.

19. 'I give your Lordship a thousand thanks for your excellent venison, I never tasted I think any so fine. It was perfectly sweet, and as fat and tender as an ortalan. I would not suffer any body that was not the *ton* to partake of it; your friend Mr Walpole was one of the company, and I think I never saw him eat so heartily, nor seem more pleased; we wanted Lady Harcourt, your Lordship, and the rest of your party to make us completely happy.

'Drinking healths it seems is quite left off except in the City, where it would have been announced—"Come, here is to the founder"—"And the confounders"— if such a health had been proposed, I suppose Mr Walpole would have been under the table, except I had acted a city lady, and given it in fun, then nobody would have laughed more than himself' (Mrs Clive to Harcourt 12 Aug. 1783, *Harcourt Papers* viii. 173–4).

20. Jane Pope (1742–1818), actress at Drury Lane from 1756 until her retirement in 1808. Two letters from her to Harcourt, 1798, 1800, are in *Harcourt Papers* viii. 191–4.

them,[21] and comforts them much under poor Mrs Mestivyer's ramblings. Lady Jerningham[22] is as deplorable: she was here one evening and insisted that there was a woman in white in one of my trees!—alas! alas! if one does not force one's self to smile like Patience on a monument,[23] one should do nothing but meditate and sigh! I have mementos in every limb and every finger—but one has lived so long as I have with little reflection, if one wants to be pulled by one's own sleeve to be put in mind of our nothingness! My letter is just a transcript of my mind—now and then pains, then foolish plagues, spirits, trifles, fooleries, pity and gloom—but it shall wear its holiday clothes at Nuneham, if you let me come thither, as I think you will. Some people invite me and press me, and I am haughty and refuse; but at Nuneham I sue for admittance, and would fly thither, if my wings were not pinioned, and the feathers battered and ruffled like those of a Shrovetide-cock. Adieu! my dear Lord!

Your most devoted

H. WALPOLE

To Harcourt, Saturday, 30 August 1783

Printed from a photostat of the MS in Lord Harcourt's possession. First printed, Cunningham viii. 404–5, reprinted, Toynbee xiii. 49–50.
Endorsed by Harcourt: Honourable Hor. Walpole August 30, 1783.

Strawberry Hill, Aug. 30th 1783.

I HAVE been much afraid, my dear Lord, that I should be disappointed at last of the happiness of seeing Nuneham once more. I have been plagued with a rheumatic fever, which I began to think nothing would remove, and which destroyed my sleep and my spirits.[1] It is much lessened within these few days; and as old folks should seize Time by the hind-lock, leaving the fore one for the young, I am determined to wait on your Lordship on Wednesday

---

21. She left about the 12th (*Harcourt Papers* viii. 175).
22. Mary Plowden (d. 1785), m. (1733) Sir George Jerningham, 5th Bt.
23. *Twelfth Night* II. iv. 119.

1. 'I have a constant rheumatic fever every night, which ruins my sleep, though almost all I have lived upon for a century' (HW to Lady Ossory 27 Aug. 1783, OSSORY ii. 413).

or Thursday next, lest I should never have another opportunity, or should wait till I might say with Cardinal Wolsey, 'Father Abbot, I am come to lay my *bones* amongst you.'[2] Indeed I may always say that with propriety, for I bring nothing else but *bones,* and those aching.

I ought to thank your Lordship for the Catalogue of Nuneham,[3] but how can I thank you for what makes me blush? You have been pleased to record the silver pennies that I have presumed to offer at your shrine,[4] you that have loaded me with ingots! Fie on you!

Sir Edward[5] says I shall be mighty happy with meeting my Lord of Oxford,[6] who is often at Nuneham, for Lord H. is very good to him. I smiled—and fear it was the only mark of joy I could bring myself to hang out.

Another of my *loyal* blood,[7] who is with me, is to have Gov. Johnstone[8] and his wife[9] tomorrow, to show my house to them. I said, '*You* may show it to them to be sure if you please, but I promise you *I* will not; *I* will not see Governor Johnstone.'

A *friend*[10] of the Governor and the Bishop (though I think one does not hear so much of the—*friends*[11] lately) on a debate some days ago[12] whether convicts could not again be sent to Virginia, said 'Oh! I should like that; it is all the commerce I desire to have with America.'—No doubt, *commerce* with America was a terrible load, but we have happily got rid of it!—I need not sign my name; I believe your Lordship would guess the writer by any paragraph in this letter.

2. Spoken at Leicester Abbey, 26 Nov. 1530; Wolsey died there three days later.

3. *Nuneham-Courtenay,* 1783. HW (with Sir Joshua Reynolds) prepared the catalogue of pictures; see *ante* HW to Harcourt 17 Aug. 1773, n. 8.

4. Presents from HW mentioned are portraits of Lady Hervey 'in crayons, painted at Paris' (p. 5); of Philippe de Vendôme (p. 6; *ante* HW to Harcourt May 1781); and of Giles Bruges, 3d Lord Chandos (p. 11). HW's description of the park at Nuneham is also quoted on p. 2, and a portrait of him 'by Gogain, after Ramsay' is mentioned on p. 5.

5. Sir Edward Walpole.

6. Bishop John Butler. See *ante* HW to Harcourt Oct. 1779, n. 8, 2 Sept. 1780.

7. Probably Conway.

8. George Johnstone (1730–87), naval officer; gov. of West Florida, 1763; M.P.; supported the government in the American war and was given the command of a small squadron off the Portuguese coast with rank of commodore, 1779.

9. Deborah Charlotte Dee (d. 1813), m. 1 George Johnstone; m. 2 (1790) Charles Edmund Nugent, Capt., R.N., later Adm. (BERRY ii. 81, n. 18).

10. The King.

11. The 'King's friends.'

12. Not a Parliamentary debate, Parliament having been prorogued from 16 July to 9 Sept. (Cobbett, *Parl. Hist.* xxiii. 1122).

From HARCOURT, April 1784

Missing. Mentioned as an 'obliging note,' *post* 20 April 1784.

To HARCOURT, Tuesday 20 April 1784

Printed from a photostat of the MS in Lord Harcourt's possession. First printed, Cunningham viii. 470–1, reprinted, Toynbee xiii. 144–5.
Endorsed by Harcourt: Walpole April 20th 1784.

Berkeley Square, April 20, 1784.

I HAD a person with me on particular business, which prevented me from answering the honour of your Lordship's obliging note immediately, and thanking you for the sight of Prior's[1] picture, which is indeed an uncommonly fine head. I was prevented from waiting on your Lordship's ancestors, as I have been at Strawberry Hill and returned but yesterday late: and I do not pretend to dispute Sir Joshua's skill, as he must know better than I do the pencilling of different masters. At first sight I merely supposed the Prior was painted by old Dahl,[2] but I dare to say Sir Joshua is in the right.

If inclination were to govern me, I should have no occasion to give a promise of visiting Nuneham; but as in second infancy as well as in the first, one is in the power of one's parents; Father Age and Mother Gout do not allow me to enter into positive engagements, and I dare only pledge myself to do, with their good pleasure, what I shall certainly wish while I have the honour of being

Your Lordship's most obliged and
obedient humble servant,

HOR. WALPOLE

1. Matthew Prior (1664–1721), poet.
2. Michael Dahl (1656–1743), born in Stockholm, was a portrait painter in London after 1688. In the 1806 *Description of Nuneham-Courtenay*, p. 14, and the *New Oxford Guide*, 1785, p. 123, the painting is attributed, apparently correctly, to Dahl. It was once Prior's own property, then Lord Oxford's, who presented it to Harcourt. It is reproduced, etched by G. W. Rhead, as the frontispiece to *Selected Poems of Matthew Prior*, ed. Austin Dobson, 1889; the provenance is given in a note on the leaf preceding the plate. It was sold at the Harcourt Sale, Christie's, 11 June 1948, lot 102; and was bought by the National Portrait Gallery, where it was first attributed to Richardson, and then re-attributed to Dahl.

From HARCOURT, ?ca January–March 1785

Printed from MS now WSL. It was among the MSS left by Mrs Damer to Sir Wathen Waller, 1st Bt, and was sold at the first Waller Sale, Sotheby's, 5–6 Dec. 1921, lot 139, to Wells, who gave it to Thomas Conolly, from whom WSL acquired it in 1937. First printed, Toynbee, *Supp.* iii. 295.

Dated conjecturally, following Dr Toynbee, from the reference to HW's illness, mentioned in his letters of this period.

LORD Harcourt having been informed by Lord Waldegrave at Windsor that Mr Walpole still continued ill, will not trouble him with a visit. He is not ignorant of Mr Walpole's dislike to receiving presents, but as four paving-tiles cannot possibly come under that denomination, he requests a place for them in Mr Walpole's china-room. They were dug out of the foundation of the Abbey Church of Pipwell in Northamptonshire, the estate belonging to which Lord Harcourt is in possession of: the small piece of sculptured brass, likewise found there, he imagines was a part of the Abbot's cross.

From HARCOURT, ca Thursday 30 August 1787

A missing letter of appreciation for the maps presented by HW, mentioning the inscription and frieze in their honour, and enclosing Lady Craven's letter to Harcourt. See next letter.

To Harcourt, Saturday 1 September 1787

Printed from a photostat of the MS in Lord Harcourt's possession. First printed, Cunningham ix. 104–6, reprinted, Toynbee xiv. 14–16.

Harcourt, in a letter to Mason of ca Sept. 1787, writes of this interchange of letters: 'A most absurd, and I think the most impudent letter I ever saw, came from Lady Craven who, I flattered myself, had dropped my correspondence and at last discovered that she and I had never been even on the foot of intimate acquaintance, oblig[ing] me at her request to write to your Merchant [HW], which I did with the utmost civility, but with nothing more. This however produced an answer sparkling as champagne, and warm and cordial as Tokay' (MASON ii. 360–1).

Strawberry Hill, Sept. 1st 1787.

I HAVE just received the honour of your Lordship's letter with the enclosed *Apology* of Lady George Anne Belle Amie,[1] which I return, and which your Lordship charitably only calls *absurd*. You will preserve it, I hope, not merely as a chef d'œuvre, but as a proof that you have been enrolled in the new Académie de belles-lettres without your knowledge.

You are pleased, my Lord, to ask my advice how to avoid that honour. I wish I knew, being condemned to the same distinction![2] The only probable way, I think, may be by not answering the letter, and then the Foundress may punish you by expulsion. I cannot promise that my nostrum will answer: I have dropped her correspondence for still *graver* reasons—and yet she heaps coals of fire on my head. Indeed I do not see how your Lordship can answer her without resenting the freedom she takes so very improperly with Lady Harcourt.[3]

1. George Anne Bellamy (? 1731–88), actress. Her *Apology for the Life of George Anne Bellamy* appeared in six volumes in 1785. HW is alluding to Lady Craven's long letter of 12 Aug. 1787 to Lord Harcourt (printed in *Harcourt Papers* viii. 332–5), in which she tells of acting in a play. The letter begins, 'It is a long time since I have had the honour of hearing from you, but I think this letter will be well worthy of an answer, as it is nothing less than a proposal for you and Lady Harcourt to become members of a very honourable society, which, though in its infancy at present, may be-

come as useful and agreeable to absent *confrères* as it is pleasant to us. To speak plainer, I have established a literary society here, at the which presides the Margrave [of Ansbach] and all his *noblesse* that delight in the muses.'

2. 'I have little time to write, and, therefore, I beg you will inform Mr Walpole of this new academy, and tell him I shall insert his name near mine' (ibid. viii. 333).

3. The only reference to Lady Harcourt in the letter is that quoted in n. 1 above.

For my part I must submit, if she chooses to make me ridiculous. I have been so foolish as to be an author (of which I most heartily repent). It is not only exposing one's self, but giving others an opportunity to expose one; and therefore being already one of that general set of fools, it matters little if I am ranged in any particular class. I scratched my name out of the Society of Antiquaries[4]—and what was I the better? Lord Buchan chose me into his congregation of wiseacres[5] at Edinburgh!—nay, I have been called names; I have been styled in magazines *an ingenious* and *learned* author![6] now I am to be a Fellow of an Academy in Germany—I wish I do not live to be member of a beefsteak club in Rosemary Lane![7]—but these are idle distresses. It is very seriously that I am ashamed of the real honours that your Lordship has showered upon me, and of which I am so very unworthy! I wish I could command any words that would distinguish real from affected modesty; yet when I am seventy years of age, surely I may be believed to speak truth. I have spoken too much in my life, and would not willingly when I am dropping to earth, assume a new character. Sincerely, my Lord, I blush to come to Nuneham to behold compliments to myself—nay, should prefer the most palpable grimace of modesty to impudent vanity—still I feel that it would wear the air of impertinent ingratitude, if I refused to obey your Lordship's commands. I shall go to Park Place soon, and will thence send over to know whether my visit would be inconvenient,—and yet, if there is veracity in man, I do heartily wish the circumstances of the frieze were effaced. I am happy that the tapestry[8] pleased your Lordship enough to bestow a room on it—

4. In 1772; see 'Short Notes,' GRAY i. 47.

5. The Society of Antiquaries of Scotland. See HW to Buchan 10 Feb. 1781 (DALRYMPLE 150–1) and to Mason 9 Feb. 1781 (MASON ii. 107).

6. An instance is the review of HW's *Historic Doubts* in the *Political Register*, March 1768, which described it as 'a very learned and ingenious performance' (ii. 185).

7. I.e., a literary club meeting in a low quarter of the city.

8. Tapestry maps bought by HW at the Sheldon sale in 1781, and presented to Lord Harcourt, who built a special room for them in 1787. HW's arms appeared in the frieze of the room. See CHATTERTON 195, n. 2, and *Harcourt*

Papers iii. 284–5. The maps which are described in Gough's *British Topography*, 1780, ii. 309–10, now belong to the Yorkshire Philosophical Society. In HW's annotated copy of his *Des. of SH*, 1774 (now WSL, formerly in the Spencer Collection, New York Public Library), HW added to p. 7: 'A two-leafed fire-screen composed of part of a map of England in tapestry, being a piece of the first manufacture of that kind made in this country. It came from Mr Sheldon's at Weston in Warwickshire, whose ancestor imported the art. The rest of the original hangings were purchased by Mr H. W. and given by him to the second Earl of Harcourt, and are now at Nuneham in Oxfordshire.'

but surely so trifling and cheap a present,[9] and so inadequate to the many valuable ones I have received from your Lordship, could in no light merit an inscription! and to a name so insignificant as mine! —and which will every day grow more obscure, or be remembered only by my follies—and then, depend upon it, your Lordship will wish you had taken my advice, and blotted out your legend. Consequently I infinitely prefer doing justice on myself, to occasioning your Lordship being reproached with misplacing your favour. I have the honour to be with great respect, my Lord,

Your Lordship's most obedient humble servant,

HOR. WALPOLE

To HARCOURT, ca September 1787

Missing. Mentioned by Harcourt to Mason ca Sept. 1787 as 'a short note, of which every other word was *honour* and *Lordship,* and without a *dear* being tacked to the title of *Lord,* announcing his approaching arrival near Henley and his intention of paying his *respects* at Nuneham' (MASON ii. 361).

To HARCOURT, ca September 1787 *bis*

Missing. Mentioned by Harcourt to Mason ca Sept. 1787 as a 'note of inquiry after Lady H. who had a cold, still more distant and formal than the former one, and as if it had been addressed to an acquaintance of yesterday' (MASON ii. 361).

9. HW paid £30 for the maps (MS cited Toynbee, *Supp.* ii. 176).

To Harcourt, Saturday ?5 June 1790

Printed from a photostat of the MS in Lord Harcourt's possession. First printed, Cunningham ix. 106 (as Sept. 1787), reprinted, Toynbee xv. 444 (as n.d.).

Dated conjecturally by the endorsement and the reference to Westminster Hall.

Endorsed by ?Harcourt: June 1790.

Saturday night.

My good Lord,

MAY I take the liberty of asking a favour of you, provided you will refuse without the least difficulty? it is to beg a ticket for Westminster Hall on Monday next[1]—not for myself, the Lord knows, who go into no crowds,[2] but for a young lady[3] for whom I am much interested. Most probably your Lordship's tickets are all engaged, but I could not refuse to solicit for her, and I flatter myself your Lordship will excuse it with your usual indulgence to

Your Lordship's most obedient humble servant,

HOR. WALPOLE

1. On Monday 7 June in Westminster Hall, Fox began his summary of the evidence on the charge against Warren Hastings (*Daily Adv.* 9 June 1790). On Wednesday 9 June the 'trial was . . . adjourned to the first Tuesday in the next session of Parliament' (ibid. 10 June 1790).

2. 'I have written very bad English for I have said the Lord goes into no crowds, which though divines say so, I hope is not true' (HW's note).

3. Perhaps Mary or Agnes Berry. Mary Berry wrote to HW 'Saturday afternoon' (conjecturally dated 18 April 1789) about tickets to the trial (BERRY i. 9–10).

To Harcourt, Thursday 4 October 1792

Printed from a photostat of the MS in Lord Harcourt's possession. First printed, Cunningham ix. 392–3, reprinted, Toynbee xv. 152–3.
Endorsed by ?Harcourt: Earl of Orford 1792.

Strawberry Hill, Oct. 4, 1792.

My dear Lord,

IF I am taking too great a liberty, I trust your Lordship will forgive it, as I flatter myself its object will contribute to your satisfaction, since its consequence will be doing—I will not say honour, but, justice to Nuneham.

Mr Farrington[1] the painter (who married a cousin[2] of mine) is, as your Lordship already knows, engaged on making drawings for a superb set of views on the course of the Thames.[3] Nuneham being one of his loveliest features, it would be pity that you yourself, my Lord, should not point out and preside over what he shall execute, and therefore I hope I do not ask too much, my Lord, in begging your patronage for him.

I do not know how soon his progress will allow him to arrive at Nuneham, but I know his purpose is to reach it in this, the painter's month, and if four months of deluge bid one expect four weeks of good weather, he may see Nuneham in all its autumnal charms— a month sooner he could only have painted pictures for Noah's new house after the flood. I have the honour to be,

My Lord, your Lordship's most obedient humble servant,

ORFORD

1. Joseph Farington (1747–1821), painter and diarist.

2. Susan Hamond (d. 1800), related to HW through both her father and her mother; see DALRYMPLE 240, n. 2.

3. Published by Boydell 1794–6 in two volumes, *An History of the Principal Rivers of Great Britain: . . . River Thames* with text by William Combe. Farington's views of Stanton Harcourt and Nuneham appear in vol. i. pp. 66 and 190. His view of SH is the frontispiece to vol. ii. HW's copy is Hazen, *Cat. of HW's Lib.*, No. 3566.

From Harcourt, ca Monday 6 January 1794

A missing letter, enclosing Haggitt's compliments, answered in the next letter.

To Harcourt, Tuesday 7 January 1794

Printed from a photostat of the MS in Lord Harcourt's possession. First printed, Cunningham ix. 430–1, reprinted, Toynbee xv. 279–80.

Berkeley Square, January 7th 1794.

My dear Lord,

I WISH I knew how to distinguish my gratitude to your Lordship from vanity, but warm as the former is, you must allow me to say that the latter has not digestion strong enough to swallow the excessive compliments Mr Hagget[1] has paid to my tragedy, which besides the gross fault in choosing such a subject, has many defects that deserve his censure. His too great partiality deprives me of the pleasure of doing full justice to his *Villeroi*,[2] as that justice would in me be supposed to flow from the prejudice of self-love—yet it would be too unjust to the author not to confess his great merit and abilities both in the construction and execution, and not to own how powerfully the interest rises the farther the plan is carried.

I am sorry for many reasons that it is not to be performed, both for the sake of the author and the public, though I see reasons why neither the managers might choose to venture it, nor the Chamberlain's office; and I am more sorry to think that the greater the author's merit, the more bitter enemies he would raise to himself— even in this country—to its shame! One or two passages I will take the liberty of saying I wish had been omitted, as the accusations urged by the Convention against the late King, for the breach of an

1. Probably the Rev. Francis Haggitt (1759–1825), D.D.; rector of Nuneham, 1786; chaplain to George III (Venn, *Alumni Cantab.*); though David Erskine Baker, Isaac Reed, and Stephen Jones, *Biographia Dramatica*, 1812, iii. 473, attribute *The Count de Villeroi* to the Rev. John Haggitt (ca 1762–1843), vicar of Madingley, Cambs, 1790–1804 (Venn, *Alumni Cantab*).

2. *The Count de Villeroi; or, the Fate of Patriotism*, 1794. It deals with the period of the French Revolution. HW's copy, now wsl, is Hazen, *Cat. of HW's Lib.*, No. 1810:55.

oath he had been forced to take to save his life, when they had kept no oath taken to him; and especially the two last lines put into the mouth of the Queen in page 14.[3] As her murderers could not prove a speck in her whole character, the most pure ever demonstrated by the longest and most rigid ordeal ever sustained by a mortal, she herself, as a mortal, might to God have accused herself of past errors, but I think no one else has a right to tax her with errors, which no man now can substantiate.

Mr Haggett I am sure will forgive my saying what truth compels me to hint, and I hope he will be assured of my respect and esteem, and your Lordship cannot doubt my being

> Your Lordship's most obliged and most
> obedient humble servant,

> ORFORD

PS. I cannot say how sensible I am of the great honour Lady Harcourt did me in having the goodness to call on me when I was gone to wait on her and your Lordship.

From HARCOURT, ca June 1795

Printed from MS now WSL. It was among the MSS left by Mrs Damer to Sir Wathen Waller, 1st Bt, and was sold at the first Waller Sale, Sotheby's, 5–6 Dec. 1921 to Wells, who gave it to Thomas Conolly from whom WSL acquired it in 1937. First printed, Toynbee, *Supp.* ii. 187.

Dated by the reference to the Queen's approaching visit to SH, 3 July 1795. *Address:* To the Earl of Orford.

My dear Lord,

I YESTERDAY waited upon the Queen, meaning to talk to H. M. upon the subject of her intended visit to Strawberry Hill,[1] but not finding her at home, I wrote at the Queen's house, and left for

3. 'May my hard fate atone my errors past,
And my wished death my mangled country heal!'

1. The Queen's letter on her visit to Lord Harcourt, is in *Harcourt Papers* vi. 46–7. She said in part, 'Independent of all the fine things which are to be seen at Strawberry Hill, the company of the host is what we one and all were the most pleased with; and I should myself

her, a long letter explanatory of your Lordship's wishes of having a week's previous notice of the said visit, that Mrs Damer might be engaged to assist your Lordship in showing the numberless interesting and beautiful curiosities with which that unrivalled repository abounds, and I moreover added, that though your Lordship wished to show her Majesty every possible mark of respect, it would be highly inconvenient, not to say dangerous, to you to wear a sword—in short, I think I said everything your Lordship could have wished me to say, but I will this morning have the honour of communicating your note[2] to the Queen, in which you express your own wishes and sentiments far better than I can pretend to express them for you.

I have the honour to be your Lordship's faithful
and *repeatedly* obliged servant,

HARCOURT

have enjoyed his presence still more, had I not continually been thinking of the fatigue our visit made him suffer. I desired and entreated him to sit down, but in vain' (*Harcourt Papers* vi. 46). See HW to Conway 2 July 1795. **Princess**

Elizabeth wrote to Harcourt, 5 July 1795 (*Letters of Princess Elizabeth of England,* ed. P. C. Yorke, 1898, p. 35): 'I can never thank you enough for having persuaded Mama to go to Strawberry Hill.'

2. Missing.

N.Dance Pinx.   J.Jackson, R.A.Del.   H.Meyer, Sculp.

GEORGE HARDINGE, Esq.   M.A. F.R.S. AND F.S.A.

Senior Justice of the Counties of   Brecon, Glamorgan, & Radnor.

Born June 22,1744: Died April 26,1816.

Published by J.Nichols & C.º March 7.1818.

THE CORRESPONDENCE
WITH GEORGE
HARDINGE

From HARDINGE,[1] Monday 16 April 1770

Printed from Nichols, *Lit. Illus.* iii. 177.

Inner Temple, Monday, April 16, 1770.

MR Hardinge presents his most respectful compliments to Mr Walpole. If Mr Walpole should have it in his power to oblige Mr Hardinge with a ticket of leave to ride through St James's Park by speaking a word to my Lord Orford,[2] it will be a serious obligation to Mr Hardinge; who flatters himself that Mr Walpole will do him the justice to believe that he does not solicit this privilege for the sake of the idle distinction that is annexed to it, but as a matter of real convenience. The truth is, that Mr Hardinge is obliged perpetually to ride to Kingston[3] upon business; and, in his way, to bump it upon the stones for upwards of two miles between the Temple and Hyde Park Corner;[4] so that such a favour is particularly desirable to him.—However, if the request should strike Mr Walpole as an improper one, he will treat it as it deserves; or, if he should not choose to lend *his* recommendation to it, Mr Hardinge hopes to be forgiven the freedom he has taken in applying; which nothing could have tempted him to do, but his experience of the flattering and kind notice Mr Walpole has honoured him with.

1. George Hardinge (1743–1816), M.P. Old Sarum 1784–1802; K.C. 1782; secretary of commissions to Lord Chancellor Camden 1766–70; commissioner of bankruptcy 1771–82; solicitor-general to the Queen 1782–94; attorney-general 1794–1816.

2. HW's nephew, the 3d E. of Orford, was Ranger and Keeper of St James's and Hyde Parks, 1763.

3. George Hardinge's branch of the Hardinge family had been settled at the manor of Canbury, including part of the town of Kingston-upon-Thames, since 1671 (W. D. Biden, *History . . . of . . . Kingston*, Kingston, 1852, p. 100).

4. From Hyde Park Corner, Hardinge presumably went through Knightsbridge to Fulham Road, down it to Putney Bridge, where he could cross the Thames, and then down Kingston Hill to Kingston itself. To be able to go through St James's Park, to the southeast of Hyde Park Corner, would be a considerable saving in distance.

From HARDINGE, Friday 20 April 1770

Printed from Nichols, *Lit. Illus.* iii. 177.

Inner Temple, April 20, 1770.

MR Hardinge is infinitely thankful to Mr Walpole for the service[1] that he has done him in so engaging a manner; a circumstance that always accompanies and heightens the good nature of Mr Walpole. The same elegance of manner that has, if possible, added to the credit of Mr Walpole's ingenuity as a writer seems to extend itself to his *friendship*—or, if that is too bold a word for Mr Hardinge upon this occasion, to his favour and obliging condescension.

From HARDINGE, ca 1771

Printed from Nichols, *Lit. Illus.* iii. 177–8, where it is dated 1771, and begins with asterisks and the explanation: 'This letter is imperfect.'

. . . the world to write well. Let me add the article of mere *style*, upon which a great deal depends; for I can by no means agree that words

Provisam rem non invita sequuntur.[1]

An Essay[2] of this kind requires great *clearness* and *precision* of language, with a certain degree of *energy*, neither too *careless*, nor too *prim*; too *simple*, nor too much *adorned*, etc.: nor is the outline of *method* a trifling circumstance; in which, by the way, there never was my Lord Mansfield's equal.—Let the call upon him be ever so abrupt and sudden, his mind immediately comprehends the whole subject, he disposes all his materials in order, and the most judicious too that could have been catered for his use by others after a month's

1. Apparently HW secured the ticket which Hardinge needed to be able to go through St James's Park.

———

1. Properly 'sequentur': 'Verbaque provisam rem non invita sequentur' ('Words spontaneously accompany the well-con-

ceived subject') (Horace, *Ars poetica* 311).
2. Hardinge's *Enquiry into the Competency and Duties of Juries in the Case of a Public Libel*, never published; the introduction alone survived (George Hardinge, *Miscellaneous Works*, 1818, i. p. xiv).

application; and this talent has great charms—it fascinates the hearer, and often passes for sound reason when it is the vehicle of arrant sophistry.

To leave the great man, and resume the little one. I have learnt the useful virtue of diffidence, and without disgrace, by compelling my own acknowledgment of the *quid ferre recusent*.[3] I have at the same time stole myself into a habit of industry, which is not amiss to correct my natural idleness—and I have conciliated your good opinion by attempting an imitation of that liberality of sentiment which accompanies what I never shall aspire to (though I am saucy enough to relish it)—an original vein of genius and wit in the writings of Mr Walpole. Who therefore has, in this view of things, more ground of respectable vanity, than, dear Sir,

Your much honoured, and most affectionate
friend and servant,

G. HARDINGE

PS. It was a favourite subject of Lord Chancellor Hardwicke's,[4] and my Lord Camden[5] has a very high opinion of it; so that I have not much fear of its reception, though it is not an interesting or amusing subject. I shall, at all events, beg to consult your friendship, which I must hope you will not refuse to me.

G. H.

3. 'Quid ferre recusent, / quid valeant umeri' ('What your strength declines, and what it is able to support') (Horace, *Ars poetica* 39).

4. Lord Hardwicke (*ante* HW to Chute 29 Sept. 1755), was involved in some of the most interesting cases of libel in the first half of the century; he was attorney-general in the cases of Rex vs. Edmund Curll (1727) for obscene libel; Rex vs. Thomas Woolston (1725, 1729) for blasphemy; Rex vs. Richard Francklin, publisher of *The Craftsman* (1731); he was in the House of Lords when Paul Whitehead was summoned before it for libel in his poem *Manners* (1739). Hardwicke's views were moderate though conservative.

5. Lord Camden (*ante* HW to Strafford 4 Oct. 1766, n. 3) was Hardinge's uncle.

One of his libel cases was his defence of William Owen, publisher of *The Case of the Hon. Alexander Murray*, 1751, when (6 July 1752) he maintained the then novel principle of the competency of juries to decide the entire question, law (whether or not there was any libel) as well as fact (whether or not something was published); the defendant was acquitted. As attorney-general, in 1758 he re-asserted this principle in prosecuting John Shebbeare for political libel. At the time of this letter, Camden was virtually the only distinguished man of law to hold this point of view, which he vainly tried to have made into law. He lived to see his principle adopted by Parliament in 1792, however.

To HARDINGE, ca April 1771

Missing. Answered in the following letter.

From HARDINGE, Tuesday 16 April 1771

Printed from Nichols, *Lit. Illus.* iii. 178.

Inner Temple, Tuesday, April 16, 1771.

Dear Sir,

YOUR very good-humoured notice and forgiveness of my bold request has obliged me extremely. I shall certainly take the first opportunity of stealing *half an hour of your frail life*[1] in a little chat, and will be sure to avail myself of your kind information as to the proper days and hours. I find you have construed my words, *deserved the hand of Lord Somers*,[2] in a different sense from that which I meant to annex to them: for you seem to collect that my Lord Somers *writ* upon this topic which I have taken up—whereas I only meant to say that he *might have* writ upon it without letting himself down, the point being of the greatest constitutional moment, though it passes through a dry medium of law reasoning and science. In short, it is an inquiry into the *competency* and *duty* of juries in the case of a public libel, introduced by a more general investigation of their *competency* and *duty* wherever *law* and *fact* are comprised in the general issue. I have been exhorted by some improvident friends to publish it, but against this rash step I am almost determined;[3] however, I shall get some copies of it printed, and will certainly present one to you, if you will deign to give it a reading.

I am, dear Sir, with the truest respect,

Your most obedient servant,

G. HARDINGE

1. Probably an echo of HW's missing letter.
2. John Somers (1651–1716), cr. (1697) Bn Somers; lord chancellor 1692–1700.
3. Hardinge may well have been de-

terred by the number of publications on the same subject which had already appeared. The libel cases arising from the printing and publishing (Rex vs. Henry Sampson Woodfall) and the reprinting

From Hardinge, Tuesday 7 May 1771

Printed from Nichols, *Lit. Illus.* iii. 178–9.

Inner Temple, Tuesday, May 7, 1771.

Dear Sir,

MANY and many after-thoughts have made such havoc in my youthful essay, that I cannot bring it yet awhile into anything like a system. However, the part I have sent you being detached from the rest, and less dry than what I am now at work upon, takes the liberty of submitting itself to the honour of your friendly criticism. To say the truth, I am not without a faint hope that, in return for my volunteer exhibition of this paltry work *in puris naturalibus*,[1] you will admit me now and then to a peep at some beautiful essay of your own; which, by the way, reminds me of Homer's arch hero,[2] who gave a suit of honest brass armour—and took one of gold in exchange. When shall I drop in upon you? Breakfast hours are the most convenient to me; but any time that may suit you best will supersede every other engagement of mine (*a fee* only excepted). Believe me, dear Sir, your most affectionate and obliged servant,

G. Hardinge

and republishing of Junius's letter to the King (Rex vs. John Almon and Rex vs. John Miller), and from the election contest of the Hon. George Onslow and the Rev. John Horne (later Horne Tooke) in Onslow vs Horne, had made the subject a much-discussed one. For example the GM 1770 xl. 37, 180, 304–7, 312–4, 364–7, 515–9, 609–11, 626, mentions libel and the function of juries. See T. H. Bowyer, *Bibliographical Examination of . . . Junius,* 1957, p. xvii.

———

1. 'In a state of nudity.'
2. Diomede, who gives a suit of armour worth nine oxen to young Glaucus in exchange for one worth a hundred oxen, in Book VI of the *Iliad*.

From HARDINGE, Wednesday 12 June 1771

Printed from MS now WSL; previously printed, Nichols, *Lit. Illus.* iii. 179, where the date of the year is supplied. Placed ca 1860 in an album by the Rev. Mr Booker; sold Sotheby's 12 April 1938 to Colbeck Radford & Co., who sold it, 1938, to WSL.

Address: The Honourable Horace Walpole Arlington Street St James's.
Postmarks: 12 IV. 13 IV. 10 o'clock IV.
In another hand: Put into the G. P. [General Post] without a Penny. C. D.
Endorsed (by Nichols): June 12.

Inner Temple, June 12.

Dear Sir,

AS I am drawing near to the conclusion of my little work, and as I have no copy of the part which I took the liberty of sending to you, I shall be obliged to you if you will be kind enough to return it. I am not without a very flattering hope to be the guest of Mr Walpole at Strawberry Hill some day this summer: but I tell you this in confidence.—It must not go any further.—Do let *him* know that I am vain enough to dream of such a distinction.

I beg you'll believe me, with the highest respect and esteem,

Dear Sir, yours etc.

G. HARDINGE

To HARDINGE, ca June 1771

Missing. Answered in the following letter.

From HARDINGE, ca Friday 21 June 1771

Printed from Nichols, *Lit. Illus.* iii. 179–80, where the date of year only is supplied.

June.

L ong as my letters are, I am not so fond of writing as you, my dear Sir, affect to believe. Yours have so agreeable and original a cast, that I would expose mine even more than you suffer me to do, for the sake of extorting from an arrant miser a little of his pelf in such valuable articles. But I will save you from the penance of any further correspondence, at least for a time, on the condition that you will permit me to make you a visit, which I have long desired, at Strawberry Hill. As to the *time,* I leave it respectfully to your own leisure, and your own humour for such *frolics;* but I must *command* you to be as quick in your invitation as the *caprice of our tempers* may appear to require. I will not even decide beforehand how soon I may be tired of you. But modesty compels me to limit your cordiality for me to one year at the farthest, commencing at the date of these presents. How ingratiating is your polite reproof to me on the subject of confining our intercourse to the ceremonious medium of the post office! The real truth is, that I am afraid equally of intruding upon you in letters and in person; but in the former case I avoid being eye-witness to your coldness, the just punishment of my forwardness.

If Dalrymple's book[1] had no other fault but *Scoto-Anglicism,* I could read it with a tithe of my disgust. May I ask what is to be collected from the whole of that work (supposing it impartial and faithful)—that, in the most critically affecting situation of politics which this country ever saw, neither side of the two leading parties produced a single public man who did not deserve to be hanged? A comfortable hearing this for us young adventurers!—*pour encourager les autres!* as Voltaire said with a most cruelly-just sarcasm, of Byng's fate.[2] I cannot persuade myself that the *liberality* (as Macaronis may call it) of exposing in the broad glare of daylight the

1. Sir John Dalrymple, afterwards Dalrymple-Hamilton-Macgill (1726–1810), 4th Bt 1771; author of *Memoirs of Great Britain and Ireland. From the Dissolution of the last Parliament of Charles II until* the *Sea-Battle off La Hogue,* 3 vols., 1771. HW's copy is Hazen, *Cat. of HW's Lib.* No. 3186.

2. The quotation is from *Candide* (1759), Chapter 23, and reads: 'mais

corrupt hearts, and the duplicity of great and favourite characters, be the liberality of a good *citizen,* or of a benevolent *man.* As to myself, base and abject as the times are, I could as readily deliver up the *sexual difference,* as the persuasion (however ludicrous it may sound) that a Patriot is a creature that has been forthcoming, and has walked upon two legs in this very island, *since the flood—* nay, that the race (though a good deal thinned) is not extinct amongst us to this day. If this creed be an erroneous one, I shall cry out, as Tully did, on the soul's immortality, *'libenter erro, nec mihi hunc errorem dum vivo extorqueri velim.'*[3] And yet, whether *'thou too, my Cobham,'* etc.[4] is not *outré* and extravagant, is matter of some doubt. Upon the death-bed indeed of *Epaminondas,*[5] *Adolphus,*[6] or *General Wolfe,*[7] one *may* conceive this heroism; but the *enthusiasm* of *action* and *pride,* though of the noblest birth, were great helps to the real virtue of those immortal men. As to myself (who am in my own estimate a patriot of the first water), I do in my conscience believe that I should not even think of the liberty of the subject, when the physician had pronounced his anathema— nay, I very much fear that, in my best health and vigour, I shall feel more anxious love towards what *Milton* calls the *charities* of a domestic circle,[8] than for the whole kingdom of England—but of this you will be so ashamed in a correspondent of yours, that I doubt you will soon disown

G. HARDINGE

dans ce pays-ci [i.e., Britain] il est bon de tuer de temps en temps un amiral pour encourager les autres.'

3. Cicero, *Cato Major de Senectute,* xxiii. 85, slightly misquoted from: 'Libenter erro nec mihi hunc errorem, quo delector, dum vivo, extorqueri volo' 'I gladly err, and I do not want this error, by which I am pleased, to be extorted from me.'

4. 'And you, brave Cobham! to the latest breath, / Shall feel your ruling passion strong in death' (Pope, *Moral Essays,* Epistle 1, ll. 262–3).

5. Epaminondas (ca 411–362 B.C.), Theban general, killed at the battle of Mantinea. He is said by Nepos to have asked, as he was dying, who had won the day; when told the Thebans, he said, 'I have lived long enough for I die unconquered.'

6. Gustavus Adolphus (Gustav II Adolf) (1594–1632), K. of Sweden 1611–32, was credited (incorrectly) by legend with having composed the hymn, 'Versage nicht, du Häuflein klein,' just before going into the battle of Lützen in which he lost his life (Nils Ahnlund, *Gustav Adolf the Great,* Princeton, 1940, pp. 144–5).

7. Whose death at Quebec, 1759, was still fresh in English memories.

8. An allusion to *Paradise Lost,* iv. 753– 7, esp. 756–7:

By thee adulterous lust was driv'n from
    men
Among the bestial herds to range, by thee
Founded in Reason, Loyal, Just and Pure,
Relations dear, and all the Charities
Of Father, Son, and Brother first were
    known.

From HARDINGE, Tuesday 18 February 1772

Printed from Nichols, *Lit. Illus.* iii. 180–1.

Temple, Feb. 18, 1772.

My dear Sir,

HOW hard it is upon me, who have admired your genius and loved your benevolence 'from the time whereof the memory of *my good taste* runneth not to the contrary,'[1] that a certain wicked disparity of age, fortune, rank, and, above all, *abilities* and *worth,* should keep me at such a distance, and oblige me to rouse your notice by the powers of teasing and sheer intrusion! Today,[2] 'Sweet Sir, a *key* or *ticket* for my horse in St James's Park.' Tomorrow, 'Could you but enable me to play the fool at a masquerade!'[3] The next day, 'Enter Mr Hardinge as an author, full of that character's affected humility:'—'The subject[4] is, to be sure, interesting, worthy of Lord Somers;—but *my* faint efforts tremble, till you condescend to undergo the penance of reading me, or, which is the same thing, to commend me unread, etc.' And all this trick upon trick, finesse upon finesse, to get little peeps at you, either in Arlington Street, or at least upon paper! But, alas! all my wits of the *sponging* sort are now bankrupt, unless you will accept of this *pretty sonnet* forsooth! writ in the Bœotian[5] atmosphere of Chancery Lane! But why is Mr Walpole, of all men living, to be the patron of this quaint pleader-like Muse? Dear Sir! and cannot you really, with your discernment, catch the grounds of this application? Well, if I must explain and explain, and lay open the plot (like Mr Bayes)[6]—marry, this it is: here is *Friendship* and *Shakespeare,* and a *Dulcinea[7] of nine years*

1. Sir William Blackstone (1723–80), *Commentaries,* Vol. I, Book I, Chap. XVIII, §473: 'Time whereof the memory of man runneth not to the contrary.'

2. See *ante* Hardinge to HW 16 and 20 April 1770.

3. This section of the correspondence is missing, but HW kept a trunk of costumes for masquerades, which Hardinge may have wanted to dip into, for borrowed finery (MANN vii. 193).

4. Hardinge's essay on juries, discussed *ante* in his letters to HW of 1771.

5. Bœotia was a district of ancient Greece proverbial for the dullness and stupidity of its inhabitants (see OED).

6. A character (ridiculing Dryden) in *The Rehearsal* (1672) by George Villiers (1628–87), 2d D. of Buckingham 1628. Bayes brings two friends to a rehearsal of his play, and explains everything to them as it progresses.

7. The name of Don Quixote's sweetheart, which had only recently, according to the OED, been introduced into English as a synonym for *mistress* or *sweetheart.*

old.[8] Well, as to *friendship* now, in the first place; why I would rather have *you my friend* than his Majesty's First Commissioner of the Treasury.[9] This, you see, makes a connection between *you* and the poem. To proceed: *Shakespeare!* why there too! how delicate a thought! Have not you vindicated *Shakespeare* from Voltaire?[10] As to the *lady,* she is the cream of the jest in point of application; for, *as you* admire and have writ sonnets (if the truth were known) to a prodigy in petticoats,[11] over whose animating genius churlish Time has no effect, *so* it is proper that you should be *countenanced* in this extraordinary attachment, by as extraordinary a one of *mine* to a female who disdains receiving any obligations from Time in the maturity of her genius; but has the same force of invention, the same accuracy and elegance of taste, the same wit and sentiment, at nine years old, in her *drawings* and *conversation,* which a travelled peer of thirty has, or thinks he has, in the design of his *vis-à-vis,*[12] or his flirting with a sentimental demirep of quality in a side-box at the Opera. Having brought the simile, through as long a sentence as any of Boccace's or Clarendon's, to a *well-turned* period, I shall only remind you of a case in point, as we lawyers term it, and conclude. *As* Sampson *lost* his strength by cutting off his *hair, so* I *recover* mine by taking Hampstead's *air.* Believe me, dear Sir,

Yours most affectionately,

G. HARDINGE

8. This sonnet is not in Hardinge's *Miscellaneous Works,* 1816, though there is one 'On a Beautiful Girl, Aged Fourteen, and a Milkmaid' (ii. 13).

9. Lord North, the prime minister.

10. In the Preface to the second edition of *The Castle of Otranto,* 1765, pp. viii–xv. See also *Notes by Horace Walpole on Several Characters of Shakespeare* (Miscellaneous Antiquities No. 16, ed. W. S. Lewis, Farmington, Conn., 1940), and HW's correspondence with Voltaire, 1768.

11. 'Mme du Deffand' (note in Nichols, *Lit. Illus.*). HW's verses on her, dated 1766, begin 'Where do Wit and Memory dwell?' (DU DEFFAND vi. 55–6). Hardinge's description, however, would better suit HW's verses on the Duchess of Queensberry (MANN vii. 299).

12. A light carriage (ibid. viii. 260, n. 4).

From Hardinge, Saturday 18 April 1772

Printed from Nichols, *Lit. Illus.* iii. 181, where the date of the year is supplied.

Temple, April 18.

Dear Sir,

THANK you, dear Sir, for your friendly and cheering goodness to me. I have always found *you* the same;—your partialities for me uniform, and your zeal in the good old cause unimpaired by the Soame Jenyns[1] of the day, who has been *legion* for many years past. Unless the ministers *choose* to be idiots, and pull caps at the cabinet for *the amusement and spirit of the conflict,* they are built for ages— they have character, wisdom, and, above all, the virtue of necessity, urging them to rouse the lion, but strangle the serpent. My share in this great national redress at present is that of good wishes alone. The time, I hope, will come, in which I may prove that, whatever my situation may be, I cannot act in public a part that looks to anything *but* the public—or make any thing but the public approbation my conduct the object of it; an approbation which is always correct and honourable if it is but *free.*

I am, dear Sir,

Yours ever most affectionately,

G. Hardinge

To Hardinge, ca April 1772

Missing. Answered in the following letter.

1. Soame Jenyns (1704–87), M.P., 1741–80; poet and heterodox theologian.

From Hardinge, Monday 4 May 1772

Printed from Nichols, *Lit. Illus.* iii. 181–3.

Inner Temple, Monday, May 4, 1772.

HOW can I thank you enough, my dear Sir, for your very affect-ing letter! As to my *warmth,* I neither disown it, nor am angry with its agreeable *witchcraft.* But if I am at all fascinated by such a *quotidianus homo*[1] as Mr. Walpole, it is by that part of him which bears me out in the highest degree of enthusiasm. Where then is the fascination? A subtle paradox this! And pray what *is* the source of my attachment to *these grey hairs,* to this *vox Cygnea*[2] of *past fifty-four?* I should insult and affront you if I were to hint at *your* vivac-ity, elegance, wit, etc. etc. This would be like Charles Townshend's arch invective against the *wicked acuteness*[3] of the present Master of the Rolls,[4] or my Lord Chatham's grave panegyric upon *the en-lightened soul of Sir John Philips.*[5] But I *may,* without flattery, say a word of your benevolence and worth—for these qualities are such a drug, that one meets with them at every turn, and one's familiarity with them makes it impossible for the merest novice to be cheated in them. Besides, to be serious, Providence has peculiarly shown its wisdom in the large characters of selfishness. He that runs may read —a coward may pass for a brave man, a weak man for a wise one; but a selfish man, by the *felo-de-se* control of his vice at perpetual enmity with his will, is *generous* in this, that he gives you fair notice of that *little* speck in his character—let him bow short or long, play the rustic or the courtier, it is all one—*fœnum habet in cornu, longe fuge:*[6] just as one sees a principled and thorough Tory Toryize

1. HW had apparently disparaged him-self as a 'common man.'
2. 'Swan's voice.'
3. During the debates over Wilkes in 1764, Sewell admitted that he had done some thinking in bed before arising on the morning on which he was speaking; Townshend regretted that Sewell did not have the same power under his wig that he had under his nightcap. The witticism is mentioned in [Archer Polson], *Law and Lawyers,* 1841, ii. 15–16, and in the DNB *sub* Sir Thomas Sewell.

4. Sir Thomas Sewell (ca 1710–84), M.P.; Kt 1764; Master of the Rolls 1764–84.
5. HW's distant cousin, Sir John Phi-lipps (1700–64), Bt, of Picton Castle, Pem-brokeshire, M.P. 1741–7, 1754–64, a Tory and formerly a Jacobite. Chatham's 'pane-gyric' was probably sarcastic.
6. Horace, *Satires,* I. iv. 34: 'He has hay on his horns [a legal warning that a bull was either mischievous or angry; give him a wide berth].' The figure of speech is applied to a poet by Horace.

throughout, in all the relative duties—a Tory parent, a Tory husband, a Tory landlord, etc. etc.

I have a great mind to attempt irony no more; for you have disgraced me. A sportive expression of mine was either dull enough or outraged enough to pass with you for an attack in sober sadness. *Your* letters *cold!* which are the most animated I ever saw—*your* expressions of good-will and friendship to me *cold* forsooth! which flatter me far beyond my warmest and vainest hopes.

You have equally disgraced me in regard to *the Patriot.*[7] I with you abhor *the false one;* but where the object is, upon the whole, chaste and sacred, like Somers and King William,[8] I cannot relish those violent lovers of historical truth who explore the faint but real blemishes of such characters, and disclose them busily to *the herd.* It is no answer to say that the main character will escape, nay brighten the more, when the attack is compelled to brood over immaterial defects. With you, and I hope with me, such a corollary is the natural one—but the herd, who are the most important observers, revolt at such inequalities; they are piqued at the loss of their hero, and yet their credulity soon grows enamoured of the unfavourable impression. I am now alluding to modern luminaries, but cannot help going further in the case of those who figured in old Greece and Rome. As a lover of ingenuous youth, I damn in my own heart the nice but *unsocial* historian[9] who, to *illustrate,* as he might call it, the character of Tully, falsely admired, but usefully admired in a distant age, should have given us the correspondence of this *little* and *timid* man, who flatters like my Lord Lyttelton, and rivals Louis Quatorze in vanity (which a Scotch pedant calls *the thin crust* of pride, an expression rather happy!) Oh, that all the letters to Atticus, and the single, but chilling letter to Lucceius,[10] were *deeper than*

7. Perhaps a reference to the title of Christopher Anstey's anonymous satire, 1767 (GRAY ii. 161, n. 13).

8. Lord Somers and William III were both identified by Hardinge with the Revolution of 1688, which he revered.

9. Titus Pomponius Atticus (109–32 B.C.), the 'publisher' of Cicero's works and the collector of his letters. His own correspondence with Cicero covers twenty-five years (68–44 B.C.), and includes one letter in which Cicero asks him to go to

Lucceius to secure the letter referred to below, as Cicero has not kept a copy of it.

10. Lucius Lucceius (d. ca 44 B.C.), minor Roman historian. There are three letters from Cicero to Lucceius among the *Epistolæ ad familiares* (V. xii, xiii, xv) but Hardinge is clearly referring to the first and longest (V. xii) in which Cicero asks Lucceius to continue his history of Rome so that it will include an account of Cicero's consulship (63 B.C.).

e'er plummet sounded![11] down falls the Patriot's name, and with it the animating exemplar of the virtues that formed it. How different was the principle of a modern author,[12] who, disdaining the vulgar shackles of a Mother Goose's tale, dishonourable to human nature, exerted his learning and his reasoning to rescue the predecessor[13] of Henry the Seventh from the extravagant lies encouraged by that narrow and attorney-like tyrant! When I declare myself a cordial admirer of this author, *obscure* as he is, need I assure Mr Walpole that I am,

　　With the highest esteem,

His affectionate friend and servant,

G. HARDINGE

To HARDINGE, ca May–June 1772

Missing. Answered in the following letter.

From HARDINGE, ca June–July 1772

Printed from Nichols, *Lit. Illus.* iii. 183–4, where the date 1772 is supplied.

Temple.

DO your worst, my dear Sir, in your healing checks to every proud foible about me, if it should even seem to endanger me, or offend others. Perhaps, where the said foible is obstinately constitutional and inoffensive, a little bit of the humourist might be allowed, and more than connived at. Sir Roger de Coverley's credulous reverence for Sir Richard Baker;[1] his desire to *'converse more at large'* with the learned and communicative tomb-shower of the Abbey;[2] his mel-

---

11. Shakespeare's *Tempest* V. i. 56–7: 'deeper than did ever plummet sound.'
12. HW, in *Historic Doubts.*
13. Richard III.

1. (ca 1568–1645), author of *A Chronicle of the Kings of England,* Sir Roger's favourite volume; see *Spectator* No. 269, 8 Jan. 1712, No. 329, 18 March 1712.
2. See ibid.

ancholy and chaste passion for the *hand and arm* of *the widow;*[3] and, above all, his very sagacious and solemn assertions of truths which are self-evident, endear him the more to us. These playful oddities relieve the starchness of Pope's *perfect monster;*[4] and one hurries with cordiality and rapture to expiate the laugh committed in a chapter of his whims and weaknesses, by reviewing and adoring him in the next chapter, for the taste of his virtues, and the winning graces of his heart.

I do not mean this preface by way of a forlorn hope (in the humourous words of *the Homer of humour*) *to blunt the cannonade of your honest friendship;*[5] and I mean it even less by way of guide or outline to your better judgment. But I thought it necessary to throw out some palliative hints by way of blinding you to my unpolite importunities. To say the truth (and I confess it with fear and trembling), where my affections are once fixed, as in the case of Mr Walpole, I have the same undisciplined warmth about me which belonged to me at 14; a boyishness this at *my* age, which has exposed me to some ridicule, and has deprived me of some valuable friends in this delicate era of apathy and decorum! And yet I cannot for my soul exert an equal degree of courage, where I most want it, in Westminster Hall; nor do I believe that even the tuition of *Bamber Gascoyne*[6] would give me what Ezekiel was furnished with, *'whose forehead was made harder than flint or adamant.'*[7] This Bamber, conceiving II *necessarily* denoted *eleven,* cited once to my Lord Mansfield *Eleventh Levinz*[8] instead of *Second.* The Bench and Bar were outrageous in their mirth; a pitying friend whispered to him, '*Second, Second,*' in vain; he persisted, with a most unembarrassed contempt for them all, 'that *Levinz* published *eleven* good and effective volumes.'

Dr Akenside's works,[9] many of which are new to the world, will,

---

3. See ibid. No. 113, 10 July 1711.

4. Addison, who was attacked by Pope in the 'Epistle to Dr Arbuthnot.'

5. Quotation not traced. The 'Homer of Humour' might be 'Joe Miller' (*post* Hardinge to HW 27 July 1772, n. 1).

6. (1725–91), M.P.; barrister of Lincoln's Inn, an unpopular politician.

7. Ezekiel, 3. 9: 'As an adamant harder than flint have I made thy forehead.'

8. Sir Creswell Levinz (1627–1701), judge. The reference is to *The Reports of Sir Creswell Levinz, Knight,* 2d edn, 2 vols., 1722.

9. Mark Akenside (1721–70), physician, poet; close friend of George Hardinge's father, Nicholas Hardinge. His *Poems* appeared in 1772; HW had a copy (Hazen, *Cat. of HW's Lib.,* No. 3063).

I hope (without any disparagement or prejudice to his undoubted superior, Mr Gray), convince you[10] that he had some very original touches of genius and poetry. Have you heard that my Lord Chatham has writ a copy of verses to Garrick?[11] I am told they are spirited, and breathe in every line a *contempt for ambition,* and a *general philanthropy. Credat Judæus!*[12]

Believe me, dear Sir,

Yours most affectionately,

G. HARDINGE

To HARDINGE, ca July 1772

Missing. Answered in the next letter.

From HARDINGE, Thursday ca 16 July 1772

Printed from Nichols, *Lit. Illus.* iii. 184, where it is undated, but placed before the letter of 27 July 1772.

Temple, Thursday.

Dear Sir,

I HAVE just received your obliging note. Although next Monday will interfere with term-possibilities, I will have the honour and pleasure to wait upon you, unless before ten on Monday morning I should have notice of any engagements which may force me to decline it. Will you be kind enough not to wait for me, nor care about me, but suffer me to see you if I can? If this is asking too much, I must be obliged to defer the meeting till Term will be over.

10. HW, in a marginal note to his copy of Pinkerton's *Letters of Literature,* said that Akenside 'has nothing original and was not even a poet' (ibid. No. 3825).

11. Chatham wrote Garrick (then at Mt Edgcumbe) an invitation in verse to visit him at Burton Pynsent. Lyttelton wrote to Chatham, 20 Feb. 1772, that he

had forwarded the poem to Garrick (William Pitt, E. of Chatham, *Correspondence,* 1838–40, iv. 196–7, where the poem is printed).

12. 'The Jew may believe this,' from 'Credat Judæus Apella, / Non ego' ('The Jew Apella may believe this, not I') (Horace, *Satires* I. v. 100–1).

I hope you will meet the Earl of Chatham at the House of Lords tomorrow; and am, dear Sir,

Most affectionately and gratefully yours,

G. HARDINGE

From HARDINGE, Monday 27 July 1772

Printed from Nichols, *Lit. Illus.* iii. 184–5.

Inner Temple, July 27, 1772.

Dear Sir,

We were in high vogue yesterday, Master, said the *Bellows-blower* to the *Organist*. You know the sequel, as it is recorded in that precious monument of humour, *Joseph Miller*.[1]

'*We* had our ingenuity, Mr Walpole, upon the subject of a certain *Gravedigger*.'[2] I gave you the naked turf, whose homeliness you have so corrected and embellished by the flowers of your wit, that I am transported with it, and owe my warmest thanks to *Richard the son of Nigell*,[3] who, by the way, is not without many curious passages. I peeped at him, in hopes of meeting with some obsolete law, more as matter of history and ornament than with any view to reason from it, in regard to the lord's right over his villein; who, it seems by him (though it was denied the other day in a very able argument of counsel), was absolutely saleable by his lord. You may guess this inquiry into villeinage took its rise from that famous question of *Anglo-Æthiopian* liberty which is now afoot, and *sub judice*, in the King's Bench, on the *habeas corpus* of a negro mutineer.[4] A very unfortunate question, let the decision fall either way! for the mis-

1. Jest-book published by John Mottley (1692–1750), playwright, biographer. He took the name from Joseph Miller (1684–1738), an actor at Drury Lane notorious for his stale jokes. *Joe Miller's Jests* was first published in 1739. In the 1836 edition, this is No. 451. When the organist had ended his recital, the organ-blower gave him this compliment, provoking the retort '*We* sirrah!' In revenge, the blower at the next recital stopped blowing, and when asked why he did not blow, replied, 'Shall it be *we*, then?'

2. HW discusses Hamlet and the grave-diggers in his *Notes . . . on Several Characters of Shakespeare*, ed. W. S. Lewis, Farmington, Conn., 1940, pp. 5–7.

3. Richard Fitzneale or Fitznigel (d. 1198), Bp of London, 1189, was the son of Nigel (d. 1169), Bp of Ely, 1133. Richard wrote *Dialogus de Scaccario*.

4. James Somerset, a negro slave, who escaped while he and his master were temporarily in England, but was captured and put on ship to be sent to Jamaica to be sold. The Court of King's Bench, 22

chief is, that we cannot *judicially* hit upon the rational medium: either the negro and his fraternity are absolute slaves in the extreme of that idea, or as free in this country as you and I. This alternation is a dilemma induced upon us by the rage for litigation of delicate points, which has taken fast hold of these times to a degree of outrage and wretched inexpediency. Before, the *negro* thought himself *bound to service*—the *masters* thought himself equally *bound* to treat his *perpetual servant,* not *slave,* humanely, or at least without flagrant inhumanity. I am persuaded, as a lawyer, that the King's Bench will be under a necessity of giving these low wretches, unfit (though it may seem invidious) for absolute liberty, a complete manumission to all intents and purposes. This will necessarily impede our commerce with the planters, who, if stripped of the parade of their blacks, will stay at home, or import themselves into some less free and more accommodating part of the world. Curse on that ungenerous maxim, fit cement of *Catilines* and *Cethegi*[6]—*Idem velle atque idem nolle, etc.*[7]

An amicable difference of opinion is the delicate flattery of true friendship. I tremble when *you* frown at a favourite of *mine;* but I respect you too much to fear your displeasure, if I should confess to you that I feel myself compelled to adhere to my sentiments of Dr Akenside as a poet, or at least a poetical writer of a very high form. Observe that I speak of him as a *writer.* His apostasy[8] in *politics,* from Cato and Aristides[9] to the Earl of Bute, was most *unpoetical,* and admits of no palliation. Your expostulation upon the *paperness* of our correspondence is very obliging, and will not be lost upon,

Dear Sir,

G. HARDINGE

June, ruled that his master had no power to compel him to board the ship or to send him to the plantations (GM 1772, xlii. 293–4; Somerset vs Stewart 14 May 1772, *English Reports,* 1900–30, xcviii. 499–510).

5. Charles Stewart, of Jamaica (*English Reports,* loc. cit.).

6. Gaius Cornelius Cethegus (d. 63 B.C.), a close associate of Catiline in the conspiracy for which he was put to death; he had joined the conspiracy in the hope of getting his debts cancelled.

7. 'Idem velle atque idem nolle, ea demum firma amicitia est' ('Agreement in likes and dislikes is what constitutes true friendship') (Sallust, *Catilina* 20).

8. At the accession of George III in 1760 Akenside followed his patron, Jeremiah Dyson, Clerk to the House of Commons, by suddenly becoming a Tory. As a result Akenside was appointed one of the physicians to the Queen in Sept. 1761 (*St James's Chronicle,* 5 Sept. 1761).

9. Cato the Censor and Aristides the Just exemplify the virtues of the Whigs whom Akenside deserted in favour of Bute.

From HARDINGE, Wednesday 23 September 1772

Printed from Nichols, *Lit. Illus.* iii. 185, where the date of the year is supplied.

Inner Temple, Sept. 23.

My dear Sir,

Memory with me has no little dependence upon the *will*[1]—for example, mine is perfectly tenacious of your promise to receive me at Strawberry Hill whenever you should be disengaged. Are *you disposed* with me to *recollect* this obliging engagement? If so, be so good as to encourage me by a line, and let me know on what particular day after Sunday next you will throw away your hospitality upon your most affectionate admirer, friend, and servant,

G. HARDINGE

To HARDINGE, ca October–November 1772

Missing. Answered in the following letter.

From HARDINGE, Tuesday 10 November 1772

Printed from Nichols, *Lit. Illus.* iii. 185–7.

Inner Temple, Nov. 10, 1772.

My dear Sir,

THERE is a word of three syllables, 'Flattery,' a word that you have conjured up against me in a former letter, at the wicked instigation of your modesty. Sure it is a little hard that I, for the mere *want* of this three-syllabled gift in *my* composition, should have lost and forfeited three or four friends, to whom (though I could not *respect* them when I found sincerity was odious to them) I was yet *partial* enough—and that now, forsooth, I should be depreciated for the possession of this very *desideratum,* and by such a dear friend

1. A reference to the three steps in Ignatian meditation: memory, understanding, will.

as Mr Walpole, whom I would not lose if I could barter him for the Seals. *Flattery!*

> ---------------Oh! fye upon it!
> -----Things rank and gross in nature
> Possess it merely![1]

Fit, extremely fit, for a duetto of rapturous compliments between *Lord Robert Bertie*[2] *and the Secretary at War,*[3] which a female acquaintance of mine (who was present) has often described with infinite vivacity and humour: every dish at the table announced a panegyric on *one* of them, which was sure to be pelted back at the *other* for this and that εὑρηκα[4] in cookery.—A scene of such low comic points out the real objects and lawful dealers in flattery. Or what think you of *Garrick* and *Murphy,*[5] dubbed, each by the other, all the best names of ancient Greece and Rome? one for a tawdry, ill-shaped suit of clothes, too big or too little, and against all chaste rules of elegance or taste (though true enough to the modern cut) ycleped his *Tragedy;*[6] the other, equally puffed in return, for a pert little nosegay, popped into the buttonhole of these clothes, a nosegay which the galleries applaud furiously, and call it his *Prologue.* So far, and in this little walk of trade, the contracting parties have a mutual advantage, and much in the same coin with poets, too, *Flattery* keeps to its proper bathos and ridicule. Horace tells you archly that *he* can always manage to be *Alcæus,* by calling his brother-poet *Callimachus.*[7] It affects one to see Pope, Swift, and my Lord Bolingbroke such glaring instances of so mean a vice. How *they* clung together, like our Scotch! If you attacked *one,* the rest of their tribe were sure to resent. In this, indeed, there was a further view, the uniting *their* phalanx to depress their contemporaries. How stiff are Pope's letters, even to little gentry! Believe *him!* no man ever had so many cordial friends and favourites; yet, I doubt, his fulsome compliments to them were understood as demanding a payment, and with interest. However, one is not much hurt hitherto at the sort of agents who do *Flattery's* work, so long as the luminaries of genius keep *their* lustre

1. *Hamlet* I. ii.
2. See *ante* HW to Chute 20 Oct. 1755, n. 13.
3. The 2d Vct Barrington (*ante* HW to Bentley 30 Sept. 1755, n. 8) was secretary at war 1755–61, 1765–78; M.P.
4. 'Discovery.'
5. Arthur Murphy (1727–1805), dramatist, actor.
6. *The Grecian Daughter,* 1772.
7. The allusion is to Horace's *Epistles,* Book II, Epistle ii, lines 99–100.

undiminished. But, alas! how does it chill one, to see this vulgar poison transferred from such little subjects to the enchanting pen of Tully, and the entire life, at least political one, of that almost inspired man, whom Dryden so affectedly but so happily describes,

> The world to BACON doth not only owe
> Its present knowledge, but the *future* too.[8]

An idea which I have seen applied more happily to 'the *prophetic eye of taste*'[9] in a certain little work just finished. But, above all, how does it mar the service of Religion, Freedom, and Learning to see or to hear the lawn sleeves of this age! '*The mitred flattery*,' which my Lord Halifax[10] rallies with such keen pleasantry as the most outrageous of any,[11] was never more extravagant and coarse than at this present writing. *The Revolution* would never have been that compendious and emphatical word in English ears, if such gossiping prelates as my Lords of Bristol,[12] Ely,[13] and Norwich,[14] and even Gloucester[15] of this day, had been solicited by James the Second, at the end of his reign, to adopt *his* notions of Law and Church. But I had almost forgot that I was a flatterer myself, that *you* had consigned me to the Murphys and Garricks. If I am one of *these professed,* it ill becomes me to descant with such irreverence upon my associates. Does not every man owe to his calling allegiance of head and of heart? Can a doctor laugh in public at the *materia medica?* or a lawyer discredit his own shop in giving himself the airs of a Whig? The misery indeed in *my* case at present is, that, being laid upon my back as *flatterer-*

---

8. Dryden's 'Epistle III. To my Honoured Friend Dr Charleton, on his Learned and Useful Works . . .' ll. 23–4. Hardinge has substituted *the* for *its* before *future* in the second line.

9. An allusion to HW's *Essay on Modern Gardening,* which had just appeared in 1771 as Chapter VII of Vol. IV of HW's *Anecdotes of Painting:* 'He [Milton] seems with the prophetic eye of taste (as I have heard taste well defined) to have conceived, to have foreseen modern gardening; as Lord Bacon announced the discoveries since made by experimental philosophy' (p. 127). A footnote to this passage in HW's *Works* ii. 527 attributes the above definition of taste to Lord Chatham.

10. George Savile (1633–95), cr. (1682) M. of Halifax.

11. 'There is a Right Reverend Flattery that hath the Precedence of all other Kinds of it. This Mitred Flattery is of all others the most exalted. It ever groweth in proportion, and keepeth pace with Power. . . .' (from 'Miscellaneous Thoughts and Reflections' in Halifax's *Complete Works,* ed. Walter Raleigh, Oxford, 1912, p. 251).

12. Thomas Newton (1704–82), Bp of Bristol, 1761.

13. Edmund Keene (1714–81), Bp of Chester 1752, of Ely 1771.

14. Thomas Hayter (*ante* HW to Chute 14 Dec. 1752, n. 3).

15. William Warburton (1698–1779), Bp of Gloucester 1759–79; writer of theological controversy; editor.

convict, I am so far like the Perjurer-convict, that I am incapable of credit though sincere, if that sincerity should happen to fall on the side of praise. Therefore, not a word can I utter of my real sentiments of your play (though I long, as much as I *ought* to long to be in favour with attorneys). Will you for this once grant a *suspending law,* a thing not without precedent, and give me just credit enough to let me be honest upon that single work?

I had writ so far, and was going to add more impertinence of this cast; but, in a visit this morning to a Dowager Countess who ought to be in your graces, . . .

From HARDINGE, Friday 17 June 1774

Printed from Nichols, *Lit. Illus.* iii. 187.

Temple, Friday, June 17, 1774.

Dear Sir,

THIS age I have not seen you! and, though I have read my Lord Chesterfield, am beast enough not to have returned your visit. Till the 26th of next month, I beg the privilege of declining the best company, and keeping the worst. Any time after that I shall be free to be wise and happy. Attendance upon chances, and possibilities of getting vent for talk without sense (now become an arrant drug, and dead upon my hands) force me to defer so long a visit (or, as I doubt it will prove, a *visit-ation*) at Strawberry Hill. Be so good as to fix a day.

Yours, my dear Sir, with the highest esteem,

G. HARDINGE

From HARDINGE, Saturday 2 July 1774

Printed from Nichols, *Lit. Illus.* iii. 187–8, where the date of the year has been inserted.

Temple, July 2.

My dear Sir,

DO I go too far, when I say that you are not averse to me, nor ashamed of admitting me to your countenance and friendship? I *'familiarize'* and *'domesticate'* myself in your company—you give me your sentiments upon men and things freely and half playfully— you let me differ with you in a sentiment here and there *de lana caprina,*[1] and bear no malice to me (whereas another supposed great man hates irreconcilably a dissentient, though upon a single occasion, or upon a topic of no importance, and though Mr Dissentient is the poorest of creatures).

Amongst other points of conflict between us, I hold *'the abstract of a good historian'* to be the most implacable—though I am not a little keen upon *Milton's prose,* which I undertake to force upon your taste before we shall be much older. I am a very Fluellin, and you shall 'eat the leek, because your appetites, look ye, are against it.'[2] (Has the tax upon America a better apology to its back?) But when I talk of *these* differences between us, I must protest against the possibility of our disagreement upon the only objects that should interest rational and social beings. This reminds me of *the good old cause;* and perhaps no part of you is more endearing to me than your goodness to me in participating that passionate warmth of sentiment *upon a certain side of the question,* which, if I thought party-politics or avarice or false ambition could ever make me forego, I could almost wish for death. If the supposition that virtue can actuate the human mind, and even my own, be false, I say, as I have said a million of times, 'May I never be undeceived!' And, by the way, it is holding false lights to a Sir William Meredith,[3] to assure him that the same wisdom that makes a courtier of him will save him from remorse. It is not so. Apostasy, though niched into office, and

1. 'About a goat's wool,' proverbial expression for 'a trifle'; see Horace, *Epistles* I. xviii. 15.

2. *Henry V,* v. i. 23–7 (inaccurately quoted).

3. Sir William Meredith (? 1725–90), Bt; M.P.; politician of no certain loyalty (cf. HW, *Last Journals,* i. 311; MASON i. 142). In 1774 he was Controller of the Household.

consoled by ministerial importance, will every now and then give a thorough heartache; and besides that this fashionable apathy, if perpetual and permanent, would incapacitate for the enjoyment of that sunshine of the soul which our native benevolence would insure to us, the intervals of the opiate (and intervals I am sure there are) afflict and disturb the most philosophical of these libertines.—I say *libertines*, for is he anything else but a *libertine*, who wilfully shuts the door against the best conceptions and emotions that God has given him?

May I be forgiven this rhapsody? or is it safe in your hands? Alas! if I were to bestow it upon my other friends, they would, in sober sadness, make due application to a certain ancient gentlewoman for a commission of lunacy against me. Interpose, I conjure you, betwixt me and the commission. Observe—in the cause of *Monro*[4] *against Hardinge*, I retain you for the defendant.

You have sometimes piqued me in calling what I said (and felt) of you by a hard name. *Flattery?* What, for its own sake? and yet, what other interest can be at the bottom of it? Have you any peculiar ascendant at Court, or over the guide and slave of it, whoever he is? Do then give me credit for dull sincerity, when I assure you that I esteem your friendship as the most fortunate acquisition of my life, and that your compositions delight me, *even* where you give them a *death's wound by reading them*—*Apropos*, let me transcribe your parody on Lord Chesterfield,[5] and lend me your polemics with Hume, etc.[6] which I long to read: this mark of your confidence you must not refuse to me.

My Lord Dacre has got a Bishop[7] to his back, the counterpart of *your* Man of God.[8] I will tell you of him at our next meeting.

I am, dear Sir, your most affectionate,

G. HARDINGE

---

4. Dr John Monro (1715–91), physician specializing in mental diseases.
5. For HW's parody, 'The New Whole Duty of Woman, in a series of letters from a mother to a daughter,' see *Works* iv. 355–60 and OSSORY i. 203, n. 6.
6. 'Narrative of what passed relative to the Quarrel between Mr David Hume and Jean-Jacques Rousseau,' written in

1767 by HW, and printed in *Works* iv. 249–56 ('Short Notes,' GRAY i. 42, n. 286).
7. Not identified.
8. Probably the 'Archbishop of Tuum' in HW's *Peach in Brandy*, 'the great wit of those times,' who 'became pope by the name of Innocent the Third, having afterwards a son by his sister' (*Works* iv. 340).

From HARDINGE, ca Thursday 7 July 1774

Printed from Nichols, *Lit. Illus.* iii. 187, where it is inserted between the letters of 17 June and 2 July.

YOU will find me in my next a suppliant, but an ingenuous one. It is a tale of distress, imparted under the seal of confidence, that you will at least have to read, if I am as dear to you as I think. All that I ask of you beforehand is, to *set* your heart (if I may use that phrase) to its favourite notes of sensibility and delicacy before you open my next letter; for you will be called upon, I assure you, not only for 'a tear of pity,' but a 'a hand'' open as day to melting charity.'[1] In the meantime, I am, with perfect and unalterable attachment,

Your admirer and servant,

G. HARDINGE

From HARDINGE, Monday 11 July 1774

Printed from Nichols, *Lit. Illus.* iii. 188–9.

Inner Temple, Monday, July 11, 1774.

My dear Sir,

TO renew the correspondence, or to endeavour to renew it, when I am to ask a favour of you, has a look in it that high spirit and delicacy have nothing to say to. But the Scriptural comment upon the Bar is beginning to be verified in miniature even in me, for my little commerce with *law* is so far *the strength of sin*[1] in its influence upon me that it enables me to say and do, upon motives of advantage, things which my natural reason and sensibilities hold in the vilest estimation; and though my villainies in this way are petty and small-ware doings enough, yet the principle is equally bad and rotten—or, as Horace distinguishes, the *damnum*[2] is less, the *facinus*[3] just the

1. 'A tear for pity, and a hand / Open as day for melting charity' (2 *Henry IV* IV. iv. 31–2).

1. I Cor. 15.56: 'The sting of death is sin; and the strength of sin is the law.'

2. 'Loss, damage, harm.'

3. 'Villainy, crime.' The reference is to the following passage: 'Nam de mille fabæ modiis cum surripis unum, / Damnum est, non facinus, mihi pacto lenius isto' ('For, when from a thousand bushels of beans

same. I have been told it is one of Aristotle's topics of eloquence,[4] to announce what is likely to displease your audience by representations in the dark, and at a distance, that make the affair worse by a thousand degrees in expectation than it will turn out in reality. The effect is natural—we are so delighted, that the real terrors or deformities of the fact, when disclosed, fall short of our violent and outraged impressions, that we give a milder reception to it than we *naturally* should have done. I practise this manœuvre now, and (like many *cunning fools*) give you notice of it.

The favour is only this, that you would lend me a ticket, to enable two or three friends of mine who have not the honour and pleasure of your acquaintance to see *Strawberry Hill.*

If this is against rule, you will be so good as to pardon me, or at least give me as gentle a rap of the knuckles as you can reconcile to the warmth of your friendship for me; for, to say the truth, I am a feeble soul, and cannot bear to be scolded in the summer months by a person so dear to me as you are.

When do you go to Paris next? or may I catch you at Strawberry Hill about a fortnight hence?

Believe me, dear Sir, yours, most affectionately,

G. HARDINGE

you filch one, the loss in that case to me, is less, but not your villainy') (*Epistles* I. 16.55–6).

4. *The Art of Rhetoric* seems not to convey these hints, but Aristotle's *Topica* begins Book VIII (on arrangement and the way to ask questions) by advising the speaker to conceal his conclusions until he has disarmed his hearers by artfully leading them from a dissimulated opening.

From Hardinge, Thursday 30 March 1775

Printed from Nichols, *Lit. Illus.* iii. 191–2, where the date of the year is supplied.

Carmarthen, March 30.

My dear Sir,

> Apollo starts, and all Parnassus shakes,
> At the rude rumbling Baralipton makes.[1]

HOW then can a solemn votary of Law have a chance of being let in at *your* door! Sir John Dalrymple very quaintly says[2] that his hero, Mr Yorke,[3] used to call himself '*a fugitive from the Muses.*' Why may not I copy Mr Yorke in the ridicule of his character, as I cannot resemble him in his knowledge of law (which I hope is no *ridiculous* attainment?) Why may not I affect now and then (if it *must* be thought *affectation*) to revisit Arcadia—and remind the author of the *Castle of Otranto* that I could have cried (*once in my life*) at the first conversation between Manfred's daughter and the imprisoned peasant[4]—that I could have loved such tears, and felt a sensual kind of enjoyment in shedding them.

Indeed, and indeed, my dear Sir, though I have been of late remiss (to my own serious loss) in paying my respects to you, my esteem for you is fresh and warm as ever. I have it much at heart, one day or another, to concert a meeting with you at my own chambers, if you can venture into so *chilling an atmosphere;* and though I do the honours of a Temple breakfast most ungracefully, yet I will risk it, if it is only to catch Mr Walpole, and cater a party for him that I think he will relish.

In the meantime let me ask an important favour of him, as I conceive it (and I am the best judge). It is, to enliven my Sisyphean labours in Wales with a letter of chit-chat and friendship, or advice to

1. 'Essay on Translated Verse,' ll. 67–8, by Wentworth Dillon (ca 1637–85), 4th E. of Roscommon, 1649.

2. In the preface to Dalrymple's *Memoirs of Great Britain and Ireland (ante* Hardinge to HW ca 21 June 1771, n. 1).

3. Hon. Charles Yorke (1722–70), attorney-general 1762–3, 1765–6; lord chancellor 1770 (for three days); M.P. He was said to

have interceded on Dalrymple's behalf once (see Mason i. 95), and so Dalrymple dedicated his work to the memory of Yorke. According to the DNB, Yorke 'was an Italian scholar, and trifled with the Muses.'

4. *The Castle of Otranto,* 2d edn, 1765, Chap. II, pp. 54–8.

me, or laugh at me, or whatever his pen cannot help writing, which (though *lame and flat in itself*) animates and delights *me,* and I (you know) am the person upon whom the cordial is to operate.

The direction is, to me *at Cardigan, South Wales;* and the letter will reach me there if writ any time before the 7th of next month.

I am, Sir, with true and sincere affection,

Your friend and most obedient servant,

G. HARDINGE

To HARDINGE, ca Monday 3 April 1775

Missing. Answered in the next letter.

From HARDINGE, Thursday 13 April 1775

Printed from MS now WSL. Previously printed, Nichols, *Lit. Illus.* iii. 192–3 with deletions in the first paragraph and date of year inserted. Sold Sotheby's, 6 Nov. 1951, Nichols Sale, lot 397, to Pickering & Chatto, who sold it in 1953 to WSL.

Cardigan, April 13.

My dear Sir,

NOT having an *ancestor* to my back, I am forced to decline the heraldical wreath which you tender with such complacency. I do indeed remember, and with profound respect, Lord Dacre's alacrity in honour of '*the Hardinges de Melburne, com. Derby,*'[1] but I doubt his partiality for his little *propositus* made him tamper a little with evidence, though perhaps not in so shameless a degree as Edmonson has done for the *Damers.*[2]

1. Hardinge was descended from a younger branch of a family long seated at King's Newton, in the parish of Melbourne and county of Derby (Nichols, *Lit. Illus.* iii. 1–3).

2. Joseph Edmondson's *Baronagium genealogicum,* 5 vols, 1764. The fifth volume,

p. 489, contained the Damer pedigree, Joseph Damer having been made Bn Milton (in the British peerage) in 1762. His ancestry is traced to 'Gilbert D'amery 15 Hen. II had lands in the County of Somerset.'

I won't let *you* suppose, my dear Sir, that even in *boyish* days I could *admire* where I could not *esteem*. But *now*, at least—at 31— a cold and cautious age, I am as phlegmatic, be assured, as Dr Samuel Clarke,[3] who, though a good man, confessed 'that he had long waited for parental tenderness to arise in his bosom, but in vain—' I canvass, I suspect, and (lawyer-like) I *cross-examine* the character before I embark with it, or call it *friend*. But *you* are proof against all my inquisitorial severities; and as to my *taste*, sure I *must* be a worshipper of *goodness*, from its impudent merit of singularity and of resisting the current. This *'honest haughtiness'*[4] of spirit in a corrupt age is a jewel that has brighter lustre than my Lord of Bellamont's[5] diamond shoe-buckles, which, I heard him say, 'very seldom lasted him above two or three *minuets*, from a certain elasticity in the muscle of his foot at a certain passage in his performance, which bent, if not broke them almost of course.'

That I am *boy* enough still to relish *talents* when they belong to an amiable mind, I cannot deny; but accuse me at your peril of mistaking the shadow for the substance! of loving Warburton because I love Hoadley,[6] or of loving Voltaire because I love his wit, without a particle of the rest, in Arlington Street—where no eloquence of style forgets *'the language of the heart.'*[7]

Your encomiums upon me would not be admissible in evidence to my character upon the Carmarthen Circuit—the *fountain* is impure and *wickedly* partial—the *stream* collects in its passage through another street more and more of the same *iniquity*. However, though it may not give the jury a better opinion of me, it will give *me* a better opinion of *myself,* and make me fancy that in future at least I must act up to the demand of this fanciful character. 'Your name is up, you may lie abed,' is a dangerous laurel, and has ruined many *fine boys* of my age—the more one *is* in favour, the more one should push on to improve the footing already acquired.

When shall I do homage at Strawberry Hill, or when *receive it,* with due solemnity, *chez moi?* Take care, my dear Sir, how you

3. Samuel Clarke (1675–1729), D.D.; metaphysician.
4. Quotation not traced.
5. Charles Coote (1738–1800), Bn Coote; cr. (1767) E. of Bellamont, son-in-law of the D. of Leinster.
6. Benjamin Hoadly (1676–1761), Bp of Bangor 1716, of Hereford 1721, of Salisbury 1723, of Winchester 1734; Whig theologian.
7. Alexander Pope, 'Epistle to Dr Arbuthnot,' ll. 398–9: 'Unlearned, he knew no schoolman's subtle art, / No language but the language of the heart.'

encourage one too far, both for *your* sake and *mine* too; for I should be a little piqued at an order given your prime vizier not to let me in above once a month.

Believe me, dear Sir, with the warmest affection and esteem,

Your friend and servant,

G. HARDINGE

To HARDINGE, ca May 1776

Missing. Answered in the next letter.

From HARDINGE, Monday 20 May 1776

Printed from Nichols, *Lit. Illus.* iii. 193–4.

Temple, Monday, May 20, 1776.

My dear Sir,

THE habits and views that engross me now are at such enmity with all that is elegant, amiable, and liberal, that I cannot, without high treason to Westminster Hall, pilfer a moment of Strawberry Hill, though I have still a wicked longing to pass two thirds of every day in that scene. *Anni prædantur euntes*[1]—a few more will have the wished-for effect of humbling my palate, which is now much too saucy for my food. The work of reformation is commenced already, and severe discipline it is, for no Methodist is more completely robbed of Garrick and Shakespeare than I am of the Muses and Graces that make part of your family. This is one honest apology for my apparent neglect of your most flattering attentions to me, in the offer of your company, advice, and friendship. The two latter no distance or disparity of our situations will ever make me surrender; the former is too high a regale for such a Carthusian regimen as mine.

1. 'Singula de nobis anni prædantur euntes' ('The advancing years rob us of one thing after another') (Horace, *Epistles* II. 2. 55).

But I have another as honest an apology *in petto;*[2] and it is, that I feel ashamed and afraid of putting your good nature to the penance of a *tête-à-tête* with an awkward pedant of a barrister, who has nothing to recommend himself in such a party but the obstinacy of his relish for ingenuous habits and sentiments, though he cannot adopt them into the system either of his manners or connections, without ruin to the politics of his trade. The result is, that you are fairly rid of an admirer who would pester you (if he were in a different sphere) from morning to night, and would drive you to the ingenuities which have been practised upon *Long Sir Thomas*[3] and his numerous fraternity of toad-eaters and prosers, when the pride of great men has taken the happy turn of shutting the door upon such visitors. And yet, after all this preface of determined banishment from your drawing-room, I am going to fancy myself domesticated there, by asking a favour, fit only to be asked by one of the initiated.

I meditate a very indecent extravagance, and, if you shall not throw a damper upon the design, propose to invest a sum which I have acquired by two or three fortunate adventures of law, in a tour through Switzerland and part of France: as Paris, Lyons, Avignon, etc. My French is not ready in conversation; and, alas! the assurance of the Bar (like all vulgar assurance) is perfectly consistent with a degree of *mauvaise honte* (most unbecoming and illiberal, as well as painful, to the owner) in good company. Besides, my object is rather to see houses, pictures, plays, etc. than to have the *entré en famille,* even if it could be compassed for me; but I wish very much to be directed by your taste and experience in the choice of the lions which I am to see.

I go further in my impertinence, and wish for a *cicerone* or two upon the spot, who for your sake would put me under his wings, and enable me to follow your hints to the best advantage—perhaps too would obtain for me some accommodations which are not permitted to travellers who have no credentials—particularly at Paris, where your name and auspices would make even *me* a figure of some consequence.

Excuse this liberty, and accept of my best thanks for a thousand

2. 'In the breast'—unrevealed. The expression was usually applied to secret creations of cardinals by popes; see, for instance, Mann to HW 20 Sept. 1774, MANN vii. 39.

3. Sir Thomas Robinson (? 1702–77), Bt (*ante* HW to Bentley 9 July 1754, n. 24; HW to Mason 5 April 1777, MASON i. 297–8).

marks of your friendly condescension already received. I shall be the happier in taking your directions by word of mouth (on my return from Hereford in four or five days) at any time that you will appoint; but, should that be inconvenient, be so good as to let me hear from you.

I am, dear Sir, with sincere respect and esteem,

Your most affectionate servant,

G. HARDINGE

From HARDINGE, Tuesday 4 June 1776

Printed from Nichols, *Lit. Illus.* iii. 194.

Temple, Tuesday morning, June 4, 1776.

Dear Sir,

THE immediate purpose of my visit in Arlington Street was defeated by more interesting topics, which you treated so *heavily* as to weigh down my *Paris* and all its rights. I shall not, however, give you up as my adviser and patron, though I do not absolutely hate you as an *acquaintance,* a character that lowers you, and raises me delightfully. Shall I beg the favour of you to write down such instructions or credentials as you think may be of use to me, either at Paris, Lyons, or Geneva? It has been intimated to me that I should be much pleased with a certain Monsieur Hubert,[1] at Geneva, if I could manage to be made known to him. Lady Ossory,[2] the Duke of Grafton,[3] and my Lord Abingdon[4] are mentioned to me as persons under whose auspices I could be effectually and readily introduced to him. The two latter I *could* reach in a roundabout way; might I presume to use your friendship in soliciting the honour of a line[5]

1. Jean Huber (1721–86), Swiss artist famous for his portraits cut out of paper with scissors. (G. Jean-Aubry, 'Jean Huber,' *Revue de Paris*, 1 June 1936, p. 623). For his silhouette of Anne, Duchess of Grafton, later Lady Ossory, see OSSORY i. 1.

2. See *ante* HW to Strafford 7 Aug. 1760, where she is mentioned as Duchess of Grafton.

3. Augustus Henry Fitzroy (1735–1811), 3d D. of Grafton; Lady Ossory's former husband with whom she made her visit to Geneva (ibid.).

4. Willoughby Bertie (1740–99), 4th E. of Abingdon, 1760.

5. See HW to Lady Ossory (OSSORY i. 307) for HW's request for this letter for Hardinge.

from the former? Adieu. Be assured always of my warmest gratitude, respect, and esteem.

I am, dear Sir, with the truest affection, yours,

G. HARDINGE

To HARDINGE, ca July 1776

Missing. Possibly the letter enclosing Lady Ossory's letter of introduction (see preceding letter).

From HARDINGE, ca July 1776

Printed from Nichols, *Lit. Illus.* iii. 195.

My dear Sir,

YOUR Lorrain High and Mightinesses[1] terrify me. I am too much of a *poliçen*[2] hitherto, at least for such luminaries. A letter for me to one reputable family at Nancy would completely satisfy my views and wishes there. But I would also beg of you to give me two or three letters for Paris to such of your friends as may be the most likely to recommend me further on in my tour, which I have, in deference to your judgment, brought back to its original plan, and have made my apologies to Belhouse.[3] Though at Paris and the other places at which I shall touch, my residence will be very short, I would yet fain smooth my way to acquaintance at any of them in future by the earliest hint of my wish to have the honour and advantage of attaching myself to their societies when I shall be more equal to them; for I mean to be very French, very Swiss, and even very German as soon as I can be a tolerable prater in French, which is the

1. Doubtless HW had offered Hardinge an introduction to the Princesse de Craon's family in Lorraine; her daughter, Mme de Boufflers, had been the friend of Stanislas I, Duc de Lorraine (MANN iv. 236).

2. Presumably Hardinge means *polisson*.

3. Belhus, Essex, the seat of Lord and Lady Dacre; Lady Dacre was Hardinge's aunt.

master-key to foreign company in all parts of Europe. Be so good as
to send the letters to my chambers, Paper-Buildings, Temple, before
the 12th of August.

I am, dear Sir, with unalterable affection,

Your friend and servant,

G. HARDINGE

To HARDINGE, ca August 1776

Missing. Letter enclosing letters of introduction for Nancy and Paris, requested in the preceding letter and acknowledged in the letter of 10 March
1777.

From HARDINGE, ca November–December 1776

Printed from Nichols, *Lit. Illus.* iii. 195. The missing portion of the letter
may have contained Hardinge's written thanks to HW for the latter's assistance
in planning his trip to the continent during the summer. Dated by Lord Lichfield's death.

. . . been a warm worshipper of King William and of my Lord
Chatham. I learnt that you were extremely out of order, and had
been even worse for a month past. I am grieved to hear it, and beg
you will let me know that you now are recovering very fast, as I cannot bear that a person in whom so many have an interest, and who
is himself so interested in the good of those who can profit by *his*
benevolence, should have anything to do with gout, or such troublesome companions. So we have lost your neighbour, Mrs Clive![1] Our
stage will never, to the end of time, replace her. I heard this morning, and from good authority enough (in the *minutiæ* of politics),

1. She retired 24 April 1769 (see MON-
TAGU, ii. 258, n. 3); in Nichols's *Lit. Illus.*,
there is added this note: 'Mrs Clive
retired from the stage in 1775, and lived
afterwards ten years in elegant retirement
near Mr Walpole's at Strawberry Hill.'
Hardinge is apparently referring, rather
belatedly, to her retirement here.

that my Lord Lichfield's[2] office is cooling its heels, till it can be filled so as to let Charles Fox into the administration. Believe me, dear Sir,

Yours, with the highest regard,

G. HARDINGE

From Hardinge, Monday 10 March 1777

Printed from Nichols, *Lit. Illus.* iii. 195–7.

Worcester, March 10, 1777.

Dear Sir,

I WAS unhappy that I could not have the honour to see you when I called upon you the other day—an event in the annals of your porter's hall too *important,* I hope, to have been suppressed in his report. Serious illness, and that worst of all disorders, lowness of spirits, as well as business of one kind or other, have deprived me since my return from the Continent of any opportunities to give you my thanks in person for the share which you took, with so much honour to me, in the conduct and plan of that expedition. I could not profit by your letters for Paris and Nancy, but I do not thank you one jot the less for them, nor will I give up the hope of employ- ing these *coaxers* hereafter to my advantage. At Geneva Lady Ossory gave me a peep at Hubert, who is a wonderful artist, and possessed of a good comic vein. He is, when grave, a little too much *ex cathedra* and sententious. In politics I had no patience with him, for I found him, in the territories of Geneva, *Toryissimorum Toryis- simum,* a *local* solecism that revolted me; but Rousseau and Voltaire have, through very different *media,* come to the same point of *en- dangering* at least the sound and sober principles of government, as well as religion, even in these happy little states. The lower class of the citizens, and the popular checks not yet removed, make one hope, however, that Astræa,[1] who has taken a fancy to them so long in her

2. Robert Lee (1706–3 Nov. 1776), 4th E. of Lichfield, 1772, custos brevium in the Court of Common Pleas.

1. Astræa, daughter of Zeus and The- mis, lived on earth until men's impiety drove her out.

old age and banishment from all other territories, will cling to them long enough to put the business of these other scenes to shame, and reprove them by her blessings there, till she warms them into that public spirit which is necessary to shake off oppression (whether it resides in the law itself, or in the conduct of the rulers) and to assert the rights of mankind.

By the way, ought I, or have I a right, to offer my respects to Lady Ossory for her goodness to me, though at your request? I have a present[2] in store for you, that will make you blush for your want of curiosity and zeal upon one of your own hobbyhorses. Whenever you can spare me a line or two upon men and things, you will do me honour, and make me happy.

Is anything in your press? When is your next volume to come out?[3] What an extraordinary creature this Chatterton![4] But how any man that has an ear, and a memory conversant in Chaucer, Spenser, and the poets of the last age, could for a moment fancy these verses to belong to an age even prior to the first, is to me inconceivable. He seems to me to have modelled himself often upon Spenser, but the modern rhythm clings to him, and baffles all his address, though he has varied it in a way to show that he had a very fine ear. Shall I beg your recommendation of some French little morsel, in their best manner, of lively and genteel, either memoirs or letters, though, after your favourites Hamilton[5] and Sévigné, one grows proud? I would fain be tolerably French, as Paris will very soon be the seat of Empire.

'I have been learning to be kicked downstairs, and thrown out of a window,' was no bad saying of a sharper at Bath in confidence to one of his coadjutors. Voltaire's letter to me, for I could not *see* him, though (as John Bull would say) *I heard him cough,* was sent open to me at Geneva on a torn and dirty inch of paper: '82 annis et 82 morbis oppressus, veniam peto si non sim visendus, sed obliviscendus.'[6]

2. See *post* Hardinge to HW 21 June 1779.

3. The next publication of the SH Press was Pont-de-Veyle's *Sleepwalker*, 1778 (Hazen, *SH Bibl.* 114–15).

4. Thomas Chatterton (1752–70), the poet. See HW's correspondence with him in vol. 16 of this edition. In 1779, HW printed at the SH Press his own *Letter* to the Editor of the Miscellanies of Thomas Chatterton (Hazen, op. cit. 116–17).

5. Anthony Hamilton (ca 1645–1720), author of *Mémoires de la Vie du Comte de Grammont*, which HW had reprinted at the SH Press (ibid. 96–9).

6. 'Oppressed by 82 years and by 82 illnesses, I beg the favour not to be seen,

I wish you better health and spirits than I have, though a ray of good humour and vivacity lights me up when I think of you, and of the infinite entertainment (serious or comic) which I owe to your pen and to your conversation. Else I am full of rheumatism and vapours; but always

Your most affectionate and most obliged,

G. Hardinge

To Hardinge, ca March 1777

Missing. Answered in the next letter, by which it appears that the address on this letter was not in HW's hand.

From Hardinge, Saturday 22 March 1777

Printed from MS now wsl; previously printed, Nichols, *Lit. Illus.* iii. 197–9. Sold, Sotheby's, 18 Nov. 1929, J. G. Nichols Sale, part of lot 239; offered 18 Dec. 1931 by G. Michelmore & Co.; sold Sotheby's 18 May 1933, part of lot 418 to Maggs Bros for wsl.

Oxford Circuit, March 22, 1777.

My dear Sir,

AN offender every day of my life against the *essential* duties of politeness, I demand from others an observance of the veriest punctilios of it—and I complain accordingly by these presents, in the Quixot spirit of your hero, my Lord Herbert,[1] that you sent me an

but to be forgotten.' Hardinge, while in Geneva the previous autumn, had sent his compliments to Voltaire, asking to see him; the epistle was composed in Latin, presumably due to his poor French but also to impress the old man, who was becoming increasingly loath to receive visitors; it is dated 22 Sept. 1776 and printed in Voltaire's *Correspondence*, ed. Besterman, Geneva, 1953–65, xcv. 77. Two other versions of Voltaire's reply are in *The Diaries of Sylvester Douglas (Lord Glenbervie)*, 1928, ii. 167, and *The Gazet-*

teer and New Daily Advertiser 10 March 1778 (cited in *Studies on Voltaire and the Eighteenth Century*, ed. Besterman, Geneva, xlix [1967]. 189–90). Voltaire repeats the same joke about 82 years of age and 82 illnesses in three letters written during the weeks immediately following Hardinge's visit (ibid. 190).

———

1. Edward, Lord Herbert of Chirbury, whose autobiography had been printed by HW at SH.

impression of a vulgar seal, value two pence, and a direction to the letter, as if not enough disgraced by the seal, in a hand that was not your own. These are freedoms, Mr Walpole, which I can discern with a hawk's eye when they are taken with me, and which I can resent with as high a sense of honour as any Irish rapier-man, Fitzgerald[2] himself not excepted.

My Lord Chesterfield (*my* Lord Coke[3]) used to shake his head upon seeing a letter ill folded up, as much [as] to say, 'The man's a vulgar, and consequently has neither a heart nor a head.' An undissembled and joyous laugh dislocated him; and an embarrassed look or sentence (often the highest beauty in male as well as female) passed universally with him as conclusive evidence of a low and disingenuous mind. But what must he have said, nay, what are his *manes* now saying, upon *your* higher offence?—which is heightened by its opposition to the general idea that you have as much politeness, and as much elegance of manners, as any man of fashion, warm from the best Parisian models—though I'm told you are almost *reprobate* enough to whisper to yourself, that libertine ethics, insincerity, and a polished address, do not constitute the *whole,* though you admit them to be *necessary* and *prevailing features* of *the fine gentleman.* But I know worse of you—that you have writ the happiest banter upon these *grâces soi-disantes,* and, as you call them (if I remember correctly), *these decorations,* which are lifted into such a farcical importance. I must own myself, however, charmed with some parts of that silly and mischievous publication. I have been looking at the second (Maty's);[4] and the *Worlds,*[5] and most of the French letters[6] delight me. Perhaps, and most probably indeed, I am not *rompée* enough in the language to be in any degree a judge of it; but these letters, I own, seem to me sweetly turned, and for ease and spirit equal to any models of that sort of thing—But *a witty and vain man of fashion* seems to be in general his portrait. He scarce went beyond it. He dealt in *prophecy,* in *characters,* and in *favourites.* Was not he sadly out in all three? Never any man so much.

2. George Robert Fitzgerald (ca 1748–86), adventurer. See HW to Mason, 3 April 1775 (MASON, i. 189 and n. 32; MANN ix. 630–1).

3. Sir Edward Coke (1552–1634), Kt, 1603; lord chief justice of the Court of Common Pleas 1606–13 and of the King's Bench 1613–16; whose *Institutes of the Laws of England* was a basic manual of legal practice.

4. The second volume of *Miscellaneous Works of the Late . . . Earl of Chesterfield,* 1777, edited by Matthew Maty (1718–76), M.D., librarian of the BM.

5. Chesterfield's contributions to *The World.*

6. Chesterfield's letters to French correspondents are described by HW to Mason 13 March 1777, MASON i. 289–92.

Your account of David's *Life*,[7] and '*as how*' my Lords the Bishops have put lawn sleeves upon his bones, pleased me infinitely. They are charming people, these Bishops—my Lord Moreton[8] had excellent fun with them in the House of Lords upon the double sense of the original Greek, from which the term *Episcopacy* came—'that in his faith and troth, he thought one of the *etymologies* very suitable to their present lives and conduct; that they were very sharp and keen *lookers-out for preferment*, and were the *best Episcopi* in that sense that any age of the world had produced.' They disgrace the Revolution[9] by the narrow ground upon which they started it—they are for blood and victory in America—they have established the Catholic religion in Canada, which is '*at the worst an outrage of that spirit* of *toleration which animates every good Protestant Church*.'[10] These are a Bishop's words; and yet these tolerants-run-mad oppress the Dissenter at the same beck of the white-wands[11] and the King's friends. They tell us then that [the] Church as well as the civil power must be supreme in spirit and control, as well as in definition; that penalties, though too harsh to be ever executed, ought still to subsist, for the parade of the thing, and as a terror to those who are out of the pale. These Bishops coquette it most unmercifully with Sandwich[12] and Dartmouth,[13] sinner and Methodist; and, if the King should have taken unto himself a Madame de Montespan,[14] we should have seen these holy men prostrate at her feet.

Your acquittal of them from the imputation of an atheistical turn in their partiality for fame, by a little change of the person of the Divinity and his place of abode, is the most ingenious manœuvre that any advocate ever struck out. It's curious to see, in one of the younger Crébillon's letters to Lord Chesterfield, a manly and serious reflection upon Voltaire's irreligion,[15] as promoting immorality,

7. *The Life of David Hume, Esq., Written by Himself*, 1777. HW's comment on it is ibid. i. 289.

8. Probably James Douglas (1702 or 3–68), 14th E. of Morton, 1738, who was representative peer for Scotland in the House of Lords for thirty years.

9. The Revolution of 1688. Archbishop Sancroft and other bishops refused to comply with James II's orders to permit religious toleration, but, when William III seized the throne, they refused to take the oath of allegiance to him.

10. In other words, English toleration of Roman Catholicism in Canada was an outrage to religious tolerance because it encouraged an intolerant church.

11. The chief officers of state, some of whom held white wands as symbols of office.

12. John Montagu, 4th E. of Sandwich, a notorious libertine.

13. The second E. of Dartmouth, noted for his piety (MONTAGU i. 273).

14. Françoise-Athénaïs de Rochechouart (1641–1707), Marquise de Montespan; mistress of Louis XIV.

15. Crébillon's letter of 26 July 1742 (Chesterfield's *Miscellaneous Works*, ed. Maty, 1777, ii. 24–31) criticizes Voltaire

while he is writing *Sophas, Angolas, Ah! quel contes!*[16] etc. etc. more generally mischievous because more generally read and felt by young people of both sexes, calculated for the purpose of giving a refined and sentimental turn to every intrigue as an improvement of it, and at the same time representing every woman as a sensualist, with only this difference, that some are more of epicures than others. This too not in frolic, not in a desultory passage or two, but in cold blood, and upon a system.

My complaint of low spirits and real indisposition is too well founded. I am approaching to you valetudinarians with an eager pace; and, if I could possess half your flights, if I could ramble as you have done upon overgrown helmets and sighing pictures, I'd readily give up my porter's legs for your gouty and thin ones: but I don't like your putting up your pen because the age has no taste, any more than I commend Lord Camden's absence from his judicial duty in the House of Lords because he has been often outvoted by white and black wands, and Scotch peers, upon a hint from the Cabinet. *Do your duties,* both of you: *Ruat Cœlum.*[17] As to my indisposition, I am whimsical upon it. I sometimes think that a certain degree of it gives a delicacy and a tenderness to the mind without enervating it, and that it's no bad school (with all deference to the superior claims of the dancing master) for that mildness of temper and those affectionate feelings which mere politeness can but ill assume. A certain Mr Shakespear, who is supposed to have known something of human nature, has lightly and sweetly touched the moral use of misery in Lear's pathetic upon the tempest:

Expose thyself to feel what wretches feel[18]

but the whole rhapsody is a masterly picture of the effect which a keen resentment of a particular injury has upon the passions, in forming them by insensible degrees to a general turn of pity for the suffering part of the species, and of hatred for the vicious—But

for lack of patriotism rather than for immorality.

16. All but *Angola* are by the younger Crébillon. *Angola,* 1746, was written by Jacques Rochette de la Morlière (1719–85) (*Comtes du Chevalier de la Morlière,* ed. O. Uzanne, 1879, pp. xv–lv). Maty in a footnote agrees that Crébillon's 'object was to expose vice. . . . but Virtue must blush that her advocate should have indulged in images and descriptions likely to inflame rather than extinguish passions' (ibid. ii. 20n).

17. 'Ruat cœlum, fiat voluntas tua,' ('Let the heavens fall, but let thy will be done')—Roman proverb. See *Putnam's Complete Book of Quotations,* ed. W. Gurney Benham, New York, 1926, p. 647a.

18. *King Lear,* III. iv. 34.

there's no end of Shakespear's beauties upon the subject of pity, which he seems to have delighted in, and to have explored in all its varieties.

How sweetly he illustrates the connection between Pity and Love, in Othello's account of his courtship to Desdemona:

> She lov'd me for the dangers I had pass'd;
> And I lov'd her, that she did pity them.[19]

I have often been fool enough to cry over these two lines. By the way, though it's the fashion to say that the mind of man is naturally and radically vicious, one may easily refute that base and pernicious doctrine by carrying a parcel of schoolboys to a deep tragedy—their tears are arguments to vindicate the genuine feelings of the heart, and outweigh folios of cold metaphysical stuff on the other side of the question.

By the way, Soame Jenyns's book[20] is a notable supplement in character with such doctrines. If I could imagine that you would read my rambling stuff upon such topics, I would say a word upon that book in my next.[21]

In the meantime I announce to you that I will take you at your word, and steal a day from you at Strawberry Hill upon my return, which I hope will be in a week—when Soame and I shall wait upon you. In my next I'll take the liberty of desiring you to name your day.

Adieu, my dear Sir.

Most affectionately yours,

G. HARDINGE

My letters entirely resemble *deeds,* [not only] in length, but in admitting of no stops.

---

19. *Othello,* I. iii. 167–8.
20. Presumably *A View of the Internal* *Evidence of the Christian Religion,* 1776.
21. Missing.

From HARDINGE, ca Monday 28 April 1777

Printed from Nichols, *Lit. Illus.* iii. 199, where the date of the year is supplied. The illness of HW's nephew, necessitating HW's absence from SH, indicates the approximate date of the month.

Temple, Monday.

My dear Sir,

I AM sincerely concerned at the occasion[1] of my disappointment, both as it will hurry your spirits and distress your feelings; but to such a heart as yours, the doing good in this melancholy case will in part compensate for trouble and uneasiness.

Strawberry Hill was upon your account very kind to me,[2] and would not send me back till this morning. Delightful as that scene cannot fail to be, I was rather hipped at the loss of your company, that so much belongs to it, and becomes it so well.

When you can spare any of your time to my little claims upon your friendship, pray do me the favour to intimate as much by a line, and, in the meantime, believe me, dear Sir,

Your most affectionate friend,

G. HARDINGE

From HARDINGE, Sunday 6 July 1777

Printed from Nichols, *Lit. Illus.* iii. 199–200.

Belhouse, July 6, 1777.

My dear Sir,

CAN I refuse myself the joy of disclosing to your good and friendly heart an event nearer and dearer to me than any of my life? A lady has accepted me in marriage, whose birth, connections,

1. A second attack of insanity suffered by HW's nephew George, E. of Orford. HW spent the last ten days of April at Barton's Mills in Suffolk, where he was only five miles from his nephew, who was staying with the Rev. Dr Ball at Eriswell, Suffolk. See HW to Sir Edward Walpole 21, 22, and 25 April 1777; HW to Mason 2 May 1777 (MASON i. 305–6); COLE ii. 43n.

2. Hardinge mentions this visit in his account of Walpole; see Appendix 4.

and habits are quite as I could wish them to have been, whose person is very beautiful, and her fortune a very good one. My friends approve highly of my taste, and I am very ambitious for your countenance to it, because there does not live the man whose criticism I respect and wish to satisfy more than yours. *Miss Long*[1] was not acquainted with me three days without knowing the esteem and relish that her good man has for your friendship. This, and a certain ingenuous taste of her own for talents and amiable qualities, make her as desirous to know you, as I am to introduce her at Strawberry Hill and sleep with her in the same sweet little bed that received me when I gave myself airs in your absence, and used every part of your scene with such cavalierness and freedom. Adieu.

Pray do me the favour to write me a line upon the subject, if it is at all interesting to you, and deserves half a minute of your time. The *Dacres* are, you may suppose, not indifferent to this good fortune of mine. They are pretty well, and desire their compliments. I am, dear Sir,

Your most obliged and affectionate servant,

G. Hardinge

To Hardinge, Wednesday 9 July 1777

Printed from MS now wsl. Previously printed, Nichols, *Lit. Illus.* iii. 200–1, Toynbee x. 78–9. Sold Sotheby's, 6 Nov. 1951 (Nichols sale, lot 428) to Maggs Bros for wsl.
Address: To George Hardinge, Esq., on the Oxford Circuit.
Postmark: Isleworth.
Endorsed: H. Walpole.

Strawberry Hill, July 9, 1777.

YOU have long been good and kind to me, dear Sir; this new instance of your friendship is the kindest of all, and is not sown in barren ground. The choice the young lady has made gives me a more favourable opinion of her than all your encomiums. I hope she will make you happy, and I will answer for your making her so; and

1. Lucy Long (d. 1820), m. (20 Oct. 1777) George Hardinge (Berry ii. 198, n. 4; DNB *sub* Hardinge).

that is a great deal in favour of the match; for I am of opinion that nine unhappy marriages in ten spring from faults on the husband's side. Women acquire liberty by marrying, find themselves happier than they were, and love the author. But men, either perfidiously do not intend to confine themselves, or grow weary of the restraint; and the chains on our side are so easily shaken off, and so little shame attends the resumption of our liberty, that it is no wonder voluntary prisoners do not remain long in prison. You see, as partial as I am to you, I shall still be ready to think you to blame, if you do not continue as happy as you seem to be at present. You are not quite young enough to have made an inconsiderate choice: the approbation of your family says you have not, and it is like your good sense to be pleased with their satisfaction. Your naming me favourably to the young lady, though a strain of friendship far beyond my merit, is another evidence of your good heart, and what I hope she will not think a mark of too much partiality in your disposition, for I wish her to respect your judgment as much as your other good qualities, and I doubt this is not the best proof you can give: yet she will have the better opinion of mine for knowing how early I received them. I can but wish you all the happiness and success I have long wished you, but I am glad you have new incitement to ambition and the exercise of your talents. A marriage is likely to improve felicity, when the wife has continual occasions of increasing her respect for her husband. I must do the ladies another piece of justice, which is to observe that the wives of great men are generally excellent wives, and attached to their glory. The inference on the contrary is, that contempt is one cause of faults in the woman. I have certainly not thought much on the subject of matrimony, and perhaps my remarks may be more new than just: perhaps too observations suggested by common sense extempore, are likely to be as true as those made on commonplace topics by premeditation. I have zeal enough to have sent you a better epithalamium. It might have had compliments better turned, but wit or poetry would not have expressed my sincerity; and I am too old to write anything but what I think. So, be congratulated as you will, you will receive none more from the heart than these warm good wishes of dear Sir,

Yours most cordially,

Hor. Walpole

From HARDINGE, Saturday 19 July 1777

Printed from Nichols, *Lit. Illus.* iii. 201.

Oxford Circuit, July 19, 1777.

Frontis ad urbanæ, etc.[1] I will risk, by a little pertness, even beyond my usual character in that line, your displeasure, for the mere *chance* of catching in some good-natured minute (*a singular one* it must be at Strawberry Hill) a defiance of etiquette, perhaps of delicacy, in my dear friend. In short, I love the *tall woman*[2] so much who has accepted of me that I cannot be happy till you send her an account that I am *sober, clean, diligent, honest, handy, etc.* Do me this favour, and say that you feel it to be wrong, but that you love me too well to refuse me. She has so good a taste that she will worship you for it, and laugh at the old women who say that she is *incorrespondabilis* to all *my* friends, till I have gone to bed to her—Stuff, that I am *boy* enough to laugh at; but you, that are an *ancient bachelor,* may take the credit of that amiable conflict between love to me and your *passion* for decency. In short, I will ask it of you, and refuse me if you dare: *Pray write to Miss Long, Hinxton, Cambridgeshire;* and take my word for it that she is worthy of *your* affection; as to *mine,* it is not worth having. *You are* (I aver it) *younger* than I am, and have more *vivacity,* etc.; yet, I thank Heaven that I (*myself I*) have not a very cold *heart* or *fancy.* But that I am warmer in *both* points, and have a better taste in *all* points, from the time that I have *known* and *admired you* (need I add the *latter?*) I can swear before a Justice of Peace.

A thousand thanks to you for your kind and spirited letter. I really at heart love my choice; else my friends (whom *à l'ordinaire* I did not *consult* till I had *resolved*) would have had no weight. God and your own *goodness* and *dullness* make you happy! May I add *Mrs Hardinge* in my next visit at Twickenham?

Yours ever, my good Sir,

G. HARDINGE

---

1. 'Frontis ad urbanæ descendi præmia' ('I have stooped for the prize of town-bred confidence') (Horace, *Epistles* I. 9. 11).

2. A pun on Miss Long's name.

From HARDINGE, July 1777

Printed from Nichols, *Lit. Illus.* iii. 201–2, where the date of the year is supplied.

July.

My dear Sir,

IN my Miss Long's house is a supposed Vandyke, and said to be the first idea for the large equestrian figure of Count Aremberg at Holkham.[1] Sir Joshua thinks it no such thing, but a copy of the upper part of that celebrated picture. He thinks it, however, a contemporary one, and good. May I send it for your inspection and opinion? I shall be in town again very soon. In the meantime a line to the Temple will be forwarded.

Ever most affectionately yours, my dear Sir,

G. HARDINGE

From HARDINGE, Friday 26 September 1777

Printed from Nichols, *Lit. Illus.* iii. 202, where the letter is misdated Thursday.

Albury, Thursday, Sept. 26, 1777.

Dear Sir,

PRAY do me the favour to let me know what *day* next week you will suffer me to trouble you with the Vandyke *soi-disant*—your *hour* too shall be most punctually observed. I will not honour you with a peep at my little personage till you can salute in the old-fashioned way a very tall wife, that must love you if she means to make me an old-fashioned husband. She dotes upon you already for your gallantry in ascribing the misconduct of the ladies to the cold-

1. 'At Holkham is a large equestrian picture of a Count D'Aremberg; both the rider and horse are in his best manner' (*Anecdotes of Painting*, ii., 1762, p. 94). The painting at Holkham is called 'Vandyck's equestrian "Duc D'Arenburg"' in Christopher Hussey's *English Country Houses: Early Georgian*, 1955, p. 141, and is depicted at the end of the Saloon, ibid. 138.

ness of their legal bedfellows.¹ Favour me with a line at Mr Vachel's,²
in Chesterfield Street. Adieu.

G. HARDINGE

To HARDINGE, ca October 1777

A missing letter of congratulation, acknowledged *post* 29 Oct. 1777.

From HARDINGE, Wednesday 29 October 1777

Printed from Nichols, *Lit. Illus.* iii. 202–3; misdated 'Thursday.'

Grove,¹ near Sevenoaks, Kent,
Thursday, Oct. 29, 1777.

THOUGH the wedding is over, my dear friend, the honeymoon
promises not only to outlive the lunar, but the madder and
longer one of the American War. Is not this *beaucoup dire?* No human being, thank heaven, was ever born with a deeper sense of the
duties and delicacies of that sacred union which has bound me for my
life to the most engaging and affectionate female that ever blessed it.
There is not a sentiment in your letter (except as to the Seals) which
I do not appropriate in my own feelings, though I could not have
expressed it with half the happiness and spirit that animates your
pen the most when it stands up for the vulgar prejudices of *good* and
fair, which the *old philosophy* loved. I shall be happier even than I
am at this moment, in the pleasure of introducing to you a modest,
but an elegant woman; whose beauty, though much admired, is a
despicable part of her, compared to her ingenuous principles, the
goodness of her heart, sweetness of her temper, and delicacy of her
sentiments. I promise you her love (pig in a poke as you are to her)

1. See *ante* HW to Hardinge 9 July
1777.
2. Presumably a relative of Lucy Long,
Hardinge's fiancée (*post* Hardinge to HW
26 Dec. 1777).

———

1. Hardinge's mother 'with two of her
daughters, had retired to the country of
Kent; and she closed her days at Grove
Hill, a pretty little seat in the vicinity of
the residence of her nephew, the present
Marquis Camden' (Nichols, *Lit. Illus.* iii.
8).

if you will do her the honour to accept of it; she loves goodness and cleverness in every shape, and I must think her, till you undeceive me (and I shall find you out, though you do not say a word), not undeserving of your protection. She has natural powers very much above par for drawing, and I mean to cultivate them, as they are ingenuous ornaments of a domestic scene. As to the Seals, the warmth of your goodness to me runs away with your gouty feet, and I must bring you back to your cut shoes upon that subject; nor indeed do you do *her* justice when you say that I shall use her ill if I should remain at the bottom of the ladder. I told her early all my hopes and fears, and discovered (which endeared her the more to me) that she was indifferent entirely to the condition of my little fames and fortunes. Indeed, she accepted me without knowing the amount of either. On the other hand, I conjure you to believe that I shall give to ambition, for her sake, every effort consistent with honour, and shall endeavour to imitate Prior's Henry[2] in the turn that he gives to Emma's fate after the severe trial to which he had exposed her, and which, by the way, is carried so far that I do not half like him when he becomes Edgar's heir, and flourishes away with his coaxer's pin-moneys, etc.

 Adieu, dear Sir. If you wish to make me worthy of your future preference, let me see you often. Your attention to me just now makes me more than ever most affectionately,

G. HARDINGE

To HARDINGE, ca November–December 1777

Missing. Answered in the next letter.

---

2. Matthew Prior's 'Henry and Emma. Poem, Upon the Model of the Nut-Brown Maid,' ll. 252–655; Henry pretends first that he is a murderer and must flee into exile and hiding. Emma offers to dress as a man and come with him. He pretends to have found another love; Emma offers to come along and help serve her. Touched by Emma's devotion, Henry finally declares his true identity as the son of the powerful Earl, and his undying attachment to Emma.

From HARDINGE, Monday 22 December 1777

Printed from Nichols, *Lit. Illus.* iii. 203.

Grove, Sevenoaks, Dec. 22, 1777.

Dear Sir,

YOU will very particularly oblige me if you will acquaint me whether *Hampden's wedding*-gloves[1] are those which he presented to his first or second wife,[2] and when and how you took possession of them, and what authority you have to fix them upon him. Many thanks to you for your obliging notice of my recommendation. You talk of consigning Shakespeare to the Americans; you say well: they have already sublime features. What think you of their terms to Burgoyne?[3] Adieu, my dear Sir.

Mrs Hardinge, who wishes to love you for yourself as well as for me, desires her most respectful compliments.

To HARDINGE, ca Wednesday 24 December 1777

Missing. Answered in the next letter.

From HARDINGE, Friday 26 December 1777

Printed from Nichols, *Lit. Illus.* iii. 203.

Grove, Sevenoaks, Dec. 26, 1777.

YOU are a most irritable and choleric antiquary. I question your authenticities? What passage in my letter denoted my suspicion of them? Hampden had two wives: the second, Edmondson says,[1]

1. HW had in the glass closet of the Great North Bedchamber at SH, 'the wedding gloves of Mrs Hampden, wife of the celebrated John Hampden [1594–1643]' ('Des. of SH,' *Works,* ii. 499). The gloves were sold SH xvi. 55 to J. H. Forbes for £4.

2. Hampden first married in 1619 Elizabeth Symeon (d. 1634); his second wife was Letitia Knollys (d. 1666), widow of Sir Thomas Vachell, Kt.

3. Gen. John Burgoyne (1722–92). The news of his surrender at Saratoga, 17 Oct., reached London on 2 Dec. (MANN viii. 340, n. 14). His troops were to go back to England on parole, on condition of not serving again in America (ibid. viii. 340–1).

———

1. *Baronagium genealogicum,* 1764, v. 412: 'second wife Lettitia Vachell dyed 1666.'

was a *Vachel;* and I wish to know whether your gloves were presented to her or to the first wife. My reason for this query is that I belong by marriage to the *Vachels,* and want to connect them with *your gloves.* I delight in your collision of Hampden with James the Second.[2] Pray honour me with a line or two; and indulge me, as I am no sceptic (save in the case of one King Richard III, and *who*[3] has taught me to *doubt* there?), with a detail of your evidence upon gloves and spurs.[4] I shall really take it as a very particular favour to, my dear Sir,

Your most affectionate,

G. HARDINGE

From HARDINGE, ca spring 1778

Printed from Nichols, *Lit. Illus.* iii. 203, where it and the next letter are placed between those of 26 Dec. 1777 and 21 June 1779.

Adelphi, Tuesday.

My dear Sir,

IF you think it necessary (which I do not) that you should give yourself the trouble of making a bow to Mrs Hardinge here before she may curtsy to you at Strawberry Hill, be it so; and let me know on what hour of Wednesday, Thursday, or Friday, you will appoint the ceremony. Our ambition is to reach your heart, and we are therefore the less tenacious of our dignities in mode and form. We shall, if you will give us leave, dine, and pass the evening with you on Sunday next upon the banks of the Thames; and, unless you will reconnoitre the lady first that you may take measure of her for the bed, I see no reason for the white-glove preliminaries—but you shall decide.

Adieu, my dear Sir. I am, as warmly as ever,

Your obliged and affectionate servant,

G. HARDINGE

2. Possibly a mistake for James I, since HW had (likewise in the glass closet in the Great North Bedchamber) 'a pair of gloves, worn by King James the First; bought out of Thoresby's museum' ('Des. of SH,' *Works* ii. 499). They were sold SH xvi. 54 to W. M. Smith for £2 12s.
3. HW himself, in *Historic Doubts.*
4. The spurs of King William III (*ante* HW to Harcourt 8 Oct. 1777).

From HARDINGE, ca 1778

Printed from Nichols, *Lit. Illus.* iii. 203–4.

Adelphi, Sunday.

Dear Sir,

MR Capell,[1] an honest and sagacious editor, has three volumes of notes upon Shakespeare that remain to be published. There is a knot of booksellers formed against him because he is (I will not say the best, but) the only editor of Shakespeare.

I have therefore advised him to accept of a subscription; to which he is averse, as being a man of a competent fortune, and a man of high spirit, though to a degree short of encountering the publication at his own expense. My Lord Dacre is a warm patron of his works, and I mention this emphatically, as it would be the height of arrogance in me to recommend him upon my own single opinion, or without the most respectable authority at my elbow. We propose to make the subscription a guinea the volume, only one guinea to be deposited now, and that in a banker's hands, to be recovered if the editor should die. May I put your name down?[2] Our list cannot receive so important an honour from any other. I wish you every blessing, and am, with the highest respect and the warmest love,

Yours, my dear Sir, most unalterably,

G. HARDINGE

1. Edward Capell (1713–81), Shakespearian scholar. His 3-vol. *Notes and Various Readings to Shakespeare* was only partly printed before his death (BM Cat.).

2. HW apparently did not subscribe, but he owned a copy of Capell's *Prolusions*, 1760 (Hazen, *Cat. of HW's Lib.*, No. 2003).

From HARDINGE, Monday 21 June 1779

Printed from Nichols, *Lit. Illus.* iii. 204.

Bedford Square, Monday, June 21, 1779.

My dear Sir,

MAY I hope that you will honour these drawings of Madame de Sévigné's favourite scene[1] with a little place in your cabinet? Accept them, I entreat you, as a mark of my attachment and affection. I am, with the highest respect and the warmest regard, my dear Sir, ever yours,

GEO. HARDINGE

To HARDINGE, ca Tuesday 29 June 1779

A missing inquiry about Hardinge's present to HW, explained in the next letter.

From HARDINGE, Thursday 1 July 1779

Printed from Nichols, *Lit. Illus.* iii. 204.

July 1, 1779.

My dear Sir,

A MERE blunder of my John Moody of a servant occasioned the detainer of my *noble present,* at the oppression of which your nerves have taken such an alarm.

> Forget you!—
> No; from the table of my memory, etc.
> I'll wipe away all trivial dull records
> That fees and law chicane have copied there.[1]

1. Grignan, in southeastern France, where Mme de Sévigné's daughter lived. HW placed them in the Breakfast Room at SH, and described them as 'Four washed views of the château de Grignan in Provence: a present from George Hardinge, Esq.' ('Des. of SH,' *Works* ii. 424).

A MS note in the Spencer copy of the *Des. of SH,* 1774, adds the date '1778.' They were sold SH xi. 107 to Lady Shelley for £2.

————

1. A paraphrase of *Hamlet,* I. v. 97–101.

I live in St Giles's, you in Arlington Street, which accounts for the difficulties of intercourse between us. The attorneys would give me half a guinea less if I were to be seen at your door, and poverty makes me think half a guinea superior to all the charms of taste and friendship. However, I will be wicked enough to be happy one day in my life, and beg you to name it. Adieu. Pray tell me what you think of Grignan.[2]

To Hardinge, Sunday 4 July 1779

Printed from Nichols, *Lit. Anec.* viii. 527 and from Anna Seward, *Letters,* Edinburgh, 1811, i. 370–1; reprinted, Cunningham vii. 218–19, Toynbee x. 435–7.

Strawberry Hill, July 4, 1779.

I HAVE now received the drawings of Grignan, and know not how to express my satisfaction and gratitude but by a silly witticism that is like the studied quaintness of the last age. In short, they are so much more beautiful than I expected, that I am *not* surprised at *your* having surprised me by exceeding even what I expected from your well known kindness to me. They are charmingly executed, and with great taste. I own too that Grignan is grander, and in a much finer situation, than I had imagined, as I concluded that the witchery of Madame de Sévigné's ideas and style had spread the same leaf-gold over *places* with which she gilded her *friends*. All that has appeared of *them* since the publication of her letters has lowered them. A single letter of her daughter,[1] that to Paulina[2] with a description of the Duchess of Bourbon's[3] toilette, is worthy of the mother.[4] Paulina's own letters contain not a tittle worth reading; one just divines that she might have written well if she had had anything to write about (which, however, would not have signified to her grandmother). Coulanges[5] was a silly, good-humoured glutton, that flat-

2. Hardinge's gift of four views of Grignan (*ante* Hardinge to HW 21 June 1779).

———

1. Mme de Grignan (*ante* HW to Bentley 24 Dec. 1754, n. 2). The letter was that of 4 Jan. 1697 (Mme de Sévigné, *Lettres,* ed. Monmerqué, 1862–6, x. 425–8).

2. Mme de Simiane (*ante* HW to Harcourt 6 Dec. 1773, n. 9).

3. Louise-Françoise de Bourbon (1673–1743), called Mlle de Nantes, m. (1685) Louis III, Duc de Bourbon (La Chenaye-Desbois iii. 761, viii. 589).

4. Cf. HW to Mme du Deffand, 22 Sept. 1768 (DU DEFFAND, ii. 141).

5. Mme de Sévigné's cousin (*ante* HW to Chute 4 Aug. 1753, n. 20). HW (DU DEFFAND loc. cit.) called him 'un gourmand, et bouffon médiocre.'

tered a rich widow for her dinners. His wife[6] was sensible: but dry, and rather peevish at growing old. Unluckily nothing more has come to light of Madame de Sévigné's son,[7] whose short letters in the collection I am almost *profane* enough to prefer to his mother's; and which makes me astonished that she did not love his wit, so unaffected, and so congenial to her own, in preference to the eccentric and sophisticated reveries of her sublime and ill-humoured daughter. Grignan alone maintains its dignity, and shall be consecrated here among other monuments of that bewitching period, and amongst which one loves to lose one's self, and drink oblivion of an era so very unlike; for the awkward bigots to despotism of our time have not Madame de Sévigné's address, nor can paint an Indian idol with an hundred hands as graceful as the Apollo of the Belvidere. When will you come and accept my thanks? will Wednesday next suit you? But do you know that I must ask you not to leave your gown behind you, which indeed I never knew you put on willingly, but to come in it. I shall want your protection at Westminster Hall[8] against the Bishops, an odious race, whether clerical or laic. You heard how infamously I have been treated by Colonel and by Ned Bishop.[9] Oh! they could not be worse if they were in orders.

Yours most cordially,

H. Walpole

6. Marie-Angélique du Gué Bagnolles (1641–1723), m. (1659) Philippe-Emmanuel, Marquis de Coulanges.

7. Charles (1648–1713), Marquis de Sévigné (NBG; Mme de Sévigné to Bussy 15 March 1648, Monmerqué, op. cit. i. 367). In 1698 he published three *Factums* or critical essays on the Latin poet Horace.

8. Where HW awaited his suit in Chancery against the heirs of Sir Cecil Bishopp or Bisshopp, from whom HW was buying Sir Cecil's former house in Berkeley Square. The purchase was delayed by a rejection from one heir, and HW complained of having to keep the purchase money uninvested during the interval (Ossory ii. 108–9, iii. 250–1). The text from this point is supplied from Anna Seward, *Letters*, i. 371, Hardinge having sent her the letter.

9. Col. Thomas Bisshopp (ca 1737–1805) and his brother Edward (d. 1792) disclaimed responsibility for HW's complaint (Ossory ii. 109, n. 2, iii. 251, 287).

From HARDINGE, Tuesday ca 6 July 1779

Printed from Nichols, *Lit. Illus.* iii. 204–5.

Bedford Square, Tuesday, July, 1779.

I AM delighted, my dear Sir, that Grignan satisfies you. The *taste* and *spirit* which you ascribe to it are '*lucro apposita.*'[1] As I could only dare to vouch for the *integrity* of the *portrait* and genuine *beauty* of the *scene*—the hope of communicating to you some part of my own enjoyment added very much to it, and I was therefore paid beforehand far above the value, so that I consider this additional *douceur* of your thanks and approbation as clear money in my pocket. You cannot hate the Bishops[2] more than I do the lawyers, though, upon the maxim of 'Employ a thief to catch a thief,' I should not dissuade recourse to the Long Robe against the Lawn Sleeves. What a cynosure in the vulgar list of *our* heroes is my Lord Somers! Can you bear with those who have committed *his* fame in a late mutilated publication?[3] Upon the same principle, 'King William, *with all his defects, deserves to be venerated,*'[4] and 'King James's principles are *exceptionable,*[5] *Dalrymple and Macpherson are commended;*'[6] and an apology is made for the Indian Idol[7] in the most vulnerable part of him, but which at St James's must not be too much abused in this reign—'Perfidy and war, upon the single plea of ambition, and this too the ambition to extend the circle of tyranny.'

1. 'Touched with gold,' an echo of HW's 'spread the same leaf-gold' (*ante* HW to Hardinge 4 July 1779). See also *ante* HW to Nuneham 6 Dec. 1773.

2. The Bisshopp family, whom HW was suing, and the bishops of the Church, whom he disliked (ibid.).

3. *Miscellaneous State Papers,* 1778, edited by Philip Yorke, 2d E. of Hardwicke; it included some of Lord Somers's papers.

4. 'If King William was guilty of any fault . . . it was the relying too little on the sentiments of his English ministry' (ibid. ii. 334).

5. James is called 'that exact and diligent Prince,' 'though his principles and his judgment were erroneous, and exceptionable, in the highest degree' (ibid. ii. 304).

6. Hardwicke identifies, as Dalrymple's

and Macpherson's, 'some late histories,' 'which in the main deserve great credit, being derived from very authentic sources' (COLE ii. 66, n. 1, quoting *Miscellaneous State Papers* ii. 304). These are Sir John Dalrymple's *Memoirs of Great Britain* (*ante* Hardinge to HW 21 June 1771) and the *History of Great Britain from the Restoration to the Accession of the House of Hannover,* 1775, by James Macpherson (1736–96).

7. Perhaps a reference to Bolingbroke who is praised in *Miscellaneous State Papers* ii. 333 for his 'manner convincing in itself and candid.' George III's tutors were said to be under Bolingbroke's influence (MANN iv. 323). HW's letter to Hardinge, *ante* 4 July 1779, had mentioned the 'Indian idol' merely as statuary.

I love your idea of running away from such an era, and hiding yourself under the petticoats of Madame de Sévigné. I often think of a sentiment in Grevile's book,[8] which he or she applies to a coxcomb, that faults often displease for being incomplete[9]—but it goes further, and makes me at this moment prefer Algiers or Constantinople to London. The ministerial highwayman of these times does not hold his pistol to us like a gentleman. He bungles, and shows that he has no civility nor honesty unless from cowardice—and his lenity upon such principles becomes an insult and a distinct species of oppression. I would go ten miles out of my way to dine with an old brickbat of a Tory who hates *Hanover rats*, and drinks, as _____ used to do, before I would go half a yard for the company of a modern Whig.

G. HARDINGE

From HARDINGE, ca May–June 1780

A 'former note,' mentioned *post* 3 July 1780.

To HARDINGE, ca June 1780

HW's missing answer to Hardinge's 'former note.' Mentioned in the next letter.

8. *Maxims, Characters, and Reflections,* 1756, by Fulke Greville (1717–ca 1805), M.P. HW's copy is Hazen, *Cat. of HW's Lib.,* No. 2009.

9. 'There are faults which as they become greater displease less' (p. 31).

From HARDINGE, Monday 3 July 1780

Printed from Nichols, *Lit. Illus.* iii. 205–6.

Bedford Square, July 3, 1780.

My dear Sir,

I SHOULD ill deserve your friendship if I took an unfair advantage of it. I told you in my former note that I was not sure whether my father[1] had obtained, or only asked, the help of your press, according to the account given me by Mr Pelham[2] as from Mr George Montagu.[3] But I *am* sure that Mr Pelham did not understand or convey to me any idea that you had *waived* it, for he rather exhorted me to make the application from what he supposed to have passed between you and my father, as represented to him by Mr George Montagu. I shall see Mr Pelham in a few days and will tell you more accurately what he supposes Mr George Montagu to have said. The 'Essay upon the Regency'[4] is not political, but historical and legal.

Whatever passed between you and my father applied, I imagine, to his English verses as well as to his Latin, for he bound them together, dated them, and explained them by notes with equal care, as if he destined them equally for the same publication.[5] But I should be sorry to build an exemption in my favour from your general plan, upon Mr George Montagu's ideas of a supposed promise, if they amount even to that, passing to me at second hand from him—when you, who have not the worst memory in the world, not only do not recollect the circumstance, and which must have made an impression even upon a *common* memory, but recollect the general cause of your determinations to have opposed any such promise, and particular instances in which you have refused the same thing to those who were more likely to have prevailed.

1. Nicholas Hardinge (*ante* HW to Bentley 5 Aug. 1752, n. 57).

2. It is not certain which Pelham this is, or when this conversation occurred. HW's friendship with Montagu lapsed in 1770.

3. Presumably HW's former correspondent, who died 9 May 1780 (COLE ii. 211, n. 3).

4. To Nicholas Hardinge's *Poems, Latin, Greek, and English,* 1818, was added 'An Historical Enquiry and Essay upon the Administration of Government in England during the King's Minority' (DNB *sub* Hardinge, Nicholas).

5. The Latin poems, edited by George Hardinge, appeared in 1780 as *Poemata auctore Nicolao Hardinge.*

The fair thing, in all such cases, is to forget one's own interest, and personate *all* the parties. The result is that, *as G.H.,* I naturally wish that I could satisfy myself. *As H.W.* or as *Lord Hardwicke,* etc. that you ought to do what I asked of you, and asked before I was aware of these difficulties. I hope you will permit me to beg your acceptance of the book, such as it is, when I have printed it; and be assured that I owe you my best thanks for the obliging manner in which you have condescended to explain yourself upon the subject. I am, dear Sir, with most affectionate and grateful esteem,

Yours ever,

G. HARDINGE

From HARDINGE, Monday 17 July 1780

Printed from Nichols, *Lit. Illus.* iii. 206–7.

Hinxton, July 17, 1780.

My dear Sir,

LORD Dacre has lately favoured me with a sight of some of my father's letters, written to him when he was abroad in 1749,[1] and in the two or three following years. In one of them, dated September, 1750, is a passage which I give to you *verbatim,* without further preface: 'During my stay there [at Kimbolton],[2] though I was disappointed in my search after political letters, etc. I met with an ancient pedigree, finely illuminated, of the Earls of Warwick, to whom, by the line of Monthermer, the Montagus pretend to be related. Have you ever seen it?[3] or have you observed the history contained in it? At the end of the roll is this title: "Thys Rol was labur'd and finishid by Master John Rows[4] of Warewyk." This Rows (Rossus Warvicensis) is commended by Leland[5] for his accuracy and fidelity. He died A.D. 1491.'

1. Thomas Barrett Lennard (later Lord Dacre) and his wife were in Italy 1749–50 (MANN iv. 75–194 *passim*).
2. Kimbolton Castle, Huntingdonshire, the seat of the Dukes of Manchester.
3. HW had seen it; Lord Sandwich borrowed the manuscript for him in 1768. For HW's description of it, see COLE, i. 133–4; GRAY, i. 177–8; 'Supplement to the Historic Doubts,' *Works,* ii. 216.
4. John Rous (? 1411–91), antiquary.
5. John Leland (ca 1506–52), antiquary.

'The figure of every hero and heroine of the family is delineated in colours. The *person* of *Richard III*, who married the heiress[6] of this family, is represented as *erect, graceful,* and *genteel*. His son's[7] face is like his own. Under the father's portrait is this character: "The moost myghty Prynce Rychard, by the grace of God, Kynge of Ynglond and of Fraunce, and Lord of Irelond, by verrey matrimony uithout dicontynewance or any defylynge yn the lawe by eyre male lineally dyscendynge fro Kynge Harre the Second—all avaryce set a syde, rewled his subjectys yn hys realme full commendabylly, punishyng offenders of hys lawes, specially extorcioners and oppressers of hys comyns and chereschyng tho that were vertues, by the whyche dyscrete guydynge he gat gret thanke of God and love of all his subjettys, ryche and pore, and gret laud of the people of all other landys about hym." '

Is not this an extraordinary character, given of Richard III after his death and in the reign of Henry VII? Carte,[8] I am told, in his new history, vindicates Richard (as Buck[9] has done before him) from at least many of the crimes imputed to him, and has attempted to demonstrate that Perkin Warbeck[10] was really the Duke of York, brother of Edward V. The portrait of Richard III in this genealogy is a confirmation of Lady Desmond's[11] report, and the character is a great coincidence in his favour. I am aware of all that you have said relative to this author in your *Historic Doubts;* and yet I cannot help thinking that such a character, drawn by him in the reign of Henry VII and for the Earl of Warwick[12] or his family, an evidence of some weight. It proves, first, that Richard III could not have maltreated Anne Beauchamp,[13] his mother-in-law, else this character

6. Anne Neville (1456–85), dau. of Richard Neville (1428–71), 16th E. of Warwick, called 'the king-maker'; she m. 1 (1470) Edward, Prince of Wales (son of Henry VI), 2 (1472) Richard, Duke of Gloucester, later (1483–5) Richard III, K. of England.

7. Edward (1473–84), Prince of Wales.

8. Thomas Carte (1686–1754), author of the *General History of England,* 1747–55.

9. Sir George Buc or Buck (d. 1623), Kt; author of the *History of the Life and Reigne of Richard the Third,* 1646. On p. 79 he defends Richard from the charge of deformity (COLE ii. 153, n. 12).

10. Perkin Warbeck (1474–99), who claimed the English throne as being Richard (1473–83 to 85), Duke of York,

son of Edward IV.

11. Catherine Fitzgerald (d. 1604) m. (between 1505 and 1534) Thomas Fitzthomas Fitzgerald, 11th E. of Desmond, 1529. She was said to have danced with Richard III whom she described as 'very well-made' (HW to Charles O'Hara 17 Sept. 1757).

12. Edward Plantagenet (1475–99), 2d E. of Warwick, n.c., was the only male holder the Warwick title in Henry VII's reign.

13. Anne Beauchamp (ca 1426–92), m. (1434) Richard Neville, 16th and 1st E. of Warwick; she was cr. (1450) Cts of Warwick, s.j. Her daughter Anne married Richard III.

would scarce have appeared in the records of *her* descendants, and when that injury must have been recent; secondly, such a *secret* and disinterested *éloge* is not inconsistent with a public testimony of the same witness, founded in the vulgar creed, and calculated for Court favour. I beg you to accept this communication as an humble mark of my attention to that curious work, *The Historic Doubts*. Be so good as to favour me with your sentiments upon the subject, by a line to me upon the Oxford Circuit. At Sir John Griffin's[14] the other day I met *your* Bentley, whom I was glad to see, as a very singular genius. I discovered, by an accident, that you are still generous to him. Believe me, dear Sir,

Your most affectionate servant,

GEO. HARDINGE

To HARDINGE, ca Thursday 20 July 1780

A missing letter, telling Hardinge that HW already knew the pedigree at Kimbolton. Answered in the next letter.

From HARDINGE, Monday 24 July 1780

Printed from Nichols, *Lit. Illus.* iii. 207-8.

Oxford Circuit, July 24, 1780.

My dear Sir,

THOUGH I am desperately piqued that you knew of my *pedigree* before, I forgive you, in consideration of your intelligence concerning a *future edition*[1] with *new evidence*. Permit me to risk your anticipation again by suggesting first, that you commend Comines[2] as being *honest,* and *well acquainted with our history,* but say nothing of such parts in him as bear hard upon Richard, though you avail yourself of him where he is favourable to that

---

14. Sir John Griffin Griffin (1719–97), K.B., 1761; 4th Bn Howard de Walden, 1784; cr. (1788) Bn Braybrooke.

1. HW's *Supplement to the Historic*

Doubts was printed in the quarto edition of HW's *Works,* 1771, but not published until 1798 (Hazen, *Bibl. of HW* 72).

2. Philippe de Comines (1445–1509), chronicler.

Prince. Secondly, that you appear to represent More[3] as having stated no pre-contract urged by the Duchess of York,[4] but that of Elizabeth Lucy;[5] whereas in truth More says[6] that the Duchess of York named Eleanor Talbot,[7] though he puts Elizabeth Lucy into Shaw's[8] mouth; and, by the way, I think *Shaw* says that *Elizabeth Lucy was named by the Duchess of York,* and it should seem, therefore, that More, after having circumstantially stated as an historical fact that the Duchess had named Eleanor Talbot, and Richard had made inquiries concerning her, could scarce mean a shift in the mention of another mistress as the object of the *same* pre-contract stated by Shaw; and the inference ought rather to be that Shaw mistook one of the mistresses for the other, and that Sir Thomas More put one of them down in the hurry of his pen, though he refers to a passage in his own work which named the other. I state these two remarks because they have struck many admirers of your work as deserving attention. Hume,[9] who cannot speak truth if he wished it, falsely says that Sir Thomas More mentions both with equal slight. In fact he mentions Eleanor Talbot's pre-contract in terms of respect, as well as Richard's inquiry concerning it. As to the Roll of Parliament, I think your observation equally forcible against More, whether he had uniformly named Eleanor Talbot or not, because the dilemma is unanswerable as you have printed it. Either he knew it, or he was ignorant of it; if he knew it, he suppressed it, which is a wilful concealment of truth; if he knew it not, what credit is due

3. Sir Thomas More (1478–1535), historian, philosopher, and saint. The passage occurs in his *History of King Richard the Third:* 'Wherefore ye kinges mother obiected openly against his [Edward IV's] mariage . . . that the kinge was sure to dame Elisabeth Lucy and her husband before god' (*Complete Works of St Thomas More,* New Haven, 1963– , ii. ed. Sylvester, 64).

4. Lady Cecily Nevile (1415–95), m. (1424) Richard, 3d E. of York; mother of Richard III. Part of her son's plot later included charging her with adultery too, making Richard III her first surviving legitimate son.

5. Elizabeth Lucy's identity has not been established (Sylvester, op. cit. ii. 243–4).

6. More apparently did not even know of Lady Eleanor's existence (ibid. ii. 243).

7. Lady Eleanor Butler was sometimes identified as the daughter of John Talbot, Earl of Shrewsbury, but this seems to be erroneous (ibid.).

8. Dr Ralph Shaw or Shaa (d. ca 1484), S.T.B.; preached a sermon at St Paul's Cross on 22 June 1483 in which the public heard for the first time the charges that Edward V and even Edward IV were illegitimate children, and that the rightful heir to the English throne was Richard, Duke of Gloucester, soon to be Richard III. Shaw, according to More (Sylvester, op. cit. ii. 66), said 'yt also dame Elisabeth Lucy was verely the wife of King Edward.'

9. David Hume. The reference is to his *History of England,* 1754–62, ii. 426, where Edward IV was said to have been privately married to 'the Lady Eleanor Talbot, daughter of the Earl of Shrewsbury.' Nothing is said about More's testimony.

to an historian ignorant of such a fact so attested? Here too, Hume deserves a good dressing, for he says roundly that neither Prince nor people, nor even the rabble, adopted this pre-contract, and that nothing like an assembly of Peers or Commons gave any countenance to it. I am not acquainted with your sentiments of Campbell, who wrote the *Lives of the Admirals*,[10] nor aware that you have or have not read the passage in that work which treats of Edward the Fifth's murder. He seems, for a dipper in the question, to make a very liberal comment. N.B. Have you seen the notes upon Buck, which are hostile to him, and impute sometimes mutilated or misrecited quotations to his partiality for his hero?

Before I conclude, suffer me to ask you two questions: first, when is the new edition to come out? and secondly, what new evidence is come to light?

I see no indelicacy in requesting this communication, as I am sure you can have no doubt of my honour if you should wish me to conceal it; but I may be wrong in asking it, as I was concerning *R.B.*[11] If I am, forgive me this additional error in judgment and refuse to indulge me in what you may perhaps think a womanish curiosity. I shall consider the subject a little and trouble you with anything new that occurs to me if I am in time. It strikes me that a few broad and clear principles of evidence in the outset would relieve the reader and facilitate his conviction. I shall try something of that sort and lay it before you. I have lately done myself high honour at Belhouse by proving that my wife is lineally descended from Henry the First, through all the Henrys and Edwards down to Edward the Third, through John of Gaunt, and this Duchess of York, etc. by the way of *Manners, Capel*,[12] *Chester* and *Long*. It is a certain fact, I assure you;

10. *Lives of the Admirals*, 1742–4, by John Campbell (1708–75). The passage is on i. 302 of the 2d edn (1750), and it merely says that Edward's being set aside ('murder' is never specified) was 'one of the darkest parts of our history.' Buck's work is called a 'panegyric rather than history,' and Buck is disparaged in footnote *k*.

11. Richard Bentley (*ante* Hardinge to HW 17 July 1780). HW evidently did not want his generosity to Bentley to be known.

12. Lady Katherine, wife of Sir Henry Capel, Kt, was granddaughter of George Manners, Lord Roos, who had married Anne, daughter of Edward IV's sister (Anne, Duchess of Exeter) by her second husband, Sir Thomas St Leger. Their daughter Anne married Sir Robert Chester, from whom descended Mrs Vachell, mother of Lucy, wife (1755) of the Rev. Richard Long (Marquis of Ruvigny and Raineval, *Plantagenet Roll . . . Anne of Exeter Vol.*, 1907, pp. 2, 30, 36, 417, 420; see also Collins, *Peerage*, 1812, i. 464–5, iii. 476–7).

and I have acquired by *contact* a partiality for these Plantagenets. Adieu, my dear Sir,

G. HARDINGE

To HARDINGE, ca July–August 1780

Missing. Answered in the next letter.

From HARDINGE, Thursday 17 August 1780

Printed from Nichols, *Lit. Illus.* iii. 208–9.

Grove, August 17, 1780.

My dear Sir,

THE first part of your letter, I own, piques me, as representing me to be capable of the folly which I described as such in my friend, and of the fear to own it if I had been answerable for it. The fact is that ages ago, when I first read your book, though in a more cursory manner than of late, I was convinced, and am now confirmed in my first impressions.

Nor do I see why you should *abandon* Richard, even to such a feeble attack as *mine,* if I had meant it, and if your defence could even have the *chance* to undeceive me because I am your friend. I have taken a good deal of pains to examine the materials and the arguments; nor do I know a thing that will give me greater pleasure than to see the additions you have made before I finish my own system, which I destine for your criticism, if you will condescend to favour me with it. I am, dear Sir,

Your most affectionate servant,

G. HARDINGE

To HARDINGE, ca September 1780

Missing. Answered in the next letter.

From HARDINGE, Sunday 10 September 1780

Printed from MS now WSL; previously printed, Nichols, *Lit. Illus.* iii. 209. Sold, Sotheby's, 18 Nov. 1929, J. G. Nichols Sale, part of lot 239; offered, 18 Dec. 1931 by G. Michelmore & Co.; sold Sotheby's 18 May 1933, part of lot 418 to Maggs Bros for WSL.
Address: The Honourable Horace Walpole Strawberry Hill Middlesex.
Postmark: 11 SE.

Hinxton, Sept. 10, 1780.

My dear Sir,

THE Dissolution,[1] that farce of state-cunning, has in some little degree deranged my politics, those of my summer-leisure in particular; and some election business in this part of the world has delayed my receipt of your obliging letter till this day; and tomorrow is the time that you have destined for my happiness at Strawberry Hill, upwards of sixty miles distant from the scene which at present engages me. I must attend the election for the County of Cambridge Thursday next,[2] and how long I may be detained in that attendance I can't foresee. Be so good therefore as to overlook me totally, but suffer me to take my chance when I can be free.

I am, with the greatest affection, dear Sir,

Your obliged and most faithful servant,

GEORGE HARDINGE

I hear your friend Mr Conway has a contest at Bury.[3] If it should produce a petition, perhaps I could have the honour to be one of his counsel by your recommendation.

1. Parliament was dissolved 1 Sept. 1780 (MASON ii. 78, n. 1).
2. On 14 Sept. 1780, Lord Robert Manners and Philip Yorke were elected M.P. for Cambridgeshire (Sir Lewis Namier and John Brooke, *House of Commons 1754–1790*, 1964, i. 218).
3. Conway defeated William Hervey at Bury St Edmunds, 12 Sept. 1780, by 18 to 13 (Namier and Brooke, op. cit. i. 378). There was no petition.

From HARDINGE, ca June 1781

Printed from Hardinge's MS copy labelled by him 'extract from a letter of G. H. to H. W.' and also labelled 'extract from a letter of mine to the last Lord Orford' (now WSL). It was sold Sotheby's, J. G. Nichols Sale 18 Nov. 1929, part of lot 239; offered 18 Dec. 1931 by G. Michelmore & Co.; and sold, Sotheby's, 18 May 1933, lot 418 to Maggs Bros for WSL. First printed Nichols, *Lit. Illus.* iii. 212–13.

Dated by the reference to C. J. Fox's note in Gibbon's book. This incident was reported in the *London Courant* 20 June 1781 (said to be from the *Morning Herald*), and in the *Public Advertiser*, the same day. HW pasted the cutting from the latter into his *Last Journals* where it is printed (ii. 367). In both newspapers, the sale of the copy of Gibbon was said to have occurred 'last week.'

Dear Sir,

NOTHING has done more injury to *civil freedom* than applying to it the images of *moral* fitness and of moral obligation.

The *'Patriot King'*[1] of *Lord Bolingbroke* would be in this light very mischievous, if it was not in itself ill-written, superficial, and weak.

Locke,[2] with intentions the noblest, and with immediate effects the most beneficial, has rather done harm than good for after ages, considered (which even in candour to him ought never to be the comment upon him) as a writer on a *subsisting* establishment, because he incorporates *natural rights* with *political duties.*

Yet I can as little bear *the Tories,* and *Blackstone* at their head, when *they* denounce their *anathemas* against those who declare a veneration of *James's*[3] doom as a noble precedent (which it is) not merely of *the facts* (much less of such a petty *item* in the account as the act of secession from the kingdom) but of elevated and constitutional *principles.*

When I read the long debates upon the mode of settling and qualifying this exemplary measure, I am hurt and piqued for the national credit of high spirit and of genius when I see *them* stoop to such political scruples of conscience.

Yet I admire (enthusiast for liberty as I am) the temper and wisdom of *Lord Somers,* who preferred humouring this Tory-cant, and

1. *Letters on the Spirit of Patriotism, on the Idea of a Patriot King . . . ,* 1749 (MANN iv. 59, nn. 20–24). *The Idea of a Patriot King* had previously been pri- vately printed by Pope, ca 1741 (ibid., n. 24).
2. John Locke.
3. James II.

with a compliment of a serious air, in preference to the loss of so important a work as the pith and substance of that *Second Magna Charta for us all*.[4]

To resume the notion of keeping *politics* detached from the rules of *domestic morality*, I must admit *one* exception, which is the article *of keeping engagements*.

The same perfidy which dishonours *the man* in his intercourse with his neighbour dishonours *the country* in its faith to another state, whether in alliance or in open war.

Yet I have seen (but with disgust) in a volume of *Parliamentary Debates*, the remark of a *Lord Say and Sele*[5] that public and private honour bore no resemblance; and Stuart,[6] a North British writer on politics, directly affirms it.

Lord Chatham was never so great as in taking the opposite ground, and in calling '*faith*' (as I heard him) 'that glorious attribute of states and of private men'—a doctrine which is not less true though our Peace at Fontainbleau[7] gives the lie to it.

Such *exceptions*, however, to the general rule of distinguishing *the man* from the *political machine* claim no stipulation or covenant. They illustrate themselves, and without prejudice to the good sense of the rule.

It is not unfair sometimes to use the argument *ad absurdum*. Let us do it here! *Sir William Temple*, in a serious mood (and without meaning it) has done it for us by one of the most extravagant Court-aphorisms that ever escaped from the pen of an able and well disciplined writer. I shall only give you his words: 'Every subject should *obey*, as he would himself *desire to be obeyed*, upon the *moral* principle of *doing* as he would *be done by*.'[8]

G. H.

4. Presumably the settlement of 1688.

5. Probably Richard Fiennes (1716–29 July 1781), 6th Vct Saye and Sele, 1742.

6. Perhaps Andrew Stuart (1725–1801), M.P., author of *Letters to the Right Honourable Lord Mansfield*, 1773.

7. The preliminary treaty between England, France, and Spain, signed 3 Nov. 1762 at Fontainebleau (MANN vi. 95, n. 1). HW commented to Mann 9 Nov. 1762 that it 'leaves the hero and heroine of Germany to scratch out one another's last eye,' and the elder Pitt condemned the treaty as, 'with respect to our allies, inglorious and dishonourable to the nation' (MANN vi. 95–6 and n. 7).

8. The complete passage is as follows: 'As every Prince should govern, as he would desire to be governed, if he were a subject, so every subject should obey, as he would desire to be obeyed, if he were a prince; since this moral principle of doing as you would be done by, is certainly the most indisputed and universally allowed of any other in the world, how ill soever it may be practised

PS. Amongst the books of Charles Fox, carried off by the indis-
criminate hands of the law, and sold under an execution,⁹ was an
odd volume of *Gibbon's History of the Roman Empire*. It sold for
three guineas, more in honour to this manuscript in the first leaf
than to the work:

I received this work from the author (on such a day).

N.B. I heard him declare at Brooks's, the day after the Rescript of
Spain¹⁰ was notified, that nothing could save this country but *six heads*
(of certain ministers whom he named) upon the table.

In fourteen days after this anathema he became *a lord of trade*,¹¹ and
has ever since talked *out* of the House as he has voted *in* it, the advocate
and champion of those ministers.

CHARLES FOX.

From HARDINGE, Wednesday 6 March 1782

Printed from Nichols, *Lit. Illus.* iii. 209.
Dated by Conway's speeches in Parliament, and by HW's answer, *post*
8 March 1782.

Great Ormond Street, Wednesday.

Sir,

THOUGH what men of this world would call business, and I
call avocations, put it out of my power to see you so often as I
wish, you must permit me upon paper to give you joy of your friend's
victory, and the personal honour which he has acquired by it. The

by particular men' ('Of Popular Discontents,' in Temple's *Works*, 1814, iii. 44).

9. 'Charles's books, which were seized, were sold this week. Gibbon's book, which contained the manuscript note by Charles, was smuggled from the sale, for, though Charles wished to have sold it, yet it never was put up. He bought in most of his books for almost nothing' (Storer to Lord Carlisle 18 June 1781, Hist. MSS Comm. 15th Report, Appendix, pt v, *Carlisle MSS*, 1897, p. 501).

10. On 16 June 1779, the 'Spanish rescript' ('Declaración . . . al ministerio Britanico') was delivered by Almodóvar to Lord Weymouth (MANN viii. 482–3, nn. 1, 2). It was a manifesto enumerating Spanish grievances against England, and it led to the declaration of war between them.

11. Gibbon, then M.P. for Liskeard, had voted with the Opposition, but hoped through Wedderburn's friendship to get a government post. On 20 June 1779, George III consented to his appointment as lord of trade (Sir Lewis Namier and John Brooke, *House of Commons 1754–1790*, 1964, ii. 495).

pitiful chicane of the first *watchman*[1] (for he cannot without abuse of terms be called *minister*), the cool apathy of John Bull, the despair of good men, the want of harmony and of dignity in opposition, the dupery and pride of country gentlemen, the corrupt baseness of contractors, and the fatality of misconduct which persecutes the Cabinet, are our present auspices.

I was not fortunate enough to hear the General in his two American propositions,[2] but I heard him upon Lord Sandwich, and thought he spoke admirably.[3] It is comparatively a point of important service to the public that we have crushed the *future* American war—but when shall we recover the *past?*

I hope soon to see you; till when believe me, Sir,

Most affectionately yours,

G. HARDINGE

To HARDINGE, Friday 8 March 1782

Printed from Nichols, *Lit Anec.* viii. 527–8; reprinted, Toynbee xii. 188–9.

March 8, 1782.

IT is very pleasing to receive congratulations from a friend on a friend's success—that success, however, is not so agreeable as the universal esteem allowed to Mr Conway's character, which not only accompanies his triumph, but I believe contributed to it. Today, I suppose, all but his character will be reversed; for there must have

1. Lord North, the prime minister.

2. On 22 Feb. 1782 General Conway introduced into the House of Commons a resolution calling for an end to the American War; at two o'clock in the morning of 23 Feb. the motion lost by one vote. On 27 Feb. General Conway introduced a similar resolution, slightly reworded in accordance with Parliamentary rules; again at two o'clock in the morning of 28 Feb. a motion to adjourn was lost by 19 votes, and the original question and an address to the King formed upon it were passed without a

division (MANN ix. 251, nn. 1–3; *Annual Register . . . 1782*, pp. 168–71).

3. On 20 Feb. 1782 Charles James Fox introduced a resolution into Parliament condemning the 'great mismanagement in the conduct of his Majesty's naval affairs' by 'a negligent and incapable minister' i.e. Lord Sandwich. It lost by 19 votes; if it had carried, Fox had announced that he would introduce a second resolution requesting the King to remove the Earl of Sandwich from his councils forever. See HW to Mason, 23 Feb. 1782, MASON ii. 187; MANN ix. 244, n. 1; *Annual Register . . . 1782*, p. 167.

been a miraculous change if the Philistines do not bear as ample a testimony to their Dagon's honour, as conviction does to that of a virtuous man.[1] In truth, I am far from desiring that the Opposition should prevail yet: the nation is not sufficiently changed, nor awakened enough, and it is sure of having its feelings repeatedly attacked by more woes; the blow will have more effect a little time hence: the clamour must be loud enough to drown the huzzas of five hoarse bodies, the Scotch, Tories, Clergy, Law, and Army; who would soon croak, if new ministers cannot do what the old have made impossible; and, therefore, till general distress involves all in complaint, and lays the cause undeniably at the right doors, victory will be but momentary, and the conquerors would soon be rendered more unpopular than the vanquished; for, depend upon it, the present ministers would not be as decent and as harmless an opposition as the present. Their criminality must be legally proved and stigmatized, or the pageant itself would soon be restored to essence. Base money will pass till cried down. I wish you may keep your promise of calling upon me better than you have done. Remember, that though *you* have time enough before you, *I* have not; and consequently must be more impatient for our meeting than you are, as I am, dear Sir,

Yours most sincerely,

H. Walpole

From Hardinge, Friday 15 March 1782

Printed from Nichols, *Lit. Illus.* iii. 209–10.

Great Ormond Street, Friday, March 15, 1782.

My dear Sir,

WHEN I wrote last, I little thought how near the ministry were to despair, and a dissolution[1] at the heel of it. Report says they are *in extremis;* and my confidence in your friendship, which has

---

1. 1 Samuel 5. 3: '. . . behold, Dagon was fallen upon his face . . . before the ark of the Lord. And they took Dagon, and set him in his place again.' HW seems to say that Dagon's party (the administration's supporters) will rally and restore him, unless a miracle occurs, just as men of conviction rallied to the virtuous Conway.

---

1. The next dissolution was in 1784.

honoured and benefited me in various ways ever since my first experiment of it, induces me to suggest a channel by which you may
do me an important service. I have no personal objects in view but
success at the Bar and credit in Parliament. As to the former, I have
reason to believe, upon recent evidence, that I have some claims
upon it. The latter will take its fate if I can obtain what I have
much at heart, a seat in the House. The share which Lord Camden
will naturally have in the new arrangement, and his kind partialities
for me, would of themselves, perhaps, insure my attainment of this
object; but I confess that I have a delicacy respecting him which
prompts me rather to carry my point through other friends, though
of course in honour to him (for I can have no claims of my own),
than by his direct and personal recommendation. I have the honour
to be one of the counsel to the Duke of Devonshire,[2] at the instance
of Lord John Cavendish,[3] who, in the handsomest manner, some
years ago sent me a general retainer for him, though he knew me
only in my professional appearance. I expressed, as I felt, my gratitude for this mark of his kind opinion. My politics, though hitherto
speculative alone, have never deviated once from those which have
distinguished his family, and I have no ambition but that of putting
them forth in the public scene. I hope too that, few as the occasions
have been which have enabled me to address a numerous audience
in the Houses of Parliament, they have done me no dishonour. But
my connection with Lord Camden, whom I should think none of
the present Opposition would be sorry to oblige, is the last and perhaps only significant card in my hands. Would you have the goodness, if the opportunity should offer, to mention me as favourably
as you can to General Conway, who might, perhaps, forward my application amongst those of the party with whom he is most connected, and who, I believe, are the Rockinghams? I should be infinitely thankful to you for this important mark of your favourable
opinion and friendship. At all events, and in every situation, believe
me, dear Sir,

Your most affectionate and most obliged,

G. HARDINGE

2. The fifth Duke (*ante* HW to Bentley   3. Uncle of the 5th D. of Devonshire
19 Dec. 1753, n. 25).   (*ante* HW to Harcourt 5 July 1782, n. 3).

To Hardinge, Friday 15 March 1782

Printed from MS now WSL. Previously printed in Nichols, *Lit. Illus.* iii. 210–11, Toynbee xii. 197–8. Sold, Sotheby's 18 Nov. 1929, J. G. Nichols sale lot 232. Sold by Francis Edwards, Ltd, to WSL, Sept. 1932.
Endorsed: H. Walpole.

Berkeley Square, March 15, 1782.

YOU need never say more than one word, dear Sir, when you wish me to do anything that is in my power to serve you. At present I believe you have largely outstripped that occasion. Lord North certainly totters; but if the Court has even a very slender majority tonight, for which they have been moving hell and earth, I am persuaded they will struggle on a little longer.[1] Should the reverse happen, I am far from thinking that a new arrangement will be easily or speedily made. In any case, I should doubt whether either side would risk dissolving the Parliament at this juncture, of which I have not heard one sober man talk.

But to come nearer to your point, should a new Parliament be called, Gen. Conway would be the most useless person to whom to recommend you. He has not the smallest inclination for coming into place; he is totally unconnected with any set of men; and even when he was secretary of state, he would on no account be concerned in any election-jobs. He has constantly declared that he is in opposition only upon the question of America, and it is my opinion that whatever change arrives, you will see him no where but where he is.

I will make you no compliments on what I think of your qualifications for Parliament, because I do not see how or where I could prove that I am sincere. *I* certainly shall have no interest with any administration; as I can answer for myself that I never will be obliged to any minister; and he who will not serve ministers, has no right to ask favours of them. As you will find that I have spoken truth about myself, I am sure you will excuse my being so sincere on all the other points; but as it is my maxim that he who speaks truth can

1. HW wrote to Mann, the next day, that 'the tax-day passed very quietly. However, it was . . . generally believed that Lord North would resign' (MANN ix. 256, and n. 14).

never be detected, I had rather speak unwelcomely, than give you hopes that it is utterly improbable I should ever be able to realize.

Yours most sincerely

H. Walpole

From Hardinge, Saturday 16 March 1782

Printed from Nichols, *Lit. Illus.* iii. 211–12.

Great Ormond Street, March 16, 1782.

My dear Sir,

I AM very thankful to you for your early and frank answer to my request. Though I cannot profit by your friend, I respect him the more for his incapacity of serving me, as you have stated it. As to yourself, every day gives me new proofs that, dear as the *Dacres* are to me upon many accounts, I have no obligation to them equal to that of owing to them your friendship.

Perhaps I may as well be out of Parliament, if it were only upon the article of temper, for I am afraid that I should not bear those two Scotch orators[1] half so patiently as the Opposition bears them. They have both avowed that interruption, though it marks the disgust of those who hear them, is of service to them and animates them the more. They assume a control over both sides of the House; make their political creed the test of the Constitution; and, if it is but intimated 'that their situation is dependent,' which is all that Powys[2] intimated last night,[3] they tear down the walls with an outcry against a calumny so illiberal.

Will Pitt scourged the Advocate last night for the impudence of his proposition, which amounted in substance to this: 'Coalition is

1. 'Mr William Adam—and Mr Dundas, lord advocate of Scotland' (Nichols, *Lit. Illus.* iii. 211 n.). William Adam (1751–1839), M.P.; Henry Dundas (1742–1811), cr. (1802) Vct Melville; lord advocate of Scotland 1775–83; M.P.

2. Thomas Powys (1743–1800), cr. (1797) Bn Lilford; M.P.

3. 'Mr Powys . . . took occasion to observe, that he would say nothing to the question before the House, until he should see some gentleman as independent as the hon. member who had made the motion, rise up to oppose it. Here he was called to order by Mr Adam, who, with great warmth, said he would never sit silent while such insinuations were thrown out' (Cobbett, *Parl. Hist.* xxii. 1186).

to save us; that coalition must include *us;* and we cannot make it so well unless we keep our places.'[4] By the way, though it may sound invidious, that young man rather disappoints me. His manner has great powers in it, and his language is brilliant; but his thoughts are not very original or copious. He picks out a topic or two ably enough, and adapted well to Parliamentary effect; he urges it forcibly, but he dwells upon it much too long, and after a time rather with new words than arguments—yet he promises great things and, for his time of day, is, to be sure, an extraordinary character. But I think *Charles Fox* many leagues beyond him, for *he* has memory, judgment, acuteness, clearness of reasoning, vigour of mind, and power of attack, in the same degree, and that a degree far beyond any man of his age. At one moment he scorns the little trammels of detail, and puts the fair question upon great and liberal grounds, which no detail can touch; at the next moment, for his purpose, he can dissect and analyse the minutest feature of the argument, with powers that a metaphysician could never have equalled in his closet. Yet, alas! he wants two great features of a consummate orator and statesman— He wants dignity of manner, which is the form, and dignity of character, which is the soul.

Adieu! I hope to wait upon you soon; till when, and ever,

Yours, etc.

G. Hardinge

To Hardinge, Thursday 18 April 1782

Printed from Nichols, *Lit. Anec.* viii. 529. Previously printed in Toynbee xii. 237.

Berkeley Square, April 18, 1782.

I HAVE great pleasure, dear Sir, in your preferment,[1] and sincerely wish you joy. I have no doubt but your abilities will continue my satisfaction as long as I can be witness to their success. I did not expect to live to see the door opened to constitutional prin-

4. Pitt's speech is outlined in Cobbett, op. cit. xxii. 1198–9.

1. As solicitor-general to the Queen (Nichols, *Lit. Illus.* iii. 12; GM 1782, lii. 207, *sub* 20 April).

ciples. That they have recovered their energy, is a proof of their excellence; and I hope that, as they have surmounted their enemies, they will not be ever betrayed by their friends.

Yours heartily,

H. Walpole

From Hardinge, ? April 1782

Printed from Nichols, *Lit. Illus.* iii. 212, where it is undated.

Dear Sir,

TO give you at once an idea of the Appellant Jurisdiction vested in the House of Peers, and *my own fame,* I beg to inform you that I made yesterday a very *able reply* to the Advocate of Scotland[1] upon a very *important* Scotch appeal.

Judges: Earl Mansfield; Bishop of Landaff;[2] a Peer with a red face, anonymous, supposed to be one of the Sixteen.[3]

Counsel: Advocate of Scotland, Solicitor General of Scotland,[4] Mr Hardinge, Mr Blair.[5]

Parties: in Scotland.

Agents: two Scotch attorneys.

Clerks and Officers of the Court: one clerk.

Hearers: from *taste* or curiosity, *none.*

Believe me, dear Sir, with unalterable respect and attachment, most affectionately yours,

G. Hardinge

---

1. Dundas.

2. Hon. Shute Barrington (1734–1826), Bp of Llandaff, 1769, of Salisbury, 1782, of Durham, 1791.

3. The representative peers of Scotland.

4. Alexander Murray (1736–95), solici-tor-general, 1775; lord of session as Lord Henderland, 1783 (*Court and City Register,* 1782, p. 243).

5. Probably Robert Blair (1741–1811) of Avontoun, a member of the bar and a friend of Dundas.

From HARDINGE, Thursday 1 May 1783

Printed from Nichols, *Lit. Illus.* iii. 212.

Great Ormond Street, May 1, 1782 [1783].[1]

My dear Friend,

I OFFER a second proof[2] of my diligence and zeal to your favourable eye; and, before I part with you, shall even trouble you with a third. What say you to Saturday fortnight for a day at Strawberry Hill? I name so distant a period that either *I or my executors* may be sure to wait upon you or yours.

To HARDINGE, Saturday 17 May 1783

Printed from Nichols, *Lit. Anec.* viii. 528–9. Previously printed, Toynbee xii. 451–2.

Berkeley Square, May 17, 1783.

THOUGH I shall not be fixed at Strawberry on this day fortnight, I will accept your offer, dear Sir, because my time is more at my disposal than yours, and you may not have any other day to bestow upon me later. I thank you for your second, which I shall read as carefully as I did the former. It is not your fault if you have not yet made Sir Thomas [Rumbold] white as driven snow to me. Nature has providentially given us a powerful antidote to eloquence, or the criminal that has the best advocate would escape. But, when Rhetoric and Logic stagger my Lords the Judges, in steps Prejudice, and, without one argument that will make a syllogism,

1. In *Lit. Illus.* iii. 212, is a cross reference from this letter dated 1 May '1782' to that of 17 May 1783 indicating that they are both part of the correspondence dealing with Hardinge's defence, 1783, of Sir Thomas Rumbold (1736–91), cr. (1779) Bt; M.P.; who was being prosecuted by Dundas, lord advocate of Scotland, for corruption in India. Counsel for and against the bill against Dundas were heard in the House of Commons, 29 April (MANN ix. 400, n. 17). Hardinge was counsel for the defence in the House (Hardinge's *Miscellaneous Works*, 1818, i. p. xvii). Hardinge's *Defence of Sir T. Rumbold* was printed in 4to, 1783, and partly reprinted as *Substance of the Defence* in his *Miscellaneous Works* i. 389–436.

2. That is, the second part of Hardinge's defence of Rumbold.

confutes Messrs Demosthenes, Tully, and Hardinge, and makes their Lordships see, as clearly as any old woman in England, that *belief* is a much better rule of *faith* than *demonstration* (a covered fling at Scripture!). This is just my case: I do believe, nay and I will believe, that no man ever went to India with honest intentions. If he returns with £100,000 it is plain that I was in the right. But I have still a stronger proof.—My Lord Coke says, 'Set a thief to catch a thief.' My Lord A[dvocate][1] says, 'Sir [Thomas Rumbold] is a rogue': *Ergo*—

I cannot give so complete an answer to the rest of your note, as I trust I have done to your pleadings, because the latter is in print,[2] and your note is MS. Now, unfortunately, I cannot read half of it; for, give me leave to say, that either your hand or my spectacles are so bad, that I generally guess at your meaning rather than decipher it, and this time the context has not served me well. You shall comment on it when I see you; till when, I am, as usually, much yours,

H. Walpole

From Hardinge, ca Sunday 20 July 1783

Printed from Nichols, *Lit. Illus.* iii. 213–14.

Ragman's Castle.

SUFFER me, dear Sir, again to throw myself upon your partialities. The whole is, I fear, to be reprinted and published. You will then be so good as to return this copy, and the two other parts, in exchange for the new volume which is to comprise the whole. Did I see you in the act of sipping coffee at Lady Di's[1] on Sunday evening? What a scene it is! N.B. I have seen the lilac festoons.[2] But will you forgive my ambition to know the artist? If that is more than I can hope to obtain, may I have the *entrée* of her sweet garden when

1. Dundas, lord advocate of Scotland, who was prosecuting Rumbold (*ante* Hardinge to HW 1 May 1783, n. 1).

2. Hardinge's *Defence* of Rumbold is not listed in HW's library.

———

1. Little Marble Hill, at Twickenham (Ossory ii. 473, nn. 32–5; Mason ii. 272, nn. 11–12).

2. 'There she painted in the boldest style, though in water-colours, a room hung with green paper, which she adorned with large festoons of lilacs' (HW's MS note cited Ossory ii. 473, n. 35). See also HW's enthusiastic description to Mason, 4 Aug. 1782, Mason ii. 272.

she is from home? Did you know that I had the honour of presenting myself at your door as a neighbour in due form yesterday se'nnight? I am to beg that you will *not* return the visit before I can give you a chair to sit upon, or mutton to eat—*your own*, for our butchers, etc. are to be the same. But where do you get your *salt? You* cannot tell me, or it would not be so good. Farewell.

Apropos of the lilac. Suffer me to explain our trespass. Mrs Hardinge and I rambled, and saw the birds were flown. We asked leave to peep, and the major-domo would have my name whether I would or no. As a misconstruction is possible, pray guard me against it.

Ever affectionately yours,

G. HARDINGE

To HARDINGE, ca Thursday 24 July 1783

A missing rebuke, answered in the next letter.

From HARDINGE, Saturday 26 July 1783

Printed from Nichols, *Lit. Illus.* iii. 214.

Lincoln's Inn Hall, July 26, 1783.

My dear Sir,

MANY thanks for your note. I am concerned that you should think me capable of intruding myself either upon Lady Di Beauclerc's acquaintance, or upon her family in her absence. I never entertained for a moment so indelicate a thought; but what I named was upon the idea that, as I am your friend and her immediate neighbour, she would not be averse to me; and that when her *whole* family, except the servants, were from home, I could now and then, without offence, drop in upon her sweet place as a part of my walk. But as I find from your account that it cannot be with propriety, I beg it as a particular favour that you will be so good as to leave me in my natural obscurities, drop no hint of my wishes to Lady Di Beauclerc, and trust to me that I shall commit no further trespass—unless now and then upon *you,* if you should have more facility and forbearance than I can hope from others, upon whose condescension I can less depend. Believe me, dear Sir,

Your most obliged and most affectionate,

G. HARDINGE

To HARDINGE, ca Thursday 31 July 1783

A missing note of regret, signed 'your obedient humble servant,' and answered in the next letter.

From HARDINGE, Saturday 2 August 1783

Printed from Nichols, *Lit. Illus.* iii. 214–15.

Ragman's Castle, Saturday, Aug. 2, 1783.

Dear Sir,

WE lament that we cannot be so happy as to see you here, and the more that indisposition is your plea. We must elope for a month in a few days, but I must hope that you will have no gout and rheumatism to interfere with our claims upon you in the course of next month. I cannot help observing that you are my *obedient humble servant* at the bottom of your note. As I am *your affectionate friend,* I had rather *you* should also be *mine.*

The Duke of York,[1] as the facetious Dalrymple remarks,[2] varied the ceremonial of his conclusion when he wrote in a bad humour to the Prince of Orange,[3] and said, 'you will believe me as kind as

---

1. Afterwards James II.
2. Though the word 'deserve' does not appear in it, Hardinge may be thinking of the letter of 2 Jan. 1684, headed 'the Duke of York to the Prince of Orange—Out of humour with the Prince,' which ends 'you may be sure I shall be as kind

to you as you have reason to expect' (Sir John Dalrymple, *Memoirs of Great Britain and Ireland,* 2d edn, 1773, ii. Appendix, 'pt i' [2d pagination], 66).
3. The Duke's son-in-law and nephew, later William III of England.

you *deserve*'—instead of '*desire*,' as upon other occasions. I do not suspect you of any resemblance to the Duke, or me of any to his correspondent; but I must in half a word say, from the bottom of my heart, that nothing will make me unhappier than to see any coolness between us; because, upon my honour, none of your numerous friends have more taste for your society, and more affection for your *unfashionable* merits of goodness and virtue, than I have, who am *not* your obedient humble servant, but your grateful and unalterably attached friend,

G. HARDINGE

From HARDINGE, ca 1783–4

Printed from Nichols, *Lit. Illus.* iii. 215.

My dear Sir,

IT will not be in our power to wait upon you tomorrow, nor till Monday next, or any day after it that you should prefer. Pray do Mrs Hardinge the justice to believe that she cannot be happier than in your company. To deserve you a little, she is cultivating her talent, and is drawing at your cabinet. If she can lie at the feet of your Aylesburys, Beauclercs, etc.[1] her ambition will take no higher flight. Adieu.

G. HARDINGE

---

1. Hardinge is referring to Lady Ailesbury's worsted-work pictures and Lady Diana Beauclerk's drawings in soot-water of scenes from the *Mysterious Mother,* in HW's collection at SH (Ossory i. 289, 294–5, iii. 15).

To Hardinge, ca 1783–4

Printed from Nichols, *Lit. Illus.* iii. 215, where it is undated, but placed before the letter of March, 1784. Reprinted, Toynbee xv. 444. This may be the letter from HW to Hardinge, one page quarto, of 1784, which was sold at Sotheby's 13 [14] July 1896 (Collectors of Autograph Letters and Historic Documents Sale), lot 434 to Barker for 13s. A letter of the same date and description was sold by Puttick and Simpson, 2 March 1897 (Valuable Collection of Autograph Letters and Documents), lot 81*. See *post* p. 632.

I SHALL be very glad of your company at dinner on Wednesday, dear Sir; but for the key of the Park,[1] I do not believe it is to be obtained. The Duke, I think, gives none, at least I remember hearing a great deal that I forget about it when he was in England; and, I dare to say, Mrs Keppel[2] nor anyone here has power to give a key; but I will inquire. I am happy to hear Mrs Hardinge is better; and, if she is at Twickenham, I shall be glad of the honour of her company too.

H. Walpole

From Hardinge, Tuesday 23 March 1784

Printed from MS now wsl. Previously printed, Nichols, *Lit. Illus.* iii. 215. Sotheby's, 6 Nov. 1951, Nichols Sale, lot 397, to Pickering and Chatto; who sold it to wsl, March 1953.
Address: The Honourable Mr Horace Walpole.

Dear Sir,

I SEND you an etching, done by Brotherton[1] from a curious drawing which I picked up two or three years ago prefixed to a very old manuscript of a treatise by *Sir John Fortescue,*[2] *Chancellor of*

1. Perhaps Hampton Court Park, of which the Duke of Gloucester was Ranger (*Court and City Register*, 1783, p. 78).
2. The Duchess of Gloucester's sister, who by 1782 lived at the Stud House in Hampton Court Park (Ossory ii. 346 and n. 4).

———

1. James Bretherton (fl. 1773–81) or

his son Charles (1760–83), engravers (Thieme and Becker). HW had a print by van der Gucht of Sir John Fortescue, sold London i. 10; Bretherton's etchings may have been among those unitemized 'other individuals of his [Henry VI's] reign,' sold London i. 9.
2. (?1394–?1476), chief justice of the King's Bench.

Henry the Sixth. A very learned, enlightened, and good man (as this Chancellor unquestionably was) deserves your favourable notice, let his exterior be ever so quaint. At least I may take refuge in the trembling humility of Heming[3] and Condel[4] when putting forth under my Lord Pembroke's[5] auspices the doubtful fame of one William Shakespear. They compare this man's works to *cheese-milk,* etc. offered by rude peasants to the lord of the village, who estimates the value not by the present itself, but the heart that makes it.[6] I am one of those peasants when I entreat your acceptance of my affectionate and grateful acknowledgments (wrapped up in the official purse of my Lord Fortescue). I have alluded to the unaccountable diffidence of Shakespear's friends in a writer above all competition or panegyric. This reminds me of a passage in Hume,[7] which imputes to Milton's age, and even to his party, an ignorance of his merit—and for proof observes that *Whitelock* calls him *one Milton, a blind man.* If you never saw the passage in Whitelock to which this *correct* and *impartial* historian refers, you will be astonished at the effrontery of such a reference.[8] Believe me ever, my dear Sir,

Your most affectionate friend and servant,

G. HARDINGE

3. John Heming (ca 1556–1630), actor; friend of Shakespeare.

4. Henry Condell (d. 1627), actor; friend of Shakespeare.

5. William Herbert (1580–1630), 3d E. of Pembroke, 1601, to whom the first folio of Shakespeare's plays is dedicated.

6. Hardinge is paraphrasing 'Country hands reach foorth milke, creame, fruites, or what they have. . . . It was no fault to approch their Gods, by what meanes they could' (2d page of the 'Epistle Dedicatorie' to the first folio, 1623, of *Mr William Shakespeare's Comedies, Histories, & Tragedies*).

7. 'It is well known that Milton never enjoyed in his lifetime the reputation which he deserved. . . . Even during the prevalence of Milton's party, he seems never to have been much regarded; and Whitlocke talks of one Milton, as he calls him, a blind man, who was employed in translating a treaty with Sweden into Latin' (Hume, *History of England,* 1864, v. 95 [Chapt. LXII]).

8. In the original passage Whitelocke is paraphrasing the Swedish ambassador's words: 'The Swedish ambassador again complained of the delays in his business, and that when he had desired to have the articles of this treaty put into Latin, according to the custom in treaties, that it was fourteen days they made him stay for that translation, and sent it to one Mr Milton, a blind man. . . . The employment of Mr Milton was excused to him, because several other servants of the council, fit for that employment, were then absent' (Bulstrode Whitelocke, *Memorials of the English Affairs from . . . Charles the First to . . . Charles the Second,* Oxford, 1853, iv. 257 [a reprint of the 1732 edition; p. 645 in the 1732 edn]).

To HARDINGE, Tuesday 23 March 1784

Printed from MS now WSL. Previously printed, Nichols, *Lit. Illus.* iii. 216, Toynbee xiii. 135. Sold, Sotheby's 18 Nov. 1929, J. G. Nichols Sale, lot 238. Sold Samuel Loveman, Jan. 1935, to WSL.
Endorsed (by ?Hardinge): Mr Hor. Walpole.

March 23d.

I AM much obliged to you, dear Sir, for the very pretty print you have sent me; but I cannot afford to hang it up, as it will be too great an acquisition to my volume of portraits. I am very sorry you can give me no better an account of the original. I have had a very slight fit of gout this winter, but I have got a very bad cold and so troublesome a cough, that I am in hopes the air of so charming a season will remove it, and I am come hither for a few days to try it in its purity—not but that I think it very possible, that a cough may be only the wind rattling through

the chinks that Time has made—[1]

and I shall be persuaded so, if it is not cured soon.

Are not you very glad of Miss Beauclerc's marriage?[2]

From HARDINGE, Saturday 16 October 1784

Printed from Nichols, *Lit. Illus.* iii. 216.

Ragman's Castle, Saturday, Oct. 16, 1784.

My dear Sir,

AS one is not immediately reminded of a *calf* by *your* conversation upon other subjects, I thought no more of your generous offer to me yesterday in a certain gallery, than Lady Di thinks of my passion for her, though I am not cured of it by her want of *taste*. But the week is not over, and I am in time to be dull *before Sunday*.

1. Edmund Waller (1606–87), 'On the Foregoing Divine Poems' ll. 13–14: 'The soul's dark cottage, batter'd and decay'd, / Lets in new light through chinks that time has made.'

2. The elder Beauclerk daughter, Mary (1766–1851), apparently did not marry until about 1795 (OSSORY ii. 334, n. 4).

The fit, however, has no occasion to be quite so long. If you can at any time spare a cow-calf, produced *bonnement* by your French beauties, and old enough to eat grass, remember me. *C'est tout dire* —no, it is not; for I have more business to do with your friendship. It is a message to the dear Lady Di. Be so good as abuse her in my name (whatever you may tell her in your own) for not liking me or Mrs Hardinge. We have seen her once for a quarter of an hour (which flew like half a quarter of a minute) in our own Castle. A little after this tantalizing peep at her, we left the neighbourhood; but a long week is past since we left our card at her door, and that was the first moment after my return that we could wait upon her. Etiquette says that we must now (to borrow a metaphor from our constant object, the Thames) lie upon our oars; that we must go to her next, and for that purpose wait for a summons from her: else I would ask her to us, or invite ourselves to her, for Mrs Hardinge and I are enchanted with her. Blanchard[1] and Sheldon[2] have just been *visible* two miles over our heads. It was a beautiful sight, and I do not care a bit for the ridicule of it, though nothing, to be sure, can be sillier. Adieu!

G. HARDINGE

To HARDINGE, Saturday 16 October 1784

Printed from Nichols, *Lit. Anec.* viii. 529, where it is undated and combined with HW's letter to Hardinge *post* ca Aug. 1785; the date and other corrections are supplied in Nichols, *Lit. Illus.* viii. 591. Reprinted in Toynbee xiii. 322–3.

Oct. 16, 1784.

Dear Sir,

I HAVE had a calf born, but it was ugly and from a *mésalliance*. But I have two more cows whose times are out, and you shall know as soon as they are delivered. When I received your note, I

1. Jean-Pierre Blanchard (1750–1809), aeronaut who ascended in a balloon at, London, 16 Oct. (MANN ix. 543, nn. 6, 7).

2. John Sheldon (1752–1808), anatomist and surgeon. He alighted from the balloon at Sunbury, when Blanchard reascended, and he is considered the first Englishman to make a voyage (as distinguished from a mere ascent) by balloon (J. E. Hodgson, *History of Aeronautics in Great Britain*, 1924, pp. 162–5, 434).

concluded it was to tell me of Lady D's message. She told me she would ask you and Mrs Hardinge tomorrow evening; and she desired I would meet you. She told me how much she admired Mrs Hardinge, and, as I agree with her Ladyship; I shall not tell *you* what she said of you.

I have just seen the balloon too; and all the idea it gave me was one I have not had since I was at school—football.

My gout, thank you, is dormant; the rest, such rest as there is, gives me no trouble.

To Hardinge, ca 1784

Printed from Toynbee xv. 445, the MS being then (1905) in Mrs Toynbee's possession. This may be the letter sold Sotheby's, 14 July 1896, or that sold Puttick & Simpson 2 March 1897. See *ante* p. 628.

Monday morning.

Dear Sir,

I THINK you go this morning to Lady Di's. Be so good as to carry the enclosed, and deliver it when Mr B.[1] is not present, which I suppose he will not be. I will trouble you too to leave her answer here as you return.

Yours, etc.,

H. W.

1. Presumably Lady Diana Beauclerk's only son by her second marriage, Charles George Beauclerk (1774–1846) (Collins, *Peerage*, 1812, i. 249; Sir Bernard Burke and A. P. Burke, *Peerage*, 1928, pp. 1580, 2016).

From HARDINGE, Tuesday ca 26 October 1784

Printed from Nichols, *Lit. Illus.* iii. 216–17 (misnumbered), see heading to next letter.

Ragman's Castle, Tuesday.

My dear Sir,

I SEND you, with many thanks, your interesting *Villars*,[1] whom I do not like the worse for *you* as a *party concerned.*[2] As to your gossiping notes,[3] I wish all my own books were so treated if *you* were the gossiper. I am an old bachelor today, and will dine with you if you will give me a bed into the bargain or insure my life between your Hill and my Castle.

I have not your *calf* after all. She is not of the little breed, and has no French blood in her veins. Ever yours, my dear friend, most affectionately and faithfully,

G. HARDINGE

From HARDINGE, ca 1784

Printed from Nichols, *Lit. Illus.* iii. 217 (misnumbered 219), where the date of the year is supplied.

Ragman's Castle, Sunday.

My dear friend,

I AM here upon a journey to Bath, and would fain have exchanged Strawberry Hill for my own desolate cottage, but I was afraid of intrusion. Pray let me know how you are, and promise that we shall be good friends when I return. I have been fighting at Norwich, in a cause of some difficulty and importance, against one of the late solicitor-generals,[1] who deported himself in a manner so

1. Probably the *Vie du maréchal duc de Villars*, ed. Anquetil, 4 vols, 1784 (Hazen, *Cat. of HW's Lib.*, No. 3387).

2. HW had noticed that Villars commented on Sir Robert Walpole's policy (ibid., quoting HW's MS 'Book of Materials').

3. HW often annotated his books. His copy of this one has not been found.

———

1. John Lee, Richard Pepper Arden, and James Mansfield had held the post of solicitor-general within the previous two years, and were all M.P.s.

illiberal that I could not, without injustice to the cause and my own personal honour, decline the painful task of setting a mark upon him. I was fortunate enough to carry the point, and ascribe the victory more to him than to myself. These are odious parts of our profession. But let us be *Dunnings*,[2] and rise to nobler heights by nobler means; then shake off the public chain and live a little to ourselves. But how long are we to enjoy that earthly heaven, the interval between glory and the tomb! Lord Ashburton's epitaph shall tell us. Well may Sir Walter Raleigh call Death *eloquent*.[3]

Farewell. I overtook your nieces[4] today, the cynosures of the Talbot Inn,[5] thanks to a peppering shower.

G. HARDINGE

To HARDINGE, Tuesday 24 May 1785

Printed from Nichols, *Lit. Illus*. iii. 217 (misnumbered 219). Reprinted Toynbee xiii. 264–5. A letter from HW to Hardinge, 1785, was sold at Sotheby's 9 July 1860 (another property sold with the John Mitford Sale), lot 119 with other letters to Waller for 6 *s.* 6 *d.*

Strawberry Hill, May 24, 1785.

MR Walpole cannot help troubling Mr Hardinge with a line on a distress he has had this morning. A company came to see his house, and said they came from Hampstead, and that Mr Hardinge had spoken to him about them; which not having happened, Mr Walpole did not know what to do. However, as they used Mr Hardinge's name, Mr Walpole (*as another set was expected*) offered them to come tomorrow, or to walk over the house now till the other company should come; but they did not choose either. Mr Hardinge knows Mr Walpole is always desirous of obliging him; but he is so teased with numerous applications, that he is forced to be as strict as possible; and was last year obliged to print his *Rules*, one of which he takes the liberty of sending to Mr Hardinge, which may save him

2. John Dunning (1731–83), cr. (1782) Bn Ashburton; one of the leaders of the Opposition in Parliament (1770–82), noted for his integrity.

3. 'O eloquent, just, and mighty Death!' (Raleigh's *History of the World*, Bk V, chapter 6, §12).

4. The Waldegraves, HW's great-nieces.

5. The inns at Twickenham were the Swan (MORE, back endpaper) and the Crown (MASON ii. 59). The Talbot Inn in London was the former Tabard, in Southwark, an unlikely place for Hardinge to meet the Waldegraves (*London Past and Present* iii. 344).

trouble too, as it will be an answer to those who may apply to him when he is not at leisure to write. Nor can Mr Walpole admit any accidental company, when a day is engaged; nor can the house-keeper[1] show the house but by a written ticket.

To Hardinge ca August 1785

Printed from Nichols, *Lit. Anec.* viii. 529 where it is combined with *ante* HW to Hardinge 16 Oct. 1784; the date and other corrections are supplied in Nichols, *Lit. Illus.* viii. 591. Reprinted Toynbee xiii. 323. Dated by the presentation of the SH edition of the Duc de Nivernais's translation of HW's *Essay on Modern Gardening*, the printing of which was completed in the final week of Aug. 1785 (Hazen, *SH Bibl.* 129).

1785.

I send you a new Strawberry Edition, which you will find extraordinary, not only as a most accurate translation, but as a piece of genuine French not metaphysicked by La Harpe,[1] by Thomas,[2] etc. and with versions even of Milton into *poetry,* though in the *French* language. The Duc[3] has had 200 copies, and I myself as many for presents: none will be sold, so their imaginary value will rise.

I have seen over and over again Mr Barrett's plans,[4] and approve them exceedingly. The Gothic parts are classic; you must consider the whole as Gothic modernized in parts, not as what it is—the reverse. Mr Wyatt,[5] if more employed in that style, will show as much taste and imagination as he does in Grecian. I shall visit *Lee*[6] next summer.

I remain, yours ever,

H. WALPOLE

1. Presumably Margaret Young (OSSORY i. 75, n. 11).

——

1. Jean-François de la Harpe (1739–1803). HW wrote to Lady Ossory 17 Sept. 1785 (OSSORY ii. 496) that Nivernais's translation was 'a most beautiful piece of French, of the genuine French spoken by the Duc de la Rochfoucault and Madame de Sévigné, and not the metaphysical galimatias of La Harpe and Thomas, etc., which Madame du Deffand protested she did not understand.'

2. Antoine-Leonard Thomas (1732–85), French poet, philosopher, critic.

3. The Duc de Nivernais (*ante* HW to Chute 3 Oct. 1765).

4. Thomas Barret (?1743–1803), M.P. HW's example inspired Barret to Gothicize his house, Lee Priory, a process which began about 1782 and was completed by 1790.

5. James Wyatt, the architect (*ante* HW to Strafford 7 Sept. 1784).

6. Lee Priory, near Canterbury, Kent. Wyatt's designs for Lee were his 'first effort to adopt the Gothic in the design of a modern mansion' (DNB). See HW to Mary Berry, 27 August 1789 (BERRY i. 59 and n. 5).

To Hardinge, ca 1789

Printed from MS now WSL. Previously printed, Nichols, *Lit. Illus.* iii. 217 (misnumbered 219), Toynbee xv. 445. Dated by the reference to the misfortune in Lady Diana Beauclerk's family. Sold by Swann Galleries, 25 Feb. 1960 lot 542, to Seven Gables Bookshop for WSL.
Endorsed: H. Walpole.

Dear Sir,

I AM now with Lady Di, who is ill from great distress by a misfortune[1] relative to her family. If you could come hither for ten minutes, you would do a great act of charity, as you can perhaps give her some advice, which I cannot do. It is not a point of law, but compassion, and yet I know not how to put her into a way of doing any good. I send you my own chaise, because it is ready, and it shall carry you back directly. You will oblige Lady Di extremely, as well as

Yours ever,

H. Walpole

From Hardinge, Friday 11 September 1795

A missing invitation to HW to meet the Archbishop of Cashel. See next letter.

To Hardinge, Saturday 12 September 1795

Missing. 'That out-pensioner of Bedlam G. H. whom I hoped I had offended in the spring by refusing him a plenary indulgence, wrote to me last night to *dine* with him on Tuesday next with the Archbishop of Cashel—I knew this was to imply '*my* cousin is Lord Lieutenant'—with all my heart! Accept I did not, however as it showed good humour, I sent a very civil sorrowful fib in return and pleaded having engaged company myself for that day' (HW to Mary Berry 10–12 Sept. 1795, Berry ii. 166).

1. The elopement of her daughter Mary (*ante* HW to Hardinge 23 March 1784) with Mary's half-brother Lord Bolingbroke, who was already married (Ossory iii. 56, n. 10).

APPENDICES

APPENDIX 1

WALPOLE'S 'INVENTIONARY' AND DESCRIPTION OF THE VYNE

An Inventionary of Alterations to be made at the Vine. JULY 1ST 1755

Within the House.

The staircase, to have four flights.

The little Strawberry parlour.

A commode. A couch, and two fly tables.

The great parlour.

Two large pictures, one at each end.

The two lesser doors to be stopped up.

Two half-length portraits of Lord and Lady Dacre on one side of the chimney.

On the other side, half-lengths of Mr J. Chute and the old Lady Dacre.

Over the doors, heads of Mr Whithed, Mr Gray, Mr Bentley, and Mr Walpole.

Drawing room within great parlour.

To be hung with green.

Over the chimney, view of Mabland.

A bedchamber and alcove to be within that.

The chimney piece of the stone gallery to be carried into . . . [MS defective] is to be a billiard room.

The great hall, to be quite plain.

For the old parlour.

Two large settees, and two coins.

The Antechapel.

To be finished as the end is.

The windows to be painted by Price with the pedigree.

The chapel.

Three pictures under the windows, of the Lord's Supper, Christ in the garden, and Christ walking on the sea. The four Evangelists in the long panels on each side.

A rich purple and silver altar-cloth, with handsome old embossed plate.

A brass eagle for a reading desk.

The walls above to be painted in a Gothic pattern: and a closet with a screen in the same pattern.

The great drawing-room one pair of stairs.

To be hung with the Chinese tapestry.

The chimney piece to be altered.

Two views of Strawberry Hill over the doors.

The green bedchamber.

To be a drawing-room with a bow window.

The gallery.

To be finished at the ends with carved wainscot.

To have two more whole lengths.

The Library.

To have the anteroom laid into it, to be finished with old wainscot, and Gothic windows.

Without doors.

A semicircular court, with a gate like Caius College.

A sheep paddock of 30 acres.

Two towers added.

The new walk continued cross the meadow to Morgason.

Opposite to the house, a Roman theatre, with an obelisk, two urns, two sphinxes.

Cypresses and cedars.

The old garden to be an open grove.

The hither wall of the kitchen garden to be pulled down, and the garden to be hid.

A spire upon the barn.

Cypresses about the summer house and the house.

Two lanes of flowering shrubs, without the garden.

The water, to be done what one can do with it.

THE VINE

At Sherborne near Basingstoke in Hampshire, the seat of William John Chute Esquire.

The house was built[1] or much enlarged by Lord Sandys, lord chamberlain to Henry VIII. He also erected the beautiful Gothic chapel, fitted up with stalls curiously carved and ornamented with capricious friezes. The windows are enriched with painted glass well preserved and taken[2] at the siege of Boulogne. The three upper lights contain Scripture histories, and below them are the portraits[3] (less than life) of Francis I, of his Queen Claude, and of his sister Margaret of Valois Queen of Navarre, who wrote the *Tales,* and who with more wit and talents, had all the amiable virtues that were so deficient in her great-niece, who bore both her name and title, and was first wife of Henry IV: each figure is kneeling at a prie-dieu.

The gallery above stairs was also fitted up by Lord Sandys, and on the panels are carved and repeated the arms of Henry VIII, Cardinal Woolsey, Archbishop Warham, and other great persons of that time.

The wood beyond the water at the back of the house still retains the name of Morguesson, a village in France near which was fought the Battle of Spours (as Mr John Chute discovered) but which has been ridiculously called by historians the Battle of Spurs, from the hasty flight, as they suppose, of the French; as if every battle in which one side retreated precipitately, might not as justly have been called so.

The Vine was purchased from the last Lord Sandys of that line by Chaloner Chute Esq. Speaker to Richard Cromwell's Parliament. He pulled down part of the ancient mansion which was much more extensive; but added the noble portico towards the garden from a design of Webbe, disciple of Inigo Jones.

Anthony Chute Esq. the last descendant but one from the Speak-

---

1. 'About 1500' (MS note, in unidentified hand).

2. 'By Lord Sands' (HW's note in his copy, now WSL, of the 2d E. of Hardwicke's *Miscellaneous State Papers,* 1778, i. 62).

3. '1543. A mistake' (MS note). The portraits are now thought to be Henry VII, his wife Elizabeth of York, and his daughter Margaret (C. W. Chute, *History of the Vyne,* 1888, p. 21).

er's eldest son, sashed the garden front, and made many alterations rather than improvements.

But the principal additional beauties to the Vine were the works of his younger brother John Chute, who was an able geometrician, and was an exquisite architect, and of the purest taste both in the Grecian and Gothic styles. He erected from his own designs the beautiful scenery of the staircase with its two vestibules, though unfortunately cramped by want of larger space. He improved the front of the house, enlarged the stoned hall, decorated the antechapel, and the chapel itself, the sides of which above the stalls were painted by Signor Roma from one of the Greek Isles; and built the pretty chapel on the right hand, to receive the fine tomb and cumbent figure in his robes of his ancestor the Speaker.

Mr John Chute enlarged the water, built the bridge, cut the walks in Morguesson and erected there the statue of the Druid; and he too made and planted the noble terrace that parts the road from his own grounds.

Mr John Chute gave the designs for the seat of Mr Andrews under Donnington Castle in Berkshire near Spinhamlands; as chaste a specimen of Gothic architecture as exists any where.

ORFORD
March 18th 1793[4]

4. This description of the Vyne was enclosed in a letter from John Cowslade to (?) Mrs Chute, 26 March 1793, beginning 'Having just received this account of the Vine from Lord Orford, I take the first opportunity of transmitting it to you.' The MSS printed in this appendix were both at the Vyne, Hants.

Eccardt pinxt   Heath Sculp.

Richard Bentley.

Published as the Act directs May 1.ˢᵗ 1798. by G.G. & J.Robinson Paternoster Row. London.

APPENDIX 2

WALPOLE'S ACCOUNT OF RICHARD BENTLEY[1]

Pieces wrote by Mr Bentley, only son to Dr Bentley.

A full and true account of the dreadful and melancholy earth-quake, which happened between 12 and 1 of the clock in the morn-ing on Thursday the fifth of April, with an exact list of such persons, as have hitherto been found in the rubbish; in a letter from a gentle-man in town to his friend in the country. 1750. This was a ridicule on the panic that was occasioned by a notion that there would be an earthquake that night. It went through seven editions. The second part was spurious. A petition to the R. H. Mr Pelham in favour of Mr Maclean, by a lady. 1750. In verse, with a declaration in old French to burlesque Warburton. An attempt towards an apology for his R. H. the Duke. 1751. A true and faithful account of the greatest wonder produced by nature these 3000 years in the person of Mr Jehan Paul Ernest Christian Ludovic Munpferdt, the surprising centaur, who will be exhibited to the public, on the first of next month (April) at the sign of the Golden Cross at Charing Cross. 1751. With a print of the centaur, designed by Mr Bentley himself, who had a very extraordinary genius for drawing and designing. In the year 1757 he translated that part of Hentznerus's travels which relate to England, which with the Latin on one side, was printed at Strawberry Hill in the autumn of that year. About the same time he wrote a copy of verses to Mr W. on the new printing press there. He wrote at Cambridge many years before, a copy of mock heroics to George Rooke, afterwards Master of Christ's College there, on the art of broiling beef-steaks.

His Drawings.

I have a large book of them, and his original designs for Mr Gray's poems. He drew the ceiling of the Library at Strawberry Hill,

1. Printed from HW's *MS Commonplace Book of Verses*, pp. 85–6.

designed the lanthorn, staircase, north front, and most of the chimney-pieces there; and other ornaments. Mr Geo. Montagu has a
few of his designs. Trevor, Bishop of Durham has some drawings of
his for alterations to the palace there. The Gothic Farm at Lady
Suffolk's at Marble Hill Twickenham, called the Priory of St
Hubert's (from Hobart, her maiden name) was partly designed by
Mr Bentley, particularly the spire, but she caused it to be executed
too low. The south side of the imaginary church there was designed
by Mr Walpole. The two square little towers were Lady Suffolk's
own. The whole was executed in 1757 and 1758. The Hon. Rich.
Bateman at Old Windsor has altered his offices in 1758 according to
a plan given by Mr Bentley. He gave Mr Churchill several designs
for his house at Chaffont, but they have not been followed exactly.
When Mr Bentley was at Jersey, he painted five or six pictures in
oil; I have four of them, one, a view of the Castle of Mont Orgueil
there, very good. A small long view of Elizabeth Castle there, begun
by him, but finished by Mr Müntz, and two others, not very good. He
designed a tomb erected at Linton in Kent for Mr Galfridus Mann
by Mr Horace Walpole, in 1758. It consists of a beautiful urn of
marble, placed in a small Gothic recess of stone, in the manner of the
ancient columbaria. It was executed by Lovel, statuary in Mortimer
Street near Oxford Road, London.

Nov. 22d 1758 was published (with a dedication by Mr W.) a
pamphlet written by Mr Bentley, called, *Reflections on the Different
Ideas of the French and English in Regard to Cruelty*, etc. This was
designed as an introduction to a bill of perpetual insolvency, designed to be brought into Parliament by Mr W. or by his means.
Sept. 8th 1760 was published in the *London Chronicle*, a letter
signed R. R. written by Mr Bentley, to expose the cruelty of killing
the dogs in London, upon a panic of their being mad.

In the same year he wrote a play, in the manner of the Italian
comedy, called *Harlequin's Mouth Opened*.

In November of the same year was published, printed at Strawberry Hill, a fine edition of Lucan in quarto, with Dr Bentley's
notes, and dedicated to the Earl of Halifax by Mr Richard Cumberland, the Doctor's grandson and Mr Bentley's nephew. The *Ad Lec-
torem* was written by Mr Bentley, and the two engravings by Grignion were from his designs.

His play of the *Wishes* or *Harlequin's Mouth Opened*, was offered to Garrick and Rich the beginning of 1761 but was refused by both. His nephew Cumberland showed it to Lord Melcomb, who carried it to Lord Bute, with a compliment in verse to that Lord by Mr Cumberland. Lord Bute showed it to the King, who sent Bentley £200 and ordered the new summer company to play [it]. There was a prologue flattering the King and Lord Bute which Foote refused to act. Two days before it was played, Cumberland wrote an anonymous pamphlet addressed to Mr Bentley, and abusing Garrick, who had refused to act Cumberland's tragedy of Cicero's banishment, which he printed this year unacted. The *Wishes* were played for the first time July 27th 1761: the 2d, 3d and part of the 4th acts were much applauded, but the conclusion extremely hissed. The epilogue concluded with a satire on Garrick. It was acted five nights. About the same time he wrote a tragedy called *Philodamas,* which he was to read to Garrick, but the latter was so angry at their treatment of him, that he declared against seeing Mr Bentley.

In 1762 he wrote an epistle in verse to Lord Melcomb on the decay of poetry. It was published in the *St James's Magazine* for March 1763.

A poem on the sonatas of Bendal Martyn; published in the *St James's Magazine* for April 1763. About the same time Lord Bute made him a commissioner of the lottery.

In November 1763, he published *Patriotism,* a mock-heroic in five cantos.

APPENDIX 3

LADY HARCOURT'S VERSES[1]

To the Honourable Horace Walpole, August, 1773, occasioned by
his approbation of the foregoing lines [to Lady Temple]:—

> To write with judgment, with correctness please,
> Unite the rules of Art with nature's ease;
> Bid lively wit and sportive fancy join
> With taste refined, and nervous sense, is thine;
> 'Tis mine at awful distance to admire,
> And wake to humbler strains an artless Lyre.
> Pleased when thy candid voice my song commends,
> More pleased to rank thee with my partial Friends.
> True merit shuns th' applause it can command,
> But lends to others a supporting hand.
> To waken Genius with the breath of praise,
> With kind indulgence every talent raise,
> Each fainter colouring of the mind display,
> O'er every dawning thought diffuse the day,
> And bid the Muse her trembling wings extend,
> Well suits the Virtues' and the Muse's friend;
> Well suits the Man whose nobly feeling heart
> Glows with the love of every liberal art.
>   Walpole, accept this tributary lay,
> To thee let gratitude her homage pay;
> Hail the kind voice unwilling still to blame,
> And giving praises which I dare not claim.

1. Printed from *Harcourt Papers* xi. 140.

APPENDIX 4

HARDINGE'S ACCOUNT OF WALPOLE[1]

Milbourne House
June 22.

Dear Sir,

I was intimate with Horace Walpole for several years. When I became familiar with his effeminacy of manner, it was lost in his wit, ingenuity and whimsical but entertaining fund of knowledge.

Though he was elegant and polished, he was not I think *well bred* in the best view of the phrase. He demanded a full stretch of admiring homage to his *bon mots,* and rather lectured in a series of prose epigrams than conversed playfully and so as to put the hearer quite at his ease.

In the course of his kind predilection for me a peculiar incident occurred, which I shall never forget. He had invited me to his Elysium (of its kind) Strawberry Hill. On my arrival I found a note—He was gone to Houghton on a sudden call, but insisted that I should pass the day and sleep under his roof and with keys of all its treasures. I did not and could not go to bed for many hours after midnight.

Dr Akenside had no *wit*—Horace Walpole had infinitely *too much.* His prose epigrams were unremitted and left the hearer no resting place. He talked, as he wrote; and one left him, at least I did, fatigued, though charmed with his enlivening sallies. They were a demand upon the animal spirits, which almost invaded the *liberty of the subject,* the liberty of being dull or of lying fallow.

When definitions are made even by such a man as Mr Locke of the boundaries, which divide wit from humour, he puzzles common readers and perhaps in part himself. But living instances are perhaps the best of all definitions. Lord Chesterfield and Mr Walpole had unexampled powers in *wit*—of humour they had no conception—

1. Extract, in an unknown hand, labelled 'Letter [to Nichols] from George Hardinge, Esq.'; here printed from a photostat of the original in the possession (1937) of F. C. Holland, West Horsley, Surrey. Printed in Nichols, *Lit. Anec.* viii. 525–6; where it is followed (pp. 526–7) by five paragraphs which are here printed from Nichols's printed text.

Fielding and Addison were preeminent examples and models of *humour,* though in different branches of it. The mock heroic irony of Addison was a more elevated cast of the power than Fielding possessed, who was only at home in the *farce of Nature.* Mr W. has often told me that he himself had no enjoyment of Tom Jones. It might be *nature* he said, it might be *humour,* but it was of a kind, that could not interest him. I pitied him, as I should pity a man, who had not all his five senses. There was a degree of quaintness in Mr Walpole's wit, but it was not unbecoming in *him* for it seemed a part of his *nature.* Some of his friends were as effeminate in appearance and in manner as himself and were as witty. Of these I remember two, Mr Chute and Mr George Montagu. But others had effeminacy alone to recommend them.

In his taste for architecture and *virtu* there was both whim and foppery, but still with fancy and with genius.

His little *jeux d'esprits* in prose (for he terribly failed in verse) are jewels and perhaps above them all his papers in *The World.* When I say that he failed in verse, I must except that striking play the *Mysterious Mother,* which in a very original vein is full of dramatic genius and of picturesque effect. The *Castle of Otranto* is a model of its kind and there is a wonderful grace in the language, which is neither too familiar, nor too elevated. It seems inseparable from the characters, the scenery, and the incidents. The *Historic Doubts* are very entertaining and well reasoned. His manner of relating a fact or of describing a character is quite his own. I never saw it equalled.

His politics were as *illegible,* if I may use that phrase, as those of Dr Akenside. His partiality for his father was amiable, but in the outrage of it absurd. He was for a time a zealot in the cause of liberty. But in the course of time that spirit cooled, and at last it flamed in the fury of his aversion, just in its principle, to all the sanguinary horrors in France, and their champions here.

His passion for *Madame du Deffand* was the most wonderful incident of his life; congenial talents and mutual vanity attached and connected them; but she was *too young for him,* though superannuated in years, and by others at least more admired than beloved. I lament, for his honour, that such a correspondence has been published.

We are told, in your entertaining *Anecdotes,* that Warburton was the best letter-writer of the age. In my judgment Horace Walpole was infinitely superior to him and all his contemporaries in that pleasing but equivocal talent. I had many of his letters for several years; and have retained some of them, which are delightfully entertaining and clever. Letters, however, especially if written by men of the world, supply no test of the writer's genuine sentiments.

I have great pleasure in sending you a copy of a letter from him [of 4 July 1779], which I think beautiful, in his best manner. The letter also which accompanies it in my packet is not inferior to it; and you are welcome to both of them.

Upon the subject of Grignan I will indulge a little egotism; it is the food of age, as music is that of love. Mr Walpole and I agreed in our passion for Madame [de] Sévigné; and when I made a little tour in 1776, that passion carried me to the Château de Grignan, where I passed a day or two, and at my own cost obtained, I think, four drawings of it, which he accepted most gracefully, and which he has done me the honour to make heirlooms at Strawberry Hill.

DATE